Business Law

AN INTRODUCTION

Lowell B. Howard

Associate Professor of Business Law
Ohio University
Member of the Ohio and Federal Bars

 BARRON'S EDUCATIONAL SERIES, INC.
Woodbury, New York

Preface

This book is intended to furnish students, businessmen, and others with a brief but reasonably complete introduction to the fundamental principles of law in the areas of contracts, sales, negotiable instruments, agency, partnerships, corporations, and property, as well as a general survey of the American legal system.

The enactment of the Uniform Commercial Code by the legislatures in a majority of the states by the end of the legislative sessions of 1963 marked what many believe to be the most important development in the commercial law field to date in this century. In full recognition of this significant event, this book presents the Code law pertaining to contracts, sales, and negotiable instruments, along with that part of the pre-Code law in these areas which remains unchanged by the Code or which is necessary as a background for making the transition to an understanding of the law as it exists under the Code. As the need arises, there is a description of the Code's impact on the law in the other areas covered in this book. Numerous references to specific provisions of the Code are included in the text and footnotes, and where it is believed necessary to an understanding of the law, sections of the official text of the Code are set forth verbatim. The 1962 Official Text of the Uniform Commercial Code, except Articles 4 and 5, is included in the Appendix. The Uniform Partnership Act is also included in the Appendix.

Throughout the writing of this book, the author has attempted to present the law in terms which would be understandable and of practical value to business law students. This objective is a reflection of the author's experience of having taught business law courses to students at Ohio University for nearly a decade, and special thanks is owed to these students. Acknowledgement of gratitude is made to Judith M. Dean, Mrs. Barbara Pierce,

Mrs. Celeste Urdahl and C. Richard Satterthwaite, all of whom helped in various stages of the preparation of the manuscript. I dedicate this book to my wife, Jeanetta.

ATHENS, OHIO   *Lowell B. Howard*

Contents

I. INTRODUCTION

II. CONTRACTS

III. SALES

IV. NEGOTIABLE INSTRUMENTS

V. AGENCY

VI. BUSINESS ORGANIZATIONS: PARTNERSHIPS AND CORPORATIONS

VII. PROPERTY

APPENDIXES

Survey and Background of the American Legal System

1

NATURE OF LAW

Definition of Law

The legal systems of the world have evolved as systematic man-made methods of administering justice impartially to the members of society in their relations with one another and society. Law in its broadest technical sense has existed for centuries, however unrefined or lacking in system or organization it may have been in some of the ancient civilizations. Legal philosophers and others have throughout recorded history contemplated and discussed the nature of law as an ever-present force in the lives of people everywhere. Yet law is so inextricably interwoven with all the other facets of human conduct and social control that it is difficult to define law simply and precisely. Indeed, law is a partial reflection of the total experience of mankind. However, one characteristic of law which other aspects of human conduct such as morals, ethics, custom, religion, economics, and science lack is that the law is enforced by organized political government. Recognition of this unique quality of law is found in Blackstone's *Commentaries on the Laws of England* in which law is defined as "a rule of civil conduct prescribed by the supreme power in a state, commanding what is right and prohibiting what is wrong." In other words the field of law is regarded as coterminous with that of organized legal sanctions recognized and enforced by the courts. This definition of law applies, whatever the source of the law may be, and it can be used to describe the law of a democratic society or that of a totalitarian state. However, in a democracy those who govern are also answerable to the law.

The lack of a complete coincidence between moral law and government-enforced law is readily apparent in most societies. For example, in the United States and elsewhere the moral law demands that a promise freely made be performed; but, as will be seen in Part Two of this book, our legal system enforces only such promises as are made in a certain form or under prescribed circumstances.

Rules of law are concerned in large measure with the adjustment of the relation of persons to other persons and to society. These interrelationships arise out of man's quest for satisfaction of his inherent longings. Chief among man's natural aspirations is the desire for food, shelter, and freedom from injury to his person and property at the hands of others. A legal relationship depends upon the existence of a government which recognizes the relationship and certain enforceable rights and duties arising therefrom.

The law is not a mass of arbitrary rules, but it consists primarily of a series of general principles and standards founded upon justice and experience and the social and religious beliefs, business habits, needs, and the cultural level of society. The law is a dynamic force, constantly changing to meet the needs of society in each era of civilization. To illustrate, before the air age courts protected landowners from superadjacent and subterranean invasion by generally adhering to the view that unauthorized entries were trespasses under the common-law maxim that he who owns the soil owns it up to the sky and down to the center of the earth. Today, exceptions to this doctrine have been worked out by courts to permit reasonable aerial flights without liability to the landowner unless actual injury to person or property results. Further adjustment of the law relating to aerial flights can be expected as man probes through outer space.

The thoughts and beliefs about the nature of law and its interrelationship with the other aspects of human nature and experience are generally classified into schools of legal thought or jurisprudence. The most prominent of these schools are the natural, the historical, the analytical, and the sociological. These philosophical approaches to an understanding of the nature of law are dealt with in depth in most of the standard works on jurisprudence.

Business Law. Business law, also referred to as commercial law, is generally defined as that part of the law within a legal system which is applicable to business transactions. However, there is no formal boundary in Anglo-American law between law as it relates to business transactions and law in general. There is, however, such a boundary in the civil law of continental European countries, which is emphasized by the existence of separate codes of commerce side by side with the civil codes.

The typical American treatises on the subject of business law are essentially texts on the law of contracts with supplementary chapters on agency, partnerships, corporations, sales, negotiable instruments and property, along with an introduction to law in general. These areas make up what might be called the central core of business law, and this book is confined to those areas. In addition many of the standard business law texts select for special treatment particular contracts such as secured transactions and suretyship or services commercially rendered, including bailments, insurance, and banking. Other topics treated less often in these texts include pertinent aspects of criminal law, torts, estates, trusts, bankruptcy, and government regulation of business.

IMPORTANCE OF A KNOWLEDGE OF LAW

A general idea of the nature and origin of law and the manner in which it controls or influences human conduct is indispensable in the complex world of today. The law touches every aspect of human activity but none more closely than those matters which are involved in business transactions. Not only is some knowledge of law necessary to the safe and confident conduct of ordinary human affairs, such knowledge is absolutely essential for those participating in the affairs of the business world where transactions have become increasingly complex and involve myriad legal rules with their exceptions and qualifications. While it is axiomatic that a person, even a member of the bar, should not attempt to act as his own lawyer, the efficient conduct of business and the wise use of the counsel and services of a practicing attorney calls for an appreciation and general understanding of the workings of our legal system. Furthermore, everyone is presumed to know the law. This familiar presumption is summed up in the legal maxim "Ignorance of the law excuseth no man."

FUNCTION OF LAW IN AMERICAN SOCIETY

The attainment of justice is the highest goal a system of jurisprudence can set for itself, and justice is the ultimate goal of the system of law which has been developed in the United States. According to Jeremy Bentham, the renowned English jurist and philosopher, a prime objective of society is to promote the greatest good for the greatest number of the members of society. Our legal system is one of the many man-made instruments or institutions employed to realize this objective.

For centuries a specific objective of law has been the preservation of peace and order, this being the primary function of the criminal branch of law. The progress of a society depends upon the harmonious cooperation of its members. Without the preservation of order, society would soon lapse into anarchy and chaos. The law has made a significant contribution to the achieving of peace and order within the separate nations of the world. In recent years the rule of law as an instrument for peace among nations has been looked to with hopefulness. Other important functions of law are the protection of society's institutions, the determination and enforcement of the rights and duties of individuals, and the regulation of those economic forces which threaten the general welfare of the people.

The fabric of the American society has woven into it certain fundamental ideas, policies, or institutions which over the years have been fostered and protected by our legal system.

¶ Important among these structural characteristics of American society are the following:

1] an economy which is basically a free enterprise system with the profit motive and competition as the essential regulators
2] right of private property
3] freedom of contract
4] inviolability of contracts
5] government of laws rather than a government of men
6] dignity of the individual person and the protection of liberties guaranteed by the U.S. Constitution and state constitutions
7] federal system of government with a national government and state governments based on written constitutions
8] theory of the separation of governmental powers among the executive, legislative, and judicial branches, with a system of checks and balances
9] doctrine of judicial review
10] tradition of religiosity of the people accompanied by certain moral standards

The day-to-day impact of law in any society is felt in the creation and protection of legal rights; or, to state it conversely, legal rights are implicit in the recognition and enforcement of legal duties, for every right implies a correlative duty to respect it. Many of the legal rights and duties of Americans are rooted in one or more of the above-enumerated characteristics or foundations of American society. Legal rights however, are not static things. Each individual has the capacity of creating, transferring, and divesting himself of legal rights. This capacity is called a legal power. This legal power is illustrated by the power a person has to produce something with his hands, with the result that he has the rights of ownership or property in the fruits of his labor. On the other hand, an exercise of power may result in a legal wrong, as, for example, when a thief steals a watch.

CLASSIFICATIONS OF LAW

Legal Wrongs

Infringement of any of the legal rights of a member of society constitutes a legal wrong. Under some circumstances a person may with legal impunity commit acts which would ordinarily be legal wrongs. For example, a person may strike another in self-defense. This immunity from the ordinary operations of the law is called a legal privilege. A legal privilege may be conferred by the law itself, as in the self-defense case, or it may be conferred by one person upon another, as when a landowner gives to his neighbor the privilege (called license) of crossing his land.

A wrong may be civil, in which case the state merely assists the injured party in obtaining a remedy; or it may be criminal, that is, an offense against society, in which case the state prosecutes and punishes the guilty wrongdoer. The civil action would be brought by the injured party, usually with the assistance of his attorney, against the defendant. The criminal action would be brought against the accused by the state, acting through a public official often called the prosecuting attorney or district attorney. A wrongful act may be both a crime and a civil wrong, as in the case of assault and battery.

Crimes. A crime is an act or omission forbidden by law and for which the offender is punished upon conviction. The rules of procedure followed in criminal cases differ in many ways from those observed in civil cases. For example, the state's burden of proof in a criminal case is that of establishing the defendant's guilt beyond a reasonable doubt, while in a typical civil case the plaintiff's burden of proof is to establish his case by a preponderance of the evidence. Crimes are defined by statutes in most states. Most of the acts defined in statutes as crimes were also recognized as crimes under the common law. All federal crimes are statutory, that is, they are defined either in the Constitution or by statutes enacted by Congress.

The essential elements of a crime at common law were (1) criminal intent and (2) a criminal act. Insane persons and infants of tender years cannot be guilty of a crime requiring criminal intent. As to others intent is determined on the basis of the "ordinary man" standard. Thus, the question is what a person would be justified in believing that an ordinary man would have intended if he had acted as the accused did under the surrounding circumstances? Under this standard the law presumes that if a person voluntarily does an act, he intended to do it and also anticipated the natural and probable consequences of the act. From this rule it follows that if A intentionally strikes B with a deadly weapon, A will be held criminally liable for B's death, even though A did not actually intend to cause B's death. However, the degree of offense committed and the penalty will usually vary depending upon the circumstances surrounding the death of one person at the hands of another. Various crimes against persons or property are graded on the basis of either the circumstances surrounding the commission of the offense or the extent of injury resulting from it, or both. For example, there is first and second degree murder and grand and petty larceny.

Many statutes of the various states prescribe regulations which have as their purpose the protection of the morals of society as well as the safeguarding of the public from the frauds of unscrupulous persons. Some statutes impose criminal penalties on an offender, irrespective of whether or not the offender intended to violate one of the statutes. For example, statutes regulating the operation of motor vehicles often make the commission of a forbidden act a crime, regardless of intention.

The common-law crimes are classified as (1) treason, (2) felonies, and (3) misdemeanors. The federal and state constitutions define treason as certain activity against the government. Felonies include serious offenses punishable by death or by imprisonment in the state penitentiary. Capital offenses are those for which the death penalty is provided. Murder, robbery, arson, grand larceny, forgery, and the like are classed as felonies. Offenses punishable by a lesser penalty, and less serious, are misdemeanors. Disorderly conduct, trespass, petty larceny, drunkenness, simple assault, and the like are some of the most common misdemeanors. There is sharp debate over whether a fourth class of crimes should be recognized for petty offenses such as those involving minor traffic violations or infractions of city ordinances. Technically these offenses are crimes and constitute misdemeanors.

Torts.   A tort is a wrongful act or omission, independent of a contract, for which the injured party may hold the wrongdoer liable. A tort is to be distinguished from a breach of contract. A tort involves the breach of a duty which is imposed by law, whereas a breach of contract is generally the result of a breach of an obligation which was voluntarily assumed by one of the contracting parties. However, the wrongful interference with the contracted rights of another person may constitute a tort. Part Two of this book contains a discussion of contract obligations and much of the remainder of the book is devoted to various other consensual or voluntary relationships.

The law protects a person from wrongful injury to his person, reputation, property, business relationships, and right of privacy. Torts may result from negligence, intentional acts, reckless and wanton acts, or the unreasonable use of one's property so as to harm another's person or property. Such unreasonable use of one's property is called a nuisance and may or may not be accompanied by negligence.

In a few unusual situations *absolute liability* for injuries is imposed against a person who carries on certain activities, despite his exercise of great caution and the absence of negligence or any intention to cause harm. This rule of strict liability (sometimes called absolute liability or liability without fault) is applied to cases involving certain lawful but extra-hazardous undertakings where injury to others is foreseeable even though the greatest precaution is taken. Strict liability has been imposed against an owner of trespassing animals, a person conducting blasting operations, and a person maintaining a fire, where in such cases injury to person or property resulted from such activities.

Every person in his contacts with others and their property is required by law to exercise the degree of care which a reasonable man of ordinary prudence would observe under the same or similar circumstances. The failure to fulfill this duty of ordinary care is termed *negligence,* and if it results in injury to another, the injured person has the right to recover money damages from the one who has been negligent. The three principal defenses to a tort action based on negligence are (1) assumption of risk, (2) contributory negligence, and (3) last clear chance.

The generally recognized intentional torts against the safety of a person or involving bodily harm are assault, battery, and false imprisonment. Assault and battery are usually found together in the same wrongful act. If a person defames another, he is liable for libel or slander. Libel is written defamation whereas slander is oral defamation. In either case there must be a publication of the defamatory statements to one other than the defamed person. Malicious prosecution is a tort committed against the good character of a person. To maintain an action for malicious prosecution, the injured party must establish that the prosecution terminated in his favor and that the prosecution was brought with malice and without probable cause.

The principal torts arising from intentional acts which interfere with property rights are trespass and conversion. While trespass can be committed against real or personal property, the term *conversion* is used to describe the wrongful appropriation of, or the unlawful dominion over, the personal property of another.

A false representation of fact made with knowledge of its falsity (or with reckless disregard of its truth or falsity), with the intention that it should be acted upon by another, and causing that other person to justifiably rely upon it to his injury, is known as deceit in the law of torts. Deceit is included within the broader term fraud which is discussed at length in Chapter 5.

Intentional interference with a person's rights under a contract is viewed as a tort for which the wrongdoer can be held liable to the injured party. Wrongful interference with a business opportunity or prospective economic advantage is a tort in certain cases. For example, intentional interference with the opportunity of a broker to earn a commission may constitute a tort.

In tort cases involving injuries other than those caused by negligence the defendant may be excused or have a justification as a defense. Such excuses or justifications include: (1) consent, (2) self-defense, (3) authority of certain public officers such as police officers, (4) entry on another's land to recapture chattels, and (5) abatement of nuisance.

Other Divisions of Law

Public Law and Private Law. The law within a particular state is often called municipal law and this law is commonly divided into two branches: (1) public law and (2) private law.

Private law governs the relationship between private citizens. It is concerned with the definition, regulation, and enforcement of rights in cases where both the person recognized as possessing the right and the person upon whom the obligation rests are private individuals. Examples of private law are the law of property and the law of contracts.

Public law includes those areas of law with which the state, that is, the public as a whole, is especially concerned. It includes criminal law, constitutional law, administrative law, and international law. Most of the legislation enacted by Congress is in the category of public law and deals with a vast and diversified number of subjects.

Substantive Law and Procedural Law.   Law is also divided into (1) substantive law and (2) procedural law. Substantive law refers to the branch of law which creates and defines legal rights and duties of individuals in relation to one another. The law of contracts is an example of one area of substantive law. In subsequent parts of this book some of the areas of substantive law which are relevant to business transactions are discussed in detail.

Procedural law, also called adjective law, refers to the legal machinery provided for within a legal system as the means of defining rights and duties in actual cases. A limited discussion of legal procedure is found in Chapter 2.

SOURCES OF LAW

The principal sources of law today are (1) the unwritten law and (2) the written law. The unwritten law is referred to as the common law, and it is found in the reported opinions of judges explaining court decisions in cases brought before the state and federal courts. The term *common law,* as will be seen, has several meanings. In addition to being used to describe judge-made rules based on precedents as distinguished from statutes, common law describes (1) the Anglo-American legal tradition as contrasted with the civil-law tradition derived from Roman law and found today in the countries of continental Europe and certain others, (2) the body of English law which was transplanted to the American Colonies, and (3) the law originally administered by the royal law courts in England as contrasted with the rules of equity administered by the Court of Chancery.

The written law exists in the federal and state constitutions and the statutes enacted by the federal Congress, the state legislatures, and the legislative bodies of local governments. Treaties are also part of the written law. The laws enacted by city councils and similar local legislative bodies of political subdivisions of a state are called ordinances, and such legislation must conform to the federal and state constitutions and state statutes.

Statutes, if not inconsistent with the constitutions or other higher law, may affirm, abrogate, or modify the common law. Systematic compilations of these statutes by a legislative body are often called codes. For example, many cities have a Traffic Code, states have Criminal Codes, and many of the federal statutes become part of the U.S. Code.

Uniform Statutes

Under our federal system of government, each state has its own statutes and courts which interpret them, and the federal government has its separate legislative and judicial branches. One result of this federal system of government has been a lack of uniformity in the law existing in the United States. This lack of uniformity did not pose a serious problem during the early period of our history. However, by 1890 it had become apparent that in the wake of the rapid development of transportation and communication along with the adding of new states, many commercial transactions involved persons residing in two or more states and the lack of uniformity in the laws of the various states became a matter of concern to lawyers, judges, bankers, and businessmen engaged in interstate business. This led to the organization of a body known as the National Conference of Commissioners on Uniform State Laws. Over the years the Commissioners, named by the Governors of the states, have prepared a great number of uniform or model laws, many of which relate to business transactions. Other groups such as trade associations and banking associations along with the American Bar Association and similar organizations have actively supported the drafting and enactment by the states of certain uniform statutes.

The earliest uniform act covered the subject of negotiable instruments. It was adopted by New York and several other jurisdictions in 1897, and it was ultimately adopted by the legislatures of all the remaining states. Ultimately, the Warehouse Receipts Act and the Stock Transfer Act were also adopted throughout the United States. Other important uniform commercial laws, including the Sales Act, Bills of Lading Act, Partnership Act, and Limited Partnership Act were adopted by a majority of the States.

Uniform Commercial Code.   Many changes in commercial practices had occurred since the early uniform statutes were drafted. Even with the widespread adoption of many of the uniform acts, nonuniformity arose among the adopting states as courts of different states, considering the same provisions of the same act, took different views as to their meaning, and handed down conflicting decisions. Efforts to restore uniformity through amendments to the uniform acts did not meet with widespread success.

The Commissioners on Uniform State Laws, along with other groups, worked on revisions of the Sales Act and the Negotiable Instruments Act in the 1930's. In the course of their work on these two statutes, the Commissioners developed the idea of incorporating into a single, modernized, and expanded uniform act all of the law relating to commercial transactions. In 1944 the American Law Institute, composed of judges, law professors, and practicing attorneys, joined with the Commissioners in the work of drafting an omnibus commercial act and sponsoring its adoption once completed. The Uniform Commercial Code appeared in 1952 as a product of this joint effort, and the first state to adopt the Code was Pennsylvania, where it went into effect on July 1, 1954, and was later amended to incorporate changes made in the Code since it was first written. As of the end of 1964 the legislatures in the following states had approved the Code and it was in effect or will take effect on the indicated dates: Alaska, Arkansas, California (Jan. 1, 1965), Connecticut, District of Columbia (Jan. 1, 1965), Georgia, Illinois, Indiana, Kentucky, Maine, Maryland, Massachusetts, Michigan, Missouri (July 1, 1965), Montana (Jan. 2, 1965), Nebraska (Sept. 2, 1965), New Hampshire, New Jersey, New Mexico, New York, Ohio, Oklahoma, Oregon, Pennsylvania, Rhode Island, Tennessee, Virginia (Jan. 1, 1966), West Virginia, Wisconsin (July 1, 1965), and Wyoming.

The Code is accompanied by detailed Comments of the drafters explaining the policy behind each section, the changes that would be made in the existing law, and many other matters. The Code purports to deal with all phases which may ordinarily arise in the handling of a commercial transaction, from start to finish. The sponsors of the Code continue to work on revisions of the original text of the Code and various amendments have been promulgated from time to time.

The Code consists of ten Articles, namely: 1. General Provisions, 2. Sales, 3. Commercial Paper, 4. Bank Deposits and Collections, 5. Letters of Credit, 6. Bulk Transfers, 7. Documents of Title, 8. Investment Securities, 9. Secured Transactions, and 10. Effective Date and Repealer. The following formerly separate uniform statutes are replaced by the Code: Sales Act, Negotiable Instruments Act, Bills of Lading Act, Warehouse Receipts Act, Stock Transfer Act, Conditional Sales Act, Trusts Receipts Act, Written Obligations Act, and Fiduciaries Act. In addition, the Code replaces miscellaneous statutes on bank collections, bulk sales, chattel mortgages, conditional sales, factors' liens, farm storage of grain, transfer of investment securities, and assignments of accounts receivables. It also codifies a variety of principles that were formerly covered only by case law or commercial custom. While the Code does not revolutionize the fundamental principles of commercial law, it does represent the greatest single development which has occurred in the commercial law field in America, and its importance increases with each new adoption of the Code.

In this book the effect the Code has had on the various topics discussed is taken into consideration, and the Code is referred to in footnotes as the UCC in the citing of particular sections of the Code relevant to topics covered in the text. The parts of this book devoted to the law of sales and negotiable instruments, Part Three and Part Four, are most affected by the Code.

LEGAL SYSTEMS

In the western world there are two principal legal systems—the civil-law system and the common-law system. The civil-law system is largely derived from Roman law and is found throughout western continental Europe and other parts of the world, especially those areas colonized by continental European countries. For example, in the United States the law of Louisiana is based primarily on the civil law system of France, while in the rest of the United States, settled principally by English colonists, the common-law system prevails.

Many countries of the world have patterned their legal systems after the Roman civil law. In a country with a civil-law system the law is formally codified, meaning that the law is systematically enacted in written form by a legislature. As a result, the term *civil law* is often used as a synonym for statutory law. A civil-law code is comprehensive and serves as the basis for all decisions of the courts in cases brought by individual citizens against one another.

The civil-law codes of today can be traced back to the most famous of the Roman codes, the Code Justinian of the 6th century A.D., which had been preceded several centuries earlier by a more unrefined codification of Roman law, called the Twelve Tables. Other codes were prepared and promulgated during the reigns of the various Roman emperors. The Germanic tribes which overran the Roman Empire also adopted codes of law, and the influence of these codes on present-day civil codes of the world can be seen.

The earliest system of written law was the Code of Hammurabi, so named in honor of its founder, the fabled King of Babylonia. It was promulgated about 2050 B.C. and contained a statement of the existing rules and customs of the land and treated justice as an inherent right of man. In other early societies of the world, codes of law were prepared, and in each case they reflected the economic, political, and social circumstances under which the people lived, and often the codes were closely related to the religion and moral standards of the people.

Common Law

The American legal system is predominantly a common-law system which was transplanted from England. Utilized by most English-speaking countries, common law is variously known also as English, Anglo-Saxon, or Anglo-American law. More specifically, the term *common law* is used to describe case law, often called judge-made law, as distinguished from statutory law. As stated before, the common law is generally described as unwritten law. However, case-precedents actually are not unwritten, they are recorded in the judicial opinions in cases which are decided and reported. These opinions are printed in bound volumes of reports and are referred to by courts, lawyers, students of the law, and other interested persons.

Recognizable courts of law existed in England following the Norman Conquest in 1066. The term *common law* was used for the law developed in the King's Courts by the royal justices from the mass of customary law which had developed in the clan courts of England following the fall of the Roman Empire.

The early history of the common law in England was influenced by the feudal system which involved the granting of land by the king to lords who in turn granted the land to lesser subjects, and the lords performed governmental functions including the holding of court to settle disputes arising under the feudal tenures. The origin of the law of real property in the United States today can be traced in large part to the feudal system established by the Norman kings in England.

In the judicial system of England with the King's Court at its head, the practice of issuing writs providing for certain legal remedies developed, the right to a trial by jury was recognized in certain cases, the doctrine of *stare decisis* became entrenched, formal written pleadings along with established legal procedures developed, a system of trial and appellate courts evolved, and a separation of law and equity occurred. All of these developments in the common-law system had evolved by the time the American colonies were established. While some modification of the English common law was made to adapt it to the needs and circumstances of the new world and further changes have been made in light of many changes occurring in America since its founding, the legal system prevailing in the United States contains most of the basic characteristics of the English common law.

Stare Decisis. The adherence to precedent by courts is summed up in the doctrine of *stare decisis*—"let the decision stand." This principle of judicial policy gives the law stability and enables a person to predict with reasonable certainty the legal effect of a course of action which has been reviewed by an appellate court in a prior decided case. The decisions of the United States Supreme Court establish rules of law which the lower federal courts follow, and within a state the courts adhere generally to the decisions of that state's court of final appeal. Where no analagous local precedents exist, the decisions of courts in other states are sometimes followed or are at least persuasive and will be cited by attorneys as authority for the positions taken by the litigants. The doctrine of *res judicata* is not to be confused with *stare decisis*. Under the doctrine of *res judicata,* once a dispute between the parties has been finally decided by a court, the parties are barred from litigating the same dispute again.

The doctrine of *stare decisis* is not a mechanical formula to be followed in all cases. On occasion a court may refuse to follow an earlier decision if a change in social and economic conditions or the equities of the present case require an opposite result. Also, in a particular case a court may have a choice of precedents or may be able to distinguish the present case from precedent. The ability of a court to depart from precedent in a proper case gives the law flexibility. It has been reported that while the U.S. Supreme Court has generally followed its previous decisions, in at least ninety decisions between 1810 and 1957, it has overruled its own previous determinations.

Equity. The remedies granted by the early common law courts of England were (1) money damages, (2) writ of replevin, and (3) writ of ejectment. The writ of replevin entitled a plaintiff to the return of his personal property withheld wrongfully, and the writ of ejectment was granted for the recovery of possession of real property. These writs are still available today, and money damages remains as the most frequently granted legal remedy. These legal remedies proved to be inadequate in many types of disputes, and as early as the fourteenth century in England the practice developed of petitioning the king for whatever remedy the king felt, in good conscience and equity, should be granted. Later these petitions for special relief were referred to the king's Chancellor, a high churchman who was an important member of the king's Council and who was known as the Keeper of the King's Conscience. Ultimately, a separate court known as the Court of Chancery was established in England to hear equity cases, and equity is now part of the common law of England and the United States, and these courts are presided over by judges drawn from the legal profession.

In the United States several states have separate equity courts on the trial level, but in most states the same court functions as both a law and equity court even though separate legal and equity principles still exist. The procedure in equity cases differs somewhat from that followed in law cases. For example, as a general rule the parties are not entitled to a jury trial although a jury may be used in some types of equity cases. Before a court will grant an equitable remedy, the party seeking it must establish that his legal rights have been invaded by the defendant and that the legal remedy available to him is inadequate. Over the years certain equitable remedies have been identified, and new ones are added from time to time in order to provide justice in new situations. Examples of widely used equitable remedies include specific performance of contracts, injunctions, reformation of contracts, rescission of contracts, accountings, foreclosure of mortgages, and divorces. Some of these remedies will be discussed later in this book as they become pertinent to the areas of law covered.

Law Merchant. The law merchant (from Latin *lex mercatoria*) is a branch of the law once applicable to the affairs of a particular class of individuals, merchants, and subsequently extended in England and in America to commercial transactions generally.

When merchants from various countries gathered at international trade fairs in countries of western continental Europe and England during the Middle Ages to transact business, they established their own informal courts to hear disputes on the basis of the general customs and usages of merchants. These merchants' courts were more like equity courts than the more rigid law courts of England. They operated without formal pleadings or records, decided cases promptly, and the law they applied became known as private international law. By about 1800 the common law courts of England had absorbed the law merchant, and the separate merchants' courts disappeared. While separate merchants' courts have never existed in America, the principles of the law merchant are part of our common law. Many of the principles of our law of contracts, sales, agency, negotiable instruments, partnerships, and other areas of commercial law can be traced to the law merchant.

Court Systems
and Procedure

2

Courts are established to administer justice fairly and impartially in cases brought before them. Courts also play an important role in the development of public policy in the United States. They not only interpret the constitution and legislative acts, but also legalize custom. A court may be presided over by one judge or several, depending upon the provisions of the statute establishing the particular court and the type of proceeding being brought before it. Generally only one judge sits in a case heard by a trial court while an appellate court will, in most cases, consist of several judges. All others who play a role in the operation of a court are called officers of the court. They include the attorneys, clerks, bailiffs, and similar persons. In the performance of its function of administering justice by deciding cases, a court declares and applies the common law and interprets and applies the statutory law in determining the rights and duties of the parties before the court.

In addition to the courts, there are many administrative tribunals and agencies at all levels of government, but especially at the federal level of government. These bodies adjudicate the rights of citizens and thus play a secondary role in the administration of justice. Strictly speaking, these agencies are outside the judicial system. Within limits established in the statutes creating them, the rulings of these agencies are reviewable by the courts.

In the United States there is a federal system of courts, and each state has a separate court system. The judges of the federal courts are appointed by the President, subject to confirmation by the Senate; and, in most instances, the judges have life tenure contingent upon their "good behavior." The pattern in the states is for judges to be elected, but a trend toward appointment of judges with a variety of selection and tenure plans is in evidence.

Jurisdiction of Courts

Any description of a judicial system will be concerned primarily with the jurisdiction of the various courts operating within the system. Jurisdiction refers to the authority of a court to hear and decide cases and involves jurisdiction over the subject matter of a case and over the parties to a case.

Jurisdiction Over Persons. In a typical civil action for money damages or other relief requiring some action on the part of the defendant, called *in personam* cases, the defendant is brought within the jurisdiction of the court by serving him with a summons within the territorial limits of the court, informing him of the suit filed against him in the particular court by the plaintiff. There are a number of "long-arm" state statutes which permit a plaintiff in certain types of *in personam* cases to obtain jurisdiction over a nonresident defendant without serving him with a summons within the state. Various "contacts" within a state are recognized as a basis for its courts to act against an out-of-state defendant. For example, a nonresident motorist involved in an accident in state A and causing injury to X may be brought within the jurisdiction of a court in state A in a suit brought by X, without the nonresident defendant being served with a summons in state A. In such cases the typical procedure is to give notice to the defendant by registered letter. *In personam* cases are to be distinguished from an *in rem* (against the thing) or *quasi in rem* suit. These latter actions permit a judgment to be taken against a defendant's property within the state by merely having the sheriff serve a writ of attachment upon the person who has physical possession of the property and then giving notice to the defendant by a published notice in a newspaper. Such "service by publication" is provided for in a variety of cases where no personal (money) judgment is involved. An *in rem* judgment binds everyone, whereas a *quasi in rem* judgment binds only the actual parties to the suit. The summons and other aspects of legal procedure and pleadings in civil cases are summarized later in this chapter.

Jurisdiction Over Subject Matter. A question concerning the subject matter jurisdiction of a court is answered by turning to those statutes which created the court and govern its operation. Jurisdiction of courts over subject matter may be classified basically as general original, specialized original, limited original, general appellate, specialized appellate, and limited appellate. No court in the United States possesses all these types of jurisdiction. The jurisdiction of one court may overlap the jurisdiction of another. This overlapping jurisdiction of courts is called concurrent jurisdiction. If a particular court is the only one authorized to hear a particular kind of case, its jurisdiction in such cases is said to be exclusive.

A court in which cases are started has original jurisdiction and is called a trial court. The U.S. District Courts are the most important courts with original jurisdiction in the federal court system. A court which hears appeals from the decisions of other courts is an appellate (review) court. The issues of fact between litigants are resolved in the trial court, often with a jury; and on appeal the appellate court simply reviews, without a jury, the record of the trial to determine if material errors were made by the trial court in the various rulings made and procedure followed during the trial. Some courts have original and appellate jurisdiction, but a court's jurisdiction will be primarily original or appellate. For example, the U.S. Supreme Court has appellate jurisdiction and certain narrow original jurisdiction as specified in Article III of the U.S. Constitution, but nearly all of its work during most terms of court is concerned with appeals. Generally the U.S. Supreme Court reviews cases in which some federal constitutional question is involved, such as the constitutionality of a statute. This judicial review of legislation and the actions of the executive branch of the government is a unique characteristic of the American legal system.

A court has either general or specialized jurisdiction. A court with general jurisdiction hears law and equity cases covering a wide range of subject matter and usually possesses both civil and criminal jurisdiction. The U.S. District Courts have this extensive general jurisdiction. Only cases placed within the specialized or limited jurisdiction of other courts to the exclusion of the court of general jurisdiction are outside the latter's jurisdiction. Courts of special or limited jurisdiction are those in which the jurisdiction is either restricted to a special class or to special classes of cases in terms of subject matter; or is limited as to amount involved, with also probably other limitations. Criminal courts are courts with specialized jurisdiction, and a civil court may be restricted to hearing only certain kinds of civil cases and thus will be a court with specialized jurisdiction. The inferior courts with a limited jurisdiction are found on the lowest tier of the judicial hierarchy and usually are not courts of record. They include county courts, municipal courts, small claims courts, justice of the peace courts, minor criminal courts, and similar courts. Appeals from such courts usually involve a trial *de novo* in a higher trial court, which means the entire case is tried again as to questions of fact and law. A court of record is usually designated as such by statute and is characterized by written pleadings, a formal record of all proceedings, and authority in the court to make final disposition of a case, subject to appeal primarily on questions of law to a higher court, if one exists.

FEDERAL COURTS

Federal Court System

On the basis of the authority for their creation originally, the federal courts are classified as (1) constitutional and (2) legislative courts. The three chief constitutional courts are the U.S. District Courts, the U.S. Courts of Appeals, and the U.S. Supreme Court. All three were created under the authority of Article III, the judiciary article of the U.S. Constitution. In its key Section 1, Article III mentions only "one supreme Court," but it goes on to authorize "such inferior Courts as the Congress may from time to time ordain and establish." The District Courts and Courts of Appeals were provided for in the Judiciary Act of 1789. No constitutional courts were added until Congress changed the status of three legislative courts—the U.S. Court of Claims, the U.S. Customs Court, and the U.S. Court of Customs and Patent Appeals—to that of constitutional courts in 1953, 1956, and 1958, respectively.

Congress has established legislative courts under Article I, Section 8, Clause 9 of the U.S. Constitution which grants to it the power "to constitute Tribunals inferior to the supreme Court." If we exclude the former legislative courts named above, the only legislative courts existing at this time are the U.S. Court of Military Appeals and the several Territorial Courts. The Territorial Courts have been created by Congress under its power to ". . . make all needful Rules and Regulations respecting the Territory or other Property belonging to the United States . . ." (Art. IV, Sec. 3, Clause 2, U.S. Constitution). The jurisdiction of the Territorial Courts is similar to that of state and local courts as well as the federal District Courts. While legislative courts are tied into the constitutional appellate judicial structure for certain purposes, they are primarily created to aid in the administration of specified federal statutes.

The U.S. Tax Court is a quasi-judicial agency which is actually more of an adjunct of the Internal Revenue Service, that is, part of the executive branch of the federal government, rather than a court in the true sense. Some persons view the Court of Military Appeals in the same way. It was created in 1950 as part of the revised Uniform Code of Military Justice. Outside the federal system of courts as discussed here, it serves as a final appellate tribunal in court-martial cases arising in the armed services.

Congress has established a great number of administrative tribunals or independent regulatory commissions, such as the Federal Trade Commission, National Labor Relations Board, Federal Power Commission, Federal Communications Commission, Securities and Exchange Commission, and Interstate Commerce Commission. While these bodies issue rulings which determine rights and duties of persons and business firms, they are not true courts. Their rulings may, in most cases, be appealed to the U.S. Court of Appeals.

Federal Courts with General Jurisdiction

U.S. District Courts.   The basic trial courts of the federal court system are called U.S. District Courts. In each state there is at least one U.S. District Court with from one to eighteen judges, the number of courts in each state and judges in each district being established by acts of Congress on the basis of the case workload. Most cases in a District Court are heard by one judge, sitting with a jury unless waived or not allowed in the particular case. Certain cases require a three judge court. In addition to the judges, personnel attached to the District Courts include district attorneys, U.S. Commissioners, marshals, clerks, referees in bankruptcy, probation officers, court reporters, and various clerical assistants. In certain types of cases, usually of an equity nature, the district judge may refer matters to the master in chancery attached to the court, for hearing and a report back of his findings to the judge who will then decide the case.

The U.S. District Courts have general original jurisdiction in a broad variety of civil, equity, and criminal cases, and their decisions are usually appealable to the U.S. Courts of Appeals, although in a few types of cases, an appeal may be taken directly to the U.S. Supreme Court.

¶ The U.S. District Courts have original jurisdiction over:

1] All criminal offenses against the United States.

2] All civil actions arising under the Constitution, laws, or treaties of the United States wherein the matter in controversy exceeds the value or sum of $10,000, exclusive of interest and costs.

3] All civil actions between citizens of different states (diversity of citizenship) or citizens and aliens wherein the matter in controversy exceeds the value or sum of $10,000, exclusive of interest and costs.

4] Admiralty, maritime, and prize cases.

5] All cases under federal statutes relating to bankruptcy, taxes, patents, copyrights, trademarks, and other cases as Congress may validly prescribe by law.

The U.S. District Courts and the state courts of general original jurisdiction have concurrent jurisdiction over the diversity of citizenship cases mentioned in the third class of cases listed above. However, if the plaintiff files such a case in the state court, the defendant may remove it to the U.S. District Court. If the amount claimed does not exceed $10,000, exclusive of interest and costs, or the diversity of citizenship requirement is not met, the state courts have exclusive jurisdiction. Generally, the other groups of cases listed above are within the exclusive jurisdiction of the federal courts, but in cases based on certain statutes not enumerated here, Congress has provided that the federal and state courts shall have concurrent jurisdiction. The

U.S. District Courts also have some authority to review and enforce orders and actions of certain federal administrative agencies and departments.

U.S. Courts of Appeals. Until 1948, the intermediate federal appellate courts were officially called U.S. Circuit Courts of Appeals. Although the word *circuit* has been dropped from the official name of these courts, they are still sometimes referred to as Circuit Courts. The United States is divided into ten circuits and there is a U.S. Court of Appeals, consisting of from three to nine judges, for each circuit plus a U.S. Court of Appeals for the District of Columbia. The Courts of Appeals have no original jurisdiction. They hear appeals from the U.S. District Courts, U.S. Territorial Courts, the U.S. Tax Court, and some District of Columbia Courts. In addition they review and enforce orders of many federal administrative tribunals and agencies.

U.S. Supreme Court. Consisting of a Chief Justice and eight associate justices, the U.S. Supreme Court has both original and appellate jurisdiction, but it exercises the former in only rare instances.

The principal jurisdiction of the Supreme Court is appellate. This appellate jurisdiction has been defined by Congress. As a general rule, appeals to the Supreme Court are a matter of privilege and not a matter of right. Most of the appeals heard by the Supreme Court involve a question concerned with some federal right, usually arising out of the U.S. Constitution. The appellate cases heard by the Supreme Court reach the Court from: (1) the state courts of last resort; (2) the U.S. Courts of Appeals; (3) the U.S. Court of Customs and Patent Appeals; (4) the U.S. District Courts; (5) the U.S. Court of Claims; and (6) the territorial or legislative courts as the laws creating them permit.

The original jurisdiction of the Supreme Court is limited by the Constitution to cases affecting ambassadors, public ministers, and consuls of foreign countries, and, in cases where a state is a party. A recent example of the exercise of the Supreme Court's original jurisdiction is the hearing of the suits between states of the Southwest over water rights.

Federal Courts with Specialized Jurisdiction

U.S. Court of Claims. Created in 1855, this court located in Washington, D.C. has original jurisdiction over cases involving certain claims by individuals against the United States. The District Courts have concurrent jurisdiction with the Court of Claims over general claims against the United States if the amount involved does not exceed $10,000. Decisions of the Court of Claims are subject to Supreme Court review in appropriate cases.

U.S. Customs Court. The present-day version of this court was created in 1926. It has its headquarters in New York, and it holds original jurisdiction over disputes between importers and the federal government arising under the federal statutes providing for duties on imports. Appeals from its decisions go to the Court of Customs and Patent Appeals, although, in a few types of cases, it is possible for an appeal to go directly to the Supreme Court.

U.S. Court of Customs and Patent Appeals. This court was created in 1910 with appellate jurisdiction over custom and tariff cases, and in 1929 its authority to review certain patent and trademark cases was added. The Court is located in Washington, D.C., and its functions are: (1) to hear appeals from decisions of the Customs Court regarding duties levied on goods imported into the United States and the classification of such goods; (2) to review Patent Office decisions on patents and trademarks; and (3) to rule on legal questions arising out of decisions of the Tariff Commission relating to import practices.

STATE COURTS

The judicial systems of the several states vary considerably in structure, jurisdiction, administration, and procedures. However, the state court systems do present a common pattern. Like the federal courts, the establishment of state courts is provided for in constitutional provisions, implemented by statutes, and the state courts can be classified on the basis of the types of jurisdiction they possess, employing the same terms as were used in the discussion of the federal courts.

Generally the state court systems provide for either a three- or four-tier judicial hierarchy. At the bottom of the system the first tier of courts is made up of trial courts with limited jurisdiction. At the next highest level the courts with general original (trial) jurisdiction and courts with important specialized original jurisdiction are found. In a minority of states an intermediate court of appeals is provided for, and it is located between the main trial courts and the court of last resort in the judicial structure. In most states the judicial structure is limited to three tiers with appeals going from the trial courts to an appellate court of last resort.

Limited Jurisdiction Courts

Although the courts at the bottom of a state court system are inferior in many respects to the upper level courts, they often are the only courts many citizens have any direct contact with, and the impression these courts leave with the persons appearing before them plays an important part in shaping the attitude of people towards courts in general. These courts often have their jurisdiction limited as to territory, subject matter, and amount of money involved.

Historically, the most prominent of these courts has been the justice of the peace court, both in England and the United States. This court and its modern counterparts, where it has been replaced, exercise jurisdiction over minor civil and criminal cases. It is not a court of record. In civil cases, contract or tort, its jurisdiction usually extends to claims for money not exceeding some fixed amount, typically a few hundred dollars. Certain types of civil cases, such as those brought to determine title to real estate, are excluded from its jurisdiction. The justice of the peace court usually may try misdemeanor cases, but in felony cases its power is limited to the holding of a preliminary hearing. Other characteristics of these courts include informal pleadings and procedure, trials without juries in most cases, and the right to a new trial in a higher court upon appeal. Over the years there has been some proliferation of inferior courts, with special courts established bearing names which suggest the nature of the cases falling within their jurisdiction. These courts include small claims courts, police courts, mayor's courts, municipal courts, county courts, and traffic courts.

Trial Courts

The state courts of general original jurisdiction are called trial courts, and it is in such courts that the bulk of the judicial legal business is transacted. The trial court with general jurisdiction hears civil (law and equity) cases without any maximum limitation as to the amount involved and hears criminal cases, however serious the crime. These courts hear cases involving a wide variety of subject matter, with only those cases the statutes place within the exclusive original jurisdiction of some other specialized court being excluded. In some states separate civil and criminal trial courts have been established. A few states maintain separate law and equity courts. The courts of general original (trial) jurisdiction are variously designated, in the different states, as courts of common pleas, circuit courts, or superior courts, and in New York, as the supreme court. Under the doctrine of *stare decisis,* the trial courts generally adhere to the rules established by the decisions rendered by the appellate courts of the state in prior cases.

At the trial court level in all states there are courts with specialized jurisdiction. One of the most prominent of these courts is the probate court, designated surrogates' or orphans' court in some states. This court has jurisdiction over the administration of decedents' estates, guardianships, adoptions, and other matters which historically have fallen within its domain.

In many states there are juvenile courts and other courts with jurisdiction restricted to cases involving certain subject matter.

Courts of Appeals

Above the state trial courts are the state courts of intermediate appeal, if such have been established by the state, and at the top of the court system is the court of last resort. The intermediate appellate courts are designated by various names, such as district or circuit courts of appeals or superior courts. These courts usually have some original jurisdiction, but their principal function is appellate. The typical civil action for money damages would not be commenced in this court.

The highest appellate court or court of last resort of a state is variously designated as the court of appeals, the supreme court of errors, the supreme judicial court, or, as in most states, the supreme court. These courts exercise general appellate jurisdiction, but, in addition, most of them have some original jurisdiction, usually confined to issuing prerogative writs, such as habeus corpus, quo warranto, and mandamus. It is this type of original jurisdiction which is also vested in the state courts of intermediate appeal. As reviewing courts, the state supreme courts sit without juries, passing on questions of law raised by the appellant in a particular case. The decisions of such courts, since inception, constitute in the main the common law in force in a particular state. The decisions of the state supreme court may be appealed to the U.S. Supreme Court if a federal question involving the U.S. Constitution, statutes, or treaties is present in the case.

LEGAL PROCEDURE

General Nature

Procedural or adjective law in civil cases is concerned with the legal machinery by which the rights and duties of persons are determined in a proceeding before a court. This branch of the law is within the special domain of the attorney and concerns such things as pleadings, process, evidence, jurisdiction, rulings of judges, trial procedure, appeals, and other aspects of the litigation process. Criminal cases involve similar procedural matters, but the prescribed procedure to be followed in criminal cases differs significantly from that which applies in civil cases. Procedure is governed by statutes in each state and these laws are not uniform. A person interested in the procedure followed in a particular state would need to examine that state's code of civil procedure or similar statutes. However, there is a common pattern of civil procedure which is used in applying the substantive law described in the succeeding chapters of this book. A brief summary of the main procedural aspects of a typical civil action follows.

Pleadings
The pleadings in a law suit consist of all the written statements filed with the clerk of the court by the parties. Functions of the pleadings include the raising of the issues in dispute between the parties, and they provide the basis for the submission of evidence at the trial.

The party who brings a law suit is called the plaintiff, and the party against whom the suit is brought is called the defendant. Once a person in consultation with his attorney has decided he has suffered a legal wrong for which a remedy is available in law or equity, and no alternative to suit remains, the attorney prepares the plaintiff's first pleading, called a declaration (petition or complaint in some jurisdictions) and files it with the clerk of the appropriate court. The declaration sets out all the allegations of fact upon which the plaintiff bases his case, describes the legal theory of the case, concludes with a prayer for relief (usually a judgment for a specified sum of money) and is signed by the plaintiff, or, in some cases, by the plaintiff's attorney. The stating of a cause of action in a declaration is referred to as stating a *prima facie* case.

Notice to the defendant of the filing of the suit and other

information about the suit, including the date by which the defendant must appear and defend, is given by means of a summons which usually must be personally served by the sheriff or other officer on the defendant within the territorial limits of the court's jurisdiction. Summons requirements are highly technical and vary from state to state and often depend upon the nature of the case. As explained at the beginning of this chapter, constructive or substitute service of the summons (notice in a newspaper) is permitted in some types of cases. Of course, a defendant may voluntarily enter his appearance and waive the service of a summons.

Unless the defendant makes an appearance by filing a pleading in response to the declaration by the specified deadline, the plaintiff may take a default judgment against the defendant. This makes it essential that a defendant take the necessary steps to defend a suit against him within the time allowed, if he has any defense to present.

In response to the declaration, the defendant will file an answer, which may be a general denial or a special denial. If the answer is in the form of a general denial, the parties are at issue on all the allegations of fact contained in the plaintiff's declaration. A special denial means that the defendant admits certain facts alleged in the declaration but denies all others, and the issue has been drawn as to those facts. The defendant may file along with his answer a cross-declaration, asking for some kind of affirmative relief.

Instead of simply filing an answer the defendant may first file one or more motions attacking the declaration in its entirety or in part. A motion attacking the sufficiency of the declaration or some other pleading is called a demurrer. The defendant filing a demurrer to the plaintiff's declaration takes the position that even if the facts alleged in the declaration are true, they do not state a cause of action. The court will either sustain or overrule the demurrer. If sustained, the plaintiff usually is permitted to amend his declaration to try to state a cause of action or he may appeal the ruling of the court. If the judge overrules the demurrer, the defendant then files his answer. Further pleadings may be necessary if the parties make further allegations or raise new questions in their exchange of pleadings. When the parties are at issue on all the facts, the case is ready for trial.

The Trial

The procedure followed in civil cases is governed by statutes in each state. These statutes are not uniform. Federal statutes prescribe the trial procedure to be followed in the federal courts. The main features of the trial of a civil case under a typical procedure are described in the following summary.

In law actions the parties are entitled to a jury trial, but in equity cases there is generally no right to a jury. Juries decide questions of fact under instructions of the judge as to the law. Questions of law are ruled upon by the court. After the jury has been selected, the attorneys make opening statements and then the evidence is presented, the plaintiff proceeding first, followed by the defendant. The plaintiff has the burden of proving his case by a preponderance of the evidence in the typical civil case. The defendant may make a motion for a directed verdict (dismissal of the suit) at the conclusion of the plaintiff's evidence. If the plaintiff has not established a *prima facie* case, the motion will be sustained; if the motion is overruled the defendant will proceed to offer his evidence. At the conclusion of the evidence, closing arguments of the attorneys are made to the jury or to the judge alone if the case is being tried without a jury.

After receiving the judge's charge, consisting of statements of the law applicable to the case, the jury will return a verdict for the plaintiff or defendant, and, if it finds for the plaintiff, fix the amount of the verdict if a recovery in money was sought. The court then enters judgment accordingly, unless the judge sustains a motion by the losing party for judgment notwithstanding the verdict. Usually the judge will not set aside the verdict of the jury, but in civil cases he may do so, upon motion by the losing party, if he feels the jury's verdict is a miscarriage of justice. An often cited reason for overruling the jury's verdict is the court's finding that the verdict is against the manifest weight of the evidence. The court's ruling on this motion, as with most other rulings, may be appealed to a higher court. Finally, the losing party may move for a new trial, and, if overruled, appeal the case. In some instances both parties may appeal, neither party being satisfied with the outcome of the case.

ENFORCEMENT OF REMEDIES

Collection of Money Judgment

The usual remedy awarded to the plaintiff in a civil case is that of a judgment for money damages. Failure of the defendant to pay the judgment does not expose him to a fine or imprisonment. However, if the defendant fails to pay the judgment, the plaintiff may seek collection of the amount due on the judgment, plus interest, by obtaining a writ of execution from the clerk of the court that rendered the judgment. A writ of execution directs the sheriff to levy against, seize, and sell at public auction property of the defendant to satisfy the plaintiff's judgment. Execution procedure is governed by state statutes which vary in detail. These statutes typically exempt from levy and execution certain types of property such as household goods of set value, personal effects within limits, a homeplace of comparatively small value, and tools of the debtor's trade.

Other important legal procedures to aid the plaintiff in collecting a money judgment are the writs of attachment and garnishment, and the judgment lien. Attachment involves the seizure of the defendant's property by the sheriff or other officer at the time the suit is commenced so that the attached property can be used to satisfy any judgment rendered in favor of the plaintiff. State statutes specify the grounds for attachment. A typical ground for attachment is the belief of the plaintiff that the defendant is planning to remove his property from the state. Generally the defendant is required to give bond to protect the defendant in the event the plaintiff does not obtain a judgment and the defendant suffers some loss as a result of the wrongful attachment.

A writ of garnishment is used to reach property or other assets of the judgment debtor which are held by third persons. Governed by state statutes, garnishment may be applied against such things as wages or salary, bank accounts, accounts receivable, and goods in storage. The statutes prescribe the amount of wages or salary which is exempt from garnishment.

Unsatisfied judgments may become a lien against any real property of the defendant under the law of many states.

Each state has a Statute of Limitations which ultimately outlaws the unpaid judgment. A judgment debtor may escape paying the judgment by having it discharged in bankruptcy, if it is a type of judgment the bankruptcy law recognizes as dischargeable.

Enforcement of Equitable Remedy

If a court grants an equitable remedy and the party against whom the court order has been issued fails to comply with the order, the court may punish the party for contempt of court. In such cases the court may impose a fine, jail sentence, or such other penalty as the court within its sound discretion deems appropriate.

ARBITRATION

Arbitration is the submission of a disputed matter to a selected person or persons for determination instead of resorting to litigation in the courts. The steady increase in the use of arbitration, especially in commercial disputes, is due to the belief that arbitration is (1) speedier, (2) less costly, (3) free from technical rules of evidence and court-room procedure, (4) able to utilize businessmen experts to decide the dispute, rather than a jury that is unfamiliar with the complex business situation involved, and (5) more likely to preserve amicable relations between the disputants. Some persons feel that arbitration has certain disadvantages such as (1) its failure to operate according to time-proven rules of legal procedure, (2) its sacrifice of fair and orderly adjudication for quick and informal decisions, (3) its overuse of the compromise device rather than a determination of the right and just decision based on reason and merit, and (4) the loss of various legal remedies and the opportunity of appeal from the arbitrator's award.

Resort to arbitration may occur as the result of a clause written into a contract that the parties will arbitrate all controversies that may arise between them relating to the contract or if no such clause was inserted into the contract, the parties may enter into a written agreement to submit to arbitration a specific controversy that has arisen. In many trades and industries the parties use standardized contracts, that is, printed contracts employed generally in that industry or trade, and almost always these standardized contracts contain an arbitration clause.

Practically all of the states have enacted arbitration statutes. The Federal Arbitration Law was enacted in 1925 to govern maritime and interstate commerce disputes. The New York statute served as a pattern for arbitration statutes in many states. Under some state statutes an agreement to submit an existing dispute to arbitration (called a *submission*) is irrevocable, but an agreement to submit future disputes to arbitration (called a *contract*) is revocable. But in New York and a number of important commercial states both types of arbitration agreements are irrevocable if in writing, and the court must specifically enforce the agreement if it is asked to do so.

Nearly all states have preserved common-law arbitration for those parties who wish to use it. Arbitration agreements which fail to meet the requirements of the arbitration statute of a state are treated as common-law arbitrations. Under common-law arbitration either party can revoke his agreement to arbitrate, and an award of arbitration can be enforced legally only by suit.

The American Arbitration Association performs an important service by making available competent arbitrators who conduct hearings and render awards in accordance with prescribed rules of procedure. Many industries maintain arbitration tribunals for settling controversies between merchants in that particular industry and arbitration facilities are provided by trade associations or similar groups.

Introduction

3

BASIC CONTRACT TERMINOLOGY

Definition and Nature

A contract is an enforceable agreement between two or more parties. Society imposes upon its members by means of its legal system a great number of duties irrespective of any real intention on the part of the individual to assume such duties. Examples of this have been seen in the law of torts. By contrast, contractual obligations are, for the most part, voluntarily assumed, the legal system merely providing the means by which the rights and duties created by the contracting parties are enforced.

Freedom to contract and the recognition by society of certain agreements as legally binding are indispensable to the efficient functioning of business enterprises in relation to the vast variety of commercial transactions in which they engage. However, it is not merely the business organization which makes use of the principles of contract law. Every individual engages to some extent almost daily in the making of contracts, whether it involves something as commonplace as a purchase of an article of merchandise from a variety store or something as important as the making of a contract with a builder for the construction of a home. The boundaries of the law of contracts are virtually limitless as its principles pervade almost every field of law. This interrelationship between contract law and other branches of law becomes evident in the other parts of this book.

The law distinguishes between those promises or agreements which are contractual, and therefore create legal obligations, from promises or agreements which create no such obligations. For example, mere social promises do not create any legal obligations. Certain elements are recognized by the courts as essential to the formation of a contract.

¶ The essential elements of a contract are as follows:

1] mutual assent (offer and acceptance)
2] consideration
3] competent parties
4] legal object

In addition, it is to be pointed out that while generally contracts are not required to be in writing, certain classes of contracts must be in writing. These special classes of contracts are described in Chapter 9. A contract which satisfies all the requirements for enforceability by a court is termed a valid contract.

The terms employed in the law of contracts must be carefully analyzed in relation to their legal meaning if a person is to understand the various principles or rules of law and underlying reasons which govern the rights and duties of parties to contracts. In this chapter many of the basic terms of contract law are defined and explained.

Classification of Contracts

Bilateral and Unilateral. A bilateral contract is one in which there is a mutual exchange of promises. Most business contracts are of this kind. A unilateral contract is one in which there is a promise on one side in exchange for an act on the other side. The most frequent example given of a unilateral contract is a promise of a reward for the return of lost property or the cap-

ture of a criminal. A contract may be both bilateral and unilateral in that the consideration on one or both sides may consist partly of promises and partly of acts.

Void, Voidable, and Unenforceable.   A void contract is a
nullity and generally creates no legal obligations. This term is
often used to describe certain illegal contracts. A contract made
by a person adjudged insane is void. In Chapter 8 on illegality
it will be seen that if the circumstances require it a court may
grant some relief, that is, recognize some obligations, even
though the illegal contract is referred to as void. A voidable
contract is one which can be avoided at the election of a party.
Examples of grounds for avoiding a contract include infancy,
insanity, fraud or misrepresentation, duress, mistake, and some
kinds of illegality. Certain contracts are neither void or voidable,
but, nevertheless, are not enforceable by one or both parties.
The law may not provide a remedy for enforcing a certain contract; some prerequisite for proving the contract may not have
been satisfied; or the remedy may have expired. An example
of the first type is certain contracts with a government. The
second type includes contracts not in writing as required by
the Statute of Frauds. The third type includes a contract against
which the period of a statute of limitations has run.

Formal and Informal.   Formal contracts are (1) those under
seal; (2) negotiable instruments; and (3) recognizances. At
one time under the common law only contracts in writing and
under seal were binding. The importance of the seal in contracts has largely disappeared. A recognizance is a special type
of contract consisting of an obligation entered into in court and
with certain formalities. Negotiable instruments, an extremely
important type of formal contract today, are dealt with at length
in Part Four of this book. Informal contracts, sometimes called
simple contracts, include all contracts falling outside the definition of formal contracts above. They may be either oral, written,
or implied. Most contracts are of the informal type.

Executory and Executed.   To the extent the obligations

called for in a contract have not been performed, the contract is executory. Conversely, to the extent a contract has been performed, it is executed. Once full performance has occurred, the contract is fully executed, or, strictly speaking, has ceased to exist.

Express and Implied Contracts

Express Contracts. An express contract is one entered into on the basis of the spoken or written words of the parties manifesting a mutual intention to contract. Implied contracts are classified as either implied in fact contracts or implied in law contracts. The implied in law contract is also referred to as a quasi contract or constructive contract.

Implied In Fact Contracts. An implied in fact contract is one inferred from the circumstances or acts of the parties. These indicia of an intention to contract may exist in combination with the words of the parties, where the words alone would be insufficient to create an express contract.

There is no generic difference between an express contract and one implied from the acts of the parties; both are true contracts and rest upon the mutual assent of the parties along with the other essential elements of a contract.

Generally when one person requests a stranger to render services without any express agreement to pay for such services, a promise to pay the reasonable value of such services is implied. The resulting contract in such a case would be an implied in fact contract. The circumstances and relationship of the parties must not suggest that the parties intended that the services were to be rendered gratuitously, as is generally the case where close relatives render services for one another.

Quasi Contracts. A quasi contract is not the result of a manifestation by the parties of an intention to create a contract, express or implied, but the law creates the contract in a proper case in order to prevent one party from enjoying benefits which in equity and good conscience he is not entitled to retain without paying some other party for them. Since no true contract exists, the law uses the term quasi contract, or contract implied in law, to describe what it has created by fiction.

The quasi-contract doctrine is designed to prevent the unjust enrichment of one party at the expense of another. This doctrine has been used in a great variety of situations, and new occasions for its use arise as justice requires. The doctrine will not be used to enlarge upon the obligations created by an actual contract, express or implied, nor is it available as a basis for recovery for benefits voluntarily conferred on another without his knowledge or consent or under circumstances indicating the benefits are a gift.

A court permitting a remedy on the quasi-contract theory will allow the plaintiff a money judgment for an amount equivalent to the unjust enrichment of the defendant. This measure of damages differs from that applied in true contract cases where the plaintiff will, as a general rule, be awarded a judgment for that amount of money which is necessary to place him in substantially the same position he would have been in had the contract been performed.

An example of a quasi contract is the case in which a payment is made under an unenforceable contract, as where a buyer has paid $1,000 under an oral agreement to buy real estate, and the seller refuses to perform and cannot be compelled to do so because the contract is not in writing as required by the Statute of Frauds. The buyer can recover his payment under the theory of quasi contract.

Mutual Assent:
Offer and Acceptance

4

INTRODUCTION

The first essential element of a contract is an agreement between the parties. This mutual assent, defined as "a meeting of the minds," is usually expressed by an offer and acceptance. It is not necessary that the parties use the words offer and acceptance in order to create a contract. The test for mutual assent to a contract is whether the words and acts of the parties along with the surrounding circumstances manifest to a "reasonable man" an apparent intention to create a legal obligation. A person's intention is determined by courts from what he says and does in relation to the surrounding circumstances, not what he secretly or actually intends. This is the so-called "objective theory" of manifestation of mutual assent as opposed to the "subjective theory."

Promissory language does not under all circumstances manifest an intent to contract. Due to the setting in which a party speaks, his statement may be made in jest, as an explosion of wrath, or for some other apparent reason which rules out any intention to make an offer. For example, services rendered by

45

members of a family for one another are presumed to be gratuitous unless it is clearly manifested by the parties that compensation for the services is intended.

An offer is a proposal by one person to enter into a legal relation with another. The one who makes the offer is called the offeror; the one to whom the offer is made is called the offeree. The offeror indicates what it is he is promising and at the same time describes what he requires in return from the offeree. An acceptance by the offeree of the offer completes the manifestation of assent.

REQUIREMENTS OF AN OFFER

An offer must be (1) made with an intention to contract as explained in the introduction above; (2) more than mere preliminary negotiation; (3) definite, reasonably certain, and complete; and (4) communicated by the offeror to the offeree.

Preliminary Negotiations

A series of conversations, letters, bargaining sessions or other forms of communications frequently take place between parties before a positive offer is made. These exchanges may at one point constitute only dickering or preliminary negotiation with no offer having yet been made.

Advertisements. Advertisements are generally interpreted as invitations to make offers rather than offers. Catalogues, circulars, display advertisements in newspapers, merchandise displays in stores, and similar descriptions of merchandise for sale are usually classified as mere invitations. However, it has been held by a court that a newspaper advertisement containing a complete description, including price, of certain merchandise for sale at a clearance sale to be held at a stated time and place followed by the words "first come, first served," constituted an offer. The test of whether an advertisement addressed to the general public is an offer is whether its contents show that some performance was promised in positive terms in return for something requested. If an advertisement is clear, definite, and explicit, and leaves nothing open for negotiation, it is an offer, acceptance of which will create a contract.

An advertisement of a reward for the return of lost property or the capture of a criminal is viewed as an offer for a unilateral contract. In the typical reward offer, the complete terms of the bargain are described in the advertisement and the nature of the offer limits the number who will be able to accept such an offer. It is the lack of this limitation on the number of persons who could accept the proposal that prevents the ordinary advertisement of goods for sale from constituting an offer. It is to be noted that in the clearance sale case described above this difficulty is overcome by the "first come, first served" provision in the newspaper advertisement.

When a Writing Is Contemplated.   There is some confusion over whether a contract is created prior to the preparation and signing of a writing in cases where such a signed writing is contemplated by the parties. Generally it is held that a contract can come into existence prior to the execution of the writing. But where it is the intention of the parties that there shall be no contract until the agreement is reduced to writing, no contract exists until the writing is executed. The test is one of intention to be bound, objectively determined. This intention is reflected by the oral and written statements of the parties, their actions, custom or trade usage, nature of the bargain, course of dealing, and all the surrounding circumstances. Courts have sometimes found that preliminary contracts of insurance have been made orally or in informal writings even though it was apparent that the parties would replace the preliminary contracts with the usual written policies. A party who intends that no obligation is to exist until a writing is signed by the parties should express this throughout the negotiations so as to remove any doubt about the legal effect of the bargaining.

Sufficiency of Terms

The offer must be sufficiently complete and definite as to all the material terms of the bargain to enable the court to determine the intention of the parties and to fix the rights and duties of the parties to the contract. Material terms include such matters as names of the parties, subject matter, price, quantity, time and place for performance, and similarly important items. In some instances a particular unexpressed material term may be supplied by trade usage or a course of dealing, that is, a customary practice prevailing in the trade or between the parties on the basis of past dealings. Omission of minor or immaterial terms from an offer will not affect its validity.

It is possible for a party to recover in quasi contract in cases where the terms of the bargain made by the parties are too uncertain and incomplete to permit recovery on an ordinary contract. In such cases the plaintiff must show that the defendant has been unjustly enriched at the expense of the plaintiff, and the plaintiff's judgment would be for the reasonable value of the benefit received by the defendant, not for the amount called for in the alleged contract.

Certainty in Contracts for the Sale of Goods.   The Uniform Commercial Code relaxes the certainty requirement in contracts for the sale of goods. See Chapter 13, page 145.

Communication of Offer

An offer is not effective until received by the offeree from the offeror or his agent. Only after such communication of the offer is an acceptance by the offeree possible. Mere assent to terms identical with those of an offer is not enough to create a contract. There must be assent to the offer. Therefore, the crossing in the mail of letters containing identical propositions will not satisfy the mutual assent requirement. Of course, one of the parties may accept the offer after receipt of the letter addressed to him. Until a letter containing an offer has been received, the offer does not become effective.

The communication of the offer requirement may be waived if the offeree's actions manifest an assent so as to deceive the offeror into the reasonable belief that his offer has been accepted. This rule is illustrated in a case where the offeree signs a contract without reading it and no misconduct by the offeror is present. In such cases the offeree cannot escape his obligations under the contract by establishing that the terms of the offer were not communicated to him.

Reward Offers. Most courts follow the communication rule in holding that where an offer of a reward has been published, one who performs the acts requested in ignorance of the existence of the offer is not entitled to recover the promised reward. Some courts do not take this view even though it is not possible to find any contractual intent by the person who renders the requested service without knowledge of the offer. These courts take the position that the offeror has received what he requested and therefore he should be required to pay. Some courts distinguish between a private reward offer and one made by the government for the capture and conviction of a criminal. In the latter case, the court may not require knowledge of the reward offer, basing its view on public policy and the notion that the reward is intended as a bounty paid by the government rather than a contractual obligation.

Tickets, Claim Checks, Etc. Tickets, parking lot checks, baggage checks, signs, invoices, bills of lading, warehouse receipts, and similar printed materials may contain, sometimes in fine print, the terms of an offer. These terms generally attempt to limit the liability of the offeror. Such an offer is not effective unless communicated to the offeree. Each case in which communication of the offer is an issue must be decided on its own facts. If the offeree actually reads the writing he receives, he is clearly bound in accordance with its terms. Most courts hold that the offeree is bound by the terms of any instrument purporting to be a contract, if he accepts it, even though he doesn't read it. The law takes the view that the offeree is under a duty to read an instrument which he knows or should know is a contract. In cases involving claim checks, such as those received at parking lots, repair shops or checkrooms, most courts have viewed such writings as nothing more than a means of identifying the holder's property which he as a bailor has placed with the bailee. Under this view the attention of the bailor must be drawn to the terms of the bailment as printed in the claim check or they will not be part of the contract between the parties. Tickets of admission to places of amusement or as evidence of a contract for transportation present a similar problem of communication. However, in such cases the party receiving the ticket is more likely to be aware of the fact that the ticket contains printed matter defining his rights and the other party's duties. The crucial question in such cases is what a reasonable man familiar with the circumstances would be justified in believing as to the nature of the writing received from the bailee.

AUCTIONS

In an ordinary auction sale, the people present at the sale make offers in the form of bids. The acceptance of such offers, resulting in a sale contract, is made by the fall of the auctioneer's hammer and the auctioneer saying "sold" in response to the highest bid. The auctioneer acting for the seller invites offers or bids from those present and is free to accept or reject the bids, unless the auction has been advertised to be "absolute" or "without reserve," in which case the auctioneer cannot withdraw the property after the bidding has commenced. Until the auctioneer indicates acceptance of a bid, a bidder may withdraw his bid.

Uniform Commercial Code
Under the Code the auctioneer in his discretion may reopen the bidding or declare the goods sold when a bid is made while the hammer is falling. The Code explains when an auction is with

or without reserve and the requirements entitling an owner to bid are set forth.[1]

BID SOLICITATIONS

Certain types of contracts are entered into on the basis of bids. Construction contracts are a common example. An advertisement for bids is viewed as an invitation to make offers. The bidders are the offerors and the party receiving the bids may accept or reject any or all the bids unless the advertisement for bids states that the contract will be let to the lowest bidder without reservation.

Governmental units such as cities, etc. are generally required by statute to solicit bids for contracts calling for certain work or materials, valued in excess of some dollar amount. The governing statute usually requires that the contract be awarded to the lowest and best bidder unless the governmental unit rejects all the bids. The pertinent statutes and their interpretation by the courts should be examined if a person plans to submit a bid in response to an advertisement by a governmental unit.

DURATION AND TERMINATION OF OFFER

¶ An offer that has been duly communicated continues in effect until it is accepted or terminates as a result of one of the following:

1] revocation by the offeror
2] terms in the offer
3] lapse of a reasonable time
4] rejection or counter-offer by the offeree
5] destruction of subject matter
6] subsequent illegality

---

[1] UCC Sec. 2-328.

7] death or insanity of either party
8] bankruptcy

Revocation

In the absence of consideration, or an offer under seal in states which have not abolished the common-law effect of the seal, an offer may be withdrawn at any time before acceptance. Courts have applied this rule even though the offeror states in his offer that it will remain open for a specified time. If the offeree furnishes consideration, often a payment of money, for the offeror's promise to keep the offer open, the offeree has a contract to keep the offer open. This type of contract, usually referred to as an option, makes the offer irrevocable for the option period.

Uniform Commercial Code Exception. For an important Code exception to the technical rule permitting an offeror to revoke his offer despite his promise to keep it open, see Chapter 13, page 144 relative to firm offers to sell goods.

Time When Revocation Is Effective. Generally a revocation is not effective until it has been received from the offeror by the offeree. However, it has been held that the knowledge on the part of an offeree that land which had been offered to him for sale had later been sold to someone else prevented him from making an effectual acceptance of the offer. Under this view it is possible for an offeree to be bound by a revocation communicated to him indirectly. An acceptance prior to a communicated revocation creates a contract.

Revocation of Public Offers. Public offers can be revoked by giving the same publicity to the revocation as was given to the original offer. In such cases the revocation is binding against the entire public, and thereafter an attempt to accept is ineffective, even if the party attempting to accept did not have actual knowledge of the revocation.

Revocation of Unilateral Offers. The unfairness of permitting an offeror to revoke his offer for a unilateral contract is apparent where the offeree has nearly completed performance of the requested acts at the time of the offeror's revocation. To avoid the hardship resulting from the application of the general rule permitting revocation at any time prior to acceptance, a court may treat the contract as bilateral or on some other theory deny the offeror the right to revoke. In any event the offeree should be able to recover in quasi contract where the offeree's part performance is beneficial to the offeror.

Terms in Offer

An offer may expressly provide for termination of the offer at a stated time or otherwise describe the time for acceptance.

If the offeror uses words of indefinite meaning or is ambiguous in stating the time for acceptance, the test for resolving the uncertainty is the objective one of the reasonable interpretation of a disinterested third person familiar with all the surrounding circumstances. For example, an offer to be accepted by return mail would not be interpreted literally. The offer could be accepted by a letter sent out the same day or even the following day where the offer was received at the close of the day, and further, the offeree could use any method of communication provided his acceptance arrived as soon as return mail would reach the offeror. What the offeror is really seeking in such cases is promptness by the offeree in accepting the offer.

A case of ambiguity arises where the offeror states a time period, such as ten days, within which the offeree may accept, but the offeror fails to state the date from which the time lapse is to be calculated. It has been argued that in view of the rule that an offer is not effective until communicated, the ten days does not begin to run until receipt of the offer. The contrary argument is that the offeror set up the time limitation for his own benefit; therefore, the ambiguity should be resolved in favor of the offeror. Under this view the time begins to run from the date the offer was written. There are cases following each of these views. The second view would appear to be a more reasonable inference of the offeror's intention, unless some contrary manifestation is present.

Lapse of A Reasonable Time

If the offer contains no terms fixing a time within which acceptance must be made, the offer terminates on the lapse of a reasonable time. What constitutes a reasonable time in a particular case is determined on the basis of such things as the nature of the offer, terms of the offer, distance between the parties, method of communication used by the offeror, trade usage or business customs between the parties, and all the surrounding circumstances. Generally, offers made in conversation terminate when the parties depart unless a contrary intention appears.

Ordinarily an offeree will not be permitted to withhold his acceptance until he has seen that risk of loss in the object of the agreement has passed. Therefore, offers to sell property which fluctuates rapidly in price or is perishable remain open a short time. On this basis an offer to buy or sell real estate remains in effect longer than an offer to buy or sell personal property, and reward offers may remain open for several years. For example, an offer of a reward for the conviction of a criminal has been viewed by a court as remaining open until the statute of limitations bars conviction.

Rejection

An offeree terminates an offer by refusing to accept it. Once the offer has been rejected it ceases to exist and cannot thereafter be accepted. However, if after an offeree has rejected an offer he communicates to the offeror what purports to be an acceptance of the rejected offer, the communication is in legal effect an offer which the original offeror, who has now become an offeree, is free to accept or reject as he wishes. Similarly, a counter-offer is a rejection, terminating the original offeror's offer and the counter-offer is also an offer which the original offeror may accept or reject.

The offeree's rejection may be a flat rejection or in the form of a counter-offer or a conditional acceptance. It is simply a matter of whether the offeree has communicated to the offeror, by words or acts, an intention not to accept the offer. A rejection does not terminate an offer until it is received by the offeror. By a careful choice of words an offeree may make an inquiry about the terms of an offer or make statements of equivocation, even a counter-offer, without rejecting the offer. For example, it has been held that a seller's reply to a buyer's purchase order containing a statement that "formal confirmation" would be sent as soon as it received confirmation from its supplier did not constitute a rejection of the offer contained in the purchase order.

Effect of Uniform Commercial Code. See Chapter 13, page 146 for a description of the Code provisions relating to conditional acceptance of offers to sell goods which are not to be viewed as rejections.

DESTRUCTION OF SUBJECT MATTER; ILLEGALITY; DEATH OR INSANITY; BANKRUPTCY

An offer may be terminated by the occurrence of an event outside the control of the parties. This kind of termination results from operation of law. If the subject matter or something essential to the performance of a proposed contract is destroyed without knowledge or fault of either party, the offer is automatically terminated by operation of law. Similarly a change in the law making illegal the performance called for in a proposed contract terminates the offer.

Death or insanity of the offeror or offeree before acceptance will terminate the offer. Bankruptcy of either party terminates an offer.

Notice of the happening of the event which terminates an offer by operation of law is not necessary in order for the termination to take effect.

ACCEPTANCE

General Requirements

The requirements for a valid acceptance are similar to those for an offer. Communication of an offer as a condition precedent to acceptance has been discussed in this chapter. The person to whom an offer is made must accept the offer if a contract is to result between the parties. Only the person to whom an offer is made can accept it. Offers, unlike many contract rights, are not assignable by the offeree to a third person without the consent of the offeror. The assignment of contract rights is discussed in Chapter 10.

Except for certain contracts required by the Statute of Frauds to be in writing, the acceptance of a contract need be in no particular form, and may be oral or may be implied from the acts of the offeree or other circumstances. The question of whether the parties are bound by an oral agreement where it is clear that they plan to prepare and sign a writing later has already been dealt with in this chapter. If an offeree has received an offer for a unilateral contract, he must perform the acts requested by the offeror in order to accept the offer. An offer for a bilateral contract is accepted by the offeree making the requested promise. The act must be performed or the promise made with the intention of accepting the offer. The offeree's intention is determined in the same manner as the intention of the offeror is determined. The test applied is that of what a reasonable man familiar with the circumstances would be justified in concluding concerning the intention of the offeree.

The acceptance by the offeree must be in strict compliance with all the material terms of the offer, and the acceptance must be communicated to the offeror.

It has been previously stated that a counter-offer or conditional acceptance is treated as a rejection which terminates the offer. Once a rejection has been received by the offeror, no subsequent acceptance by the offeree is possible. A counter-offer, of course, may be accepted by the original offeror, in which event a contract results.

Silence as Acceptance

Generally, mere silence on the part of the offeree does not amount to acceptance. For example, this rule applies to an offer in which the offeror states: "If I do not hear from you within 30 days, I will assume you have accepted this offer." Unordered merchandise is sometimes mailed to an addressee with an accompanying sales letter containing such language. In such cases the addressee's failure to reply to the offer does not create a contract unless previous dealings or other circumstances raise a duty upon the part of the offeree to reply or unless it can be established that the offeree remained silent with the intent to accept. In any case the offeree should not use the unordered merchandise if he has no intention of accepting the offer. Use of the article will ordinarily be construed as acceptance. However, the person receiving such unordered merchandise is under no duty to return it at his expense and may make a reasonable charge for its storage until claimed by the owner. He may simply refuse to receive such material from the post office or shipper.

Unordered merchandise cases are to be distinguished from those cases involving offerees who receive books, phonograph records, or similar articles from an offeror with whom the offeree has made a prior contract, often involving a club membership, calling for such merchandise to be sent to the offeree on a refusal basis. The book or record club type of contract usually creates a duty on the part of the member to take certain action to reject the offered merchandise or his silence will constitute acceptance. An authorization by an offeree to treat his silence as assent is usually present in such cases.

It has been held by a court that a failure of an insurance company to reject a life insurance policy application with reasonable promptness constituted acceptance of the application.

The silent acceptance of personal services may result in a contractual liability to pay the reasonable value of such services unless the relationship of the parties or other circumstances rule out any contractual intent.

COMMUNICATION OF ACCEPTANCE

General Requirements

If an offeror clearly states that the offeree must comply with certain instructions relating to the time, place, and method of communicating the acceptance, the offeree must comply fully with such stipulations if he wishes to accept. Any departure from such mandatory terms of the offer ordinarily constitutes a counter-offer. Most offers do not stipulate in detail the acceptance procedure the offeree must follow.

If an offeror merely suggests, expressly or impliedly, an acceptance procedure, the offeree may use a different procedure, provided his acceptance is delivered to the offeror before the offer terminates. If the offeror says nothing about the time, place, or method of communicating the acceptance, the offeree is free to accept within a reasonable time, at any place, and by any method of communication, but, again, the acceptance must reach the offeror before the offer terminates.

Unilateral Contract

In an offer for a unilateral contract the offeror is requesting the offeree to perform an act and, as a general rule, the acceptance is effective and the offeror is bound by the contract the moment the offeree performs the act, regardless of whether or not notice of the performance is given to the offeror. Usually an offeror of a unilateral contract learns of the performance of the requested act. If the nature of the requested act is such that the offeror would not be expected to learn of its performance, the offeree is under a duty to notify the offeror of the performance in order for the acceptance to be effective. The usual example given of this exceptional type of unilateral contract is the contract of guaranty. For example, A in New York, asks

B, in Chicago, to loan $1,000 to C, and A promises B that he will guarantee payment by C. A does not become liable on his promise to B unless A is given notice that the loan has been made.

Bilateral Contract

Promises are exchanged in a bilateral contract. The offeree must communicate his acceptance promise to the offeror in order to create a contract. Face-to-face or telephone transactions pose no problem as the offer and acceptance are spoken and heard almost simultaneously. But where the various other agencies of communication are used, such as the mails or telegraph, a time lag between placing of the message with the agency and the delivery of it necessarily occurs. In addition, there is the risk that the acceptance message will be lost or missent by the agency of communication and never reach the offeror. The offeror may expressly provide that the acceptance will not be effective until actually received by him at a stated time and place. However, most offers do not contain such a provision. Courts have developed rules which attempt to cope with the problems mentioned.

The general rule provides that an acceptance is effective and a contract arises when the acceptance is placed with the agency of communication, provided the offeree uses the means of communication authorized by the offeror. Therefore, while acceptances can be effective when sent, offers, revocations, and rejections are not effective until received. If the offer is silent as to what means of communication the offeree is to use in communicating his acceptance, the authorized agency is the one used by the offeror unless a contrary trade usage is present. In such a case the offeror has made the agency of communication his agent for the purpose of transmitting the offer and acceptance and, therefore, must bear the risk that the messages may be mishandled. For example, where the offeror sends his offer by letter and nothing is said as to how the answer is to be sent, authorization to communicate the acceptance by mail is implied. Where acceptance by mail is authorized, the contract is created at the moment the offeree places his properly addressed and postage-prepaid acceptance letter with the offeror's agent, the post office. If the letter is never received by the offeror, the contract exists nevertheless. The offeree has the burden of proving that the letter was mailed and he must establish the time of mailing where this is relevant as in a case where the offeror alleges revocation or some other event terminated the offer before acceptance. The offeree may find it prudent to use registered or certified mail for his acceptance letter.

If an acceptance is communicated by an unauthorized agency, courts have held it is not effective until received and is effective only if received within the time an acceptance by the authorized agency would have been received in the ordinary course.

Uniform Commercial Code
The modern view taken by some courts is to allow the offeree to close a contract by acceptance through any reasonable or customary mode of communication on the ground that the offeror impliedly permits or authorizes it. Section 2-206 of the Uniform Commercial Code adopts this view in relation to contracts between merchants for the sale of goods.

Unreal Consent

5

The validity of a contract depends upon the consent of the parties being voluntary and real. An agreement may on the surface appear to be a valid contract, but a close scrutiny of all the circumstances surrounding the formation of the agreement may reveal that the apparent assent of a party was not voluntary or genuine.

¶ Apparent consent may be unreal when it would not have been given but for the existence of any of the following:

1] Mistake
2] Fraud
3] Misrepresentation
4] Duress
5] Undue influence

The effect of any one of these interferences with a party's assent to a contract is to render the contract void or at leas voidable at the election of the party who was the victim of such a circumstance, provided he acts seasonably. The usual remedy granted in such cases is rescission which results in restoring the parties to their positions prior to the making of the contract. Other remedies may be available depending on the circumstances.

Unconscionability. The Uniform Commercial Code provides

that any unconscionable clause found in a contract for the sale
of goods will not be enforced. See Chapter 13, page 148 for a
discussion of the doctrine of unconscionability as it relates to
sales contracts.

MISTAKE

Mutual Mistake

Mistake is defined as an erroneous mental conception which
influences a person to act or to omit to act. If a mistake is
made by both parties to a contract, such a mistake is referred
to as mutual. Generally, courts will grant relief from a mutual
mistake if it is material, unintentional, free from negligence,
and no innocent third party will be prejudiced by granting the
relief. However, mutual mistake as to the quality of the subject
matter of a sale contract will not ordinarily affect the validity
of a contract. Courts will not grant relief merely because a
contract turns out to be unprofitable, burdensome, or simply
a bad bargain.

Common mutual mistake cases include mistake as to (1) the
existence of the subject matter; (2) the identity of the subject
matter; and (3) the quality of the subject matter. To illustrate
the first type of mutual mistake case, assume A sells B a horse,
but unknown to either party the horse had died before the contract was made. The contract is void because there is no subject matter upon which the minds of the parties could agree.
The second mutual mistake case is illustrated where A agrees
to sell B a farm called the Smith place located in Jackson
County. There are two farms in Jackson County generally referred to as the Smith place, the seller having in mind the one
Smith place and the buyer the other. No contract exists if
neither party was at fault. The third case is illustrated where
A sells B an old coin for a small sum, both parties admitting
they have no knowledge of the coin's true value. The coin turns
out to have great value. The contract is binding. Neither party

knew the true value of the coin, and each had an opportunity to ascertain the value before the contract was made.

Reformation of Written Instruments. A court of equity will grant the remedy of reformation to correct a written instrument which, through mistake or oversight of the parties, does not express the intention of the parties.

Unilateral Mistake

A mistake made by one party to a contract alone is a unilateral mistake. As a general rule, a unilateral mistake as to the subject matter, terms, or effect of a contract does not affect the validity of a contract unless the one party knows of the mistake of the other party and takes unfair advantage of the mistaken party. For example, A submits to B an offer to do some construction work for $5,000. B accepts the offer. Unknown to B, there was a $500 cost item omitted from A's offer. The contract is binding.

A unilateral mistake known to the other party and taken advantage of by him may enable the mistaken party to avoid the contract. However, if the opportunity of knowledge is equally open to both parties, one is not bound to reveal to the other what he has by greater care discovered. To illustrate, if A sells his land to B who knows that valuable minerals are beneath the surface of the land, the contract is ordinarily binding, even though A is unaware of the minerals and B knows this. B is not required to disclose what A has had an equal or better opportunity to discover, but B must not by any word or trick mislead A.

As indicated in the preceding illustration, if one party to a contract designedly causes the mistake of the other by willful misstatement or by trick or sometimes by silence where a duty to speak exists, this may make the contract voidable on the ground of fraud. Courts will grant relief where hardship amounting to injustice would result if relief were denied. This is particularly true if the position of the parties has changed in such a way that they cannot be restored to their original positions.

Where by mistake of fact, one pays another money that he does not owe, he may recover it back. But if a contract is made, or money paid, under a mutual or unilateral mistake as to the law of the state where the contract is made, such contract is binding, for ignorance of the law does not excuse the mistake. Everyone is presumed to know the law. This rule is not applied to hold one responsible for knowing the law of another state or foreign country.

FRAUD AND MISREPRESENTATION

Elements

The essential elements of fraud are: (1) There must be misrepresentation or concealment of a material fact. (2) The misrepresentation must be made with knowledge of its falsity or made with reckless disregard as to whether it is true or false. (3) The misrepresentation must be made with the intent of misleading the other party into relying upon it as true. (4) The other party must actually and reasonably rely upon the misrepresentation as true. (5) Injury to the other party must result from such reliance.

Courts have avoided a precise definition of fraud. This policy is designed to discourage the unscrupulous from thinking that a clever scheme could be devised so as to fall outside the definition of fraud and thus deny the victim one of the remedies for fraud. Fraud is multifarious in its forms and is always assuming new forms. Each case in which fraud is alleged requires an examination of the evidence in light of the above elements which provide a general guide as to what constitutes fraud.

A false representation may be made by words or acts. The misrepresentation must relate to a matter of existing or past fact, not promises concerning the future or the legal effect of the transaction. Expressions of opinion, judgment, estimate, and similar statements do not ordinarily constitute fraud. Statements of value are usually viewed as opinions. Sellers of goods are given considerable latitude in connection with the statements they make about their goods. This topic is explored further in the discussion of warranties in Chapter 15.

Mere failure to reveal facts is not fraud unless (1) a relationship of trust and confidence exists between the parties, or (2) the facts relate to a latent defect, not a patent defect which the other party could reasonably detect, or (3) the silent party is under a duty to speak, as where the circumstances have prevented or disarmed inquiry by the other party.

The misrepresentation must be material. This means it must be such as to render it improbable that the contract would have been entered into upon the terms in which it was made if the truth had been known.

The party asserting fraud must establish that to his injury he justifiably relied upon the fraudulent representation. One cannot rely upon a representation which he knows to be false. Generally, if the opportunity to obtain the facts is equally within reach of both parties, there is no right to rely. The courts use the reasonable-man test in determining the question of justifiable reliance.

Remedies

The victim of fraud may have a choice of remedies. If the injured party has performed, he may receive the remedy of rescission, permitting him to have back what he has paid upon his returning the consideration he has received. He may set up the fraud as a defense to a suit by the other party. Lastly, the fraud victim may bring an action for deceit, the tort name for fraud, in which case he seeks damages while not disturbing the performance of the contract.

The usual remedy for misrepresentation without fraud, as in cases of unintentional or innocent misrepresentation, is rescission of the contract. In both fraud and misrepresentation, the injured party must assert his remedy within a reasonable time after learning of the falsity.

DURESS AND UNDUE INFLUENCE

Duress exists when one person, by the unlawful act of another, is induced to make a contract under circumstances which deprive him of the exercise of his free will. There is no contract without the consent of the parties to its terms, and there is no real consent when a party's freedom to exercise his will voluntarily is overcome.

Under the early common law the only form of duress recognized was the threat of physical injury. Over the years the courts have recognized several additional forms of duress. Today, duress may consist of threats (1) to commit bodily harm against the contracting person or his close relative or deprive them of their liberty, (2) to destroy or wrongfully withhold property, (3) to bring a criminal prosecution for an improper purpose, and (4) to injure a person's business interests. Naturally, if the threat is carried out, the duress is present. Threat of a civil suit is not viewed as duress unless the suit is wholly without foundation.

The early test for duress was whether the threat of danger was sufficient to deprive a constant and courageous man of his free will. Modern courts have abandoned this objective standard in favor of a more subjective measuring stick. Under the modern view, in determining whether a course of conduct results in duress, the question is not what effect such conduct would have upon an ordinary man, but rather the effect upon the particular person toward whom such conduct is directed. In determining such effect, the age, sex, health, and mental condition of the person affected, the relationship of the parties, and all the surrounding circumstances may be considered.

The effect of duress is to render the contract of the duress victim voidable at his election. The injured party may have the contract rescinded or, if appropriate in the particular case, recover damages.

Undue influence is similar to duress in that the free will of a party to a contract has been unduly interfered with. The free agency of a person is destroyed and another person's will has been substituted. The influence must be such as to control the mental operations of a party, overcoming his independent judgment, thereby producing a disposition of property, making of a contract, or some act on his part which he would not have done if left freely to act according to his own desire.

Where parties stand in a confidential relationship or repose great trust in one another, the opportunity for undue influence arises. Such relationships include lawyer and client, doctor or nurse and patient, parent and child, and similar relationships. Any contract between such persons will be scrutinized for undue influence where the weaker of the parties complains of the bargain which appears to be rather one-sided.

The legal effect of undue influence, as in the case of duress, is to make the contract voidable at the election of the victim.

Consideration

6

INTRODUCTION

At early common law in England, before the emergence of the doctrine of consideration, only written contracts under seal were legally binding. Formality was the test used for deciding which agreements would be enforced by courts. Early seals consisted of blobs of wax bearing a distinguishing impression or mark which were placed next to the signatures of the parties to the contract. Later the forms of seals changed to the point where often it consisted simply of the letters "L.S." (which are the abbreviation for the Latin *locus sigilli* meaning the place of the seal). In most contracts entered into today the parties do not use seals, except in the case of corporations which are required to place their corporate seals on certain legal instruments. Certain public officials, such as notary publics, use seals in connection with the performance of their duties.

Today the early common law effect of a seal has been abolished in most states. This view is expressed in the Uniform Commercial Code in relation to contracts for the sale of goods or an offer to buy or sell goods.[1] As stated in the introduction to the law of contracts, Chapter 3, courts today recognize most

---

[1] UCC Sec. 2-203.

informal contracts, oral or written, as fully binding. A few states provide by statute that the presence of a seal on a contract shall be *prima facie* evidence of consideration, meaning that the party in a law suit who asserts lack of consideration, usually the defendant, has the burden of pleading and proving the lack of consideration in order to escape liability on his promise.

Agreement alone is not sufficient in most cases to create a contract enforceable by the courts. In addition to the agreement of the parties there must be consideration. As a general rule, the plaintiff suing to enforce an ordinary contract has the burden of establishing consideration along with the mutual assent of the parties to the contract.

Recent developments in the law indicate a departure from strict adherence to the technical requirement of consideration in determining the enforceability of certain kinds of contracts or promises. The main thrust of this trend is found in the Uniform Commercial Code where certain provisions of the Code substitute good faith in place of consideration as the test for enforceability of contracts falling within the scope of the Code.

As explained in Chapter 13 of this book, the Code provides that an offer by a merchant to sell or buy goods in a signed writing which by its terms gives assurance that the offer will be held open is not revocable for lack of consideration, if certain conditions as specified in the Code are met.[2] Another inroad against the consideration requirement is found in the Code's provision that a court may refuse to enforce an unconscionable contract or contract clause involving the sale of goods even though the promise for which enforcement is being sought is supported by consideration.[3] The Code further provides in its general provisions that the parties to every contract under the Code are under a duty of good faith in the performance of their obligations.[4]

---

[2] UCC Sec. 2-205.
[3] UCC Sec. 2-302.
[4] UCC Sec. 1-203.

DEFINITIONS AND THEORIES

Consideration is a kind of bargained-for price, not necessarily money or something of economic value, which one party pays or promises for the binding effect of another's promise. This means that each party to an agreement has to have something paid to him or promised him or done for him in exchange for what he pays or promises or does. Thus, a promise, oral or written, to make a gift is not binding upon the promisor. However, once a gift has been executed, that is, the property transferred to the donee, the donor cannot rescind the gift for lack of consideration. Analysis of many contract cases in which courts have found a lack of consideration reveals that often the court is saying in effect that what is present is an executory promise to make a gift. Promises to make gifts to charitable, religious, or educational groups do not come under this rule. These promises will be discussed at the end of this chapter in connection with the injurious reliance theory of consideration. The consideration requirement applies to both unilateral and bilateral contracts.

A legalistic definition of consideration widely used by courts states that consideration is detriment to the promisee or benefit to the promisor, bargained for and given in exchange for a promise. This definition of consideration is exemplified by the dominant theory of consideration, the bargain or exchange theory. Other theories recognized in certain limited situations by the courts are the promissory estoppel or injurious reliance theory and the moral consideration theory. Most of the discussion in this chapter relates to the widely followed bargain theory of consideration.

Legal Detriment

Under the bargain theory of consideration the promisor need not receive something of benefit, but the consideration found to be present in the exchange must have been bargained for by the parties. The consideration to support a promise may consist solely of a legal detriment incurred by the promisee as bargained for by the promisor. For example, in the often cited case of *Hamer v. Sidway,* 124 N.Y. 538, 27 N.E. 256 (1891), an uncle promised a nephew $5,000 on reaching majority, if the nephew would refrain, until he reached 21 years of age, from drinking liquor, using tobacco, swearing, and playing cards or billiards for money. After the nephew had so refrained, the uncle's estate refused to pay the sum promised, on the ground that no benefit was received by the uncle from the forbearance by the nephew, and hence there was no consideration to support the uncle's promise. The court held that the nephew's refraining from doing the described acts constituted consideration because it represented a legal detriment; that is, the giving up of a right as bargained for by the uncle. The uncle's estate was held liable to the nephew.

Adequacy of Consideration

The amount of benefit to the promisor or detriment to the promisee essential to constitute consideration is immaterial. Any amount of either one is enough if it is what the parties have bargained for. However, a great disparity between the benefits received by the parties to a contract may require a court to scrutinize the bargain for evidence of fraud or other misconduct by the party receiving the vastly greater benefit. The general rule that the courts will not inquire into the adequacy of the consideration does not apply to a promise to pay money founded solely on a pecuniary consideration, since a pecuniary consideration is capable of exact and definite measurement. For example, if A agrees to pay $10 to B in exchange for $5 from B, A's promise is not binding. The case involves in effect a promise to make a gift.

Nominal Consideration. The parties may provide for a nominal consideration such as $1.00 and it will be recognized by courts as a valid consideration if the parties intend it to be consideration. Generally the $1.00 must actually be paid. Nomi-

nal consideration cases are illustrated by written instruments
which contain such a statement as, "In consideration of $1.00
to me in hand paid, the receipt of which is hereby acknowl-
edged, I promise to. . . ." In such cases there is often actual
consideration beyond the $1.00 recited in the contracts.

Pre-existing Obligations

Neither the promise to do a thing nor the actual doing of it
will constitute a sufficient consideration to support a contract
if it is merely a thing which the party is already bound to do
either by law or by a subsisting contract with the other party.

Legal Obligations. The performance by a public official of
his official duty is not a legal detriment and not sufficient consideration to support a promise. As a result, a sheriff cannot
claim a reward for capturing and helping convict a criminal
wanted for a crime committed within the county where the
sheriff holds office. Public policy as well as lack of consideration
prevents the office holder from claiming payments from individuals for performance of their official duties. If such payments
could be claimed, public officials would be tempted to neglect
their duties until promises of such payments were forthcoming
and favoritism might be shown by the officials on the basis of
such payments. If a public official does something in excess of
what is required by law, this act may be a legal detriment and
thus constitute consideration.

A bargain to refrain from committing a crime or tort does
not create a legal detriment and cannot be sufficient consideration to support a promise, as each citizen is already under a
duty to refrain from such wrongdoing.

Contractual Obligations. Generally a promise to pay additional compensation for the doing of that which the promisee
is already under contract to do is not supported by consideration. Under this rule a builder cannot enforce against an
owner the latter's promise to pay an additional sum for completing work the builder was already obligated to do under the
original contract. In such a case there is no legal detriment to

the builder or benefit to the owner arising out of the agreement for additional compensation, since the owner was already entitled to have the work done. If the builder assumes new duties, as in cases where the manner, mode, or time of performing is altered to the detriment of the builder or to the advantage of the owner, the owner's promise to pay more money is binding.

An exception to the general rule is recognized in cases where a party is promised additional compensation after refusing to complete his contract because of exceptional circumstances or unforeseen difficulties and burdens which would justify such party in rescinding the contract. This exception has been applied in building contracts where an owner promises the builder more money in return for the builder's agreement to complete the work originally called for but now made substantially more difficult because of circumstances which were not within the contemplation of the parties when the original contract was made. Another possibility is the cancellation of the original contract and the substitution of an entirely new contract in its place in which case the consideration problem may be overcome.

Uniform Commercial Code.   Section 2-209 (1) of the Code provides that a contract for the sale of goods may be modified by agreement without any consideration being required to make the modification agreement binding.

DISCHARGE OF A LARGER SUM BY PAYMENT OF A LESSER SUM

Liquidated Debt

The general rule is that when a debt is liquidated, that is, not indefinite in amount or in dispute, payment of part of the debt at the place the debt is payable and at or after the due date in return for the creditor's promise to take the part payment in full satisfaction of the debt does not discharge the debt. The creditor's promise is not supported by consideration; therefore, he can repudiate his promise and collect the unpaid portion in most states. The payment of the lesser sum is performance of a pre-existing contractual obligation and so no legal detriment has been suffered by the debtor nor has any benefit to which he wasn't already entitled been received by the creditor. It follows from this rule that a merchant may accept and cash a check that his customer has marked "payment in full" and still collect from the customer any amount still due.

If the debtor furnishes any additional bargained-for consideration along with the lesser sum in exchange for the creditors promise to accept it in full payment, the debt is discharged. The additional consideration may take the form of payment before the due date, payment at a place other than originally agreed upon, or anything of value which the creditor is willing to accept.

It is possible for a creditor to accept a lesser sum and make a gift to the debtor of the balance admittedly owed to the creditor. This must be established by clear and convincing evidence, a certificate of gift delivered to the debtor or his agent being sufficient. A mere receipt marked "payment in full" and delivered to the debtor would not constitute a gift of the balance due.

Unliquidated Debt

The general rule applicable to liquidated debts does not apply where at the time the lesser sum is paid, an honest and bona fide dispute exists over the amount due. In such cases the debt is said to be unliquidated, that is, disputed. A *compromise* of the dispute by the creditor agreeing to accept a certain sum in full payment, followed by the payment will be recognized as binding. This is referred to as an *accord and satisfaction*. The legal detriment to the debtor in such cases is the giving up of his legal right to go to court and litigate the question of his liability to the creditor. This will support the promise of the creditor to take the lesser sum in full payment.

COMPOSITION OF CREDITORS

If a number of creditors of a single debtor mutually agree with the debtor that each creditor will accept a certain percentage of his claim in full satisfaction of his claim, the arrangement is called a *composition of creditors*. Composition agreements are binding on the basis of public policy, and some courts hold that they are supported by consideration; other courts simply make an exception to the rule that a promise to accept part payment in full satisfaction of a liquidated debt is void for lack of consideration.

FORBEARANCE TO SUE

Forbearance to sue on a claim made in good faith is sufficient consideration to support a promise made by the party threatened with the suit or by a third party. The promisee need not establish the validity of his claim before being permitted to sue on the promise which settled his claim. However, the promisee must reasonably believe he has a claim and must not merely give up suing on a wholly groundless claim.

MUTUALITY IN BILATERAL CONTRACTS

A promise by one party may constitute sufficient consideration to support the promise of the other party to a contract. But in order that a promise may be supported by a promise there must be mutuality of obligation. In other words, the promised performance must not be left to the election of the promisor. If a promise doesn't really bind a promisor to anything, his promise is *illusory,* and unless both parties are bound, neither is bound in a bilateral contract.

Output and Requirements Contracts

"Output" and "requirements" contracts must be examined to see if they meet the mutuality requirement. To illustrate, if A promises to deliver to B all the yeast B desires to order for use in his bakery during the next month, B's obligation is illusory, thus the contract lacks mutuality and A's promise isn't supported by consideration. If B had promised to take a definite quantity of yeast or to order from A all the yeast he might need during the month and A had agreed to furnish the same, both parties would have been bound. A similar view is taken with respect to "output" contracts. Section 2-306 of the Uniform Commercial Code provides that where a party agrees to sell his output or to buy his requirements, that future output or requirements must bear some reasonable relation to estimates given or to past output or requirements.

Right to Cancel

If a party has the right to cancel the contract at any time prior to the time for performance, the contract lacks mutuality and isn't binding unless the right to cancel is conditional on some event beyond the control of the party possessing such right.

PAST CONSIDERATION

A promise made in consideration of a prior act or forbearance on the part of the promisee, for which there was no expressed or implied promise to pay at the time, is not supported by a sufficient consideration. For example, if goods are sold without any warranty, and later the seller gives a warranty to the buyer, no new consideration having passed, the price originally paid for the goods without a warranty will not support the warranty subsequently made.

Past Obligations Distinguished

Past consideration cases are to be distinguished from the case where a present promise is made to pay a sum certain to discharge an existing obligation but which had been indefinite as to amount. To illustrate, a present promise is supported by consideration where A promises to pay a certain sum to B for services rendered by B at some prior time, if the services were performed under circumstances manifesting that the parties intended that B was to be compensated.

MORAL CONSIDERATION

General Rule
Generally, a mere moral obligation does not constitute sufficient consideration to support a promise. In the past consideration cases a moral duty to pay for what was received may be present, but this will not make the obligation legally binding.

Exceptions
Exceptions are made to the preceding rule in cases where a promise is made to fulfill an obligation which has been discharged by operation of law. For example, promises to pay claims barred by the running of the statute of limitations or by a bankruptcy proceeding are binding without any new consideration. Many states require such promises to be in writing. This exception is not applied to promises to pay a debt discharged by a composition agreement, for the reason that a composition agreement discharges the debt by the contract of the parties, not by operation of law.

INJURIOUS RELIANCE

A promise which the promisor should reasonably expect to induce action or forbearance of a definite and substantial character on the part of the promisee and which does induce such action or forbearance is binding if injustice can be avoided only by enforcement of the promise. Based on the principles of estoppel, this view of consideration is called the injurious reliance or promissory estoppel theory of consideration. The injurious reliance theory of consideration differs from the bargain theory in that under the injurious reliance theory it is not required that the detriment incurred by the promisee be a detriment which was requested by the promisor. Most courts follow the bargain theory of consideration, refusing to apply the injurious reliance theory as the test for consideration in business contracts unless equity and justice requires it. A few extreme cases have arisen where the injurious reliance doctrine has been applied to business contracts.

Charitable Subscriptions

Promises to make gifts to charitable, educational, religious, and similar institutions are generally enforced in the United States on the basis of the injurious reliance theory of consideration. Under this theory the donor or subscriber becomes bound on his promise or subscription once the promisee has incurred some obligation in reliance on the promise or subscription. Some courts sustain the validity of such promises on the theory that the promise of each subscriber is the consideration for the promises of the others. In charitable subscription contracts there is a strong underlying public policy favoring the enforceability of such promises.

Capacity of Parties

7

INTRODUCTION

At least two parties are necessary to a contract, and, as stated in the list of essentials of a contract in Chapter 3, the parties must be competent.

A competent person is one who has the legal and mental capacity to make a contract enforceable against him at law. Capacity or competency is presumed, and the burden of proving incompetency is usually upon the party alleging it. Those classes of persons about which the question of capacity to contract may arise under the law include the following: (1) infants (legal term for minors); (2) insane persons; (3) intoxicated persons; (4) married women; (5) corporations; and (6) aliens. In addition, the contracts of governments raise problems with respect to capacity. The right of sovereign governments to enter into contracts, to sue on their contracts, and to be sued thereon is recognized. These matters are governed by statutes in each state.

INFANTS' CONTRACTS

Definition and Legal Status of Infants

Infants are defined in most states as all persons under the age of twenty-one years. In a few states women become of age at eighteen, and in some states one or both sexes attain the rights of adults upon marriage. Under the common law a person is of full age at the beginning of the day preceding the twenty-first anniversary of his birth. This view still prevails in most states, but a few states provide by statute that an infant reaches his majority on his twenty-first birthday.

A child does not have the power to bind a parent on a contract simply by virtue of the parent and child relationship. The party seeking to hold the parent liable for a contract made by a child of the parent must establish that the child was acting as the agent of the parent under the ordinary rules of agency as described in Part Five of this book. An exception is made resulting in liability of a parent for necessaries furnished a child on the credit of the parent, provided the parent has not met his legal duty to support the child.

An infant cannot personally bring or defend an action in court. An action on his behalf must be brought either by his guardian or by a next friend. Suits against an infant must be defended by a guardian.

Voidable Contracts Rule

Society, speaking through our legal system, takes the view that infants need protection from their immaturity, inexperience, and from those adults who would take unfair advantage of infants in business dealings. Therefore, as a general rule, an infant's contracts, except for necessaries, are voidable at his option, not void. The infant may if he wishes treat his contract as fully binding and the adult party to the contract with the infant will be bound. Of course, certain unusual contracts such as enlistments in the armed forces and executed marriage contracts generally cannot be avoided by an infant. Some states have enacted statutes limiting the power of an infant to disaffirm his contracts, but these statutes have limited application. Statutes in many states grant to minors, particularly to those eighteen years of age or older, the power to bind themselves in certain specified legal transactions. The statutes of a particular state should be examined to determine the exact nature of these exceptions to the general rule under which minors' contracts are voidable as explained below. The right to disaffirm is personal to the infant, but it can be set up for his benefit by his legal representatives, such as his heirs, executor or administrator, and his guardian. The right to disaffirm is not available to an adult party to a contract with an infant.

The right of an infant to disaffirm his contracts is based exclusively on his minority. The personal qualities of a particular infant do not override his incapacity. The fact that a minor is married, well educated, experienced, engaged in business, emancipated, or acts like an adult, does not usually enlarge upon his capacity to contract. The law intends, however, that the infant use the right to disaffirm as a shield and not as a sword. Abuse by some minors of their right to disaffirm has led to some cutting down in a few states of their legal protection, either by statute or court decision.

A disaffirmance of a contract by an infant is irrevocable and must apply to the entire contract.

Business Contracts. An infant's right to disaffirm extends to contracts relating to a business operated by the infant, even though he is dependent on the income from the business for his livelihood and that of his family, if he is married. Some modification of this general rule has been made by statutes or court decisions in a few states, but the general rule is still followed widely. An infant may be held liable for the reasonable value of tools of a trade under the common law necessaries exception to the general rule, but this exception has not been expanded to include contracts for the purchase of vehicles, machinery, equipment used in an infant's business, or business contracts generally. Similarly, an infant's purchase of stock in a corporation may be disaffirmed, and he may recover the purchase price in full with no deduction being made for capital impairment, in the absence of the corporation's insolvency.

Infant Partners. An infant may be a partner in a partnership and possess the same rights and duties as any partner, but he may withdraw as a partner without liability for breaching his contract of partnership. Also, the infant partner can disaffirm his personal liability as a partner to the creditors of the partnership. Upon disaffirmance an infant partner may recover from the adult partner the amount of the infant's capital contribution, minus any previous withdrawals and subject to creditors' rights.

Personal Property Transfers. Personal property sold by an infant cannot be recovered by the infant from a person who had purchased it in good faith from the one to whom the infant had transferred it. Both the Uniform Sales Act and Uniform Commercial Code embrace this rule which is contrary to an early common-law view.[1]

Emancipation

Emancipation is a common-law concept under which the parent's common-law right to a child's services and therefore to his earnings, is terminated due to the parent's release of custody and dominance over the child. A payment made to the child will not discharge the employer from liability to the parent unless the child has been emancipated. The emancipation of a child may be expressed by the parent, implied from the acts of the parent, or based on the provisions of a statute governing emancipation in the particular state. Generally the marriage of a minor results in emancipation. Emancipation does not enlarge the general capacity of an infant to contract. However, after emancipation a child's parents do not usually furnish necessaries for the child and as a result the child will be in a position to make contracts for necessaries which he cannot disaffirm. Also, some states now have statutes dealing with the legal rights of an emancipated minor.

Disaffirmance

Time of Disaffirmance. As a general rule, an infant's contract may be disaffirmed by him either before becoming of age,

---

[1] USA Sec. 24, UCC Sec. 2-403.

or reaching majority, or within a reasonable time thereafter. Failure to disaffirm within a reasonable time after majority results in ratification. An infant may not disaffirm his contract affecting title to real estate until he reaches majority. A reasonable time after majority is determined on the basis of the nature of the contract and surrounding circumstances. Courts have held that a reasonable time in which to disaffirm a contract is longer in the case of a sale of real property as compared to a sale of personal property.

Form of Disaffirmance. No particular form or manner of disaffirmance is required. Any act which clearly shows an intent to disaffirm a contract is sufficient. To illustrate, an intention to disaffirm may be manifested by the infant's notice to the other party of the infant's purpose to disaffirm, by the bringing of a suit to recover back the consideration he has parted with, or by the setting up of infancy as a defense in an action brought against him on the contract.

Executed and Executory Contracts. A wholly executory contract is one which has not been performed by either party. The disaffirmance of such a contract by a minor is quite simple. In such a case the infant merely indicates his intention to disaffirm the contract and thereafter he cannot be required to perform, even if the contract is for necessaries.

In the case of an executed contract, the infant has the right to disaffirm and get back the consideration which he has given the other party. As a general rule, an infant who disaffirms a contract must return the consideration he has received, provided he still has it. But, under the majority view, if he has squandered, used, destroyed, or no longer has the consideration he received, he may still disaffirm the contract even though the parties cannot be put in status quo. To illustrate, an infant may purchase an automobile and after it is demolished in an accident, disaffirm his contract and demand from the seller the full amount he paid for it.

Some courts seek to ameliorate the hardship to the adults in such cases by holding that on disaffirmance the infant can recover the consideration paid only in excess of the value of the use of the property to him plus its depreciation in value through such use. Carrying this view further, some courts require an infant who returns goods sold to him to compensate the seller for injuries to the goods sustained while in his possession. These conditions to disaffirmance are not recognized by most courts despite the apparent hardship caused the adult in some cases, unless the infant misrepresents his age.

Misrepresentation of Age. The fact that an infant misrepresents his age does not as a general rule bar him from disaffirming his contract. However, under the modern view, an equity court will estop an infant from avoiding a transaction in which he has misrepresented his age and the other party has justifiably relied on such misrepresentation to his detriment unless the infant restores to the other party any consideration received by the infant and still in his possession, and, in addition, accounts for the value he received from its use and its depreciation in value.

A few states have enacted statutes providing that an infant cannot disaffirm if he engages in business as an adult, misrepresents his age, and the other party has good reason to believe him capable of contracting.

Misrepresentation by the infant of his age will permit the other party to rescind the contract as in other cases of misrepresentation.

Ratification

If, after becoming of age, an infant ratifies a contract made during his minority, it becomes binding upon him and his right to disaffirm is terminated. Ratification of a contract by an infant cannot occur until after he reaches majority. The rule that denies an infant full capacity to make a binding contract also precludes him from binding himself by any ratification while still an infant.

Ratification may be express, or it may be implied from the

acts of an infant. Examples of an infant's conduct from which ratification is implied include the infant's keeping and using for an unreasonable time after majority property acquired under a contract made during infancy, receiving and accepting performance in whole or in part after the infant reaches his majority, and performance by the infant after reaching majority. Mere acknowledgement of the existence of the contract by the minor does not amount to ratification.

It is not necessary to a binding ratification that the infant be aware at the time of his act of ratification that he had a legal right to avoid the contract.

Necessaries

Liability for Necessaries. An infant may make himself liable for necessaries. An infant's liability for necessaries is quasi contractual rather than arising from the promise of the infant. Accordingly, an infant is liable for the reasonable value or whatever he agreed to pay, whichever is less. In any case an infant is liable only for the necessaries actually furnished him. Therefore, an infant is not bound by his executory contract to buy necessaries. If the contract is in part executed, the infant is liable for the value only of that part of the necessaries actually furnished to him.

In order for the infant to be held liable, the necessaries must have been furnished on the credit of the infant, not the credit of the parent. The liability of the parent for necessaries furnished a child has been discussed previously in this chapter.

What Are Necessaries? Necessaries is a relative term depending on the infant's social position and situation in life and his actual requirements at the time of delivery. The same thing may be necessary to one person under certain circumstances and unnecessary to another person under other circumstances. Luxuries would not constitute necessaries. Only those items essential to the infant's continued existence and general welfare or that of his wife and children are considered necessaries. Generally recognized categories of necessaries include (1) food, (2) clothing, (3) shelter, (4) medical care, (5) education, and (6) tools of trade.

If an infant is already supplied either by his parent or guardian, or by previous purchases with sufficient necessaries, no further purchases on credit of articles of the same kind can bind him. An infant living with his parent or guardian who is able and willing to furnish him with everything suitable and necessary to his position in life, cannot make a binding contract, even for necessaries.

INFANTS' TORT LIABILITY

In general, an infant is liable for his torts and crimes unless in the commission of the wrong there is required to exist some element which the infant is incapable of possessing because of his age.

An infant will not be liable in tort if the effect of holding him liable actually results in the enforcement of a contractual liability. The tort for which an infant is held liable must be a distinct wrong which is independent of a contract. Many courts do not follow this limitation on an infant's tort liability in cases where the infant is sought to be held for a misrepresentation committed while negotiating a contract.

Generally, a parent is not liable for a child's tort, except where this rule has been modified by statute. If the child commits a tort while acting as the parent's agent, the parent may be held liable as principal under the law of agency. Also, if a child commits a tort at the direction of the parent or in the presence of the parent when the child should have been controlled, the parent can be held.

INSANE AND INTOXICATED PERSONS

Contracts made by a person who has been judicially declared insane by a court of competent jurisdiction are absolutely void and not merely voidable.

If an insane person has not been judicially declared insane, his contracts are voidable only, and in most cases the rules governing infants' contracts apply, including those with respect to disaffirmance, ratification, and necessaries. However, where an insane person has had the benefits of the contract, and the sane party had no knowledge or reason to know of the insanity of the other party, and there is no unfairness, the insane party cannot disaffirm the contract unless he can put the sane party in *statu quo*.

The prevailing test of insanity in contract cases is whether the alleged insane person had sufficient reason to understand the nature and effect of the transaction in dispute.

If intoxication is so extreme as to produce legal incapacity, that is, the person is so intoxicated as to be incapable of understanding the nature of the transaction being negotiated, the effect is generally held to be the same as that of insanity and the same rules apply.

MARRIED WOMEN, CORPORATIONS, ALIENS

Married Women

At common law married women did not have capacity to contract. Thus, any contracts they entered into were treated as void. Most states have enacted statutes abolishing or greatly modifying the common-law rules relative to married women's contracts. Under these married women's statutes, a married woman possesses, in many states, the same right to contract as possessed by anyone else. These statutes should be consulted if a person is concerned with the law of a particular state.

Corporations

A corporation has in general, only those powers, including the power to contract, as are conferred upon it by the state which issued the corporation its charter. The powers of a corporation are discussed in Chapter 30.

Aliens

In most states aliens have substantially the same capacity to contract as citizens unless a state of war exists between the nations to which the contracting parties owe their allegiance. In time of war the federal statute forbidding "trading with the enemy" may also apply. Some states have statutes restricting aliens from owning real property and any contract contrary to such statutes would be void. Treaties affecting an alien's right to contract may also exist.

Illegality

8

NATURE OF ILLEGALITY

Legality of subject matter is one of the essential elements of a valid contract. The parties to contracts enjoy considerable freedom in choosing the subject matter and objectives of their contracts. However, a contract must not either by its creation or its performance be injurious to the public interest or inimical to the general social welfare. A contract is illegal and usually unenforceable if it is criminal, tortious, or in violation of society's concept of morality or public policy. While an illegal contract may involve a criminal act, most illegal contracts are not criminal in nature.

Courts and writers on the subject of illegal agreements recognize the following, sometimes overlapping, classes of illegal agreements: (1) agreements in violation of positive law, (2) agreements declared void by statute, and (3) agreements contrary to public policy. A contract may be legal in one state and illegal in another. Certain contracts are viewed as illegal in all or most states, and it is these contracts which are identified and discussed in this chapter. Covering a wide range of subject matter, illegal contracts include agreements to obstruct justice, agreements in unreasonable restraint of trade and employment, agreements to stifle bidding at public sales, agreements involving the unauthorized practice of law, agreements promoting immorality, agreements interfering with the duties of public officials, agreements to defraud, and agreements interfering with marital or parental relations.

EFFECT OF ILLEGALITY

Generally a court will not enforce an illegal contract. Some courts refer to an illegal contract as void. This means that usually a court refuses to grant relief to either party, leaving the parties where it finds them, whether the contract is executory, executed, or partly executed. As a result, a party to an illegal contract who has fully performed his part of the bargain may not be permitted to enforce the promise of the other party, recover for benefits conferred, or force a return of his consideration. The purpose of this rule is the protection of the public interest rather than the punishment of the party who made the illegal contract.

If the court finds that the public interest would be promoted by granting a remedy to one of the parties, the court will make an exception to the general rule and grant relief. A person who belongs to the group a regulatory statute is designed to protect may recover for breach of a contract entered into with a person who failed to comply with the statute. For example, failure of a builder to possess a contractor's license required by state law will not prevent an owner who contracts with the unlicensed contractor for certain construction work from holding the builder liable for breach of contract.

Mere lack of knowledge on the part of both parties that the contract is illegal will not permit the parties to enforce the illegal contract unless the circumstances of the particular case require that some relief be granted as a matter of public policy or justice. Knowledge of a seller that the other party plans to use a sold article for an illegal purpose does not make the sale contract illegal unless the seller is a participant in the wrongful act or the article is to be used in committing a serious crime. This same rule applies to a loan agreement. On this basis, a loan of money to a known gambler would be valid even though the lender knew the money was to be used illegally for gambling, and the lender could recover the borrowed money unless he was a participant in the illegal gambling venture.

Where parties are not *in pari delicto,* that is, not equally guilty, the courts may grant relief to the less guilty party as a matter of public policy or because abstract principles of justice as they apply to the facts of the particular case require that some relief be granted. This exception to the general rule of leaving parties to an illegal contract where the court finds them is illustrated by cases where one party conceives an illegal scheme or venture and induces another person to enter into an illegal agreement by fraud, undue influence, or duress.

If a contract contains both legal and illegal provisions, the courts will enforce the legal provisions, provided such enforcement does not have the effect of enforcing either directly or indirectly the illegal parts.

The policy of the law is to encourage timely repentance by those who enter into illegal contracts. If, prior to the performance of an illegal act called for in a contract, one of the parties repents and wishes to rescind the contract, he may usually recover any consideration he has given. For example, a party to a bet on the outcome of an athletic contest may withdraw his money from the stakeholder before the contest has taken place.

Many states have statutes governing the rights of persons who lose money gambling. Under these statutes the person who has lost money gambling often may recover it.

REPRESENTATIVE ILLEGAL BARGAINS

Contracts to Commit Crimes and Torts

An agreement which involves the commission of a crime or which tends to induce the commission of a crime is illegal as contrary to positive law. Thus, an agreement to commit assault, larceny, arson, or any act defined by society as a crime cannot be enforced.

Similarly, an agreement which cannot be performed without the commission of a tort is illegal and unenforceable. Mere commission of a tort in the course of performing a contract does not make the contract illegal. For example, the construction of a building pursuant to a contract may involve one of the workmen causing injury to neighboring property due to the workman's negligence. This would not make the construction contract illegal. The contract is not illegal unless it has as its objective or purpose the commission of a tort. Examples of contracts calling for the commission of torts include an agreement to interfere with a third person's contract, an agreement to commit fraud against a third person or to injure his person, property, or business.

Statutes and Illegal Contracts

Wagers.   Wagering contracts are generally illegal as a matter of public policy and are prohibited or strictly regulated by statutes in all states.

A gambling contract is one in which the parties agree that a certain sum of money or some other thing shall be paid or delivered to one of them upon the happening or not happening of an uncertain event. In true gambling agreements the parties either create the determining event or create the risk involved in the wager. Betting by participants on the outcome of a card game illustrates creating the event out of which the winning or losing is to result. Wagers on the outcome of political elections or college football games are examples of parties creating the risk as a vehicle for gambling. These bargains in the nature of a bet or wager are generally prohibited by wagering statutes.

While gambling contracts are illegal, risk-shifting, and speculative, bargains are legal. Insurance policies are legal risk-shifting bargains which serve the economy and are socially desirable. Where the insured has no interest in the property insured, the policy is a mere wager instead of a contract for indemnity against loss and as such is void. Insurable interest, speaking generally, is such a legal or equitable interest in property as gives the insured a direct pecuniary interest in its preservation. An owner of property has such an interest, but an insurable interest may be less than complete ownership as in the case of the security interest held by a mortgagee in property which has been mortgaged to the mortgagee as security for a debt. The insurable interest in life insurance policies is present if the relationship between the insured and the person buying the insurance is such as to rule out an intention to speculate in human life. If the insured and the person obtaining the insurance are the same person, an insurable interest is clearly present. In other cases close relationship by blood, marriage, or contract between the insured and the party obtaining the life insurance satisfies the insurable interest requirement. An insurable interest based on a contractual relationship is present where a creditor obtains insurance on the life of his debtor, with the amount of the insurance equal to the indebtedness.

Contracts made in good faith to purchase stocks or commodities on an exchange or board of trade are not illegal even though highly speculative in nature. Such transactions play a necessary part in the operation of a market economy. However, if neither party intends that the stock or commodity shall be actually delivered, but that there shall be a settlement by the payment merely of the difference between the contract price and the market price on the day set for delivery, such a transaction is illegal and void as a mere bet or wager upon the rise or fall of the market.

Usury. A contract is usurious if it provides for a rate of interest in excess of the maximum allowed by the usury statute of the state. The maximum lawful per annum rate ranges from 6 to 30 per cent in the various states which fix a maximum, with 8 per cent or 10 per cent set as the maximum in most states.

Licensed lenders such as small loan associations or companies and pawnbrokers who make small loans are not subject to the usury statute, but are governed instead by Small Loan Laws in most states. These statutes permit such licensed lenders to charge higher interest rates in recognition of the higher risk involved and other factors. The average rate permitted under these laws is in the range of 2½ to 3 per cent a month on the unpaid balance, with the maximum lawful rate usually dependent on the amount loaned. Also, the law fixes a maximum amount which such a lender can loan to any one borrower.

The usury laws are not uniform either as to the maximum lawful contract rate of interest or as to the consequences of violating the statute. In some states the statute declares the entire usurious contract void, and the lender forfeits both the principal and the interest, in others the creditor forfeits all interest, in still others only the interest above the legal rate is forfeited. In a number of states the usury laws do not apply to loans to corporations.

The legal rate of interest in a state is to be distinguished from the maximum lawful contract rate (usury law), the legal rate being a rate applicable by statute upon debts due and upon loans on which interest is to be charged, but the rate of which is not fixed by the parties. The legal rate of interest fixed by most states is 6 per cent per annum.

Sunday Laws. The statutes of the different states declaring Sunday contracts illegal differ considerably in their language and effect. Many Sunday laws, often called "blue laws," have fallen into disuse or have been beclouded by confusing and conflicting interpretations by courts. Some of the statutes expressly declare Sunday contracts void unless they are for advancement of religion, or charity, or for works of necessity or mercy. Other statutes prohibit labor or business of one's "ordinary calling," while others prohibit "all work or labor" on Sunday. Some statutes prohibit certain business transactions such as sales of merchandise, but list the rendering of certain services and the sale of certain articles of merchandise, usually necessities, as excepted from the prohibition.

Bargains negotiated on Sunday but closed or performed on a

secular day are not illegal. If an agreement is made and fully performed on Sunday, most courts will not disturb the executed contract. Marriage contracts, either the engagement to marry or the marriage ceremony, entered into on Sunday are valid. Generally legal instruments such as checks, notes, deeds, and mortgages executed on Sunday are valid and enforceable. However, any question relating to the legal effect of a Sunday law on a contract must be answered on the basis of the language of the Sunday statute, if any, of the state involved, the courts' interpretations of any such law, and the circumstances of the particular case.

Regulatory Licensing Statutes. Statutes have been enacted under the police power in most states to require a license before a person can practice certain professions, such as law or medicine, or carry on a particular business or trade, such as that of a stockbroker, real estate broker, beautician, contractor, or pawnbroker. If the purpose of the licensing law is to protect the public against dishonest and incompetent persons, a contract made by an unlicensed person to perform the particular service or to enter into the regulated business transaction is void and such person cannot enforce the contract or collect for his services. In addition, these statutes usually provide for a penalty against the unlicensed person.

If the purpose of a licensing statute is to raise revenue rather than to protect the public by regulating the entry into the business involved, a contract in violation of the statute is generally held valid. For example, failure of an ordinary merchant to obtain a required vendor's license would not preclude the merchant from enforcing an otherwise valid sale contract against a buyer.

Contracts Against Public Policy

Contracts which are contrary to public policy are illegal. Public policy is the community common sense and common conscience applied to matters of public morals, health, safety, and general welfare. Any contract in contravention of a statute may be against public policy. However, even in the absence of a statute the courts of a state may decide that a particular contract is against public policy and thus void under the common law. A few of the more common types of contracts held by courts to be contrary to public policy are discussed in the remainder of this chapter. Others were briefly mentioned at the beginning of the chapter. These contracts may also be prohibited or at least regulated by statutes in some states. The primary concern of the courts in ruling on the validity of agreements under attack on public policy considerations is the effect such agreements have upon the general welfare of society.

Contracts in Restraint of Trade. Contracts in direct restraint of trade or which have as their primary purpose the creation of a monopoly in a line of commerce are against public policy and illegal as an undue interference with free competition. Agreements not to compete in business, to divide a market or profits, to control prices, or to limit production are examples of such illegal bargains. In addition to such agreements being unenforceable under the common law, antitrust legislation has been passed both by Congress and by the states declaring monopolies and restraints of trade illegal, and these statutes subject those who make such agreements to civil and criminal penalties. The discussion which follows deals with some of the common-law aspects of agreements in restraint of trade.

The law is clear that restrictive covenants against competition, though in partial restraint of trade, are enforceable if they are reasonable to the covenantee, covenantor, and to the public. Covenants in partial restraint of trade are generally valid when they are agreements (1) by the seller of property or a business not to compete with the buyer in such a way as to injure the value of the property or business purchased, (2) by a retiring or prospective partner not to compete with the firm, (3) by the buyer or lessee of property not to use it in competition with the business retained by the seller or lessor, and (4) by an employee not to compete with his employer after the termination of his employment.

The underlying justification for permitting restrictions to be placed upon an individual's right to engage in a business of his choice arises from the fact that in the sale of his business he has transferred, he has been compensated for the goodwill which existed therein. In order to be valid the bargain in restraint of trade must be ancillary, that is, incidental to the main contract, must have as its purpose the protection of interests created by the contract, and must be no greater than is reasonably necessary to protect those interests. For example, a contract in which A sells his restaurant business to B and in the sale agreement, A promises not to enter the restaurant business in the same locality for five years is a legal contract even though it calls for a partial restraint of trade. The territory and time restrictions must not be greater than what is reasonably necessary to protect the buyer. The modern trend is to enforce restrictive covenants by the seller of a business even though they are unlimited as to time if they are reasonable in all other respects. In recent cases the courts have followed a more liberal consideration of the vendee's right and the tendency is to permit greater contractual restraints to be imposed upon the vendor. As a general rule, a contractual restriction against an employee competing with his former employer must be limited as to both territory and time.

Although a covenant is found to be unreasonable, it may be severed and enforced to the extent of giving reasonable protection to the covenantee. A growing number of states permit the partial enforcement of "divisible" covenants in contracts for the sale of a business, if the part of the area in which enforcement would be reasonable is by the wording of the contract readily ascertainable.

Contracts to Influence Governmental Action.   An agreement which has as its objective the improper influencing of a government official or employee in the performance of his duties is against public policy and illegal. Professional persons, such as lawyers, may make valid contracts calling for the performance of their special services in relation to matters pending before the executive, legislative, or judicial branches of government.

Bona fide lobbying agreements designed to promote or oppose the enactment of legislation are valid so long as they do not call for objectionable methods and are consistent with statutes controlling lobbies. Bargains to pay public officials bribes are clearly illegal. Any corrupting bargain which brings or tends to bring a public servant's personal interests in conflict with his duties to the public are illegal. The question of the validity of such a contract does not depend on whether it can be shown that the public has actually suffered any detriment or loss.

Limitation of Liability. Courts oppose on the ground of public policy an agreement which has as its purpose the relieving of one person from liability for overt wrongs, such as fraud, willful negligence or intentional torts against the person or property of another. However, a bargain relieving one person from liability for his nonwillful negligence is valid, provided no duty to the public is owed by the relieved party and no evidence of misconduct such as fraud, duress or undue influence is present.

Common carriers, parking lot operators, warehousemen, and others holding out their services to the general public may not, by contract, exempt themselves entirely from liability for their own negligence, but such parties may bargain to limit to a reasonable degree the amount of damages recoverable for injury to property, but not to the person, resulting from ordinary negligence. These matters are often covered by state statutes and, if interstate commerce is involved federal statutes are applicable.

Writing and Interpretation

9

STATUTE OF FRAUDS

Origin and Purpose of Statute of Frauds

In 1677 the English Parliament enacted a statute entitled "A Statute for the Prevention of Frauds and Perjuries," usually referred to today by its short title, Statute of Frauds. Most of the sections of this statute which relate to the necessity of a signed writing for certain classes of contracts have been adopted, with local variations, in each state. A contract may fall within more than one of the classes of contracts listed in the statute.

The purpose of the Statute of Frauds is to require written proof of claims based on certain kinds of promises, which because of their nature and on the basis of experience, are susceptible to perjury by the promisee and his witnesses. To accomplish its purpose, the statute provides that certain specific classes of contracts are not enforceable unless evidenced by a writing signed by the party to be bound thereby or his agent. A few states provide that contracts which fail to comply with the statute are void, but most states treat such contracts as merely unenforceable and only if the party against whom the oral contract is sought to be enforced pleads the statute as a defense at his earliest opportunity. If an oral contract which comes within the Statute of Frauds has been fully performed, neither party will be permitted to rescind the contract. If the oral nature of the contract is not objected to by a party, the court will not do so. Thus, it is frequently said that the statute does not go to the existence of a contract but merely affects the matter of procedure or proof. The statute is sometimes criticized on the basis that the requirement of a signed writing for certain types of contracts has not entirely eliminated the evils it is directed against. Others argue that it makes possible the immoral but legal escape from obligations where in fact a contract exists but is unenforceable because it is oral and falls within the statute.

Classes of Contracts Under the Statute of Frauds

¶ Briefly summarized, the following are the classes of contracts usually included in the Statute of Frauds by the various states.

1] Contracts of an executor or an administrator to pay out of his own funds the debts of the estate.

2] Contracts to answer for the debt or default of another.

3] Contracts made in consideration of marriage, except that mere mutual promises to marry need not be in writing.

4] Contracts for the sale of an interest in land.

5] Contracts which by their terms cannot be performed within one year from their formation.

6] Contracts for the sale of goods or choses in action of a value above a certain amount ($500.00 minimum under the Uniform Sales Act and the Uniform Commercial Code section containing the Code's statute of frauds covering sales of goods). Certain exceptions to the requirement of a writing for sales contracts are listed in the Uniform Sales Act and the Uniform Commercial Code. The Code exceptions are described in Chapter 13.

In addition to the contracts listed in the Statute of Frauds, many states have statutes that require the following contracts to be in writing: (1) a promise to make a will, (2) a promise to pay a debt barred by the statute of limitations or a discharge in bankruptcy, (3) a contract to pay a broker a commission for finding a buyer of real estate. A particular state's statutes and their interpretation by the courts of the state must be examined in order to learn precisely what contracts are required to be in writing in that state.

Contracts of Executors or Administrators

A deceased person's estate is administered by an executor if the decedent left a will naming an executor. If a person dies intestate (without a will) or no executor is named in a will, an administrator is appointed to handle the estate. Administrators and executors cannot be held liable on any promise to pay from their own funds any debt of the estate which they are administering unless such a promise is in writing and signed by the promisor. Such promises are simply specific examples of guaranty contracts which make up the second class of contracts under the Statute of Frauds.

Contracts to Pay Debt of Another

Original and Collateral Promises Distinguished. An oral promise by A to B that if B would extend credit to C "I will pay you if C does not" is not binding. The contract by A is a collateral or secondary undertaking, referred to technically as a contract of guaranty or surety, and such contracts must be in writing and signed by the guarantor. However, if A orally promised C, the debtor, that A would pay C's debt to B, A's promise would be original and not within the statute. C could sue on the oral promise as the promisee or B could sue as a creditor beneficiary.

If A said to B: "Let C have goods up to $100 and I'll pay the bill," A's promise would be an original promise and no writing is necessary. In such a case the credit has been extended directly to A, and this makes A's promise primary or original rather than collateral. The promisor A has agreed to pay in all events, obligating himself absolutely, instead of promising to pay if C does not. If A had requested B to sell the goods to C on the credit of C and had followed this with his (A's) oral promise to pay the bill, the oral promise would be within the statute and unenforceable. The intention of the parties is a critical factor in distinguishing between original and collateral promises. The particular words employed by the promisor do not in themselves determine whether the statute applies. All the surrounding circumstances must be considered along with the form of the promise.

An agreement substituting one debtor for another does not fall within the statute. Such a contract is called a novation and no writing is required. Where a promisor agrees to pay from funds he holds belonging to the debtor if the debtor does not pay, the contract is original. A contract of indemnity does not fall within the statute, provided the promisee is not a creditor.

A promise by a buyer of property to pay the balance owed by the seller to a holder of a mortgage against the property is viewed as an original promise. In such cases the seller remains liable to the mortgagee unless he is released. Again, a novation results if the mortgagee agrees to release the original mortgagor and it is agreed by the parties that the buyer is obligated for the balance owed.

Main Purpose Rule.   Courts hold that a promisor who stands to gain materially from his oral promise to pay a debt of another if the debtor does not, is bound on his oral promise. This is called the main purpose rule. For example, a del credere agent's oral promise to pay for goods purchased on credit if the buyer does not is enforceable. In such cases the agent is viewed as making the promise primarily to enhance his prospects for commissions by encouraging his principal to employ him. An assignor who orally guarantees to the assignee that a claim he has assigned will be paid is bound on the oral promise on the theory that the assignor has made the guaranty to get a larger price for the assignment, for his own benefit, and not to benefit the debtor. This principle also applies to oral promises of executors or administrators to pay the debt of the decedent or his estate, where the main purpose of the promise is to benefit the promisor.

Marriage Contracts

This provision of the Statute of Frauds does not apply to mutual promises to marry. It requires a writing for agreements involving marriage as a consideration for a promise to pay money, transfer property, or a settlement of the rights of the parties in each other's property. Such antenuptial agreements are not enforceable unless in writing. Breach of promise-to-marry suits have been abolished by statute in many states.

Contracts for Sale of Land

The law surrounds the transfer of the ownership of real property with certain formalities, including the Statute of Frauds provision. Agreements for the sale of land or for any interest in or concerning land are unenforceable unless they are in writing and signed. Included within this class of contracts are mortgages, easements, and leases, except that leases of short duration, usually not in excess of one year, may be oral in most states. Many states require that where an agent is to sign the writing, his authority must be evidenced by a signed writing.

Contracts to construct buildings, to insure buildings, to loan money with which to buy land, and other contracts merely relating to land are not within this class under the statute, because they do not affect an interest in the real property. Oral contracts for the sale of the produce of land such as timber are treated as sales of personal property if the trees are to be cut before the ownership passes from the seller to the buyer.

Part Performance. Under some circumstances part performance of an oral contract for the sale of real property may justify a court in refusing to apply the statute. A typical case where this is the result is the case where under an oral contract a purchaser of real property goes into possession of the property with the consent of the seller and makes extensive improvements to it. Mere payment of the price by the purchaser is not sufficient part performance to entitle him to specific performance of the contract. Payments made in reliance on an oral contract which is not enforceable under the statute may be recovered in quasi contract.

Contracts Not to be Performed Within One Year

A contract which by its terms cannot be performed within one year from the date it is made must be in writing. The actual time it takes for the performance of a contract or the time the parties expect it will take for the performance is immaterial. For example, an oral agreement by A to work for B for two years from the date of the agreement is unenforceable. The time lapse is calculated from the date of the entering into of the contract, not from the date performance is to commence. Thus, an oral agreement made July 1, calling for employment for one year from July 10, is unenforceable. However, if the employee hired for one year is to start working the day following that on which the contract is made, it is generally held that the statute does not apply. An oral agreement by A to take care of B, an invalid, as long as B lives, in return for B's payment of $5,000 to A is binding, even though the period of performance is uncertain. The same result applies where A orally agrees to employ B for B's life. In either case it would be possible for the contract to be performed within one year, because, as envisaged by the wording of the contract, B might die within a year from the date of the agreement. The fact that B may live many years is immaterial. However, some states have modified their Statute of Frauds to require that lifetime contracts must be evidenced by a writing. In such states, an oral agreement to hire a person for life is unenforceable.

Contracts For Sale of Goods and Personal Property

The Uniform Commercial Code contains provisions that describe the writing requirement relative to contracts for the sale of goods and other kinds of personal property in those states which have adopted the Code. The Code's provisions in relation to contracts for the sale of goods are discussed in Chapter 13 of this book.

Compliance With the Statute of Frauds

Any kind of writing, including such things as letters, telegrams, and memoranda, will satisfy the Statute of Frauds, if the writing describes the names of the parties, the subject matter of the contract, all other material terms of the contract, and in most states, the consideration supporting the contract. The required memorandum may consist of separate papers if they can be connected on the basis of a reference within each paper to another.

Only the party against whom enforcement is sought or his authorized agent must sign the writing. In most cases this means that only the defendant must sign.

See Chapter 13 for the rules which govern compliance with the sale of goods provision of the Uniform Commercial Code's statute of frauds.

PAROL EVIDENCE RULE

The best evidence of what the parties intended to include in their contract is their written agreement if one has been prepared. For this reason the parol evidence rule prohibits the testimony of the parties or other witnesses concerning oral understandings if the effect of such evidence is to alter, add to, or vary the terms of a written contract. The parol evidence rule has no application to a suit involving an oral contract.

The parol evidence rule is not violated if oral or other extrinsic evidence is offered in evidence (1) to establish that the agreement lacks one of the essential elements of a contract; (2) to prove that the contract is invalid due to fraud, misrepresentation, mistake, duress, or undue influence; (3) to supply a missing term of an incomplete contract; (4) to prove that the writing was not to take effect until an agreed, uncertain future event happened; and (5) to clear up ambiguities or the meaning of technical terms or words used in the written contract.

INTERPRETATION OF CONTRACTS

Once the terms of a contract have been established, a further question may arise as to how the terms of the contract are to be interpreted or construed so as to carry out the intention of the parties in light of the circumstances surrounding the making of the contract. If the agreement has been reduced to writing, the meaning of the language used in the writing must be determined. The courts have evolved certain common sense standards or rules of construction to aid them in the interpretation of contracts. A sampling of some of the basic rules of construction follows.

1] All the provisions of a written contract must be construed together in determining the meaning and intention of any particular words, clause, or provision of the contract.

2] If there is doubt or ambiguity in the language of a contract, the document is to be construed strictly against the party who prepared it or selected its language and in favor of the party who took no part in its preparation or in the selection of its language. This rule is often applied against insurance companies where it is necessary to construe an ambiguous provision of a policy prepared and issued by the company.

3] Where there is a conflict between any of the printed provisions of a contract and those inserted in writing at the time the contract is executed, the latter will control. Typewritten phrases are given effect over printed phrases if there is any inconsistancy between them.

4] Ordinary words are to be interpreted according to their common and usual meaning unless the circumstances show that a different meaning was intended by the parties.

5] Technical words are given their technical meaning unless a contrary intention is shown. Where a word has a special meaning in a particular business, it must be interpreted as ordinarily used in that business.

6] It is a general rule that where there are general and special provisions in a contract relating to the same thing, the special provisions control.

7] If the amount involved in a contract is expressed both in words and in figures and they are in conflict as to amount, the amount stated in words will be taken as correct.

Rights of Third Persons

10

ASSIGNMENT OF CONTRACTS

Nature of Assignment

Rights and duties are created by the formation of a contract. An assignment of contract rights is the transfer by a party to the contract of his rights, all or part of them, to a third person. The party making the transfer is called the assignor; the third person to whom the transfer is made is called the assignee. In the absence of statute or of requirements expressed in the contract, an assignment need not be in any particular form and may be made with or without consideration. Generally a gratuitous assignment can be revoked by the assignor giving notice to the obligor prior to performance of the assigned obligation.

Assignment in General

Under the early common law a contract was viewed by courts as personal to the parties who created the contract. For this reason contract rights were not assignable unless the promisor consented. Today most contract rights are assignable without the consent of the promisor unless the terms of the contract prohibit assignment. However, if the contract is personal in nature or the obligations of the promisor will be materially increased or altered by requiring him to perform for the assignee, the contract is not assignable.

Assignment by Operation of Law. While most contract assignments result from action of the parties, a contract may be assigned by operation of law in the event of (1) death or (2) bankruptcy of a party to a contract. If a party who has made a contract dies, most contracts which he might have assigned during his lifetime pass to his executor or administrator who may sue or be sued upon them. Contracts for personal services do not survive the death of either party. When a person becomes bankrupt, his rights and obligations under contracts pass to his trustee in bankruptcy. At common law, a man upon his marriage became entitled by operation of law to his wife's personal property and could enforce her claims arising out of contract. This rule has been abolished by statutes.

Assignment Under the Uniform Commercial Code. The Code provides that a right to damages for breach of the whole contract for a sale of goods or a right arising out of the assignor's due performance of his entire obligation can be assigned despite agreement otherwise.[1] Section 2-210 of the Code states the extent to which duties may be delegated and rights assigned under sales contracts. Assignment of contract rights in general is not governed by the Code.

Assignable Contracts

Claims for money are freely assignable. Other types of contracts which have been held assignable include a contract to sell land or goods, and an agreement not to compete with the buyer of a business or with an employer. The latter type of contract was discussed in Chapter 8 in relation to legality.

The assignment of wages and salaries is regulated by statutes in most states. Some of the statutes require a writing and other formality, limit the percentage of wages that may be assigned, and require both spouses to sign the assignment agreement if

---

[1] UCC Sec. 2-210 (2).

the wage earner is married. A few states prohibit the assignment of future wages.

Non-assignable Contracts

Contracts involving a personal relationship or a high degree of trust and confidence between the parties are not assignable unless the person against whom the right is to be enforced consents. Such contracts include those for personal services, a property insurance policy, and a contract for the purchase of property on credit without any security for the seller. It can be seen in such cases that to permit the assignment over the objection of the obligated party would thrust the latter into a personal relationship with a stranger or materially increase his burden or risk as compared to what was contemplated at the time he made the contract.

Delegation of Duties

Contract duties are not assignable, but impersonal duties can be delegated unless the contract prohibits delegation. However, the delegating party remains liable for any breach of the contract. For example, a builder under contract to construct a building could normally delegate his duties thereunder to workmen and subcontractors, but he could still be held liable for breach of the contract if the party to whom the duties are delegated fails to perform.

Rights of the Assignee

An assignee is entitled to the rights of the assignor, but no more. This means that the assignee takes the assigned rights subject to any defenses or counterclaims the obligor under the contract could have raised against the assignor.

An assignor is not liable to an assignee if the obligor merely refuses to perform or becomes insolvent and thus is unable to perform the assigned obligation. Although the assignor does not guarantee to the assignee that the obligor will perform his obligation, the law recognizes certain implied warranties by the assignor for the benefit of the assignee when an assignment is made for a valuable consideration. The assignor impliedly warrants that (1) the assigned claim is genuine, valid, and not subject to defenses, (2) he has passed good title to the assignee, and (3) he will do nothing which will interfere with the performance of the contract for the benefit of the assignee. The first warranty covers such things as capacity of the parties to the assigned contract, legality of the contract, and defenses such as previous performance, fraud, duress, and the like. The third warranty is breached and the assignor is liable to the assignee if the assignor accepts performance from the original obligor or makes a subsequent assignment resulting in loss to the assignee. The implied warranties may be eliminated by express agreement of the assignor and assignee.

Notice of Assignment
While an assignment is effective as between the assignor and assignee the moment it is made, it does not bind the obligor until he has notice of it. Therefore, it is essential that the assignee promptly notify the obligor of the assignment.

The obligor after learning of the assignment must render to the assignee any performance due the assignor with whom he contracted. If the obligor renders performance to the original obligee (assignor) before notice of the assignment, the obligor is discharged, and the only recourse of the assignee is against the assignor for having breached an implied warranty as explained above. Further, if after assignment but before notice, some matter of defense has risen, the assignee may be unable to require performance by the obligor.

Prompt notice of an assignment is also necessary in order to protect the assignee in cases where the assignor wrongfully assigns the same right to two or more assignees. Courts confronted with the case of successive assignments of the same contract right to assignees who take for value and without knowledge of a prior assignment have not reached uniform decisions. Under the so-called "American Rule," some courts have held that the first assignee has the superior right on the basis of the rule of property law that once a right has been assigned nothing remains for the assignor to transfer to the subsequent assignees. Other courts follow the rule, known as the "English Rule," which gives the first assignee to give notice of assignment the superior claim to the contract right. In any case involving successive assignments of the same contract right, a careful balancing of the equities of the parties is required.

CONTRACTS FOR BENEFIT OF THIRD PERSONS

Classes of Third-party Beneficiaries

A person who is not a party to a contract may nevertheless receive some benefit from the performance of the contract. Such a person is called a third-party beneficiary. Third-party beneficiaries are classified as (1) donee beneficiaries, (2) creditor beneficiaries, and (3) incidental beneficiaries.

Donee Beneficiaries

Where performance of a promise in a contract will benefit a person other than the promisee, that person is a donee beneficiary if it appears that the primary intention of the parties of the contract was to make a gift to the beneficiary. Generally a donee beneficiary can hold the promisor liable for failure to perform as promised. Also, the promisee has a cause of action against the promisor who breaches the contract. A typical donee beneficiary contract is the life insurance policy.

Creditor Beneficiaries

A third person falls within the designation of creditor beneficiary if performance of a promise made in a contract will operate to discharge a real or a supposed debt or obligation owed by the promisee (debtor) to the third person (creditor). A third person who is a creditor beneficiary may generally maintain an action at law on a promise made for his benefit by another. A common third-party creditor beneficiary contract is involved where A owns property upon which B holds a mortgage and A sells the land to C, who agrees in the sale contract with A to assume and pay to B the balance owed by A on the mortgage, as part of the purchase price of the property. B is a third-party creditor beneficiary of the contract between A and C. B may sue C on his promise. If C does not pay B and A does, A may then recover from C the amount he has paid B.

Incidental Beneficiaries

In order that a third person may enforce a promise made for his benefit, the parties to the contract must have included the promise directly or primarily for the benefit of such third person. Both parties must manifest in their contract an intention to bestow a benefit on the third party. An incidental or indirect benefit to the third person is not sufficient to give him a right of action for nonperformance of the promise. This principle was applied in a very early case in which a number of shopkeepers in a community had agreed to close their shops on Sundays, and for any breach it was agreed that the violator of the agreement would pay $100 to a specified charitable society. The court in holding that the society could not recover on the contract took the view that the purpose of the penalty provision in the contract was not to benefit the society but to enforce compliance with the Sunday closing provision of the contract for the benefit of the parties to the contract.

Discharge, Performance
and Breach

11

DISCHARGE OF CONTRACT

When the parties to a valid contract are no longer obligated and have no further rights under the contract, the contract is said to be discharged. In some cases the entire contract is discharged and the parties are released from all obligations created by the contract. In other cases only one of the parties may be discharged of his duties under the contract and the other party may still be obligated to perform. Thus, there may be a total or partial discharge of the parties to a contract.

Methods of Discharge
The principal methods by which a contract may be discharged include (1) performance, (2) breach, (3) nonoccurrence of a condition precedent, (4) occurrence of a condition subsequent, (5) impossibility, (6) agreement, (7) cancellation or renunciation, and (8) operation of law.

PERFORMANCE AND BREACH

Performance of Contracts
Most contracts are discharged by the faithful performance of the obligations of the parties. The parties to a contract are ex-

pected to co-operate with one another in making performance possible. The failure of one party to fulfill his duty to co-operate or an unjustified affirmative act of one of the parties which prevents him or the other party from performing constitutes a material breach of the contract. Whenever this happens, either prior to the time of performance or after performance has commenced, the injured party may treat the contract as discharged and sue for breach of contract. Further discussion of breaches of contract appears later in this chapter.

Tender of Performance. A tender of performance is an offer or effort to perform made by a party who is prepared fully to perform his contractual obligations. It may be (1) an attempt to pay money as required by the contract, or (2) an attempt to do some act called for by the contract, such as the delivery of goods or the rendering of services.

If the other party refuses the tender of acts called for under the contract, the tendering party is usually discharged from any further obligations on the contract and he may bring an action for breach of contract. But where a party is obligated to pay a sum of money, his tender of the money, though in strict accordance with the contract, does not discharge the debt. However, such a tender and its refusal does (1) stop the accrual of interest from the date of tender, (2) make the creditor responsible for court costs if the creditor brings suit on the debt, and (3) release any pledge, mortgage, or other security given for the debt.

A tender of money to be valid must be for the exact amount due and the money must be legal tender. All coins and currencies issued by the United States government have been declared by act of Congress to be legal tender. Checks or other negotiable instruments are not legal tender, and they do not discharge a debt unless the parties understand that the instrument is being given and accepted as payment. In the absence of such an understanding, the acceptance of a check is treated as a conditional payment and the debt for which the check is given is not discharged until the check is actually paid by the bank upon which it was drawn. A check which has been paid is evidence of payment of the obligation noted on the check. A receipt for payment is acceptable evidence of payment, but it may be rebutted by evidence showing it to be in error, a forgery, or to have been given under mistake.

A debtor who is indebted on several obligations to his creditor is free at the time of payment to designate which of his obligations he is paying, and the creditor who receives such payment must follow the instructions given. In the absence of instructions, the creditor is free to apply the payment on any of several obligations due, or he may spread the payment among several obligations, or he may apply the payment against a claim which has been barred by the statute of limitations. However, in the latter case the outlawed claim is not revived where other obligations existed against which the payment could have been applied.

Doctrine of Substantial Performance.   At common law nothing less than complete performance would discharge a contract. This rigid rule has been relaxed to some extent by the equity courts which recognize that in some cases a performance which falls slightly short of perfect or literal compliance with the contract may nevertheless give the promisee what he could reasonably expect under the circumstances and thus entitle the party who substantially performed to recover on the contract. In such cases an allowance is made to the victim of the minor breach to compensate him for the slight defect in performance by the other party.

The doctrine of substantial performance is frequently applied to construction contracts and similar contracts where a promisee is not justified in expecting perfect performance by the promisor. The doctrine has no application to promises calling for the payment of money or to other promises which are by their nature recognized generally as capable of being performed exactly as promised.

If a contractor who has agreed to construct a building attempts in good faith to erect the building, and does so substantially, he may recover from the other party to the contract in spite of slight or trivial defects, for which compensation can be made by allowance to the other party. But the failure to perform must not be substantial, or willful, or due to bad faith.

Courts permit a party to recover on the theory of *quantum meruit* (as much as he deserves) for the value of his good faith performance which falls below that which would be considered substantial, unless the party who received the defective performance chooses to return it, if this is possible.

Time of Performance. Time of performance is said to be "of the essence" in a contract when failure of a party to perform upon a certain date or within a specified time, as the case may be, is a material breach, that is, it deprives the other party of something vital. In such cases the time of performance is treated as a condition precedent, and failure to comply with the condition discharges the injured party from his obligations on the contract and gives him the right to sue for breach of contract.

If the parties expressly provide in their contract that "time is of the essence," courts will enforce such a provision unless it is found that to do so would result in undue hardship and injustice. The controlling test used in determining whether time of performance is vital in a particular case is the intention of the parties as gathered from the terms of their contract, the nature of the subject matter of the contract, and the surrounding circumstances. On this basis a court may hold that time is of the essence even though the contract does not expressly so provide. For example, a party to an option contract must, due to the nature of the contract, exercise his option by the deadline provided for in the contract. Similarly, courts may imply that time is of the essence in certain mercantile contracts, such as those calling for delivery of goods by a certain date, the seller having knowledge that the buyer wants the goods so he can sell them during a certain season of the year. By contrast, the time of performance by a builder under a construction contract containing a specified completion date would not generally be construed to be of the essence. Therefore, the builder's tardy performance could fall within the substantial performance doctrine entitling him to recover the contract price for his performance less an amount necessary to compensate the other party for losses caused by the late performance.

As a general rule, if no time is specified for the performance of a contract, the law allows a reasonable time. What is a reasonable time depends upon the facts and circumstances of the particular case.

Personal Satisfaction Contracts. A contract may expressly provide that a party is to perform to the personal satisfaction of the other party who need not pay for the performance unless he is satisfied with it. In deciding whether a party's performance meets the personal satisfaction requirement, courts classify such contracts as either (1) contracts involving personal taste or judgment, or (2) contracts involving mechanical fitness, utility, or marketability for a particular purpose. A typical illustration of the first is a promise to paint a portrait to the personal satisfaction of the promisee. Applying a subjective test to such contracts, courts generally hold that the promisee is not required to pay for the portrait so long as he establishes that he is honestly dissatisfied with the portrait. To escape liability, his dissatisfaction must be actual and not feigned.

Courts apply an objective ("reasonable man") test to contracts involving mechanical fitness, utility, or marketability and hold that the performing party is entitled to payment if a reasonable person would be satisfied with the performance rendered or tendered. This test has been applied to construction and repair contracts.

Breach of Contracts

A breach of contract is a failure without legal excuse to perform an obligation under a contract. In addition, it has been pointed out earlier in this chapter that an act of a party which has the effect of preventing performance is treated as a breach of contract. If a material breach of contract is committed, the injured party is discharged from his duty to perform and has a right of action for damages or other appropriate relief. Breaches less than material give the victim a cause of action for damages. Of course the offended party may, if he chooses, accept the defective performance without objection. In such cases the aggrieved party is deemed to have waived the breach of contract.

Divisible and Indivisible Contracts. A contract may be divisible or indivisible, that is, capable of separation into independent parts or one which must be treated as a whole in terms of what a party must do to entitle him to performance by the other party. Where the promises on each side are mutually dependent and the contract is indivisible, a breach of performance by one party of a part of the contract will discharge the other party and give the latter an action for damages against the one in default. If, however, the contract is a divisible one, or the transaction is made up of a series of contracts, then the breach of a divisible part will not discharge the other parts and the party who has performed one of the severable parts may recover for that portion from the other contracting party. But, the promisor permitted to recover will be held responsible for any damage caused by his failure to perform all parts of the contract.

It is often difficult to determine whether a contract is divisible or indivisible. The governing principle is the manifested intention of the parties as gathered from the words, conduct, and circumstances which entered into the making of the contract. Where such intention is not discernable, courts simply decide the cases on the basis of fairness and common sense. As a general rule, if the payment of a lump sum is to be made for several articles, the contract is treated as indivisible. The Uniform Commercial Code follows this rule as is pointed out in Chapter 16 of this book.

Contracts to render personal services for a specified term,

such as one year, are held divisible when the compensation is stated as payable at specified shorter periods or can be so construed.

Anticipatory Breach.   Anticipatory breach occurs if one of the contracting parties clearly indicates in advance that he will not perform or be able to perform when the time for performance as called for in the contract has arrived. Anticipatory breach is sometimes called renunciation or repudiation. Generally, if an anticipatory breach occurs, the aggrieved party may immediately treat the repudiated contract as though it had already been breached; thus the injured party may rescind the contract or sue for damages without waiting for the arrival of the time for performance set by the contract. This rule does not apply to a promise to pay a money debt, including a negotiable instrument. For example, if the maker of a negotiable promissory note announces before the due date that he will not pay it when due, the holder must wait until the due date of the note before taking action against the maker.

An anticipatory breach may be retracted unless the party entitled to performance has acted on the basis of the anticipatory breach by canceling the contract or materially changing his position.

The Uniform Commercial Code's treatment of anticipatory breach of sales contracts, or repudiation as it is called in the Code, is discussed in Chapter 16 of this book.

CONDITIONS

Conditions Generally

Although a contract may create certain rights and duties, the enjoyment of the rights by the parties and the performance of their duties may be conditional and thus not enforceable until all the conditions have been satisfied. A promise which is unconditional is referred to as an *independent promise*.

Conditions may be created by the manifested assent of the

parties, express or implied; or they may be implied by the law without any manifestation of assent or intention by the parties to create them. *Express conditions* are those provided for by the words of the parties to a contract, oral or in writing. Those conditions which are a necessary part of the contract in view of its inherent nature are called *conditions implied in fact* and are viewed by the courts as having been intended by the parties, though not expressed. For example, a landlord's covenant to repair, with no right of entry reserved in the lease, is impliedly conditional upon notice from the tenant that the premises are out of repair. *Conditions implied in law* are called constructive conditions, and courts read them into contracts as a matter of justice or to avoid hardship in a particular case, apart from any manifested intention of the parties.

Conditions Precedent. A condition precedent provides for the occurrence of some event or the existence of some fact before there is a right to performance of some obligation created by the contract. For example, a contract for the sale of real estate may provide that the contract is contingent upon the buyer being able to obtain financing according to certain specified terms, thus creating an express condition precedent. This condition would raise an implied promise on the part of the buyer to make a reasonable effort to secure the financing. Thus, satisfaction of the implied condition precedent by the buyer would be necessary before he could escape his obligation to buy the property by claiming the benefit of the express condition precedent.

Construction contracts often provide that the progress payments and final payment called for in the contract are dependent upon the furnishing of a certificate of a named architect or engineer. Courts treat such provisions as creating conditions precedent and deny the contractor who sues on the contract the right to recover unless the certificate has been furnished or excused. Failure to furnish the certificate is excused by courts if the architect or engineer has died or is incapacitated, or there is fraud or collusion involved in the withholding of the certificate, or the withholding is clearly unreasonable or wholly arbitrary. Courts do not generally substitute their judgment for that of the professional person concerning the construction work performed, provided the professional person has acted honestly and for good reason in withholding the certificate.

Conditions Subsequent.   A condition subsequent provision in a contract extinguishes a party's duty of performance on the happening of some event or the coming into existence of some fact. A casualty insurance policy which provides that the insured shall give notice of a loss within a stated period or the company is discharged from liability for such loss illustrates a typical condition subsequent.

Conditions Concurrent.   If the parties to a contract intend that they are to perform their obligations simultaneously, such an intention creates concurrent conditions. This type of contract is illustrated by a contract for the sale of goods where payment and delivery are to occur at the same time. The party seeking to enforce the contract against the other party must be ready, able, and willing to perform his obligations, although actual performance in such cases is not a prerequisite to relief. Only a tender of performance is required.

IMPOSSIBILITY

Impossibility Generally

Impossibility may prevent a contract from being created, or it may discharge a contract after it has come into existence. Impossibility which prevents the creation of a contract has been discussed in Chapters 4 and 5 in connection with mutual assent and mistake. It was seen that if the performance of the contract is physically or legally impossible at the time it is made, no contract is created and neither party becomes obligated.

Foreseeable Burdens Distinguished From Impossibility. Foreseeable intervening events which merely make the performance of a contract more burdensome for a party do not, as a general rule, excuse such party from his duty to perform, even though holding him liable subjects him to great financial loss. Under this rule such things as strikes, inability to get laborers or materials, price increases, unavoidable accidents, floods, fire, acts of God, inability to perform because of incapacity, and the like, do not excuse performance unless the contract provides that their occurrence will excuse performance. A contract provision which excuses performance under certain specified circumstances is called an *exculpatory clause*.

IMPOSSIBILITY AND EXCUSED PERFORMANCE

There are three types of impossibility which the courts have traditionally recognized as excuses for nonperformance. These exceptions to the general rule are (1) death or serious illness of a promisor of personal services, (2) destruction of essential subject matter, and (3) subsequent illegality.

Death or Serious Illness in Personal Service Contracts. If a contract provides for the personal services of a particular person, the death or incapacitating illness of that person discharges him and his estate from liability on the contract. To illustrate, if A agrees to perform in a dramatic production and owing to illness he is unable to perform, A is excused from liability for nonperformance.

Personal service contracts must be distinguished from contracts in general, because the latter survive the death of the contracting party unless the contract contains a provision terminating the contract on the death of one of the parties during the term of the contract. For example, the death of a debtor does not discharge his money debt, the debtor's estate being liable for the debt.

Destruction of Essential Subject Matter. Where the continued existence of a specific thing is essential to performance, the contract is discharged if the thing is destroyed through no fault of either party. For example, a builder who contracts to repair an existing building is excused from his duty to perform if the building is destroyed by fire without fault on his part. In such cases most courts permit the builder to recover for the value of the labor and material incorporated into the property up to the time of impossibility resulting from the fire. Recovery by the builder for materials purchased by him for the repair work but not attached to the property at the time of the fire is not allowed even where it is shown that the materials would be no value to him on another job and have no resale value.

A contract to construct a new building is not discharged by the destruction of the partially completed building. In such cases performance is still possible even though the performance will involve additional burden, perhaps ruinous financial loss, to the builder. If a builder is to be excused from performance where foreseeable burdens such as those caused by fire or other disasters arise, the contract must so provide.

Cases have arisen involving the destruction of the source of performance thus making it burdensome but not physically impossible for a party to perform his contract. The general rule of nonexcuse has been applied unless the source was expressly mentioned in the contract as essential to performance. To illustrate, under the strict rule a party contracting to sell and deliver certain equipment would not be discharged from his obligation to perform if the factory in which he planned to manufacture the equipment was destroyed by fire. The particular factory was not a specific thing essential to the performance of the contract. However, if the parties understood that the equipment was to be manufactured in the particular factory, then its destruction by fire would excuse the equipment manufacturer from performing unless the fire could be attributed to his wrongful act. Some courts have departed from application of the strict rule of nonexcuse by holding that the continued existence of the means of performance is an implied condition of contractual liability unless the destruction of the means of performance is the fault of the party seeking escape from the contract.

Subsequent Illegality.   If a change in the law after a contract has been created makes the performance of the contract illegal, the promisor is excused from performance. The change in the law must have the effect of preventing performance. If the law change merely makes performance more difficult or burdensome, the promisor is not excused. The change in the law may result from enactment of a statute, court decision, or promulgation of a government regulation. Various executive orders have been issued in wartime which have made certain contracts more burdensome for one of the parties. The courts have applied the general rule of nonexcuse to such cases unless the contract provides for excuse or can be interpreted in such a way that the party is excused. For example, a lease of a storeroom is not terminated by the wartime issuance of an executive order prohibiting the sale of the goods (such as new tires) the tenant is selling in the business being conducted on the site of the leased premises. Although it may be burdensome to do so, the lessee could use the storeroom for some purpose not restricted by the executive order. These cases are often referred to as *commercial frustration* cases, and the courts generally deny relief to the party who complains merely because his business has become less profitable. However, a lease containing a provision restricting the use of the premises to the sale of the goods described in the subsequent executive order prohibiting the sale of such goods would be terminated by legal impossibility, and the lessee would be excused from any further payment of rent.

DISCHARGE BY AGREEMENT

Contracts are created by agreement and generally they may be terminated by agreement. A contract made for the benefit of a third person may not be terminated without the third person's consent if he has changed his position in reliance on the contract. The agreement which discharges a contract may take the form of (1) mutual promises to terminate or rescind, (2) a substitute contract, (3) a novation, and (4) waiver.

Mutual Termination and Rescission

In considering how contracts may be discharged by an agreement to cancel or rescind, it is necessary to distinguish between *executory* and *executed* contracts. If a contract is wholly executory, that is, completely unperformed, it may be terminated by a mutual agreement of the parties to abandon their rights to performance. The exchange of legal detriments resulting from each party giving up his right to performance constitutes the consideration needed to support the promises to abandon the contract.

If the contract is executed, fully or partly, the parties may agree to return to each other the performance received and such an agreement to rescind is supported by consideration in the form of the return by each party of what he has received from the other. Of course, if both parties have fully performed their obligations, the contract is already discharged by performance. The promise of one party who has performed to forego his right to require performance by the other party, is not binding unless supported by some new consideration. In some states a written release of a party to a contract is recognized as binding. The few states which still recognize the efficacy of the seal do not require any new consideration in order for a written release under seal to be binding.

Modification of sales contracts in states which have adopted the Uniform Commercial Code is governed by Section 2-209 of the Code and is discussed in Chapter 13 of this book.

Substitute Contract

A contract may be discharged wholly or in part by a subsequent agreement intended to replace the old agreement. As a general rule, the evidence must be clear and convincing that the parties intend to substitute the new contract for the old before a discharge of the former contract will result. Even then the substituted agreement, like all contracts, generally must be supported by a valid consideration. The mutual agreement of the parties to a bilateral executory contract to terminate it and to replace it with a new contract is supported by consideration in the form of the new advantages or burdens contained in the new contract and the giving up of the rights created by the old.

Novation

A novation is a multilateral agreement between the parties to a contract and a third person whereby the third party is substituted for either the obligor or obligee in the original contract. For example, A sells to B an automobile upon which A owes a balance of $500 to C, the party from whom A had purchased the automobile originally. B agrees to pay to C the $500 balance owed by A in consideration of C's promise to release A. With the assent of all the parties, a novation has been created and the contract between A and C has been discharged. The novation has discharged the obligor, A, from his obligation to C and has substituted a new obligor, B, in place of A. In other cases a novation may replace an obligee with a new party.

Novation is sometimes broadly defined to include any agreement which extinguishes an existing agreement and substitutes a new one in its place. This definition embraces the bilateral agreement substituting a new contract for an old one, with no change in the parties. This type of contract was discussed under discharge of contracts by agreement.

Waiver

A waiver is the voluntary surrender of a known right or claim. A common form of waiver is the failure of the victim of a breach of contract to seasonably object to the defective performance. For example, if a purchaser of a piano fails to complain about the known damaged condition of the piano at the time of delivery and pays for the piano without objection, the purchaser by his conduct has waived his right to rescind the sale contract. A waiver may be express or implied.

CANCELLATION AND RENUNCIATION

Contracts in the form of a legal instrument, such as a contract under seal or a formal document, may be discharged by a cancellation or surrender of the instrument and need not be supported by any consideration. Destruction or mutilation of the written instrument or writing the word "cancelled" or a similar notation on the document by the obligee with the intention of relinquishing his rights under the contract constitutes cancellation. Surrender is the giving back of the contractual document by the obligee to the obligor with the intention of cancelling the rights therein and is sometimes referred to as a renunciation.

Discharge of negotiable instruments by cancellation or renunciation is provided for and described in Section 3-605 of the Uniform Commercial Code.

OPERATION OF LAW

The methods of discharging contracts which are usually classified under operation of law include (1) the running of the statute of limitations, (2) bankruptcy, (3) merger, and (4) material alteration of a written contract.

Statute of Limitations

A statute of limitations fixes a time limit within which suit must be commenced after a cause of action arises. Actions for breach of contract must be brought within the time prescribed by statute. Once the time period has run, the right of action upon the contract is "outlawed," that is, barred by the statute. The policy of the law is to bar suits on rights which are asserted after an undue delay. Such delay usually is accompanied by the disappearance of evidence and the death of witnesses. Each state has its own statutes of limitations establishing time limits on the various kinds of legal actions. Suit on an oral contract is barred, in many states, after three years; on a written contract, such as a promissory note, suit is barred in many states after six years. As will be pointed out in Chapter 16, the Uniform Commercial Code provides for a four year statute of limitations in the case of sales contracts and authorizes the parties to reduce, by their original agreement, the period of limitation to not less than one year but they may not extend it.[1]

A cause of action accrues when one person has the right to commence suit against another person. In the case of contracts generally, a cause of action accrues in favor of the aggrieved party when a breach occurs. The Code specifies when a cause of action accrues in the case of a sale contract breach.[2] On open accounts and similar contracts, the time is computed from the time the last payment or charge is made. Therefore, a voluntary payment by the debtor or a charge to his account is said to "toll the statute" and to start it running anew from the date of such transaction for the full period fixed by the statute. This result makes it advantageous for a creditor to accept from his debtor even a very small payment which might be viewed as a nuisance in the absence of the tolling effect.

The aggrieved party is excused from bringing an action against the breaching party within the time fixed by statute if certain circumstances arise which are beyond his control. For example, the period of time a creditor or debtor is a minor or is insane is usually eliminated from the period prescribed by statute, as is the period during which the debtor is absent from the state.

As pointed out in Chapter 6 on consideration, a new promise made by a debtor after the statute has run may be enforceable. Some states require such a new promise to be in writing, particularly where the barred obligation was in writing.

---

[1] UCC Sec. 2-725 (1).
[2] UCC Sec. 2-725 (2).

Bankruptcy

A discharge in bankruptcy releases the debtor from all provable and properly scheduled claims arising out of contract. Technically the contract itself is not discharged, as the bankruptcy discharge merely acts as a bar to any action on the contract claims discharged in the bankruptcy proceedings heard in the U.S. District Court under the Federal Bankruptcy Act. A subsequent agreement by the debtor to pay his creditor may revive the creditor's claim on the contract that had been discharged in bankruptcy, if the revival agreement meets the requirements of the particular state.

The Congress has enacted laws on bankruptcy pursuant to authority granted to it by the federal constitution. The purpose of bankruptcy law is to secure the equitable distribution of insolvent estates among creditors and to relieve honest but unfortunate debtors from the burden of debts so they can have a fresh start in their economic enterprises. If the debtor files a petition in bankruptcy, the proceeding is known as a voluntary bankruptcy. A petition filed by creditors puts the debtor into what is known as involuntary bankruptcy.

Merger

Discharge of a contract by merger occurs where one contract is merged into a contract or obligation of a "higher degree or order" by operation of law. For example, a judgment on a contract automatically merges the contractual obligation in the judgment and discharges the contract. Another example is the case of a debtor on an open account giving the creditor a promissory note to take the place of the account. The legal result is a merger of the open account into the obligation created by the promissory note.

Material Alteration

A material alteration of a written contract by one of the parties without the prior or subsequent consent of the other party will normally discharge the contract. Of course the non-altering party may, if he wishes, insist on the performance of the contract in accordance with its original tenor. The alteration must be intentional, not accidental, and it must be a material alteration. The alteration is material if it changes the legal effect of the instrument, that is, alters the rights or duties of the parties. If the alteration is made by a third party and without the knowledge and consent of either of the contracting parties, the contract is not discharged and the rights of the parties are not affected.

Remedies

12

INTRODUCTION

Objective and Classes of Remedies

The objective of the law of remedies in relation to a breach of contract is to put the aggrieved party, in so far as is practical, in the position he would have occupied had the contract been fully performed. Generally parties enter into a business contract with the expectation of realizing an economic gain or profit from the transaction. In most cases a money judgment will most nearly give the victim of a contract breach the benefits he expected to enjoy as the result of the performance of the contract by the other party. Therefore, the legal remedy of money damages is the remedy usually granted for a breach of contract.

Money damages may not provide an adequate remedy for a breach of contract. In such cases a court may as a matter of sound discretion grant appropriate equitable relief to the injured party. The principal equitable remedies which are often applied to breach of contract cases are (1) specific performance, (2) injunction, and (3) rescission or restitution. The enforcement of remedies, legal and equitable, was discussed in Chapter 2.

For a discussion of remedies available to buyers and sellers of goods under the Uniform Commercial Code, see Chapter 16

Declaratory Judgment

If issues about the meaning of a written contract have arisen, a party to the contract may bring an action for a declaratory judgment even though no breach of the contract has occurred. In such cases the court will declare what are the rights and duties of the parties under the contract. This procedure is governed by the Uniform Declaratory Judgments Act in a number of states.

Election of Remedies

A breach of contract victim may be entitled to one of several alternative remedies. In such cases he may be required to choose from the remedies available to him. For example, if the plaintiff brings an action for damages, he is barred from seeking restitution. Similarly, the remedies of specific performance and restitution are mutually exclusive. As a general rule, the plaintiff may seek the legal remedy of money damages as well as the equitable remedy of specific performance in the same suit. In any case where the injured party's choice of a particular remedy is followed by a material change in position by the other party in reasonable reliance thereon, the injured party may be estopped from obtaining some other remedy.

CLASSES OF MONEY DAMAGES

Damages in relation to breaches of contract are classified as (1) nominal, (2) compensatory, (3) consequential or special, and (4) liquidated.

Nominal Damages

If a breach of contract has occurred but the victim has suffered no measurable loss or injury as a result of the breach, the plaintiff will be awarded a judgment for nominal damages, usually one dollar, and the court costs will be assessed against the defendant. In such cases the plaintiff is likely to be "out of pocket" as it is the rule in most civil cases, including the typical breach of contract action, that each litigant must pay his own attorney fees.

Compensatory Damages

Compensatory damages are awarded to a victim of a breach of contract to compensate him for the ordinary losses suffered and gains prevented as a result of the breach.

The prevailing theory of the law of damages in relation to a breach of contract is that of compensating the victim, not that of punishing the breaching party. *Punitive* or *exemplary* damages are rarely granted in breach of contract cases, even where the breach was willful. Historically, such damages were sometimes awarded for a breach of promise to marry.

Measuring Damages. Examples of how compensatory damages are measured can be presented by looking at some typical contracts and their breach. If a unilateral contract has been fully executed by the plaintiff, the measure of damages is the value of the performance promised by the defendant. Generally in a bilateral contract which is either wholly executory or partly performed by either party, the measure of damages is the value of the unfulfilled performance less the cost to the injured party of completing his performance. To illustrate, in a contract for the sale of goods, if title to the goods has passed, the seller is entitled to recover the purchase price in most cases. Where title to the goods has not passed to the defaulting buyer, the measure of damages is the difference between the contract price and the market value of the goods at the time and place of delivery as provided for in the contract. The same formula is applied in measuring the damages incurred by the buyer in the ordinary case of breach by the seller of an executory contract for the sale of goods.

Loss of Profits. Difficulty arises in assessing profits or other gains which the injured party claims he was denied by a contract breach. The amount claimed must not be speculative or remote, that is, the loss must be established with reasonable certainty. Under this standard loss of profits probably could not be established if a contract involved a new or speculative enterprise. However, if loss of profits is claimed in relation to an established business with acceptable accounting records showing a history of profits which have been directly interfered with by the breach of contract, the loss could be allowed as part of the injured party's recovery.

Consequential Damages

Consequential damages or special damages are those damages awarded to the injured party for unusual losses arising because of the special or unusual circumstances of the particular contract which were readily foreseeable by the breaching party. For example, a breach of warranty by the seller of goods may have consequences causing the buyer losses far beyond the ordinary loss of the difference between the value of the goods if they had been as warranted and their value in the actual condition when received by the buyer.

Liquidated Damages

A contract provision which stipulates the amount of damages to be recovered by the injured party in the event of a breach of the contract is a liquidated damages provision. This stipulated amount may be recovered unless the court finds it to be a penalty, that is, the provision having been inserted in the contract to coerce the party to perform rather than having been designed as a reasonable approximation of the loss the injured party would suffer from the breach. If the court finds the stipulated amount to be a penalty, the court will instruct the jury, in a jury case, to determine the actual amount of damages, if any, to be awarded the plaintiff. Contracts for the construction of buildings often provide for a specified amount to be paid by the builder to the owner for each day performance is late. The validity of the provision would be determined by applying the above principles.

MITIGATION OF DAMAGES

The law imposes a duty upon the victim of a breach of contract to minimize his damage. For example, an employee discharged without cause before his term of employment has expired must exercise reasonable diligence in finding similar employment in the same locality. Similarly, in some states a lessor must make a reasonable effort to rent his property vacated by the tenant in violation of a lease. A manufacturer given notice of cancellation of a contract for the manufacture and sale of goods must not incur further costs if such will add to the manufacturer's damages.

EQUITABLE REMEDIES

Specific Performance

A judgment for money does not provide an adequate remedy for a breach of contract in certain exceptional cases. In such cases an equity court may as a matter of discretion grant a decree of specific performance which orders a party to a contract to carry out his contractual obligations precisely as promised. For example, specific performance of a contract to sell and convey land is generally granted at the request of either the buyer or the seller. The buyer is granted specific performance for the reason that each tract of land is unique and, therefore, money damages would be an inadequate remedy. Based upon the equitable doctrine that the remedies ought to be mutual, the seller in such cases may usually receive specific performance, as well as the buyer.

Specific performance of contracts for the sale of personal property is seldom granted. As pointed out in the discussion in Chapter 16 of a buyer's remedies under the Uniform Commercial Code, exception is made where the personal property has no market value or has some unique quality which makes it unobtainable on the market. Such would be the case of a work of art, an heirloom, and similar articles.

Because of the policy against forcing persons into a personal relationship, specific performance of contracts for personal services is not granted. A construction contract is not a proper subject of a specific performance decree as it would impose the intolerable burden upon the equity court of prolonged and detailed supervision of the performance of the contract. Also, specific performance will be withheld if it would cause undue hardship. In all cases the primary prerequisite for the granting of specific performance or any other equitable remedy is the inadequacy of the legal remedy.

Injunction

In certain unusual breach of contract cases, a court may grant an injunction to the injured party. The injunction is an equitable remedy which orders the party against whom it is directed to either take some affirmative action or to refrain from committing certain acts, under penalty of being punished for contempt of court if the order is violated. This remedy is granted where irreparable harm to property or other rights is threatened by a breach of contract. While specific performance of a personal services contract will not be granted, a *negative covenant* in such contract may be enforced by means of an injunction, which may have the indirect effect of bringing about the performance of the promised personal services. For example, a professional athlete who has agreed to perform his skilled services for the other party to the contract and no other party may be restrained by injunction from breaching his negative covenant, although a court would not enforce his promise of affirmative performance.

Rescission

As an alternative to the recovery of damages for a breach of contract, the victim may ask for rescission of the contract, or restitution, as this remedy is sometimes called. Unlike damages which are designed to place the injured party as nearly as possible in the position he would have occupied had the contract been performed, the object of rescission is to put the parties back in the positions they were in before the contract was made. Like all equitable remedies the granting of restitution rests within the sound discretion of the court.

Sales Contracts

13

INTRODUCTION

The law of sales consists of a body of law which governs the rights and duties arising out of those contracts which make up the largest class of contracts in the business world—contracts which have as their subject matter the sale of goods. These important commercial transactions involved in the marketing of goods affect everyone, but buyers and sellers of goods are especially concerned.

Development of Uniform Laws

Uniform Sales Act. Prior to the widespread adoption in recent years of the Uniform Commercial Code (states which have adopted the Code, as of the end of 1964, are listed in Chapter 1 of this book), sales transactions were governed in more than two-thirds of the states by the Uniform Sales Act, promulgated in 1906 by the National Conference of Commissioners on Uniform State Laws and patterned after England's Sale of Goods Act of 1894. The Uniform Sales Act will be referred to here simply as the Sales Act. Before these statutory developments, the law of sales was judge-made, first, in the special commercial courts in England (referred to as the law merchant courts) and, later, in the common-law and equity courts of England and the United States. An intolerable lack of uniformity in the decisions of the courts of the various states in this country led to the drafting and enactment of uniform state legislation to overcome the conflicts and confusion in the law. The Sales Act codified much of the law of sales as it had evolved under the common law and abrogated or modified some of the common-law rules. It was one of a series of uniform commercial laws prepared and offered to the state legislatures for adoption in an attempt to bring about uniformity in the law being applied to commercial transactions in the various states.

Uniform Commercial Code. Article 2 of the Uniform Commercial Code, entitled "Sales," replaces the Sales Act which had become outmoded both in terms of organization and substance. The Sales Act was no longer responsive to the needs of those engaging in sales transactions, and, in some instances, was actually out of harmony with established commercial practices. A further problem had been created by the nonuniform interpretation of many of the Sales Act provisions by courts of different states. The Code adopts many of the principles contained in the Sales Act as well as those found in court decisions and gives the force of law to what are viewed as generally accepted commercial practices, all with the aim of permitting buyers and sellers to enjoy reasonable expectations and to carry out their objectively manifested intentions. The Code is replete with a great number of specific rules designed to provide a framework within which disputes arising out of sales transactions can be resolved by arbitration or litigation. Many of these rules will be discussed in this book, along with certain fundamental concepts found in the Sales Act and court decisions which remain part of the law of sales.

Definitions and Distinctions

Sale. A sale is defined as a contract whereby a person called the seller (or vendor) transfers the general property interest in goods to another person called the buyer (or vendee) for a consideration called the price. The term title is often used to describe the general ownership of property.

Sale v. Bailment and Security Transaction. The general property interest or title may be described as the general or beneficial ownership in goods as distinguished from a restricted interest, such as a security interest or mere possession which are regarded as special property interests. For example, a bailment is distinguished from a sale in that in a bailment the owner (bailor) merely turns over the temporary possession of the property to the bailee, the bailor retaining the ownership and the bailee assuming a duty to return the property or dispose of it as instructed by the bailor. The law of bailments is discussed in Chapter 34 of this book. The interest a mortgagee holds in relation to property mortgaged to him by the owner (mortgagor) is an illustration of a security interest.

Sale v. Contract to Sell. A contract to sell differs from a contract of sale or present sale in that in a contract to sell the title is not transferred by the mere agreement. In a contract to sell, the seller assumes a contractual obligation to transfer the title at a future time. The Code's definition of a "contract for sale" includes both a present sale and a contract to sell goods at a future time.

Goods and Related Terms. Section 2-105 of the Uniform Commercial Code defines "goods" and certain related terms as follows:

1] "Goods" means all things (including specially manufactured goods) which are movable at the time of identification to the contract for sale other than the money in which the price is to be paid, investment securities (Article 8) and things in action. "Goods" also includes the unborn young of animals and growing crops and other identified things attached to realty as described in the section on goods to be severed from realty (Section 2-107).

2] Goods must be both existing and identified before any interest in them can pass. Goods which are not both existing and identified are "future" goods. A purported present sale of future goods or of any interest therein operates as a contract to sell.

3] There may be a sale of a part interest in existing identified goods.

4] An undivided share in an identified bulk of fungible goods is sufficiently identified to be sold although the quantity of the bulk is not determined. Any agreed proportion of such a bulk or any quantity thereof agreed upon by number, weight, or other measure may to the extent of the seller's interest in the bulk be sold to the buyer who then becomes an owner in common.

5] "Lot" means a parcel or a single article which is the subject matter of a separate sale or delivery, whether or not it is sufficient to perform the contract.

6] "Commercial unit" means such a unit of goods as by commercial usage is a single whole for purposes of sale and division of which materially impairs its character or value on the market or in use. A commercial unit may be a single article (as a machine) or a set of articles (as a suite of furniture or an assortment of sizes) or a quantity (as a bale, gross, or carload) or any other unit treated in use or in the relevant market as a single whole.

It is important to note that certain types of personal property are expressly excluded from the above definition of goods. Contracts for the sale of real property or for the furnishing of a service are not governed by the law of sales but, in some respects, the governing rules parallel one another.

Sale v. Gift.   The definition of a sale expressly indicates that the transfer of the general property interest in the goods must be for a consideration called the price. Although the price in a sales transaction is usually in the form of money, the price may be made payable in any personal property. Unless a price is or is to be paid, the transaction is not a sale although it may result in title to goods passing from one person to another. For example, a gift of personal property passes title but the transaction is gratuitous, the donee not paying any price, and the transaction is governed by the law of gifts as described in Chapter 33.

Merchants and Non-Merchants. A major departure from the approach taken by the Sales Act is found in the Code's scheme of applying certain rules to disputes between merchants and different rules if a non-merchant is involved. Under the Sales Act all buyers and sellers generally are treated alike, although courts in some cases have found occasion to recognize the peculiar characteristics of one or both the parties to the controversy. According to Section 2-104 (1) of the Code, " 'merchant' means a person who deals in goods of the kind or otherwise by his occupation holds himself out as having knowledge or skill peculiar to the practices or goods involved in the transaction or to whom such knowledge or skill may be attributed by his employment of an agent or broker or other intermediary who by his occupation holds himself out as having such knowledge or skill." It can be seen that this definition of merchant is broad enough to include not only persons in the business of selling goods, but almost anyone dealing regularly in the business world. If both of the parties to the sales transaction are merchants, the parties will be given great liberality and flexibility in the giving of effect to the terms of their agreement. On the other hand, if one of the parties to the sale is not a merchant, the contractual requirements and provisions will be more strictly controlled. The basis for this distinction is that business needs require that merchants be given great freedom in arranging their transactions, and ordinarily merchants will be nearly on a parity in bargaining position and commercial knowledge. Non-merchants, however, need more protection and are more likely to be in a disadvantageous bargaining position due to their inexperience in the market place. Further significance of the distinction between merchants and non-merchants will become apparent in the discussion of specific rules of sales law in this part of the book.

SALES CONTRACTS UNDER THE UNIFORM
COMMERCIAL CODE

Formation of the Sales Contract

A contract is the legal vehicle for engaging in a sales transaction.
Most of the basic rules of general contract law, as discussed
in Part Two of this book, apply in sales transactions. For instance, a sales contract must satisfy the four essential elements
of a contract, described as mutual assent, consideration, competent parties, and legality. Also, the assent must be real and genuine, that is not based on mistake, fraud, duress or undue
influence, and there is a statute of frauds applicable to sales
contracts. A further requirement added by the Code is that the
agreement must not be unconscionable. This requirement is discussed later in this chapter.

The Code makes important changes in the practice of applying traditional contract rules to consideration and offer and acceptance problems arising in sales transactions. These depar-
tures from general contract law are discussed below. They
demonstrate that the policy of the Code is to have the law conform with mercantile practice and understanding and to recognize the existence of a contract whenever the parties have clearly
expressed an intent to be bound and a reasonably certain basis
for granting an appropriate remedy can be found.

Revocability of Offers. As pointed out in Chapter 4, page
52, it is a general rule of contract law, usually followed in most
states, that an offeror has the right at any time to withdraw or
revoke his offer before it is accepted, even if he had promised
in a signed writing not to do so, unless he had received consideration for such a promise. The Code abandons this rule
partially by providing that an offer by a merchant to buy or
sell goods in a signed writing which gives assurance that it will
be held open needs no consideration to be irrevocable for a
reasonable time or during a stated time, but in no event for a

time exceeding three months.[1] A firm offer provision contained in a form supplied by the offeree must be separately signed by the offeror to make the Code rule applicable. Offers by non-merchants to sell goods do not fall within the Code rule, and thus, come under the general rule and are revokable unless supported by consideration. Some courts have worked out tenuous modifications of the general rule applicable to firm offers, but it remained for the Code to provide a clear-cut statutory statement of an exception to the long-standing general rule. Prior to the Code, statutes had been enacted in some states, including New York, to modify the general rule in order to make promises to keep offers open binding without consideration under certain circumstances.

Certainty of Terms. Seeking to relax the application of the contract rule that generally a bargain must be definite, certain, and complete as to all material terms, Section 2-204 of the Code provides:

1] A contract for the sale of goods may be made in any manner sufficient to show agreement, including conduct by both parties which recognizes the existence of such a contract.

2] An agreement sufficient to constitute a contract for sale may be found even though the moment of its making is undetermined.

3] Even though one or more terms are left open, a contract for sale does not fail for indefiniteness if the parties have intended to make a contract and there is a reasonably certain basis for giving an appropriate remedy.

Due to the fact that under the Code a sales contract may be created even though all the terms are not agreed upon, rules of construction are set forth in Sections 2-305 to 2-311, inclusive, of the Code to aid the parties and courts in supplying these missing terms. For example, there are rules of construc-

---

[1] UCC Sec. 2-205.

tion applying to open-price terms, output, requirements, exclusive dealings, absence of place for delivery, absence of time of performance, open time for payment or running of credit, and other matters relating to performance of the contract.

Acceptance. Under the Code, the parties to a sales transaction can have a binding contract even though the acceptance contains additional or different terms from those contained in the offer. Section 2-207 of the Code provides:

1] A definite and seasonable expression of acceptance or a written confirmation which is sent within a reasonable time operates as an acceptance even though it states terms additional to or different from those offered or agreed upon, unless acceptance is expressly made conditional on assent to the additional or different terms.

2] The additional terms are to be construed as proposals for addition to the contract. Between merchants such terms become part of the contract unless:

A] the offer expressly limits acceptance to the terms of the offer;

B] they materially alter it; or

C] notification of objection to them has already been given or is given within a reasonable time after notice of them is received.

3] Conduct by both parties which recognizes the existence of a contract is sufficient to establish a contract for sale although the writings of the parties do not otherwise establish a contract. In such case the terms of the particular contract consist of those terms on which the writings of the parties agree, together with any supplementary terms incorporated under any other provisions of this Act.

A basic rule of contract law requires that an acceptance of an offer for a contract comply strictly with the terms of the offer with respect to the mode and time of acceptance as well as all other material terms prescribed in the offer. This rule when applied to ambiguously worded offers has in some cases unfairly deprived a party of a contract. Some courts have avoided such unfair results by holding that if the mode of acceptance is not clearly suggested or prescribed, the acceptance may be made in any manner that is reasonable, taking into consideration such things as the subject matter of the offer, custom, and prior dealings. This approach to the problems created by ambiguous offers is found in Section 2-206 of the Code which provides:

1] Unless otherwise unambiguously indicated by the language or circumstances
    A] an offer to make a contract shall be construed as inviting acceptance in any manner and by any medium reasonable in the circumstances;
    B] an order or other offer to buy goods for prompt or current shipment shall be construed as inviting acceptance either by a prompt promise to ship or by the prompt or current shipment of conforming or nonconforming goods, but such a shipment of nonconforming goods does not constitute an acceptance if the seller seasonably notifies the buyer that the shipment is offered only as an accommodation to the buyer.

2] Where the beginning of a requested performance is a reasonable mode of acceptance an offeror who is not notified of acceptance within a reasonable time may treat the offer as having lapsed before acceptance.

It can be seen that under Subsection 2-206 (1) (b) of the above-quoted Code provision a shipment of goods in response to an order to which it does not conform is an acceptance and at the same time a breach, and the seller cannot escape liability by setting up the traditional contract rule that a failure to comply with the terms of an offer constituted a rejection of the offer, thus preventing the formation of a contract. This provision of the Code also makes it possible for the seller to send a nonconforming shipment as an accommodating substitution rather than having the shipment constitute an acceptance and breach.

Unconscionability

Generally the Code permits the parties to control completely all of the terms of their sales contracts so long as the terms are not unconscionable. Section 2-302 of the Code provides that if a sales contract or one of its clauses is found by a court to be unconscionable as a matter of law, the court may refuse to enforce the contract, disregard the clause, or limit the application of the clause. This important change in the approach to unduly harsh or oppressive contracts allows the courts to decide cases directly on the basis of unconscionability rather than on the basis of a strained construction of some concept of contract law or on the basis of the illogical construction of the wording of the contract. The basic test of unconscionability, as used in the Code, is whether, in the light of the general commercial background and the commercial needs of the particular trade or case, the clauses involved are so one-sided as to be unconscionable under the circumstances existing at the time of the making of the contract. A similar philosophy pervades the entire Code and finds expression in such phrases as "good faith," "best efforts," "reasonable time," and "commercial reasonableness."

Modification and Waiver

The Code provides that a sales contract may be modified without consideration, but the sales contract may require any modification to be in writing, and, except as between merchants, such a requirement on a form supplied by the merchant must be separately signed by the other party and the Statute of Frauds provision of the Code must be satisfied if applicable.[2] Under the Code an ineffective modification may nevertheless operate as a waiver unless retracted prior to a material change in position by the other party in reliance on the waiver.[3] Any modification would have to be grounded in good faith as Section 1-203 of the Code provides: "Every contract or duty within this

---

[2] UCC Sec. 2-209 (1) (2) (3).
[3] UCC Sec. 2-209 (4) (5).

Act imposes an obligation of good faith in its performance or enforcement."

Statute of Frauds Under the Uniform Sales Act

In Chapter 9 the operation of the statute of frauds was discussed with respect to contracts generally. As we have seen, the Statute of Frauds was first enacted by the English Parliament in 1677 and later became part of the law of each state in America.

Section 17 of the English Statute of Frauds was made a part of the Uniform Sales Act. Section 4 of the Sales Act provides: "A contract to sell or a sale of any goods or choses in action of the value of $500 or upwards shall not be enforceable by action unless the buyer shall accept part of the goods or choses in action so contracted to be sold or sold, and actually receive the same, or give something in earnest to bind the contract, or in part payment, or unless some note or memorandum in writing of the contract or sale be signed by the party to be charged or his agent in that behalf." While $500 was the most common minimum amount fixed in the various states' statutes, the amount has varied in other states from $30 in one state to $2,500 in another. The Code in its statute of frauds provision relating to sales of goods fixes the minimum amount at $500, and defines the amount as the "price" of the goods rather than their "value."

Statutes of Frauds Under the Uniform Commercial Code

First, it is important to recognize that the Code contains four different "statutes of frauds" as follows: (1) Section 2-201 dealing with the sale of goods; (2) Section 8-319 relating to the sale of investment securities; (3) Section 9-203 dealing with the sale of accounts receivable, contract rights and chattel paper; and (4) Section 2-209 dealing with the sale of any other kind of personal property. Only the statute of frauds provision dealing with the sale of goods is involved in the following discussion of the Code requirements.

Compliance with the Code's Statute of Frauds for the Sale of Goods. Under the Code, a contract for the sale of goods for the price of $500 or more is not enforceable unless there is a writing indicating a contract has been made, the quantity of goods involved in the sale, and the writing must be signed by the party against whom enforcement is sought or by his authorized agent or broker.[4] Unlike the Sales Act statute of frauds provision which includes both "goods" and "choses in action," the Code statute of frauds section relating to the sale of goods applies only to "goods," with money, investment securities, and things in action being excluded by definition.[5]

Under the pre-Code law, there was substantial judicial authority that the writing had to contain all of the material terms of the contract such as the price of the goods, the quantity of the goods involved, the credit terms, the delivery terms, and others. Under the Code, however, the only requirements are that the writing (1) indicate that a contract for sale exists between the parties, (2) the quantity of goods involved in the sale, and (3) the party to be held must have placed his name on the writing. Since the memorandum is not the contract but only evidence of it, the signing by only one party is not lack of mutuality as discussed in Chapter 6. This rule conforms to the policy of the Code with respect to the liberal approach to the certainty requirement as noted previously in this chapter.

The customary writing used by the parties to a sale is called a *bill of sale* which usually is limited to a description of the personal property being transferred, the names of the seller and buyer, the price; and it is signed by the seller.

Exceptions. The exceptions to the writing requirement of the Code's statute of frauds governing the sale of goods are as follows:

1] Specially manufactured goods.
2] Admissions by pleading or otherwise in court.

---

[4] UCC Sec. 2-201 (1).
[5] UCC Sec. 2-105 (1).

3] Goods for which payment has been made and accepted or which have been received and accepted.

4] Confirmatory writing, if between merchants.

Specially Manufactured Goods. Contracts for goods which "are to be specially manufactured for the buyer and are not suitable for sale to others in the ordinary course of the seller's business" need not be evidenced by a writing, but the oral agreement is enforceable only if the seller "before notice of repudiation is received and under circumstances which reasonably indicate that the goods are for the buyer, has made either a substantial beginning of their manufacture or commitments for their manufacture or procurement." [6] A common example of such specially manufactured goods is calendars whose face carry the name and advertisement of the buyer.

Admissions in Court. The Code provides that the statute of frauds is satisfied "if the party against whom enforcement is sought admits in his pleading, testimony, or otherwise in court that a contract for sale was made, but the contract is not enforceable under this provision beyond the quantity of goods admitted." [7] This rule raises the possibility that a party who can show no compliance with the statute of frauds might still bring suit on the oral contract, and, if the defendant then admits the oral contract in the court proceedings, the statute becomes satisfied. The interesting question has been raised as to whether upon cross-examination a party could be forced to admit the existence of a sales contract and thus satisfy this provision of the Code.

Payment or Delivery. An oral sales contract is enforceable to the extent that the seller has accepted payment for the goods or to the extent that the buyer has received and accepted the goods.[8] Before the Code, courts interpreted part performance

---

[6] UCC Sec. 2-201 (3) (a).
[7] UCC Sec. 2-201 (3) (b).
[8] UCC Sec. 2-201 (3) (c).

as taking a sales contract completely out of the statute of frauds provision of the Sales Act and, under this view, the contract was enforceable in its entirety. Under the Code, the oral contract is enforceable only to the extent that there has been payment for or receipt and acceptance of the goods. Thus, under the Code rule, if an oral contract called for delivery of 100 units (total price $500 or more) and only 75 units had been received and accepted by buyer, the seller could recover from the buyer only for the 75 units. The seller could not recover damages for the buyer's refusal to accept the remaining 25 units. Conversely, if the buyer had paid for only 75 units, he could enforce the contract against the seller for only 75 units. The buyer would have no remedy in court for the seller's refusal to deliver the remaining 25 units.

Confirmatory Writing. Between *merchants,* a written confirmation of an oral contract of sale may be sent within a reasonable time and if the party receiving it fails to give written notice of objection within ten days, he will have waived the statute of frauds.[9] This rule is designed to preclude the unscrupulous recipient of a letter confirming an oral sales order from being able to stand by and watch the fluctuations in the market price of the goods and declare the contract enforceable or unenforceable as his best interests dictate. While this Code rule is applicable only between merchants, the Code definition of merchant is sufficiently broad to cover most persons dealing in the business world.

Parol Evidence Rule

The Code adopts in most respects the parol evidence rule applicable to contracts generally.[10] This rule of evidence which bars the admission of oral testimony to vary the terms of a written contract was described, along with its exceptions, in Chapter 9.

---

[9] UCC Sec. 2-201 (2).
[10] UCC Sec. 2-202.

Assignment and Delegation

Assignment of rights and delegation of duties in a sales contract are permitted under the Code unless the contract provides otherwise or unless a substantial interest in having performance by the promisor exists, and the Code clarifies the effect of clauses in the sales contract which attempt to limit such transfers.[11] An assignment delegating performance creates reasonable grounds for insecurity, and the other party may demand assurances from the assignee.

BULK SALES

Background

A bulk sale is the transfer in bulk and not in the ordinary course of the transferor's business of a major part of the transferor's stock in trade. Before the enactment of Bulk Sales Acts, creditors were sometimes victimized by the fraudulent merchant who would sell his business, including his unpaid-for inventory of merchandise, and then disappear with the proceeds before the creditors learned of the sale. The common-law rules regarding fraudulent transfers of assets by a debtor would not permit the creditors of the debtor (seller) to reach the goods in the hands of the buyer if the buyer was a bona fide purchaser. To qualify as a bona fide purchaser the buyer must have paid value for the goods and must not have participated in the scheme to defraud the creditors or taken the goods with knowledge of the fraud.

Bulk Sales Acts Prior to the Uniform Commercial Code

In an effort to give creditors a measure of protection from fraudulent bulk sales, all states enacted Bulk Sales Acts of varying types. These statutes declare that sales in bulk shall be deemed fraudulent and void as against the creditors of the seller unless the creditors are notified of the details of the proposed

---

[11] UCC Sec. 2-210.

bulk sale a certain number of days before it occurs. In addition to the notice requirement, the acts usually require that the buyer obtain from the seller a complete and detailed inventory of the goods showing the cost to the seller of each article to be sold, and the buyer is required to retain the inventory for a specified period of time for inspection by the seller's creditors. Further, the seller is required to furnish the buyer with a written list, certified by the seller under oath, of the names and addresses of the seller's creditors with the amount owing to each of them. It is the duty of the buyer to notify the creditors of the proposed sale, and of the price, terms and conditions thereof. The New York act, since replaced in that state by the adoption of the Uniform Commercial Code, was copied by many states. It required five days' notice to creditors before the sale was completed. The statutes of several states required 10 days' notice, and others fixed varying periods. The notice to the creditors was designed to give the creditors an opportunity to take steps to protect their interests, including the bringing of suits. Under the New York type act, failure to comply with the act resulted in the creditors being permitted to proceed against the goods in the buyer's hands, even where the latter qualified as a bona fide purchaser.

The pre-Code Pennsylvania form of Bulk Sales Act, was adopted by several states. It went further by requiring that the buyer distribute the proceeds of the sale to the creditors.

Many bulk sales statutes made the giving of a false list of creditors by the seller a criminal offense. Failure to comply with the bulk sales statutes does not make the sale void as between the buyer and seller, but it exposes the buyer to claims against the goods by the seller's creditors. Parties to a bulk sale should become familiar with the requirements of the statutes of the state where the sale is to take place.

Bulk Sales Under the Uniform Commercial Code
Article 6 of the Uniform Commercial Code has as its purpose the simplification and making uniform the law of bulk sales, but

it retains many of the features of the old bulk sales statutes it replaces.

The Code defines bulk transfers and protected creditors, lists transfers excepted from the operation of the Code, describes the remedies of creditors in case of non-compliance, and declares what must be done to comply with the act. The requirements relate to listing of property and creditors, notice to creditors, and application of sale proceeds, leaving it up to the legislature of each state to decide whether the transferee must distribute the proceeds of the sale to the creditors. The Code requires that the transferee give notice to each creditor at least 10 days before he takes possession of the goods or pays for them, whichever happens first. The Code sets up a six months statute of limitations in regard to actions arising out of bulk sales. The Code also contains special provisions covering auctions involving bulk sales.

Title, Risk and
Related Matters

14

TITLE CONCEPT

Sales transactions result in the transfer of the ownership of goods from seller to buyer. Once the ownership of the goods (usually referred to by lawyers and judges as title to the goods) has passed in a sales transaction, the buyer normally enjoys the benefits and bears the risks of such ownership, except where the risks have been shifted by insurance or other agreement. As a general rule, risk follows title, which means that in a sales transaction he who has the title bears the risk of loss of or damage to the goods even though the price may not have been paid, nor delivery made. Historically, disputes involving sales transactions have often been resolved under the Uniform Sales Act and existing case law on the basis of whether the property in the goods (title) had passed to the buyer. For example, the passing of the title to the buyer meant (1) the seller could recover the price, not merely damages, (2) the risk of loss of or damage to the goods was on the buyer, (3) the buyer had the remedies of an owner of personal property, such as replevin to gain possession of the goods or an action of trover to recover a money judgment for the value of the goods, if the seller wrongfully refused to deliver the goods and thus had converted the buyer's property. If title had not passed, and either party defaulted, the other party usually had no remedy except to sue for damages. The question of the ownership of the goods also governed, in many cases, with respect to (1) who had an insurable interest in the goods, (2) the rights of creditors of the buyer and seller, with respect to being able to levy against the goods or attach them, (3) the choice of governing state law, (4) the application of tax laws, and other matters related to the goods which constituted the subject matter of the sale.

TITLE TRANSFER AND RISK UNDER
THE UNIFORM SALES ACT

The Uniform Sales Act's prime rule relating to the transfer of property as between seller and buyer is that the title to the goods passes when the parties intend it shall pass. Responsibility for the goods and the risk of loss or damages rests with the party holding title to the goods in the absence of an agreement to the contrary. An exception to the general rule that risk follows title occurs when the seller retains title as security for payment of the purchase price. If the parties expressly agree as to when the title is to pass or who is to bear the risk of loss, that understanding will control. But sales contracts generally are silent on such property matters and the court must decide the question, if a controversy arises. The Sales Act declares that the intention of the parties shall be ascertained from the terms of the contract, the conduct of the parties, usages of trade, and the circumstances of the case.

In some sales transactions it is relatively clear as to when the parties intended the title to pass. For example, in a typical cash-and-carry sale the title passes as the goods are handed across the counter in exchange for the price. But in more complicated sales transactions, the intention of the parties concerning the time of title passing is often obscure. Section 19 of the Sales Act sets forth the following five rules of presumption as to the unexpressed intention of the parties with respect to when the title shall pass:

Section 19.   *Rules for Ascertaining Intention.*   Unless a different intention appears, the following are rules for ascertaining the intention of the parties as to the time at which the property in the goods is to pass to the buyer.

Rule 1.   Where there is an unconditional contract to sell specific goods, in a deliverable state, the property in the goods passes to the buyer when the contract is made and it is immaterial whether the time of payment, or the time of delivery, or both, be postponed.

Rule 2.   Where there is a contract to sell specific goods and the seller is bound to do something to the goods, for the purpose of putting them into a deliverable state, the property does not pass until such thing be done.

Rule 3.   1] When goods are delivered to the buyer "on sale or return," or on other terms indicating an intention to make a present sale, but to give the buyer an option to return the goods instead of paying the price, the property passes to the buyer on delivery, but he may revest the property in the seller by returning or tendering the goods within the time fixed in the contract, or, if no time has been fixed, within a reasonable time.

2] When goods are delivered to the buyer on approval or on trial or on satisfaction, or other similar terms, the property therein passes to the buyer:

A] When he signifies his approval or acceptance to the seller or does any other act adopting the transaction;

B] If he does not signify his approval or acceptance to the seller, but retains the goods without giving notice of rejection, then if a time has been fixed for the return of the goods, on the expiration of such time, and, if no time has been fixed, on the expiration of a reasonable time. What is a reasonable time is a question of fact.

Rule 4.   1] Where there is a contract to sell unascertained or future goods by description, and goods of that description and in a deliverable state are unconditionally appropriated to the contract, either by the seller with the assent of the buyer, or by the buyer with the assent of the seller, the property in the goods thereupon passes to the buyer. Such assent may be expressed or implied, and may be given either before or after the appropriation is made.

2] Where, in pursuance of a contract to sell, the seller delivers the goods to the buyer, or to a carrier or other bailee (whether named by the buyer or not) for the purpose of transmission to or holding for the buyer, he is presumed to have unconditionally appropriated the goods to the contract, except in the cases provided for in the next rule and in Section 20. This presumption is applicable, although by the terms of the contract the buyer is to pay the price before receiving delivery of the goods, and the goods are marked with the words "collect on delivery" or their equivalents.

Rule 5.   If the contract to sell requires the seller to deliver the goods to the buyer, or at a particular place, or to pay the freight or cost or transportation to the buyer, or to a particular place, the property does not pass until the goods have been delivered to the buyer or reached the place agreed upon.

It can be seen that these rules of presumption depend in part upon the classification of the goods as specific, unascertained, or future; in part upon the performance of the contract such as putting the goods into a deliverable condition or state, or delivery of the goods to a common carrier or to the buyer at some place other than the seller's place; and upon whether the sales contract is conditional or unconditional.

Fungible Goods.   Title to a designated quantity of fungible goods, in existence and owned by the seller will pass at the time the contract is made if the parties intend a present sale. In such a case, the buyer becomes an owner in common with the owner or owners of the remaining shares, the title to an undivided share of the goods passing to the buyer even though no specific portion of the goods has been physically separated from the mass and identified as belonging to the buyer. Fungibles are goods which are treated commercially as composed of units each of which is like any other unit. They are usually sold by weight or measure and include such things as coal, grain, oil, sugar, and similar chattels.

Definitions

Specific goods are those which are (1) in existence, (2) owned by the seller, and (3) identified as the subject matter of the contract. Unascertained goods are those which are in existence at the time the contract is made, but which have not been identified either by the buyer or by the seller with the assent and authority of the buyer so as to be distinguished from other goods of the same kind belonging to the seller. Future goods are those which are not in existence at the time of the bargain, or not then owned by the seller. Goods are in a deliverable state if the seller needs to do nothing to the goods to make them comply with the contract. Where weighing, counting, or measuring is not necessary to establish the identity of the goods, but merely to fix the price, such actions are not essential to the passing of title. A contract is unconditional if it contains no provisions postponing the passing of title. An example of a conditional contract which would delay or prevent altogether the passing of title is found in the statement of Rule 3 (2) describing a sale on approval which is discussed and contrasted with a sale or return later in this chapter. A provision in a contract postponing the date of payment or the date of delivery, or both, does not prevent the passing of the title to the goods prior to the occurrence of such events.

Summary of Sales Act Rules

The Uniform Sales Act in Rule 1 of Section 19 provides that the title passes to the buyer at the time the contract is made if the goods are specific and in a deliverable state, and if the contract is unconditional. According to Rule 2 of Section 19 of the

Sales Act, where the seller is bound to do something to the goods for the purpose of putting them into a deliverable state, title does not pass until such thing is done. Title to unascertained or future goods passes from the seller to the buyer when the goods are "unconditionally appropriated to the contract."

Appropriation is defined by courts to mean a mutual assent of the parties that the property interest in particular identified goods is transferred to the buyer in compliance with the contract. Rules 4 and 5 of Section 19 of the Sales Act set up presumptions of appropriation which govern the passage of title to unascertained goods, with the result that under these rules the title to such goods will pass when the goods have been delivered to the buyer or reached the place agreed upon.

In a sale or return, title and risks of ownership pass to the buyer on delivery, with the buyer having the option to pass title back to the seller (Rule 3 (1), Sec. 19, U.S.A.). In a sale on approval, title and risk remain in the seller until the buyer indicates his approval or fails to return the goods within the agreed time for trial, or if no time is stated, within a reasonable time (Rule 3 (2), Sec. 19, U.S.A.). The buyer as a bailee in a sale on approval is responsible for loss of or damage to the goods resulting from his negligence or intentional wrongful act. Sales or return and sales on approval under the Uniform Commercial Code are discussed later in this chapter.

TITLE TRANSFER UNDER
THE UNIFORM COMMERCIAL CODE

An important change made by the Code in the law of sales is the Code's shift away from an emphasis on the importance of locating the title (ownership) to the goods as a solution of sales problems. Article 2 of the Code attempts to provide specific rules designed to solve specific problems arising in sales transactions, without regard to title. The Code adopts the "contractual approach" as a substitute for the "title approach" in the belief that most disputes arising out of sales transactions can be resolved by deciding whether the sales contract has been properly performed. However, under the "title approach" of the Sales Act the passing of title generally depends upon whether the seller has performed his contract, so, to a large extent, the legal results are the same under either the "title approach" or "contract approach."

Where specific matters are not covered by other provisions of Article 2 of the Code, Section 2-401 of the Code provides that "matters concerning title become material." This important section sets forth the following rules:

Section 2-401 . . . 1] Title to goods cannot pass under a contract for sale prior to their identification to the contract (Section 2-501), and unless otherwise explicitly agreed the buyer acquires by their identification a special property as limited by this Act. Any retention or reservation by the seller of the title (property) in goods shipped or delivered to the buyer is limited in effect to a reservation of a security interest. Subject to these provisions and to the provisions of the Article on Secured Transactions (Article 9), title to goods passes from the seller to the buyer in any manner and on any conditions explicitly agreed on by the parties.

2] Unless otherwise explicitly agreed, title passes to the buyer at the time and place at which the seller completes his performance with reference to the physical delivery of the goods, despite any reservation of a security interest and even though a document of title is to be delivered at a different time or place; and in particular and despite any reservation of a security interest by the bill of lading

A] if the contract requires or authorizes the seller to send the goods to the buyer but does not require him to deliver them at destination, title passes to the buyer at the time and place of shipment; but

B] if the contract requires delivery at destination, title passes on tender there.

3] Unless otherwise explicitly agreed where delivery is to be made without moving the goods,

A] if the seller is to deliver a document of title, title passes at the time when and the place where he delivers such documents; or

B] if the goods are at the time of contracting already identified and no documents are to be delivered, title passes at the time and place of contracting.

4] A rejection or other refusal by the buyer to receive or retain the goods, whether or not justified, or a justified revocation of acceptance revests title to the goods in the seller. Such revesting occurs by operation of law and is not a "sale."

RISK OF LOSS UNDER THE CODE

The Code provides that risk of loss rests with the owner of the goods, unless there has been a breach of the sales contract, in which case the risk of loss is placed on the party who has breached the contract. The risk of loss, however, only remains on the breaching buyer for a reasonable period of time. Under some circumstances the Code places the risk of loss on the party in possession of the goods regardless of whether or not he has title to the goods. These rules are set forth in Sections 2-509 and 2-510 of the Code as follows:

Section 2-509 . . . 1] Where the contract requires or authorizes the seller to ship the goods by carrier

A] if it does not require him to deliver them at a particular destination, the risk of loss passes to the buyer when the goods are duly delivered to the carrier even though the shipment is under reservation (Section 2-505); but

B] if it does require him to deliver them at a particular destination and the goods are there duly tendered while in the possession of the carrier, the risk of loss passes to the buyer when the goods are there duly so tendered as to enable the buyer to take delivery.

2] Where the goods are held by a bailee to be delivered without being moved, the risk of loss passes to the buyer

    A] on his receipt of a negotiable document of title covering the goods; or

    B] on acknowledgment by the bailee of the buyer's right to possession of the goods; or

    C] after his receipt of a non-negotiable document of title or other written direction to deliver, as provided in subsection (4) (b) of Section 2-503.

3] In any case not within subsection (1) or (2), the risk of loss passes to the buyer on his receipt of the goods if the seller is a merchant; otherwise the risk passes to the buyer on tender of delivery.

4] The provisions of this section are subject to contrary agreement of the parties and to the provisions of this Article on sale on approval (Section 2-327) and on effect of breach on risk of loss (Section 2-510).

Section 2-510 . . . 1] Where a tender or delivery of goods so fails to conform to the contract as to give a right of rejection the risk of their loss remains on the seller until cure or acceptance.

2] Where the buyer rightfully revokes acceptance, he may to the extent of any deficiency in his effective insurance coverage treat the risk of loss as having rested on the seller from the beginning.

3] Where the buyer as to conforming goods already identified to the contract for sale repudiates or is otherwise in breach before risk of their loss has passed to him, the seller may to the extent of any deficiency in his effective insurance coverage treat the risk of loss as resting on the buyer for a commercially reasonable time.

SELECTED MATTERS UNDER THE CODE

Sale On Approval and Sale Or Return

The Code distinguishes between a sale on approval and a sale or return on the basis of the intended use of the buyer. If the goods are delivered primarily for use, it is a sale on approval. On the other hand, if the goods are delivered primarily for re-sale, it is a sale or return. In either case the buyer may return the goods to the seller, even though they conform to the contract. The Code then specifically spells out the risk of loss, rights of buyer's creditors, passage of title and acceptance by the buyer with respect to both a sale on approval and a sale or return.[1] The principles of law governing a sale on approval and a sale or return under the Uniform Sales Act were set forth earlier in this chapter. These principles have been incorporated into the Code provisions referred to above.

Insurable Interest

Under the Code, the buyer obtains an insurable interest in the goods on their identification to the contract, and thus may obtain protection from risks which may arise prior to the passage of title.[2] The seller retains an insurable interest in the goods until title passes, default, insolvency, or notification to the buyer of final identification.[3]

Identification can be made at any time and in any manner agreed to by the parties. In the absence of explicit agreement, identification occurs when the contract is made if it is for the sale of goods already existing and identified. It occurs when the goods are shipped, marked, or otherwise designated by the seller as goods to which the contract refers if the contract is for the sale of future goods. Crops are identified when planted or otherwise become growing crops, and animals are identified when conceived, subject to agreement of the parties and provided the contract is for the sale of unborn young to be born within one year after making the contract, or for the sale of crops to be harvested within one year or the next normal harvest season after contracting, whichever is longer.

---

[1] UCC Sec.'s. 2-326 and 2-327.
[2] UCC Sec. 2-501 (1).
[3] UCC Sec. 2-501 (2).

Good Faith Purchasers

The Code continues the provisions of the Sales Act and the common-law rules under which a person with a voidable title can transfer a good title to a good faith purchaser. The protection of the good faith purchaser results in an exception to the general rule of property law that a seller cannot transfer better title to property than the title he holds.

Section 2-403 of the Code describes the power to transfer good title to good faith purchasers as follows:

> Section 2-403 . . . 1] A purchaser of goods acquires all title which his transferor had or had power to transfer except that a purchaser of a limited interest acquires rights only to the extent of the interest purchased. A person with voidable title has power to transfer a good title to a good faith purchaser for value. When goods have been delivered under a transaction of purchase, the purchaser has such power even though
>
> A] the transferor was deceived as to the identity of the purchaser, or
> B] the delivery was in exchange for a check which is later dishonored, or
> C] it was agreed that the transaction was to be a "cash sale," or
> D] the delivery was procured through fraud punishable as larcenous under the criminal law.
>
> 2] Any entrusting of possession of goods to a merchant who deals in goods of that kind gives him power to transfer all rights of the entruster to a buyer in ordinary course of business.
>
> 3] "Entrusting" includes any delivery and any acquiescence in retention of possession regardless of any condition expressed between the parties to the delivery or acquiescence and regardless of whether the procurement of the entrusting or the possessor's disposition of the goods have been such as to be larcenous under the criminal law.

"Buyer in ordinary course of business" and "good faith" are defined by the Code as follows.

Section 1-201 (9) "Buyer in ordinary course of business" means a person who in good faith and without knowledge that the sale to him is in violation of the ownership rights or security interest of a third party in the goods buys in ordinary course from a person in the business of selling goods of that kind but does not include a pawnbroker. "Buying" may be for cash or by exchange of other property or on secured or unsecured credit and includes receiving goods or documents of title under a pre-existing contract for sale but does not include a transfer in bulk or as security for or in total or partial satisfaction of a money debt.

Section 1-201 (19) "Good faith" means honesty in fact in the conduct or transaction concerned.

Shipping Terms and Documents

F.O.B., F.A.S., C.I.F. Over the years certain shipping terms used in sales transactions have become standardized through mercantile practice. Therefore, the parties to sales contracts usually employ shipping symbols like F.O.B., F.A.S., C.I.F., or C.&F. instead of spelling out in detail an agreement with respect to the delivery of the goods, including the matter of who is to pay the freight.

Under pre-Code law, the rules of the common law and the Uniform Sales Act looked to the particular shipping terms used by the parties to a sale of goods in determining when the title passed, and on that basis, the rights and duties of the parties were governed. A brief summary of the pre-Code definitions and effect of these delivery terms follows. For example, if the contract calls for the goods to be shipped F.O.B. (free on board) or F.A.S. (free alongside), the seller is obligated to deliver to the carrier goods which conform to the contract and which are properly packed, and he is required to make a reasonable contract of carriage in behalf of the buyer who is to pay the freight. Title to the goods passes to the buyer when the goods are turned over to the carrier if the seller has performed all his duties, and the seller is entitled to payment for the goods on tender of the shipping documents.

If the contract calls for shipment "F.O.B. destination" or F.O.B. at a designated place, the title passes to the buyer when the goods are delivered to the buyer at destination or at the specified place.

The letters C.I.F. in a sales contract stand for the words, "cost, insurance, and freight," and mean that the seller assumes the following obligations:

1] Deliver conforming goods, properly packed, to the carrier and take out a bill of lading to the buyer's order or to the seller's order indorsed in blank and prepay the freight;

2] Take out insurance for the buyer's account covering the goods in transit, and himself pay the insurance premium;

3] Make out an invoice in which it is stated that the buyer is indebted to the seller for the cost price, plus the freight prepaid by the seller, and plus the insurance premium paid by the seller;

4] Mail the shipping documents to the buyer, including the bill of lading, the receipt for the freight, the insurance policy, the receipt for the premium, and the invoice.

As soon as the seller has properly performed these obligations, title and risk of loss pass to the buyer, and the buyer is bound to pay the price on receipt of the shipping documents even though the goods have not yet arrived. The term C.&F. means the same as C.I.F. except that the buyer will take care of the insurance.

Shipping Terms Under the Uniform Commercial Code.   As previously stated, the Code has greatly reduced the importance of the title concept. The approach taken by the Code is to set forth legal rights and duties in specific situations. One example of this is the treatment of delivery terms in Sections 2-319 to 2-324, inclusive, of the Code. These sections in addition to setting forth specific definitions of commercial delivery terms, spell out the obligations and rights of the parties, including the expense of loading and shipment and the risk of loss. The definitions of delivery terms set forth in the Code are the first codification of terms of shipment. The following terms are included in the Code: F.O.B. (free on board) place of shipment; F.O.B. place of destination; F.O.B. vessel, car or other vehicle; F.A.S. vessel (free alongside) at named port; C.I.F. (cost, insurance, and freight); C.&F. (cost and freight); C.I.F. or C.&F., net landed weights; payment on arrival, warranty of condition on arrival; ex-ship (from the carrying vessel); and No arrival, No sale. In addition, these sections of the Code provide that in F.O.B., F.A.S., C.I.F. and C.&F. sales, unless otherwise agreed, the buyer must make payment on the tender of the required documents, and the goods may not be substituted for the documents.

Bills of Lading. When goods are delivered to a common carrier for shipment, the carrier signs a paper called a bill of lading which is a receipt for the goods and a contract of shipment. There are two types of bills of lading, the negotiable and the nonnegotiable. If the bill of lading is negotiable in form, that is, states that the carrier will deliver the goods named therein to a certain person or to his order, it is a document of title. By this is meant that the goods back of the bill of lading may be sold or pledged by transferring or indorsing the bill of lading without delivery of the goods themselves.

The negotiable bill of lading may be either an order bill or a bearer bill. In the case of an order bill of lading, the carrier agrees to deliver the goods to the named consignee or to his order, that is, to any person to whom the consignee indorses and transfers the bill of lading. A bearer bill of lading provides that the carrier will deliver the goods to any person presenting the bill of lading, and indorsement to a new holder is not necessary: delivery of the bill to him is enough.

A nonnegotiable bill of lading is also called a straight bill of lading, and in it the carrier promises merely to deliver the goods to the named consignee. Presentment of the straight bill of lading is not necessary to obtain the goods. It is only necessary that the consignee identify himself when calling for the goods.

Sellers often use negotiable bills of lading as a means of retaining control over the possession of the goods after shipment in order to make sure the buyer does not get the goods until he has paid the price for them or made some satisfactory arrangement for payment in the future. A common procedure followed by a seller is to consign the goods to the order of himself or his agent, such as a bank or finance company, at the destination; to draw a bill of exchange, often called a draft, on the buyer for the price, payable to himself, or his agent; to attach the draft to the bill of lading, indorsed if necessary, and to send both to the collecting agency at the city in which the buyer is located. The buyer must pay the draft if it is a "sight" draft or accept it if it is a "time" draft, and he must receive delivery of the bill of lading, accompanied by any necessary indorsement, before he has the right to claim the goods from the carrier. The use of this procedure by the seller for the purpose of securing the payment of the purchase price does not prevent the title to the goods and the risk from passing to the buyer when the goods are delivered to the carrier as provided for in the rules explored previously in this chapter. Section 2-505 of the Code governs the right of a seller to reserve a security interest in goods which have been shipped.

Other Matters Under the Code

The following matters are listed here as to their subject along with a reference to the pertinent provisions of the Uniform Commercial Code: suits against third persons for injury to goods, Section 2-722; buyer's right to the goods on the seller's insolvency, Section 2-502; rights of seller's creditors against sold goods, Section 2-402; and rights of financing agency, Section 2-506.

Warranties

15

The maxim *caveat emptor* (let the buyer beware) was applied by the courts to sales contracts during the early history of the law of sales. The circumstances surrounding sales of goods during the early period were such that nearly all statements made by a seller were viewed by the law as mere sales talk or puffing and not binding on him unless he expressly said that he warranted the goods.

Today, while buyers are expected to exercise reasonable caution in their dealings with sellers, the law does recognize express and implied warranties for the protection of buyers unless properly disclaimed against by agreement of the parties. In general, a warranty refers to the assumption by the seller of some responsibility with respect to the quality, character, or suitability of the goods he sells. A warranty may be created by an express provision of the sales contract, it may be implied from the agreement, and it may be imposed by law in certain cases even though contrary to the manifest intention of the parties. Court decisions, as well as the Uniform Sales Act and the Uniform Commercial Code, classify warranties as express and implied obligations. This breakdown is used in the discussion of warranties in this chapter.

EXPRESS WARRANTIES

An express warranty is an affirmation of fact or promise made by the seller concerning the goods and which becomes part of the basis of the bargain between the seller and buyer.[1] In addition, the Code includes within its definition of express warranty two of the warranties, description and sample, which are listed in the Uniform Sales Act as warranties implied by law. These two warranties will be discussed here under express warranty.

No particular phraseology is necessary to constitute an express warranty, and the seller need not intend his statement or representation to be a warranty. It is not essential to the binding effect of a warranty that the seller should know it is false. The good faith of the seller is no defense to an action for breach of warranty. If, however, a seller makes a fraudulent (intentional) misrepresentation of fact about his goods to induce the buyer to purchase, both an express warranty and deceit are present, and the buyer will have an election of remedies. The elements of fraud or deceit were enumerated in Chapter 5. If the seller has committed deceit, the buyer may seek his remedy in tort or pursue his remedy for breach of warranty. The element called *scienter* (guilty knowledge) is present in deceit, but not in the case of mere misrepresentation.

A seller's sales talk, statements of opinion concerning the goods being sold, and his claims concerning the value of the goods do not fall within the definition of express warranty. The law permits a seller a certain amount of leeway in "puffing" and exaggerating about his goods, recognizing that, although the buyer may be influenced by it, he should know that it may or may not be true. It is often difficult to distinguish opinion from statement of fact. It has been held that the following statements were, or could reasonably be found to be, express warranties: a statement in an advertisement to sell a second-hand baby

---

[1] UCC Sec. 2-313 (1) (a).

grand piano in "good condition, excellent tone"; a statement that a used car was "in good operating condition"; advertisement and labeling of a home permanent hair curling product as "very gentle"; and a statement by a sales clerk, in selling a fur coat, that the coat was warranted to stand all weather. In other cases, it was held that the following were not affirmations of fact and were therefore not express warranties: a claim by the seller of a radio that foreign stations could be reached; a representation by the seller of accessory mouldings for used automobiles, to make them appear more recent models, that these mouldings were readily salable merchandise and that there should be a demand for it; a statement by the seller of a suit of clothes that the "suit will wear like iron"; and a statement that a patented article was "a valuable and useful improvement." Such statements as "These goods will make you rich," "These goods are A-1," and "Our goods are strictly high class" are viewed as "sales talk" for which the seller is not legally responsible.

Where the buyer has had a chance to examine the goods before purchase and does examine the goods, he cannot rely on any warranty either express or implied, as to patent defects, that is, those visible and apparent on inspection. However, any latent (hidden) defects would be covered by such warranties.

Warranties in Sale by Description or Sample. The Sales Act implied warranties that goods sold by description or sample shall correspond with the description or sample are classified under the Code as express warranties. Subsection 2-313 (1) (b) of the Code provides: "Any description of the goods which is made part of the basis of the bargain creates an express warranty that the goods shall conform to the description," and Subsection 2-313 (1) (c) provides, "Any sample or model which is made part of the basis of the bargain creates an express warranty that the whole of the goods shall conform to the sample or model."

IMPLIED WARRANTIES

Implied Warranty of Title

Unless the parties manifest a contrary intention, the law, as stated in the Code, protects the buyer of goods with the implied warranties that the seller has a good title to the goods and that the goods are free from encumbrances other than those known to the buyer.[2] In addition, unless otherwise agreed a merchant seller regularly dealing in goods of the kind sold impliedly warrants against patent or trademark infringement claims by third persons, but a buyer who furnishes specifications to the seller must hold him harmless against any infringement claim which arises out of compliance with the specifications.[3]

The Code provides that the warranty of title will only be excluded by specific language or by circumstances which give the buyer reason to know he is only getting such title as the seller has.[4] For example, sales by sheriffs, executors, foreclosing lienors, pawnbrokers, etc. are of such a nature that a buyer is not entitled by virtue of the sale alone to the personal obligation of the seller respecting clear title to the goods.

Implied Warranty of Merchantability

The Code continues, with certain changes, the implied warranty of merchantability provided for under the Sales Act and court decisions. The Code provides: "Unless excluded or modified . . . , a warranty that the goods shall be merchantable is implied in a contract for their sale if the seller is a merchant with respect to goods of that kind."[5] This warranty is not limited, as under the Sales Act, to situations in which the goods are bought by description from a seller who deals in goods of that

---

[2] UCC Sec. 2-312 (1).
[3] UCC Sec. 2-312 (3).
[4] UCC Sec. 2-312 (2).
[5] UCC Sec. 2-314 (1).

description. The Code limits the warranty to sales made by "merchants," but it broadens the scope of the warranty by omitting the requirement that the sale be by description.

Generally the courts have defined "merchantable" to mean "fair, average quality." Subsection (2) of Section 2-314 of the Code sets out specific standards for determining whether or not goods are merchantable.

Food and Drink Served in Restaurants. Courts have disagreed as to whether or not the serving of food or drink in restaurants is a sale or merely the furnishing of a service which would rule out any warranties with respect to the quality of the food, including the implied warranty of merchantability. The majority view taken by courts in this country has treated such transactions as sales with warranties attaching for the protection of the buyers. Some courts have held that a sale of food or drink was a sale only if the food or drink was consumed off the premises. The Code resolves this controversy by providing that "the serving of food or drink to be consumed either on the' premises or elsewhere is a sale," with the result that the server may be held liable for the breach of an implied warranty of merchantability if the food or drink is unfit for consumption and causes injury.[6] Of course, servers of harmful food or beverages continue to be liable as before for their negligence where injury results.

Implied Warranty of Fitness for Particular Purpose

When the buyer wants the goods for some particular purpose and makes known that fact to the seller and the buyer relies upon the seller's judgment to furnish an article which will meet the particular purpose, the implied warranty of fitness for a particular purpose attaches and the seller becomes liable in damages if the goods are not reasonably fit for the purpose.

The Code continues this implied warranty and eliminates the patent or trade name exception provided for in the Sales Act.

---

[6] UCC Sec. 2-314 (1).

Under the Sales Act, a buyer ordering goods by use of a trade or patent name is denied the protection of the warranty of fitness for the particular purpose on the theory that he relied on his own skill and judgment in selecting the goods and not on the seller's skill and judgment. As provided for in the Code, the fact that the goods are described by a patent or a trade name in the sales contract will not be conclusive, but this fact will be relevant in determining whether the buyer relied on the seller's skill and judgment.

PERSONS PROTECTED BY WARRANTIES

Privity of Contract Doctrine

As a general rule, courts have held that a seller is liable for damages for breach of warranty to his immediate purchaser, and that the benefit of the warranty does not extend to any other persons even though they use or come in contact with the goods. The requirement that the plaintiff and defendant be in a contractual relationship in order for the plaintiff to recover for breach of warranty is called the privity doctrine. If this view is followed, the absence of privity of contract between the plaintiff and defendant means that the only remedy the plaintiff has for injury caused by defective goods is to bring suit and prove that the defect was caused by the defendant's negligence. In most cases, such proof is very difficult to establish. Therefore, plaintiffs prefer to sue for breach of warranty, for all they need to prove is the contract of sale, the presence of the defect or injurious substance in the product, and the resulting injury.

Privity Exceptions and Uniform Commercial Code. Growing criticism of the privity of contract requirement in cases involving personal injuries from defective goods has resulted in many courts holding that lack of privity will not defeat a plaintiff's action for breach of warranty where the goods in question involve those used in or on the human body. On this basis, courts have held manufacturers and processors of such things as food, beverages, drugs, cosmetics, soap, clothing, tobacco products, and similar articles liable to the ultimate consumer for damages for breach of warranty. A variety of theories have been relied on by the courts to support abandonment of the privity doctrine, but a common theme in the cases is the recognition that public policy dictates that in view of the hazard to the general public, the various parties involved in the manufacture or distribution of certain goods must be held to a high standard of performance for the protection of consumers. Other theories upon which some courts base the consumer's recovery from the manufacturer are (1) the third party beneficiary doctrine, (2) treating the warranty of fitness for consumption as running with the article like a covenant running with the land and (3) the view that the act of the manufacturer in placing the goods upon the market, accompanied by the usual advertising found on labels, is an offer by the manufacturer which is accepted by the subvendee upon making a purchase. Objections to these theories are raised on the ground that they are drawn from contract or property principles which do not fit the sale situation. In most states statutes impose on a manufacturer or producer the duty not to sell adulterated food products. Since that duty is statutory, no privity of contract is necessary to enable a person injured by the breach of that duty to recover from the manufacturer or producer. The breach of such a statutory duty is usually termed negligence as a matter of law.

The Code extends the protection of the seller's warranty, express or implied, "to any natural person who is in the family or household of his buyer or who is a guest in his home if it is reasonable to expect that such person may use, consume, or be affected by the goods and who is injured in person by breach of the warranty. A seller may not exclude or limit the operation of this section." [7]

---

[7] UCC Sec. 2-318.

EXCLUSION OR MODIFICATION OF WARRANTY

Under the common law the parties to a sale contract are free to provide in their contract that the seller has no warranty obligations, either express or implied. However, courts have often refused to enforce disclaimers of warranty liability in cases where the disclaimers were found to be unconscionable, based on deception by the seller, or otherwise unfair.

Uniform Commercial Code.   The Code permits the exclusion or modification of warranties, express or implied, but sets up important limitations and specific requirements which must be complied with by those drafting a sales contract.[8] These limitations and requirements are summarized in the following discussion.

Under the Code, the warranty of title may be excluded or modified "only by specific language or by circumstances which give the buyer reason to know that the person selling does not claim title in himself or that he is purporting to sell only such right or title as he or a third party may have." Therefore, a general exclusion of all express and implied warranties will not exclude a warranty of title. An express exclusion of this warranty is required.

The Code requires that express warranties and exclusion clauses in sales contracts be construed as consistent with one another, but that subject to the parol evidence rule, the express warranties will prevail over the negation or limitation clause where they are in conflict.

The exclusion of the implied warranty of merchantability must mention merchantability and if in writing must be conspicuous. Subsection (10) of Section 1-201 of the Code defines conspicuous as follows:

> "Conspicuous": A term or clause is conspicuous when it is so written that a reasonable person against whom it is to

---

[8] UCC Sec's. 2-312; 2-316; 2-317.

operate ought to have noticed it. A printed heading in capitals (as: NONNEGOTIABLE BILL OF LADING) is conspicuous. Language in the body of a form is "conspicuous" if it is in larger or other contrasting type or color. But in a telegram any stated term is "conspicuous". Whether a term or clause if "conspicuous" or not is for decision by the court.

Exclusion or modification of the warranty of fitness for a particular purpose must be accomplished by a writing and which is conspicuous. The clauses, "there are no warranties which extend beyond the description on the face hereof," "as is," "with all faults," and other similar language will operate to exclude all implied warranties.

Examination by the buyer or the refusal by the buyer of a direct demand by the seller for the buyer to examine the goods will exclude recovery for defects which the examination ought to have revealed, according to the Code. Also, a course of dealing, course of performance or usage of trade may also exclude an implied warranty.

REMEDIES FOR BREACH OF WARRANTY

If a breach of warranty occurs, a buyer may elect from the following remedies: (1) refuse to accept the goods and bring an action for damages for breach of warranty, (2) keep the goods and assert his claim for damages by way of recoupment or counterclaim when sued by the seller for the purchase price, (3) keep the goods and sue for damages, or (4) rescind the contract. The Code treats goods which breach a warranty as nonconforming goods and gives the buyer rights which embrace the above remedies.

The buyer has a right to maintain an action for damages for breach of a warranty without returning or offering to return the goods, but the buyer must give notice of the defect in the goods to the seller within a reasonable time after its discovery.

The measure of ordinary damages for a breach of warranty is the difference between the value of the goods delivered to the buyer and their value had they been as warranted. Special or consequential damages may be claimed by the buyer in accordance with the principles governing damages in breach of contract cases generally as described in Chapter 12.

The buyer's right to rescind for breach of warranty depends upon the buyer notifying the seller within a reasonable time of his election to rescind. On rescission the buyer is entitled to the return of any purchase money he has paid and he must return or offer to return the goods to the place of delivery, subject to the buyer's right to a lien on the goods as security for the return of his purchase money. The buyer's lien in this instance means that the buyer has the right to refuse to return the goods until any purchase money he has paid is restored to him.

Limitation of Remedies for Breach of Warranty.   The buyer and seller may contractually establish in advance by means of a liquidated damage clause the amount of damages the buyer can claim for a breach of warranty, provided the amount fixed is reasonable in light of all the circumstances.[9] The Code provides that the agreement of the buyer and seller may limit "the buyer's remedies to return of the goods and repayment of the price or to repair and replacement of non-conforming goods or parts." [10] If the remedy set forth in the agreement is to be exclusive, the agreement must so state. Further, the Code restricts contractual modification or limitation of remedies by providing that the limitation may not be effective if it fails of its essential purpose, the rule against unconscionable clauses must be considered, and the limitation of consequential damages for personal injury on consumer goods is prima facie unconscionable.

The Code's statute of limitations on a breach of warranty action is found in Section 2-725 which provides that unless

---

[9] UCC Sec. 2-718.
[10] UCC Sec. 2-719.

future performance is involved, a cause of action for breach of warranty arises when a tender of delivery is made, regardless of the party's lack of knowledge thereof. Where a warranty extends to future performance of the goods and discovery of the breach must await the time of such performance, the cause of action accrues when the breach is or should have been discovered. The period of limitation for breach of warranty is four years, subject to reduction by the original agreement of the parties to not less than one year.

Performance, Breach
and Remedies

16

PERFORMANCE

Delivery and Acceptance

Seller's Performance.   A sale contract creates a general obligation on the part of the buyer to pay the price and on the
seller to deliver the goods. Section 2-503 of the Uniform Commercial Code describes in detail the manner in which the seller
must tender delivery when the seller has a duty to deliver to a
carrier or to a definite destination, when the goods are in the
possession of a bailee, and when the contract requires the seller
to deliver documents. If the tender is improper and the time for
performance has not expired, the seller may notify the buyer of
his intention to cure the tender and then perform within the
contract time. Where the buyer rejects a tender that seller had
reasonable ground to believe would be accepted, the seller, on
prompt notification to the buyer, will be granted a further reasonable time to make a conforming tender.[1]

---

[1] UCC Sec. 2-508.

Unless otherwise agreed, the seller must ordinarily tender the goods in a single delivery, but if the circumstances give either party the right to make or demand delivery in lots, the price if it can be apportioned may be demanded for each lot.[2] An installment contract requires delivery in separate lots.[3] This Code provision remedies the injustice of the rule at common law and under the Sales Act which permitted buyers to force their sellers to breach by making surprise rejections of the goods because of some minor nonconformity at a ·time at which the seller could not cure the deficiency within the time for performance.

Where the seller is authorized to ship the goods to the buyer but is not required to deliver them at the destination, the seller must deliver the goods to a carrier, obtain the proper shipping documents for buyer to obtain possession, and notify the buyer.[4] Special delivery terms such as F.O.B., etc. were referred to in Chapter 14.

Buyer's Performance. A proper tender of the goods by the seller entitles him to have the buyer's acceptance of the goods and payment of the purchase price in accordance with the contract, and the buyer's right to retain or dispose of the goods is conditional upon his making any payment that is due.[5] Payment may be made in any manner "current in the ordinary course of business." If the seller demands payment in legal tender, he must give buyer a reasonable time to procure cash.[6] Thus, the Code prevents the seller from forcing the buyer to breach the contract as permitted under the common law and Sales Act view that in the absence of agreement to the contrary, the parties contemplated a "cash payment," and a buyer tendering a check would be in default, and his breach would at least permit the seller to terminate the contract. A payment by check is con-

---

[2] UCC Sec. 2-307.
[3] UCC Sec. 2-612 (1).
[4] UCC Sec. 2-504.
[5] UCC Sec. 2-507.
[6] UCC Sec. 2-511 (2).

ditional and defeated between the parties by dishonor of the check on due presentment.[7]

Buyer's Acceptance and Inspection. A buyer accepts goods by signifying his acceptance to seller; by failure to reject after a reasonable opportunity to inspect; and by doing any act inconsistent with seller's ownership; and acceptance of a part of any commercial unit is acceptance of that entire unit.[8]

When the buyer accepts the goods: (a) he must pay for them; (b) he may not reject the goods; (c) he must notify the seller of any breach within a reasonable time; and (d) he must notify the seller of litigation involving seller's duties and in case of infringement litigation for which the seller would be liable, the buyer must on demand turn over control of the case to the seller.[9] The Code permits a buyer to revoke his acceptance under certain conditions.[10]

Section 2-513 of the Code governs the buyer's right to inspection of the goods. Unless otherwise agreed, the buyer has a right before he accepts or pays for the goods to inspect them at any reasonable place and time and in any reasonable manner. If the contract provides for "C.O.D." delivery or for payment against documents of title, the buyer has no right of inspection unless the agreement so provided. The buyer must bear the expense of the inspection, but he may recover the expenses from the seller if the goods do not conform and are rejected.

Either the buyer or the seller on reasonable notice to the other may preserve evidence of goods in dispute by inspecting, testing and sampling the goods in the possession or control of the other, and the buyer and seller may provide for a third party inspection to determine the conformity of the goods.[11]

---

[7] UCC Sec. 2-511 (3).
[8] UCC Sec. 2-606.
[9] UCC Sec. 2-607.
[10] UCC Sec. 2-608.
[11] UCC Sec. 2-515.

BREACH

Buyer's Rights and Duties Upon Seller's Breach

The buyer's principal rights and duties upon the seller's breach are contained in Sections 2-601 to 2-605, inclusive, of the Code and they are summarized in the following discussion. Except in the case of installment contracts, if the goods fail to conform to the contract, the buyer may reject the whole; accept the whole; or reject part and accept part. In order to reject the goods, the buyer must seasonably notify the seller, must not exercise ownership of the goods after rejection, and must hold them with reasonable care at the seller's disposition. If the seller has no agent or place of business at point of rejection, a merchant buyer must follow any reasonable instructions given by the seller, and the buyer may demand indemnification for expenses as a condition precedent to following instructions. When the buyer sells the goods, he is entitled to recover out of the proceeds the reasonable expenses of care and sale and a reasonable sales commission. If the seller gives no instructions, the buyer must make reasonable efforts to sell perishables and goods which threaten to decline in value speedily and may store, reship, or resell nonperishables.

The buyer must particularize the defects to which he is objecting where the seller could have cured the defect seasonably, or as between merchants where the seller has demanded particularization.[12] This provision of the Code affords protection to the seller and also protects the buyer from a waiver of claim by failing to state all the defects in the original notice.

Installment Contracts. An installment contract requires delivery in separate lots. If the nonconformity or default on any installment impairs the value of the whole contract, the nonconformity or default constitutes a default of the whole con-

---

[12] UCC Sec. 2-605.

tract; otherwise if the seller gives adequate assurance of its cure, the buyer must accept the installment.[13]

Repudiation

When either party repudiates the contract, the other party may await performance for a commercially reasonable time, or resort to any remedy for breach, and in any case may suspend his own performance.[14] Repudiation of a sales contract as described in the Code is essentially the same as an anticipatory breach of an ordinary contract. The repudiating party may retract his repudiation before his next performance is due and before the aggrieved party has materially changed his position or indicated he is treating the repudiation as final. The retraction must include any assurance justifiably demanded and retractions reinstate the repudiating party's rights subject to due excuse and allowance to the aggrieved party.[15]

Assurance

Either party to a sale contract who has reasonable grounds for insecurity may make written demand for adequate assurance of due performance. A party properly demanding assurance may suspend his performance until assurance is given, and if assurance is not forthcoming within a reasonable time, not in excess of thirty days, the failure to give assurance is a repudiation of the contract.[16]

Excuse for Nonperformance; Unforeseen Events

When identified goods suffer a casualty before the risk of loss passes to the buyer or on a "no arrival, no sale" contract, the buyer may avoid the contract whether the loss is total or partial. If the casualty loss is only partial, the buyer may demand in-

[13] UCC Sec. 2-612.
[14] UCC Sec. 2-610.
[15] UCC Sec. 2-611.
[16] UCC Sec. 2-609.

spection and elect to accept the goods with due allowance for the loss.[17]

Sections 2-614 and 2-615 of the Code make provision for a substituted performance under certain conditions and excuse of the seller from his obligation to perform where his performance is prevented by certain unforeseen events.

CANCELLATION AND TERMINATION

The terms "cancellation" and "termination" are defined and interrelated in Subsections 2-106 (3) and (4) of the Code, in relation to contracts for the sale of goods, as follows:

(3) "Termination" occurs when either party pursuant to a power created by agreement or law puts an end to the contract otherwise than for its breach. On "termination" all obligations which are still executory on both sides are discharged but any right based on prior breach or performance survives.

(4) "Cancellation" occurs when either party puts an end to the contract for breach by the other and its effect is the same as that of "termination" except that the cancelling party also retains any remedy for breach of the whole contract or any unperformed balance.

REMEDIES UNDER THE CODE

Seller's Remedies

Depending upon the circumstances surrounding the buyer's breach of the sales contract, the seller may have, under the Code, one or more of the following remedies:

1] action for the price of the goods plus incidental or consequential damages
2] action for damages

---

[17] UCC Sec. 2-613.

3] right to withhold delivery of the goods

4] right to stoppage of the goods in transit

5] right to reclaim the goods within ten days after their receipt if buyer becomes insolvent

6] right of resale, including the sale of unfinished goods in the process of being manufactured

7] right to cancel

A complete description of these remedies, including the conditions necessary for their existence and the limitations upon their exercise is found in Sections 2-701 to 2-710, inclusive, of the Code.

Measure of Damages.   The measure of damages for the buyer's nonacceptance of the goods or repudiation of the contract is the difference between the market price at the time and place of tender and the unpaid contract price and incidental damages, less expenses saved due to the buyer's breach. If the damages will not properly compensate the seller for his losses, the seller may recover the profit that would have been enjoyed if the contract had been performed, including overhead and incidental damages. Incidental damages include any commercially reasonable charges, expenses, or commissions resulting from buyer's breach. Sections 2-723 and 2-724 of the Code spell out in detail the manner and methods of proving market price.

Buyer's Remedies

Right to Reject or Revoke Acceptance of Nonconforming Goods.   In the absence of a contrary agreement, a buyer is not required to accept a delivery of the goods if they fail to conform to the contract, and he may revoke an acceptance of such goods.[18] As stated before, an exception is made in the case of nonconforming installment deliveries which do not substantially impair the value of that installment. The buyer's rights and duties in the event of the seller's breach were discussed earlier

---

[18] UCC Sec.'s. 2-601; 2-608.

in this chapter. As a general rule, if nonconforming goods are delivered, the buyer may (1) reject the whole, (2) accept the whole, or (3) accept any commercial unit or units and reject the rest. Acceptance of nonconforming goods does not necessarily result in a loss of other remedies available to the buyer, including damages. Sections 2-601 to 2-608, inclusive, of the Code govern such matters as rejection, the manner and effect of rightful rejection, the waiver of rejection and breach by buyer's failure to particularize defects upon which rejection is based, acceptance of the goods, revocation of acceptance, and related subjects.

Damages. The Code asserts the buyer's right to damages for a breach of the sales contract, but does not require the buyer to elect the remedy of damages to the exclusion of other remedies, including rescission of the contract. Election was required under the prevailing pre-Code rule. Where the seller fails to deliver or repudiates the contract or the buyer rightfully rejects or revokes, the buyer may cancel and in addition to recovering of so much of the price as has been paid, may "cover" and have damages, or recover damages for nondelivery.[19]

The Code rules governing the buyer's damages are contained in Sections 2-713 to 2-715, inclusive, and these rules are summarized in the following discussion. The measure of damages for nondelivery or repudiation is the difference between the market price at the time the buyer learned of the breach and the contract price, together with incidental and consequential damages, less expenses saved.

Where the buyer has accepted the goods but given notification of their nonconformity, he may recover the loss ordinarily resulting from the seller's breach. As pointed out in the discussion in Chapter 15 of the buyer's remedies for breach of warranty, in the absence of special circumstances, the recovery for breach of warranty is the difference between the value of the goods accepted and the value if the goods had been as warranted. Inci-

---

[19] UCC Sec. 2-711 (1).

dental and consequential damages caused by the seller's breach of a sale contract may be recovered in a proper case. Incidental damages include reasonable expenses arising out of or connected with the seller's breach. Consequential damages include loss from buyer's general or particular requirements of which the seller had reason to know and which could not have been reasonably prevented by the buyer. Personal injury and property damage proximately resulting from a breach of warranty are included in consequential damages.

On notification to the seller, the buyer may deduct any part of the damages from any part of the purchase price still due on the contract.[20]

Replevin.   The buyer may obtain possession of the goods by bringing an action in replevin if the goods have been identified to the contract, and if, after reasonable effort, he is unable to effect "cover." Replevin may also be had when goods are shipped under reservation and satisfaction of the security interest is made or tendered.[21]

Specific Performance.   If the goods are unique or other proper circumstances exist, the buyer may have specific performance.[22] It is provided that "the decree of specific performance may include such terms and conditions as to payment of the price, damages, or other relief as the court may deem just."[23]

Right to Cover.   After a breach by the seller, the buyer may, at his option, in good faith and without unreasonable delay, purchase goods in substitution for those due under the contract.[24] This remedy is referred to as *cover*. In addition to cover the buyer may claim damages if a loss from the seller's breach can be established.

Right to Security Interest and Recovery of Deposit.   If the

---

[20] UCC Sec. 2-717.
[21] UCC Sec. 2-716 (3).
[22] UCC Sec. 2-716 (1).
[23] UCC Sec. 2-716 (2).
[24] UCC Sec. 2-712.

buyer rightfully rejects or revokes, he has a security interest in the goods to the extent of his payments and expenses.[25] In cases where the seller justifiably withholds delivery because of the buyer's breach, the buyer is entitled to restitution of any excessive payments he has made to the seller as defined in Section 2-718 of the Code.

Liquidation or Limitation of Damages or Remedies

The Code permits reasonable liquidated damage clauses in sales contracts.[26] A liquidated damages clause in a contract is one which defines the amount an aggrieved party may recover in the event of a breach. Limitations of remedies, if reasonable, may be included in a sale contract, but such a clause must state that the remedy provided is exclusive or resort to the specified remedy or remedies will be viewed as optional and thus will leave other remedies open to the aggrieved party.[27]

Consequential damages may be limited or excluded if the provision is not unconscionable. As pointed out in Chapter 15, the Code provides that a limitation on damages for personal injuries in the case of consumer goods is prima facie unconscionable.

Statute of Limitations

Under the Code, the period of limitations for breach of a contract is four years.[28] Before the Code, states fixed by statute the period of limitation for actions on contracts generally, and sales contracts were grouped together with other kinds of contracts. These statutes of limitations remain in effect but, in those states which have adopted the Code, sales contracts will be governed by the four year statute of limitations. States often have set a longer period of limitation for written contracts than for oral contracts. This distinction is not made in the Code. If a case

---

[25] UCC Sec. 2-711 (3).
[26] UCC Sec. 2-718.
[27] UCC Sec. 2-719 (1).
[28] UCC Sec. 2-725.

for breach of a sales contract is dismissed otherwise than on the merits, another action may be commenced within six months, according to the Code. A state's laws which toll the running of statutes of limitations under certain circumstances as described in Chapter 12 also apply to sales contracts.

A cause of action accrues on the occurrence of a breach regardless of lack of knowledge. As pointed out in Chapter 15, this means that the cause of action accrues on tender of delivery of the goods in a breach of warranty situation.

The Code permits the parties in the original agreement to reduce the limitation period to not less than one year, but the parties may not extend the period of limitation beyond four years.

Introduction

17

BACKGROUND AND DEVELOPMENT

Business transactions are immeasurably facilitated by the use of a vast variety of legal instruments. A legal instrument is a formal expression in writing of some agreement or obligation, or of some act on which the rights of the parties are dependent. Today, many business transactions are settled by the transfer of legal instruments which are classified as negotiable instruments, sometimes referred to as commercial paper. Having discussed in Part Two of this book the rules generally applicable to all contracts, we will now discuss negotiable instruments, a special class of contracts possessing unique characteristics, including the quality of negotiability.

A negotiable instrument, defined in terms of its elements, is an instrument in writing, signed by the maker or drawer, containing an unconditional promise or order to pay a sum certain in money on demand or at a definite future time to order or to bearer; and when the instrument is addressed to a drawee, is one in which he is named or otherwise indicated therein with reasonable certainty. The above elements of a negotiable instrument are discussed in detail in Chapter 18 dealing with the requirements of negotiability.

Types of negotiable instruments were used in the ancient societies and became prevalent during the Middle Ages. Evidence has been found of a promissory note payable to bearer of the approximate date of 2100 B.C., and foreign bills of exchange were used by the Florentine and Venetian merchants of the twelfth and thirteenth centuries as a means of transmitting credit from one country to another without actually transferring metallic money. Negotiable instruments were often used as substitutes for money in commercial transactions and, by the understanding and usage of those employing them, were closely assimilated to money.

Commercial paper has always been subject to well-defined usages and rules which make up part of the law merchant. Although the law merchant originated separate from the common law in England, it has been pointed out that it was later engrafted into the common law and became part of it. Founded on the customs and usages of merchants, the law regulating negotiable instruments is today the combined result of reason and experience, slowly modified by the necessities and changes in commercial practices. The law governing negotiable instruments today is found in statutes and court decisions.

Uniform Statutes

As pointed out in the beginning of this book, the Commissioners on Uniform State Laws have, either alone or in collaboration with others, prepared and sponsored a number of uniform acts relating to various subjects both in the commercial law field and in other fields of law. The earliest uniform act promulgated by this group was the Uniform Negotiable Instruments Act, referred to in this book as the N.I.L. Modeled largely on the English Bills of Exchange Act of 1882, the N.I.L. was adopted by New York in 1897, and it was ultimately adopted by all the states.

Many changes in commercial practices occurred since the drafting of the N.I.L., and courts of different states had handed down conflicting decisions as to the meaning of certain provisions of the N.I.L. As a result, a complete overhauling and modernization of the N.I.L. was undertaken and ultimately became Article 3 of the Uniform Commercial Code, referred to in this book as the Code. Article 3 of the Code, however, applies only to notes, drafts, checks, bills of exchange, and certificates of deposit. Unlike the N.I.L., it does not apply to corporate debt obligations, such as bonds and debentures. These instruments are covered in Article 8 of the Code. Article 4 of the Code deals with bank collections and certain phases of bank deposits. The latter article takes the place of the American Bankers Association Bank Collection Code. Article 5 covers letters of credit.

The discussion which follows in this part of the book relates primarily to Article 3 of the Code. However, substantial reference is made to the old N.I.L. and the case law thereunder for the reason that the Code continues much of this law. And in states which have not adopted the Code, the N.I.L. is still in effect.

NEGOTIABILITY BENEFITS

Negotiability Contrasted with Assignability

The rights under a contract may usually be assigned, that is, transferred, so that the assignee of them may sue and recover if the party from whom he derived his rights could. But, as we saw in Chapter 10, the assignee of ordinary contract rights is subject to be met in the enforcement of his claim by whatever defenses existed or arose between the debtor and original creditor (assignor), not only at the time of assignment, but down to the time when the debtor had notice of the assignment.

EXAMPLE 1. A owes B $100 arising out of a sale of goods by B to A. B assigns the $100 claim to C. Upon suit by C against A, A establishes the defense that B never delivered the goods as called for in his contract with B. A will prevail. Any defense which A would have had against B may be set up against C, even though C has paid value and is innocent of the defense.

The same result as explained above prevails where a non-negotiable instrument is transferred. If an instrument is negotiable, then its transfer is effected by a procedure called negotiation and the transferee, called a holder, takes the instrument free from many of the defenses which might have been set up against his transferor; provided the holder qualifies as a holder in due course. Generally, a holder in due course is not subject to personal defenses, but is subject to real defenses. The holder in due course concept and the various defenses to negotiable instruments are explained in Chapter 20.

EXAMPLE 2.   A issues a negotiable promissory note to B for $100. B indorses and delivers the note to C, a holder in due course. C may recover from A on the note despite A's defense of lack of consideration or any other personal defense he may have which would have defeated B's right to collect from A. If B had forged A's name to the note, then B would have the defense of forgery (a real defense) which he could assert against any holder, even a holder in due course.

A negotiable instrument is thus analogous to money, for one who without misconduct receives money from a thief or finder without knowledge of the loss or theft, giving value for it, can hold it against the world, including the one who lost the money or was the victim of the thief. This rule as to theft or finding applies to negotiable instruments which, being payable to bearer or indorsed in blank, are transferred like money by mere delivery.

The rules of negotiability are grounded upon both commercial custom and public policy which demands that both money and the instruments used as its substitute should be taken fearlessly, so that their circulation will be encouraged and promoted. As a result, a holder in due course of a negotiable instrument is able to occupy a position superior to that of a mere assignee of a contract right. However, the holder in due course is still subject to two major risks: (1) the presence of a real defense as illustrated by the forgery illustration in Example 2 above, and (2) insolvency of the parties from whom collection is attempted. The person receiving a nonnegotiable instrument is in the position of a mere assignee and his rights are determined by ordinary contract law.

Presumption of Consideration

If a contract is in the form of a negotiable instrument, there is a presumption that it was given for a consideration, which means that ordinarily in a suit between the immediate parties— as where a payee sues the maker of a note, for example—the maker has the burden of proving a lack of consideration. In a suit on an ordinary contract, the party who brings the action must prove that the promise he is seeking to enforce rests upon a consideration. And once a negotiable instrument is negotiated to a holder in due course, the question of consideration can no longer be inquired into, so far as the holder in due course or one claiming through him is concerned. Other procedural advantages may be made available to the holder of a negotiable instrument, depending upon the statutes of the state in which suit is brought.

TYPES OF NEGOTIABLE INSTRUMENTS

Broadly classified, negotiable instruments calling for the payment of money consist of (1) promissory notes and (2) bills of exchange or drafts. Over the years as commercial transactions have become more complex, variations of the two basic types of negotiable instruments have been developed and continue in use up to the present time. The N.I.L. classifies negotiable instruments as notes, bills of exchange, and checks, while the Code defines four classes: (1) notes, (2) drafts, (3) certificates of deposit, and (4) checks. The terms bill of exchange and draft are often used interchangeably, and a certificate of deposit is a type of promissory note.

Promissory Notes
A promissory note is an unconditional promise in writing made by one person (called the maker) and signed by him, promising to pay on demand, or at a definite future time, a certain sum in money to the order of another person (called the payee) or to bearer. No particular words must be used but the illustration which follows will serve as an example of a negotiable promissory note.

$500.00   Athens, Ohio,   May 15, 19 64

Thirty days _____ after date for value received, we, or either of us,

promise to pay **THE ATHENS NATIONAL BANK**   Athens, Ohio, or Order,

Five Hundred and no/100 _____ **Dollars,**

for value received, with interest at 6 per cent.

No. 1

Due June 14, 1964

Stephen Williams
Julia Williams

Promissory Note

Secured Notes. The original parties to a promissory note may find it expedient to combine one or more security contracts with the maker's promise to pay. The usual types of such notes are collateral note, mortgage note, title-retaining (conditional sale) note, and cognovit note. A collateral note is one in which the maker pledges personal property, often securities, to the payee as security. A mortgage note combines a note with a mortgage on real property or chattels (tangible personal property) as security. In the event of default the payee can foreclose his mortgage. A title-retaining note combines a note with a conditional sale contract so as to permit the payee to retain title of certain goods until the maker has paid the note. The chattel mortgage and title-retaining notes are frequently used in the financing of retail sales of goods. Cognovit notes, also called judgment notes, contain a provision authorizing the holder to take judgment against the maker without service of summons or trial if the maker defaults. The cognovit note has been banned or restricted by statute in many states.

Certificates of Deposit

A certificate of deposit is issued by a bank to one who deposits money and takes the certificate of the bank for it. Courts have held the certificate of deposit to be a negotiable promissory note, provided the usual elements of negotiability are present. It may be made payable on demand or it may be made payable at a fixed future time with interest. The Code classifies the certificate of deposit as a negotiable instrument.

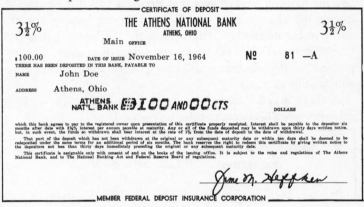

Certificate of Deposit

Bills of Exchange or Drafts

A bill of exchange is an unconditional written order by one person upon another, directing him to pay to a third person, or to his order, or to the bearer, a sum certain in money. The term draft is sometimes used as the equivalent of bill of exchange.

The party who draws and signs a bill of exchange is called the drawer; the party upon whom it is drawn is called the drawee,

Bill of Exchange or Draft

and the party in whose favor it is drawn is called the payee. A foreign bill of exchange is a bill drawn in one state or country and payable in another state or country; an inland bill is one drawn and made payable in the same state or country. The importance of this distinction will be explained later in connection with liability of parties.

A check may be defined as a brief order or draft drawn by a depositor upon his bank, payable on demand.

Check

While a check has most of the characteristics of a bill of exchange, it possesses unique qualities which will be described in detail in Chapter 22. A cashier's check is a bill of exchange drawn by a bank upon itself and accepted by the act of issuance. Certification of a check by the drawee bank is equivalent to an acceptance and renders the bank primarily liable. A voucher check contains a statement of the debt paid by the check. A bank draft is a draft by one bank upon another with which the drawing bank has funds or credit. If payable on demand, such a draft is treated as a check; if payable at a future time, it is a bill of exchange.

A trade acceptance is a draft or bill of exchange drawn for goods purchased, and accepted by the purchaser. It recites upon its face that it arises out of such purchase. Trade acceptances have not come into universal use. They were created to supersede the ordinary open or book account so as to give the seller of goods a negotiable instrument which could be discounted with his bank. A bank acceptance is a draft or bill of exchange drawn on and accepted by a bank.

Requirements for Negotiability

18

FORM OF NEGOTIABLE INSTRUMENTS

Under both the Negotiable Instruments Law and the Uniform Commercial Code, an instrument must meet certain formal requirements before it is recognized as a negotiable instrument. ¶ Under both it must

1] be in writing and signed by the maker or drawer;
2] contain an unconditional promise or order (and, under the Code, no other promise, order, obligation, or power except as authorized by Article 3 of the Code);
3] be payable in a sum certain in money;
4] be payable to order or bearer;
5] be payable on demand or at a definite time under the Code (at a fixed or determinable future time under the N.I.L.);
6] name the drawee or otherwise indicate with reasonable certainty in the instrument who the drawee is, if the instrument is addressed to a drawee.

The requirements for negotiability are listed in Section 1 of the N.I.L., and the Code's version of the requirements for negotiability are listed in Section 3-104 (1) of the Code. An instrument may be negotiable, that is, it meets all the formal requirements, and yet be invalid and unenforceable because it does not meet one or more of the essential elements of a binding contract. This will be made apparent when defenses are examined in Chapter 20.

As indicated above, the requirements for negotiability as stated in the Code are not precisely the same as those found in the N.I.L. However, they are substantially the same. The sixth requirement, which applies only to bills of exchange, does not appear in the Code, but from its nature this requirement would seem to be implied nevertheless. Some of the divergencies between the N.I.L. and the Code will be referred to in the detailed discussion of these formal requisites which follows.

Writing and Signed

The law does not prescribe any particular kind of writing or particular material upon which the writing must be placed in order to create a negotiable instrument. Writing includes handwriting, printing, typewriting, or other intentional reduction to tangible form. Although it would not be a good business practice to do so, the instrument could be written and signed with a lead pencil.

Signature. An instrument to be negotiable must be signed by the maker in the case of a promissory note; the drawer must sign in the case of a bill. The signature may be handwritten, typed, printed, or made by a mark, commonly an "X," and it need not appear in any particular place on the paper. It may consist of a trade or assumed name. The test for the signing requirement is whether the party sought to be held intended the signature or mark as his signature. For example, a promissory note was written in duplicate by placing carbon paper between two sheets of paper. It was held that the carbon duplicate, bearing a carbon copy of the maker's signature was not a negotiable instrument, but was simply a carbon copy of the instrument.

The signature of any party to a negotiable instrument may be made by an authorized agent. If a party's signature is forged or written without authority, he is not liable on it, unless he ratifies it or is precluded from denying liability by the doctrine of estoppel.

Promise or Order Must be Unconditional

Promise or Order Requirement. To be negotiable, a promissory note must contain a promise. Although the word promise need not appear in the note, language equivalent to a promise must be used. The Code states: "A promise is an undertaking to pay and must be more than an acknowledgement of an obligation."[1] "I.O.U. twenty dollars" is not a promise but a mere acknowledgement. So also, "Due you twenty dollars" is unsufficient, but "Due John Doe or order $100 payable July 1st" has been held to be a promise to pay.

To be negotiable, a bill of exchange or check must contain an order. The Code provides: "An order to pay is a direction to pay and must be more than an authorization or request."[2] Where the instrument read: "Mr. Little: Please to let the bearer have seven pounds and place it to my account, and you will oblige your humble servant R. Slackford," the English court held that this language did not constitute an order. Words of politeness such as "Please pay" do not impair the force of an order. The words used must import an absolute intention that the money should at all events be paid.

Unconditional Promise or Order. Negotiable instruments must be unconditional if they are to be readily accepted as a substitute for money and as vehicles of credit. An express condition, as where the maker of a note promises to pay "if A graduates from the university," is fatal to negotiability. Even performance of the condition does not cure the defect, since negotiability is determined by what appears on the face of the instrument. The requirement of an unconditional promise or order is stated in the N.I.L. in loose, general language, while Section 3-105 of the Code sets forth in more precise terms what

---

[1] UCC Sec. 3-102 (1) (c).
[2] UCC Sec. 3-102 (1) (b).

does and what does not constitute conditions. The provisions of Section 3-105 are summarized in the following paragraphs.

The negotiability of an instrument is not affected by a mere reference on its face to the transaction out of which it arose. Similarly, a mere reference in the instrument to a separate agreement, or that it was given in return for an executory promise, or that it is secured by a mortgage described in a security agreement does not impair negotiability.

A promise or order is not unconditional when the instrument states it is subject to or governed by some other agreement. But, the Code provides that an instrument which states that "the promise or order is made or the instrument matures in accordance with or 'as per' " the transaction out of which it arose meets the unconditional requirement.

An instrument which recites that it is to be paid out of a particular fund is not negotiable, the general credit of the obligor not being pledged. In such instruments the obligation has been made conditional upon the existence of such fund at the maturity of the instrument and upon its then being sufficient in amount. The fact that at the time the instrument falls due, there is such a fund and it is then sufficient, does not change the rule, for as pointed out before, a negotiable instrument must be negotiable on its face, and not by force of extrinsic facts. To illustrate, a promise in a note which reads: "I promise to pay to the order of A five hundred dollars out of sale proceeds of 85 Park Avenue" is conditional and therefore makes the note nonnegotiable.

The Code modifies and clarifies the particular fund doctrine by providing that (1) if the instrument is issued by a government or governmental agency or unit, payment may be limited to a particular fund without impairing negotiability; and (2) an instrument is negotiable although payable only out of the assets of a partnership, an unincorporated association, a trust, or an estate. Under the N.I.L., courts were split over the negotiability question in the latter case.

Although an instrument payable from a particular fund is

nonnegotiable, a promise or order to pay is unconditional though coupled with an indication of (1) a particular fund out of which reimbursement is to be made, or (2) an account which is to be charged. Reimbursement or charging an account contemplates the obligor paying from his own funds and then after payment, reimbursing himself or making the charge. In such cases, the obligor binds himself to pay regardless of the sufficiency or even the existence of the fund or account. For example, an order which provides: "Pay to the order of A five hundred dollars and charge to account of Hillcrest Farm" is unconditional because it merely indicates the fund from which the paying party is to get back his money.

Sum Certain and Money

In order for an instrument to be negotiable it must be payable in money and its sum must be certain. These requirements promote certainty in ascertaining the present value of an instrument, thus helping these instruments serve as substitutes for money. A promise to pay money and do something else is not negotiable. The same result occurs where the obligor is given the option of paying money or doing something else. Under the N.I.L. a promise or order to pay money or do something else at the holder's option is negotiable. No such provision appears in the Code.

Money is defined in the Code as "a medium of exchange authorized or adopted by a domestic or foreign government as a part of its currency." [3] Under this statement, money is not limited to legal tender, but it is not so broadly defined as to include whatever happens to be a medium of exchange in a particular community. The test of money is that of government sanction.

The Code provides that an instrument calling for payment of a stated sum in a foreign currency, even though payable in the United States, is payable in a "sum certain in money" and, ". . . unless a different medium of exchange is specified in the

---

[3] UCC Sec. 1-201 (24).

instrument, may be satisfied in payment of that number of dollars which the stated foreign currency will purchase at the buying sight rate for that currency on the day on which the instrument is payable or, if payable on demand, on the day of demand.[4]

Generally, provisions in instruments calling for stated installment payments, stated discounts, stated interest, exchange at a fixed rate or at the current rate, attorney fees, collection costs, or acceleration of obligor's obligation upon his default do not make the sum uncertain.[5] Although a provision in an instrument for the payment of an attorney's fee or costs does not render the instrument nonnegotiable, some states view the provision itself as contrary to public policy and unenforceable. A promise to pay the principal sum "together with all taxes and charges . . . that may be levied upon this note" has been held to provide for an uncertain sum and made the note nonnegotiable.

Certainty of Time of Payment

The Code provides that a negotiable instrument must "be payable on demand or at a definite time." Like the other requirements for negotiability, this requisite contributes to the rational determination of the present value of an instrument. More particularly, this requirement permits a holder to know (1) when the obligor can be compelled to pay, (2) when the obligation of secondary parties will arise, (3) when the statute of limitations will start to run, and (4) whether he can qualify as a holder in due course. Also, the duration of an obligation described in a negotiable instrument is a determinant of discount rates and credit risks.

Demand instruments are defined by the Code as including "those payable at sight or on presentation and those in which no time for payment is stated." [6]

---

[4] UCC Sec. 3-107 (2).
[5] UCC Sec. 3-106.
[6] UCC Sec. 3-108.

Definite time is defined in Section 3-109 of the Code as follows:

1] An instrument is payable at a definite time if by its terms it is payable
   A] on or before a stated date or at a fixed period after a stated date; or
   B] at a fixed period after sight; or
   C] at a definite time subject to any acceleration; or
   D] at a definite time subject to extension at the option of the holder, or to extension to a further definite time at the option of the maker or acceptor or automatically upon or after a specified act or event.
2] An instrument which by its terms is otherwise payable only upon an act or event uncertain as to time of occurrence is not payable at a definite time even though the act or event has occurred.

In its definition of definite time the Code differs significantly in some respects with the N.I.L. For example, the Code provides that the certainty of time payment is not affected by "any acceleration" clause, whether acceleration is at the option of the maker or the holder or is automatic. This provision eliminates the distinction formerly made between acceleration provisions conditioned upon the happening of an event which is either within the control of the obligor or not within the control of the parties, and those giving the holder an unrestricted power to accelerate. Under the N.I.L. most courts have held that an instrument payable "at the option of the holder if he deems himself insecure," provides for an uncertain time of payment which destroys negotiability; a contrary result prevails under the Code. However, the holder must act in good faith in exercising such option.[7]

---

[7] UCC Sec. 1-208.

The Code also changes the law concerning instruments payable after events certain to happen although the time of happening be uncertain. For example, a promissory note payable at a fixed period of time after the death of the maker or some other person would be negotiable under the N.I.L., but not under the Code. It would appear, however, that negotiable postobituary notes are possible under the Code because of the validity given to "any acceleration" clause. For example, a note, "I promise to pay six weeks after my Uncle George's death," would be nonnegotiable under the Code, but a note, "I promise to pay 100 years from date, but payment shall be accelerated by the death of my Uncle George to a point of time six weeks after said death" would be negotiable under the Code.

Words of Negotiability

A negotiable instrument must be payable to order or to bearer. In using such language or its equivalent the parties to an instrument indicate an intention to issue a negotiable instrument. Sections 3-110 and 3-111 of the Code define what is meant by payable to order and payable to bearer.

The usual language employed in creating order paper is "pay to the order of X" or "pay to X or order." The intention is that X is to receive payment if he holds the paper, but if X wishes he may name someone else to receive payment. The typical bearer language is "pay to bearer" and the intention is that any person who is in possession of the instrument is entitled to payment. Mere use of the word *bearer* may not be enough to meet the words of negotiability requirement. The context in which the word is used must be examined. For example, an instrument payable "to the bearer X" is nonnegotiable because an intention is expressed that only one specific person is to receive payment. Any words evincing an intention that the instrument is negotiable will satisfy the words of negotiability requirement, but, of course, the instrument would also have to meet the other requirements of negotiability in order to be negotiable.

MATTERS NOT AFFECTING NEGOTIABILITY

The negotiability of an instrument is not affected by (1) omission of statement of consideration for the instrument or place where the instrument is drawn or payable; (2) statement of collateral, provision for maintenance of collateral, and authorization to sell same upon default; (3) a confession of judgment clause or waiver of rights given by statute to obligor; (4) a full satisfaction indorsement provision; (5) a statement in a draft drawn in a set of parts to the effect that the order is effective only if no other part has been honored; (6) the fact that the instrument is undated, antedated, or postdated; and (7) presence or absence of a seal.[8]

RULES OF CONSTRUCTION

Section 3-118 of the Code provides for certain rules of construction to be applied where an instrument contains ambiguous terms or where there are certain omissions in the instrument, as follows:

¶ The following rules apply to every instrument:

    A] Where there is doubt whether the instrument is a draft or a note, the holder may treat it as either. A draft drawn on the drawer is effective as a note.

    B] Handwritten terms control typewritten and printed terms, and typewritten control printed.

    C] Words control figures except that if the words are ambiguous figures control.

    D] Unless otherwise specified a provision for interest means interest at the judgment rate at the place of payment from the date of the instrument, or if it is undated from the date of issue.

---

[8] UCC Sec's. 3-112; 3-113; 3-114.

E] Unless the instrument otherwise specifies two or more persons who sign as maker, acceptor or drawer or indorser and as a part of the same transaction are jointly and severally liable even though the instrument contains such words as "I promise to pay."

F] Unless otherwise specified, consent to extension authorizes a single extension for not longer than the original period. A consent to extension, expressed in the instrument, is binding on secondary parties and accommodation makers. A holder may not exercise his option to extend an instrument over the objection of a maker or acceptor or other party who in accordance with Section 3-604 tenders full payment when the instrument is due.

DELIVERY

A negotiable instrument must be delivered in order to be issued originally or subsequently negotiated. As between immediate parties, such as maker and payee, indorser and indorsee, this rule is absolute; but as between a prior party, such as a maker of a note, and a subsequent holder in due course, a valid delivery is presumed. For example, A makes a negotiable promissory note payable to the order of B and leaves it on his (A's) desk. B takes possession of the note without A's consent. B cannot recover against A on the note, because there was no delivery. If, however, B negotiates the note to H, a holder in due course, H can recover against A. Lack of delivery as a defense is discussed further in Chapter 20 dealing with holder in due course and defenses.

Negotiation

19

Transfer By Negotiation

The term *transfer* when used in its broad legal sense means any act by which the owner of a thing delivers it to another with the intent of passing his rights in it to the new owner. The two types of negotiable instrument transfers which are recognized by the law are referred to as negotiation and assignment. We have seen that the transfer of the rights in an ordinary contract is referred to as an assignment.

If a negotiable instrument is negotiated, the person receiving it becomes a holder and may qualify as a holder in due course with all the rights such a holder enjoys. The requirements for negotiation of a negotiable instrument depend upon whether the instrument is a bearer or an order instrument.

Negotiation of Bearer and Order Instruments

A person becomes a holder of bearer paper by receiving delivery of it. If the paper is order paper, a proper indorsement and delivery are essential for negotiation of the paper to a holder.

An order instrument is defined in Section 3-110 of the Code as follows:

> 1] An instrument is payable to order when by its terms it is payable to the order or assigns of any person therein

specified with reasonable certainty, or to him or his order, or when it is conspicuously designated on its face as "exchange" or the like and names a payee. It may be payable to the order of

A] the maker or drawer; or

B] the drawee; or

C] a payee who is not maker, drawer, or drawee; or

D] two or more payees together or in the alternative; or

E] an estate, trust or fund, in which case it is payable to the order of the representative of such estate, trust or fund or his successors; or

F] an office, or an officer by his title as such in which case it is payable to the principal but the incumbent of the office or his successors may act as if he or they were the holder; or

G] a partnership or unincorporated association, in which case it is payable to the partnership or association and may be indorsed or transferred by any person thereto authorized.

2] An instrument not payable to order is not made so payable by such words as "payable upon return of this instrument properly indorsed."

3] An instrument made payable both to order and to bearer is payable to order unless the bearer words are handwritten or typewritten.

Bearer instruments are defined in Section 3-111 of the Code as follows:

An instrument is payable to bearer when by its terms it is payable to

A] bearer or the order of bearer; or

B] a specified person or bearer; or

C] "cash" or the order of "cash," or any other indication which does not purport to designate a specific payee.

Transfer By Assignment

Negotiable instrument transfers which do not constitute negotiations are viewed as assignments. A mere assignee is not a holder and thus cannot be a holder in due course. But, as explained in the next chapter, an assignee may be a successor to a holder in due course and as such not subject to the personal defenses of prior parties. Further, the assignee (also called transferee) of a negotiable instrument may rise to the position of a holder by exercising his right to compel his transferor to negotiate the instrument. Once the negotiation occurs, the transferee may qualify as a holder in due course in his own right. This situation arises when order paper is transferred for value but without indorsement.[1]

INDORSEMENTS

Indorsements in General

An indorsement has a twofold legal effect. The indorsement of the instrument along with delivery of it (1) passes title to the instrument to the indorsee, and (2) the indorsement puts the indorser under liability to the indorsee and subsequent holders of the instrument. The extent and nature of the indorser's liability will be discussed in Chapter 21.

An indorsement must be written on the instrument by or on behalf of the holder, but if there isn't space for the indorsement on the instrument, the indorsement may be written on an attached paper (called an allonge). When the name of the payee or indorsee is misspelled or otherwise incorrectly written, he may sign his name as it appears in the instrument, adding, if he wishes, his proper signature; but signature in both names may be required by a person paying or giving value for the instrument.[2] While an indorsement is usually on the back of the

---

[1] UCC Sec's. 3-201 and 3-202.
[2] UCC Sec. 3-203.

instrument, it may be placed on the face. Any form of signature is sufficient for an indorsement. The signature of the indorser without further words is sufficient. Words of negotiability are not necessary in the indorsement.

The indorsement must be of the entire instrument, but if any part of the amount called for by the instrument has been paid, an indorsement of the residue is permitted. The Code treats an indorsement of only part of the sum due on the instrument as an assignment.[3]

If the instrument is payable to two or more payees or indorsees jointly, e.g., "to the order of A and B," all must indorse unless they are partners, or unless one has authority from the other or others to indorse for all. An instrument payable to two or more payees or indorsees severally, e.g., "to the order of A or B," may be negotiated by the indorsement of any one of the payees or indorsees as the case may be. If the instrument is payable to "A and/or B," it is payable in the alternative to A, or to B, or to A and B together, and it may be negotiated, enforced, or discharged accordingly.

Under the Code an indorsement or negotiation is effective to pass title even if it is obtained by fraud, duress, or mistake; made in breach of duty; made by a minor, a corporation exceeding its powers, or any other person without capacity; or occurs as part of an illegal transaction.[4] The Code permits the defrauded party, the minor, etc., to rescind the transfer but until he does, he leaves the transferee in a position to negotiate the instrument to a holder in due course which will cut off the right to rescind.

Kinds of Indorsements

Indorsements may be either special or in blank, and may be unqualified or qualified, restrictive or non-restrictive, conditional or unconditional. The discussion of each of the types of indorse-

---

[3] UCC Sec. 3-202 (3).
[4] UCC Sec. 3-207.

ments which follows is concerned primarily with the effect they have on further negotiation. The effect on indorser liability of a qualified and unqualified indorsement is taken up in Chapter 21.

Special and Blank Indorsements. The subject of special and blank indorsements is covered by Section 3-204 of the Code. This section provides:

1] A special indorsement specifies the person to whom or to whose order it makes the instrument payable. Any instrument specially indorsed becomes payable to the order of the special indorsee and may be further negotiated only by his indorsement.

2] An indorsement in blank specifies no particular indorsee and may consist of a mere signature. An instrument payable to order and indorsed in blank becomes payable to bearer and may be negotiated by delivery alone until specially indorsed.

3] The holder may convert a blank indorsement into a special indorsement by writing over the signature of the indorser in blank any contract consistent with the character of the indorsement.

This Code provision overrules the rule prevailing under Section 40 of the N.I.L. which courts generally interpreted as providing in effect that an instrument bearer on its face remains negotiable by delivery alone despite a special indorsement thereon. The Code makes clear that the last indorsement controls as to whether the instrument is a bearer or order instrument.

A blank indorsement usually consists of the signature of the indorser alone. For example, "John Jones" is a blank indorsement. Its effect is to make the instrument payable to bearer. The blank indorsement may or may not be restrictive, qualified or conditional, depending upon the words the indorser adds to his signature.

A special indorsement consists of the indorser's signature and words naming the person to whom the instrument is payable. For example, "Pay to the order of A. (signed) B"; or "Pay to A or order. (signed) B"; or "Pay to A. (signed) B" are special indorsements. Indorsement by the special indorsee in addition to delivery of the instrument by him is necessary for further negotiation. The special indorser may add words making his special indorsement restrictive, qualified or conditional.

Qualified Indorsement. A blank or special indorser of an instrument remains secondarily liable on the instrument, that is, such an indorser can be required to pay the instrument if the primary party defaults and the holder takes certain steps as explained in Chapter 21. This indorser liability as a guarantor can be eliminated by the indorser writing a qualified indorsement. The usual words employed in a qualified indorsement are "without recourse." While the Code does not include the qualified indorsement within its classification of indorsements, it does make provision for it in Section 3-414 with the same effect as existed under pre-Code law.

A qualified indorsement has no effect on the further negotiability of the instrument. Such an indorsement merely eliminates the indorser's guaranty contract but, as pointed out later, the qualified indorser remains liable on certain warranties. In effect, a qualified indorsement constitutes the indorser a mere assignor of the title to the instrument.

Restrictive and Conditional Indorsements. Section 3-205 of the Code defines the restrictive indorsement as follows:

An indorsement is restrictive which either
A] is conditional; or
B] purports to prohibit further transfer of the instrument; or
C] includes the words "for collection," "for deposit," "pay any bank," or like terms signifying a purpose of deposit or collection; or
D] otherwise states that it is for the benefit or use of the indorser or of another person.

Section 3-206 of the Code makes some major changes in the law governing the effect of restrictive indorsements. In summary, the changes (1) make it possible for a restrictive indorsee to be a holder in due course; (2) permit intermediary banks to disregard the restrictive indorsement except that of its immediate transferor; and (3) permit further negotiation despite a restrictive indorsement.

Examples of restrictive indorsements include: "Pay to A only. (signed) B"; "Pay to X bank for collection only. (signed) B"; and "Pay to A in trust for C. (signed) B." As can be seen, these examples illustrate Subsections (b), (c), and (d), respectively of Section 3-205 of the Code.

As can be seen from reading Subsection (a) of Section 3-205 of the Code, conditional indorsements are included in the Code's definition of restrictive indorsements. Used very rarely, a conditional indorsement imposes a condition upon further negotiation. For example, "Pay to the order of A if he sells my house. (signed) B" is a conditional indorsement.

A conditional indorsement does not affect further negotiation of the instrument. The party obligated on the instrument may disregard the condition and pay the holder without incurring any liability to the conditional indorser, but the holder holds the proceeds subject to the rights of the conditional indorser. Pursuant to Section 3-206 of the Code, the transferee under a conditional indorsement can become a holder in due course free of the conditional indorser's claim.

Holder in Due Course
and Defenses

20

HOLDER IN DUE COURSE

Introduction

A person receiving a negotiable instrument may be (1) a holder in due course, that is, one who is able to satisfy certain requirements and thus enjoy certain advantages, or (2) a mere holder who is unable to qualify as a holder in due course. The holder in due course enjoys the preferred position of taking the instrument free and clear of many defenses which would be available to a prior party. A holder who cannot qualify as a holder in due course is subject to any defense a prior party may be able to assert. However, as explained later, a holder who derives his title from a holder in due course may acquire all the rights of a holder in due course, although he may not personally satisfy the requirements of one.

Requirements for Qualification as a Holder in Due Course

The N.I.L. in Section 52 provides that in order to qualify as a holder in due course a holder must acquire a negotiable instrument (1) complete and regular on its face, (2) for value,

(3) in good faith, and (4) before the instrument is overdue. In a condensed and modified manner the Code in Section 3-302 (1) defines a holder in due course as a holder who takes the instrument "(a) for value; and (b) in good faith; and (c) without notice that it is overdue or has been dishonored or of any defense against or claim to it on the part of any person."

Value Requirement. The Code continues the requirement of the N.I.L. that the holder purchase the instrument, but the Code is more specific and detailed than the N.I.L. as to what constitutes value. Taking for value is defined in Section 3-303 of the Code as follows:

> A holder takes the instrument for value
>> A] to the extent that the agreed consideration has been performed or that he acquires a security interest in or a lien on the instrument otherwise than by legal process; or
>> B] when he takes the instrument in payment of or as security for an antecedent claim against any person whether or not the claim is due; or
>> C] when he gives a negotiable instrument for it or makes an irrevocable commitment to a third person.

If a negotiable instrument is negotiated as a gift, the donee does not give value for the instrument and cannot qualify as a holder in due course.

The usual value furnished is money and the amount of money does not need to be the face amount of the instrument. A holder who buys an instrument for less than the face value is deemed to have given value and is entitled to recover the full amount of the instrument provided the holder is in good faith and meets the other requirements for a holder in due course. A pledge of, or one who has a lien on, an instrument is deemed a holder for value to the extent of the lien.

An executory promise is not value sufficient to make the promisor a purchaser for value. To the extent a purchaser of an instrument has performed his obligation before he learns of a defense, he is a holder in due course.

Under the Code, a bank which had credited the proceeds of a note or other instrument to the account of its customer will be a holder for value to the extent that the credit had been drawn against. If the bank should learn of some defense to an instrument after it has credited the proceeds of the instrument to its customer's account, the bank would not be a holder in due course with respect to any sum which the customer had not actually withdrawn from his account. Most courts apply the "first in, first out" tracing rule, that is, that the first debits to the depositor's account are charged to the first credits, in determining the exact moment at which the bank pays the proceeds over to the depositor for purposes of the bank qualifying as a holder in due course.

It can be seen from the Code definition of value that if a bank should acquire a security interest in an instrument by taking it as collateral for a loan, it would be a holder for value immediately, whether or not the customer had drawn on the proceeds of the loan. Security interest means an interest in personal property or fixtures which secures payment or performance of an obligation.

A bank would also be a holder for value of any instrument it might take in payment of or as security for an antecedent claim against its customer whether or not that claim was due. Also, a bank would be a holder for value of any instrument which the bank itself might issue, such as a cashier's check, or that might be given to it in return for an irrevocable commitment to some third person, such as a letter of credit or an undertaking to honor a draft.

Good Faith Requirement. A purchaser of a negotiable instrument must take the instrument in good faith in order to qualify as a holder in due course. Good faith means that at the time the purchaser takes the instrument he must have acted honestly and fairly under the facts and circumstances within his knowledge with respect to the rights of prior parties. The rights of the holder are to be determined by the simple test of honesty and good faith and not by a speculative issue as to his diligence or negligence. The Code and N.I.L. are in basic accord as to the above subjective test of good faith.

The Code lists some suspicious circumstances which prevent a person from becoming a holder in due course, regardless of his actual state of mind at the time he acquired the instrument. The Code provides, "A holder does not become a holder in due course of an instrument: (a) by purchase of it at a judicial sale or by taking it under legal process; or (b) by acquiring it in taking over an estate; or (c) by purchasing it as part of a bulk transaction not in the regular course of business of the transferor." [1]

Mere knowledge of the fact that the person negotiating the instrument is or was a fiduciary does not *per se* give the purchaser notice of a defense or claim.[2] But the purchaser has notice of a claim against the instrument when he has knowledge that a fiduciary has negotiated the instrument in payment of or as security for his own debt or in any transaction for his own benefit or otherwise in breach of a duty.[3]

Knowledge of the purchaser of an instrument that the consideration for it was an executory contract does not prevent his becoming a good faith holder, unless there has been a breach of the contract to the knowledge of such purchaser.[4]

Complete and Regular On Its Face. The holder in due course requirement of the N.I.L. that the instrument must be "complete and regular on its face" is not included in the Code section on holder in due course, but appears in the Code section on "notice." The Code provides in Section 3-304 (1) (a): "The purchaser has notice of a claim or defense if the instrument is so incomplete, bears such visible evidence of forgery or alteration, or is otherwise so irregular as to call into question

[1] UCC Sec. 3-302 (3).
[2] UCC Sec. 3-304 (4) (e).
[3] UCC Sec. 3-304 (2).
[4] UCC Sec. 3-304 (4) (b).

its validity, terms, or ownership or to create an ambiguity as to the party to pay." Thus, incompleteness and irregularity are important in their relationship to the "notice" requirement of the Code. In addition, they come within the Code's broadened concept of good faith.

¶ Section 3-115 of the Code provides for the completion of incomplete instruments as follows:

> 1] When a paper whose contents at the time of signing show that it is intended to become an instrument is signed while still incomplete in any necessary respect it cannot be enforced until completed, but when it is completed in accordance with authority given it is effective as completed.

> 2] If the completion is unauthorized, the rules as to material alteration apply (Section 3-407), even though the paper was not delivered by the maker or drawer; but the burden of establishing that any completion is unauthorized is on the party so asserting.

The Code includes an important departure from the N.I.L. by providing that knowledge "that an incomplete instrument has been completed," does not of itself give the purchaser notice of a defense or claim, unless he has "notice of any improper completion." [5]

The following are examples of instruments which the courts have held under the N.I.L. to be incomplete on their face because of omissions or unfilled blanks:

> 1] "_____ after date."
> 2] "On or before four _____ after date."
> 3] "I promise to pay to the order of _____."
> 4] "To _____. Accepted January 1, 1955."

It can be seen that incompleteness consists of the omission of material terms such as the due date in time instruments,

---

[5] UCC Sec. 3-304 (4) (d).

amount, name of the payee of an order instrument, or the drawee of a bill.

Failure to insert a pronoun or connective word will not make an instrument incomplete, and the same result follows where an instrument expresses the amount payable in words but not in figures.

The Code continues the N.I.L. view that a purchaser of an incomplete instrument takes the instrument subject to all defenses available to the prior parties irrespective of whether or not the defenses have anything to do with the blank terms.

Courts have held instruments irregular in cases: (1) where the instrument was stamped "paid" or "payment refused"; (2) where the word "canceled" was written on the face of the instrument; (3) where a usurious rate of interest was charged and this fact appeared on the face of the instrument; (4) where an instrument is made out to an officer of a corporation and signed by the same officer as agent of the corporation. For example, if A, President of M Corporation, issues the corporation's note, payable to himself, signing it "M Corporation, by A, President," the note is irregular.

Irregularities such as alterations, erasures, or insertions relating to material terms on the face of the instrument are likely to preclude the purchaser from becoming a holder in due course if a person of reasonable prudence would have detected the irregularity. The following, either on the basis of a Code provision or court decisions, do not constitute irregularities: (1) postdating; (2) antedating; (3) differences in the handwriting, in the body of the instrument; (4) difference between the handwriting in the signature and the handwriting in the body of the instrument; (5) the amount in figures and not in writing; (6) omission of revenue stamps in states where such are required by statute.

Requirement of Taking Without Notice that the Instrument is Overdue. Section 52 (2) of the N.I.L. provides: "A holder in due course is a holder who has taken the instrument under the following conditions: . . . that he become the holder of it before it is overdue, and without notice that it had been previously dishonored, if such was the fact." The basis for this rule is that a person taking an overdue instrument should suspect that something is probably wrong with the instrument, for otherwise it would have been paid when due. Of course, if the instrument has been dishonored and the purchaser knows this, he cannot be a holder in due course.

An instrument maturing on a fixed date is overdue the day following the due date. Days of grace were abolished by the N.I.L.

Although a demand instrument is due at the moment of delivery and generally the statute of limitations begins to run at that time, such an instrument is intended to circulate for some period of time. Demand instruments are overdue if they have been outstanding more than a reasonable length of time. What is a reasonable length of time is a question of fact, depending upon (1) the nature of the instrument, (2) usages of trade or business, and (3) the facts of the particular case.

Demand notes are intended to circulate for a longer period of time than demand bills of exchange and checks. Demand bills of exchange are intended to circulate for a longer period of time than checks. In connection with the requirement that a holder take the instrument before it is overdue in order to qualify as a holder in due course, a rule of thumb is that a reasonable time is measured in months for demand notes, in weeks for demand bills of exchange, and in days for checks. It has been held that a purchaser of a demand note 3 months and 6 days after its issue was a purchaser before maturity; but that a purchaser 7 months after date was not a purchaser before maturity. Each case must be left to be determined upon its own peculiar circumstances. For example, a demand note circulating in a rural area would be expected to have a longer life than one issued in an urban community.

As we have seen, the Code continues the requirement that a holder in due course must take the instrument before it is overdue. However, the Code attempts to explain in more specific terms the meaning of the requirement by providing in Section 3-304 (3) as follows:

The purchaser has notice that an instrument is overdue if he has reason to know

A] that any part of the principal amount is overdue or that there is an uncured default in payment of another instrument of the same series; or

B] that acceleration of the instrument has been made; or

C] that he is taking a demand instrument after demand has been made or more than a reasonable length of time after its issue. A reasonable time for a check drawn and payable within the states and territories of the United States and the District of Columbia is presumed to be thirty days.

Without Notice of Infirmities or Defects. A holder cannot qualify as a holder in due course if at the time of acquisition he knew of some infirmity in the instrument or of any defect in the title of his transferor. Infirmities refer to defenses parties may have to the instrument. Title defects may arise from obtaining instruments or signatures thereon by fraud, duress, or other unlawful means. The kind of facts which under the Code prevent due course holding were summarized previously.

PAYEE MAY BE A HOLDER IN DUE COURSE

The Code adopts the majority view under the N.I.L. that a payee may qualify as a holder in due course. A technical difficulty under the N.I.L. caused some courts to take the view that a payee cannot be a holder in due course. This view is based on Section 52 (4) of the N.I.L. which seems to require that a holder in due course take by negotiation, and Section 30 of the N.I.L. defines "negotiation" in terms of the further transfer of instruments already issued.

Usually, the payee will not be a holder in due course, because he will be dealing directly with the obligor and thus will be a party to any defenses and claims. But, if a payee meets the requirements of value, good faith, and acquisition prior to maturity, he becomes a holder in due course, whether he takes the instrument by purchase from a third person or directly from the obligor.

The Code expressly adopts this view.[6]

SUCCESSORS TO HOLDER IN DUE COURSE

Section 58 of the N.I.L. reads: "In the hands of any holder other than a holder in due course, a negotiable instrument is subject to the same defenses as if it were nonnegotiable. But a holder who derives his title through a holder in due course, and who is not himself a party to any fraud or illegality affecting the instrument, has all the rights of such former holder in respect of all parties prior to the latter."

This principle raises the position of the holder in due course to a high level by making the rights he holds salable to anyone except a person actually involved in wrongdoing with respect to the paper. Mere knowledge of a defense to the instrument, failure to give value, or taking an overdue instrument, will not preclude a transferee from taking the rights of a holder in due course from or through a holder in due course. It is to be emphasized that a transferee who cannot personally qualify as a holder in due course because of his inability to meet the requirements may nevertheless enjoy the rights of a holder in due course.

The Code continues this rule by providing that once a defense is cut off by negotiation to a holder in due course, the defense

---

[6] UCC Sec. 3-302 (2).

is not restored if the instrument is later transferred to a non-culpable person who is not a holder in due course.[7] For example, if A procures a note from B by fraud in the inducement, and transfers it to H, a holder in due course, who then transfers the note to X, X has the rights of a holder in due course and as such is not subject to B's defense of fraud unless X was a party to the fraud. A could not take rights of a holder in due course by reacquiring the note from H or a subsequent party.

DEFENSES

Introduction

It was pointed out earlier in this chapter that certain defenses cannot be set up against a holder in due course of a negotiable instrument. Defenses to negotiable instruments are classified as personal defenses and real defenses. The holder in due course is not subject to personal defenses, but he is not protected from real defenses. Both types of defenses are effective against a holder who is not a holder in due course or against the holder of a nonnegotiable instrument. Such a holder is in much the same position as an assignee of a simple contract. Generally personal defenses arise out of the transaction which caused the instrument to be voluntarily issued or negotiated, though because of the circumstances it is voidable except against a holder in due course. Real defenses exist in cases where the negotiable instrument lacks legal efficacy at its inception and thus is void even though transferred to a holder in due course. The following discussion classifies and explains the most common types of personal and real defenses.

Personal Defenses

Absence, Failure, or Illegality of Consideration. The obligation created by a negotiable instrument must be supported

---

[7] UCC Sec's. 3-201 and 3-306.

by consideration as in any other contract. But a lack of consideration is no defense against a holder in due course, since consideration is conclusively presumed in favor of such a holder. The same result occurs in cases where consideration is provided for in the transaction creating the instrument but the promisor fails to perform what he has promised in exchange for the maker's or acceptor's obligation. A breach of warranty in a contract for the sale of goods is similarly treated.

The fact that an instrument arose out of an illegal transaction is ordinarily a personal defense not available against a holder in due course for the reason that one may not assert his own participation in an illegal transaction in defense to a suit by an innocent party. However, if a statute makes an instrument founded upon a specified illegal consideration such as usury or a gambling debt void, the illegality is a real defense and can be set up against a holder in due course. For example, if A issues his negotiable promissory note to B to bribe a certain public official, the note is based on an illegal consideration and B could not recover on the note. But, if the note is negotiated to a holder in due course, A cannot use the illegal consideration defense against such a holder.

The usury law of the particular state should be consulted to determine the exact effect of a negotiable instrument calling for interest in excess of the maximum parties may legally contract for in that state. The Code provides that illegality may be a real or personal defense depending upon whether the statute or common law of the state declares the illegal contract to be void and not merely rendered voidable.[8]

Fraud in the Inducement.   Two distinct types of fraud must be kept separate in discussing the effect of fraud on the rights of a holder in due course of a negotiable instrument. Fraud in the inducement is a personal defense while fraud in the execution, discussed later, is a real defense.

A negotiable instrument issued on the strength of a false

---

[8] UCC Sec. 3-305 (2) (b).

representation is merely voidable. The misrepresentation is an example of fraud in the inducement. This is not a valid defense against a holder in due course. In such cases the fraud victim understands he is signing the instrument and he intends to sign a negotiable instrument. For example, if A induces B by a false representation to buy some shares of stock and B gives to A his promissory note for $1,000, A cannot hold B on the note, but if A negotiates the note to H, a holder in due course, H is not subject to the personal defense of fraud in the inducement.

Payment Before Maturity.   Payment before maturity is a discharge of the instrument to the extent of the payment only as between the immediate parties and not as against a holder in due course.

Generally it is the duty of one paying commercial paper before maturity, if in part, to have the payment indorsed thereon, or, if in full, to take reasonable precaution to prevent its further circulation by accident or fraud. The mere taking of a receipt by the one paying the instrument will not discharge this duty. The person paying a negotiable instrument should take it up. For example, if A pays in full his negotiable promissory note to B thirty days before it is due, leaving the note in B's hands and before it is due, B negotiates it to H, a holder in due course, A must pay it again, this time to H. The same rule applies where a payee grants a release or extension of time to the maker. As to a holder in due course taking the instrument it is still subsisting as a legal obligation in accordance with its terms.

Set-off or Counterclaim.   It is a rule under the common law that the right to a set-off or counterclaim by the maker of a negotiable instrument against the payee is not available to such maker in an action on the instrument by a holder in due course. However, where the plaintiff is not the payee, but a subsequent holder, the maker may set off a demand which he has against such holder, even though the latter is a holder in due course.

Duress and Undue Influence.   Duress and undue influence are closely related to fraud. Obtaining a negotiable instrument or any signature thereto by force, fear, or improper influence usually creates a personal defense in favor of the victim but which cannot be set up against a holder in due course. However, if the duress is extreme as in the case where one's hand is forcibly taken by another and his signature written in the instrument by force, there is duress in the execution which renders the instrument void in everybody's hands.

Non-delivery of a Completed Instrument. The N.I.L. provides in Section 16: "Every contract on a negotiable instrument is incomplete and revocable until delivery of the instrument for the purpose of giving effect thereto . . . But where the instrument is in the hands of a holder in due course, a valid delivery thereof by all parties prior to him so as to make them liable to him is conclusively presumed." From this provision it follows that if a bearer instrument, complete and regular on its face, is lost or stolen and is negotiated to a holder in due course, the non-delivery of the instrument by the prior party may not be set up against the holder in due course. This result applies only in the case of a bearer instrument which permits further negotiation by delivery alone. The finder or thief of an order instrument could not negotiate it further without forging an indorsement, and such forgery would be a real defense against any holder.

The Code continues the rule that non-delivery of a completed instrument is a personal defense,[9] but contrary to the N.I.L., the Code makes non-delivery of an incomplete instrument a personal defense rather than a real defense.[10]

Real Defenses

Real defenses generally exist where the negotiable instrument lacks legal efficacy at its inception, and they may be asserted against any holder, including a holder in due course. In the discussion of personal defenses, it was pointed out that under certain circumstances illegality or duress may be a real defense. As

---

[9] UCC Sec. 3-306 (c).
[10] UCC Sec's. 3-115 (2) and 3-407 (3).

already stated, the Code declares non-delivery of an incomplete instrument a personal defense while under the N.I.L. it is a real defense. The Code includes in its list of real defenses a discharge in bankruptcy or other insolvency proceedings and any other discharge of which the holder has notice when he takes the instrument.[11]

In addition to the above, the most common types of real defenses recognized under pre-Code law and under the Code include fraud in the execution, forgery, incapacity, and material alteration.

Fraud in the Execution.   Fraud in the execution occurs in cases where the signature of a party is obtained by fraud or trickery; the signing party does not know that the paper he signs is a negotiable instrument; and he has no intention of issuing such an instrument. In such cases the signing party has a defense which can be asserted against any holder, including a holder in due course, unless the signing party was negligent. For example, assume that M, a friend of P, is asked by P to serve as a witness to P's will. P folds the paper so as to conceal its contents. M signs on the line indicated to him by P, who states the paper is his will. The paper is in fact a negotiable promissory note which P negotiates to H, a holder in due course. M has the real defense of fraud in the execution which can be set up against H, there being no negligence by M under the circumstances.

If a person voluntarily signs a negotiable instrument, supposing it to be an obligation of a different character, but has full means of information as to the paper's true character and neglects to avail himself thereof, he cannot set up such ignorance and mistake as defense against a holder in due course. Generally a party will be negligent where he signed a paper without reading it, or if unable to read, failed to call for assistance from someone who could read and explain the nature of the paper to him.

---

[11] UCC Sec. 3-305.

Forgery. No obligation is created against a party whose signature is forged to the writing upon which a claim is based. Therefore, forgery is a real defense and a person whose name is forged to a negotiable instrument cannot be held liable upon it, even by a holder in due course. Such an instrument is a nullity unless the one denying the genuineness of his signature is estopped from asserting the forgery as a defense or has ratified the unauthorized signature.[12]

Incapacity. The principles of law applicable to ordinary contracts entered into by those suffering from some form of incapacity apply with equal force to negotiable instruments. The person under disability is favored over the holder in due course. For example, if a minor signs a negotiable instrument in any capacity, his act may be disaffirmed even against a holder in due course, unless the minor signed the instrument for necessaries. However, as indicated in Chapter 19, an indorsement of a negotiable instrument by one lacking full capacity passes the property therein, notwithstanding that because of incapacity the indorsing party incurs no liability thereon.

A holder in due course may hold a minor liable on a negotiable instrument for necessaries provided the holder can meet the various contract law requirements for holding a minor liable for necessaries as described in Chapter 7 where the contracts of minors and others lacking full capacity to contract are discussed.

The Code recognizes incapacity as a real defense, but leaves the question of whether infancy, insanity, or marriage amount to incapacity to the individual states to determine under other law.

Material Alteration. Unless the parties liable on a negotiable instrument give their assent, a material alteration according to the N.I.L. discharges the entire instrument in the hands of the holder who makes the alteration. But if an instrument is materially altered and thereafter negotiated to a holder in due

---

[12] UCC Sec. 3-404.

course, he may enforce the instrument as to its original, unaltered terms. For example, if M issues a negotiable promissory note to P for $10 and P alters the note to read $100 and negotiates it to H, a holder in due course, H may recover $10 from M on the instrument. P could recover nothing on the note.

The Code follows the above material alteration rule except that, unlike the N.I.L., the Code makes a distinction between those material alterations innocently made and those fraudulently made.[13] Under the Code a material alteration does not discharge any party unless it is made for a fraudulent purpose.

A material alteration is any change in the date, the sum payable (principal or interest), the time or place of payment, the number or relation of the parties, the medium of currency, adding of place of payment, or any change or addition in the legal effect of the instrument as a contract.

---

[13] UCC Sec. 3-407.

Liability of Parties

21

The contractual liability of a party to a negotiable instrument is either primary or secondary, and the parties can be classified on this basis. Primary parties include (1) makers of promissory notes and (2) drawees who have accepted bills of exchange, including drafts and checks. Secondary parties include (1) drawers of bills of exchange and (2) indorsers of negotiable instruments. No demand of payment or satisfaction of other conditions precedent is necessary to fix the liability of a primary party. The liability of a secondary party, apart from his warranty liability, is not fixed until the conditions precedent of presentment, dishonor, and notice of dishonor have been satisfied. The warranty liability of secondary parties to negotiable instruments appears at the end of this chapter.

Questions concerning interest on negotiable instruments are resolved by Sections 3-118 (d) and 3-122 (4) of the Code. The Code contains specific provisions governing the running of the statute of limitations. This is done by stating in Section 3-122 of the Code when a cause of action accrues on the various instruments, demand and time.

LIABILITY OF PRIMARY PARTIES

Contract of Maker and Drawee-acceptor

Under the Code the maker of a promissory note or a drawee who accepts a draft contracts unconditionally that he will pay it according to its tenor at the time of his engagement or as completed pursuant to Section 3-115 of the Code.[1] This liability continues until the statute of limitations runs against the instrument. No step need be taken by the holder, such as a demand for payment after the note or draft is due, in order to fix the maker's or acceptor's liability. However, the Code provides that "any party making tender of full payment to a holder when or after it is due is discharged to the extent of all subsequent liability for interest, costs, and attorney's fees," and "where the maker or acceptor of an instrument payable otherwise than on demand is able and ready to pay at every place of payment specified in the instrument when it is due, it is equivalent to tender." [2] The effect of a place of payment provision in an instrument is discussed later.

In addition to the maker's or acceptor's unconditional liability, the maker or acceptor "admits as against all subsequent parties including the drawee the existence of the payee and his then capacity to indorse." [3]

Identification of Parties

Makers, drawers, drawee-acceptors, and indorsers customarily sign in a certain place on negotiable instruments. For example, makers and drawers usually place their signatures in the lower right-hand corner of the instrument; drawees normally write their acceptance across the face of the instrument, while indorsers ordinarily sign on the reverse side of the instrument. Although a person's signature may appear in the place usually reserved for one of the parties named above, the liability of the person may be that of one of the other parties because this was intended. The law is interested in the substance of the party's undertaking, not the form in which it appears. The test is substantive, not impressionistic. This requires that an instrument

---

[1] UCC Sec. 3-413 (1).
[2] UCC Sec. 3-604.
[3] UCC Sec. 3-413 (3).

be read carefully to correctly identify the capacity in which a party has signed.

A similar problem results where an agent or other representative signs an instrument without clearly indicating that the principal alone is intended to be liable on the instrument. The Code provides certain rules of construction and of liability to govern such ambiguous forms of signature by agents.[4] In dealing with a signature in an ambiguous capacity, the Code provides: "Unless the instrument clearly indicates that a signature is made in some other capacity it is an indorsement.[5]

Acceptance of Drafts

The drawee of a draft or check is not liable on the instrument until he agrees to pay it. The drawee's agreement to pay is called an acceptance in the case of the draft, and a certification in the case of a check.

Under the N.I.L. an acceptance or certification could be written on the instrument or in a separate writing, called a "collateral acceptance." In addition, the N.I.L. provided that where a drawee to whom a bill (check or draft) is delivered for acceptance destroys the same, or refuses within twenty-four hours after such delivery, or within such other period as the holder may allow, to return the bill accepted or non-accepted to the holder, he will be deemed to have accepted the same. Some courts have applied this "constructive acceptance" provision to presentments for payment, with the result that banks have been deemed to have certified checks which have been presented for payment, unless they dishonor them within twenty-four hours from the time the checks are delivered. The Code requires that an acceptance be written on the instrument itself, thus outlawing a "collateral" or "constructive" acceptance as permitted under the N.I.L. The acceptance may consist simply of the drawee's signature on the instrument. The instrument

---

[4] UCC Sec's. 3-403 and 3-404.
[5] UCC Sec. 3-402.

may be accepted although it has not been signed by the drawer or is otherwise incomplete or is overdue or has been dishonored. The Code's basic provisions concerned with acceptance are found in Sections 3-409 to 3-413, inclusive.

Domiciled Instruments

If an instrument states it is payable at a bank or other special place, it is referred to as a "domiciled instrument." A tender of payment by the obligor on the date and at the place of payment called for by the instrument stops the running of interest. Under the Code, the failure of a holder to present a bank-domiciled instrument to the domiciliary bank on the due date gives makers and acceptors of such an instrument a position of secondary liability with the result that the maker or acceptor is discharged to the extent they are injured by the delay.[6] Insolvency of the bank subsequent to the due date of the instrument is the typical event which may result in loss to the obligor through failure of the holder of the instrument to make a timely presentment for payment. This Code provision extends to makers and acceptors the same protection that the N.I.L., as interpreted by most courts, gives to drawers of checks. Under the N.I.L. no presentment or notice of dishonor is necessary to charge any maker or acceptor. This rule could work a hardship because if an instrument was payable at a bank and the maker or acceptor placed funds in the bank for payment of the instrument, the maker or acceptor could be seriously prejudiced if the instrument was not presented at maturity and later the bank failed. Nevertheless, under the N.I.L. the maker or acceptor in this situation continued liable to the holder of the instrument. Presentment and notice of dishonor of notes and drafts which are not payable at a bank are still not necessary in order to hold the maker or acceptor liable.

In the case of an instrument payable at a bank, the Code gives the states a choice as to whether such a bank-domiciled

---

[6] UCC Sec. 3-502 (1) (b).

instrument is an order on the bank to pay or merely states a place of payment.[7] In New York and surrounding states the first interpretation has prevailed, whereas in the South and West the second interpretation has been followed.

LIABILITY OF SECONDARY PARTIES

Nature of Liability of Secondary Parties

Drawers of a draft or check and the unqualified indorsers of all negotiable instruments are secondarily liable. This means that they will not be required to pay the instrument unless the person primarily liable defaults or unless the instrument is dishonored on its presentment to the drawee. There are conditions precedent to the liability of a secondary party. This kind of liability is sometimes referred to as conditional or collateral liability.

The conditions precedent to the liability of a secondary party are (1) presentment, (2) dishonor, and (3) notice of dishonor. Unless they are waived or excused, these conditions must be met by the holder of an instrument in order to make any secondary party liable. A person secondarily liable may waive these conditions either at the time he becomes a party to the instrument or afterwards. Where the waiver is written in the instrument itself, it is binding upon all parties, but where it is written above the signature of an indorser, it binds him only. The Code provides a number of excuses for failure to take the formal steps necessary to hold parties secondarily liable.[8]

In addition to the conditional liability of a secondary party, as described above, such a party may be obligated on a warranty contract and on any underlying obligation which was responsible for the transfer or issuance of the negotiable instrument by the secondary party. Warranty liability is discussed later in this chapter. The Code provides that if a party's liability on the in-

---

[7] UCC Sec. 3-121.
[8] UCC Sec. 3-511.

strument is discharged, he is also discharged on the underlying obligation.[9]

A person who signs or indorses an instrument as a guarantor, using such words as "payment guaranteed" or "collection guaranteed," is not entitled to presentment or notice of dishonor. However, if a party adds the words "collection guaranteed" to his signature on the instrument, he engages to pay only after judgment and execution has been returned unsatisfied against the maker or acceptor or upon a showing that the maker or acceptor has become insolvent or that it is useless to proceed against him. If the words "payment guaranteed" are used, the party adding such words to his signature engages to pay the instrument without resort to any other party.[10]

Presentment for Acceptance and Payment

Presentment is a demand for acceptance or payment made upon the maker, acceptor, or other payor by or on behalf of the holder. The Code provides that "presentment for acceptance is necessary to charge the drawer and indorsers of a draft where the draft so provides, or is payable elsewhere than at the residence or place of business of the drawee, or its date of payment depends upon such presentment.[11] The holder is given the option of presenting for acceptance any other draft payable at a stated date. Presentment for acceptance is not relevant to promissory notes or bills of exchange payable on demand.

Presentment for payment from the primary party is necessary in order to hold any indorser.[12] The Code provides "in case of any drawer, the acceptor of a draft payable at a bank or the maker of a note payable at a bank, presentment for payment is necessary, but failure to make presentment discharges such drawer, acceptor, or maker only as stated in Section 3-502 (1)

---

[9] UCC Sec. 3-802.
[10] UCC Sec. 3-416.
[11] UCC Sec. 3-501 (1) (a).
[12] UCC Sec. 3-501 (1) (b).

(b)." [13] As we have seen, the latter provision limits the discharge to the extent of injury caused by the failure to present. This rule differs from the N.I.L. which provides that drawers of drafts are completely discharged by the failure of the holder to make proper presentment. As can be seen, the Code applies the N.I.L. check rule of pro tanto discharge to the drawers of all drafts, whether or not they are payable at banks.

The requirements for presentment for acceptance or payment are stated in Sections 3-503 to 3-507, inclusive of the Code in terms of how, where, when, by whom, and to whom the presentment must be made. As compared to the N.I.L. rules, the Code rules are simpler and more liberal, but the Code makes a few significant changes.

The Code defines presentment as a demand for acceptance or payment made upon the maker, acceptor, or other payor by or on behalf of the holder. Summarized, the Code's requirements for presentment for acceptance or payment are as follows:

How and Where. Under the Code any demand upon the party to pay is a presentment no matter where or how. A mere demand for acceptance or payment is a sufficient presentment if the primary party unqualifiedly refuses the demand. Presentment may be made by mail or through a clearing house or in any other reasonable manner. Normally presentment will be made at the primary party's place of business or at the place stated in the instrument. However, presentment may be made at some other place, except "a draft accepted or note payable at a bank . . . must be presented at such bank." The Code does provide that the party to whom presentment is made may require certain things including exhibition of the instrument and the holder is given a reasonable time in which to comply. If the primary party does not assert these rights, a presentment to him is sufficient no matter how or where made, except for instruments which must be presented at a bank.

When. Time instruments must be presented on the due date.

---

[13] UCC Sec. 3-501 (1) (c).

Demand instruments must be presented within a reasonable time after the date of issue. The Code contains some ground rules for determining reasonable time and rules of presumption as to what constitutes a reasonable time in specific situations are also spelled out. The Code states: "Presentment to be sufficient must be made at a reasonable hour, and if at a bank, during its banking day." This provision rejects the N.I.L. rule which permits "presentment at any hour before the bank is closed. . . ." The N.I.L. rule permits a holder to make a presentment after regular banking hours so long as the bank's personnel are in the bank winding up the day's business. Due dates falling on shortened or non-business days, such as Saturdays or holidays, are handled by the Code section which provides that "Where any presentment is due on a day which is not a full business day for either the person making presentment or the party to pay or accept, presentment is due on the next following day which is a full business day for both parties." Section 3-503 (1) (b) of the Code continues a N.I.L. rule by providing that "where an instrument is payable after sight it must either be presented for acceptance or negotiated within a reasonable time after date or issue whichever is later." Acceleration paper must be presented within a reasonable time after acceleration or secondary parties will be discharged. However, the Code provides that such a discharge is not effective against a subsequent holder in due course unless he knows the instrument is overdue by virtue of the operation of the acceleration clause.[14]

By Whom and To Whom. Presentment may be made by the holder or anyone authorized by him to receive payment for him. As indicated in the discussion above of how the presentment can be made under the Code, it is not required that the presentment be made by the holder or his agent in person.

The Code provides that presentment may be made "to any one of two or more makers, acceptors, drawees or other payors." The N.I.L. rule is different in that it requires that presentment

---

[14] UCC Sec. 3-602.

be made to each of two or more makers, acceptors, or drawees unless they are partners or one has authority to act for the others.

Notice of Dishonor

If a negotiable instrument after presentment to the primary party is dishonored by non-payment (or non-acceptance), the holder must then give notice of that fact to the drawer and to each indorser. Once the notice has been duly given, the holder has an immediate right of recourse against the parties so notified. Failure to give such notice will discharge the secondary parties.

Section 3-508 of the Code provides in detail as to how, when, where, by whom, and to whom the notice must be given. The purpose of the requirement of notice of dishonor is to give the secondary parties the material facts upon which their liability is founded, and so that they may take the necessary steps of preserving their right of reimbursement from prior indorsers and against the drawer. As pointed out before, the notice of dishonor, as with presentment, may be waived or even excused under certain circumstances. Summarized, the requirements for notice of dishonor are as follows:

How and Where. The Code provides that notice of dishonor may be given in any reasonable manner, and that it may be oral or written, and in any terms which identify the instrument and state that it has been dishonored. It specifically provides that returning the instrument itself bearing a stamp, a ticket, or some other writing stating that payment has been refused, or sending a debit notice with respect to the instrument, is sufficient to satisfy the requirements of the Code.

If an address is stated in the instrument, notice should be sent to such address. If no address is listed, the notice can be sent to the party's residence or business address, if known. If these addresses are not known, notice may be sent to the post office, where he is accustomed to receive his letters. The Code permits notice to be sent to the last known address of a party who is dead or mentally incompetent. Under the N.I.L., the practice is to send such notice to the administrator or executor of the deceased party. In any case, if notice is actually received within the time allowed it will be effective, though it may not have been sent to the prescribed place.

When. Section 3-508 (2) of the Code sets the time limits on notice of dishonor. Notice of dishonor must be given by a bank by its midnight deadline (midnight of the next banking day after dishonor) and by any other person by midnight of the third business day after dishonor or receiving notice of dishonor. Compared to the N.I.L. the Code permits a longer time in which to give notice of dishonor, and the Code sets up separate time limits for banks and non-banks. Written notice is given when sent although it is not received, and when mailed, the notice is sent and effective when deposited in the mail.

By Whom and To Whom. Section 3-508 (1) of the Code states, "Notice of dishonor may be given to any person who may be liable on the instrument by or on behalf of the holder or any party who has himself received notice, or any other party who can be compelled to pay the instrument. In addition an agent or bank in whose hands the instrument is dishonored may give notice to his principal or customer or to another agent or bank from which the instrument was received." This provision enlarges upon the category of parties who may give notice of dishonor as defined in the N.I.L.

Protest

Under the N.I.L., protest is required to charge any party secondarily liable on a draft which on its face was drawn in one state or country and payable in another state or country. The Code eliminates the requirement of protest except with respect to drafts drawn or payable outside the United States, its territories, or the District of Columbia. Of course, protest may be made even though in a particular instance the law does not require it, and protest of interstate checks and drafts is likely to continue for some time in order to avoid conflict of law problems which may arise when a state which has not adopted the Code is involved.

Protest is a sworn statement, an affidavit, in which it is declared that the instrument described was on a certain day presented for payment or acceptance and that such payment or acceptance was refused. The reason for dishonor, if given, is stated in the protest statement, and usually included is a statement that notice of dishonor has been sent to the secondary parties. The protest is usually made for the holder by a notary public or some similar public official.

Protest provides a method for proving that an instrument has been dishonored and that the steps precedent to holding secondary parties have been taken.

WARRANTY LIABILITY

General Nature of Warranty Liability

A party negotiating a negotiable instrument is selling property. As in a sale of goods, the law implies certain warranties on the part of the seller of an instrument. The liability of the seller on these warranties is a primary liability; and the conditions precedent (presentment, dishonor, and notice) to fixing the secondary liability of a drawer or indorser are not necessary to impose the liability of a seller of a negotiable instrument for breach of these implied warranties.

Warranties provide a wide range of protection, but they do not protect against what is probably the greatest hazard of all, that of mere economic inability of a party to pay. Warranties do not guarantee payment, but they do give protection as described below.

Warranties of Indorsers and Transferors

Under the Code certain warranties are provided for whether the indorsement is qualified (without recourse) or unqualified, or the transfer of the negotiable instrument is by mere delivery.[15] It will be recalled that bearer paper can be negotiated by delivery alone, while indorsement in addition to delivery is required to negotiate order paper.

¶ These warranties are as follows:

1] That the transferor or indorser has good title to the instrument or is authorized to obtain payment or acceptance on behalf of one who has good title and the transfer is otherwise rightful.

2] That all signatures are genuine or authorized.

3] That the instrument has not been materially altered.

4] That he has no knowledge of any insolvency proceedings instituted with respect to the maker or acceptor or the drawer of an unaccepted instrument.

In addition, the Code provides that the unqualified indorser and the mere transferor of a negotiable instrument warrants that no defense of any party is good against the party taking the instrument. By indorsing "without recourse" (qualified indorsement) the indorser merely warrants that he has no knowledge of any defense, and, of course, the qualified indorser also makes the four warranties listed in the preceding paragraph.

It can be seen from the above summary of the Code's statement of warranties made by those transferring a negotiable instrument that the warranty liability of a mere transferor is broader than in the case of a qualified indorser. This is a significant change from the N.I.L. rule which treats mere transferors and qualified indorsers alike in terms of their warranty liability. However, the N.I.L. rule limiting the mere transferor's warranty liability to his immediate transferee is continued by the Code. If the transfer is by indorsement, whether qualified or unqualified, the indorser makes the above described warranties "to any subsequent holder who takes the instrument in good faith."

---

[15] UCC Sec. 3-417 (2).

As in the case of warranties in connection with sales, the parties to negotiable instruments can by agreement disclaim or supplement any of the warranties described above. In the case of an indorser, such a disclaimer must be shown by the indorsement and parol proof is not admissible as against a subsequent party. Finally, it is important to note that warranties are present only where an instrument is transferred for a consideration. They are not present where an instrument is transferred as a gift.

Warranties on Presentment

The Code states separately, but in the same Code section, the warranties arising in connection with acceptance and payment, that is, presentment, and those arising in connection with the transfer of the instrument. The warranties on transfers were listed above. The warranties on presentment are stated in Section 3-417 (1) of the Code as follows:

> 1] Any person who obtains payment or acceptance and any prior transferor warrants to a person who in good faith pays or accepts that
>> A] he has a good title to the instrument or is authorized to obtain payment or acceptance on behalf of one who has a good title; and
>> B] he has no knowledge that the signature of the maker or drawer is unauthorized, except that this warranty is not given by a holder in due course acting in good faith
>>> *i*) to a maker with respect to the maker's own signature; or
>>> *ii*) to a drawer with respect to the drawer's own signature, whether or not the drawer is also the drawee; or
>>> *iii*) to an acceptor of a draft if the holder in due course took the draft after the acceptance or obtained the acceptance without knowledge

that the drawer's signature was unauthorized; and

c] the instrument has not been materially altered, except that this warranty is not given by a holder in due course acting in good faith

i) to the maker of a note; or

ii) to the drawer of a draft whether or not the drawer is also the drawee; or

iii) to the acceptor of a draft with respect to an alteration made prior to the acceptance if the holder in due course took the draft after the acceptance, even though the acceptance provided "payable as originally drawn" or equivalent terms; or

iv) to the acceptor of a draft with respect to an alteration made after the acceptance.

The obligations imposed by this section of the Code are particularly relevant to the position occupied by the drawee-bank where checks paid by it contain a forged signature of the drawer or an indorser or contain a material alteration. The Code rules governing such cases are covered in the next chapter dealing with checks.

The last provision of Section 3-417 of the Code provides that "A selling agent or broker who does not disclose the fact that he is acting only as such gives the warranties provided in this section, but if he makes such disclosure warrants only his good faith and authority."

LIABILITY OF ACCOMMODATION PARTIES

An accommodation party is one who signs a negotiable instrument in any capacity for the purpose of lending his name and credit to another party to it.[16] The person seeking credit or a

---

[16] UCC Sec. 3-415 (1).

loan may not have any collateral security to pledge or mortgage, but may have a friend or business associate whose credit standing is such that the other party may be willing to accept his accommodation signature on the debtor's instrument. A person may be an accommodation party whether or not he is paid for executing the instrument.

Under the Code, an accommodation party is treated as a surety, but his liability to anyone who has taken the instrument for value before it is due is determined by the capacity in which he signs even though the taker knows of the accommodation.[17] The accommodation party can sign a note as a maker or indorser, or he can sign a bill of exchange as a drawer, acceptor, or indorser. An accommodation maker or acceptor is primarily liable and the fact that he is a surety does not require that the holder first proceed against the principal debtor. As an indorser or drawer, an accommodation party is secondarily liable and therefore liable only if there is presentment, notice of dishonor, and, in an appropriate case, protest.

An accommodation maker can set up any defense that the law of contracts or suretyship gives him, but such a defense is personal and will be cut off by a holder in due course. Under the law of suretyship, an extension of time of payment, release of collateral, or other changes in the principal debtor's obligations without the consent of the surety will discharge the surety. The same result can occur with reference to the obligation of an accommodation party, even if he is a maker of a note or an indorser who has waived presentment and notice of dishonor.

The Code provides that if a party is a holder in due course and has no notice of the accommodation, oral proof is not admissible to give the accommodation party the benefit of discharges which depend upon the suretyship character of his obligation.[18] If the party is not a holder in due course, or knows of the accommodation even though he is a holder in due course,

---

[17] UCC Sec. 3-415 (2).
[18] UCC Sec. 3-415 (3).

an oral proof may be used to show the accommodation character of the obligation of the accommodation party. The Code further provides that an indorsement which shows that it is not in the chain of title is always notice of its accommodation character.[19] For example, if a party is the holder of a note payable to himself, which has been indorsed by someone other than the maker, the holder is on notice that the indorser is an accommodation party who will be discharged under the law of suretyship if the holder grants an extension of time or other indulgence to the maker without the indorser's consent.

In conclusion the Code states, "An accommodation party is not liable to the party accommodated, and if he pays the instrument has a right of recourse on the instrument against such party." [20]

DISCHARGE

Nature and Methods of Discharge

A contract is said to be discharged when it loses its force and effect as a legal obligation. A negotiable instrument may be in physical existence and held by someone, yet be discharged. It is to be emphasized that discharge is only a personal defense which is cut off by a holder in due course. Of course most acts of discharge, due to their very nature, preclude a subsequent purchaser from being a holder in due course. For example, a party taking an instrument which has been paid previously is likely to take the instrument after maturity and thus not be able to qualify as a holder in due course. Negotiable instruments are usually discharged by payment, but there are other methods of discharge.

¶ The recognized ways of discharge are listed in subsection (1) of Section 3-601 of the Code as follows:

---

[19] UCC Sec. 3-415 (4).
[20] UCC Sec. 3-415 (5).

1] payment or satisfaction
2] tender of payment
3] cancellation or renunciation
4] impairment of right of recourse of collateral
5] reacquisition of the instrument by a prior party
6] fraudulent or material alteration
7] certification of a check
8] acceptance varying a draft
9] unexcused delay in presentment or notice of dishonor or protest.

In addition, subsections (2) and (3) of Section 3-601 of the Code provide:

2] Any party is also discharged from his liability on an instrument to another party by any other act or agreement with such party which would discharge his simple contract for the payment of money.

3] The liability of all parties is discharged when any party who has himself no right of action or recourse on the instrument (a) reacquires the instrument in his own right; or (b) is discharged under any provision of this Article, except as otherwise provided with respect to discharge for impairment of recourse or of collateral.

The Code contains provisions explaining in some detail each of the above forms of discharge and the relevant Code sections should be examined if a question arises relating to a particular method of discharge. Several of the Code rules governing discharge differ significantly from those found in the N.I.L.

Checks

22

General Nature of Checks

The Code defines a check as a draft drawn on a bank and payable on demand.[1] Historically, checks have fallen within the broad definition of a bill of exchange, a check being a special type of bill of exchange. A check is distinguished from other bills of exchange in that (1) the drawee of a check is always a bank; (2) a check is usually demand paper; and (3) a check is drawn against funds deposited by the drawer with the drawee bank in a checking account.

The law views a check as a conditional payment of the debt or obligation for which it is given. If the check is not paid, the person who received it is remitted to his original rights against the drawer. The mere delivery of a donor's check of itself does not constitute a valid gift, as it is revocable, either by stop payment order or by death of the drawer before the check is presented for payment.

The requirements for negotiability which are applicable to negotiable instruments generally make it essential that a check satisfy these form and content requirements if it is to have the characteristics of negotiability. Most of the general law applicable to bills of exchange payable on demand applies to checks,

---

[1] UCC Sec. 3-104 (2) (b).

but both the N.I.L. and the Code contain provisions applicable solely to checks. Article 4 of the Code deals with bank collections and certain phases of bank deposits; while Article 3, as pointed out previously, applies to commercial paper generally. In addition, certain commercial practices and related common-law principles and rules have developed with respect to checks which makes it convenient, if not necessary, to describe the law of checks apart from the law applicable to negotiable instruments in general. This chapter is devoted to a discussion of some of the legal aspects of checks.

Relationship Between Depositor and Bank

The legal relationship between the depositor of funds in a checking account and the bank is both (1) that of creditor and debtor and (2) that of principal and agent. The bank becomes the debtor of the depositor (creditor) to the extent of the amount deposited. The bank also becomes the depositor's agent with a duty to pay out the funds on deposit to such person or persons as the depositor (principal) orders in the form of checks drawn upon the bank.

The bank is under a contractual obligation to honor the depositor's checks when properly presented, if his bank balance permits their payment. The obligation of the bank is to pay the checks in the order of their presentment, not in the order of their issuance. If a number of checks are presented to the drawee bank simultaneously and the drawer's balance on deposit is insufficient to pay the total of the checks, the bank owes a duty to pay as many of the checks as the depositor has credit to meet, and the bank has the right to pay the checks in any order convenient to the bank. If a depositor's check is not honored, without justification, the bank is liable for any resulting loss suffered by the depositor.[2] Substantial injury to the depositor's credit is a kind of injury for which the drawer of the check could recover damages. Also, the damages may include those caused by the

---

[2] UCC Sec. 4-402.

arrest or prosecution of the customer, or other consequential damages, if they are proved and shown to have been proximately caused by the wrongful dishonor.

The "stale check" problem is met by a Code provision which declares that a bank is under no obligation to pay a check, other than a certified one, which is presented more than six months after its date, but it may charge its customer's account for a payment made thereafter in good faith unless a valid stop payment order was in effect.[3]

The holder of a check has no right to compel the bank on which it is drawn to pay it unless the check has been certified by the bank. A check is not an assignment of funds which the drawer has on deposit in the bank. As stated before, a check is merely an order to the bank to pay. Under this principle, when the bank pays a check, it need not be concerned whether the drawer wrote other checks first. Also, the nonassignment rule means that the drawer has the right to stop payment, which he would not have if the check were an assignment, completed by delivery of the check.

Death or Incompetence of Drawer

The Code continues the rule that the death of a customer does not revoke the bank's authority to pay checks drawn by him or collect items for him or account for proceeds of collection until the bank knows that he has died and has reasonable opportunity to act on such knowledge. Similarly, the Code makes the additional provision that the incompetence of a customer likewise does not revoke the bank's authority until the bank knows of an adjudication of insanity.[4]

The Code goes further in permitting a bank, even though it has knowledge that a customer has died, to pay or certify, for a period of ten days after the date of his death, checks drawn by the customer prior to his death, unless the bank is ordered

[3] UCC Sec. 4-404.
[4] UCC Sec. 4-405 (1).

to stop payment by a person claiming an interest in the deceased customer's account. This provision permits some of the decedent's current debts to be paid promptly by checks drawn and issued shortly before death without the necessity of and delays involved in the executor or administrator issuing new checks.[5]

Stop Payment Orders

A drawer of a check may revoke the order given to the bank to pay funds from the drawer's account. This revocation of the order on and authority given to the bank is called a stop payment order. Drawers stop payment in most instances because the check has been lost, or because they have not received or are not going to receive the consideration for which they gave the check in payment.

The Code provides that the stop payment order must be received at such time and in such manner as to afford the bank a reasonable opportunity to act on it prior to the payment or certification of the check, or some similar step.[6] Under the Code an oral stop payment order is binding upon the bank for only fourteen days unless the customer confirms it in writing within that period. Generally banks require written confirmation of a stop payment order. A written order is effective for only six months unless it is renewed in writing. The stop payment order must identify the check in question. This is done by describing the number, date, payee, and amount as written on the check.

The drawer has the burden of establishing the amount of his loss resulting from the payment of a check contrary to a stop payment order. This means that if the drawer would have been liable to the holder of a check if payment had been refused, as would be the case where the check was given in payment of some enforceable debt of the drawer to the payee or where the check had reached the hands of a holder in due course, the drawer

---

[5] UCC Sec. 4-405 (2).
[6] UCC Sec. 4-403.

cannot recover anything from the bank for its failure to obey a stop order. In such cases the drawer cannot establish that he has suffered any damage by reason of such failure.

The Code provides that no agreement can disclaim a bank's responsibility or limit the measure of damages for its own failure to exercise ordinary care.[7] Such disclaimer agreements sometimes appear in the printed stop payment order furnished by a bank to its customers. Since most failures to obey stop payment orders are the result of negligence, such a disclaimer would rarely excuse the bank from liability in a Code state. In states where no relevant statute is in effect the same result is likely to prevail on the basis of public policy.

Certification of Checks

A certified check is a regular check drawn on a bank by a depositor and certified by the bank. Certification makes the bank primarily liable on the check; it is similar to an acceptance of a bill of exchange by the drawee. The drawer's account is debited with the amount of the check at the time of certification, and a special account usually called the "certified check account" is credited. Certification removes for the benefit of the payee the risk of the check's nonpayment because of insufficient funds in the checking account of the drawer.

The Code requires certification to be written on the check.[8] No particular form of words is required. The usual form consists of the word *certified* written or stamped across the face of the check over the signature of the proper bank officer.

Certification may be obtained by the drawer, payee, or subsequent holder of a check and is governed by Section 3-411 of the Code. If the drawer has the check certified, the bank becomes primarily liable, and the drawer continues secondarily liable. If the payee procures the certification, the bank becomes

---

[7] UCC Sec. 4-103 (1).
[8] UCC Sec. 3-410 (1).

primarily liable and the drawer is discharged. Therefore, if the certifying bank becomes insolvent before the check is presented for payment, there can be no recourse against the drawer. If the check is certified at the request of the holder, the bank becomes primarily liable, and the drawer and indorsers are discharged. The release of the drawer and indorsers is based on the election of the payee or holder to take the promise of the bank in lieu of cash. Herein lies a major difference between the law regarding ordinary bills of exchange and that regarding checks. The drawer of an ordinary bill of exchange remains secondarily liable if the holder obtains acceptance of the bill.

Liability of Drawer of Check to Holder

Upon failure of the drawee bank to pay the amount of the check to the holder who presents it for payment at the bank, the holder may sue the drawer on the check. This liability of the drawer of a check is not dependent upon the holder's complying with the presentment, dishonor, and notice requirements for holding secondary parties liable. However, it is necessary that the holder present the check for payment within a reasonable time after its issue or the drawer will be discharged from liability to the extent of the loss caused by the delay. On an uncertified check which is drawn and payable within the United States and which is not a draft drawn by a bank, a reasonable time for presentment or to initiate bank collection to hold the drawer is thirty days after date of issue of the check, whichever is later.[9] If no loss is caused the drawer by the holder's delay, the only time limitation against the holder being able to collect from the drawer is the statute of limitations.

Historically the principal cause of loss to the drawer from a delay in presentment has usually been the insolvency of the drawee bank. In such case the drawer loses in the bank failure the funds he had available for meeting the check. The time for

---

[9] UCC Sec. 3-503 (2) (a).

presentment rule is designed to protect drawers from this bank failure loss and, in addition, it expedites the banking business and protects drawers against "stale" outstanding checks.

In order to hold prior indorsers liable on a check, the holder must make proper presentment followed by proper notice of dishonor. If he fails to take the necessary steps, the indorsers of the check will be released, just as in the case of indorsers of an ordinary bill of exchange. The Code specifies that the presentment for payment of a check must be made within seven days after an indorser's indorsement and notice of dishonor given in order for a holder to fix the indorser's liability.[10] The rules governing the liability of secondary parties in general was discussed in Chapter 21.

Forgeries and Alterations

Forged Signature of Drawer.   The drawer of a check, the drawee bank, and the party receiving payment on a check possess certain rights and duties with respect to forgeries and alterations. A drawee bank which pays a check on which the drawer's signature is forged must recredit the drawer's account with the amount so paid out. This rule is based on the fact that the drawee bank has on file a card or other record containing a specimen of the drawer's signature which can be compared with the signature on the check presented for payment. Generally the drawee bank which pays a check on which the drawer's signature is forged cannot recover back from the person who received the money paid out, unless, of course, the bank has paid the check to the forger.[11] By paying the check, the bank admits the existence of the drawer, his capacity and authority to draw the check, and the genuineness of his signature.

Forged Indorsement.   A drawee bank is liable to the drawer for paying a check on which the payee's indorsement, or the indorsement of any subsequent indorser whose indorsement is

---

[10] UCC Sec. 3-503 (2) (b).
[11] UCC Sec. 3-418.

essential to the negotiation of the check, is forged. In such cases the drawee bank has not complied with the drawer's order. In forged indorsement cases the law generally permits the drawee bank to recover back from the party who presented the check bearing the forged indorsement any payment it has made, even though the party who received payment had no connection with the forgery. This is based on the warranty of good title made by the presenting party and those who indorsed the instrument subsequent to the forged indorsement. This rule prevails under the Code and existed under prior law.[12]

Alterations. A bank which pays a check which has been altered by raising its amount cannot charge the drawer's account with the full amount which it has paid out, but the bank may, if in good faith, charge the drawer's account with the amount for which the check was originally drawn.[13] The Code permits the bank to recover from the person it paid on the altered check the excess payment made on an altered uncertified and unaccepted instrument. The basis for this recovery by the bank is breach of warranty. The warranty against material alterations and the limitations upon its scope as it applies for the benefit of a paying bank are described in Sections 4-207 and 3-417 of the Code.

Duty of Drawer to Report Forgeries; Effect of Drawer's Negligence

When a bank makes a statement of a depositor's account available to him, the customer is under a duty to examine promptly the statement and cancelled checks to discover any forgeries or alterations and then to notify the bank promptly of any discrepancies. Section 4-406 of the Code states this general duty and describes in detail the various rights and duties of a bank and its depositors relative to forgeries, alterations, unauthorized signatures, raised or altered checks, and fictitious payees. This

---

[12] UCC Sec. 3-417 (1) (a).
[13] UCC Sec. 4-401 (2) (a).

Code provision sets up an absolute bar to asserting unauthorized drawer's signatures or alterations against a bank more than one year after the statement of a customer's account and paid items are furnished, and a three year bar on forged indorsements.

The Code permits a bank to charge to the account of its customer an altered check or one bearing a forged signature of the drawer or a forged indorsement if the bank can show that its customer had been negligent and that his negligence was the proximate cause of the loss. For example, a drawer must take care to avoid leaving blank spaces in a check which could be filled in without detection. Also, a drawer engaged in operating a business must conduct his business affairs and supervise his employees so it cannot be said that forgeries of his checks resulted from his negligence.

Fictitious Payees

A variation of the forgery problem is the fictitious or nonexistent payee case. Section 9 (3) of the N.I.L. provides that a check drawn payable to the order of a fictitious or nonexistent payee is payable to bearer, provided the fact that the named payee is a fictitious or non-existing person was known to the person making it so payable. As a bearer instrument such a check requires no indorsement in order for it to be negotiated. Therefore, if such a check has the name of the designated payee indorsed on it by some dishonest person, this is not treated by the courts as a forged indorsement so as to preclude the drawee bank from charging the drawer's account. This result has imposed no hardship on the drawer in cases where he personally prepared and signed the fictitious or nonexistent payee check.

A second type of fictitious payee case which has caused a great deal of difficulty and confusion is the one in which the check payable to a fictitious or nonexistent payee has been drawn by the drawer's agent or employee, who had authority to draw checks on the employer's account; and the employee, in furtherance of a dishonest scheme to defraud his employer, made the check payable to the order either of a person who he knew did not exist, or who he intended should never have any interest in the instrument. Courts have generally held, under the N.I.L., that such checks, like those in the first case, were payable to bearer, thus required no indorsement, and could be charged to the drawer's account if they were paid by the drawee bank.

A third type of fictitious payee case has arisen in the situation where the dishonest agent or employee did not sign the check himself, but merely furnished or filled in the name of the payee, handed the check to his employer or to some honest employee acting for the employer, and the resulting check was signed by the employer or the honest employee acting as agent. Under the N.I.L. the courts have generally held that the check in this situation was not payable to bearer, with the result that the drawee bank could not charge the check to the account of the drawer, because the payee's indorsement had been forged. Dissatisfaction with placing the loss on the bank in this case has been based on the fact that it was the drawer's dishonest employee who brought about the loss. A number of states amended the fictitious payee provisions of the N.I.L. so as to require the drawer to bear such a loss rather than placing it on the bank. The Code rule protects the bank in this fictitious payee case and the others discussed above.[14] In all of the cases described above, the party acting fraudulently is subject to civil and criminal liability.

Impostor Cases

If a drawer issues a check to a person, in the belief that the person is the same person whose name is written on the check as payee, when in fact the person receiving the check is an impostor, the question arises as to whether the drawee bank can legally charge the drawer's account after paying the check. Most courts have taken the view that in such cases the drawer intends the person with whom he is dealing to become the

---

[14] UCC Sec. 3-405 (1) (b) (c).

owner of it and that, on this basis, the indorsement by the impostor of the payee's name is valid in so far as permitting the drawee bank to charge the drawer's account after paying the check. To this extent the indorsement is not viewed as a forgery.

Some courts have distinguished between the case where the drawer of the check and the impostor are dealing face to face and the case where the drawer and impostor are dealing by mail, telegram, or telephone, permitting the drawee bank to charge the check in the former case but refusing to permit the charge in the latter case.

The Code handles the impostor situations by adopting a single rule which provides that an indorsement by any person in the name of the named payee is effective if an impostor, by use of the mails or otherwise, has induced the drawer to issue the check to him or to his confederate in the name of the payee.[15]

Subrogation Rights of Bank

Section 4-407 of the Code gives the payor bank rights of subrogation in the event it pays an item contrary to a stop-payment order or otherwise improperly, in order "to prevent unjust enrichment and only to the extent necessary to prevent loss to the bank by reason of its payment . . ." The rights to which the bank would be subrogated would be (a) those of any holder in due course against the maker or drawer; (b) those of the payee or any other holder against the drawer or maker, either on the item or under the underlying transaction; (c) those of the drawer or maker against the payee or other holder under the underlying transaction.

---

[15] UCC Sec. 3-405 (1) (a).

Nature, Creation and Authority of Agents

23

NATURE OF EMPLOYMENT RELATIONSHIPS

One of the oldest and most common legal relationships is that of agency. Corporations carry on all their business through agents or employees, and other types of business organizations as well as individuals find it necessary or convenient to employ the services of others. The agency relationship is present when one person, the agent, is authorized to act for and under the control of another person, the principal, in business dealings of a contractual nature with third persons. Generally, an agent can be authorized to do anything which the principal himself could lawfully do. The purpose of the agency must not be criminal, immoral, or against public policy. Also, certain acts such as voting, making a will, and making a sworn statement require the personal action of the person doing them and thus, due to their nature, cannot be delegated to others.

The legal consequences of employing a person or business firm to render services depends to a large extent on the type of employment relationship created. The relationship may be that of principal and agent, employer and employee (often referred to in legal parlance as master and servant), or the person or firm employed may be an independent contractor. Generally, a principal or employer is liable for the acts of his agent or employee, if such acts are within the scope of the employment. In most cases an employer is not liable to third persons for the acts of an independent contractor, and various rights and duties associated with the other employment relationships do not exist where an independent contractor is employed. For these reasons it is vital to be able to distinguish between the various employment relationships.

KINDS OF EMPLOYMENT RELATIONSHIPS

Principal and Agent

An agent deals with third persons in respect to business transactions, usually the making of contracts, entrusted to him by his principal, and the agent is under the control of the principal in relation to such transactions. An agent is a fiduciary in that he possesses powers and rights to be exercised for the benefit of his principal. As a fiduciary, an agent is held to a high standard of loyalty, honesty, and good faith. The rights and duties which exist between principals and agents are discussed in Chapter 24.

Although the possible agency relationships are infinite, typical agents include a salesman who sells his principal's goods to third persons, a purchasing agent who buys goods from others for his principal, and a corporation executive carrying on the business of a corporation. The term agency is often used incorrectly to describe a business organization which sells the products or handles the advertising for the products of a particular manufacturer. This use of the term *agency* is a misnomer in relation to the technical legal meaning of agency as stated above. For example, an automobile "agency" does not usually act as an agent of the manufacturer from which the dealer buys his cars, and the typical advertising "agency" is not an agency in the legal sense, but, instead, is an independent contractor in relation to its accounts.

Employer and Employee

The law of employer and employee, or master and servant, runs parallel, in many respects, to that of principal and agent, and the same rules often apply to either relation. The relationship of employer-employee and principal-agent are distinguished on the basis of the nature of the services rendered. Unlike an agent, who is a business representative for the purpose of bringing his principal into legal relations with others, an employee is employed to perform manual tasks, skilled or unskilled, under the direction of his employer. A factory worker is a good example of an employee. An employee executes the commands of his employer, chiefly in reference to things, but occasionally with reference to persons when no contractual obligation is to result. The same person may at one time, and as to certain things, act as an employee, while at another time, or as to other things, he acts as an agent. For example, a janitor may be authorized to buy fuel or cleaning supplies. While making such purchases the janitor acts as an agent and while performing cleaning services he acts as an employee. An employee does not ordinarily have authority to obligate his employer to third persons on contracts.

An employee may be in the general employ of one employer, yet, while performing a particular act which results in injury to a third person, the employee may be acting under the direction of another person. Where an employee has two employers, a general and a special one, the latter, if having the power of control over the employee's activities, is the one responsible for the employee's actions, including his torts. For example, a nurse in the general employ of a hospital may at the moment of committing a tort which causes injury to a patient being treated in the hospital be under the control and direction of the patient's doctor, who may not be an employee of the hospital. The tort of the nurse could be imputed to the doctor who was the special employer of the nurse, and as such, the doctor is liable for the tort of the nurse, commited within the scope of the special employment.

Employer and Independent Contractor

An independent contractor is a person who contracts with another to produce a certain result for him but who is not controlled by the other nor subject to the other's right to control with respect to the means and methods used in the performance of the undertaking. The *control test* is the most important criterion for distinguishing the agent or employee from the independent contractor. For example, a building contractor who contracts to build a house according to the terms of a contract is usually an independent contractor. He furnishes his own equipment, tools, and employees; and he often obtains the materials used in completing the work called for in the contract. The owner does not ordinarily control the day-to-day performance of the work by the builder and his employees.

As stated before, the employer is not liable for the torts of the independent contractor or of the latter's employees; nor does the independent contractor have authority to obligate the employer on contracts. If the employer is negligent in selecting the independent contractor, or retains him after it is demonstrated that he is likely to cause loss or injury to others, the employer may be held liable for the contractor's torts and those of his employees. In such cases it is the negligence of the employer which provides the basis for imputing the wrongful act causing the injury back to the employer.

Classes of Agents

Agents are divided into a variety of classes depending upon (1) the nature and extent of their authority, (2) the character of their calling, and (3) the obligations they assume.

An agent may serve for compensation or he may be an agent who acts gratuitously, serving voluntarily without any expectation of payment for his services. The legal consequences, including the duties of the principal and agent, are substantially the same in either case, except that a gratuitous agent may quit at any time he chooses without incurring liability to the principal for doing so.

Classified on the basis of the extent of the actual authority conferred on agents by their principals, agents are general, special or universal. An agent with no actual authority but who, as a result of the principal's words or conduct, is held out to a third person as possessing an apparent authority, is called an ostensible or apparent agent. This type of agency is called agency by estoppel and will be discussed later.

General Agent. A general agent is one authorized to transact all the business of his principal of a certain kind or in a certain place. A person employed to operate and manage a retail store for the principal is a general agent. In addition to his express authority, a general agent will possess a wide range of implied powers ordinarily incidental to the operation of such an agency and any express limitations by the principal on the customary or ostensible authority of the general agent will not be binding upon third persons who do not know and should not know of such limitations on his authority.

Special Agent. A special agent is one authorized to act only in a specific transaction or a number of disconnected transactions. A person authorized to buy a particular tract of land is an example of a special agent. The incidental or implied authority of a special agent is necessarily much more narrow in scope than that of a general agent. Thus, a third person dealing with a special agent must be especially careful to determine the extent of the agent's authority and stay within it, otherwise the principal will not be bound.

Universal Agent. Theoretically there may be universal agents, who are authorized to perform all things the principal may properly and legally authorize an agent to do. Such agents, however, rarely, if ever, exist.

Professional Agents. In certain specialized transactions the services of a person engaged in a professional calling may be employed. A professional agent is in business for himself, usually serves many different principals, and while he is subject to the principal's control with respect to the particular transaction he is handling for him, he is not under the control of the principal in regard to his physical acts. Factors, brokers, attorneys, and auctioneers fall into the classification of professional agents. Generally these professional agents must obtain a license or certificate before engaging in business and, as pointed out in the law of contracts, failure to have the required license usually precludes them from collecting compensation for their services. Also, a person acting without a required license subjects himself to various penalties.

A factor, sometimes called a commission merchant, is an agent who sells, for a commission called factorage, goods belonging to his principal and who is given possession of the goods and deals with the buyer much as the principal would if he sold the goods direct. A *del credere* agent is a factor who, for an extra compensation or commission, undertakes to his principal that the party to whom he sells the principal's goods will pay for them.

A broker sells property or contractual rights for his principal but does not have possession of the things he is to sell. A real estate broker is a good example of such an agent.

Attorney in Fact. An attorney in fact is an agent who is given authority under a power of attorney to perform a particular act not of a legal nature. The attorney in fact is not to be confused with an attorney at law who is employed to perform legal services. Of course, the attorney at law or lawyer may also serve as an attorney in fact if authorized by his client to do so. Auctioneers are agents whose business it is to sell property publicly to the highest bidder.

CAPACITY TO BE PRINCIPAL OR AGENT

Any person competent to act for himself may act through an agent. The rules which relate to the capacity of persons to make contracts apply to the appointment of agents. Minors and insane persons not officially adjudged insane may appoint agents, but the appointments and the contracts negotiated by their agents are voidable at the election of such principals. Married women may appoint agents, pursuant to their statutory powers to contract. Corporations, partnerships, and other types of business organizations with capacity to contract may appoint agents. Unincorporated associations may not appoint agents, but the individual members of such a group who authorize or ratify an appointment of an agent or his acts may be treated as principals and held liable to third persons.

Any person capable of performing the act in question may serve as an agent even though he does not have full capacity to contract for himself. For example, a minor may be an agent and negotiate a binding contract for his principal. The legal status of the contract is determined by the principal's capacity to contract, not the agent's. This rule recognizes that the party to the contract is the principal, not the agent who is merely serving as the conduit through which the principal directs the making of the contract. It has been stated previously that most professional agents are required to obtain a license before they can act.

CREATION OF AGENCY AND AUTHORITY OF AGENT

The relationship of principal and agent and the authority of an agent may be created by (1) express appointment, (2) implication, (3) estoppel, (4) operation of law, and (5) ratification. In addition, the authority of agent may arise by virtue of necessity or an emergency. This kind of authority will be discussed in connection with implied authority.

The burden of proving the existence of an agency relationship is on the party who asserts it. In lawsuits involving agency the crucial question is often concerned with whether the agency relationship existed or whether the agent has or has not exceeded his authority. A general discussion of the various types of authority follows. In the next chapter, under the heading of Principal and Third Persons, authority will be discussed in relation to specific types of transactions engaged in by agents for principals.

Express Agency and Authority

Most agencies are created by an employment contract, written or oral, in which the principal expressly confers certain authority upon the agent. However, as already pointed out, an agent may act gratuitously, and without any enforceable contract of agency in existence between him and his principal; yet, such an agent is capable of obligating his principal to third persons, and his duties toward his principal are much the same as those owed by a paid agent.

The authority of an agent may be described in language which specifies the rights and duties of the parties to the agreement, or the authority may be stated briefly in general terms, leaving much of the agent's authority to be implied on the basis of general custom, trade usage, and past practices of the principal. The actual authority of an agent is comprised of his express and implied authority.

A formal appointment of an agent is made by means of a legal instrument called a power of attorney, and it will be construed as granting only those powers which are expressly specified and such others as are essential to carry into effect the express powers. Powers of attorney may be general or special. A general power of attorney vests in the agent a wide range of powers so that he can do, in general, whatever the principal could do were he present to act. In a special power of attorney the agent's authority is limited to a specified transaction or a limited class of transactions. A general power of attorney should not be granted unless it is clearly needed.

Ordinarily an agent may be appointed orally, even when the contract he is to make for his principal must be in writing under the Statute of Frauds. Because of the Statute of Frauds, a contract of agency which by its terms cannot be performed within one year from its date must be in writing. Most states require that if an agent is appointed to convey an interest in real property, such authority must be in writing. Similarly, many states provide that an agent's authority to contract for the sale of an interest in real property must be in writing. At common law an agent could not execute an instrument under seal unless authorized to do so by an instrument under seal. This rule still prevails in the few states which still recognize the efficacy of the seal.

Implied Agency and Authority

The conduct or acts of a person may manifest an intention to appoint an agent. The legal basis of an implied agency is similar to that of an implied in fact contract which was discussed in the law of contracts. The authority of an agent may be similarly implied.

Courts generally hold that where authority is expressly conferred upon an agent, he has by implication such incidental authority as is necessary, reasonable, and proper to carry his power into effect and complete the business he is authorized to do. The test for determining the scope of an agent's implied authority is the justified belief of the agent. This standard is applied in relation to the nature of the agency, whether general or special, trade usages, general customs, past dealings between the principal and agent, and all other facts and circumstances which are material in the particular case.

Authority by Necessity. A special type of implied authority arises if an emergency arises and an agent is unable to contact his principal for instructions. In such cases an agent or employee, in some instances, may exercise his own judgment and take whatever action is necessary to handle the emergency. A common example is the implied authority of a train conductor to secure medical assistance for passengers injured in a train wreck.

Agency and Authority by Estoppel

The agency itself and the authority of an actual or apparent agent may be established on the basis of estoppel. An agent's acts or contracts within the scope of his apparent authority may be binding on the principal even though no actual authority, express or implied, to do such acts or to make such contracts has in fact been conferred upon him. Apparent or ostensible authority may be greater than, less than, or the same as an agent's actual authority. In apparent authority cases, a person held liable as a principal is said to be estopped from denying that the person he held out possessed the authority in question.

In order to use the doctrine of estoppel as a basis for apparent agency or authority there must be (1) willful or negligent conduct by the principal which (2) reasonably caused the third person to believe that authority existed, and (3) the third person must have relied on the apparent authority to his injury. For example, a person who repeatedly recognized his liability upon promissory notes signed by another person will be estopped to deny authority for a subsequent signing, as against one who deals in good faith on the basis of the previous apparent authority.

Apparent authority of an agent cannot be established by the words, acts or conduct of the agent alone, but must be traced to some act, conduct, or words of the principal. Not only must there be fault imputed to the principal because of some act or omission on his part, but the other party dealing with the apparent agent must be free from negligence and must have acted in good faith, respecting every restriction on the agent's authority of which he may have notice.

Agency and Authority by Operation of Law

In certain instances an agency is said to be created by operation of law. For example, a wife is an agent for her husband in purchasing necessaries if he has wrongfully failed to supply her with such things and she has no means herself with which to obtain the necessaries. On the same basis some states have held that a minor child may be deemed an agent of his parents for the purpose of purchasing necessaries if his parents have failed to furnish such necessaries. A notice by a husband or father to third persons not to extend credit to his wife or children does not relieve the husband or father from liability for necessaries properly supplied to them, although the notice could terminate an actual agency to buy on the husband's or father's credit. The implied in law agency recognized in such cases is grounded in the legal responsibility of the husband or father to support his family.

Agency and Authority by Ratification

An agency may be created by ratification where a person with no actual or apparent authority to act as agent represents that he is the agent of another person and engages in a transaction in the other person's name. Ratification may also occur where an agent does some act beyond the scope of his actual authority. The purported principal's subsequent approval of the unauthorized acts is called ratification and makes him liable, just as if the transaction had been authorized from the first whether it be a contract or a tort. The ratification relates back to the time of the act in question, curing the absence of authority. As a result the agent is released from liability to both his principal and third persons for having acted without authority.

In order to have a valid ratification the following requirements must be met: (1) the party ratifying must have been in existence and capable of doing or authorizing the act at the time it was performed, (2) the party ratifying must have been capable of doing or authorizing the act at the present time, (3) the purported principal must have been named or otherwise designated so that he may be ascertained, (4) the one who acted without authority must have done so as agent of his principal or the person represented to be his principal, (5) the ratifying party must have full knowledge of all the material facts at the time he ratifies, (6) the act to be ratified must be legal,

(7) the entire transaction must be ratified, (8) the third party must not have withdrawn from the transaction, (9) the rights of third persons must not have intervened prior to the attempted ratification, and (10) usually an unauthorized act must be ratified by the same means necessary to confer authority to do it in the first place.

Ordinarily ratification may be expressed, or it may be implied from the conduct of the principal. If a person with full knowledge of all the material facts takes the benefits of an unauthorized act done on his behalf, he will be bound on the transaction. For example, a person with such knowledge who accepts goods bought for him without authority, or unreasonably retains or uses them, or sells them, will be liable for the price. Similarly, ratification may result when a person brings a suit based on an unauthorized act, or, knowing about an unauthorized act, remains silent beyond a reasonable length of time in cases where a duty exists to speak out in repudiation of the unauthorized act.

Ratification need not be communicated to the third person, to take effect, and it is irrevocable when once made.

Secret Limitations on Authority

A principal may, from time to time, by special instructions, limit the authority of his agent. While these instructions will bind both the agent and third persons from the time they have notice of them, the principal cannot, as against a third person who has dealt with the agent in good faith within the scope of his actual or apparent authority, escape liability by showing that he had previously, but unknown to the third person, modified or limited the agent's authority by secret instructions.

Principal and Agent

24

DUTIES AND LIABILITIES OF AGENT

The law recognizes the fiduciary nature of the relationship between a principal and agent by implying certain duties owed by an agent to his principal. These duties are in addition to those stated in the employment contract or gratuitous appointment of an agent, and they are subject to any valid agreement the principal and agent may have made with references to them. If an agent commits a material breach of any of his duties he may (1) be discharged, (2) forfeit his compensation, and (3) be held liable to the principal in damages.

¶ The implied duties of an agent toward his principal include the duty

1] To be loyal.
2] To obey all lawful instructions except in emergency.
3] To exercise ordinary care and skill.
4] To communicate all notices and disclose all pertinent knowledge.
5] To perform his duties personally where discretion is involved.
6] To account for money and property.
7] To refrain from commingling the principal's property with his own.

The agent's duty to perform his duties personally will be discussed in the next chapter in relation to the authority of an agent to delegate his duties, and the duty of the agent to communicate with his principal will be described in connection with the statement of the rule that generally notice to or knowledge of the agent is notice to or knowledge of the principal. The remaining duties listed above will be discussed in this chapter.

Duty of Loyalty

The agent's duty of undivided loyalty to his principal is based on the fact that the agent is serving as a fiduciary for the benefit of the principal. The agent's duty to be loyal includes the duty not to (1) divulge the principal's business secrets or confidential information, (2) buy from or sell to himself without the principal's consent, (3) serve his principal and another principal in the same transaction without their consent, and (4) compete with his principal.

An agent must not use, either while employed by his principal or after his employment is terminated, confidential information and trade secrets belonging to his principal, for the purpose of advancing his personal interest to the detriment of the principal. This rule extends to customer lists, secret formulas or processes, and other confidential information of a similar nature. However, an agent may, upon leaving the employ of his principal, put to use for his benefit and that of a subsequent employer the skill and general knowledge the agent acquired while working for his former principal.

If an agent buys from or sells to himself, either directly or indirectly through a "strawman" or "dummy," without the full knowledge and consent of his principal, the principal may rescind the transaction even though the price was the best obtainable and no bad faith on the part of the agent was involved. This inflexible right of the principal to set aside the transaction is designed to remove every possible temptation for unfaithfulness from the path of an agent. The rule against an agent serving two principals in the same transaction, unless both principals consent, is applied in the same manner. For example, a real estate broker who acts as an agent for both the buyer and seller without their knowledge and consent is not entitled to compensation for his services and the contract, even though fully performed, is not binding on the parties. If one of the parties knows of the dual agency, the party with such knowledge may not rescind the contract and he will usually be liable to the agent for his compensation. However, the party without knowledge of the dual agency may repudiate the contract and he is not liable to the agent for his compensation.

The principal may claim from his agent all profits or commissions, rebates, bonuses, and similar payments received from a third person by the agent in connection with any violation of the agent's duty of loyalty. The fact that the contract negotiated by the agent is favorable to the principal does not preclude the principal from avoiding the contract, if he wishes, and claiming the secret profits from his agent. Profits made by an agent from a sideline carried on during time when the agent should have been working for his principal may be claimed by the principal.

Duty to Obey Instructions

It is the duty of an agent to follow faithfully all reasonable instructions and directions of the principal. For example, if an agent instructed to sell for cash sells for credit, or, being instructed to buy or sell, neglects to do so, he is liable for any ensuing loss and may be discharged and may forfeit any right that he may otherwise have to compensation.

Exceptions are made to the general rule that it is the agent's duty to obey instructions if (1) obeying the instructions require the agent to commit an unlawful or criminal act, or (2) a sudden emergency makes it necessary for the agent to depart from the instructions and it isn't possible to consult with the principal before proceeding. A gratuitous agent is under no duty to follow his principal's instructions, but if he proceeds to perform, he must follow strictly the instructions.

In general, ratification by the principal relieves the agent from all liability for disregarding instructions, and prevents a forfeiture of his compensation, unless the principal has no choice but to ratify or incur greater loss.

Duty to Exercise Care and Skill

An agent is under a duty to use at least ordinary care and skill in the performance of his duties. The failure of the agent to exercise such care is negligence, and the agent is liable for any loss caused thereby.

The agent's duty to exercise ordinary care and skill includes the duty (1) of a collecting agent to collect only in money unless otherwise authorized, (2) to remit by the usual means unless otherwise instructed, (3) to check the credit standing of a credit buyer or borrower.

Professional agents, such as lawyers, accountants, and others who hold themselves out as possessing special skills must possess and exercise the degree of care and skill possessed and exercised by agents performing such professional services in the locality.

Duty to Account; Commingling

An agent must keep regular accounts of all his actions on behalf of his principal, preserve all records pertaining to the agency, and, whenever reasonably requested, make and present to his principal a full statement of his dealings.

Any of the principal's money or property intrusted to the agent must be accounted for to the principal. The agent must not so mingle the property or money of the principal with his own that they cannot be distinguished. If he does so, any loss to the property or money will fall upon the agent. Therefore, an agent should, in depositing his principal's money in a bank, either deposit it in his principal's name, or indicate in some other manner, that the money belongs to the principal. If he does so, using due care to select a safe and solvent bank, any loss of the funds must be borne by the principal. But if the agent deposits them in his own name and account he will be absolutely liable if they are lost by the failure of the bank.

The law may impose a constructive trust, for the benefit of the principal, against the agent's estate if the agent has misappropriated the principal's property or money by using it in purchasing other property for the agent's personal benefit. An agent who misappropriates the principal's property may be charged with the crime of embezzlement, and the principal may bring a tort action in trover against him for conversion.

DUTIES AND LIABILITIES OF PRINCIPAL

¶ The duties of a principal toward his agent include the following:

    1] To compensate the agent;
    2] To reimburse the agent;
    3] To indemnify the agent.

In addition to having the right to enforce these duties by suit, an agent has a lien upon the principal's property and money in his possession as a means of helping him enforce the principal's duties.

Compensation

The principal must pay to the agent the agreed compensation. If the amount of compensation has not been fixed by agreement, the agent is entitled to the customary compensation for such services. If no customary compensation can be established, the principal must pay the agent the reasonable value of his services. No compensation can be claimed by the agent if the circumstances indicate that his services were rendered gratuitously. An agent may be deprived of compensation if he has breached some duty owed to the principal, he abandons his employment, or the purpose of the agency is illegal.

Professional agents such as real estate brokers and lawyers are often employed on a contingent fee basis, that is, their compensation is dependent on accomplishment of a certain result. For example, a real estate broker usually takes a listing of real property an owner wishes to sell with the understanding that the broker must produce a buyer before the broker is entitled to his commission. The broker is said to earn his commission in the typical case when he finds a buyer who is ready, willing, and able to buy on the terms contained in the listing agreement. Compensation for most professional agents is usually standardized in the community where they are employed. The selling agent is usually paid a percentage of the selling price. It is important to examine carefully the contract employing a professional agent to determine what basis for compensation is provided for in the agreement. Some states require that contracts employing certain types of professional agents be in writing in order for the agent to recover compensation.

If the principal breaches a bilateral contract of agency by wrongfully discharging the agent, the agent may sue to recover the agreed compensation. However, the discharged agent must mitigate his damages by seeking similar employment in the same locality.

Reimbursement and Indemnity

The principal must reimburse the agent for all expenses necessarily incurred by the agent in the discharge of the agency, unless the agent's regular compensation is intended to cover these expenses.

If an agent suffers some loss while following the principal's instructions, the principal is obligated to indemnify the innocent agent for such loss.

TERMINATION OF AGENCY

Methods of Termination

An ordinary agency may be terminated by the (1) act of one or both of the parties, or (2) by operation of law. Special termination rules relating to agencies coupled with an interest are discussed at the end of this chapter.

Act of Parties. Termination of an agency by act of the parties may result from: (1) mutual agreement, (2) expiration of time period specified in contract, (3) accomplishment of the objectives of the agency, (4) action of either party where no time period is specified, (5) action of either party prior to expiration of specified time period. These methods of termination are explained briefly in the following discussion.

The parties may terminate an agency contract, as any other contract, by mutual agreement.

An agency terminates automatically upon expiration of the time period specified in the agency contract, or upon accomplishment of the purposes for which the agency was created. If the parties continue the agency relationship, without a new contract, beyond the period specified, the law implies that the agency has been renewed for a further period of the same duration, embodying the terms of the original contract.

If an agency contract doesn't specify a date for termination, the agency is one at will, and either the principal or agent is free to terminate the agency provided the terminating party acts in good faith.

The principal or agent possesses the power to terminate an ordinary agency at any time even where the agency contract provides for a specified term, but the right to terminate does not exist in such cases unless, of course, a breach of duty by one of the parties justifies termination by the other party. The wrongful termination subjects the terminating party to liability for damages as pointed out in the discussion of the duty of a principal to compensate his agent for the contract period and the duty of an agent to fulfill his promise to render services.

Operation of Law. The events which terminate an agency by operation of law are: (1) death of either principal or agent, (2) adjudged insanity of either principal or agent, (3) the bankruptcy of principal or agent, in most cases, (4) subsequent illegality of the objective of the agency, (5) destruction or loss of the subject matter of the agency, (6) the disqualification of principal or agent (as where either loses his license when a license is required), or (7) impossibility of performance.

The occurrence of any of the events listed above automatically terminates an ordinary agency according to the view of most courts. Transactions of the agent after a termination by operation of law are void even though the acting parties have no notice or knowledge of the event which caused the termination. An exception is made in the case of a bank receiving its customer's check for payment from his account after the death of the customer but before the bank learns of the death. In such a case the law provides that the bank may charge the customer's account and not be liable to the customer's estate for the amount of the check. This is explained further in Chapter 22 of this book.

Death of either party not only terminates the agent's authority, it discharges the surviving party and the deceased party's estate from further obligation on the agency contract. Dissolution of a corporation has the same effect as death of a natural person serving as a principal. Bankruptcy of the principal terminates the agent's authority, and bankruptcy of the agent has the same effect where the bankruptcy interferes with the agent's ability to execute his authority.

Notice of Termination

If an agency is terminated by operation of law, notice to third persons is generally not necessary. However, if the principal becomes insane, his agent's contracts are binding on the principal unless he has been officially adjudged insane or the third party knows of the principal's mental illness. If an agency is terminated by act of the parties, it is the duty of the principal to notify all third persons who know of the agency, or the principal may, on the basis of apparent authority, be held liable to a third party on some future transaction negotiated by the former agent. The type of notice which the principal must use to protect himself depends on whether the third person had dealt with the principal through the agent or merely knew of the agency. Actual notice, in any form, to the third person who had dealt with the agency is necessary, while constructive notice to the third person who had not dealt with the agency is sufficient. Constructive notice may take the form of a notice published in a newspaper in the locality involved. The fact that the third person, who knows of the agency but had not dealt with the agency, doesn't actually read the newspaper notice is immaterial. Such person is bound by the public notice and cannot thereafter hold the principal liable on contracts made by the former agent.

Agency Coupled with an Interest

An agency coupled with an interest, also called power given as security, is irrevocable by the principal and is not terminated by the death or insanity of either party. To constitute an agency coupled with an interest the agent must have a legal or equitable property interest in the subject matter of the agency, and the power is granted for the purpose of protecting such interest. For example, a power given as security such as a power of sale contained in a mortgage is an agency coupled with an interest. The mortgagee who is the holder of the mortgage and power is a kind of agent who is authorized, upon the mortgagor's default, to sell the mortgaged property and apply the proceeds toward the payment of the debt. The discharge of the debt terminates the power given as security.

A mere interest in the results or proceeds of an agency, by way of compensation, does not constitute an agency coupled with an interest. For example, if a person is authorized to sell certain property for another and to have a commission out of the proceeds, an ordinary agency results, and the authority is revokable at will. The same is true where a person is authorized to collect a debt and is promised one-half of any sum collected for his services.

Principal, Agent and Third Persons

25

LIABILITY ON CONTRACTS

Disclosed Principal and Authorized Contracts

A disclosed principal is one who is at the time of the transaction revealed as a party to the transaction which the agent is presumably carrying on in his behalf. An agent who acts in the name of his principal and within the scope of the agent's authority binds the principal and third person. As explained before in the general discussion of authority, an agent's basic authority may consist of one or more of the following kinds: express, implied, and apparent. If no authority is present, the principal may make himself and the third person liable by ratification. The principal is not liable to the third person on contracts made by an agent without authority unless they are ratified by the principal. An agent is not personally liable and may not ordinarily sue on a contract made by him for a disclosed principal unless the agent has made himself a party to the contract or has a special interest or property in the contract.

Undisclosed Principal

Liability of Principal and Agent. A principal is said to be undisclosed when the agent does not disclose to the third person the existence of the agency and the identity of the principal. An agent for an undisclosed principal will necessarily enter into contracts in his own name and on the strength of the agent's credit. For these reasons, an agent is liable on contracts made by him for an undisclosed principal. The third person may elect to hold the undisclosed principal if the agent acted within the scope of his authority. An agent for an undisclosed principal will have an apparent authority as wide as the scope of the business he is transacting.

There can be no ratification of a contract made for an undisclosed principal because one of the requirements for ratification is that the agent must make the contract in the name of the principal.

Third Person's Right of Election. As a general rule, the third party, upon discovery of the existence of the agency and the identity of the principal, may elect to hold either the agent or the undisclosed principal liable. Both the principal and the agent cannot be held on the contract. Once the third party has elected to hold the principal or agent, the other party is discharged.

Ordinarily, election by the third party cannot take place until he learns the identity of the undisclosed principal. No right to hold the undisclosed principal will arise if the third person has received full performance from the agent before the agency is revealed. Election consists of express declaration or conduct by the third person, after disclosure of the principal, which indicates an intention to hold the particular party.

Most courts hold that an undisclosed principal who in good faith and before disclosure pays his agent for the benefit of the third party is not liable to the third party in cases where the agent fails to turn the money over to the third person.

Liability of Third Person. The liability of the third person to the undisclosed principal on contracts made for the latter's benefit by the agent is recognized in most cases. However, if the contract stipulates it is made exclusively with the agent or is one which is based on the personal qualities of the agent and which would not have been entered into but for these qualities, the principal cannot claim the contract for himself. The rules of contract law which provide that certain types of contracts are not assignable or certain duties cannot be delegated apply here.

The third person who enters into a contract with an agent for an undisclosed principal is liable to the agent for breach of the contract. However, the right of the principal to sue on the contract is superior to that of the agent, provided the contract is a simple contract, that is, not a contract under seal or a negotiable instrument.

When the undisclosed principal seeks to take advantage of a contract which his agent has entered into without disclosing the principal, he must do so subject to all the rights, equities, and defenses which the third person could have established against the agent. For example, the third person may set off against the undisclosed principal a claim due the third person from the agent and the set-off need not have arisen out of the transaction being claimed by the undisclosed principal. Also, payment made by the third person in good faith to the agent of an undisclosed principal before disclosure is generally a good defense against the principal.

As stated previously, the third person is not ordinarily liable to the agent on a contract negotiated for a disclosed principal.

Liability on Writings

An agent signing a written contract for his principal should sign in the following manner: "AB by his agent, CD," or "AB by CD," for it is generally recognized that the signing of the principal's name, followed by the name of the agent, separated by the word "per" or "by," is a proper method of excluding personal liability of the agent.

If an ordinary simple contract is signed by the agent in a manner which does not name the principal, as where he signs "CD, Agent," a court will examine the terms of the entire writing and will admit parol evidence to determine the parties to the contract. However, if the writing is a negotiable instrument, no person can be held on it unless his name appears on the instrument. Under this rule of negotiable instruments law, an undisclosed principal cannot be held upon a negotiable instrument by the holder of the instrument.

Agent's Authority in Particular Matters

Authority to Collect. The general rule is that an agent authorized to negotiate a sale transaction has no implied authority to collect or receive payment, and a third person who makes payment to the agent will bear any loss resulting from the defalcation of the agent, in the absence of other circumstances indicative of authority to receive payment. Where, however, the agent is entrusted with possession of the goods which he is authorized to sell, he is generally deemed to have implied authority to collect for them at the time of delivery. A traveling salesman is held to have implied authority to accept a down payment or deposit at the time he takes an order, but he may not ordinarily collect future payments as they come due. Authority to collect money does not include implied authority to accept some other medium of payment, or to compromise the debt, or to extend the time of payment.

Authority of an agent to collect payments may also be implied from representations or acquiescence of the principal, past transactions involving the parties, or from custom or usage.

If a principal has made a loan through an agent and left the borrower's promissory note with the agent, authority of the agent to receive payment and discharge the note may be implied.

Of course, if an agent has actual authority to collect, the principal will be liable for a payment by the third person to the agent even though the third person may not know of such actual authority.

Authority in Relation to Negotiable Instruments. Authority of an agent to sign or indorse negotiable instruments in the principal's name does not exist unless expressly conferred, or the nature of the business entrusted to the agent makes it essential that such authority be implied, or facts exist in the particular case which vest apparent authority in the agent to sign such instruments.

Authority to Purchase on Credit. A special purchasing agent authorized to buy property, and supplied with funds, has no implied authority to buy on credit, unless such is the usage of the trade in which he is employed. But if an agent, authorized to buy, is not furnished with necessary funds, he has implied authority to buy on the principal's credit. A general agent given authority to manage a business is said to have the power to purchase those things essential to the carrying on of a business, either on credit or for cash.

Liability for Agent's Misrepresentations. Ordinarily where an agent has authority to negotiate a contract for his principal, the statements, representations, and admissions with reference to the business he is authorized to transact are as binding upon the principal as if the latter had made them personally. Therefore, if an agent has made misrepresentations on which the third person has reasonably relied, the third person has the right to rescind the contract even though the representations were unauthorized or expressly forbidden by the principal.

Liability for Agent's Warranties. Generally an agent employed to sell goods has no implied authority to give a warranty which will bind his principal unless the goods are of a kind usually sold with warranty. It is generally held that an agent selling a principal's goods has implied authority to make warranties which are no more extensive than those implied in law in connection with a sale of the particular goods. Implied warranties in sales contracts were discussed in Chapter 15.

Liability of Agent on Unauthorized Contracts

An agent of a disclosed principal impliedly warrants to the third person (1) his authority to represent his principal in the transaction and make the contract with the third person for his principal and (2) the existence and competency of his principal. This liability attaches even though the agent acted in good faith and honestly believed he was authorized. These warranties do not apply in the undisclosed principal case.

If lack of authority is present in a disclosed principal case, most courts hold that the agent is not liable to the third person on the contract itself, but the agent is liable either (a) for breach of warranty of his authority, or (b) the agent is liable in a tort action for deceit, if the agent fraudulently misrepresented his authority. The measure of recovery is the damage suffered by the third person. If the circumstances permit a tort action, the third person may sue either in tort for deceit or may elect to sue for damages on breach of implied warranty of authority.

If an agent acts for a nonexistent or wholly incompetent principal, the third person may hold the agent liable as a party to the contract. Generally if an agent acts for a principal who does not have full capacity to contract, such as a minor, the agent is not held liable to the third person unless he misrepresents or conceals the status of the principal's capacity.

An agent is not liable to the third person for breach of warranty of authority if (1) the principal ratifies the unauthorized contract; or (2) the third person knows, or under the circumstances should as a person of ordinary prudence know, of the lack of authority; or (3) the agent makes a full disclosure before contracting of the uncertainty of his authority; or (4) the principal could not be bound on the contract even if the agent possessed the authority to negotiate it. An example of the last basis for the agent's escaping liability is where a contract is not evidenced by a writing as required by the Statute of Frauds.

Delegation of Authority

Most agents are employed because of the special trust and confidence which their principals repose in their integrity, skill, and experience. For this reason, it is generally held that an agent may not delegate his authority which involves the agent's discretion or skill, unless it is otherwise agreed as between the principal and agent. But an agent may, without express authority, employ a subagent to do such acts as are purely ministerial.

Authority to employ a subagent may be implied from the nature of the agency and the practical necessities of the case. For example, a person placed in general charge of a business requiring the help of many subordinate employees usually has implied authority to employ them.

If an agent employs a subagent without authority, the latter is not the agent of the principal. In such cases, the subagent merely represents the agent who appointed him, and the principal will not be bound to third persons by the acts or contracts of the subagent. Also, the principal will not be liable to the subagent for his compensation.

The principal may ratify a delegation of authority, and he may be bound by the acts of the subagent under the rules of estoppel, that is, on the basis of apparent or ostensible authority as discussed previously.

KNOWLEDGE OF OR NOTICE TO AGENT

A principal is chargeable with and bound by the knowledge of or notice to his agent received from responsible sources by the agent in the course of his employment, with reference to matters to which his authority extends, even though such knowledge or notice is not actually communicated to his principal. This principle is based on (1) the duty of the agent to disclose to his principal all notice and knowledge which he may possess and which is necessary or material to the protection of the principal's interests and (2) the presumption that an agent ordinarily discharges that duty. Another basis for the rule is the theory of the legal identity of the principal and agent. This rule has been applied in certain cases to knowledge acquired prior to the creation of the agency.

Applying this rule, it has been held that notice given to the agent by the purchaser of land, of an encumbrance on the land is notice to the principal. Similarly, notice to an agent employed to purchase goods, of false representations of the seller concerning the goods, is notice to the principal, and it has been held that the agent's failure to rescind the contract in such a case precluded the principal from later rescinding.

Well established exceptions to the knowledge and notice rule provide that a principal is not charged with having knowledge of what is known by his agent: (1) when the agent is acting adversely to his principal's interest, (2) when the agent is under a duty to another principal to conceal his knowledge, or (3) when the third party acts in collusion with the agent to defraud the principal. In such cases the presumption is that the agent is not likely to communicate knowledge which would reveal his misconduct to his principal.

TORT LIABILITY

Liability of Principal

The principal is liable for the torts of his agent if the tort is committed within the scope of employment, even though the wrongful act was not authorized by the principal or may be contrary to the principal's instructions. This rule also applies to the employer and employee relationship. Before a court will impute the tort of an agent or employee to the principal or employer, the injured party must be able to prove that the agency or employment relationship existed and that the tort was committed by the agent or employee while engaged in the performance of the duties of his employment. All types of torts fall within this rule, including negligence, trespass, fraud, assault and battery, false imprisonment, and so on. The fact that the agent commits the tort maliciously and willfully does not relieve the principal from liability, provided the tort was committed within the scope of his employment.

The theory of the liability of a principal for the tortious conduct of his agent is referred to as the doctrine of respondeat superior. It is founded on the superintendence and control which the principal is supposed to exercise over the agent.

The test for determining whether a tort of an agent is within the scope of employment is whether the wrongful act was done while the agent was in the service of, and acting for, the principal in the carrying on of the principal's business. If the agent has departed from the scope of the employment and then commits a tort while on a "frolic of his own" the principal is not liable. For example, if a bakery truck driver drives some distance away from his route to see a friend and on the way negligently runs the principal's truck into X, the principal is not liable.

Liability of Agent

The rule which makes the principal liable for his agent's torts does not relieve the agent from liability to the injured third party. In general, the agent is personally liable for his torts whether they were within the scope of his employment or not. The principal and agent are jointly and severally liable, which means they may be sued in the same legal action or in a separate action. Of course, the injured party is entitled to only one satisfaction and once compensated for his injuries, whether as a result of an action against the principal or agent, he cannot then sue the other party.

There are instances in which an agent merely serves as an innocent conduit through which his principal commits a tort. In such cases the principal is liable to the third person but the innocent agent is not. For example, if an agent passes along to the third person a misrepresentation by his principal and the agent doesn't know or could not be expected in the exercise of ordinary prudence to know that the representation he makes is false, the agent is not personally liable. This same rule, excusing the agent but not the principal from liability, has been followed where a third person is injured as a result of the agent's using a defective instrument furnished by the principal where the agent did not know and by the exercise of reasonable care would not know of the defect in the instrument. However, an agent is liable for the conversion of the personal property of a third person even though he is merely following the instructions of his principal in taking possession of the property and has no reason to know that his acts are wrongful.

Generally an agent is not liable for injuries to third persons resulting from the breach of some duty owed by the agent to the principal. For example, B employs A, a C.P.A., to prepare an audit of B's business and to prepare certified financial statements reflecting the financial condition of B's business. On the basis of the financial statements, C makes a loan to B. Upon the failure of B to repay the loan, A is not liable to C for ordinary negligence in making the audit and preparing the financial statements which gave an erroneous impression of the financial condition of B's business. However, it has been held by courts that A is liable to C if the public accountant's negligence is gross and of such a degree that it could support an inference of fraud.

If an agent's tort is innocently committed while performing his duties as instructed by his principal, the principal is obligated to indemnify the agent for any amount he may be required to pay to the injured third person. Similarly, the principal can hold his agent liable for damages the principal is required to pay to a third person injured by the wrongful act of the agent, unless the agent in committing the tort was merely carrying out the instructions of the principal.

A third person who commits a tort against an interest of the agent is liable to the agent for his injury or loss. The tort may be unrelated to the agency, or it may be related to the agency, as where there is a malicious interference by a third person with the agent's employment contract or where a third person may induce another person to breach a contract which the agent negotiated for his principal and thereby causes loss to the agent.

Introduction to Business Organizations; Nature and Creation of Partnership

26

INTRODUCTION TO BUSINESS ORGANIZATIONS

The principal forms of business organization available in the United States are as follows: (1) single proprietorship, (2) partnership, (3) corporation, (4) limited partnership, (5) statutory or limited partnership association, (6) unincorporated association, the most familiar example of which is the joint stock company, and (7) the Massachusetts or business trust. The most frequently used business forms are the single proprietorship, the partnership, and the corporation.

Other types of business organizations which involve variations of some of the above include the joint venture, mining partnership, syndicate, and cooperative. A joint venture is a business enterprise limited to a single transaction or a particular undertaking, such as a real estate development, and it is generally subject to the same principles of law as partnerships. A mining partnership engages in the development of a mine claim, with the partners viewed as having more limited authority than in a general partnership. A syndicate is an association formed to conduct a business transaction, ordinarily of a financial nature. It is similar to a joint venture and is treated as a partnership, unless incorporated. A cooperative is an association of individuals or enterprises, often farmers or consumers, to further some common enterprise. Cooperatives are often incorporated and they are regulated by statutes.

Only the ordinary general partnership and the corporation business forms are discussed at length in this book. However, a brief description of each of the other principal forms of business organizations follows.

Single Proprietorship

The simplest form in which a business can be conducted is the single proprietorship. The proprietor is the sole owner of the business and has complete control over it. Taking the risks present in the enterprise, the proprietor enjoys the profits and bears the losses. He is personally liable on the contracts of the business and is responsible for torts committed by his employees within the scope of the enterprise's activities.

Limited Partnership and Partnership Association

Limited partnerships and limited partnership associations contain partners who enjoy limited liability. These forms of partnership were unknown at common law, their creation being provided for by statute. They make possible the attracting of capital from those not disposed to engage actively in business, but who are willing to invest with the hope of profit, provided their risk of loss is limited to their capital contribution. A limited partnership is characterized by a valid statute providing for its creation, a contract between the partners, one or more general partners along with one or more limited partners, and compliance with the statute. At the heart of these statutes is the requirement that the organizers of a limited partnership draw up articles of limited partnership and file a copy of those articles with a public official.

Limited partnership acts have been enacted in all states, with most states adopting the Uniform Limited Partnership Act. Under the latter law, a limited partnership can carry on any business which could be carried on by an ordinary partnership, unless specific exception is stated in the statute. Some states have excluded banking and insurance. The limited partnership is often used by brokerage firms. A general partner in a limited partnership is similar to the partner in an ordinary partnership with the same powers and subject to the usual liabilities of general partners. The limited partner may exercise only those rights and powers prescribed by statute, and his liability is limited to his capital contribution. A limited partner is usually liable as a general partner if his surname appears in the firm name, or he takes part in the control of the business, or the firm fails to comply with the statute. The solution of any problem with reference to a limited partnership requires a study of the pertinent statutes.

Limited Partnership Association. A few states have statutes which provide for limited partnership associations, also called statutory associations. These statutes generally provide for transferable shares of the member, subject to approval by the other partners of the new member; the liability of the members is limited to their invested capital; the word *limited* is used in the association name; and the association is considered a separate legal entity in the state where it is organized. Unlike the limited partnership, there are no general partners in a limited partnership association, all the members being limited or special partners with the shield of limited liability. The protection acquired by the members of a properly organized and operated association is almost that of stockholders in a corporation. The federal government recognizes the statutory association as a corporation for tax purposes.

Failure to comply with certain statutory requirements will result in loss to the members in such an association of their personal immunity beyond their capital invested. Other distinct disadvantages exist with respect to these associations, with the result that the corporate form of doing business is preferred.

Unincorporated Association (Joint Stock Company)

The term unincorporated association is usually used to describe a combination of persons for the furtherance of a common non-profit purpose. Social clubs, fraternal associations, and political party organizations are common examples of such groups. However, the form of business organization known as the joint stock company and organized for profit is also classified as an unincorporated association. Members of a joint stock company, where it is recognized, are able to arrange by contract with one another a business organization with perpetual existence, freely transferable shares, and centralized management. In these respects it is like a corporation and differs from a partnership. The principal disadvantage which the joint stock company has in common with the partnership is that the associates do not have limited liability. As a result, the joint stock company form of business association is rarely used in the United States.

Business Trust

The business trust or "Massachusetts" trust is a business organization created by a deed or declaration of trust so as to secure limited liability for those contributing capital to the enterprise, without the necessity of incorporation. The contributors of capital transfer assets to one or more persons, called trustees, who manage and operate the business for the benefit and profit of the contributors who are called beneficiaries. The trustees have legal title to the property in trust and the beneficiaries have the equitable or beneficial interest in the property, their interests in the trust estate being evidenced by trust certificates which are transferable like shares in a corporation. The chief risk assumed by those investing in a business trust is that they will not obtain limited liability if the trust is defectively created or if the beneficiaries reserve the right to control or control in fact the actions of the trustees and the management of the business. In such cases the trust will be viewed as a partnership or simply an association, with unlimited liability attaching to the beneficiaries. Some states refuse to recognize the business trust as a separate form of business organization and apply to it the rules governing partnerships or joint stock companies.

INTRODUCTION TO PARTNERSHIPS

Definition

The Uniform Partnership Act, adopted in nearly all states, defines a partnership as "an association of two or more persons to carry on as co-owners a business for profit." [1] This concise definition is implemented by other provisions of the U.P.A. which will be summarized later in this chapter. Associations formed for nonprofit purposes are not partnerships. Such associations include religious organizations, clubs, college and school classes, fraternal societies, political groups, and trade associations. However, these associations may act through agents, and their members may incur personal liability for such transactions on the basis of agency law.

Partnership law is the result of a fusion of principles which had their origin in the civil law, the law merchant, equity, and the common law. Although certain rules of law are peculiar to partnerships, many partnership matters are governed by the principles of the law of contracts, property, and especially agency. The law of partnerships defines the rights and duties and regulates the conduct of these voluntary associates among themselves and in their relations with third persons.

Characteristics

Aggregate Theory v. Entity Theory. Basically, a partnership is not, as contrasted with a corporation, a legal entity or

---

[1] UPA Sec. 6.

person having a legal existence separate and apart from the persons composing the firm. This view of the nature of a partnership is called the "aggregate theory" as opposed to the "entity theory." However, for certain purposes a partnership is treated as an entity under various statutes, and it is similarly viewed as a legal unit by businessmen and courts under some circumstances. To illustrate, businessmen and lawyers refer to the partnership as having rights and obligations distinct from those of its members; partnership accounts are recognized; the partners act as agents of the firm; the Internal Revenue Code and the Federal Bankruptcy Act recognize partnerships as entities; and state statutes dealing with various subjects view partnerships as persons. Despite the modern tendency to view the partnership as an entity, for the purpose of individual liability of the partners for partnership obligations, the aggregate theory prevails. Civil law countries, either by provisions of their commercial codes or by judicial usage, treat partnerships as legal persons. The U.P.A. does not explicitly state that the partnership is a person, but many of its provisions are consistent with the legal person concept, especially those dealing with partnership property and insolvency. Certain of these sections of the U.P.A. will be referred to later.

Primary Features of Partnerships. In addition to the lack of general recognition of the partnership as a legal entity, the principal legal features of a partnership are (1) mutual agency in that the partners act as agents for one another and the firm within the scope of the firm's business; (2) each partner has unlimited personal liability for the firm's obligations; (3) formation of a partnership is achieved by simple agreement or acts of the parties; and (4) dissolution of the partnership results if a partner ceases to be a partner.

Partnership *v.* Corporation

The advantages of the partnership form of business organization include informality and economy of organization, freedom from special governmental regulations and restrictions, and freedom from certain taxes or the minimization of taxes in some cases. Many business enterprises are created as a sole proprietorship or a partnership, later evolving to the point where the owner or owners find it is desirable to incorporate.

The corporation as a form of organization for carrying on a business affords advantages over the partnership. These include liability of the stockholders limited to the capital subscribed, continuous life irrespective of a stockholder's death, bankruptcy, disability, or transfer of his stock, free transferability of the stockholder's interest in the corporation, facilitation of acquiring large amounts of capital, efficient centralized management organization, and recognition of the corporation as a legal person. Despite the apparent advantages of the corporation, a consideration of all the factors involved in a particular case may result in the conclusion that the business can best be conducted as a partnership or as a proprietorship. Today, the tax consequences are often a dominant consideration in any such decision. The limited liability advantage of the corporation will not exist where creditors of the corporation refuse to extend credit to it unless financially responsible stockholders pledge their personal liability as surety.

CLASSES OF PARTNERSHIPS AND PARTNERS

Partnerships are often classified as (1) ordinary partnerships, (2) limited partnerships and (3) limited partnership associations. The latter two classes of partnerships were described previously.

Ordinary Partnerships

The ordinary partnership is the typical form of partnership. They may be classified according to their scope as (1) universal, (2) general, and (3) special. A universal partnership exists when the partners unite all their property and services and share all profits, however made. This form of partnership is rare today. A general partnership exists when partners engage in transactions of a particular class, such as the continuing conduct of a business or profession. A special partnership is also known as a joint venture or adventure and has been described before.

Trading v. Nontrading Partnerships. Ordinary partnerships are further classified as trading and nontrading. A trading partnership is one engaged in buying and selling goods. A nontrading partnership is one which renders services, such as a partnership engaged in the practice of a profession. The importance of this distinction will be brought out in subsequent discussion of the implied authority of partners.

Classes of Partners

Partners are sometimes referred to with qualifying terms of which some of the most important are general, silent, secret, dormant, nominal or ostensible, limited, and subpartner.

A general partner is the usual type, active in the conduct of the business and liable for the firm's obligations without limitation as to amount. A silent partner is one who is known to the public but who is inactive in the conduct of the business. A secret partner is active in the conduct and control of the firm but is not known to the public as a partner. A dormant partner is both silent and secret. A nominal partner is a partner by estoppel in that he permits himself to appear to be a partner even though he is not in fact a partner. Limited partners were described previously. A subpartner is not actually a partner but merely a person who agrees to share the profits or bear the losses suffered by an actual partner in a partnership.

Self-explanatory terms describing other kinds of partners include retiring, incoming, managing, surviving, and liquidating or winding-up partners.

CREATION OF PARTNERSHIPS

Introduction

No formalities need be complied with in forming a partnership. A partnership agreement may be oral, unless the objectives of the partnership fall within the Statute of Frauds as explained in Chapter 9 of this book and referred to briefly at the conclusion of this chapter. Whether a particular written agreement establishes a partnership poses a question of law to be decided by the court. If the facts in a case are disputed and more than one inference may be drawn from them, then the question of whether a partnership exists is one of fact for the jury, under proper instruction from the judge. Typical provisions of a written partnership agreement, referred to as articles of partnership, are described at the conclusion of this chapter.

The primary test for determining if a partnership exists is the legal intention of the parties as evidenced by their written or oral agreement, if any, and the acts of the parties. The legal intention of parties is measured objectively rather than subjectively. Therefore, the personal feelings or beliefs of the parties, expressed or unexpressed, about the nature of their relationship is not conclusive. Parties may call themselves partners, yet the law will not necessarily view them as such. Conversely, parties may expressly stipulate that their contract does not create a partnership; yet the law may find that one exists on the basis of legal intent. However, courts do give some weight to what the parties call their contract.

As a general rule, courts view the active managerial stockholders of a corporation so defectively created as to be neither *de jure* nor *de facto* personally liable as partners.

The U.P.A. provides that ". . . persons who are not partners as to each other are not partners as to third persons," with the one exception of "partnership by estoppel." [2] Partnership by estoppel is discussed later in this chapter.

---

[2] UPA Sec. 7 (1).

Tests of Existence of Partnership

Certain basic rules for determining whether a partnership exists
have evolved in the law of partnerships. These tests along with
their limitations are codified in Section 7 of the U.P.A. as
follows:

> In determining whether a partnership exists, these rules
> shall apply:
> 1] Except as provided by Section 16, persons who are
> not partners as to each other are not partners as to third
> persons.
> 2] Joint tenancy, tenancy in common, tenancy by the
> entireties, joint property, common property, or part owner-
> ship does not of itself establish a partnership, whether such
> co-owners do or do not share any profits made by the use
> of the property.
> 3] The sharing of gross returns does not of itself estab-
> lish a partnership, whether or not the persons sharing them
> have a joint or common right or interest in any property from
> which the returns are derived.
> 4] The receipt by a person of a share of the profits of
> a business is prima facie evidence that he is a partner in the
> business, but no such inference shall be drawn if such profits
> were received in payment:
> > A] As a debt by instalments or otherwise,
> > B] As wages of an employee or rent to a landlord.
> > c] As an annuity to a widow or representative of a
> > deceased partner.
> > D] As interest on a loan, though the amount of pay-
> > ment vary with the profits of the business.
> > E] As the consideration for the sale of the good-will
> > of a business or other property by instalments or
> > otherwise.

As has been seen, the U.P.A. definition of a partnership requires that the partners (1) carry on a business; (2) as co-
owners; (3) for a profit.

¶ In summary, an ordinary partnership generally depends upon the existence of the following four elements:

    1] voluntary nature of the association
    2] community of interest in the profits
    3] community of interest in the ownership of the business
    4] community of managerial authority over the business.

Partnership by Estoppel

It has been pointed out that the U.P.A. provides that persons who are not partners as to each other are not partners as to third persons, but under certain conditions, one who is not actually a partner may be what is referred to as a partner by estoppel. Section 16 of the U.P.A. describes the conditions for imposing liability upon a person as though he were a partner as follows:

    1] When a person, by words spoken or written or by conduct, represents himself, or consents to another representing him to any one, as a partner in an existing partnership or with one or more persons not actual partners, he is liable to any such person to whom such representation has been made, who has, on the faith of such representation, given credit to the actual or apparent partnership, and if he has made such representation or consented to its being made in a public manner he is liable to such person, whether the representation has or has not been made or communicated to such person so giving credit by or with the knowledge of the apparent partner making the representation or consenting to its being made.

        A] When a partnership liability results, he is liable as though he were an actual member of the partnership.

        B] When no partnership liability results, he is liable jointly with the other persons, if any, so consenting to the contract or representation as to incur liability, otherwise separately. . . .

Summarized, if a person holds himself out, or permits himself to be held out as a partner, he is estopped from denying he is a partner if a third person, justifiably relying upon such holding out, incurs a loss. Courts disagree as to whether a person who merely learns that he is being falsely held out as a partner is under a duty to third persons to take affirmative steps to deny that he is a partner.

Capacity to Be a Partner

Generally, any person with capacity to contract may become a partner. The question of capacity to become partners has arisen, principally with respect to *infants, insane persons, married women, aliens,* and *corporations.* Trust estates or unincorporated associations cannot become a member of a partnership because there is no legal entity capable of entering into the relationship. Partnerships may, with the consent of their members, enter into partnership with other firms or individuals.

Infants (minors) and insane persons may become members of a partnership, but they have the right to disaffirm the partnership agreement and their personal liability to firm creditors. However, it is generally held that the minor cannot withdraw his capital contribution if injury to partnership creditors will result, nor will the adult partners be required to reimburse him for the loss of his capital contribution. In some states the right of an infant partner to disaffirm liability on his partnership agreement and firm obligations has been restricted by statute. While the partnership relation remains in effect, an infant partner has the usual powers of a partner.

Today, the capacity of a married woman to enter into a partnership is provided for in the Married Women's Property Act or similar statutes. Some states still impose limitations, such as forbidding the married woman from entering into a partnership agreement with her husband. At common law, although a married woman could not participate as a partner in a business and thus be held liable as a partner, her capital contribution was subject to the rights of the firm's creditors. Thus, at common law the result was that, in effect, a married woman could be a limited partner, but not a general partner.

An alien whose country is not at war with our own may become a partner. In the event of war between the countries of which partners are citizens, the partnership agreement would become void as against public policy, just as contracts generally between such persons become illegal.

As a general rule, in the absence of specific authority conferred upon corporations by statute or provision in the corporation's articles, it is beyond the power (*ultra vires*) of a corporation to become a general partner, because it would turn over to persons other than the officers and directors of the corporation the exercise of power to incur obligations, dispose of corporate assets, and otherwise carry out the corporation's purposes. Corporations may enter into joint adventures or become a limited partner where the business venture is within the power of the corporation as determined by its charter.

A corporation cannot avail itself of the plea of *ultra vires* to escape liability as a partner to innocent third parties who have performed their side of a contract relying on the holding out by the corporation of itself as a partner.

PARTNERSHIP ARTICLES

Although a partnership may be informally created and its existence proved by manifestations of the parties, it is customary to embody the terms of association in a written document called articles of partnership or co-partnership. Certain terms of a partnership agreement may require a writing because of the Statute of Frauds. For example, an agreement between A and B to form a partnership, and for A to transfer his ownership of certain land to the partnership, is within the Statute of Frauds, and not enforceable unless in writing. Similarly, a contract forming a partnership which, by its terms, is not to be performed within one year from the date it is made is unenforceable unless it is in writing. An oral partnership contract within the Statute of Frauds creates a partnership at will and the partnership continues until one or more of the partners choose to terminate it. In any event, carefully drafted written articles are desirable as a means of limiting the possibility of fraud or controversy.

Partners enjoy considerable freedom in defining their rights and duties by contract, but they cannot by provisions in the partnership articles eliminate their personal liability to third persons or relieve themselves of the fiduciary duty the partners owe to one another. Typical provisions of partnership articles include (1) name of partnership and names of partners, (2) description of the business, (3) location of the business, (4) term of the partnership, (5) capital contributions of each partner, (6) description of partnership property, (7) how the profits and losses will be shared, (8) management of the business, keeping of books, etc., (9) duties and powers of the partners, (10) agreement not to carry on any other business, (11) salaries and drawing accounts of partners, (12) withdrawal of partners, (13) dissolution and winding up of the business, (14) plan for continuation of business after the death of one of the partners and (15) arbitration. General partnership law applies to situations arising for which no provision is made in the articles of partnership.

Partnership Property; Relations of Partners

27

PARTNERSHIP PROPERTY

What Constitutes Partnership Property

Anything capable of being owned may be partnership property. Determining what property belongs to the partnership is especially important when both the firm and the partners are insolvent, because partnership creditors have first claim on partnership property and the creditors of an individual partner have first claim against his individual property.

Intention Test. The intention test is used to determine whether particular property belongs to the partnership. Under this test it is a matter of arriving at the intention of the members of the partnership with respect to who was to be the owner of certain property. The intention of the partners is revealed by their conduct, by the provisions of the partnership agreement or any agreement preliminary thereto, by the terms of written instruments transferring the property, by entries in the partnership books, and by the use made of the property.

The capital in the form of money or other property contributed to the firm by the partners, additions to capital, property acquired by the firm in the course of carrying on firm business, and the resulting business will belong to the partnership. The U.P.A. provides: "Unless the contrary intention appears, property acquired with partnership funds is partnership property." [1] Property which is used by the firm is not necessarily partnership property. Such property may have been loaned or leased to the firm by a partner or others.

Generally the good will of a partnership, including its name, is treated as partnership property, to be viewed as existing for the common benefit of the partners as their respective rights in the partnership may appear.

Title to Partnership Property

Personal property, including tangible property such as motor vehicles or other chattels, and intangible property such as negotiable instruments, may be transferred to or by a partnership in the firm name. On the contrary, at common law the legal title to real estate could not be acquired, held, or conveyed in the partnership name. This rule was based on the common-law theory that title to real property could only vest in a person, either natural or artificial, such as a corporation. Under this rule, a partnership was not deemed to be a person, natural or artificial, but rather an aggregation of individuals. The U.P.A. changes this rule in providing: "Any estate in real property may be acquired in the partnership name. Title so acquired can be conveyed only in the partnership name." [2] It is apparent that with respect to title to real property, the U.P.A. adopts the entity concept of a partnership.

Nature of Partner's Interest in Partnership Property

The U.P.A. in Section 25 defines the partners' co-ownership of partnership property, real and personal, as a tenancy in partnership. Section 25 describes the incidents of tenancy in partnership as follows:

---

[1] UPA Sec. 8 (2).
[2] UPA Sec. 8 (3).

A] A partner, subject to the provisions of this act and to any agreement between the partners, has an equal right with his partners to possess specific partnership property for partnership purposes; but he has no right to possess such property for any other purpose without the consent of his partners.

B] A partner's right in specific partnership property is not assignable except in connection with the assignment of the rights of all partners in the same property.

C] A partner's right in specific partnership property is not subject to attachment or execution, except on a claim against the partnership. When partnership property is attached for a partnership debt the partners, or any of them, or the representatives of a deceased partner, can not claim any right under the homestead or exemption laws.

D] On the death of a partner his right in specific partnership property vests in the surviving partner or partners, except where the deceased was the last surviving partner, when his right in such property vests in his legal representative. Such surviving partner or partners, or the legal representative of the last surviving partner, has no right to possess the partnership property for any but a partnership purpose.

E] A partner's right in specific partnership property is not subject to dower, curtesy, or allowances to widows, heirs, or next of kin.

The U.P.A. also provides that "a partner's interest in the partnership is his share of the profits and surplus, and the same is personal property." [3] Thus, the interest of a partner in real estate owned by the firm is viewed for legal purposes as personal property. Except in the case of a conveyance of partner-

---

[3] UPA Sec. 26.

ship real estate, appearing in the name of the partner or partners individually, to a purchaser for value without notice of the firm's ownership of the property, the legal title to partnership property cannot be conveyed as the individual property of any of the partners. Neither can it be devised by will or inherited in such manner. These rules apply though the title was put in the name of the partners or any of them without reference to the firm, if it was acquired as partnership property within the meaning of the U.P.A. However, the rights of bona fide purchasers of the real estate or of creditors are governed by the recorded deed, rather than the intention of the purchasing partners, as to the question whether or not the real estate is firm property. The estate of a deceased partner is entitled to receive the value of the deceased partner's interest in the partnership as a personal chose in action, including the value of his interest as a partner in the firm real estate.

Effect of Transfer of Partner's Interest

Section 27 of the U.P.A. describes the effect of an assignment of a partner's interest in the partnership as follows:

1] A conveyance by a partner of his interest in the partnership does not of itself dissolve the partnership, nor, as against the other partners in the absence of agreement, entitle the assignee, during the continuance of the partnership, to interfere in the management or administration of the partnership business or affairs, or to require any information or account of partnership transactions, or to inspect the partnership books; but it merely entitles the assignee to receive in accordance with his contract the profits to which the assigning partner would otherwise be entitled.

2] In case of a dissolution of the partnership, the assignee is entitled to receive his assignor's interest and may require an account from the date only of the last account agreed to by all the partners.

Creditors of Individual Partner

Creditors of an individual partner may under the U.P.A., reach the partner's interest in the partnership and its property by means of a "charging order." Section 28 of the U.P.A. provides that on "due application to a competent court by any judgment creditor of a partner, the court which entered the judgment, order or decree, or any court may charge the interest of the debtor partner with payment of the unsatisfied amount of such judgment with interest thereon." A receiver may be appointed by the court for the purpose of satisfying the judgment. Unlike the procedure followed when the common-law writ of execution is issued, no specific property of the partnership is attached in the charging order proceeding, and the partnership continues, with the receiver, if one has been appointed, satisfying the judgment from the debtor partner's interest in the firm.

RELATIONS OF PARTNERS TO ONE ANOTHER

Rights

Part IV of the U.P.A. defines the rights and duties of partners in relation to their partnership and in relation to one another. In the discussion which follows, these rights and duties are summarized.

The partnership agreement may define, within limits, the rights, duties, and powers of the partners. As stated previously, the agreement may not relieve the partners of the fiduciary duty they owe to each other or the unlimited liability they owe to third persons. Unless the partnership agreement provides otherwise, a partner has the right to (1) share in the profits and the surplus; (2) share in the management of the partnership; (3) inspect the firm's books and have them kept at the firm's place of business and receive information about its affairs; (4) contribution and indemnity; (5) interest on advances or loans to the partnership; (6) return of advances and capital; (7) an accounting of partnership affairs if certain circumstances exist. In addition to these rights the partners have rights with respect to partnership property as described previously in this chapter.

Profits and Losses. Equal sharing of the profits, surplus, and losses is the rule, in the absence of contrary agreement. This rule applies even though the partners have contributed unequal amounts of capital or services. If the agreement provides for an unequal sharing of profits but fails to specify how losses are to be shared, then losses are shared in the same proportion as profits.

Compensation. No right to salary or wages for a partner exists in the absence of agreement, but a surviving partner is entitled to reasonable compensation for his services in winding up the partnership affairs. Generally, the no-compensation rule applies despite the fact that a partner's services are extraordinary, he devotes more time to the firm as compared to the other partners, or he performs all the services because of a partner's illness. This rule is based on the premise that each partner has a duty to devote his time and energies to the partnership with his reward to consist of sharing in the profits. By an agreement, express or implied, a partner may be entitled to remuneration for services rendered.

Management. Equal voice in the management and conduct of the partnership business is the rule, unless the partnership agreement provides otherwise; each partner having one vote regardless of his capital contribution. Routine decisions may be made by a simple majority vote, if the majority is acting in good faith and within the scope of the partnership, but unanimous agreement of the partners is required for fundamental changes in the partnership, such as changing the nature or location of the business, reducing or increasing the capital of the partners, and admitting new members to the firm. Unanimous consent of the partners is also necessary for any action in contravention of any agreement between the partners. Dissolution of the partnership may become necessary if the partners are equally divided on a matter which could be decided under the majority-decision rule and the articles of partnership make no provision for such a contingency.

Contribution and Indemnity. A partner's right of contribution rests upon the broad principle that common burdens should be equally borne. The liability of partners for firm obligations is by nature joint, and when one partner satisfies more than his pro rata share of this obligation, he has to that extent performed a duty rightly owed by his partners, and is entitled to reimbursement from his partners for the excess.

The partner's right to indemnity arises from a breach of a partner's duty to conform to the partnership agreement. It is a right to recover for losses sustained by one partner through such breach by another. For example, where one partner substitutes the partnership for his individual indorsement on an accommodation note, he is personally liable for the consequent loss. Neither contribution nor indemnity is available to the partner who has himself breached a duty to the partnership.

Interest on Payments, Advances, and Capital Contributions. Ordinarily a partner contributing capital is presumed to look to profits rather than to interest on the capital, and it is accordingly held that no interest will be allowed upon capital in the absence of special agreement.

The U.P.A. provides that unless the parties agree otherwise, a partner who in the aid of the partnership makes any payment or advance beyond his agreed-upon capital contribution is entitled to be paid interest from the date of the payment or advance; but a partner is entitled to receive interest on the capital contribution by him only from the date when repayment should be made.[4]

Return of Advances and Capital. Each partner is entitled to the return of his advances or similar payments and contributions to the firm capital except where such payments were made necessary by his own culpable act. In settling accounts between

---

[4] UPA Sec. 18 (c) (d).

partners after dissolution, advances will take priority in the order of payment out of the partnership assets over the capital contributions.

Duties

Fiduciary Relationship and Obligations. A fiduciary relationship of mutual trust, loyalty, and confidence exists between partners. The law imposes upon partners the highest standard of integrity and good faith, as it does upon agents generally. Each partner owes his copartner the duty to inform him as to partnership matters, and to consult him in regard to all unusual or unexpected questions of substantial importance not covered by the partnership agreement. A partner who sells his interest in the firm to a copartner owes a duty to disclose to the buying partner all the facts which bear upon the value of the interest being sold and which are not available to the buying partner. The same duty of full disclosure is owed by the buying partner to the selling partner.

It follows from the fiduciary nature of the relation between partners that a partner must not, without the consent of the other partners, (a) make a personal or secret profit at the expense of the partnership or partners, (b) sell to or buy from himself for the firm, (c) act as agent for a third party in a contract with the firm, (d) apply firm property to his own use, (e) engage in a business in competition with that of the firm, and (f) permit his personal interest to conflict with that of the partnership.

Other Duties. In transacting partnership business each partner owes a duty to exercise reasonable care and skill and not to exceed the authority granted him by the partnership agreement. However, a partner is not liable to his partners or the firm for honest mistakes or errors in judgment.

It is apparent that certain correlative duties of partners to one another arise out of their rights as described above, including the duty to conform to the partnership agreement.

Remedies

Accounting. As a general rule, partners cannot maintain an action at law against each other on a claim involving a partnership transaction, nor can the partnership sue the individual partners on partnership claims. Such claims must be adjusted, in most cases, by means of the equitable proceeding called accounting, which is usually an incident to a decree of dissolution and the winding up of the partnership affairs. Partners may sue each other at common law if there is no necessity of going into their mutual obligations as partners.

Section 22 of the U.P.A. provides for the remedy of accounting as follows:

Any partner shall have the right to a formal account as to partnership affairs:

    A] If he is wrongfully excluded from the partnership business or possession of its property by his co-partners.

    B] If the right exists under the terms of any agreement,

    C] As provided by Section 21,

    D] Whenever other circumstances render it just and reasonable.

Section 21 of the U.P.A. provides that a partner holds as trustee any benefit or profit he obtains in violation of the fiduciary duty he owes to the other partners, and he is held accountable to the partnership for such gains.

Partners and Third Persons; Dissolution and Termination

28

AUTHORITY OF PARTNERS

Partners as Agents

A mutual agency relationship exists among partners, with each partner empowered to bind the firm, himself, and his partners to third persons on transactions within the scope of the partnership business. The liability of one partner for the acts of his copartner is founded on the principles of agency, each partner acting as both an agent and a principal. A partner's authority, like that of an agent, may be (1) express, (2) implied, and (3) apparent. The authority of partners may be expressly granted or limited by the partnership agreement, and such an agreement binds the partners between themselves and also is binding upon third persons who have notice of it.

Implied Authority

The law recognizes that it is customary for partners to make contracts and engage in certain types of transactions in the course of carrying on in the usual way the business of the partnership. Unless third persons have notice of a partnership agreement to the contrary, partners in an ordinary partnership have implied authority to enter into the following transactions, subject to the limitations noted and also subject to local business customs or usages.

Borrowing Money and Executing Negotiable Instruments. In an ordinary trading or commercial partnership, that is, a partnership whose business consists of buying and selling, each partner has authority to borrow money for partnership purposes. To effectuate this authority, a partner may execute negotiable instruments in the firm name and give security, such as a mortgage or pledge of the personal property of the firm, for the repayment of the loan. A subsequent misapplication of the borrowed money to the individual use of the borrowing partner will not deprive the lender of his remedy against the partnership and the other members of the firm, provided the lender acted in good faith. However, money borrowed by one partner, on his individual credit, will not become a debt of the firm by being used in its business. A partner in a nontrading partnership does not ordinarily possess the authority to borrow money and execute negotiable instruments. However, in a particular nontrading partnership such authority may be expressly conferred or it may fall within the usual course of the partnership business.

Sales and Purchases. A partner has implied authority to sell any part of the partnership property which is held for the purpose of sale. Incidental to such transactions, a partner has authority to execute the documents necessary to transfer the title and to make the usual warranties concerning the property.

A partnership is bound by a purchase made in its behalf by one partner in the ordinary course of its business, and the purchasing partner may pledge the credit of the firm. The firm remains liable even though the partner converts the property to his personal use.

Other Transactions. Ordinarily a partner has implied authority to settle, compromise, release, and receive payment in money or negotiable instruments (but not property) of debts and other claims of the firm; to settle, compromise, and pay out of firm funds or property bona fide claims against the firm; to obtain insurance, casualty and life, and handle transactions related to the insurance policies issued; to engage employees and agents to render services needed in the carrying on of the business; to bring suits at law and engage attorneys to defend suits. brought against the partnership; and to perform all other acts essential to the normal operation of the type of business in which the partnership is engaged. Generally a partner has no implied authority to bind the firm on a guaranty or surety contract. However, it has been held that the firm is liable if such a contract was made in furtherance of the purposes of the partnership.

Estoppel, Admissions, Ratification

Estoppel and Apparent Authority. As pointed out in the previous chapter, the common-law estoppel doctrine with respect to the creation of an apparent partnership has been incorporated into the U.P.A. As a result, a person who is in fact not a partner, but who is held out as a partner with his consent, may be held liable to third persons just as if he were actually a partner. Similarly, where an actual partner acts without authority or in excess of his authority, the partnership and the other partners may be estopped to deny that the partner had authority so to act. The essential elements of authority by estoppel, also called apparent or ostensible authority, are the holding out of a partner, with his consent, as having an authority, and reliance thereon in good faith by a third person with resulting loss to such person if the transaction is not held binding against the firm and the apparent partners.

Admissions. It is an established principle in the law of evidence, that a person's admissions or declarations against his own interest are admissible as an exception to the hearsay rule. Applying this principle to partnerships, courts have held and the U.P.A. provides that an admission or representation made by a partner concerning partnership affairs within the scope of his authority is evidence against the partnership.[1] To illustrate, an admission by a partner of an amount due from the firm, made during negotiations with the third person creditor, will bind the firm. However, statements of an alleged partner are not admissible to prove the existence of a partnership. Independent evidence must be relied on to show the existence of the partnership, after which the admissions rule applies as described above.

Ratification. The originally unauthorized acts of a partner may become binding on the firm and its members by subsequent ratification. The general rules of agency law governing ratification by the principal of the unauthorized acts of an agent are applicable to partnerships. The essentials of an effective ratification of a partner's acts are that the act must have been lawfully done by a person purporting to act as a partner having the appropriate authority for identifiable copartners who have later adopted it with full knowledge of all material facts. Ratification will not be applied to defeat the bona fide claims of third persons acquired in the interval.

Notice to or Knowledge of Partner

The U.P.A. follows the common-law rule in providing that notice to any partner of any matter relating to partnership affairs, and the knowledge of the partner acting in the particular matter, acquired while a partner or then present in his mind, operate as notice to or knowledge of the partnership, except in the case of a fraud on the partnership committed by or with the consent of that partner.[2]

LIMITATIONS ON AUTHORITY

Partners may by agreement expressly limit the authority each partner possesses in relation to his dealings with third persons.

---

[1] UPA Sec. 11.
[2] UPA Sec. 12.

The U.P.A. provides: "No act of a partner in contravention of a restriction on authority shall bind the partnership to persons having knowledge of the restriction." [3] In addition to taking notice of apparent limitations on a partner's authority, the third person must determine if a partnership actually exists, unless the estoppel doctrine can be applied to impose liability for the benefit of the third person.

In the discussion of the management rights of partners it was pointed out that the decision of the majority of the members binds the partnership with respect to ordinary matters, unless the action taken is contrary to the partnership agreement of which the third person has notice. The resulting contract binds the firm and all the partners even though a dissenting partner gives notice of his dissent to the person with whom the majority are dealing. Of course, the majority must act in good faith and the contract must be within the scope of the partnership business.

As seen previously, fundamental changes in the internal affairs of a partnership such as adjustment in the capital accounts of the partners, changes in the nature or location of the business, and admission of new partners requires approval of all the partners. This same rule applies to transactions with third persons where the transaction is unusual or could interfere with the continuation of the partnership business. Specifically, the U.P.A. provides that, unless authorized by the other partners or unless they have abandoned the business, one or more but less than all the partners have no authority to (1) assign the partnership property in trust for creditors or on the assignee's promise to pay the debts of the partnership; (2) dispose of the good will of the business; (3) do any other act which would make it impossible to carry on the ordinary business of a partnership; (4) confess a judgment; or (5) submit a partnership claim or liability to arbitration or reference. [4]

---

[3] UPA Sec. 9 (4).
[4] UPA Sec. 9 (3).

LIABILITY OF PARTNERS

Kinds and Nature of Liability

A partnership and its members may incur liability on the basis of (1) contracts, (2) torts, and (3) crimes.

Contracts. A contractual obligation of a partnership is the debt of each individual member of the firm as well as the debt of the firm.

At common law a partner's obligation on firm contracts was generally held to be part of a joint obligation; thus all partners, with some exceptions, had to be served with a summons in order for the plaintiff to proceed to judgment against the partnership. Many states have modified this common-law rule by statute in order to permit a partnership creditor to take judgment against those partners upon whom service of summons has been obtained. Under this procedure the creditor may satisfy his judgment out of partnership assets or out of the assets of the individual partners who were brought before the jurisdiction of the court by proper service of summons.

Torts. A partnership and the partners are liable to injured third persons for the torts of a partner committed within the scope of the firm's business. Each partner is liable under this rule despite a lack of participation, knowledge, or ratification of a particular partner in relation to the wrongful act by the acting partner. This vicarious liability is grounded in the law of agency and relates to the full gamut of torts, including negligent and willful acts and deceit.

The tort liability of partners is joint and several. If a partner commits a tort while acting within the scope of the partnership business, all of the partners are collectively and individually liable to the injured party who may sue and recover from any or all of the partners, as well as the partnership. Of course, the injured party is entitled to only one satisfaction.

Crimes. A partnership, since it is not a legal person or entity separate from its members, cannot be held criminally liable for the criminal acts of a partner, and the other partners are not liable unless they have participated in the criminal acts. If a partnership business is organized for an illegal purpose, all the partners are held criminally responsible. Some criminal statutes, such as those requiring a license before engaging in certain transactions, place liability upon the firm itself where a partner violates the statute while acting in behalf of the partnership.

DISSOLUTION; WINDING UP; TERMINATION

Introduction

Dissolution of a partnership results when any partner ceases to be a member of the firm or the membership of the firm changes for any reason. The U.P.A. recognizes the closing of a partnership as a three-step process: (1) dissolution, (2) winding up, and (3) termination.[5] After dissolution of a partnership, the business may be carried on by a new business organization, usually a new partnership, a corporation, or an individual proprietorship. The winding up of a partnership business may follow dissolution, and it involves liquidating the assets of the firm, paying firm debts, and distributing the capital and profits, if any, to the partners. Termination occurs automatically upon completion of the winding-up process and marks the end of the partnership's legal existence.

Causes of Dissolution

The various causes of a partnership dissolution may be classified and discussed under the following headings: (1) act of one or more of the partners without violation of the partnership agreement; (2) act of one or more of the partners in violation of the partnership agreement; (3) operation of law; and (4) court decree.

Dissolution without Violation of Agreement. The U.P.A. provides that a partnership is dissolved without violation of the

---

[5] UPA Sec's. 29 and 30.

partnership agreement in the following cases: (a) by the termination of the definite term or the accomplishment of the particular undertaking specified in the partnership agreement; (b) by the express will of any partner when no definite term or particular undertaking is specified; (c) by the mutual agreement at any time of all the partners who have not assigned their interests or had their interests subjected to a charging order for their separate debts; and (d) by the bona fide expulsion of any partner from the business in accordance with the partnership agreement.[6]

Dissolution Contrary to Agreement. A partner may withdraw from the firm and thus cause dissolution of the partnership even though in doing so he violates the partnership agreement and he may be held liable to the other partners for wrongfully terminating the partnership relationship. In such cases it is said that the right to dissolve may not exist but the power to dissolve always exists.[7]

Dissolution by Operation of Law. Dissolution by operation of law is caused (a) by any event which makes the business of the partnership or the conduct of the partnership unlawful; (b) by the death of any partner; or (c) by the bankruptcy of any partner or the partnership.[8]

Dissolution by Court Decree. The U.P.A. provides that a court of equity may, upon application by or for a partner, order dissolution upon a showing of (a) insanity; (b) incapacity; (c) misconduct; (d) material violation of the partnership agreement; (e) failure of the business; (f) other circumstances which render a dissolution equitable.[9] Also, provision is made for dissolution by court decree on application of an assignee of a partner's interest or a judgment creditor with a charging order.[10]

---

[6] UPA Sec. 31 (1).
[7] UPA Sec. 31 (2).
[8] UPA Sec. 31 (3) (4) (5).
[9] UPA Sec. 32 (1).
[10] UPA Sec. 32 (2).

Notice of Dissolution and Authority

Generally dissolution of a partnership terminates all authority of the partners to bind the firm, except on transactions relating to the winding up of the affairs of the partnership, including unfinished business. For example, partners in a dissolved retail firm could sell and liquidate the stock of merchandise on hand but usually would have no authority to contract for new merchandise. Section 35 of the U.P.A. describes the rules governing the power of a partner to bind the partnership to third persons after dissolution. The notice aspect of these rules is summarized in the following discussion.

Notice to Third Persons. Under the U.P.A., third persons are entitled to notice of the dissolution of a partnership, unless the partnership is dissolved because it is unlawful to carry on the business or the dissolution is caused by the bankruptcy of a partner and the third person deals with the bankrupt partner. At common law, notice of dissolution was not generally required when dissolution was caused by operation of law or court decree; notice being necessary when dissolution resulted from the act or agreement of the partners.

The U.P.A., in describing the *kind of notice* required, divides third persons into two groups. The first group consists of those third persons who had extended credit to the partnership prior to dissolution. Those in the first group are entitled to actual notice. Any medium of communication may be used, but the notice must be actually received to take effect. The second group is composed of third persons who knew of the partnership but had not extended credit to the partnership before dissolution. As to those in the second group, notice by publication is sufficient. This latter notice, called constructive notice, is usually given by placing in a newspaper of general circulation in the place where the partnership was located, an advertisement to the effect that the partnership has been dissolved. Third persons who did not know of the partnership are not entitled to notice. Until proper notice is given, a partner may bind all the partners on contracts with third persons entitled to notice, provided the contracts are within the scope of the business.

Notice to Partners.   The U.P.A. provides that where dissolution is caused by the act, death, or bankruptcy of a partner, each partner is liable to his copartners for his share of any liability created by subsequent contracts, unless the partner acting for the partnership as if the partnership had not been dissolved had knowledge or notice of the dissolution.[11] Therefore, it is important for a partner withdrawing from a firm or for the representative of the estate of a deceased or bankrupt partner to give notice to the other partners of the event which causes the dissolution.

CHANGES IN MEMBERSHIP

The effect of changes in the membership of a partnership in relation to the liability of the parties involved to third persons is governed by general rules of law which can be described in terms of a hypothetical partnership consisting of A, B, and C. Assume A withdraws, dies, or otherwise ceases to be a partner and B and C continue the operation of the partnership business. Under the U.P.A., the new partnership is liable for the debts of the old firm. A remains liable, along with B and C, on the old debts; and A will be liable on the obligations of the new firm, unless proper notice of the dissolution, if required, is given.

In the second assumed situation, A sells his interest in the partnership to a third person, D, who is accepted by B and C as a partner and the partnership business is continued. The liability positions of A, B, and C are the same as in the first situation. However, if the creditors of the old firm agree to release A from the liabilities of the old firm in return for a promise by the new partner, D, to make himself liable on such obligations, a novation results and A is released from liability to the

---

[11] UPA Sec. 34.

old creditors. Notice of A's withdrawal will be necessary to prevent A from being liable for the obligations of the new partnership. The new partner, D, is not liable for the obligations of the old partnership, unless he agrees, as part of the agreement making him a partner, to assume such obligations. This would result in the creditors of the old firm becoming creditor beneficiaries of the purchase agreement. Similar results would follow where A, B and C simply added a new partner rather than replacing one of their number with a new partner.

WINDING UP AND DISTRIBUTION

Winding Up Rights and Procedure

On dissolution, a partnership is not terminated but continues until the winding up of partnership affairs is completed. Section 37 of the U.P.A. provides: "Unless otherwise agreed the partners who have not wrongfully dissolved the partnership or the legal representative of the last surviving partner, not bankrupt, has the right to wind up the partnership affairs; provided, however, that any partner, his legal representative or his assignee, upon cause shown, may obtain a winding up by the court." A court may appoint a receiver to wind up the business if the partners are in disagreement.

In the absence of an agreement to the contrary, the partners entitled to wind up the partnership after the retirement or death of a partner are not to continue operation of the partnership without settling accounts with the retiring partner or estate of the deceased partner. Section 42 of the U.P.A. states: "When any partner retires or dies, and the business is continued . . . without any settlement of accounts . . . , unless otherwise agreed, he or his legal representative . . . may have the value of his interest at the date of dissolution ascertained, and shall receive as an ordinary creditor an amount equal to the value of his interest in the dissolved partnership with interest, or, at his option . . . in lieu of interest, the profits attributable to the

use of his right in the property of the dissolved partnership."
In the earlier discussion of partnership property it was seen
that on the death of a partner title to all partnership property,
including real property owned by the firm, vests in the surviving
partner or partners for the purpose of winding up the partnership affairs. They must, within a reasonable time, collect and
preserve the assets, pay the debts, and make an accounting to
the deceased partner's estate for the deceased partner's interest
in the partnership. This accounting procedure is often provided
for in detail by the partnership articles, along with a provision
for insurance on the lives of the partners, with the insurance
proceeds used to pay the estate of a deceased partner for his
interest in the dissolved partnership.

Winding up a partnership's affairs includes completing transactions unfinished upon dissolution, auditing partnership accounts, collecting moneys due, selling the partnership property,
and other acts necessary to liquidate and distribute the partnership assets.

Rules for Distribution of Assets

Section 40(b) of the U.P.A. declares: "The liabilities of the
partnership shall rank in order of payment, as follows:

"I. Those owing to creditors other than partners,
"II. Those owing to partners other than for capital and
       profits,
"III. Those owing to partners in respect of capital,
"IV. Those owing to partners in respect of profits."

No particular difficulty is present in the distribution of a partnership's assets if the firm is solvent. As indicated previously the
partners share equally in the profits, unless their partnership
agreement provides otherwise.

If a partnership is insolvent but the partners are solvent in
their individual estates, the partners must contribute funds sufficient to satisfy the claims of partnership creditors. The losses

must be shared equally, unless the partners have agreed otherwise.

If both the partnership and one or more of the partners are insolvent, the rival claims of the creditors of the partnership and the creditors of the individual partners are subject to the general rule that firm creditors have first claim on firm assets and individual creditors have first claim on individual assets.

Corporations: Nature, Creation and Termination

29

INTRODUCTION

Predominance of the Corporation

Modern industrial enterprises are usually incorporated, and persons engaged in economic activity in general often find it advantageous to use the corporate form of business organization. The business corporation is the predominant institution of the private sector of our economy. Studies conducted have revealed that corporations in the United States today generate more than one half of the national income in the form of wages and salaries, interest and dividend payments, tax payments, and retained earnings. The corporations in this country provide jobs for more than 30 million people, almost as many as all other forms of business, professional, farm, and government employment combined. There are more than 1 million corporations in the United States, and they account for more than 90 per cent of the sales in the manufacturing, transportation, and utilities industries; more than 75 per cent in finance, insurance, real estate, wholesale trade, and mining; and more than 50 per cent in retail trade and construction. Only in farming and a miscellaneous group of services does the corporation play a minor role.

History

Prior to 1600, the corporate device was used primarily by nonprofit groups such as churches and by eleemosynary organizations devoted to charitable and educational causes. Local governmental units such as the towns in England were also incorporated at an early date. During the period of exploration and colonization in the new world, important foreign trading companies were chartered by the Crown or by special acts of Parliament in England. Familiar to students of economic history are the East India Company, chartered in 1600; the Hudson Bay Company, chartered in 1670; and similar trading companies which were organized in England to exercise monopolistic trading privileges and, at the same time, perform functions of a governmental nature in the newly established colonies abroad.

The first business corporations in the United States were chartered by special state legislation, but abuses of this method led to adoption of general statutes under which corporations could be formed. The forerunners in the adoption of such general enabling legislation were North Carolina (1795), Massachusetts (1799), and New York (1811). Today, each state has a general corporation act under which most businesses may be incorporated, not as a matter of special privilege granted by the legislature, but on the basis of complying with the procedure prescribed in the statute. Major revisions in the state corporation acts have occurred from time to time. For example, in New York a new Business Corporation Law went into effect September 1, 1963. Certain special types of businesses such as banks, savings and loan associations, insurance companies, and railroads are incorporated in most states under separate state corporation acts designed for such businesses. Non-profit corporations are usually chartered under a non-profit corporation act.

The state corporation statutes are not uniform, but they do follow a general pattern. The Commissioners on Uniform State Laws proposed a Uniform Business Corporation Act in 1928 which was subsequently adopted by four states, and many states patterned some provisions of their corporation acts after parts of the uniform act. It was later decided that uniformity in the various states with respect to corporation law was not essential and the designation of the uniform act was changed to model act. Subsequently, the American Bar Association and others sponsored the drafting of the Model Business Corporation Act which has been adopted or is the basis for the business corporation act in several states and continues to influence legislation in other states. As a result of this development, the Commissioners withdrew their model act.

In those states which have adopted the Uniform Commercial Code (see Chapter 1, page 14 for a list of adopting states to date), Article 8 of the Code replaces existing statutes governing the transfer of corporation shares of stock, including the Uniform Stock Transfer Act.

NATURE OF CORPORATION

The idea of a corporation as a fictitious legal person, distinct from the human beings who compose it, can be traced to the ancient civilizations where evidence of definite conceptions of group existence separate from the members making up the group can be found.

In 1819, Chief Justice Marshall defined a corporation as an "artificial being, invisible, intangible and existing only in contemplation of law." [1] A corporation is recognized by law as having an existence separate and apart from the individuals who create and own it, even where all the stock of a corporation is owned by one individual. This concept of the corporation as a distinct legal entity is at the heart of the prevailing rule that generally shareholders are not personally liable on the debts of the corporation. Rights, duties, and other legal relations arising out of the enterprise are adjusted as though the corporation

---

[1] *Trustees of Dartmouth College v. Woodward* 4 Wheat. 517, 4 L. Ed. 629 (1819).

were a separate entity. The shareholders have in theory only an indirect interest in the assets of the corporation, which is manifested in their right to share in dividends and in the distribution of corporate assets on liquidation. As a legal person, a corporation may, in its own name, enter into contracts; own, buy and sell property; sue and be sued. The separateness of the corporation is also generally recognized for tax purposes, the corporation being considered a "tax entity."

Corporations may claim the protection afforded to persons by certain provisions of the Federal Constitution, but corporations are not generally permitted to assert constitutional safeguards set up for the protection of citizens. For example, courts treat a corporation as a person under the "due process" and "equal protection" clauses of the Fourteenth Amendment, but a corporation cannot claim the "privileges and immunities" benefit accorded citizens under Article 4, Section 2 of the Constitution. Therefore, unlike a natural person, it does not have a constitutional right to do business in any state it chooses without first complying with the foreign corporation statutes of each foreign state in which it proposes to do business. However, a corporation is a citizen of the state in which it is incorporated for the purpose of applying the diversity of citizenship requirement in civil actions brought in the Federal courts as described in Chapter 2.

EFFECT OF WRONGFUL USE OF CORPORATION

While courts generally adhere to the concept that the corporation has a legal identity separate from that of the shareholders who own and control it, the separateness of the corporation entity and the shareholders will be disregarded in cases where the corporate device is used as a cloak for fraud, or to avoid a legal obligation, or to gain an unjust advantage. In such cases justice requires that the "corporate veil be pierced" and that the individual members be held personally liable to the injured third persons for the obligations of the corporation. A common illustration is the case of a person who sells his business and agrees in the contract with the buyer to refrain from competing with the buyer in the same neighborhood for ten years. The seller could not escape his restrictive covenant by forming a corporation to carry on a business in competition with the buyer.

In cases where it is found that a parent corporation has completely dominated a subsidiary and has used it as a shield for wrongdoing, courts will refuse to recognize the separateness of the two corporations and will hold the parent liable for the acts and debts of the subsidiary.

Creation of a corporation for the purpose of obtaining limited liability for the shareholders is not illegal per se. Some wrongful use of the corporate device must be present before a court will disregard the separateness of the corporation and the shareholders.

ADVANTAGES OF THE CORPORATION

Reference was made in Chapter 26 to some of the advantages and disadvantages of the corporate form of business organization as compared to the other forms, especially the partnership. The traditional advantages of the corporation are summarized as follows: (1) *Limited Liability*. The liability of a shareholder for debts of the corporation, and therefore his risk, is limited to the amount he pays for his shares. (2) *Management*. The management of the business can be centralized in a board of directors thereby permitting selection of experts as managers of the business, irrespective of whether they are shareholders, and the exclusion from management of shareholders who do not possess desired skills or experience. (3) *Continuity*. The corporate enterprise can have continuous existence, that is, the business organization is not dissolved by the death, insanity, or withdrawal of an owner. (4) *Transferability*. An interest in the business, evidenced by a stock certificate, is freely transferable, thus usually permitting a dissatisfied owner to withdraw from the enterprise easily without serious financial loss. (5) *Capital.* Capital can be attracted in large amounts and usually more readily than is possible when some other type of organization is used. There are or may be also, from time to time, depending upon the applicable laws, numerous advantages, and also some disadvantages from the standpoint of taxation, but no attempt is made here to deal with this subject.

CLASSES OF CORPORATIONS

General Classifications

Corporations are broadly classified as (1) corporations for profit, (2) corporations not for profit, and (3) governmental corporations. The corporations in the first two classes are often described as private corporations and those in the third class as public corporations.

Profit. A corporation for profit is the ordinary business corporation which is operated to make a profit and which issues stock to shareholders who anticipate that profits will be distributed to them as dividends. The corporation for profit, often called private business corporation, will be discussed primarily in this book.

Nonprofit. Nonprofit corporations generally serve some religious, charitable, social or educational purpose and include churches, lodges, clubs, schools, and similar groups or institutions not operated for the purpose of making a profit. Nonprofit corporations are private in nature and do not ordinarily issue stock, membership being acquired by being admitted as a member pursuant to the constitution and bylaws of the organization. States generally have a nonprofit corporation act separate from the general corporation act under which corporations for profit are chartered.

Governmental. Governmental corporations, also called public corporations, are organized under state or federal law for governmental purposes. Municipalities are incorporated under state laws. Congress has created a number of corporations to carry out specific federal functions. Examples include the Federal Deposit Insurance Corporation, The Tennessee Valley Authority, and the Commodity Credit Corporation. A recent example is the Communications Satellite Corporation created by Congress in 1962.

Domestic and Foreign Corporations

A corporation is a domestic corporation with respect to that state under whose laws it is incorporated. It is a foreign corporation in every other state. Thus, a corporation chartered in New York is a domestic corporation in New York, but in all other states it is a foreign corporation. Similarly, a corporation created under the law of one nation is a foreign or alien corporation in other countries.

Regulation of Foreign Corporations. Foreign corporations must comply with the foreign corporation statutes of each state in which they do business. Although doing business in a state has not been clearly defined, it is broadly defined as carrying on intrastate business as opposed to interstate business and requires some regularity and continuity of activity within the state rather than casual or isolated transactions. The Model Foreign Corporation Act and the statutes of many states set forth basic principles and specific examples which can be used as a guide in determining what does and does not constitute doing business in a state.

A foreign corporation doing business in a state is required to obtain a license from that state, comply with regulations, pay taxes and fees, and submit to the jurisdiction of the courts in suits brought against it within the state. Failure to obtain the required license subjects a foreign corporation to penalties prescribed by the statutes of the foreign state. These penalties may take the form of fines levied against the corporation or its officers, directors, or agents; a ban against the corporation doing business within the state; the corporation is usually denied the right to sue in the courts of the state to enforce contracts made there; and, in some cases, the officers, directors and stockholders may be held liable as partners on all intrastate business.

The extent or nature of a foreign corporation's activity or presence within a state may be sufficient to subject it to suit in the state's courts or to subject it to certain taxes, without the corporation's being required to comply with the foreign corporation licensing statute of the state.

INCORPORATION

Choice of State of Incorporation

If an enterprise plans to do business within one state, it will probably be incorporated in the state in which its activities are to be confined, particularly if the corporation is to be a small closely held one. The organizers of a corporation which plans to operate interstate and, thus take on a national character, with perhaps a public offering of stock, will incorporate in the state which has corporation statutes best suited to the purposes of the proposed corporations.

Deciding where to incorporate is based on three primary considerations: (1) liberality of the state's corporation law with respect to giving the managers of a corporation freedom of action, especially in regard to the financing of the corporation; (2) cost of incorporating and maintaining a corporation in the particular state, including initial fees and annual franchise fees and taxes; and (3) stability of the state's corporation law in terms of being able to predict with reasonable certainty the legality of any course of action the corporation may wish to take. Historically, the state of Delaware has provided corporation statutes attractive to those seeking a state in which to incorporate a business. As a result, almost one third of all the corporations listed on the New York Stock Exchange are Delaware-chartered corporations, and it is estimated they account for probably half of the value of all shares listed on the New York Stock Exchange.

If incorporation is contemplated in a state other than the one where the corporation is to carry on its business, it is, of course, necessary to determine the cost of qualifying as a foreign corporation in the state where it will be doing business.

Incorporation Procedure

A corporation is a "creature of statute." This means that a corporation can only be formed by compliance with requirements set forth in the corporation statutes of the state where the corporation is being organized.

Articles of Incorporation. The basic incorporation document is called the "articles of incorporation." In some states this document is called the "certificate of incorporation" and is referred to generally as the "charter." The articles must be executed by the incorporators and filed with a specified state official, usually the Secretary of State. Upon the filing and approval of the articles and payment of the required fee, the legal existence of the corporation usually commences, and a certificate or some kind of document is issued by the state official to indicate the incorporation has occurred. Some states require local recording of the articles in addition to their filing with the designated state official. Public notice of the incorporation is required in some states.

The usual provisions of the articles describe the name of the corporation; the address of the principal place of business within the state; the object and purposes of the corporation; the capital structure, that is, the total number of shares the corporation is authorized to issue, the classes of stock, whether shares are to be with par value or no par value; the minimum capital with which the corporation will commence business; the duration of the corporation (usually perpetual); the designation of an agent to receive service of legal papers for the corporation; and the names and addresses of the incorporators. In some states the names of those persons who are to serve as directors until the first meeting of stockholders must be included in the articles. Each state specifies the minimum contents of the articles, and generally the organizers are permitted to include such other provisions as they desire, provided they are not contrary to law. Changes in the provisions of the articles must be made by the process of amending the articles in accordance with formalities prescribed by statute.

Incorporators. Generally there must be three or more incorporators who are natural persons of lawful age and at least a majority of whom are citizens of the United States. The incorporators may or may not also be promoters of the corporation, and in most states they need not be subscribers to the stock of the corporation. As a matter of fact, the incorporators often are mere "dummies" who play no other role in relation to the corporation, stepping aside and turning the newly formed corporation over to the shareholders who proceed to complete the organization and control the operation of the corporation.

Completing Corporate Organization

After the corporation charter has been duly filed with the state, organization meetings are held and other steps are taken to complete the structure of the corporation and to put it into operation as a business enterprise. This procedure usually embraces such matters as obtaining subscriptions to shares and issuing of stock, meetings of the incorporators and stockholders, adoption of bylaws, election of directors, meetings of the board of directors, election of officers and fixing of their salaries, adoption of pre-incorporation contracts made by promoters, and authorization of payment of expenses of incorporation. Care must be taken to comply with the state statutes and provisions of the articles of incorporation with respect to giving proper notice to those entitled to receive notice of the various organization meetings unless waivers of notice are obtained.

Promoters

Function. A promoter is a person who engages in activities necessary to create a corporation. Typical activities of promoters include planning the organization of the corporation, soliciting subscriptions to stock, negotiating and contracting for property and employees, preparation of the articles of incorporation, and performing all other functions involved in the pre-incorporation process. Established principles of law govern the relationship of the promoter, third persons, and the corporation, and their rights and duties with respect to one another.

Fiduciary Relationship. Promoters stand in a fiduciary or trust relationship toward the proposed corporation, to their fellow promoters, and to those who subscribe to the stock of the corporation. As a fiduciary, promoters owe a duty of utmost good faith to the corporation being promoted and to those involved therein. This duty requires a promoter to make a full disclosure of all the material facts and circumstances relating to any property he transfers to the corporation; and he will be liable for any loss suffered by the corporation and the interested parties if he takes a secret profit.

Promoters often receive shares of stock from the newly formed corporation in exchange for property transferred to the corporation by the promoter or for services rendered by the promoter. Where the promoter is issued fully-paid shares with a certain par value and the promoter has not paid the full par value of the stock because the consideration for the shares was overvalued, the promoter's stock is said to be "watered." A similar scheme of overvaluation of assets and stock can occur with respect to no par shares. In such cases, the promoter has breached his fiduciary duty and will be held liable to the corporation, to existing creditors of the corporation, and to subscribers and stockholders injured by the promoter's fraud. However, the fiduciary relation of the promoter does not extend down to future shareholders and future creditors. It is in this way that promoters are sometimes able to obtain overvalued or "watered" stock and enjoy a "windfall" by selling it to anyone who will buy it at the price set by the seller. Any liability of the promoter arising out of such subsequent sales must be based on a showing of fraud in accordance with the common-law principles which govern actions for fraud. State and federal securities laws, known as "blue sky" laws, provide a substantial measure of protection to the public from the fraudulent manipulation of stock by promoters and corporation insiders.

Compensation and Reimbursement. Promoters are not entitled to receive compensation for their services or reimbursement for their expenses incurred in behalf of the proposed corporation in the absence of express agreement. It behooves a promoter to arrange for his compensation and reimbursement by contract with those for whom the promoting work is done. Otherwise, the promoter will have to depend upon the newly formed corporation's agreeing to compensate and reimburse him. As a general rule, a promoter has a right of action against his fellow promoters for contribution for the legitimate expenses of the promotion; but he has no right, in the absence of express contract, to hold other promoters liable for remuneration.

Liability on Pre-Incorporation Contracts. Promoters are not agents of the corporation they are promoting, since no principal exists until the corporation is created. Therefore, the corporation is not liable on pre-incorporation contracts made for it by promoters, unless it adopts such contracts either by express action of the board of directors or by implication after the corporation is chartered. Implied adoption is manifested by a corporation receiving and accepting the benefits of a pre-incorporation contract.

Courts have generally held the promoter liable on a pre-incorporation contract whether the contract was made in the name of the promoter or in the name of the proposed corporation, provided there was no clear indication of intention that the promoter was not to be liable. Adoption of the contract by the corporation does not by itself relieve the promoter of liability, and the release of the promoter by the corporation does not relieve the promoter from his liability to the other contracting party unless the latter consents.

DE JURE AND DE FACTO CORPORATIONS

De Jure Corporations.   If the incorporators fully or substantially meet all the mandatory requirements under the statutes of the state in which a business is incorporated, the corporation is called a corporation *de jure,* meaning that it is a corporation as a matter of law. Minor defects in the incorporation do not prevent a corporation from having a de jure existence. The existence of a de jure corporation is not subject to attack even in a direct action by the state.

De Facto Corporations.   Deviation from the prescribed legal procedure for incorporation may be so substantial that a corporation is not de jure, nevertheless, there may be sufficient compliance with the law to create, as to third persons, a *de facto* corporation, that is, one existing in fact. The requirements for a de facto corporation are (1) a valid statute under which the corporation could have been properly organized; (2) a good faith attempt by the incorporators to comply with the statute; and (3) use of the corporate powers granted by the charter.

The legal existence of a de facto corporation is not subject to collateral attack. This means that in a suit to which the corporation is a party neither party will be permitted to escape liability by setting up the invalidity of the corporation's existence arising out of some technical defect in its incorporation. The shareholders of a de facto corporation usually enjoy limited liability. The de facto corporation is subject to direct attack by the state in a quo warranto proceeding brought by the Attorney General to revoke the corporation's charter because of the defects. As long as the state permits a de facto corporation to exist, the corporation has all of the rights, privileges, and responsibilities of a de jure corporation. Requiring all corporations to be de jure would not serve the public interest.

If any of the three requirements for a de facto corporation are not satisfied, the persons who purport to operate the business as a corporation will generally be held liable as partners to third parties. In some cases courts have applied the principles of estoppel in order to prevent a party from unfairly escaping liability by asserting that a corporation did not have a legal existence.

DISSOLUTION AND TERMINATION

The dissolution of a corporation terminates its corporate existence, except that the statutes which govern dissolution generally provide that for a fixed period of time the corporation continues for the limited purpose of winding up its affairs. Winding up includes the collection and payment of claims, the sale of assets, the bringing and defending of suits, and similar transactions, but the dissolved corporation must not engage in new business.

Dissolution of a corporation may result from (1) voluntary surrender of its charter; (2) expiration of the time limit specified in its charter; (3) judicial or involuntary dissolution upon suit by minority stockholders or by creditors; (4) forfeiture of its charter; (5) repeal of charter by the state, if such right was reserved to the state; and (6) merger, consolidation, or reorganization.

Surrender of Charter. The shareholders and officers may voluntarily dissolve the corporation and surrender its charter to the state by following the procedure prescribed in the statutes of the state of incorporation.

Expiration of Term. If the corporation charter specifies that the corporation is to continue for a certain period of time or until the happening of some named event, the corporation is automatically dissolved upon the expiration of the stated period or happening of the stated event. Most corporations have a perpetual existence as provided for in the corporation statutes of today. If a corporation charter expires, a renewal of the old charter or obtaining a new charter can prevent interruption of the business of the corporation.

Suit by Stockholders. Corporation statutes in each state usually describe causes for which a corporation may be dissolved upon petition to a court by minority stockholders, and, in some cases, by creditors. The procedure to be followed is set out in the statutes and provision is made for the appointment of a receiver to administer the property and affairs of the corporation for the benefit of all the interested parties.

Forfeiture of Charter. Statutes prescribe the grounds of forfeiture whereby the Attorney General of the state of incorporation may bring a quo warranto proceeding in the name of the state to have a corporation's charter cancelled. Typical grounds of forfeiture are failure of a corporation to use its charter, misuse by the corporation of its powers, nonpayment of taxes, and failure to file reports required by state statutes.

Repeal of Charter. If the state reserves the right to repeal a corporation's charter, either by statute or by state constitutional provision, the state may dissolve the corporation by repeal of its charter. In exercising the right of repeal, the state must not impair vested rights, such as the stockholders' and creditors' rights in the assets of the corporation. In the absence of a reservation to the state of a right to repeal a corporation's charter, no right to repeal exists; because the charter is not viewed as a mere license or privilege but rather a contract between the state and the corporation, the obligations of which cannot be impaired by unilateral act of the state.

Merger, Consolidation, Reorganization. Merger of two corporations occurs when one surrenders its charter and merges with the other corporation. In a consolidation of two or more corporations, all the corporations surrender their charters and are consolidated into a new corporation. Reorganization of a corporation usually refers to insolvency proceedings under the federal bankruptcy laws. The reorganization of a corporation does not necessarily result in its dissolution.

Corporation Powers
and Liabilities

30

POWERS AND LIMITATIONS

General Powers

The articles of incorporation of a corporation and the statutes under which it is incorporated each contain an express enumeration of powers the corporation may exercise in the carrying on of activities incidental to its corporate existence. In addition to its express powers, a corporation has those implied powers which are reasonably necessary and proper for carrying out its express powers. The early rule applicable to the interpretation of the extent of the powers conferred upon the corporation was that the powers should be strictly construed. This view has given way to a more liberal interpretation of a corporation's express and implied powers.

The principal powers granted to corporations by statute or recognized as existing by necessity include the power (1) to have a name; (2) to have a corporate seal; (3) to have perpetual existence; (4) to provide for its financing, management and operation under bylaws and through various officers and agents; (5) to sue and be sued; (6) to make contracts; and

(7) to acquire and transfer property in order to carry out the purposes of the corporation.

General Limitations

The powers of a corporation are limited by statutes and by the statement of the corporation's purposes contained in the articles of incorporation. Unlike a natural person who has the inherent power to do any act not prohibited by law, a corporation, being a creature of the state, possesses only the powers granted to it by the state. Also, the fact that a corporation is an artificial creature of the law and not a natural person precludes it from engaging in certain human activities such as, for example, marriage and voting. Of course, corporations do merge with one another and they lobby for legislation, so, in a sense, corporations engage in some activities generally thought of as peculiar to natural persons.

Purpose Limitations

The statement of purposes in the articles of incorporation acts as a self-imposed limitation on the powers of the corporation in that it defines the type of business the corporation will conduct. Any transaction engaged in by the corporation must be reasonably related to the purpose and business of the corporation. For example, a corporation which describes its purpose as the operation of an automobile dealership would not have the power to operate a bakery.

Professional Service Corporations. State law traditionally has prohibited corporations from having as their purpose the practice of a profession such as, for example, law, medicine, dentistry, or accounting. The view is held that the public interest requires that such professionals be restricted to natural persons who obtain a license granted on the basis of their education, skill, and character.

Recently more than half the states have enacted legislation to let groups of doctors and other professionals form corporations or associations taxable as corporations. The main appeal of these new state laws is that practitioners, as corporation employees, would owe no income tax on income set aside in United States Treasury approved retirement plans until paid back to them as benefits. When the professional service corporation statutes were enacted, the states kept in mind the public policy considerations which had previously caused the corporate form to be considered unsuitable for professional practice. Therefore, the state legislatures modified the corporate form for professional use in order to safeguard the traditional relationships between the professional and his clients, the public, and other professionals. In some states, for example, a professional service corporation does not provide limited liability for its shareholders. Thus, such a professional service corporation is a hybrid and not a true corporation. Serious questions have been raised about the legality and propriety of legislation permitting lawyers to practice law as a corporation.

Name Limitations

Name. The name selected for a corporation must not infringe upon the name of an existing corporation or mislead the public. Usually, the name of the corporation must end with or include the word Company, Corporation, Incorporated, or an abbreviation thereof. The purpose of this requirement is to give notice to the public that the business is incorporated. Statutes generally prohibit the use of such words as "Bank," "Trust," "Insurance," etc., in the name of a corporation chartered under a general corporation statute. Such words are reserved for use in the names of corporations formed under special statutes making provision for incorporation of enterprises engaged in the type of activity suggested by the particular word. A change in the name of a corporation is effected by amendment to the articles of incorporation.

Specific Powers

Bylaws. The shareholders of a corporation generally have the power to adopt and change bylaws. In many states, the articles of incorporation may delegate to the board of directors the authority to adopt, amend, and repeal bylaws. Bylaws complete the corporate structure by providing rules for the regulation and management of the corporation's internal affairs, and usually include such things as the time and place and manner of conducting meetings of shareholders and directors, the powers and duties of officers, and how shares are to be transferred.

Bylaws of a corporation are invalid if they conflict with the articles of incorporation, the constitution, or statutes of the state of incorporation, and they must not violate the vested rights of stockholders. Valid bylaws are binding upon the stockholders, directors, and officers regardless of whether they know of their existence or were among the majority who approved them. Bylaws are not binding on third persons unless they have knowledge or notice of their content. Third persons are presumed to have knowledge of the provisions of a corporation's articles for the reason that the articles are, unlike a corporation's bylaws, a matter of public record.

Property Transactions. A corporation generally has in relation to the carrying out of its lawful purposes the power to purchase or otherwise acquire, lease as lessor or lessee, encumber, sell, exchange, transfer, hold as trustee, and dispose of property or any interest therein. In some states there are statutory or constitutional limitations and restrictions imposed on the corporate ownership of property, especially real estate.

A corporation may make reasonable donations for the public welfare or for charitable, scientific, or educational purposes. A sale of the corporation's entire assets is generally governed by statutes which typically require consent of all or a substantial majority of the corporation's shareholders.

Guaranty Contracts. In the absence of express authority contained in its articles, a corporation does not generally have the power to act as a surety or guarantor, or an accommodation party. Such power exists where the guaranty takes the form of indorsement on negotiable paper in furtherance of the corporation's business or where the lending of its credit to another is incidental to the carrying out of its purposes.

Membership in Partnerships and Joint Ventures. Express authority in its articles is necessary before a corporation can enter into a partnership, but a corporation may participate in a joint venture, in connection with the corporation's business, without express authority. The rule against participation in a partnership is based on the idea that a partner could expose the corporation to wide-ranging liability, contrary to the concept of the management of the corporation resting with its directors and officers.

Borrowing. Borrowing money is within the power of a corporation, either express or implied, where it is necessary for the conduct of the corporation's business. The corporation may pledge or mortgage its property to secure the repayment of borrowed money and issue promissory notes and bonds in connection with its borrowing transactions. Stockholder approval may be required before certain obligations against the corporation can be created. The authority question must be resolved in each instance on the basis of an examination of the relevant statutes and provisions of the articles and bylaws of the corporation.

Stock Acquisitions. Corporation codes generally authorize corporations to become the owner of shares of another corporation where such an acquisition furthers the objectives of the acquiring corporation. Through such stock acquisitions a corporation is able to act as a holding company which controls the other company, and it may create operating or subsidiary companies which it can control unless contrary to statutes such as the antitrust laws or public utility holding company laws.

As a general rule, a solvent corporation has the power to purchase its own stock, but such purchases must be made from surplus and must not impair the rights of stockholders or creditors. A corporation may receive its stock as a gift or in payment of a debt. Reacquired stock is called treasury stock, and, unless cancelled, is treated as still being issued or outstanding. Treasury stock may be resold by the corporation at any price it will bring, not being subject to the rule that an original issue of shares cannot be sold for less than par, and it may be issued in connection with profit-sharing or incentive plans, or as part of a stock dividend. As treasury stock, the shares cannot be voted by the corporation, nor can dividends be declared on them.

ULTRA VIRES ACTS

Definition

Any act of a corporation that goes beyond the powers given to it by the state is an *ultra vires* act. The term is a Latin one which means "beyond the powers."

Effect of Ultra Vires Contracts

Court decisions and corporation statutes no longer treat all ultra vires transactions of corporations as necessarily illegal and thus void. A contract of a corporation may be ultra vires, yet not be illegal in the sense of being contrary to the public welfare. Naturally, any illegal contract a corporation might make would also be ultra vires and its effect would ordinarily be determined on the basis of principles of law relating to illegal contracts in general as discussed in Chapter 8.

While courts are not in agreement on the effect of an ultra vires contract which is not also illegal in the sense of being against the public interest, the following generalizations have been made with respect to the rights of the parties to the ultra vires contract.

1] If the contract is fully executed, both parties having completed their performances, the court will not interfere and will refuse to grant relief to either party, leaving the parties where it finds them.

2] If the contract is wholly executory, neither party having performed, either party may escape liability by raising the defense of ultra vires to a suit by the other party.

3] If the contract is fully executed by only one of the parties, there is a conflict of authority as to the legal effect of the contract, but most state courts hold that the party who has rendered performance may recover upon the contract. Permitting the defendant to raise the defense of ultra vires and thereby retain the performance he has received and to refuse to perform on his part would be inequitable and work a hardship. In some states the party who has performed can recover in quasi contract but not on the contract itself. This requires the other party to pay the reasonable value of what he has received or return it. This rule has been followed by the federal courts as well as a minority of the state courts.

Since a corporation charter is a contract between the corporation and the state of incorporation and between the corporation and its stockholders and the corporation has impliedly agreed to stay within its powers, ultra vires acts are a breach of contract and provide a basis for objection by the state and the stockholders. The state may bring suit in equity to obtain an injunction against the commission of ultra vires acts, or, in an aggravated or extreme case, ask in a quo warranto proceeding that the charter of the corporation be forfeited. Stockholders may enjoin a corporation from performing an ultra vires act, and the directors and officers responsible for the commission of an ultra vires act which causes loss to the corporation may be held personally liable to the corporation for such loss.

LIABILITIES OF CORPORATIONS

Contracts

Due to their artificial nature and lack of any physical existence, corporations must necessarily act through their agents in making contracts and performing all the acts necessary for the conduct of the corporation's business. The contractual liability of the corporation is determined on the basis of the general principles of contract law and agency law, with the added consideration of those legal principles governing the powers of a corporation, including the doctrine of ultra vires.

Torts

A corporation is liable in the same manner as a natural principal or employer for the torts of its officers, agents, and servants committed in the course and within the scope of the employment. The doctrine of ultra vires cannot be invoked by a corporation as defense in order to defeat liability for an injury resulting from the tort of its agent or employee. The authority of the agent of a corporation can be express, implied, or apparent. The tort liability of a corporation extends to such torts as deceit, negligence, nuisance, trespass, assault and battery, false imprisonment, conspiracy, libel and slander.

Crimes

The generally accepted modern rule is that a corporation may be held liable for the criminal acts of its officers, agents, and employees; except that a corporation is incapable of committing those crimes which have as one of their elements the requirement of criminal intent or which involve an act of personal violence.

Many state and federal statutes are directed against the criminal activities of corporations as well as natural persons. Examples include provisions of the antitrust laws, the unemployment and workmen's compensation laws, the Securities Acts of 1933 and 1934, tax laws, and the Bankruptcy Act. All these and similar laws impose duties upon corporations to do, or not to do, certain acts, and criminal penalties are specified for failure to comply with the law. Of course, a corporation cannot be punished by imprisonment, but it can be subjected to the fine provided for in nearly all criminal statutes.

Corporation Management and Finance

31

MANAGEMENT

Directors

Function and Powers. The determination of the basic policies related to the carrying on of the usual and ordinary operations of a corporation is vested in the board of directors elected by the shareholders. The powers of the directors may be described in the articles and will include the authority to appoint officers, to make contracts, to declare dividends, and to act generally as agents and managers of the corporation business. The directors act for the shareholders but they are not their agents since they are not under the control of the shareholders in the sense a principal controls his agent. The shareholders indirectly reflect their wishes concerning the management policies of the corporation by exercising their right to elect the members of the board of directors. A direct control over the affairs of the corporation rests with the shareholders in the requirement that fundamental changes in the corporation and unusual or extraordinary transactions be approved by the shareholders. Corporation statutes often require that amendments to the articles of incorporation to change the name, purpose, powers, or capital structure of the corporation must be approved by the holders of two-thirds or in some states three-fourths, of the voting stock of the corporation. Similar consent of the shareholders is usually necessary to sell all the assets of the corporation or to effect a merger or consolidation, or to dissolve or reorganize the corporation. Except for such basic matters affecting the rights of shareholders, there is an increasing trend to place more and more management control and discretion over the affairs of corporations in the hands of the directors. The duties of a director involve skill and discretion and, therefore, cannot be delegated by the directors to others.

Qualifications, Election, Removal, Compensation. Directors generally need not be residents of the state of incorporation or shareholders of the corporation unless the articles of incorporation or bylaws so require. In some states a director must own at least one share of stock in the corporation. The articles or bylaws may prescribe other qualifications for directors. Nearly all states provide by statute that a minimum of three directors is required and only a few states specify the maximum permitted. Within these statutory limits the articles or bylaws of a corporation may establish the exact number of directors.

Directors are elected by the stockholders. However, under the corporation statutes of several states the first board of directors must be named in the articles of incorporation. The state may require, or the articles may permit, a shareholder to cumulate his votes for directors as explained in Chapter 32. The articles or bylaws may establish the term of office of the directors, but they remain in office until their successors are elected and qualified.

The shareholders may remove a director for cause such as fraud or neglect of duty. Improper removal of a director will subject the corporation to liability for breach of contract. Directors may not remove a fellow director who has been elected by the shareholders unless the power of removal is expressly conferred on the directors in the articles or in the bylaws. The articles or bylaws usually provide for removal of directors in accordance with the provisions of the statute. Directors are free to resign from office when they please. A vacancy in the board may be filled by the other members pending the holding of a meeting of the shareholders to elect a director to fill the vacancy.

The general rule is that directors are not entitled to compensation for exercising their regular duties as directors. However, it is customary for directors to receive some compensation as well as reimbursement for expenses incurred in attending meetings. If a director performs services for the corporation which are not within the normal scope of his duties as director, he is entitled to a reasonable compensation. In many cases a director also serves as an officer for which he is compensated. Generally the directors cannot fix their own salaries unless authorized by the articles, bylaws, or shareholders. The shareholders may authorize the payment of compensation to the directors and, in many cases, the directors are authorized by the articles or bylaws to fix their own compensation.

Meetings of Directors. The directors of a corporation must ordinarily act as a board or body and not individually in making management decisions for the corporation. Thus, the separate and individual action of one or more, even all, of the directors is not the action of the board and will not be effective unless subsequently ratified at a meeting of the board. A director may not vote by proxy at a board meeting.

Meetings of the directors may be held within or without the state of incorporation unless the articles or bylaws provide otherwise. The bylaws usually specify the time and place of the regular meetings of the board of directors and no notice of such meetings is required. Notice to each director of the time, place, and purposes of special meetings is generally required. Defects in the notice procedure followed in calling a board of directors' meeting may be waived by the directors. A quorum for a valid directors' meeting consists of a majority of the number of directors specified in the articles or bylaws as composing the board. The articles or bylaws may state what constitutes a quorum.

Liability of Directors.   Directors assume a fiduciary obligation to the corporation when they take office and owe a duty of utmost good faith and loyalty in the performance of their duties as directors. Occupying positions of trust, directors are required to deal with the corporation's property and conduct its business with prudence and good faith. While directors are not personally liable for losses caused by their honest mistakes of business judgment as long as they exercise reasonable care and skill, the board or the individual directors may be liable for losses incurred by the corporation, shareholders, or, in some cases, creditors, if the losses result from the directors neglect of duty, negligence in the performance of their duty, bad faith, or fraud.

A director who has a personal interest in a transaction entered into by the corporation has the burden of showing that the transaction was proper and not unfair to the corporation. Generally, this means that a director must refrain from participating in the consideration by the board of directors of a matter in which the director has a financial interest, and he must make a full disclosure of any facts concerned with the transaction. It is a breach of a director's fiduciary duty of loyalty for a director to receive a secret profit at the expense of the corporation or shareholders or to place himself in a position where his personal interest would prevent him from acting for the best interests of the corporation or the shareholders.

Directors are personally liable to the corporation for any losses caused to it by the directors knowingly and intentionally entering into *ultra vires* transactions. Shareholders may ratify an *ultra vires* transaction, if the transaction is not illegal. Directors may be held liable to creditors for knowingly paying an unlawful dividend to the shareholders. Statutes often contain provisions covering the liability of directors, and some statutes make provision for a director to save himself from liability, in certain cases, by recording his dissent to action taken at a meeting of the board of directors or by absenting himself from the meeting.

Officers

Officers in General. In most states the corporation statutes require that a corporation have a president, secretary, and treasurer and authorize the corporation to have vice-presidents and such other officers, assistant officers, managers, and agents as it may desire. It is common for a large corporation to have all of the above officers as well as a chairman of the board of directors. Each of the vice-presidents is often placed in charge of some important department or division of the corporation, such as production, sales, public relations, legal, labor relations, and the like.

The officers of a corporation are generally appointed by the board of directors at its annual meeting for one-year terms. It is required by statute in most states that the president also be a director, and it is common, but not necessary, for the other officers to serve also on the board of directors. Within limitations specified by statute or the bylaws, an officer may hold more than one office. The officers, unlike directors, are entitled to receive reasonable compensation for the performance of their official duties. Generally the directors fix the salaries and other compensation of the officers, but, in some cases, they are referred to the shareholders for approval. If the compensation paid to officers is excessive, that is, it bears no reasonable relation to the value of services rendered, the shareholders may bring suit to have the compensation reduced.

Authority of Officers. Most state statutes do not set out in detail the authority and duties of officers, leaving that matter to be determined in the bylaws or by the board of directors. Of course, the board of directors cannot delegate to the officers any of its policy-making functions, such as the authority to declare dividends.

Corporate officers are agents and their authority, like that of agents generally, may be (1) actual (express or implied), or (2) apparent, or (3) derived from ratification.

Express authority stems from statute, the articles of incorporation, or, most frequently, from bylaws and the resolutions of the board of directors.

Implied authority is present by virtue of the function of a particular office and arises from general custom, the practice of the particular corporation, or as incidental to express authority.

Apparent authority, also called ostensible authority, often arises by estoppel, as where a corporation clothes an officer or agent with apparent authority, which is reasonably relied upon in good faith by third persons, the corporation is estopped from denying such authority. Where there is apparent authority, the absence of actual authority, express or implied, is immaterial.

Unauthorized acts of officers which could have been previously authorized by the board of directors may be thereafter ratified by the board. Ratification may be express, such as a resolution of the board of directors approving the transaction, or ratification may be implied. An implied ratification usually results from acceptance of benefits with knowledge of the facts.

Third persons are bound by limitations imposed upon the authority of corporate officers by the articles of incorporation, but limitations on authority contained in the bylaws or resolutions of the board of directors are not binding upon third persons unless they have notice or knowledge of the limitations. This distinction is made because the provisions of the articles are matters of public record while the bylaws and directors' resolutions are not.

Liability of Officers. The duties owed by corporate officers and agents to the corporation are essentially the same as those of directors and agents generally. Like the directors, the officers are fiduciaries in relation to the corporation. Thus, they are liable to the corporation for any secret profit they receive at the expense of the corporation or any other gains arising from a breach of their duty of loyalty to the corporation. Officers are generally liable to the corporation for losses arising from *ultra vires* transactions engaged in by the corporation through its officers. The officers are liable to the corporation for losses caused by their failure to exercise ordinary care and skill in the handling of corporate business, but are not liable for good faith mistakes of judgment made while performing their discretionary authority. As pointed out in the next chapter, legal cause of action for losses suffered by the corporation due to acts or omissions of the directors, officers, and others belongs to the corporation, but if the corporation fails to bring suit, the shareholders may bring a *derivative* suit for the benefit of the corporation.

Officers are not personally liable on contracts they make for the corporation if they have the authority to make such contracts and they make clear to the other party that they are acting for the corporation. However, as is true of agents generally, corporate officers are liable for their torts which cause injuries to others. The general principles of agency law apply in determining the relationship of corporate officers and agents to third persons.

State and federal laws regulating the sale of securities by corporations provide for the liability of the officers and directors to investors who incur losses as a result of the violation of such laws.

FINANCE

Capital Structure

The capital structure of a corporation must be described in the articles of corporation. This provision of the articles states the amount of capital stock the corporation is authorized to issue, whether it is to consist of one or more classes or kinds of stock, what each class of stock shall be, the number of shares of each class authorized to be issued, whether the shares are to be par value or no par value, the par value of any par value shares, and the rights, preferences, restrictions, and liabilities attaching to each class or kind of stock.

Terminology

Certain basic terms related to the capital structure and financial operations of corporations are defined here. Other terms of this nature are defined as they arise in the discussion of shareholder rights and liabilities in the next chapter.

Stock Certificate

Share of Stock and Stock Certificate.   A share of stock is intangible personal property (a chose in action) giving the owner, called shareholder, a fractional undivided interest in the corporation, including such rights as participation in the control of the corporation, the right to receive dividends when declared, and the right to share in the distribution of the corporate assets upon dissolution of the corporation. A shareholder does not have a specific property interest in the assets of the corporation, because, under the entity concept, the assets belong to the corporation. The extent of a shareholder's rights and obligations is a matter of contract between the shareholder and the corporation. The terms of the contract are gathered from the statutes of the state of incorporation, the articles of incorporation, and the bylaws. The shareholder's rights and obligations are summarized in his stock certificate.

A stock certificate is the tangible evidence of the ownership of a stated number of shares of stock in a corporation. The certificate is not the share itself, but only evidence of it. Stock certificates are in the form of negotiable instruments issued by the corporation under its seal and signed by its authorized officers and the transfer of stock certificates is effected in the manner prescribed by law. The provisions which must be included in stock certificates are prescribed by state law.

Stated Capital and Capital. Modern corporation statutes define the term stated capital, also referred to as capital stock, as the aggregate par value of issued shares with a par value and, in the case of shares without par value, the consideration received therefor except to the extent that part of such consideration is allocated to capital surplus by the board of directors or by the articles of incorporation. The stated capital is reflected in the balance sheet of the corporation as an obligation to the shareholders and is viewed as a fund to be retained for the protection of creditors. Dividend payment or purchases by a corporation of its own stock must not invade the stated capital.

The term capital is usually used to refer to the net worth of the corporation, but the term is also used at times to describe the total assets of the corporation or that portion of the assets derived from shareholder's purchases of stock from the corporation or derived from earnings of the corporation.

Authorized Capital Stock. Authorized capital stock is the amount of stock of all classes which the corporation is authorized, by its articles of incorporation, to issue.

Issued Stock. The term *issued stock* describes the amount of stock which is actually issued to the shareholders of the corporation and includes treasury stock.

Outstanding Stock. Outstanding stock is stock which has

been issued and is in the hands of individual shareholders and, unlike issued stock, does not include treasury stock.

Treasury Stock. Treasury stock means shares of a corporation which have been issued, have been subsequently acquired by and belong to the corporation, and have not been cancelled or restored to the status of authorized but unissued shares. They are viewed as issued but not outstanding shares. Treasury shares are dormant in that they may not be voted or receive dividends, but they may be sold by the corporation or otherwise disposed of for some valid purpose.

Bonds. A bond is a type of legal instrument evidencing a debt and is a device often used by corporations for borrowing money. The holders of corporate bonds are creditors of the corporation and, therefore, they ordinarily have priority over the shareholders who are not creditors of the corporation but have a proprietary interest in the corporation. If a bond issue is secured by a lien (often a mortgage) on the assets of the corporation, the bondholders would have priority over general creditors as to the assets covered by the lien. Secured bonds take a variety of forms. One example is a *collateral trust bond* which is secured by a pledge of certain corporation property with a trustee who holds the pledged property for the benefit of the bondholders. Unsecured bonds are called *debentures* and the holders of such bonds, upon the insolvency of the corporation, would participate on a pro rata basis with general creditors in the corporation's assets. Bonds which yield interest only if the corporation makes a profit are called *income bonds.* A *participating bond* entitles the holder to share with shareholders in the corporate profits. A *convertible bond* entitles the holder to convert it into stock of the corporation as specified in the bond.

Kinds of Stock

The two basic kinds of stock issued to finance a corporation are common stock and preferred stock. A corporation may provide for two or more classes of the same kind of stock in its capital structure, and the various rights of shareholders such as those relating to voting and dividends are distributed among the classes as the articles of incorporation designate. The rights and liabilities of shareholders are discussed in detail in the next chapter but some of the basic features of common and preferred stock will be summarized here.

Common Stock. Common stock is the basic or ordinary stock in the financial structure of a corporation. It usually gives the holder the right to vote, to receive dividends, and to share in the distribution of the corporation's assets upon dissolution, but it is usually inferior to preferred stock with respect to certain rights, usually in the matter of priority in the receipt of dividends.

Preferred Stock. The basic feature of preferred stock is its priority over common stock with respect to dividends. For example, $100 par value preferred stock bearing 7 per cent dividends would entitle the holder to receive annual dividends of $7 for each share before any dividends are paid on the common stock. Preferred stock usually has priority over common stock in the distribution of assets upon dissolution. Ordinarily the articles of incorporation will specify that preferred stock is nonvoting. In the absence of such a provision, preferred stock has the right to vote.

Preferred stock is usually issued as par value stock and it may be *cumulative* or *noncumulative*. Also, it may be *participating* or *nonparticipating*. Cumulative preferred stock means the holder has the right to receive all arrears of dividends not paid in prior years before dividends can be paid on other stock. Most courts have held that preferred stock is cumulative unless the articles of incorporation provide that it is noncumulative. Participating preferred stock gives the holder the right to additional dividends after the fixed preferred dividend is received. The majority of courts have held that preferred stock is nonparticipating unless the articles specify that it is participating.

Redeemable preferred stock gives the corporation the option of calling in the stock and redeeming it usually at its par value. *Convertible* preferred stock gives the holder the right to convert the stock into another kind or class of stock, usually common.

Par Value and No Par Value Stock. Par value stock is designated as such and has its par value share stated in the articles of incorporation and the certificates issued to the owners of such stock. The placing of a par value upon shares has been generally regarded as some kind of a representation that the corporation has received value at least equal to the par value of each share issued. Therefore, statutes have attempted to protect investors and creditors by requiring that par value shares shall be issued only for money, property or services of a value at least equal to the par value of shares issued. Of course, par value stock may be issued at a price above par. It is readily apparent that the aggregate par value of outstanding shares has no necessary relation to the net worth of a corporation after the corporation has operated for a time. Therefore, the par value of the stock of a going corporation is not very meaningful. The problem of "watered stock" in relation to par value stock is discussed in the next chapter. The statutes usually provide that promissory notes or uncertified checks shall not be accepted in payment for stock issued by a corporation.

No par value stock has no nominal value, its price usually being set by the directors in accordance with the requirements specified in the statutes of the state of incorporation. The price at which no par stock is issued will vary from time to time, depending on the market and the intrinsic value of each share as representing a fractional interest in the corporation. The discretion of the directors in setting the price for no par value shares must not be exercised in a fraudulent or discriminatory manner.

Stock Subscriptions

A stock subscription is an offer or an agreement to purchase a stated number and kind of shares of stock in a corporation already organized or to be organized.

Writing Requirement. A subscription agreement for stock in a corporation not yet formed or for stock to be issued in the future by an existing corporation does not, under the majority view, come within the Statute of Frauds and therefore need not be in writing. On the other hand, a contract for the transfer of existing shares in a corporation comes within the Statute of Frauds in non-Code states or falls under Section 8-319 of the Uniform Commercial Code in states which have adopted the Code, and therefore such contracts must be in writing or satisfy the substitutes for a writing as provided for in the statutes. No other formalities are prescribed for subscription contracts.

Subscriptions before Incorporation. A subscription to the stock of a proposed corporation is an offer which when accepted by the corporation upon or after incorporation ripens into a binding contract. Prior to incorporation, and until the subscription offer is accepted, the subscriber is free, under the majority common-law rule, to revoke his offer. A minority of courts have held that subscriptions are irrevocable on the theory that the subscription agreement constituted a contract among the subscribers to become shareholders upon formation of the corporation. Statutes in several states make stock subscriptions irrevocable for some specified length of time, typically six months. In some states the acceptance of a subscription by the corporation occurs automatically at the moment the corporation charter is acquired, but the view in most states is that the corporation must take some action to accept expressly or impliedly the subscription before the subscriber is bound.

Subscriptions after Incorporation. Subscription for the un-issued shares of stock in an existing corporation are governed by general rules of contract law. If the subscription agreement takes the form of an offer by the subscriber, the acceptance by the corporation creates a binding contract and makes the subscriber a shareholder in the corporation at that time, even though the delivery of the stock certificate and payment of the purchase price of the stock are postponed. A subscription agreement may be so worded as to make the corporation the offeror and the subscriber the offeree so that a contract results upon the subscriber's acceptance.

Conditions in Subscription Agreements. A subscription agreement for stock in an existing corporation may contain conditions unless they are contrary to the articles of incorporation or statute. Usually the condition will be a condition precedent which makes the subscriber's obligation dependent upon the performance of some act or the happening of some event. Courts have been careful to examine conditional subscriptions closely for the reason that they can serve as instruments for fraud against other shareholders and the creditors of the corporation.

Compliance by the corporation with its statement of purposes as stated in its articles of incorporation is viewed as a kind of implied condition precedent to the subscriber's liability. Therefore, if there is a material variance between the description of the corporation as stated in the subscription agreement and the purpose as stated in the articles or the actual nature of the corporation as it is organized and operating, the subscriber is not bound by the subscription agreement.

"Blue Sky Laws"

The state governments have used their police power and the federal government has used its constitutional power to regulate interstate commerce and the use of the mails to enact statutes, called *blue sky laws,* to regulate the issuance and sale of corporate securities. The name that is given to these laws suggests the evil at which they are aimed. Before these laws were adopted, unscrupulous promoters of corporations had been known to make such fraudulent and extravagant statements about the securities of the corporation or the corporation itself that the statements had no limit except the blue sky itself or the statements of the promoters were said to "have no more basis than so many feet of blue sky."

The most common type of state blue-sky law requires that the securities to be sold to the public be qualified or registered with the state and that dealers in securities be licensed. Qualification of new securities ordinarily consists of filing data about the issuing corporation and the proposed stock issue with the regulatory body. The information disclosed by the data filed is a matter of public record and thus available to any interested investor. The laws usually impose criminal penalties and provide for civil remedies in cases involving fraudulent practices.

The Federal Securities Act of 1933 and the Federal Securities Exchange Act of 1934 are the basic federal laws which regulate the sale of securities and the operation of security exchanges involving interstate commerce or the use of the mails. These laws do not provide for government approval of securities or exchange operations in the sense of assuring an investor of the safety of his investment. They do require registration of certain security issues and a full disclosure of information about the securities. They also prohibit certain practices which had been used in manipulating markets to the detriment of investors.

Transfer of Stock

A shareholder has the right to transfer his shares in a corporation just as he has the inherent right to transfer any other property he may own. However, any reasonable restriction on the transfer of stock is binding upon a shareholder, provided the restriction is stated upon the certificate. Any restriction which makes the stock nonnegotiable is void. The rules governing the validity of restrictions upon the transfer of stock are discussed in the next chapter.

Large corporations employ a *transfer agent* to handle the details of stock transfers, and a *registrar* is designated to see that no stock certificates are issued for shares in excess of the number authorized by the articles of incorporation. These functions are performed by the corporation's secretary in small corporations.

Stock transfers are governed by statutes in all states. The statutory rules applicable to transfers of shares of stock are contained in the Uniform Stock Transfer Act and in Article 8 of the Uniform Commercial Code. The Code repeals and replaces the U.S.T.A. in each of the states which have adopted it. The U.S.T.A. remains in effect in the other states.

In general, the ownership of shares is transferred either by the delivery to the transferee of the stock certificate indorsed by the owner in blank, or to a specified person, or by the delivery of the certificate by the owner accompanied by a separate assignment or power of attorney executed by the owner. Stock certificates have an assignment form printed on the back of the certificate which can be used to indorse and transfer the certificate under the first method. The transfer by either method is binding as between the transferor and transferee even though the transfer has not been registered upon the books of the corporation. Until a transferred stock certificate is presented to the corporation or its transfer agent for registration, the corporation may treat the registered owner (the transferor) as the person who has the right to vote, to receive dividends, and all other rights of a shareholder. If all the legal formalities necessary to transfer a stock certificate from the transferor to the transferee have been complied with, the corporation has a duty to register the transfer. Wrongful refusal by the corporation to transfer the stock makes the corporation liable to the transferee. Any lien held by the corporation against the stock for some indebtedness of the shareholder must be noted conspicuously on the certificate in order for the lien to be valid against a purchaser of the stock and thus justify the corporation's refusal to register the transfer until the indebtedness is removed.

Negotiability. In Section 8-105 (1) of the Code it is declared that investment securities, of which corporation stock is an example, are negotiable. This means that if a person purchases stock in good faith and for value, he takes good title to the stock free and clear of most defenses or claims that may be raised by former owners or other claimants. The Code further provides that the rights and duties existing between parties to negotiable instruments such as notes, bills of exchange, checks, and the like as discussed in Part Four of this book are also generally present where the instrument is a stock certificate or other investment security as defined in the Code.

Article 8 of the Code establishes rules which relate to such problems or matters as forged or unauthorized signature on issue of stock, forged or unauthorized indorsement on stock certificates, sale of stock through a broker, attachment of stock by a creditor, and the replacement of lost, destroyed, or stolen stock certificates.

Shareholder Rights and Liabilities

32

INTRODUCTION

Status of Shareholders

Definition. A shareholder is defined as one who is a holder of record of shares in a corporation. The term record refers to the stock register of the corporation. The fact that the shares have not been paid for or that a share certificate has not been issued does not ordinarily prevent the shareholder relationship from arising. The share certificate is merely evidence of ownership, and not the shares themselves. It is important to note that while in so far as the corporation is concerned, shareholders are those whose names appear as such upon the corporation's books, a person may, as to others, have the status of a shareholder. For example, as between a transferor of shares and the transferee who has not had the shares transferred into his name upon the corporation's books, the transferee is the shareholder and entitled to all the rights and privileges appended thereto.

Creation of Shareholder Relationship. The shareholder relationship arises either by a subscription of a purchase of shares from the corporation, or by a purchase from a shareholder, or by gift, bequest, or inheritance. The decision as to whom the corporation will sell its shares rests with the corporation. As a matter of practice, shares of a corporation are usually sold to anyone. The corporation may provide for a limited restriction upon the transfer of its shares, and to the extent that the restrictive provision does not constitute an unlawful restraint upon alienation it will be effective as a qualification for membership as a shareholder. A valid restriction often found in small corporations where the stock is held by few persons is the provision that in the event a shareholder desires to sell any of his shares, or in the event of his death, the shares must first be offered to the corporation or other shareholders at a price agreed upon or at a price to be determined by the parties. Restrictions which impose a permanent impediment to the transfer of the corporation's shares or which unduly restrict their transfer are void. For example, a restriction which requires the approval of a corporation or of its directors or shareholders before a transfer can be had is void. Any restrictions on the right to transfer shares must be stated on the certificate representing the shares.

Principal Rights of Shareholders. The principal rights of shareholders are as follows: (1) the right to receive notice of shareholders' meetings and to vote at such meetings for the election of directors and on other matters, (2) the right to share in dividends and, upon dissolution, the right to share in the corporation's assets, (3) the right to inspect the books and records of the corporation, (4) preemptive rights, and (5) the right to bring suit in behalf of the corporation under certain circumstances.

The rights of a shareholder are viewed as contractual. This contract consists of the applicable provisions of the state and Federal Constitutions, statutes of the state of incorporation, and the articles of incorporation.

Right to Attend Meetings and Vote

Shareholders do not have the right to manage and control directly the day-to-day operation of the corporation. The general management of the corporation is vested in a board of directors elected by the shareholders. Fundamental actions affecting the corporation, such as amendment of the articles to change the capital structure, purpose, or name of the corporation may be taken only with the approval of the shareholders. Other major transactions such as assumption by the corporation of long-term indebtedness, merger or consolidation, and reorganization must be referred to the stockholders for their consent.

Meetings.   Actions by shareholders as a group must ordinarily be taken in a regular, or properly called special meeting. Most corporation statutes and bylaws provide for the holding of at least one shareholders' meeting annually, with the time and place usually being specified in the bylaws. Most states do not require that the shareholders' meetings be held within the state of incorporation.

Statutes in a majority of states require that notice be given of regular as well as special meetings of shareholders. The notice must comply with any time and manner of transmission requirements which may be specified, and notice of a special meeting must describe the subject matter to be acted upon at the meeting. If some unusual action, such as dissolution of the corporation, is to be taken at a regular meeting, the notice must make mention of that fact. Failure to comply with the notice requirements invalidates the action taken at the meeting. Shareholders may waive notice of meetings or ratify action taken at an improperly held meeting.

A quorum of shareholders must be present or represented by proxy in order for the action taken at a meeting to be valid. At common law two or more shareholders present in person constituted a quorum, but under the statutes or bylaws of today the quorum requirement is generally a majority of the voting stock, present in person or represented by proxy. The quorum requirement and the other rules relating to shareholders' meetings, such as notice, required percentage of shareholders' votes to approve various actions, and the rules governing the conduct of meetings vary from state to state and from corporation to corporation. Any problem with respect to these matters must be resolved by an examination of the state statutes and the various documents controlling the operation of the corporation, especially the articles of incorporation and the bylaws. Subject to some limitations, a common policy found in the statutes is to specify a rule which is to be applied unless the corporation establishes a rule of its own. The aim of the law is to preserve the autonomy of the corporation, to facilitate the efficient conduct of the affairs of the corporations, and yet, at the same time, protect the interests of shareholders.

Voting in General. At common law shareholders were entitled to one vote per person. Today the prevailing rule is that each shareholder is entitled to as many votes as he owns shares of stock with voting rights. All classes of shares have voting rights unless the articles provide otherwise. If the right to vote has not been expressly denied by a provision of the articles, the right to vote exists and cannot be taken from a stockholder by the bylaws. Ordinarily the articles will grant voting rights to the common stock and provide that the preferred shares have no vote or will grant restricted voting rights to such shares. In some cases the articles provide that preferred shareholders may vote if the corporation has defaulted in the payment of their dividends for a specified time, and bondholders may be given voting rights if the interest payments on the bonds are in arrears for a specified time. In any case involving a transaction which would infringe on a stockholder's fundamental rights, the affected stockholder will have the right to vote on the transaction even though he holds nonvoting stock.

Unlike a director, a stockholder is not in a fiduciary relationship with his corporation. Thus, a stockholder who has a personal interest in a matter to be decided by the stockholders' meeting may attend the meeting and vote on the matter. If, however, a majority of the stockholders intend to transact some business clearly detrimental to the corporation or to the minority stockholders, the action may be enjoined by the parties who would be injured by it.

Generally, only shareholders of record at the time of the shareholders' meeting, or on a specified date prior to the meeting, are entitled to vote at a shareholders' meeting. The general rule is that the legal owner of shares is entitled to vote them. Therefore, trustees, executors, and administrators are entitled to vote the shares owned by their estates. If stock is pledged as collateral security, the legal title remains with the pledgor and he ordinarily has the right to vote the stock. However, the contract of pledge may provide that the pledgee is to vote the stock. The intention of the parties controls the right to vote if a dispute arises.

Treasury shares and the unissued shares of a corporation may not be voted, but a corporation may vote stock which it holds in other corporations. In some states a subsidiary is not permitted to vote stock it holds in the parent corporation for the reason that the result would be similar to permitting the parent to vote its treasury stock, in that the parent dominates the subsidiary and would dictate how it voted.

An understanding of the rules pertaining to the exercise of voting rights by the shareholders of a particular corporation is possible only after a careful analysis of the statutes of the state of incorporation, the articles, and the bylaws of the corporation.

Proxy Voting. A shareholder may vote either in person or by proxy. Voting by proxy involves a shareholder's designating someone to vote his shares in his stead. A solicitation of proxies often accompanies a struggle for control of the board of directors of a corporation. In most states proxy appointments must be in writing, they are revocable with certain limitations, and they are not valid beyond a specified time, typically eleven months.

Cumulative Voting. Cumulative voting is the method of voting for candidates to the board of directors of a corporation by which shareholders may cast a number of votes equal to the number of shares multiplied by the number of directors to be elected. These votes may be cast for one candidate or distributed among any number of candidates up to the number to be elected at the election. The cumulative voting plan is designed to give minority shareholders the opportunity to gain representation on the corporation's board of directors. For example, using the cumulative voting method the holders of twenty-five per cent of the shares voting plus one share, can elect one of three directors; twenty per cent of the shares voting plus one share can elect one of four directors; and forty per cent plus one share can elect two of four directors. Under straight voting a majority of the shares voting could elect the entire board. Nearly all states make provision for cumulative voting for directors, with some providing for mandatory cumulative voting and others having permissive cumulative voting. Courts disagree on the validity of the device of impairing the effect of cumulative voting by providing in the articles for the election of the directors by classes, as for example, when directors serve for three years and one third of the directors are elected each year.

Voting Agreements and Trusts. The voting trust is a device that is used principally in connection with corporation reorganizations, to insure control of the corporation by certain persons, and other similar situations where the objective is continuity of management over a period of years. The shareholders create a voting trust by transferring their stock to a trustee or a board of trustees for a specified time and receive in return trust certificates which give them all the rights of a stockholder, except voting rights which are exercised by the trustee or trustees. Most states recognize the validity of a voting trust so long as there is no fraud or unfairness to minority stockholders. Statutes in many states provide for the creation, regulation, and operation of voting trusts, and they usually set a time limitation of 10 years on their operation.

Dividends

Nature of Dividends. A legally declared dividend gives a shareholder the status of a creditor of the corporation and the right to share pro rata with the other shareholders in the profits.

net earnings, or surplus of the corporation. The capital structure provision of the articles of incorporation describes the dividend rights of shareholders in relation to one another with respect to preferences, accumulation of dividends, and participation. As general creditors, the shareholders enjoy no priority in proceedings against the assets of a bankrupt corporation to collect their duly declared but unpaid dividends. Once a fund for the payment of dividends has been set aside, if the corporation becomes bankrupt, the fund might be treated as a trust fund to which the shareholders entitled to the dividends would have priority.

A corporation may not rescind a dividend once its declaration has been made public unless the payment of the dividend would be illegal. Courts have held that a stock dividend may be rescinded before payment even though its declaration has been made public.

Form of Dividends.   Dividends may be paid in money, scrip, stock, bonds, or property. Dividends are usually paid in money, but in order to free the corporation's cash for other corporate purposes, the directors may pay one of the other types of dividends. Scrip is a form of promissory note promising to pay the holder cash at a specified later date. Such certificates are usually interest-bearing.

When a corporation pays a dividend in its stock there is a capitalization of surplus. A stock dividend is not taxable as income to the stockholder at the time it is received. Although similar in some respects, there are basic differences between a stock dividend and a stock split. Stock splits are often used to bring shares into a relatively popular price range and for the beneficial effect they sometimes have on the price of the shares on the market. Neither a stock split or a stock dividend changes the proportionate interest of each stockholder.

Payment of a dividend in the form of bonds makes the shareholders receiving the bonds creditors of the corporation. A bond dividend must not impair the rights of creditors of the corporation or its capital stock. A property dividend may be paid in stock owned by the corporation in another corporation or it may take the form of some physical asset of the paying corporation.

Tests for Valid Dividends. Legal restrictions on the payment of dividends by corporations are designed to protect the rights of the creditors of the corporation and the various classes of shareholders in relation to one another. The general rule is that dividends must be paid out of surplus. Stated conversely, the rule is that dividends may not be paid out of capital. Also, a corporation may not pay a dividend if it is insolvent, or if the dividend payment will render the corporation insolvent. The terms *surplus* and *capital* are not uniformly defined, and further confusion results from exceptions made to the surplus requirement on the basis of the nature of the surplus a dividend is being paid from, what form of dividend is being paid, and the nature of the corporation itself. An example of the latter exception is the wasting asset corporation, e.g., mining companies, which under typical statutes may declare dividends which are in fact a return of capital, provided certain restrictions are observed.

Most states have statutory tests for determining the validity of corporation dividends. Certain observations can be made concerning these tests. Generally surplus is defined as the amount of the corporation's assets in excess of its liabilities and its stated capital. A surplus may be created in various ways. The usual kinds of surpluses are (1) earned surplus, (2) paid-in surplus, (3) revaluation surplus, and (4) reduction surplus.

An earned surplus results from the profitable operation of the corporation and will provide a source for valid dividends in any form. A corporation may not have earned a profit during the current year, yet it may have an earned surplus accumulated from prior earnings and thus can pay a dividend. The statutes in some states permit a corporation to pay a dividend from current net profits, without regard to the existence of an earned surplus.

A paid-in surplus is a type of capital surplus resulting from the corporation's selling its par value stock at a premium, that is, above par, or from the designation by the board of directors of a portion of the price received for no par value stock to the paid-in surplus account. Dividends may usually be paid from paid-in surplus, but some states require that the shareholders be informed of the type of surplus from which the dividend was paid, if other than earned surplus.

A revaluation surplus results from a revaluation of the assets of the corporation to reflect the increase in value of the corporation's assets resulting from a rise of the level of prices since the assets were acquired or from other factors.

A reduction surplus is created by reducing the capital stock or "stated capital" of the corporation. State statutes often restrict the payment of dividends from a reduction surplus to a stock dividend.

Since the state statutes regulating the payment of dividends are exceedingly diverse, it is necessary to consult the local statutes and court decisions if a question arises concerning the validity of a dividend.

Directors' Discretion as to Dividends. The dividend policy of a corporation is determined by its board of directors under the board's authority to conduct the ordinary affairs of the corporation. Only under extreme circumstances or upon evidence of bad faith is a court likely to reverse the decision of the board of directors with respect to such questions as to how much will be paid in dividends and when they will be paid. The courts generally believe that their arbitrary ruling should not be substituted for the discretion of the directors.

One of the few cases where the court compelled the payment of additional dividends is that of *Dodge v. Ford Motor Company.*[1] The company had $2 million capital stock, $18 million debts and an accumulated surplus of $112 million. Its potential net earnings for the year were $60 million, and $54 million of

---

[1] 204 Mich. 459, 170 N.W. 668 (1919).

its surplus was in liquid assets. Dividends of $1.2 million had been decided upon by the directors. This represented 60 per cent of the $2 million nominal capital but only about 1 per cent of the $114 million net assets and considerably less than the annual net earnings or the dividends which had been paid in the past. The directors planned to use the remaining potential annual net earnings for expansion and to reduce the price of the automobile from $440 to $360. The company was able to sell at $440 all the cars it could produce. Declaring that a business corporation was operated primarily for the profit of the stockholders, the court ordered a dividend of $19 million, equal to one-half the "cash surplus."

Dividends on Preferred Stock. Although preferred shareholders are entitled to some priority as to dividends over other classes of stock, the board of directors determines whether the specified preferred dividend will be paid, and its decision will not be disturbed by a court in the absence of bad faith or a clear abuse of discretion. Thus, the preferred shareholders enjoy a priority with respect to dividends but not a guarantee.

Cumulative preferred stock means that the directors are not authorized to pay a dividend on junior stock, usually common, until the current and all past dividends are paid on the cumulative preferred stock. If the preferred stock is noncumulative and if the dividends are not paid during a given period, the holder of such shares is no longer entitled to receive them. However, some courts have permitted noncumulative preferred shareholders to claim passed dividends upon a showing that the directors wrongfully retained in the corporation funds from which the noncumulative preferred shareholders could have received their specified dividend. This rule is likely to be invoked where the directors favor the common shareholders with a dividend drawn from a surplus accumulated over a period of years during which time the noncumulative preferred dividend was passed.

As a general rule, preferred stock carries all the rights of the common stockholders if there are no limitations to the contrary. Thus, preferred stock is assumed to be cumulative unless the articles of incorporation provide otherwise. Notice of restrictions on the rights of shareholders is printed on each stock certificate.

Participating preferred stock is given the right to receive additional dividends after it has received its stated amount or percentage of dividends and after a like dividend is paid to common stockholders. Such preferred stock may be designated as fully participating, or the participation feature may be limited. Participation may also be applied to the distribution of a corporation's assets upon liquidation.

Effect of Transfer of Stock on Right to Dividend. As between the transferor and transferee of corporation stock, the general rule is that if the dividend is in cash or property other than the corporation's own stock, the person who was the owner of the stock on the date the dividends were declared, not the date of payment, is entitled to the dividends. On the contrary, the general rule is that the person who owns the stock at the date of distribution, not the date of declaration, is the person entitled to a stock dividend where a transfer has occurred. The corporation by action of the board of directors may specify in the declaration of a dividend that it will be payable to those who will be holders of record on a specified date. If this action is taken the right to the dividend will be determined accordingly. Also, the transferor and transferee may fix by agreement who is entitled to a dividend and such an agreement will control. In any case the corporation discharges its duty if it pays dividends to the shareholders appearing on its records as such on the controlling date. Of course, the corporation must heed any notice of transfer duly received and enter such transfer on its records. If a dividend is distributed by the corporation to a shareholder of record in accordance with this rule, the corporation is discharged. But any transferor receiving such dividend contrary to his agreement with his transferee is liable to the transferee for the money or property received. Sales of stock on the New York Exchange are subject to an exchange rule which provides that stock will, as a general rule, be sold ex dividend beginning four business days before the date of payment of the dividend.

Right to Distribution of Assets
When a corporation is dissolved, the assets of the corporation must first be used to pay its creditors and any balance remaining is shared by the stockholders. Certain classes of stock may have a preference or priority in this distribution.

Inspection of Books
Both at common law and under corporation statutes a shareholder has the right to inspect corporate books and records in order to protect his economic interest in the corporation. This important right is governed by statute in nearly all states. The shareholder is required to exercise his right of inspection for a proper purpose and at a reasonable time and place. The shareholder may employ an attorney, accountant, or other agent to conduct the inspection and may extract copies of pertinent records. His request for an inspection must be in writing and some states require that generally the shareholder own some minimum per cent of the outstanding shares, typically 5 per cent, and some states require that the shareholder own his shares for some minimum period of time before he can assert the right of inspection.

A writ of mandamus is the usual remedy available to a shareholder seeking to compel a corporation to comply with his legitimate inspection request, and penalties against the corporation and officers who deny the inspection right are provided for in some states. Generally the corporation has the burden of showing that a shareholder has an improper motive for wanting to inspect the records. Examples of an improper purpose include an intention of the shareholder to use the obtained information in an enterprise in competition with the corporation, a request to inspect in order to obtain a list of shareholders to be used in a direct mail selling campaign unrelated to the corporation, and a request for inspection as a matter of idle curiosity.

Pre-emptive Rights

As a general rule, each shareholder is entitled to an opportunity to maintain his proportionate control and interest in the corporation. To implement this opportunity, each shareholder has a pre-emptive right to subscribe to a new issue of stock, in proportion of his holding of outstanding shares, before the newly allotted shares are offered to the public. Where capital stock is reduced, a stockholder may require the corporation to redeem a proportionate part of the stock held by him and the other shareholders similarly situated.

The pre-emptive right is applicable to new authorizations of stock and has been applied in some cases to a new allotment of stock previously authorized, especially where a considerable lapse of time had occurred after the original issue.

The pre-emptive right is evidenced by transferable *stock warrants* issued to the shareholders, and these warrants are separately quoted and traded as *stock rights* on the stock exchanges if the stock is listed.

Generally the pre-emptive right does not extend to a reissue of treasury shares, to shares issued for property or services, or to fulfill conversion or option rights granted by the corporation, or to accomplish a merger or consolidation.

A variety of state statutes deal with the pre-emptive right. Most states permit a corporation to deny to the shareholders the preemptive right by an appropriate provision in the articles of incorporation. Assuming that the right is provided for by statute or the articles, recognition of this right by a court will depend upon whether an issue of shares to the public without first giving a shareholder an option to buy will deprive him of some valuable right he has in the corporation, usually with respect to voting or dividends.

Shareholder Suits

The right to bring suit for injuries to the corporation belongs to the corporation, not the shareholders. An exception to this rule is made where the officers or directors of the corporation fail to enforce the corporation's rights or are themselves involved in the wrongful acts injurious to the corporation. In such cases a shareholder may bring what is called a *derivative suit* on behalf of the corporation, but only after exhausting his remedies within the corporation by demanding that the directors or officers bring suit in the name of the corporation and obtaining their refusal to do so. This demand is excused where the corporation is operating under the domination of the wrongdoers, because in such cases a request for suit would be a vain and useless gesture. Any judgment or recovery obtained in a derivative suit will be for the benefit of the corporation, and indirectly all its shareholders and creditors.

One or more shareholders of a certain class may bring a *class suit* against the corporation, its directors, or officers, to protect the rights of all those shareholders holding the particular kind or class of stock. A common example is a suit by a holder of noncumulative preferred shares to enjoin the directors from passing dividends on such shares when ample earnings are available from which the preferred dividend could be paid.

While generally minority shareholders must accede to the actions of the majority in the conduct of the affairs of the corporations, they may bring suit in certain extreme cases where the action of the majority amounts to fraud and not mere poor judgment. Statutes have been adopted in some states to define the rights of minority shareholders under certain circumstances, including the right of the minority to have their shares purchased by the corporation at a fair price. Of course, an individual shareholder may bring suit to enforce any personal right he has under his contract as a shareholder. Examples are suits to collect duly declared dividends or to enforce any of the rights of shareholders discussed in this chapter.

LIABILITY OF SHAREHOLDERS

General Rule of Limited Liability

As a general rule, a shareholder in an ordinary corporation is not personally liable for the debts and liabilities of the corporation. The risk of the shareholder is limited to the amount of his original capital investment. If a shareholder's stock is assessable and an assessment is made, the shareholder will be liable to the corporation for the amount of the assessment. Most corporations do not issue assessable stock.

Special Cases of Shareholder Liability

Subscription Contracts.   A subscriber who fails to pay for his shares in full is liable to the corporation on his subscription contract for the balance owed. Any subsequent transferee who knows that the shares he receives were not fully paid may be held liable to the corporation for the unpaid balance. Creditors of an insolvent corporation may enforce the liability of a subscriber or transferee for any deficiency.

Watered Stock.   Watered stock is stock issued in return for cash, properties, or services equal in value to less than the stock's par value. Courts have disagreed on the test to be used for determining if corporate capital is overvalued. However, most courts use the *good faith test* to determine if full value has been given for stock. Under this test, proof of overvaluation of the consideration received for stock is insufficient unless lack of good faith on the part of the corporation directors who established the value of the consideration can be shown. If watered stock is issued, it is viewed by courts as a misrepresentation of the corporation's capital, and on this basis creditors who relied on the misrepresentation are permitted to recover from the holders of watered stock. Under some state statutes the holder of watered stock is liable to creditors of the corporation whether or not they have relied on an overvaluation of corporate capital.

Illegally Received Dividends. If a dividend has been illegally declared and paid, the shareholders are liable for repayment of such dividends to the corporation or the creditors of an insolvent corporation may require the repayment.

Statutory Liability for Wages. Several states have statutes which impose personal liability upon shareholders for unpaid wages due from the corporation to employees.

Personal Property

33

NATURE OF PROPERTY

Attributes of Private Ownership

The word *property* as commonly used means all things, tangible and intangible, that are capable of being owned. For example, an automobile, shares of stock in a corporation and the like are referred to as property. However, in the legal sense, the term *property* does not mean the thing itself that is owned but refers to the rights or interests that a person has in a thing, such as land or an automobile, or it may refer to legal rights not connected with a physical object, such as a franchise, patent, copyright, and other intangible property interests. An owner of property has the exclusive right to own, possess, use, enjoy and dispose of objects or rights in any manner consistent with the law. The person who has this "bundle of rights" is said to have the ownership of or title to property.

As noted in Chapter 1, private ownership of property is a fundamental characteristic of the American society and is closely related to our free competitive economy in which the individual is able to produce things of value to society and, at the same time, enjoy the private ownership of the fruits of his labor. The enjoyment of private property rights depends upon the existence of a government that provides the legal machinery necessary to protect those rights. In this connection, we have seen that the efficacy of law itself depends upon its enforcement by organized society. The Fourteenth Amendment to the Constitution of the United States declares that no state shall "deprive any person of life, liberty, or property without due process of law."

The property rights of an individual and his legal rights in general are not absolute. They are limited by the legal proposition that an individual must not pursue a course of action in asserting his rights that will interfere with the rights of others or be detrimental to society. For example, an owner of land must not use his land in such a manner as to create a nuisance that causes injury to another person or his property or causes injury to the public at large. The law thus simultaneously protects and limits property rights by enforcing corresponding duties.

In seeking to bring about benefits for the group, governments limit through their powers of taxation, police power, and eminent domain the right of an owner to use his real property. An owner of real property must pay the taxes and assessments levied upon his property; the state may, under its police power, regulate the use of property in order to protect the health, safety, morals, and general welfare of its citizens; and the government may take private property for a public purpose by virtue of its power of eminent domain, provided the owner is paid a just compensation. The government may implement the constitutional guarantee of "civil rights" by enacting legislation forbidding certain discrimination among members of the public making use of public accommodations made available on private property.

Ownership and Possession

Ownership is not to be confused with the term *possession*. Ownership (sometimes called title) and possession need not be held by the same person. They are often severed as, for example, where A leases or loans his property to B or leaves it with B for repair. The ownership of the property remains with A, but B has possession. Possession may be actual or constructive. A person who owns a watch has actual possession, or possession in fact, of the watch when he is wearing it or has it within his manual control. If the owner leaves the watch at home while he is away at his office, he does not have actual possession of the watch, but does have constructive or legal possession. In either case there is an intention of the owner that he is to exercise control over the watch. Both kinds of possession, actual and constructive, whether held by the owner of the property or by someone else, are protected by the law.

Custody is a type of physical control over property without having possession of it. For example, a stockroom employee has custody of the merchandise placed under his control, but his employer has the legal or constructive possession.

CLASSIFICATION OF PROPERTY

Property is classified as (1) real and personal, (2) tangible and intangible, and (3) public and private. It will be seen from the definitions of these classes that a particular item of property may, due to its characteristics, fall within more than one classification.

Real and Personal Property

Real property, also called realty or real estate, includes the interest one may have in land and in such objects attached to the land as to be regarded as a part of it. Realty is permanent, fixed, and immovable. It includes the land itself, the space above the land, minerals and natural resources under the soil, timber, buildings and similar permanent attachments to the land called fixtures. Legal questions concerning real estate, such as the manner of transferring title, the regulation of the land's use, the imposition of taxes, and other problems are governed by the law of the state in which the realty is located, and it is immaterial whether the owner lives in that state or not.

In general, personal property includes all property that is not real property and its most important characteristic is its mobility. Personal property is temporary in nature and may be taken from place to place by the owner. Examples include vehicles, clothing, books, negotiable instruments, stocks, and bonds. It is regarded as having its situs at the owner's domicile for some purposes—such as taxation—although it may actually be located elsewhere.

The law recognizes three kinds of personal property. They are chattels real, chattels personal in possession, and chattels personal in action. Chattels real are those interests in real property that are less than a freehold estate. The freehold estates are identified in Chapter 34. A lease of land for a period of years is an example of a chattel real. Chattels personal in possession are those tangible (also called corporeal) objects which may be transferred from hand to hand and include such things as vehicles, clothing, and books. Chattels personal in action, also called "choses in action," include such intangible (incorporeal) property as negotiable instruments, stocks, bonds, contract rights, patents, and copyrights. The owner of intangible personal property usually holds possession of a paper evidencing his rights, but he may have to bring a legal action to reduce his property, often a claim for money, to possession.

Personal property or real property may be converted to the other. For example, when minerals are severed from the earth they become personal property and when lumber is incorporated into a house it is converted from personal property to real property.

The distinction between real and personal property is of vital importance in the solution of legal questions concerned with such matters as taxation, administration of decedent's estates, complying with the Statute of Frauds in contracts for the sale of property, and the requirements for the transfer of title to property.

Tangible and Intangible Property

Things which are of a physical nature and thus capable of being handled, seen, and possessed are tangible, also called corporeal property. Real estate is, of course, tangible property. Goods, or chattels, constitute an important type of tangible personal property.

Intangible, or incorporeal property, includes those rights or interests that cannot be perceived by the senses because they are invisible and do not have a tangible existence. Examples include corporation stock and bonds, rights under a contract, leaseholds, and franchises.

Public and Private Ownership

Property owned by the federal, state, or local government is classed as public property and includes parks, highways, office buildings, military installations, school buildings, etc. Private property is that property owned by individuals, a group of individuals, corporations, or some other type of business organization. The fact that privately owned property is used for some public purpose does not change the basic nature of the property from private to public.

METHODS OF ACQUIRING OWNERSHIP

The ownership of, or title to, personal property may be acquired by means of: (1) purchase, (2) original creation, (3) original possession, (4) gift, (5) will or inheritance, (6) finding, (7) confusion, (8) accession, and (9) operation of law.

Purchase

The purchase of personal property is the most common method of acquiring ownership of such property. The law regulating the sale and purchase of goods is covered in Part Three of this book.

Original Creation

A person may acquire the ownership of personal property by producing or creating it through his own labor, mental or physical. Examples include intellectual creations such as inventions, paintings, books, and musical compositions. The rights of the creator of such things are protected by patent, copyright, and trademark laws.

Original Possession

Wildlife and fish in their natural habitat are unowned and become the property of the person who reduces them to his possession, provided there is no violation of a "game law" or trespass against the rights of a landowner. If a captured wild creature escapes and returns to its natural state, it is again unowned and can be reduced to possession by another person who will become the owner. The owner of a domesticated animal does not lose his ownership if his animal strays from his land and becomes lost.

Gift

A gift is the voluntary transfer of property from the donor to the donee without any consideration being given for the transfer. As pointed out in Chapter 6, a promise between individuals to make a gift is not binding, since it is unsupported by consideration.

A gift *inter vivos* (between living persons) is a gift of property, real or personal, which takes effect during the lifetime of the donor, and once executed it is irrevocable. The two basic requirements for a gift are (1) an unconditional delivery by the donor of the property to the donee, or to some third person, who holds the property for the donee, and (2) a present intention on the part of the donor to vest title to the property in the donee. Of course, the gift must be accepted to make it complete. If the donor suffers from some incapacity, such as being a minor, he may disaffirm the gift. The problems created by having a donee who is a minor and thus able to disaffirm his transfers of the property after he receives it are alleviated somewhat in nearly all states by the adoption of the Uniform Gifts to Minors Act.

Delivery may be actual, that is, in the form of a manual handing over of the property from the donor to the donee, or the third person acting for the donee. Where the property is intangible or is not physically present at the place and time of the intended gift, a constructive or symbolical delivery is sufficient to satisfy the delivery requirement. For example, a key to a lock box containing the subject of the gift may be delivered or some document of title, such as a stock certificate, negotiable instrument, or pass book to a bank account may be delivered. An indorsement of the document may be required with some instruments. A deed of gift may be used as a means of evidencing by a legal instrument the making of a gift of property. It is necessary that the donor divest himself of all dominion and control over the property.

A gift *causa mortis* (in anticipation of death) is a gift made by one in peril of imminent death and is executed by transferring the possession of the personal property to the donee, but upon the condition that if the donor survives the peril he may revoke the gift and reclaim the property. Also, such a gift may be revoked by the donor before he dies and the death of the donee before the donor's death revokes the gift. For a valid *causa mortis* gift, the intention and delivery requirements for an *inter vivos* gift must be met, and the testamentary nature of the gift must be present. Unlike the *inter vivos* gift, a *causa mortis* gift is in a sense revocable and is restricted to personal property.

Will or Inheritance

A person may leave a will in which he designates, within limits specified by the law of the state, who shall acquire title to the decedent's property upon his death. A gift of personal property by will is called a legacy or bequest and a gift of real property by will a devise.

When a person dies without a will, that is, intestate, his personal property after administration of the estate by the personal representative (administrator or executor) passes "by distribution" to his next of kin, and his real property descends to his heirs as provided for in the state statutes of descent and distribution. Both types of property are broadly referred to as having been acquired by inheritance where they have come from a relative who dies intestate.

Finding Lost, Misplaced, or Abandoned Property

One of the most familiar principles of personal property law is that the finder of lost property acquires good title to the property against the whole world except the true owner. Under the common law, the owner who lost the article can recover it from the finder or from anyone who has taken possession through the finder. The finder is guilty of larceny if he, with knowledge of the identity of the true owner, appropriates the property to his own use. If he simply doesn't know the identity of the owner and does not have reasonable means of discovering his identity and uses the property, he is liable to the owner in conversion for the value of the property. The finder cannot claim a reward for finding and returning the article unless a reward had been offered and the finder knew of the offered reward. Some states have statutes which establish a procedure the finder can follow and obtain title to the property. The usual statute requires the finder to advertise the fact that he has found the property and wait a specified time before the rights of the true owner are extinguished.

The law distinguishes between *lost, misplaced,* and *abandoned* property. The abandonment of property is the relinquishing of all ownership, possession or claim to the article, as when someone discards clothing on a trash dump or a ship is abandoned on a reef. An abandoned article becomes the property of the first person who takes possession of the article with the intention of becoming the owner of it.

If A finds a wallet laying in the aisle of a store, the wallet will generally be classed as lost property and A is entitled to possession of the wallet and its contents until the true owner claims them. An article is said to be lost when the owner has involuntarily parted with the possession of it, and it is found in a place and under circumstances to suggest to the finder that the owner's will was not employed in placing the article there.

If A finds a wallet on a counter in a store, the wallet is presumed to be mislaid, not lost, and the owner of the store is viewed as a gratuitous bailee of the wallet and as having the right and duty to take possession of it and hold it for the owner. A mislaid article is one voluntarily placed somewhere by an owner who expects to pick it up later, but afterward forgets where he put it. Again, the place where the article is subsequently found, aisle and counter in the above examples, suggests the nature of the property, lost in the aisle and mislaid on the counter.

The problem of "abandoned" bank accounts and other monies in financial institutions is met by state statutes. For example, under the Abandoned Property Law of New York, banks in New York must advertise annually accounts having $25 or more, for which owners or their heirs have not made claim for 10 years, or on which no deposits or withdrawals have been made or interest collected. If no claim is made as a result of the advertisement, or the tracing efforts of the bank, the money is turned over to the state and it ceases to be a liability of the bank. However, a claimant can always make claim to the state for such money. Funds over and above a reserve set up to handle such claims are available for state purposes. In a recent year, the state of New York collected nearly $6 million under the abandoned property law.

Confusion

Confusion is the mixing of goods owned by different persons so that the property of each can no longer be distinguished and separated. Grain, oil, coal, and similar fungibles are examples of the kinds of property that are liable to confusion. If the confusion results from common consent or accident not due to the negligence of one of the parties, each party will be deemed the owner of a proportionate share of the mass, and any loss to the goods will be shared by the co-owners in proportion to their undivided interests in the goods. If the mixing results from the tortious act of one of the parties, the title to the entire mass will be viewed as resting with the innocent party to the extent necessary to protect his interest. If the confusion is caused by the negligence of a party, he must bear any resultant loss.

Accession

Property permanently added to other property and forming a minor part of the total value of the resulting property becomes, in most instances, the property of the owner of the original article. This is the general rule of accession and it is applied to permit an owner of an automobile to claim the new parts and value added to the vehicle pursuant to a repair contract. Similarly, if A furnishes raw materials to B, a manufacturer, under a contract whereby B is to make an article out of the materials, A owns the finished article unless B has added a significantly large proportion of the materials and value which has gone into the finished product.

Difficult problems arise when the accession occurs without any contract with the owner for the improvements of the original article or without his consent. Generally if property is stolen and labor or materials, or both, are then added to it by the thief, the owner of the original property may recover it in its improved state, without compensation to the thief for the improvements, even though the value of the added property exceeds that of the stolen article and even though the property has been transferred by the thief to a bona fide purchaser. However, if the bona fide purchaser of the previously stolen property greatly enhances its value by adding property to it, the original owner loses title to the property as against the innocent purchaser, but the original owner has the right to recover the value of the original article from either the innocent purchaser or the thief. Of course, if the innocent purchaser is held for this amount, he can then collect from the thief for this loss, if he can be found.

Operation of Law

The title to personal property may be transferred by operation of law. Examples include a sale of personal property under order from a court and a sale of the property of a bankrupt by a trustee in bankruptcy for the benefit of creditors.

Bailments

34

Definition and Creation

A bailment is the legal relationship created by the transfer of the possession of personal property from one person called the bailor to another person called the bailee for some special purpose, the goods to be returned to the bailor or otherwise disposed of by the bailee according to instructions from the bailor. Examples of bailments include loaning an automobile, checking a coat, storing furniture in a warehouse, delivering an appliance to a repairman for repairs, delivering goods to a carrier to be transported, delivering raw materials to a manufacturer for processing, pledging of property, consigning of goods and, in some cases, parking a car in a parking lot.

Essential Elements. The essential elements of a bailment are:

1] the retention of the title to the personal property by the bailor,

2] the placing of the possession of the property with the bailee, and

3] the duty of the bailee to return the property to the bailor or dispose of it as directed by the bailor.

The relationship of bailor and bailee usually results from a contract, express or implied. It follows, therefore, that a person may not ordinarily be made a bailee against his will. In most cases there will be an actual delivery and acceptance of the property that is the subject of the bailment. The word *bailment* comes from the French word *bailler,* to deliver. Actual delivery is the manual transfer of the property by the bailor to the bailee. However, the delivery or acceptance of property so as to create a bailment need not be actual or express; they may be implied by law from the circumstances and, as a result, a person may have the duties and liabilities of a bailee imposed upon him without previous contract. For example, if a person finds a lost or mislaid article and takes it into his custody, he is a bailee for the unknown owner, although he had no contract with him. In such cases the bailment is referred to as a constructive bailment. A similar bailment arises where a person steals or converts property belonging to another. The wrongdoer is a bailee and the law creates for him a promise to return it to the owner. An involuntary bailment may be created when a person's goods are cast by flood or tornado upon another's land or where his animals stray onto the premises of another. The owner of the premises goes into possession of the property although there is no actual delivery, no acceptance, and no express contract. The law imposes upon the person in possession a duty to exercise some care as to the property and he has an obligation to turn it over to the owner. Some courts have held in such cases that no bailment arises.

While actual delivery of the subject matter of a bailment is not always necessary in a contractual bailment, there must be at least a constructive delivery, such as handing over to the bailee some symbol or representative of the goods which controls possession of them, as, for example, a negotiable bill of lading or a negotiable warehouse receipt for the goods. The possession of the goods may be delivered to the bailee without any manual handling of the goods; such as when a buyer leaves his purchased goods temporarily in the seller's possession, the

seller having possession of the goods first as owner and then, as
a result of the sale and the retention of the goods for the buyer,
as a bailee.

The possession element of a bailment is satisfied if it can be
established that the alleged bailee either expressly or impliedly
assumed control over the property. To illustrate, a bailment
arises when a patron of a restaurant checks his hat and coat
with the attendant in charge of the restaurant checkroom, but,
if a person merely hangs his hat and coat on a hook or rack
along the wall of the restaurant, usually no bailment is created.
It has been held that if a person parks his automobile in a parking lot, retaining the keys and having the privilege of getting
it himself whenever he wishes, the transaction is a lease of the
parking space and does not create a bailment. By contrast, if
the auto is surrendered to a parking lot attendant who parks
it and returns it to the owner when he calls for it, the necessary
control over the automobile rests with the parking lot operator
and a bailment is created.

Subject Matter of Bailments.   The subject matter of a bailment must be some form of personal property, tangible or intangible. Thus, the bailed property may consist of chattels such
as an automobile, a book, or jewelry, or it may consist of
money, shares of stock, bonds and other securities. There can
be no bailment of real property.

Who May Be Bailor.   Any person who has possession of
personal property may be a bailor. Usually, a bailor will be the
owner of the property, but all that is necessary is that the bailor
have the right to possession as against all persons except the
true owner. Thus, a thief or finder may be a bailor as to a
third person, even though while in possession he may be a bailee
in relation to the true owner.

Pledge.   A pledge is a bailment of personal property as security for a debt or performance of some obligation, with a
power in the pledgee to sell the property in the event of default
by the debtor or obligor. Property commonly pledged by a
pledgor includes shares of stock, bonds, savings bank books,

negotiable instruments, insurance policies, bills of lading, warehouse receipts, and tangible property such as jewelry. As can be seen from these examples, the property delivered in a pledge transaction may be the tangible property itself or documentary symbols of the property. The property in a pledge is returned to the pledgor when the debt is paid or the obligation performed. If the possession of property used as security for a debt is to remain with the owner-debtor, a chattel mortgage will be used, because, in a mortgage, possession of the property need not be delivered to the mortgagee.

Banks often make loans to borrowers who furnish collateral security in the form of a pledge. The collateral security in such loan transactions is often stocks and bonds. The rights of the parties in such a pledge are governed by the agreement of the parties, which is usually set forth in a promissory note called a collateral note. Pawnbrokers are in the business of making loans secured by pledges and they are regulated by statutes.

Bailment and Other Transactions Distinguished

Sale. In a bailment, the title to the property usually is in the bailor and possession is in the bailee and it is not intended that title shall vest in the bailee. By contrast, in a sale the object is to transfer title and possession to the buyer. In a *conditional sale* possession of the goods is passed to the buyer but the title is reserved in the seller as security and, on payment of the purchase price, will pass to the buyer. Such questions as who bears the risk of loss or damage to the property are often answered on the basis of whether there has been a sale or a bailment. The general rule is that risk of loss or damage rests with the owner. Thus, if a sale has occurred the risk of loss is on the buyer. Also, as a general rule, the buyer's creditors may attach the goods, the buyer can resell the goods, and he must pay taxes on the goods.

Where possession of goods is given to a person with the understanding that he may, if he likes, buy the goods instead of returning them, the transaction is called a *bailment with an option to buy.* This type of transaction is also called a *sale on approval* and is discussed in Chapter 14. In a *consignment sale* the consignee is a bailee and agent of the consignor to sell the goods.

Barter. If A takes his grain to a mill and is to receive in exchange meal already ground a barter has occurred, not a bailment. A barter is a transaction where goods are exchanged for goods. In a bailment the bailor gets back the identical goods or in some agreed upon altered form. The bailment of goods to be altered is illustrated by the case in which the bailor delivers raw materials to a manufacturer or processor with the understanding that the form of the materials is to be changed before they are returned.

Fungibles. There may be a bailment of fungible goods even though there is to be no return of the identical goods or some processed form of them. For example, if A delivers grain to a grain elevator and it is understood that an equal amount of grain of the same kind and quality is to be returned to A, the transaction is a bailment even though with A's consent his grain is mingled with the other grain and the identity of the mass of grain in the elevator is continually changing, by being added to and taken from. If, however, the elevator operator is given the option of returning the grain or paying the market price for A's grain, the transaction is interpreted as a sale, since the elevator operator may do what he likes with the grain deposited with him, the same as an owner of it might do. If A is given the option of demanding either grain or the market price, the transaction is regarded as a bailment until A exercises his option to sell by taking money instead of grain. It then becomes a sale.

Debt. The distinction between a bailment and a debt is substantially identical with the distinction between a bailment and a sale. Where the transaction is a loan the title passes to the borrower, and he is under no obligation to restore the specific money borrowed. The bailor is not a creditor of the bailee; he is the owner of the goods that are temporarily in the possession of the bailee for a particular purpose. The bailee's solvency or insolvency will in no way affect the bailor's right to recover possession of the goods.

Bank Deposits. The relation between an ordinary depositor and the bank receiving his funds for general deposit is not one of bailor and bailee but rather one of creditor and debtor. The depositor, along with the bank's other creditors, would be entitled to only a proportionate share of the bank's assets in the event of its insolvency. Of course, the risk of loss to the depositor is minimized in most banks by the Federal Deposit Insurance Corporation insurance of deposits up to $10,000.00 or some similar type of insurance.

If a bank receives funds from or for a customer and it is agreed that the identical funds are to be turned over to the customer, a bailment results and the funds are considered a special deposit rather than a general deposit.

Safe Deposit Box and Night Depository. The use of a safe deposit box or night depository by a bank customer is viewed by most courts as creating a bailment, but some courts say that there is a mere rental of space and, thus, the relationship between the customer and the bank is that of lessee and lessor, not bailor and bailee. In such cases the issue over the nature of the relationship between the customer and the bank is complicated by the fact that neither party has exclusive control over the box and its contents. However, the express written contract between the bank and the customer may define the nature of the transaction and contain a provision relieving the bank from liability for loss, subject to local statutes.

Custody of Servant or Agent. Delivery of goods by a master to his servant does not, as a general rule, create a bailment. The servant is said to have custody of the goods, not possession. Whether an agent is deemed to have custody or possession of his principal's goods will depend upon the circumstances of the case. If the agent has custody of the goods, the rights of the parties will be determined by the application of the law of agency; if the agent has possession, such rights will be determined by the law of bailments.

CLASSIFICATION OF BAILMENTS

Broadly classified, bailments are either ordinary or extraordinary. The extraordinary bailment is present where the bailee is a person who is ready and willing to serve the public generally, such as the common carrier and the innkeeper or hotelkeeper. The legal aspects of these two extraordinary bailments involve unusual rights and duties, and they are discussed at the end of this chapter. All other bailments are classified as ordinary bailments and the discussion which follows is concerned with such bailments.

RIGHTS, DUTIES AND LIABILITIES
OF BAILOR AND BAILEE

Introduction

Traditionally, courts approached the problem of determining whether the bailee in an ordinary bailment was liable for damage to or loss of the bailed property by recognizing three classes of bailments. These three classes of bailments, the duty usually owed by the bailee in each and the corresponding degree of negligence for which the bailee is liable are summarized as follows: In a bailment for the *sole benefit of the bailee* the bailee owes a duty of *great care* and will be liable for injury to or loss of the property caused by *slight negligence*. In a bailment for the *sole benefit of the bailor* the bailee owes a duty of *slight care* and is liable only for *gross negligence*. In a *mutual benefit* bailment the bailee owes a duty of *reasonable care* and is liable for *ordinary negligence*. Since courts today do not regularly follow the above formula-like approach in determining whether a bailee is liable for damage to or loss of the bailed property, the duties of bailors and bailees in all kinds of ordinary bailments will be discussed with reference to the nature of the bailment made where this is relevant to the particular duty being described.

The parties to an ordinary bailment may establish by agreement their rights and duties to one another in relation to the bailed property. However, in many bailment contracts the parties fail, wholly or in part, to spell out their obligations to one another. The law imposes on the parties to a bailment certain duties and recognizes that they have certain rights, subject to the agreement of the parties.

Bailor's Duties

Subject to the express provisions of the bailment agreement, the bailor is under the duty (1) to perform his agreement, (2) to make certain repairs, (3) to warn of defects, and (4) to reimburse the bailee. As indicated in the following discussion, the existence of each of these duties may depend upon the nature of the bailment present, that is, whether the bailment is a mutual benefit bailment, a bailment for the sole benefit of the bailee, or a bailment for the sole benefit of the bailor.

Duty to Perform Agreement. The bailor in a bailment for hire usually agrees that the bailee is to have possession of the bailed property for a specified time. An example of a bailment for hire is the renting of an automobile. The bailor must not disturb the bailee's possession of the property or repossess it unless the bailee's conduct endangers the property or the bailee has abandoned it. The bailor is responsible for any loss caused the bailee by the bailor's wrongful repossession of the bailed property or other losses caused by the bailor's breach of the contract with the bailee.

Duty to Repair. Ordinary repairs to bailed property, that is, those due to ordinary wear and tear, are the responsibility of the bailee in a mutual benefit bailment, such as the rental of an item of equipment. Repairs that are extraordinary in nature, and not due to the neglect or fault of the bailee, are the responsibility of the bailor.

Duty to Warn of Defects. In a bailment for the sole benefit of the bailee, such as the lending of an automobile, the bailor has a duty to warn the bailee of defects or conditions in the loaned property which might make it dangerous to the bailee and which are known to the bailor. By contrast, in a mutual benefit bailment, such as the renting of an automobile, the bailor has a duty to exercise ordinary care to inspect the bailed property for dangerous defects, and either to make the article safe for its intended purpose or to inform the bailee of any unsafe condition he discovers. The bailor impliedly warrants in a bailment for hire and use that the property is reasonably suitable for the purpose for which it is to be used, as revealed by the bailment agreement. This implied warranty of reasonable fitness is founded upon the same principles underlying the same implied warranty in the law of sales as contained in the Uniform Sales Act and as incorporated into the scope of express warranties under the Uniform Commercial Code, as explained in Chapter 15 of this book.

Duty to Reimburse. If a bailee incurs expense in preserving the bailor's property, the bailor must reimburse the bailee unless the expense was due to the bailee's negligence, misconduct, or misuse of the property.

Bailee's Duties

Subject to the express provisions of the bailment agreement, the bailee is under a duty (1) to perform his agreement, (2) to preserve and protect the property, (3) to return the property, (4) to refrain from misuse of the property. The extent of each of these duties depends upon the nature of the bailment as well as the terms of the bailment agreement.

Duty to Perform Agreement. The bailee is liable for losses suffered by the bailor as a result of the bailee's breach of the bailment contract. Failure of the bailee to return the bailed property as provided for in the contract makes the bailee liable in tort for conversion of the property. If the bailee is to perform some service in respect to the property, such as repair a watch, he must perform with ordinary care and skill, and failure to do so subjects him to liability for any resulting loss.

Duty to Preserve and Protect Property. We saw previously

that courts at one time generally took the view that the bailee's duty of care for the bailed property depended upon whether the bailment was solely for his benefit (in which case he must use great care and is liable for slight negligence), or solely for the benefit of the bailor (in which case he need use but slight care and is liable for gross negligence), or for the mutual benefit of the parties (in which case he must use ordinary care and is liable for ordinary negligence). The modern trend is toward the more flexible standard of care that in all bailments the bailee is under a duty to exercise that degree of care a reasonable man would exercise considering the circumstances, including the nature of the goods, the creation of the bailment, and the purpose of the bailment. In any case a bailee is not liable for loss or damage to the property unless he is negligent or, of course, willfully injures or misuses the property. The bailee is not liable as an insurer unless such liability is provided for in the bailment contract. However, the bailee by virtue of his possession of the bailed property has an insurable interest in the property and may enter into a contract of insurance in respect to the property.

Where property is delivered to a bailee and is returned to the bailor in a damaged state or is not returned at all, the law presumes the bailee's negligence or other fault to be the cause, that is, the bailor has a prima facie case against the bailee. To escape liability the bailee has the burden of showing that the loss was due to other causes consistent with due care on his part.

Generally the parties may, by express contract, increase or decrease the obligations of bailment normally implied by law. Clauses in bailment contracts which expressly limit the bailee's liability, or relieve him from liability completely, for his negligence are not against public policy, but such exculpatory clauses are ineffective against gross negligence or bad faith. The use of general words, such as "not responsible for loss or damage," will be insufficient to eliminate liability, but words excusing from some specific peril, such as "not responsible for loss or damage due to negligence" will be effective as a release from the particular peril. Contract provisions excusing a bailee from liability for negligence will be closely scrutinized by courts and must indicate a clear intention to excuse the bailee before they will be enforced. Also, in some states the extent to which such provisions can operate is governed by statutes.

Duty to Return the Property. The bailee is under a duty to return the property to the bailor, or otherwise account for it according to the contract, upon the termination of the bailment. If the bailee fails to return or account for the bailed property, the bailor may maintain an action for the value of the property. The contract may determine the time and place for return of the property. If not expressed in the contract, the property must be returned as soon as the purpose of the bailment has been accomplished, and it must be returned to the bailor's residence, place of business, or at the place of delivery to the bailee, according to the custom in the locality. As a general rule, a bailee is excused from his duty to return the property if it was lost, stolen, or destroyed without negligence or fault on his part or if the property is taken from him under legal process resulting from litigation between some third person and the bailor.

Duty to Refrain from Unauthorized Use of Property. Due to the nature of a bailment for the sole benefit of the bailor, the bailee has no right to use the property unless the use becomes necessary in order to preserve the property. Where use of the property by the bailee is provided for, the bailee has a duty not to go beyond the authorized use, and he is liable for all damage to the property emanating from any use not authorized expressly or impliedly by the bailment contract, whether or not the damage was caused by his negligence or fault.

Bailee's Right to Compensation

No right of the bailee to compensation exists in a bailment for the sole benefit of the bailee. The bailee's right to compensation in a bailment for the sole benefit of the bailor or in a mutual benefit bailment depends upon the terms of the agreement of the parties. The bailment may be a gratuitous bailment for the sole benefit of the bailor, the clearly expressed intention being that the bailee is to receive no compensation, as where a neighbor stores in his garage another neighbor's automobile with no expectation by either party of a charge being made for the storage of the automobile. In commercial contracts for the storage or repair or rendering of some other service in respect to the bailed property, the bailee is entitled to the contract price for his services. If no price for the services is agreed upon, and the circumstances do not indicate that the service of the bailee shall be gratuitous, the bailee is entitled to recover from the bailor the reasonable value of the services rendered.

Bailee's Lien.   At common law the bailee has an artisan's lien as security for his reasonable charges where he has enhanced the value of the bailed property by spending money or rendering services upon it. Under this lien the bailee may retain the property until his charges are paid, and statutes in most states give a lienor the right to sell the property if his charges are not otherwise satisfied. A bailee's lien is not a general lien, but a special lien that extends only to the property bailed and not to the bailor's property in general. The lien is possessory in that it is lost if the bailee voluntarily parts with the possession of the property. The right to a lien is waived by the bailee if the bailment contract contains a provision granting credit to the bailor or provides for redelivery of the goods without at the same time receiving compensation for the services expended upon the property.

The common-law lien of a bailee may be superior to prior liens on the property or other interests in the property. For example, a mechanic who renders necessary repairs to a mortgaged automobile at the request of the owner-mortgagor in whose possession the automobile had been left by the mortgagee, has a lien superior to the mortgage lien on the ground that since the repairs preserve the security, the mortgagee must be deemed to have consented to their being done. Also, the bailee lienholder may retain possession as against the claims of judgment creditors of the bailor who seek to levy execution or attachment against the property.

Rights Against Third Persons

In all classes of bailments, whether for mutual benefit or for either the bailee's or the bailor's sole benefit, a bailee in possession of personal property has such an interest in the property that he may recover damages against a third person for conversion of, or any injury to, the property bailed while in his possession, or he may maintain an appropriate action to recover possession of the property.

Sale of Property by Bailee

A bailee may not dispose of the bailed property unless authorized by the bailor. Thus, a bailee cannot ordinarily transfer a valid title to a third party by sale of the property which is the subject of the bailment. The sale of the property without the consent of the bailor is a conversion for which the bailee can be held liable. Mere possession, unaccompanied by other circumstances giving it a special character or creating an estoppel, is not such evidence of ownership as to prevail against the true owner. Hence, even if the bailee sells the property to a bona fide purchaser for value, the owner can nevertheless recover the property or its value from the purchaser. However, the bailor is estopped from asserting his ownership as against a good faith purchaser where the bailor has by his words or conduct made it appear to such purchaser that the bailee was the owner or had authority to sell the property.

Bailment for Manufacture

A bailment for manufacture is illustrated by the case in which the bailor delivers raw materials to a manufacturer or processor with the understanding that the form of the materials is to be changed before they are returned. As pointed out in Chapter 33, any materials and enhancement of value added by the bailee to the bailor's property in the manufacturing process becomes the property of the bailor by accession. The manufacturer bailee cannot remove the added materials if the bailor fails to pay for the manufacturing services. The remedies available to the unpaid bailee are either to deliver the property and sue for compensation or to withhold delivery, asserting an artisan's lien, until he is paid the price of his services.

Bailor Not Liable for Bailee's Negligence

A bailor is not liable to third persons for acts of negligence committed by a bailee or the bailee's employee while they are using the property bailed. The negligence of the bailee cannot be imputed to the bailor as in an agency relationship where the torts committed by the agent while within the scope of the agency are imputed to the principal. To illustrate the bailment rule, where the owner of a car delivers it to a garage for repairs, and the garageman agrees to deliver the car to the owner after the repairs, a bailment relationship is created and continues until the car is delivered to the owner, and the garageman does not, while delivering the car, become a servant or agent of the owner so as to make the owner liable for injuries to a third person caused by the negligence of the driver. Statutes in some states impose liability upon the owner of a vehicle for damages negligently caused by a person using the vehicle with the owner's permission. Of course, in any case where the owner of a vehicle who loans it to a person, knows or should have known that the bailee was a careless driver or otherwise unfit to drive, the owner, because of his negligence, can be held liable to third persons injured by the driver while negligently operating the vehicle.

EXTRAORDINARY BAILMENTS

Common carriers and innkeepers make their services available to the public generally, and they are classified as extraordinary bailees, with duties and liabilities greater than those of ordinary bailees.

Common Carriers

A common carrier is one who is in the business of transporting for a compensation the goods of any person who may apply for such service. Railways, steamship companies, motor truckage companies, and air freight lines serving all members of the public are common carriers. A private carrier is one who carries goods only for those whom he chooses.

Both common carriers and private carriers are bailees, but the common carrier is held to a higher standard of responsibility than the private carrier. A private carrier is liable only as an ordinary bailee for hire. But common carriers are insurers of the goods they accept for transportation against all losses except those resulting from certain specified causes. This extraordinary liability of a common carrier originated at a time when the government afforded inadequate protection to goods in transit and when robberies were of frequent occurrence and the danger of collusion between the carrier and the robber was present. For these reasons, the general rule developed that a common carrier is liable for loss or theft or damage to the goods without proof of negligence on the part of the carrier, except that caused by (1) an act of God, (2) an act of the public enemy, (3) an act of the state, (4) an act of the shipper, or (5) the inherent nature of the goods. An act of God is some natural phenomena not caused nor contributed to by man and includes such things as hurricanes, unusual floods, earthquakes, lightning, and landslides. Fire, unless caused by lightning, is not an act of God. Common carriers are regulated by federal and state laws administered by government commissions. These laws permit the carriers to limit their liability by contract with the shipper under certain circumstances.

Innkeepers

An innkeeper or hotelkeeper is one who holds himself out as ready and willing to furnish lodging to all members of the public, usually travelers, who are willing to pay reasonable charges. The term "innkeeper" is construed to mean those who operate "motels," but it does not include operators of apartment, boarding, or rooming houses.

As an extraordinary bailee, an innkeeper is generally liable under the common-law rule for all loss of, or damage to, guests' property except for losses caused by (1) an act of God, (2) an act of a public enemy, (3) the inherent nature of the goods, or (4) negligence of the guest or his servants. Under this rule of strict liability, the guest need not establish that the loss was caused by the negligence of the innkeeper. The liability of the innkeeper for loss of, or damage to, the guests' property is absolute unless the innkeeper can prove that the loss was caused by one of the excepted causes.

Statutes in most states now permit an innkeeper to limit his liability for a guest's property. These statutes typically provide that an innkeeper may limit his liability by furnishing a safe or vault where a guest's money and valuables may be placed for safekeeping and by posting a notice informing the guest of the safekeeping service and further informing him that if the guest does not avail himself of the service, the liability of the innkeeper in case of loss shall not exceed a stated sum.

Real Property

35

INTRODUCTION

The law of real property is highly complex and formalized in comparison with other areas of law. This can be explained in large part by the fact that English land law, on which our present-day real property law is based, is itself based on the complex system of land tenure of feudalistic times which began with the Norman Conquest. The feudal concepts and terminology, although modified to conform to the social, political, and economic structure in America, remain as the basis of real property law in the United States.

ESTATES IN REAL PROPERTY

The two major classes of estates in real property are: (1) freehold estates, and (2) leasehold or less than freehold estates.

Freehold Estates
The freehold estates combine the right of immediate possession with ownership at least for life and are of two kinds: (1) fee simple estates, which may be absolute or determinable, and (2) life estates.

Fee Simple. A fee simple estate, also called fee simple absolute, is the highest possible estate or interest a person can have in real property. This estate gives the owner full dominion over the particular real estate for an unlimited duration of time and all other estates must be carved from it. The owner of real property in fee has the unconditional power to dispose of the property or any of the rights pertaining thereto during his lifetime; the property may be devised by the owner by will; and if the owner dies intestate (without a will) the property descends to his heirs as provided for in the state statutes of descent and distribution. When a person is referred to as the owner of land, it is usually meant that the person has a fee simple estate in the land. The two chief characteristics of the fee simple estate are (1) the owner's power of alienation, or voluntary disposal, and (2) the inheritability of the estate.

A *determinable fee simple estate* (also referred to as a qualified fee or base fee) is an estate in fee which will continue until the happening of some possible event. Upon the happening of the named event, the property will revert to the owner who conveyed the determinable fee, or if he is deceased, to his heirs. For example, a grant of land to a church "so long as the land is used for church purposes" conveys a determinable fee simple estate title to the church. If the possibility of the named event occurring is removed, the determinable fee ripens into a fee simple absolute estate and no reversion can occur. A determinable fee can be created either by deed or by will.

Life Estate. A life estate is an estate the duration of which is limited to the life of the person holding it or to the life or lives of another or others. The owner of a life estate is called a life tenant, and he has the right to use the property for the duration of the estate. He must not commit waste, that is, do anything with the property which will result in permanent injury to it. The life tenant is limited to using the property in the manner to which it was accustomed to being used by the person who created the life estate. Subject to the terms of the instrument creating the estate, the life tenant may operate existing mines and oil or gas wells for his benefit, and where the property involved is rental property such as apartments and houses, the life tenant is entitled to the rents and profits. In addition to refraining from committing waste, the life tenant is under a duty to make ordinary repairs, to pay the ordinary taxes on the property, and to pay the interest on any outstanding mortgage or other encumbrance against the property in so far as the income from the property permits. Although under no duty to do so, a life tenant may insure the premises for his own benefit. A life tenant may sell, lease, or mortgage his life estate.

Life estates are classified as conventional and legal. A conventional life estate is created by the deed or the will of the owner of the fee simple estate. A legal life estate is created by the operation of law, usually for the benefit of the surviving spouse of a deceased owner of land. This kind of life estate exists in those states which recognize the right of dower or curtesy or some similar property right. At common law dower referred to the widow's life estate and curtesy to the widower's life estate and the requirements for the vesting of the estates differed. Today curtesy has been abolished in most states and a dower interest substituted in its place. Another form of property interest sometimes referred to as a legal life estate is the homestead right. The homestead right is granted by statute in most states to permit the head of a family to occupy land of a given area or value exempt, in most cases, from forced sale to satisfy his debts.

The property interest left over after the termination of a life estate or a leasehold estate is called a *future estate* and it may be either a *remainder* or a *reversion*. For example, if A grants a life estate to B for B's life, A is a reversioner because the reversion, that is, the residue left in A will revert to him or his heirs, upon the termination of the life estate. If the conveyance of an estate provides that a third party is to come into possession of the property after a preceding estate has ended, the future estate is called a reminder. For example, if A grants a life estate to B for B's life and upon B's death the property is to pass to C, a remainder interest has been created in favor of C.

Leasehold Estates

The leasehold estates (also called less than freehold estates) are (1) estates for years, (2) estates from year to year, (3) estates at will, and (4) estates at sufferance.

Estate for Years. An estate for years is a leasehold for a definite period of time. For example, a business storeroom leased for a period of one year creates an estate or tenancy for one year and at the end of the fixed term the tenancy terminates automatically with no notice required of either tenant or landlord unless the lease agreement provides otherwise. Although referred to as an estate for years; the period of this form of leasehold estate can be for any fixed term, even less than one year.

Estate from Year to Year. An estate from year to year is created to run from one fixed period to another and thus is often called a periodic tenancy. The fixed period may be from week to week, month to month, or such other period as the parties designate in their agreement. A common example of a periodic tenancy is the renting of a house, for no definite period, but the tenant agrees to pay a certain rental each month. A periodic tenancy is created in such case, and it continues to renew itself from month to month, indefinitely, until it is terminated at the expiration of one of the months by a notice given by one of the parties in accordance with the law. The typical statute requires a thirty-day written notice be given in order to terminate a month to month tenancy.

Estate at Will. An estate or tenancy at will has no fixed term and may be terminated by the landlord or tenant at any time he wishes. At common law notice was not required to terminate a tenancy at will, but statutes today generally require a thirty-day notice.

Estate at Sufferance. An estate or tenancy at sufferance is one in which a tenant holds over without the landlord's consent, after the expiration of his term or other rightful possession. For example, a tenant who continues in possession of real property after the expiration of the term of his lease without the landlord's consent or a mortgagor who holds over after default, foreclosure, and expiration of the redemption period is a tenant at sufferance and is not entitled to notice to vacate the premises unless a notice is required by statute.

CO-OWNERSHIP OF PROPERTY

Types of Co-ownership

An owner of real property has an estate in severalty when he is the only owner of a specific parcel of real estate. Co-ownership of real property is present when more than one person owns the title to a particular piece of real estate. The principal forms of co-ownership are the tenancy in common and the joint tenancy. Other forms of co-ownership are the tenancy by the entirety, community property, the tenancy in partnership, and the condominium.

Tenancy in Common. In a tenancy in common each co-owner has a separate undivided share in the property and upon the death of a co-owner, his share passes to his heirs and not to the other co-owners. Each co-owner in a tenancy in common is said to hold an undivided fraction of every particle of the whole in common with his co-tenant or co-tenants.

A tenancy in common may be created by will or by deed. It also arises when several persons inherit real property by descent from a person who dies intestate (without a will). In most states if a deed grants property to "A and B" or to "A, B, C, and D" a tenancy in common is created. The law favors the tenancy in common over the joint tenancy as a matter of public policy because, as will be seen, in the joint tenancy the survivorship feature makes it possible to disinherit the natural objects of the joint tenant's bounty and affection such as his wife and children. Thus, to create a joint tenancy the parties must clearly express such an intention. If the intention of the parties is not clear, the law generally provides that the co-ownership will be treated as a tenancy in common.

A tenant in common may convey, lease, or mortgage his interest to another co-tenant or to a third party, and the interest of a tenant in common may be reached by his creditors, either before or after the death of the co-tenant.

The co-owners may voluntarily partition the property, or one or more of the co-owners may bring a partition action in court to have the real property physically divided between or among the co-tenants. If physical division of the property is not practicable, the property will be sold and the proceeds of the sale will be shared by the co-owners, after deduction of the costs of the partition proceeding.

Joint Tenancy. In a joint tenancy each person owns an undivided interest in the property and upon the death of a joint tenant, his share passes to the surviving joint tenant or tenants and not to the deceased tenant's heirs, as in the case of a tenancy in common. The right of survivorship is the chief characteristic of the joint tenancy. It must be created by express language in the instrument, usually a deed or will, setting up the co-ownership. In a deed or other instrument the wording usually used to create a joint tenancy is: "to A and B as joint tenants with the right of survivorship," and the phrase "not as tenants in common" is sometimes added. Personal property such as money on deposit in a financial institution and stock in a corporation, as well as real property, is often the subject matter of a joint tenancy.

If a joint tenant conveys by deed his interest in real estate to an outside party, the joint tenancy is destroyed and a tenancy in common is created. A joint tenant cannot, because of the right of survivorship, devise by will his interest in the joint tenancy, nor can his interest be inherited.

While the joint tenancy exists, the interest of a joint tenant may be taken to satisfy his debts, but on the death of one of the joint tenants the surviving joint tenant becomes the owner of the whole property, free of all claims originating in the acts of the deceased joint tenant. Therefore, it is important that a person extending credit to a co-owner of property determine the nature of the co-ownership and take whatever steps may be necessary to make the property subject to the creditor's claim.

Tenancy by the Entirety. A tenancy by the entirety is a form of joint tenancy between a husband and wife. Neither spouse can convey his or her interest in the property so as to defeat the title of the survivor to the whole property or estate. A judgment-creditor of one of the co-tenants cannot have execution levied against the property held in a tenancy by the entirety. If the creditor has taken judgment against both the husband and wife on a joint obligation, the property is subject to execution. In case of divorce the parties become tenants in common. In most states the tenancy by the entirety is no longer recognized, but a husband and wife may accomplish a similar result, at least as to the right of survivorship feature, by creating a joint tenancy.

Community Property. In several states, chiefly in the West and Southwest, there is established by statute a type of co-ownership of property between husband and wife called community property. Under the community property laws the husband and wife are regarded as equal owners of all property, real and personal, acquired during the marriage except that acquired by gift, devise, or descent, or owned by either spouse before marriage. Generally, the husband has the right to manage and control community property, but some state statutes require the wife's consent for certain transactions with respect to land.

Tenancy in Partnership. The tenancy in partnership was described in Chapter 27, and as pointed out there, its incidents are set out in Section 25 of the Uniform Partnership Act.

Condominium. A number of states have recently enacted statutes to legalize the condominium which is a form of co-ownership of real property. In a condominium involving an apartment building each co-owner owns outright his own apartment and also owns an undivided share in the common facilities such as the land, parking space, elevators, and the building itself.

EASEMENTS AND LICENSES

An easement is an irrevocable nonpossessory right held by one person to use in a limited way land possessed by another or the right to limit the use of another person's land. For example, an owner of land may grant by written agreement a right of way over his land to another person. This illustrates what is known as an *affirmative easement*. If A acquires from B, an adjoining property owner, an easement of light and air over B's property, A has a *negative easement* which gives him the right to have B refrain from erecting on his land a structure that would cut off light and air from A's property.

An *easement appurtenant* is created for the purpose of benefiting the land possessed by the owner of the easement and is illustrated by the above examples. The benefited land is called the *dominant tenement* and the land subject to the easement is called the *servient tenement*. If the dominant tenement is transferred, the easement appurtenant passes with it to the new owner. In such cases the easement is said to "run with the land" and may not be sold or devised separate from the land to which it is appurtenant, but it must be conveyed only with such land.

When an easement is not appurtenant to any dominant tenement, it is called an *easement in gross* and generally it is not transferable. Easements to utility companies are usually easements in gross and they are illustrated by a landowner's grant of an easement to a power company to maintain its transmission lines across the land.

A *profit a prendre* is an easement that permits a person to enter the land of another and remove something. For example, a landowner may grant to another person the right to come on the grantor's land and remove sand and gravel or other described natural resources or minerals. A *profit in gross* arises where the property to be removed is not appurtenant to a dominant tenement owned by the grantor, as in the case where the owner of coal under a parcel of land sells the coal but does not own the surface.

Easements are created (1) by express grant, (2) by exception or reservation in a deed by a person conveying land, (3) by implication, (4) by estoppel, (5) by necessity, and (6) by prescription. The usual method of creating an easement is by an express grant in the form of a deed executed as prescribed by the statutes of the state in which the property is located.

A *license* is similar to an easement; however, technically it grants no interest in the land and so may be created orally. Since a contract for an easement calls for the transfer of an interest in land, the Statute of Frauds requires that the contract be in writing. A license is revocable at the will of the person granting the license unless the license is coupled with an interest. A typical example of a license is where a landowner gives a person permission to enter on the land to hunt or fish.

ACQUISITION OF TITLE TO REAL PROPERTY

The principal means employed in transferring title to real property are (1) by deed, (2) by will, and (3) by descent. Among other methods of acquiring title to real property are (1) public grant or patent, (2) adverse possession, (3) operation of law through execution and judicial sales, and (4) accretion.

Deeds

Most transfers of title to real property result from purchase agreements. The actual transfer of title to real property from one selling the property to a purchaser or giving it to a donee is accomplished by means of a deed executed and delivered by the grantor to the grantee in accordance with the formalities prescribed by the statutes of the state where the real estate is located. In general, the requirements of a deed include (1) the names of the grantor and grantee; (2) a recital of the consideration for the deed; (3) words of conveyance; (4) description of the property conveyed; (5) exceptions or reservations; (6) the covenant of warranty and other convenants; (7) execution, including the date, the signatures of the grantor and witnesses and an acknowledgment; and (8) delivery and acceptance.

The two types of deeds in general use in the United States are (1) the *warranty deed* and (2) the *quitclaim deed.* Either type of deed is sufficient to transfer a grantor's title, but the warranty deed provides greater protection to the grantee. Thus, a purchaser of real property should usually insist on receiving a warranty deed. A warranty deed is the type of deed used in most transactions involving a sale of title to real property. In a warranty deed the grantor warrants that a good title to the real estate described in the deed is being conveyed and that no encumbrances exist such as taxes, assessments, a mortgage or other liens except those set forth in the deed. Specifically, the usual warranties in a warranty deed are (1) the covenant of seisin, (2) the covenant for quiet possession, and (3) the covenant against encumbrances. If the title is defective, the grantee may hold the grantor liable on his warranties.

In a *general warranty deed* the grantor warrants against all title defects regardless of whether they arose before or after the grantor acquired the title, while in a *special warranty deed* the grantor warrants the title against only those defects that arose after the grantor acquired title.

A quitclaim deed does not contain a warranty relative to the grantor's title but conveys to the grantee whatever title or interest the grantor has, if any, in the property. Quitclaim deeds are frequently used in removing a "cloud" from the title to real estate, as where a deed is obtained from a spouse who had failed to release a dower interest in a prior deed. They are also frequently used when real estate is being transferred as a gift or when a tenant in common conveys his interest to the other tenants in common.

Once a deed has been delivered it is important that the grantee file his deed for recording in the proper office at the court house in the county in which the property is located. The recording of a deed serves as constructive notice to everyone of the title acquired by the grantee. Therefore, if the grantor should sell or mortgage the same property to another person, the first grantee will be protected if he recorded the deed, even though the subsequent grantee were an innocent purchaser or mortgagee for value and without actual notice of the prior conveyance. An unrecorded deed is effective only between the grantor and grantee and as to others who have actual notice of it.

Before closing a contract for the sale of real estate, the buyer will ordinarily have the title examined to determine that the title is good. It is usually required by the sale contract that the seller must furnish the buyer with an abstract of title certified to date. An abstract is a summary of the history of the title to the property. It does not guarantee the title but is merely a source of information about the title from which an attorney can give an opinion as to the title held by the grantor. The buyer may have the title insured by a title company in order to protect himself against losses which may result later from title defects, even those which would not ordinarily be discovered by a "search" of the title and an examination of the abstract.

In a number of states the "Torrens System" of land registration has been adopted. Under this system an owner of land in fee follows a prescribed procedure to obtain a certificate of title from a designated official, and all liens and encumbrances against the property are noted on the certificate of title. Transfers of title are accomplished by delivery of a deed accompanied by the certificate of title to the new owner who submits them to the designated official who records the transaction and issues a new certificate of title to the grantee. Fees paid for the certificates are held by the state in a fund to protect persons, who without negligence on their part, sustain loss or damage after the original proceeding of registration by another person as owner as a result of fraud, mistake, error, or misdescription of the property on the public records.

Will and Descent

The property interests of a deceased person descend by his will, if he left one, or by terms of the state statutes of descent and distribution, if he died intestate (without a will). Of course, the property left by a decedent is subject to the claims of creditors.

A person may devise his interests in real estate to such persons as he wishes, subject to the claim of a surviving spouse as provided for by the law of the state concerned. The person making a will (the testator, if a man; testatrix, if a woman) must take care to comply with the formal requirements for making a will as prescribed by state statutes. In general, a will must be in writing, signed by the person making it, attested to by two (in some states three) witnesses, and published, that is, declared by the testator or testatrix to the witnesses as his or her will. To insure that a will is prepared and executed according to law, it should be drafted by an attorney.

If a person dies intestate (without a will) his property goes to his heirs and next of kin as described in the state statutes of descent and distribution. Personal property of the decedent is distributed according to the statutes of the state of his residence; real property according to the statutes of the state in which it is located. Although the statutes in the various states are not uniform, they follow the pattern of designating as heirs those persons most closely related to the deceased person, on the assumption that if a will had been left such persons would probably have been named as beneficiaries. Where no heirs survive, the property of the decedent *escheats* to the state.

Other Methods of Acquiring Title

Public Grant or Patent. Title to real property owned by the government is transferred to a buyer by a public grant or patent. For example, the homestead laws provide for a patent to be issued by the federal government to those wishing to settle on and become the owner of certain designated public land made available for such purpose.

Adverse Possession. A person may acquire title to another's real property by means of possession which must be open, continuous, and hostile to the exclusion of the owner for a period of time. The period during which the land must be held adversely in order to gain title varies in the different states. In several states the period is fixed by statute as twenty or twenty-one years, whereas in others the period is less. The periods of time land is possessed adversely by several different persons may be tacked together if there is privity between them, as when one adverse possessor conveys or devises to another his interest in the land. The title acquired by adverse possession may involve a fee simple title or it may involve a lesser interest. The acquisition of an easement by adverse possession is referred to as *prescription.* As a practical matter, it is very difficult to satisfy all the requirements for obtaining title by adverse possession.

Operation of Law. A purchaser of real property at an execution or judicial sale may acquire title to the property even though the owner has not consented to the sale. Such sales often take place in the administration of an estate, or to satisfy a creditor's judgment against the landowner, or to satisfy the claim of a mortgagee or other lienholder seeking foreclosure, or to collect unpaid taxes levied by the government against the property or owner.

Accretion. Title to land is acquired or lost as it is added or eroded away by the action of water upon land bordering a stream or body of water. The enlargement of property by this method is called accretion. Sudden or violent changes in the channel or flow of water do not change the ownership of the affected land. For example, if a river suddenly follows a different channel, the titles of the owners of the land on each side of the river are not affected where the river had been described as the boundary between the two tracts of land.

FIXTURES

Definition and Nature

Included within the definition of real property is anything affixed to the soil by the hand of man so as to become part of it. If what is otherwise personal property is attached to or used in association with land under such circumstances that it becomes part of the land, it is called a fixture and belongs to the owner of the land. Therefore, when a person sells real estate such as his house, the fixtures, including such things as the installed plumbing, garbage disposal, heating system, storm windows, trees, shrubs, and fences pass with the land to the new owner although no mention is made of them in the deed or purchase agreement.

Tests of a Fixture

Historically the courts have used three general tests to determine whether an article is a fixture. These tests are; (1) attachment of the article to the land or something appurtenant to the land, (2) adaptation of the article to the use of the property to which it is attached, and (3) intention of the annexing party to make the article a permanent accession to the land.

The early view taken by courts was that attachment of the article of personal property was the decisive factor in determining whether the article had become a fixture. Today the chief value of the attachment or annexation test is its use by courts in arriving at the intention of the parties involved in a dispute over the nature of the thing in question and who owns it. Articles incorporated into the structure of a building so as to become an integral part of the building lose their character as personal property and become part of the real estate, irrespective of any expressed intention of the parties. If the removal of an article would cause injury to the real property to which it is attached and would substantially destroy the article, courts generally consider such an attachment as strong evidence that the parties intended the article to become a fixture and the owner of the land can claim it. On the other hand, slight attachment to the real property is evidence of an intention that the article was to remain personal property. However, the mode of attachment is not conclusive. An article held in place by gravity alone, as in the case of a statue weighing several tons placed in the court-yard of a residence or stones placed on the top of the ground to form a patio in the yard of a residence, may be a fixture when all the circumstances are considered. Relevant circumstances include the use made of the annexed item as it relates to the real estate and the relationship between the annexing person and the real estate where the annexation occurred.

Portable items such as keys to doors, storm windows, and window screens are by their nature and common acceptance generally considered as essential to the use and enjoyment of buildings and "go with the land" as fixtures. Applying the adaptation test to such articles, courts have held that if the article is essential to the purpose for which the land or building is used it is presumed that it was intended as a permanent im-provement, although its attachment with the land is such that it may be severed without injury to the article or the land. On this basis, a court has held that items of equipment such as refrigerators, stoves, cabinets, and in-a-door beds installed in an apartment building were fixtures.

The intention of the party attaching a chattel to real prop-erty is the controlling test under the modern rule which governs whether the chattel has become a fixture. Where the annexing party's intention is expressly declared, usually in an agreement with another party, the expressed intention will ordinarily con-trol the status of the chattel. Thus, the parties to a lease or a contract of sale may expressly provide, in the lease or contract, with respect to the ownership of each item of property. In the absence of an expressed intention, the courts arrive at the an-nexing party's intention by applying the objective test of what a reasonable man familiar with the circumstances of the case would be justified in concluding about the nature of the property in question. The facts which must be considered in applying this standard are the nature of the article, the nature of the property to which the article is attached, the mode of its attachment, the adaptation of the article to the use of the premises involved, and the relation of the parties who are claiming the article, both their relation to the premises and to one another.

If the party who annexes personal property to land is the owner of the land, there is a strong presumption that he intends to make a permanent addition to the land, but if the annexor has only a limited interest in the land—such as a tenant under a lease, a life tenant, or a licensee—it will be presumed that the annexation was only for his comfort or convenience and he intended to take it with him when he left the land.

Trade, Domestic and Agricultural Fixtures

In the absence of a contrary agreement, courts generally hold that a tenant who has added trade, domestic, or agricultural fixtures may remove them as his personal property, provided their removal will not materially injure the landlord's property. If the lease is for a definite term, the tenant must remove the fixtures before the term provided for in the lease expires unless the lease provides when the fixtures may be removed. Where the tenancy is of uncertain duration, such as a tenancy for life or a tenancy at will, the tenant has a reasonable time after the termination of the tenancy to remove such property. Trade, domestic, and agricultural fixtures are defined as articles installed by a tenant on the leased property to facilitate its use for some business or farming purpose or, in the case of residential property, to make it more comfortable or attractive.

LANDLORD AND TENANT

Leases

Definition. A lease of real property is a contract under which one person called, the lessor, grants to another, the lessee, the right to use and possess certain real property for a consideration called rent. The parties to a lease are also referred to as landlord and tenant and, as we have seen, the estate created by a lease is less than a freehold estate. Although a lease is a conveyance of an interest in land, the leasehold estates are treated for some purposes as personal property and are technically known as chattels real.

Elements of a Lease. The essential elements of a lease are: (1) the tenant's possession of the land must result from the express or implied consent of the landlord; (2) the occupation of the land by the tenant must be subordinate to the title of the landlord; (3) the tenant must have the right to the present possession of the land to the exclusion of others; and (4) a reversionary interest must remain in the landlord giving him the right to regain the possession of the property upon the expiration of the lease.

Under the Statute of Frauds most states require that a lease for more than one year must be in writing. In some states a lease for a term of three years or less need not be evidenced by a writing to be enforceable. Since a lease is a contract, it must satisfy the requirements applicable to contracts generally as discussed in Part Two of this book. In addition, lease agreements in general must contain provisions which cover at least the following matters: (1) the names of the parties, (2) a description of the property leased, (3) a designation of the term for which the tenancy is to exist, and (4) the price agreed upon as rental. Other provisions taking the form of covenants by the lessor and lessee are often included in leases. Covenants in leases create contractual obligations which if breached give the aggrieved party the right to certain remedies including the right to terminate the lease and to hold the breaching party liable for damages. Examples of matters often covered by covenants are the use and restrictions on the use to be made of the leased premises, responsibility for erecting structures and making other improvements or alterations to the property, designation of who has the duty to make repairs, rights of the parties upon destruction of or damage to the premises without fault of either party, option of the lessee to renew or extend the tenancy or purchase the property, right of the lessee to assign or sublease, and termination of the lease.

Rights, Duties and Liabilities of Landlord and Tenant

Possession and Use of Premises. The landlord impliedly warrants that he will give possession of the leased premises to the tenant, who has the right to the exclusive possession and use of the property for the term of the lease. If the landlord or others interfere with the tenant's possession or use of the property or cause injury to it, the tenant may maintain an action against such persons. Unless the lease agreement provides otherwise, the landlord has no general right to enter onto the premises during the term of the lease, and if he does, he is a trespasser. However, the law implies that a landlord may go on premises leased to a tenant to collect rent or to otherwise protect or enforce his interests as landlord.

The tenant's use of the leased premises must be lawful, and the use must be consistent with the use for which they were intended by the parties or to which they have been put, subject to any valid condition in the lease concerning the use of the property. The tenant is under a duty to pay the rent specified in the lease, and at the expiration of the lease he must surrender the premises in good condition, except for ordinary wear and tear.

Condition of Premises and Repairs. The common law rule is that a lessee takes the premises as he finds them unless the lease provides otherwise. In the absence of statute or express provision in the lease to the contrary, a tenant is under a duty to make ordinary repairs, but not structural repairs or repairs to parts of the property used in common with other tenants.

Destruction of Premises. At common law, if a leased building was destroyed by fire or the elements, neither the landlord nor tenant had any obligation to rebuild, in the absence of agreement, but tenant's duty to pay rent continued until the term expired on the theory that the lessee's estate in the land remained. Statutes have been enacted in several states to provide that when a leased building is destroyed or made untenantable, without fault of the lessee, by fire or the elements, and no express agreement to the contrary has been made, the lessee may surrender the premises and be excused from liability for rent subsequent to the surrender. In all states the same result can be accomplished by provision in the lease.

Assignment and Subletting. A lessee may assign or sublease the premises without the consent of the lessor unless the lease or some statute prohibits such action. It is common practice for a lease to contain a provision prohibiting assigning or subletting without the written consent of the lessor.

An assignment is a conveyance by the tenant of his entire interest in the premises. The assignee assumes the status as tenant with all the rights and duties of the assigning tenant whose interest ceases, but the assigning tenant continues liable for the rent and for the performance of the other covenants of the lease unless he is released by his lessor.

A sublease is a conveyance by the tenant of only part of the premises or only a portion of the term of the lease. The relationship of landlord and tenant between the sublessor and sublessee is created by subletting, but the sublessee is not a tenant of the original landlord and is liable only on the covenants of his own sublease and has no responsibility to the lessor on the original lease.

Termination of Lease

A lease may terminate as a result of the following causes: (1) expiration of the term of the lease, if the lease is for a definite period of time; (2) voluntary surrender of the premises by the lessee, with the consent of the lessor to release the lessee from his obligations under the lease; (3) forfeiture of the lease due to breach of a covenant, as provided for in the lease; (4) loss of the lessor's title due to a taking of the property by eminent domain or other judicial proceeding such as foreclosure under a prior mortgage, and (5) by statute, as illustrated by the case discussed earlier involving destruction of the premises without fault of the tenant.

APPENDIXES

SELECTED BIBLIOGRAPHY

The books included in this bibliography have been selected to assist the reader who wishes to make a further study of business law, particularly with reference to the law as it exists under the Uniform Commercial Code. Most of the listed books contain extracts from court opinions in actual cases which provide further illustrations of the application of many of the principles discussed in this book.

Anderson, Ronald A.	*Anderson's Uniform Commercial Code* 2 Vols.	Lawyers Co-op.	1961
Anderson, Ronald A. and Kumpf, Walter A.	*Business Law: Principles and Cases*	South-western	1963
Dillivou, Essel R. and others	*Principles of Business Law:* Alternate 7th Edition, Uniform Commercial Code	Prentice-Hall	1964
Dykstra, Gerald O. and Dykstra, Lillian G.	*Business Law: Text and Cases*	Pitman	1958
Gillam, Cornelius W., editor	*Foundations of Law in a Business Society Series*	Prentice-Hall	1963
Houghteling, James L., Jr. and Pierce, George G.	*The Legal Environment of Business*	Harcourt, Brace & World	1963
Lavine, A. Lincoln	*Modern Business Law*	Prentice-Hall	1963
Lusk, Harold F.	*Business Law: Principles and Cases*	Irwin	1963
Mounce, Earl Winfield and Dawson, Townes Loring	*Business Law: Text and Cases*	Heath	1958
Smith, Len Young and Roberson, G. Gale	*Business Law: Uniform Commercial Code Edition*	West	1962
Thompson, George C. and Brady, Gerald P.	*Law in a Business Environment*	Wadsworth	1963
Votaw, Dow	*Legal Aspects of Business Administration*	Prentice-Hall	1961
Wyatt, John W. and Wyatt, Madie B.	*Business Law: Principles and Cases*	McGraw-Hill	1963

Uniform Commercial Code

ARTICLE 1: GENERAL PROVISIONS

Part 1

Short Title, Construction, Application and Subject Matter of the Act

§1–101. Short Title. This Act shall be known and may be cited as Uniform Commercial Code.

§1–102. Purposes; Rules of Construction; Variation by Agreement. (1) This Act shall be liberally construed and applied to promote its underlying purposes and policies.

(2) Underlying purposes and policies of this Act are

(a) to simplify, clarify and modernize the law governing commercial transactions;

(b) to permit the continued expansion of commercial practices through custom, usage and agreement of the parties;

(c) to make uniform the law among the various jurisidictions.

(3) The effect of provisions of this Act may be varied by agreement, except as otherwise provided in this Act and except that the obligations of good faith, diligence, reasonableness and care prescribed by this Act may not be disclaimed by agreement but the parties may by agreement determine the standards by which the performance of such obligations is to be measured if such standards are not manifestly unreasonable.

(4) The presence in certain provisions of this Act of the words "unless otherwise agreed" or words of similar import does not imply that the effect of other provisions may not be varied by agreement under subsection (3).

(5) In this Act unless the context otherwise requires

(a) words in the singular number include the plural, and in the plural include the singular;

(b) words of the masculine gender include the feminine and the neuter, and when the sense so indicates words of the neuter gender may refer to any gender.

§1–103. Supplementary General Principles of Law Applicable. Unless displaced by the particular provisions of this Act, the principles of law and equity, including the law merchant and the law relative to capacity to contract, principal and

Reprinted with permission of the National Conference of Commissioners on Uniform State Laws.

433

agent, estoppel, fraud, misrepresentation, duress, coercion, mistake, bankruptcy, or other validating or invalidating cause shall supplement its provisions.

§1–104. Construction Against Implicit Repeal. This Act being a general act intended as a unified coverage of its subject matter, no part of it shall be deemed to be impliedly repealed by subsequent legislation if such construction can reasonably be avoided.

§1–105. Territorial Application of the Act; Parties' Power to Choose Applicable Law. (1) Except as provided hereafter in this section, when a transaction bears a reasonable relation to this state and also to another state or nation the parties may agree that the law either of this state or of such other state or nation shall govern their rights and duties. Failing such agreement this Act applies to transactions bearing an appropriate relation to this state.

(2) Where one of the following provisions of this Act specifies the applicable law, that provision governs and a contrary agreement is effective only to the extent permitted by the law (including the conflict of laws rules) so specified:

Rights of creditors against sold goods. Section 2–402.

Applicability of the Article on Bank Deposits and Collections. Section 4–102.

Bulk transfers subject to the Article on Bulk Transfers. Section 6–102.

Applicability of the Article on Investment Securities. Section 8–106.

Policy and scope of the Article on Secured Transactions. Sections 9–102 and 9–103.

§1–106. Remedies to Be Liberally Administered. (1) The remedies provided by this Act shall be liberally administered to the end that the aggrieved party may be put in as good a position as if the other party had fully performed but neither consequential or special nor penal damages may be had except as specifically provided in this Act or by other rule of law.

(2) Any right or obligation declared by this Act is enforceable by action unless the provision declaring it specifies a different and limited effect.

§1–107. Waiver or Renunciation of Claim or Right After Breach. Any claim or right arising out of an alleged breach can be discharged in whole or in part without consideration by a written waiver or renunciation signed and delivered by the aggrieved party.

§1–108. Severability. If any provision or clause of this Act or application thereof to any person or circumstances is held invalid, such invalidity shall not affect other provisions or applications of the Act which can be given effect without the invalid provision or application, and to this end the provisions of this Act are declared to be severable.

§1–109. Section Captions. Section captions are parts of this Act.

Part 2

General Definitions and Principles of Interpretation

§1–201. General Definitions. Subject to additional definitions contained in the subsequent Articles of this Act which are applicable to specific Articles or Parts thereof, and unless the context otherwise requires, in this Act:

(1) "Action" in the sense of a judicial proceeding includes recoupment, coun-

terclaim, set-off, suit in equity and any other proceedings in which rights are determined.

(2) "Aggrieved party" means a party entitled to resort to a remedy.

(3) "Agreement" means the bargain of the parties in fact as found in their language or by implication from other circumstances including course of dealing or usage of trade or course of performance as provided in this Act (Sections 1–205 and 2–208). Whether an agreement has legal consequences is determined by the provisions of this Act, if applicable; otherwise by the law of contracts (Section 1–103). (Compare "Contract".)

(4) "Bank" means any person engaged in the business of banking.

(5) "Bearer" means the person in possession of an instrument, document of title, or security payable to bearer or indorsed in blank.

(6) "Bill of lading" means a document evidencing the receipt of goods for shipment issued by a person engaged in the business of transporting or forwarding goods, and includes an airbill. "Airbill" means a document serving for air transportation as a bill of lading does for marine or rail transportation, and includes an air consignment note or air waybill.

(7) "Branch" includes a separately incorporated foreign branch of a bank.

(8) "Burden of establishing" a fact means the burden of persuading the triers of fact that the existence of the fact is more probable than its non-existence.

(9) "Buyer in ordinary course of business" means a person who in good faith and without knowledge that the sale to him is in violation of the ownership rights or security interest of a third party in the goods buys in ordinary course from a person in the business of selling goods of that kind but does not include a pawnbroker. "Buying" may be for cash or by exchange of other property or on secured or unsecured credit and includes receiving goods or documents of title under a pre-existing contract for sale but does not include a transfer in bulk or as security for or in total or partial satisfaction of a money debt.

(10) "Conspicuous": A term or clause is conspicuous when it is so written that a reasonable person against whom it is to operate ought to have noticed it. A printed heading in capitals (as: Non-Negotiable Bill of Lading) is conspicuous. Language in the body of a form is "conspicuous" if it is in larger or other contrasting type or color. But in a telegram any stated term is "conspicuous". Whether a term or clause is "conspicuous" or not is for decision by the court.

(11) "Contract" means the total legal obligation which results from the parties' agreement as affected by this Act and any other applicable rules of law. (Compare "Agreement".)

(12) "Creditor" includes a general creditor, a secured creditor, a lien creditor and any representative of creditors, including an assignee for the benefit of creditors, a trustee in bankruptcy, a receiver in equity and an executor or administrator of an insolvent debtor's or assignor's estate.

(13) "Defendant" includes a person in the position of defendant in a cross-action or counterclaim.

(14) "Delivery" with respect to instruments, documents of title, chattel paper or securities means voluntary transfer of possession.

(15) "Document of title" includes bill of lading, dock warrant, dock receipt, warehouse receipt or order for the delivery of goods, and also any other document which in the regular course of business or financing is treated as adequately evidencing that the person in possession of it is entitled to receive, hold and dispose of the document and the goods it covers. To be a document of title a document must purport to be issued by or addressed to a bailee and purport to cover goods in the bailee's possession which are either identified or are fungible portions of an identified mass.

(16) "Fault" means wrongful act, omission or breach.

(17) "Fungible" with respect to goods or securities means goods or securities of which any unit is, by nature or usage of trade, the equivalent of any other like unit. Goods which are not fungible shall be deemed fungible for the purposes of this Act to the extent that under a particular agreement or document unlike units are treated as equivalents.

(18) "Genuine" means free of forgery or counterfeiting.

(19) "Good faith" means honesty in fact in the conduct or transaction concerned.

(20) "Holder" means a person who is in possession of a document of title or an instrument or an investment security drawn, issued or indorsed to him or to his order or to bearer or in blank.

(21) To "honor" is to pay or to accept and pay, or where a credit so engages to purchase or discount a draft complying with the terms of the credit.

(22) "Insolvency proceedings" includes any assignment for the benefit of creditors or other proceedings intended to liquidate or rehabilitate the estate of the person involved.

(23) A person is "insolvent" who either has ceased to pay his debts in the ordinary course of business or cannot pay his debts as they become due or is insolvent within the meaning of the federal bankruptcy law.

(24) "Money" means a medium of exchange authorized or adopted by a domestic or foreign government as a part of its currency.

(25) A person has "notice" of a fact when

(a) he has actual knowledge of it; or

(b) he has received a notice or notification of it; or

(c) from all the facts and circumstances known to him at the time in question he has reason to know that it exists.

A person "knows" or has "knowledge" of a fact when he has actual knowledge of it. "Discover" or "learn" or a word or phrase of similar import refers to knowledge rather than to reason to know. The time and circumstances under which a notice or notification may cease to be effective are not determined by this Act.

(26) A person "notifies" or "gives" a notice or notification to another by taking such steps as may be reasonably required to inform the other in ordinary course whether or not such other actually comes to know of it. A person "receives" a notice or notification when

(a) it comes to his attention; or

(b) it is duly delivered at the place of business through which the contract was made or at any other place held out by him as the place for receipt of such communications.

(27) Notice, knowledge or a notice or notification received by an organization is effective for a particular transaction from the time when it is brought to the attention of the individual conducting that transaction, and in any event from the time when it would have been brought to his attention if the organization had exercised due diligence.

(28) "Organization" includes a corporation, government or governmental subdivision or agency, business trust, estate, trust, partnership or association, two or more persons having a joint or common interest, or any other legal or commercial entity.

(29) "Party", as distinct from "third party", means a person who has engaged in a transaction or made an agreement within this Act.

(30) "Person" includes an individual or an organization (see Section 1–102).

(31) "Presumption" or "presumed" means that the trier of fact must find the existence of the fact presumed unless and until evidence is introduced which would support a finding of its non-existence.

(32) "Purchase" includes taking by sale, discount, negotiation, mortgage, pledge, lien, issue or re-issue, gift or any other voluntary transaction creating an interest in property.

(33) "Purchaser" means a person who takes by purchase.

(34) "Remedy" means any remedial right to which an aggrieved party is entitled with or without resort to a tribunal.

(35) "Representative" includes an agent, an officer of a corporation or association, and a trustee, executor or administrator of an estate, or any other person empowered to act for another.

(36) "Rights" includes remedies.

(37) "Security interest" means an interest in personal property or fixtures which secures payment or performance of an obligation. The retention or reservation of title by a seller of goods notwithstanding shipment or delivery to the buyer (Section 2–401) is limited in effect to a reservation of a "security interest". The term also includes any interest of a buyer of accounts, chattel paper, or contract rights which is subject to Article 9. The special property interest of a buyer of goods on identification of such goods to a contract for sale under Section 2–401 is not a "security interest", but a buyer may also acquire a "security interest" by complying with Article 9. Unless a lease or consignment is intended as security, reservation of title thereunder is not a "security interest" but a consignment is in any event subject to the provisions on consignment sales (Section 2–326). Whether a lease is intended as security is to be determined by the facts of each case; however, (a) the inclusion of an option to purchase does not of itself make the lease one intended for security, and (b) an agreement that upon compliance with the terms of the lease the lessee shall become or has the option to become the owner of the property for no additional consideration or for a nominal consideration does make the lease one intended for security.

(38) "Send" in connection with any writing or notice means to deposit in the mail or deliver for transmission by any other usual means of communication with

postage or cost of transmission provided for and properly addressed and in the case of an instrument to an address specified thereon or otherwise agreed, or if there be none to any address reasonable under the circumstances. The receipt of any writing or notice within the time at which it would have arrived if properly sent has the effect of a proper sending.

(39) "Signed" includes any symbol executed or adopted by a party with present intention to authenticate a writing.

(40) "Surety" includes guarantor.

(41) "Telegram" includes a message transmitted by radio, teletype, cable, any mechanical method of transmission, or the like.

(42) "Term" means that portion of an agreement which relates to a particular matter.

(43) "Unauthorized" signature or indorsement means one made without actual, implied or apparent authority and includes a forgery.

(44) "Value". Except as otherwise provided with respect to negotiable instruments and bank collections (Sections 3–303, 4–208 and 4–209) a person gives "value" for rights if he acquires them

(a) in return for a binding commitment to extend credit or for the extension of immediately available credit whether or not drawn upon and whether or not a charge-back is provided for in the event of difficulties in collection; or

(b) as security for or in total or partial satisfaction of a pre-existing claim; or

(c) by accepting delivery pursuant to a pre-existing contract for purchase; or

(d) generally, in return for any consideration sufficient to support a simple contract.

(45) "Warehouse receipt" means a receipt issued by a person engaged in the business of storing goods for hire.

(46) "Written" or "writing" includes printing, typewriting or any other intentional reduction to tangible form.

§1–202. **Prima Facie Evidence by Third Party Documents.** A document in due form purporting to be a bill of lading, policy or certificate of insurance, official weigher's or inspector's certificate, consular invoice, or any other document authorized or required by the contract to be issued by a third party shall be prima facie evidence of its own authenticity and genuineness and of the facts stated in the document by the third party.

§1–203. **Obligation of Good Faith.** Every contract or duty within this Act imposes an obligation of good faith in its performance or enforcement.

§1–204. **Time; Reasonable Time; "Seasonably".** (1) Whenever this Act requires any action to be taken within a reasonable time, any time which is not manifestly unreasonable may be fixed by agreement.

(2) What is a reasonable time for taking any action depends on the nature, purpose and circumstances of such action.

(3) An action is taken "seasonably" when it is taken at or within the time agreed or if no time is agreed at or within a reasonable time.

§1–205. **Course of Dealing and Usage of Trade.** (1) A course of dealing is a sequence of previous conduct between the parties to a particular transaction which is fairly to be regarded as establishing a common basis of understanding for interpreting their expressions and other conduct.

(2) A usage of trade is any practice or method of dealing having such regularity of observance in a place, vocation or trade as to justify an expectation that it will be observed with respect to the transaction in question. The existence and scope of such a usage are to be proved as facts. If it is established that such a usage is embodied in a written trade code or similar writing the interpretation of the writing is for the court.

(3) A course of dealing between parties and any usage of trade in the vocation or trade in which they are engaged or of which they are or should be aware give particular meaning to and supplement or qualify terms of an agreement.

(4) The express terms of an agreement and an applicable course of dealing or usage of trade shall be construed wherever reasonable as consistent with each other; but when such construction is unreasonable express terms control both course of dealing and usage of trade and course of dealing controls usage of trade.

(5) An applicable usage of trade in the place where any part of performance is to occur shall be used in interpreting the agreement as to that part of the performance.

(6) Evidence of a relevant usage of trade offered by one party is not admissible unless and until he has given the other party such notice as the court finds sufficient to prevent unfair surprise to the latter.

§1–206. Statute of Frauds for Kinds of Personal Property Not Otherwise Covered. (1) Except in the cases described in subsection (2) of this section a contract for the sale of personal property is not enforceable by way of action or defense beyond five thousand dollars in amount or value of remedy unless there is some writing which indicates that a contract for sale has been made between the parties at a defined or stated price, reasonably identifies the subject matter, and is signed by the party against whom enforcement is sought or by his authorized agent.

(2) Subsection (1) of this section does not apply to contracts for the sale of goods (Section 2–201) nor of securities (Section 8–319) nor to security agreements (Section 9–203).

§1–207. Performance or Acceptance Under Reservation of Rights. A party who with explicit reservation of rights performs or promises performance or assents to performance in a manner demanded or offered by the other party does not thereby prejudice the rights reserved. Such words as "without prejudice", "under protest" or the like are sufficient.

§1–208. Option to Accelerate at Will. A term providing that one party or his successor in interest may accelerate payment or performance or require collateral or additional collateral "at will" or "when he deems himself insecure" or in words of similar import shall be construed to mean that he shall have power to do so only if he in good faith believes that the prospect of payment or performance is impaired. The burden of establishing lack of good faith is on the party against whom the power has been exercised.

Article 2: Sales

Part 1

Short Title, General Construction and Subject Matter

§2–101. Short Title. This article shall be known and may be cited as Uniform Commercial Code—Sales.

§2–102. Scope; Certain Security and Other Transactions Excluded From This Article. Unless the context otherwise requires, this Article applies to transactions in goods; it does not apply to any transaction which although in the form of an unconditional contract to sell or present sale is intended to operate only as a security transaction nor does this Article impair or repeal any statute regulating sales to consumers, farmers or other specified classes of buyers.

§2–103. Definitions and Index of Definitions. (1) In this Article unless the context otherwise requires

(a) "Buyer" means a person who buys or contracts to buy goods.

(b) "Good faith" in the case of a merchant means honesty in fact and the observance of reasonable commercial standards of fair dealing in the trade.

(c) "Receipt" of goods means taking physical possession of them.

(d) "Seller" means a person who sells or contracts to sell goods.

(2) Other definitions applying to this Article or to specified Parts thereof, and the sections in which they appear are:

"Acceptance". Section 2–606.
"Banker's credit". Section 2–325.
"Between merchants". Section 2–104.
"Cancellation". Section 2–106(4).
"Commercial unit". Section 2–105.
"Confirmed credit". Section 2–325.
"Conforming to contract". Section 2–106.
"Contract for sale". Section 2–106.
"Cover". Section 2–712.
"Entrusting". Section 2–403.
"Financing agency". Section 2–104.
"Future goods". Section 2–105.
"Goods". Section 2–105.
"Identification". Section 2–501.
"Installment contract". Section 2–612.
"Letter of Credit". Section 2–325.
"Lot". Section 2–105.
"Merchant". Section 2–104.
"Overseas". Section 2–323.
"Person in position of seller". Section 2–707.
"Present sale". Section 2–106.

"Sale". Section 2–106.

"Sale on approval". Section 2–326.

"Sale or return". Section 2–326.

"Termination". Section 2–106.

(3) The following definitions in other Articles apply to this Article:

"Check". Section 3–104.

"Consignee". Section 7–102.

"Consignor". Section 7–102.

"Consumer goods". Section 9–109.

"Dishonor". Section 3–507.

"Draft". Section 3–104.

(4) In addition Article 1 contains general definitions and principles of construction and interpretation applicable throughout this Article.

§2–104. Definitions: "Merchant"; "Between Merchants"; "Financing Agency". (1) "Merchant" means a person who deals in goods of the kind or otherwise by his occupation holds himself out as having knowledge or skill peculiar to the practices or goods involved in the transaction or to whom such knowledge or skill may be attributed by his employment of an agent or broker or other intermediary who by his occupation holds himself out as having such knowledge or skill.

(2) "Financing agency" means a bank, finance company or other person who in the ordinary course of business makes advances against goods or documents of title or who by arrangement with either the seller or the buyer intervenes in ordinary course to make or collect payment due or claimed under the contract for sale, as by purchasing or paying the seller's draft or making advances against it or by merely taking it for collection whether or not documents of title accompany the draft. "Financing agency" includes also a bank or other person who similarly intervenes between persons who are in the position of seller and buyer in respect to the goods (Section 2–707).

(3) "Between merchants" means in any transaction with respect to which both parties are chargeable with the knowledge or skill of merchants.

§2–105. Definitions: Transferability; "Goods"; "Future" Goods; "Lot"; "Commercial Unit". (1) "Goods" means all things (including specially manufactured goods) which are movable at the time of identification to the contract for sale other than the money in which the price is to be paid, investment securities (Article 8) and things in action. "Goods" also includes the unborn young of animals and growing crops and other identified things attached to realty as described in the section on goods to be severed from realty (Section 2–107).

(2) Goods must be both existing and identified before any interest in them can pass. Goods which are not both existing and identified are "future" goods. A purported present sale of future goods or of any interest therein operates as a contract to sell.

(3) There may be a sale of a part interest in existing identified goods.

(4) An undivided share in an identified bulk of fungible goods is sufficiently identified to be sold although the quantity of the bulk is not determined. Any agreed proportion of such a bulk or any quantity thereof agreed upon by

number, weight or other measure may to the extent of the seller's interest in the bulk be sold to the buyer who then becomes an owner in common.

(5) "Lot" means a parcel or a single article which is the subject matter of a separate sale or delivery, whether or not it is sufficient to perform the contract.

(6) "Commercial unit" means such a unit of goods as by commercial usage is a single whole for purposes of sale and division of which materially impairs its character or value on the market or in use. A commercial unit may be a single article (as a machine) or a set of articles (as a suite of furniture or an assortment of sizes) or a quantity (as a bale, gross, or carload) or any other unit treated in use or in the relevant market as a single whole.

§2–106. Definitions: "Contract"; "Agreement"; "Contract for Sale"; "Sale"; "Present Sale"; "Conforming" to Contract; "Termination"; "Cancellation". (1) In this Article unless the context otherwise requires "contract" and "agreement" are limited to those relating to the present or future sale of goods. "Contract for sale" includes both a present sale of goods and a contract to sell goods at a future time. A "sale" consists in the passing of title from the seller to the buyer for a price (Section 2–401). A "present sale" means a sale which is accomplished by the making of the contract.

(2) Goods or conduct including any part of a performance are "conforming" or conform to the contract when they are in accordance with the obligations under the contract.

(3) "Termination" occurs when either party pursuant to a power created by agreement or law puts an end to the contract otherwise than for its breach. On "termination" all obligations which are still executory on both sides are discharged but any right based on prior breach or performance survives.

(4) "Cancellation" occurs when either party puts an end to the contract for breach by the other and its effect is the same as that of "termination" except that the cancelling party also retains any remedy for breach of the whole contract or any unperformed balance.

§2–107. Goods to Be Severed From Realty: Recording. (1) A contract for the sale of timber, minerals or the like or a structure or its materials to be removed from realty is a contract for the sale of goods within this Article if they are to be severed by the seller but until severance a purported present sale thereof which is not effective as a transfer of an interest in land is effective only as a contract to sell.

(2) A contract for the sale apart from the land of growing crops or other things attached to realty and capable of severance without material harm thereto but not described in subsection (1) is a contract for the sale of goods within this Article whether the subject matter is to be severed by the buyer or by the seller even though it forms part of the realty at the time of contracting, and the parties can by identification effect a present sale before severance.

(3) The provisions of this section are subject to any third party rights provided by the law relating to realty records, and the contract for sale may be executed and recorded as a document transferring an interest in land and shall then constitute notice to third parties of the buyer's rights under the contract for sale.

Part 2

Form, Formation and Readjustment of Contract

§2–201. Formal Requirements; Statute of Frauds. (1) Except as otherwise provided in this section a contract for the sale of goods for the price of $500 or more is not enforceable by way of action or defense unless there is some writing sufficient to indicate that a contract for sale has been made between the parties and signed by the party against whom enforcement is sought or by his authorized agent or broker. A writing is not insufficient because it omits or incorrectly states a term agreed upon but the contract is not enforceable under this paragraph beyond the quantity of goods shown in such writing.

(2) Between merchants if within a reasonable time a writing in confirmation of the contract and sufficient against the sender is received and the party receiving it has reason to know its contents, it satisfies the requirements of subsection (1) against such party unless written notice of objection to its contents is given within ten days after it is received.

(3) A contract which does not satisfy the requirements of subsection (1) but which is valid in other respects is enforceable

(a) if the goods are to be specially manufactured for the buyer and are not suitable for sale to others in the ordinary course of the seller's business and the seller, before notice of repudiation is received and under circumstances which reasonably indicate that the goods are for the buyer, has made either a substantial beginning of their manufacture or commitments for their procurement; or

(b) if the party against whom enforcement is sought admits in his pleading, testimony or otherwise in court that a contract for sale was made, but the contract is not enforceable under this provision beyond the quantity of goods admitted; or

(c) with respect to goods for which payment has been made and accepted or which have been received and accepted (Section 2–606).

§2–202. Final Written Expression: Parol or Extrinsic Evidence. Terms with respect to which the confirmatory memoranda of the parties agree or which are otherwise set forth in a writing intended by the parties as a final expression of their agreement with respect to such terms as are included therein may not be contradicted by evidence of any prior agreement or of a contemporaneous oral agreement but may be explained or supplemented

(a) by course of dealing or usage of trade (Section 1–205) or by course of performance (Section 2–208); and

(b) by evidence of consistent additional terms unless the court finds the writing to have been intended also as a complete and exclusive statement of the terms of the agreement.

§2–203. Seals Inoperative. The affixing of a seal to a writing evidencing a contract for sale or an offer to buy or sell goods does not constitute the writing a sealed instrument and the law with respect to sealed instruments does not apply to such a contract or offer.

§2–204. Formation in General. (1) A contract for sale of goods may be made in any manner sufficient to show agreement, including conduct by both parties which recognizes the existence of such a contract.

(2) An agreement sufficient to constitute a contract for sale may be found even though the moment of its making is undetermined.

(3) Even though one or more terms are left open a contract for sale does not fail for indefiniteness if the parties have intended to make a contract and there is a reasonably certain basis for giving an appropriate remedy.

§2–205. Firm Offers. An offer by a merchant to buy or sell goods in a signed writing which by its terms gives assurance that it will be held open is not revocable, for lack of consideration, during the time stated or if no time is stated for a reasonable time, but in no event may such period of irrevocability exceed three months; but any such term of assurance on a form supplied by the offeree must be separately signed by the offeror.

§2–206. Offer and Acceptance in Formation of Contract. (1) Unless otherwise unambiguously indicated by the language or circumstances

(a) an offer to make a contract shall be construed as inviting acceptance in any manner and by any medium reasonable in the circumstances;

(b) an order or other offer to buy goods for prompt or current shipment shall be construed as inviting acceptance either by a prompt promise to ship or by the prompt or current shipment of conforming or non-conforming goods, but such a shipment of non-conforming goods does not constitute an acceptance if the seller seasonably notifies the buyer that the shipment is offered only as an accommodation to the buyer.

(2) Where the beginning of a requested performance is a reasonable mode of acceptance an offeror who is not notified of acceptance within a reasonable time may treat the offer as having lapsed before acceptance.

§2–207. Additional Terms in Acceptance or Confirmation. (1) A definite and seasonable expression of acceptance or a written confirmation which is sent within a reasonable time operates as an acceptance even though it states terms additional to or different from those offered or agreed upon, unless acceptance is expressly made conditional on assent to the additional or different terms.

(2) The additional terms are to be construed as proposals for addition to the contract. Between merchants such terms become part of the contract unless:

(a) the offer expressly limits acceptance to the terms of the offer;

(b) they materially alter it; or

(c) notification of objection to them has already been given or is given within a reasonable time after notice of them is received.

(3) Conduct by both parties which recognizes the existence of a contract is sufficient to establish a contract for sale although the writings of the parties do not otherwise establish a contract. In such case the terms of the particular contract consist of those terms on which the writings of the parties agree, together with any supplementary terms incorporated under any other provisions of this Act.

§2–208. Course of Performance or Practical Construction. (1) Where the contract for sale involves repeated occasions for performance by either party with knowledge of the nature of the performance and opportunity for objection to it by the other, any course of performance accepted or acquiesced in without objection shall be relevant to determine the meaning of the agreement.

(2) The express terms of the agreement and any such course of performance, as well as any course of dealing and usage of trade, shall be construed whenever reasonable as consistent with each other; but when such construction is unreasonable, express terms shall control course of performance and course of performance shall control both course of dealing and usage of trade (Section 1-205).

(3) Subject to the provisions of the next section on modification and waiver, such course of performance shall be relevant to show a waiver or modification of any term inconsistent with such course of performance.

§2-209. Modification, Rescission and Waiver. (1) An agreement modifying a contract within this Article needs no consideration to be binding.

(2) A signed agreement which excludes modification or rescission except by a signed writing cannot be otherwise modified or rescinded, but except as between merchants such a requirement on a form supplied by the merchant must be separately signed by the other party.

(3) The requirements of the statute of frauds section of this Article (Section 2-201) must be satisfied if the contract as modified is within its provisions.

(4) Although an attempt at modification or rescission does not satisfy the requirements of subsection (2) or (3) it can operate as a waiver.

(5) A party who has made a waiver affecting an executory portion of the contract may retract the waiver by reasonable notification received by the other party that strict performance will be required of any term waived, unless the retraction would be unjust in view of a material change of position in reliance on the waiver.

§2-210. Delegation of Performance; Assignment of Rights. (1) A party may perform his duty through a delegate unless otherwise agreed or unless the other party has a substantial interest in having his original promisor perform or control the acts required by the contract. No delegation of performance relieves the party delegating of any duty to perform or any liability for breach.

(2) Unless otherwise agreed all rights of either seller or buyer can be assigned except where the assignment would materially change the duty of the other party, or increase materially the burden or risk imposed on him by his contract, or impair materially his chance of obtaining return performance. A right to damages for breach of the whole contract or a right arising out of the assignor's due performance of his entire obligation can be assigned despite agreement otherwise.

(3) Unless the circumstances indicate the contrary a prohibition of assignment of "the contract" is to be construed as barring only the delegation to the assignee of the assignor's performance.

(4) An assignment of "the contract" or of "all my rights under the contract" or an assignment in similar general terms is an assignment of rights and unless the language or the circumstances (as in an assignment for security) indicate the contrary, it is a delegation of performance of the duties of the assignor and its

acceptance by the assignee constitutes a promise by him to perform those duties. This promise is enforceable by either the assignor or the other party to the original contract.

(5) The other party may treat any assignment which delegates performance as creating reasonable grounds for insecurity and may without prejudice to his rights against the assignor demand assurances from the assignee (Section 2–609).

Part 3

General Obligation and Construction of Contract

§2–301. General Obligations of Parties. The obligation of the seller is to transfer and deliver and that of the buyer is to accept and pay in accordance with the contract.

§2–302. Unconscionable Contract or Clause. (1) If the court as a matter of law finds the contract or any clause of the contract to have been unconscionable at the time it was made the court may refuse to enforce the contract, or it may enforce the remainder of the contract without the unconscionable clause, or it may so limit the application of any unconscionable clause as to avoid any unconscionable result.

(2) When it is claimed or appears to the court that the contract or any clause thereof may be unconscionable the parties shall be afforded a reasonable opportunity to present evidence as to its commercial setting, purpose and effect to aid the court in making the determination.

§2–303. Allocation or Division of Risks. Where this Article allocates a risk or a burden as between the parties "unless otherwise agreed", the agreement may not only shift the allocation but may also divide the risk or burden.

§2–304. Price Payable in Money, Goods, Realty, or Otherwise. (1) The price can be made payable in money or otherwise. If it is payable in whole or in part in goods each party is a seller of the goods which he is to transfer.

(2) Even though all or part of the price is payable in an interest in realty the transfer of the goods and the seller's obligations with reference to them are subject to this Article, but not the transfer of the interest in realty or the transferor's obligations in connection therewith.

§2–305. Open Price Term. (1) The parties if they so intend can conclude a contract for sale even though the price is not settled. In such a case the price is a reasonable price at the time for delivery if

(a) nothing is said as to price; or

(b) the price is left to be agreed by the parties and they fail to agree; or

(c) the price is to be fixed in terms of some agreed market or other standard as set or recorded by a third person or agency and it is not so set or recorded.

(2) A price to be fixed by the seller or by the buyer means a price for him to fix in good faith.

(3) When a price left to be fixed otherwise than by agreement of the parties fails to be fixed through fault of one party the other may at his option treat the contract as cancelled or himself fix a reasonable price.

(4) Where, however, the parties intend not to be bound unless the price be

fixed or agreed and it is not fixed or agreed there is no contract. In such a case the buyer must return any goods already received or if unable so to do must pay their reasonable value at the time of delivery and the seller must return any portion of the price paid on account.

§2–306. Output, Requirements and Exclusive Dealings. (1) A term which measures the quantity by the output of the seller or the requirements of the buyer means such actual output or requirements as may occur in good faith, except that no quantity unreasonably disproportionate to any stated estimate or in the absence of a stated estimate to any normal or otherwise comparable prior output or requirements may be tendered or demanded.

(2) A lawful agreement by either the seller or the buyer for exclusive dealing in the kind of goods concerned imposes unless otherwise agreed an obligation by the seller to use best efforts to supply the goods and by the buyer to use best efforts to promote their sale.

§2–307. Delivery in Single Lot or Several Lots. Unless otherwise agreed all goods called for by a contract for sale must be tendered in a single delivery and payment is due only on such tender but where the circumstances give either party the right to make or demand delivery in lots the price if it can be apportioned may be demanded for each lot.

§2–308. Absence of Specified Place for Delivery. Unless otherwise agreed

(a) the place for delivery of goods is the seller's place of business or if he has none his residence; but

(b) in a contract for sale of identified goods which to the knowledge of the parties at the time of contracting are in some other place, that place is the place for their delivery; and

(c) documents of title may be delivered through customary banking channels.

§2–309. Absence of Specific Time Provisions; Notice of Termination. (1) The time for shipment or delivery or any other action under a contract if not provided in this Article or agreed upon shall be a reasonable time.

(2) Where the contract provides for successive performances but is indefinite in duration it is valid for a reasonable time but unless otherwise agreed may be terminated at any time by either party.

(3) Termination of a contract by one party except on the happening of an agreed event requires that reasonable notification be received by the other party and an agreement dispensing with notification is invalid if its operation would be unconscionable.

§2–310. Open Time for Payment or Running of Credit; Authority to Ship Under Reservation. Unless otherwise agreed

(a) payment is due at the time and place at which the buyer is to receive the goods even though the place of shipment is the place of delivery; and

(b) if the seller is authorized to send the goods he may ship them under reservation, and may tender the documents of title, but the buyer may inspect the goods after their arrival before payment is due unless such inspection is inconsistent with the terms of the contract (Section 2–513); and

(c) if delivery is authorized and made by way of documents of title otherwise than by subsection (b) then payment is due at the time and place at which the buyer is to receive the documents regardless of where the goods are to be received; and

(d) where the seller is required or authorized to ship the goods on credit the credit period runs from the time of shipment but post-dating the invoice or delaying its dispatch will correspondingly delay the starting of the credit period.

§2–311. Options and Cooperation Respecting Performance. (1) An agreement for sale which is otherwise sufficiently definite (subsection (3) of Section 2–204) to be a contract is not made invalid by the fact that it leaves particulars of performance to be specified by one of the parties. Any such specification must be made in good faith and within limits set by commercial reasonableness.

(2) Unless otherwise agreed specifications relating to assortment of the goods are at the buyer's option and except as otherwise provided in subsections (1) (c) and (3) of Section 2–319 specifications or arrangements relating to shipment are at the seller's option.

(3) Where such specification would materially affect the other party's performance but is not seasonably made or where one party's cooperation is necessary to the agreed performance of the other but is not seasonably forthcoming, the other party in addition to all other remedies

(a) is excused for any resulting delay in his own performance; and

(b) may also either proceed to perform in any reasonable manner or after the time for a material part of his own performance treat the failure to specify or to cooperate as a breach by failure to deliver or accept the goods.

§2–312. Warranty of Title and Against Infringement; Buyer's Obligation Against Infringement. (1) Subject to subsection (2) there is in a contract for sale a warranty by the seller that

(a) the title conveyed shall be good, and its transfer rightful; and

(b) the goods shall be delivered free from any security interest or other lien or encumbrance of which the buyer at the time of contracting has no knowledge.

(2) A warranty under subsection (1) will be excluded or modified only by specific language or by circumstances which give the buyer reason to know that the person selling does not claim title in himself or that he is purporting to sell only such right or title as he or a third person may have.

(3) Unless otherwise agreed a seller who is a merchant regularly dealing in goods of the kind warrants that the goods shall be delivered free of the rightful claim of any third person by way of infringement or the like but a buyer who furnishes specifications to the seller must hold the seller harmless against any such claim which arises out of compliance with the specifications.

§2–313. Express Warranties by Affirmation, Promise, Description, Sample. (1) Express warranties by the seller are created as follows:

(a) Any affirmation of fact or promise made by the seller to the buyer which relates to the goods and becomes part of the basis of the bargain creates an express warranty that the goods shall conform to the affirmation or promise.

(b) Any description of the goods which is made part of the basis of the bargain creates an express warranty that the goods shall conform to the description.

(c) Any sample or model which is made part of the basis of the bargain creates an express warranty that the whole of the goods shall conform to the sample or model.

(2) It is not necessary to the creation of an express warranty that the seller use formal words such as "warrant" or "guarantee" or that he have a specific intention to make a warranty, but an affirmation merely of the value of the goods or a statement purporting to be merely the seller's opinion or commendation of the goods does not create a warranty.

§2–314. Implied Warranty: Merchantability; Usage of Trade. (1) Unless excluded or modified (Section 2–316), a warranty that the goods shall be merchantable is implied in a contract for their sale if the seller is a merchant with respect to goods of that kind. Under this section the serving for value of food or drink to be consumed either on the premises or elsewhere is a sale.

(2) Goods to be merchantable must be at least such as

(a) pass without objection in the trade under the contract description; and

(b) in the case of fungible goods, are of fair average quality within the description; and

(c) are fit for the ordinary purposes for which such goods are used; and

(d) run, within the variations permitted by the agreement, of even kind, quality and quantity within each unit and among all units involved; and

(e) are adequately contained, packaged, and labeled as the agreement may require; and

(f) Conform to the promises or affirmations of fact made on the container or label if any.

(3) Unless excluded or modified (Section 2–316) other implied warranties may arise from course of dealing or usage of trade.

§2–315. Implied Warranty: Fitness for Particular Purpose. Where the seller at the time of contracting has reason to know any particular purpose for which the goods are required and that the buyer is relying on the seller's skill or judgment to select or furnish suitable goods, there is unless excluded or modified under the next section an implied warranty that the goods shall be fit for such purpose.

§2–316. Exclusion or Modification of Warranties. (1) Words or conduct relevant to the creation of an express warranty and words or conduct tending to negate or limit warranty shall be construed wherever reasonable as consistent with each other; but subject to the provisions of this Article on parol or extrinsic evidence (Section 2–202) negation or limitation is inoperative to the extent that such construction is unreasonable.

(2) Subject to subsection (3), to exclude or modify the implied warranty of merchantability or any part of it the language must mention merchantability and in case of a writing must be conspicuous, and to exclude or modify any implied waranty of fitness the exclusion must be by a writing and conspicuous. Language to exclude all implied warranties of fitness is sufficient if it states, for example, that "There are no warranties which extend beyond the description on the face hereof."

(3) Notwithstanding subsection (2)

(a) unless the circumstances indicate otherwise, all implied warranties are excluded by expressions like "as is", "with all faults" or other language which in common understanding calls the buyer's attention to the exclusion of warranties and makes plain that there is no implied warranty; and

(b) when the buyer before entering into the contract has examined the goods or the sample or model as fully as he desired or has refused to examine the goods there is no implied warranty with regard to defects which an examination ought in the circumstances to have revealed to him; and

(c) an implied warranty can also be excluded or modified by course of dealing or course of performance or usage of trade.

(4) Remedies for breach of warranty can be limited in accordance with the provisions of this Article on liquidation or limitation of damages and on contractual modification of remedy (Sections 2–718 and 2–719).

§2–317. Cumulation and Conflict of Warranties Express or Implied. Warranties whether express or implied shall be construed as consistent with each other and as cumulative, but if such construction is unreasonable the intention of the parties shall determine which warranty is dominant. In ascertaining that intention the following rules apply:

(a) Exact or technical specifications displace an inconsistent sample or model or general language of description.

(b) A sample from an existing bulk displaces inconsistent general language of description.

(c) Express warranties displace inconsistent implied warranties other than an implied warranty of fitness for a particular purpose.

§2–318. Third Party Beneficiaries of Warranties Express or Implied. A seller's warranty whether express or implied extends to any natural person who is in the family or household of his buyer or who is a guest in his home if it is reasonable to expect that such person may use, consume or be affected by the goods and who is injured in person by breach of the warranty. A seller may not exclude or limit the operation of this section.

§2–319. F.O.B. and F.A.S. Terms. (1) Unless otherwise agreed the term F.O.B. (which means "free on board") at a named place, even though used only in connection with the stated price, is a delivery term under which

(a) when the term is F.O.B. the place of shipment, the seller must at that place ship the goods in the manner provided in this Article (Section 2–504) and bear the expense and risk of putting them into the possession of the carrier; or

(b) when the term is F.O.B. the place of destination, the seller must at his own expense and risk transport the goods to that place and there tender delivery of them in the manner provided in this Article (Section 2–503);

(c) when under either (a) or (b) the term is also F.O.B. vessel, car or other vehicle, the seller must in addition at his own expense and risk load the goods on board. If the term is F.O.B. vessel the buyer must name the vessel and in an appropriate case the seller must comply with the provisions of this Article on the form of bill of lading (Section 2–323).

(2) Unless otherwise agreed the term F.A.S. vessel (which means "free alongside") at a named port, even though used only in connection with the stated price, is a delivery term under which the seller must

(a) at his own expense and risk deliver the goods alongside the vessel in the manner usual in that port or on a dock designated and provided by the buyer; and

(b) obtain and tender a receipt for the goods in exchange for which the carrier is under a duty to issue a bill of lading.

(3) Unless otherwise agreed in any case falling within subsection (1) (a) and (c) or subsection (2) the buyer must seasonably give any needed instructions for making delivery, including when the term is F.A.S. or F.O.B. the loading berth of the vessel and in an appropriate case its name and sailing date. The seller may treat the failure of needed instructions as a failure of cooperation under this Article (Section 2–311). He may also at his option move the goods in any reasonable manner preparatory to delivery or shipment.

(4) Under the term F.O.B. vessel or F.A.S. unless otherwise agreed the buyer must make payment against tender of the required documents and the seller may not tender nor the buyer demand delivery of the goods in substitution for the documents.

§2–320. C.I.F. and C. & F. Terms. (1) The term C.I.F. means that the price includes in a lump sum the cost of the goods and the insurance and freight to the named destination. The term C. & F. or C.F. means that the price so includes cost and freight to the named destination.

(2) Unless otherwise agreed and even though used only in connection with the stated price and destination, the term C.I.F. destination or its equivalent requires the seller at his own expense and risk to

(a) put the goods into the possession of a carrier at the port for shipment and obtain a negotiable bill or bills of lading covering the entire transportation to the named destination; and

(b) load the goods and obtain a receipt from the carrier (which may be contained in the bill of lading) showing that the freight has been paid or provided for; and

(c) obtain a policy or certificate of insurance, including any war risk insurance, of a kind and on terms then current at the port of shipment in the usual amount, in the currency of the contract, shown to cover the same goods covered by the bill of lading and providing for payment of loss to the order of the buyer or for the account of whom it may concern; but the seller may add to the price the amount of the premium for any such war risk insurance; and

(d) prepare an invoice of the goods and procure any other documents required to effect shipment or to comply with the contract; and

(e) forward and tender with commercial promptness all the documents in due form and with any indorsement necessary to perfect the buyer's rights.

(3) Unless otherwise agreed the term C. & F. or its equivalent has the same effect and imposes upon the seller the same obligations and risks as a C.I.F. term except the obligation as to insurance.

(4) Under the term C.I.F. or C. & F. unless otherwise agreed the buyer must make payment against tender of the required documents and the seller may not tender nor the buyer demand delivery of the goods in substitution for the documents.

§2-321. C.I.F. or C. & F.: "Net Landed Weights"; "Payment on Arrival"; Warranty of Condition on Arrival. Under a contract containing a term C.I.F. or C. & F.

(1) Where the price is based on or is to be adjusted according to "net landed weights", "delivered weights", "out turn" quantity or quality or the like, unless otherwise agreed the seller must reasonably estimate the price. The payment due on tender of the documents called for by the contract is the amount so estimated, but after final adjustment of the price a settlement must be made with commercial promptness.

(2) An agreement described in subsection (1) or any warranty of quality or condition of the goods on arrival places upon the seller the risk of ordinary deterioration, shrinkage and the like in transportation but has no effect on the place or time of identification to the contract for sale or delivery or on the passing of the risk of loss.

(3) Unless otherwise agreed where the contract provides for payment on or after arrival of the goods the seller must before payment allow such preliminary inspection as is feasible; but if the goods are lost delivery of the documents and payment are due when the goods should have arrived.

§2-322. Delivery "Ex-Ship". (1) Unless otherwise agreed a term for delivery of goods "ex-ship" (which means from the carrying vessel) or in equivalent language is not restricted to a particular ship and requires delivery from a ship which has reached a place at the named port of destination where goods of the kind are usually discharged.

(2) Under such a term unless otherwise agreed

(a) the seller must discharge all liens arising out of the carriage and furnish the buyer with a directon which puts the carrier under a duty to deliver the goods; and

(b) the risk of loss does not pass to the buyer until the goods leave the ship's tackle or are otherwise properly unloaded.

§2-323. Form of Bill of Lading Required in Overseas Shipment; "Overseas". (1) Where the contract contemplates overseas shipment and contains a term C.I.F. or C. & F. or F.O.B. vessel, the seller unless otherwise agreed must obtain a negotiable bill of lading stating that the goods have been loaded on board or, in the case of a term C.I.F. or C. & F., received for shipment.

(2) Where in a case within subsection (1) a bill of lading has been issued in a set of parts, unless otherwise agreed if the documents are not to be sent from abroad the buyer may demand tender of the full set; otherwise only one part of the bill of lading need be tendered. Even if the agreement expressly requires a full set

(a) due tender of a single part is acceptable within the provisions of this Article on cure of improper delivery (subsection (1) of Section 2-508); and

(b) even though the full set is demanded, if the documents are sent from abroad the person tendering an incomplete set may nevertheless require payment upon furnishing an indemnity which the buyer in good faith deems adequate.

(3) A shipment by water or by air or a contract contemplating such shipment

is "overseas" insofar as by usage of trade or agreement it is subject to the commercial, financing or shipping practices characteristic of international deep water commerce.

§2–324. "No Arrival, No Sale" Term. Under a term "no arrival, no sale" or terms of like meaning, unless otherwise agreed,

(a) the seller must properly ship conforming goods and if they arrive by any means he must tender them on arrival but he assumes no obligation that the goods will arrive unless he has caused the non-arrival; and

(b) where without fault of the seller the goods are in part lost or have so deteriorated as no longer to conform to the contract or arrive after the contract time, the buyer may proceed as if there had been casualty to identified goods (Section 2–613).

§2–325. "Letter of Credit" Term; "Confirmed Credit". (1) Failure of the buyer seasonably to furnish an agreed letter of credit is a breach of the contract for sale.

(2) The delivery to seller of a proper letter of credit suspends the buyer's obligation to pay. If the letter of credit is dishonored, the seller may on seasonable notification to the buyer require payment directly from him.

(3) Unless otherwise agreed the term "letter of credit" or "banker's credit" in a contract for sale means an irrevocable credit issued by a financing agency of good repute and, where the shipment is overseas, of good international repute. The term "confirmed credit" means that the credit must also carry the direct obligation of such an agency which does business in the seller's financial market.

§2–326. Sale on Approval and Sale or Return; Consignment Sales and Rights of Creditors. (1) Unless otherwise agreed, if delivered goods may be returned by the buyer even though they conform to the contract, the transaction is

(a) a "sale on approval" if the goods are delivered primarily for use, and

(b) a "sale or return" if the goods are delivered primarily for resale.

(2) Except as provided in subsection (3), goods held on approval are not subject to the claims of the buyer's creditors until acceptance; goods held on sale or return are subject to such claims while in the buyer's possession.

(3) Where goods are delivered to a person for sale and such person maintains a place of business at which he deals in goods of the kind involved, under a name other than the name of the person making delivery, then with respect to claims of creditors of the person conducting the business the goods are deemed to be on sale or return. The provisions of this subsection are applicable even though an agreement purports to reserve title to the person making delivery until payment or resale or uses such words as "on consignment" or "on memorandum". However, this subsection is not applicable if the person making delivery

(a) complies with an applicable law providing for a consignor's interest or the like to be evidenced by a sign, or

(b) establishes that the person conducting the business is generally known by his creditors to be substantially engaged in selling the goods of others, or

(c) complies with the filing provisions of the Article on Secured Transactions (Article 9).

(4) Any "or return" term of a contract for sale is to be treated as a separate

contract for sale within the statute of frauds section of this Article (Section 2–201) and as contradicting the sale aspect of the contract within the provisions of this Article on parol or extrinsic evidence (Section 2–202).

§2–327. Special Incidents of Sale on Approval and Sale or Return. (1) Under a sale on approval unless otherwise agreed

(a) although the goods are identified to the contract the risk of loss and the title do not pass to the buyer until acceptance; and

(b) use of the goods consistent with the purpose of trial is not acceptance but failure seasonably to notify the seller of election to return the goods is acceptance, and if the goods conform to the contract acceptance of any part is acceptance of the whole; and

(c) after due notification of election to return, the return is at the seller's risk and expense but a merchant buyer must follow any reasonable instructions.

(2) Under a sale or return unless otherwise agreed

(a) the option to return extends to the whole or any commercial unit of the goods while in substantially their original condition, but must be exercised seasonably; and

(b) the return is at the buyer's risk and expense.

§2–328. Sale by Auction. (1) In a sale by auction if goods are put up in lots each lot is the subject of a separate sale.

(2) A sale by auction is complete when the auctioneer so announces by the fall of the hammer or in other customary manner. Where a bid is made while the hammer is falling in acceptance of a prior bid the auctioneer may in his discretion reopen the bidding or declare the goods sold under the bid on which the hammer was falling.

(3) Such a sale is with reserve unless the goods are in explicit terms put up without reserve. In an auction with reserve the auctioneer may withdraw the goods at any time until he announces completion of the sale. In an auction without reserve, after the auctioneer calls for bids on an article or lot, that article or lot cannot be withdrawn unless no bid is made within a reasonable time. In either case a bidder may retract his bid until the auctioneer's announcement of completion of the sale, but a bidder's retraction does not revive any previous bid.

(4) If the auctioneer knowingly receives a bid on the seller's behalf or the seller makes or procures such a bid, and notice has not been given that liberty for such bidding is reserved, the buyer may at his option avoid the sale or take the goods at the price of the last good faith bid prior to the completion of the sale. This subsection shall not apply to any bid at a forced sale.

Part 4

Title, Creditors and Good Faith Purchasers

§2–401. Passing of Title; Reservation for Security; Limited Application of This Section. Each provision of this Article with regard to the rights, obligations and remedies of the seller, the buyer, purchasers or other third parties applies irrespective of title to the goods except where the provision refers to such title.

Insofar as situations are not covered by the other provisions of this Article and matters concerning title become material the following rules apply:

(1) Title to goods cannot pass under a contract for sale prior to their identification to the contract (Section 2–501), and unless otherwise explicitly agreed the buyer acquires by their identification a special property as limited by this Act. Any retention or reservation by the seller of the title (property) in goods shipped or delivered to the buyer is limited in effect to a reservation of a security interest. Subject to these provisions and to the provisions of the Article on Secured Transactions (Article 9), title to goods passes from the seller to the buyer in any manner and on any conditions explicitly agreed on by the parties.

(2) Unless otherwise explicitly agreed title passes to the buyer at the time and place at which the seller completes his performance with reference to the physical delivery of the goods, despite any reservation of a security interest and even though a document of title is to be delivered at a different time or place; and in particular and despite any reservation of a security interest by the bill of lading

(a) if the contract requires or authorizes the seller to send the goods to the buyer but does not require him to deliver them at destination, title passes to the buyer at the time and place of shipment; but

(b) if the contract requires delivery at destination, title passes on tender there.

(3) Unless otherwise explicitly agreed where delivery is to be made without moving the goods,

(a) if the seller is to deliver a document of title, title passes at the time when and the place where he delivers such documents; or

(b) if the goods are at the time of contracting already identified and no documents are to be delivered, title passes at the time and place of contracting.

(4) A rejection or other refusal by the buyer to receive or retain the goods, whether or not justified, or a justified revocation of acceptance revests title to the goods in the seller. Such revesting occurs by operation of law and is not a "sale".

§2–402. Rights of Seller's Creditors Against Sold Goods. (1) Except as provided in subsections (2) and (3), rights of unsecured creditors of the seller with respect to goods which have been identified to a contract for sale are subject to the buyer's rights to recover the goods under this Article (Sections 2–502 and 2–716).

(2) A creditor of the seller may treat a sale or an identification of goods to a contract for sale as void if as against him a retention of possession by the seller is fraudulent under any rule of law of the state where the goods are situated, except that retention of possession in good faith and current course of trade by a merchant-seller for a commercially reasonable time after a sale or identification is not fraudulent.

(3) Nothing in this Article shall be deemed to impair the rights of creditors of the seller

(a) under the provisions of the Article on Secured Transactions (Article 9); or

(b) where identification to the contract or delivery is made not in current course of trade but in satisfaction of or as security for a pre-existing claim for money, security or the like and is made under circumstances which under any rule of law of the state where the goods are situated would apart from this Article constitute the transaction a fraudulent transfer or voidable preference.

§2–403. Power to Transfer; Good Faith Purchase of Goods; "Entrusting". (1) A purchaser of goods acquires all title which his transferor had or had power to transfer except that a purchaser of a limited interest acquires rights only to the extent of the interest purchased. A person with voidable title has power to transfer a good title to a good faith purchaser for value. When goods have been delivered under a transaction of purchase the purchaser has such power even though

(a) the transferor was deceived as to the identity of the purchaser, or

(b) the delivery was in exchange for a check which is later dishonored, or

(c) it was agreed that the transaction was to be a "cash sale", or

(d) the delivery was procured through fraud punishable as larcenous under the criminal law.

(2) Any entrusting of possession of goods to a merchant who deals in goods of that kind gives him power to transfer all rights of the entruster to a buyer in ordinary course of business.

(3) "Entrusting" includes any delivery and any acquiescence in retention of possession regardless of any condition expressed between the parties to the delivery or acquiescence and regardless of whether the procurement of the entrusting or the possessor's disposition of the goods have been such as to be larcenous under the criminal law.

(4) The rights of other purchasers of goods and of lien creditors are governed by the Articles on Secured Transactions (Article 9), Bulk Transfers (Article 6) and Documents of Title (Article 7).

Part 5

Performance

§2–501. Insurable Interest in Goods; Manner of Identification of Goods. (1) The buyer obtains a special property and an insurable interest in goods by identification of existing goods as goods to which the contract refers even though the goods so identified are non-conforming and he has an option to return or reject them. Such identification can be made at any time and in any manner explicitly agreed to by the parties. In the absence of explicit agreement identification occurs

(a) when the contract is made if it is for the sale of goods already existing and identified;

(b) if the contract is for the sale of future goods other than those described in paragraph (c), when goods are shipped, marked or otherwise designated by the seller as goods to which the contract refers;

(c) when the crops are planted or otherwise become growing crops or the young are conceived if the contract is for the sale of unborn young to be born within twelve months after contracting or for the sale of crops to be harvested within twelve months or the next normal harvest season after contracting whichever is longer.

(2) The seller retains an insurable interest in goods so long as title to or any security interest in the goods remains in him and where the identification is by the seller alone he may until default or insolvency or notification to the buyer that the identification is final substitute other goods for those identified.

(3) Nothing in this section impairs any insurable interest recognized under any other statute or rule of law.

§2–502. Buyer's Right to Goods on Seller's Insolvency. (1) Subject to subsection (2) and even though the goods have not been shipped a buyer who has paid a part or all of the price of goods in which he has a special property under the provisions of the immediately preceding section may on making and keeping good a tender of any unpaid portion of their price recover them from the seller if the seller becomes insolvent within ten days after receipt of the first installment on their price.

(2) If the identification creating his special property has been made by the buyer he acquires the right to recover the goods only if they conform to the contract for sale.

§2–503. Manner of Seller's Tender of Delivery. (1) Tender of delivery requires that the seller put and hold conforming goods at the buyer's disposition and give the buyer any notification reasonably necessary to enable him to take delivery. The manner, time and place for tender are determined by the agreement and this Article, and in particular

(a) tender must be at a reasonable hour, and if it is of goods they must be kept available for the period reasonably necessary to enable the buyer to take possession; but

(b) unless otherwise agreed the buyer must furnish facilities reasonably suited to the receipt of the goods.

(2) Where the case is within the next section respecting shipment tender requires that the seller comply with its provisions.

(3) Where the seller is required to deliver at a particular destination tender requires that he comply with subsection (1) and also in any appropriate case tender documents as described in subsections (4) and (5) of this section.

(4) Where goods are in the possession of a bailee and are to be delivered without being moved

(a) tender requires that the seller either tender a negotiable document of title covering such goods or procure acknowledgment by the bailee of the buyer's right to possession of the goods; but

(b) tender to the buyer of a non-negotiable document of title or of a written direction to the bailee to deliver is sufficient tender unless the buyer seasonably objects, and receipt by the bailee of notification of the buyer's rights fixes those rights as against the bailee and all third persons; but risk of loss of the goods and of any failure by the bailee to honor the non-negotiable document of title or to obey the direction remains on the seller until the buyer has had a reasonable time to present the document or direction, and a refusal by the bailee to honor the document or to obey the direction defeats the tender.

(5) Where the contract requires the seller to deliver documents

(a) he must tender all such documents in correct form, except as provided in this Article with respect to bills of lading in a set (subsection (2) of Section 2–323); and

(b) tender through customary banking channels is sufficient and dishonor of a draft accompanying the documents constitutes non-acceptance or rejection.

§2–504. **Shipment by Seller.** Where the seller is required or authorized to send the goods to the buyer and the contract does not require him to deliver them at a particular destination, then unless otherwise agreed he must

(a) put the goods in the possession of such a carrier and make such a contract for their transportation as may be reasonable having regard to the nature of the goods and other circumstances of the case; and

(b) obtain and promptly deliver or tender in due form any document necessary to enable the buyer to obtain possession of the goods or otherwise required by the agreement or by usage of trade; and

(c) promptly notify the buyer of the shipment.

Failure to notify the buyer under paragraph (c) or to make a proper contract under paragraph (a) is a ground for rejection only if material delay or loss ensues.

§2–505. **Seller's Shipment Under Reservation.** (1) Where the seller has identified goods to the contract by or before shipment:

(a) his procurement of a negotiable bill of lading to his own order or otherwise reserves in him a security interest in the goods. His procurement of the bill to the order of a financing agency or of the buyer indicates in addition only the seller's expectation of transferring that interest to the person named.

(b) a non-negotiable bill of lading to himself or his nominee reserves possession of the goods as security but except in a case of conditional delivery (subsection (2) of Section 2–507) a non-negotiable bill of lading naming the buyer as consignee reserves no security interest even though the seller retains possession of the bill of lading.

(2) When shipment by the seller with reservation of a security interest is in violation of the contract for sale it constitutes an improper contract for transportation within the preceding section but impairs neither the rights given to the buyer by shipment and identification of the goods to the contract nor the seller's powers as a holder of a negotiable document.

§2–506. **Rights of Financing Agency.** (1) A financing agency by paying or purchasing for value a draft which relates to a shipment of goods acquires to the extent of the payment or purchase and in addition to its own rights under the draft and any document of title securing it any rights of the shipper in the goods including the right to stop delivery and the shipper's right to have the draft honored by the buyer.

(2) The right to reimbursement of a financing agency which has in good faith honored or purchased the draft under commitment to or authority from the buyer is not impaired by subsequent discovery of defects with reference to any relevant document which was apparently regular on its face.

§2–507. Effect of Seller's Tender; Delivery on Condition. (1) Tender of delivery is a condition to the buyer's duty to accept the goods and, unless otherwise agreed, to his duty to pay for them. Tender entitles the seller to acceptance of the goods and to payment according to the contract.

(2) Where payment is due and demanded on the delivery to the buyer of goods or documents of title, his right as against the seller to retain or dispose of them is conditional upon his making the payment due.

§2–508. Cure by Seller of Improper Tender or Delivery; Replacement. (1) Where any tender or delivery by the seller is rejected because non-conforming and the time for performance has not yet expired, the seller may seasonably notify the buyer of his intention to cure and may then within the contract time make a conforming delivery.

(2) Where the buyer rejects a non-conforming tender which the seller had reasonable grounds to believe would be acceptable with or without money allowance the seller may if he seasonably notifies the buyer have a further reasonable time to substitute a conforming tender.

§2–509. Risk of Loss in the Absence of Breach. (1) Where the contract requires or authorizes the seller to ship the goods by carrier

(a) if it does not require him to deliver them at a particular destination, the risk of loss passes to the buyer when the goods are duly delivered to the carrier even though the shipment is under reservation (Section 2–505); but

(b) if it does require him to deliver them at a particular destination and the goods are there duly tendered while in the possession of the carrier, the risk of loss passes to the buyer when the goods are there duly so tendered as to enable the buyer to take delivery.

(2) Where the goods are held by a bailee to be delivered without being moved, the risk of loss passes to the buyer

(a) on his receipt of a negotiable document of title covering the goods; or

(b) on acknowledgment by the bailee of the buyer's right to possession of the goods; or

(c) after his receipt of a non-negotiable document of title or other written direction to deliver, as provided in subsection (4) (b) of Section 2–503.

(3) In any case not within subsection (1) or (2), the risk of loss passes to the buyer on his receipt of the goods if the seller is a merchant; otherwise the risk passes to the buyer on tender of delivery.

(4) The provisions of this section are subject to contrary agreement of the parties and to the provisions of this Article on sale on approval (Section 2–327) and on effect of breach on risk of loss (Section 2–510).

§2–510. Effect of Breach on Risk of Loss. (1) Where a tender or delivery of goods so fails to conform to the contract as to give a right of rejection the risk of their loss remains on the seller until cure or acceptance.

(2) Where the buyer rightfully revokes acceptance he may to the extent of any deficiency in his effective insurance coverage treat the risk of loss as having rested on the seller from the beginning.

(3) Where the buyer as to conforming goods already identified to the con-

tract for sale repudiates or is otherwise in breach before risk of their loss has passed to him, the seller may to the extent of any deficiency in his effective insurance coverage treat the risk of loss as resting on the buyer for a commercially reasonable time.

§2-511. Tender of Payment by Buyer; Payment by Check. (1) Unless otherwise agreed tender of payment is a condition to the seller's duty to tender and complete any delivery.

(2) Tender of payment is sufficient when made by any means or in any manner current in the ordinary course of business unless the seller demands payment in legal tender and gives any extension of time reasonably necessary to procure it.

(3) Subject to the provisions of this Act on the effect of an instrument on an obligation (Section 3–802), payment by check is conditional and is defeated as between the parties by dishonor of the check on due presentment.

§2-512. Payment by Buyer Before Inspection. (1) Where the contract requires payment before inspection non-conformity of the goods does not excuse the buyer from so making payment unless

(a) the non-conformity appears without inspection; or

(b) despite tender of the required documents the circumstances would justify injunction against honor under the provisions of this Act (Section 5–114).

(2) Payment pursuant to subsection (1) does not constitute an acceptance of goods or impair the buyer's right to inspect or any of his remedies.

§2-513. Buyer's Right to Inspection of Goods. (1) Unless otherwise agreed and subject to subsection (3), where goods are tendered or delivered or identified to the contract for sale, the buyer has a right before payment or acceptance to inspect them at any reasonable place and time and in any reasonable manner. When the seller is required or authorized to send the goods to the buyer, the inspection may be after their arrival.

(2) Expenses of inspection must be borne by the buyer but may be recovered from the seller if the goods do not conform and are rejected.

(3) Unless otherwise agreed and subject to the provisions of this Article on C.I.F. contracts (subsection (3) of Section 2–321), the buyer is not entitled to inspect the goods before payment of the price when the contract provides

(a) for delivery "C.O.D." or on other like terms; or

(b) for payment against documents of title, except where such payment is due only after the goods are to become available for inspection.

(4) A place or method of inspection fixed by the parties is presumed to be exclusive but unless otherwise expressly agreed it does not postpone identification or shift the place for delivery or for passing the risk of loss. If compliance becomes impossible, inspection shall be as provided in this section unless the place or method fixed was clearly intended as an indispensable condition failure of which avoids the contract.

§2-514. When Documents Deliverable on Acceptance; When on Payment. Unless otherwise agreed documents against which a draft is drawn are to be delivered to the drawee on acceptance of the draft if it is payable more than three days after presentment; otherwise, only on payment.

§2–515. Preserving Evidence of Goods in Dispute. In furtherance of the adjustment of any claim or dispute

(a) either party on reasonable notification to the other and for the purpose of ascertaining the facts and preserving evidence has the right to inspect, test and sample the goods including such of them as may be in the possession or control of the other; and

(b) the parties may agree to a third party inspection or survey to determine the conformity or condition of the goods and may agree that the findings shall be binding upon them in any subsequent litigation or adjustment.

Part 6

Breach, Repudiation and Excuse

§2–601. Buyer's Rights on Improper Delivery. Subject to the provisions of this Article on breach in installment contracts (Section 2–612) and unless otherwise agreed under the sections on contractual limitations of remedy (Sections 2–718 and 2–719), if the goods or the tender of delivery fail in any respect to conform to the contract, the buyer may

(a) reject the whole; or

(b) accept the whole; or

(c) accept any commercial unit or units and reject the rest.

§2–602. Manner and Effect of Rightful Rejection. (1) Rejection of goods must be within a reasonable time after their delivery or tender. It is ineffective unless the buyer seasonably notifies the seller.

(2) Subject to the provisions of the two following sections on rejected goods (Sections 2–603 and 2–604),

(a) after rejection any exercise of ownership by the buyer with respect to any commercial unit is wrongful as against the seller; and

(b) if the buyer has before rejection taken physical possession of goods in which he does not have a security interest under the provisions of this Article (subsection (3) of Section 2–711), he is under a duty after rejection to hold them with reasonable care at the seller's disposition for a time sufficient to permit the seller to remove them; but

(c) the buyer has no further obligations with regard to goods rightfully rejected.

(3) The seller's rights with respect to goods wrongfully rejected are governed by the provisions of this Article on Seller's remedies in general (Section 2–703).

§2–603. Merchant Buyer's Duties as to Rightfully Rejected Goods. (1) Subject to any security interest in the buyer (subsection (3) of Section 2–711), when the seller has no agent or place of business at the market of rejection a merchant buyer is under a duty after rejection of goods in his possession or control to follow any reasonable instructions received from the seller with respect to the goods and in the absence of such instructions to make reasonable efforts to sell them for the seller's account if they are perishable or threaten to decline in value speedily. Instructions are not reasonable if on demand indemnity for expenses is not forthcoming.

(2) When the buyer sells goods under subsection (1), he is entitled to reimbursement from the seller or out of the proceeds for reasonable expenses of caring for and selling them, and if the expenses include no selling commission then to such commission as is usual in the trade or if there is none to a reasonable sum not exceeding ten per cent on the gross proceeds.

(3) In complying with this section the buyer is held only to good faith and good faith conduct hereunder is neither acceptance nor conversion nor the basis of an action for damages.

§2–604. Buyer's Options as to Salvage of Rightfully Rejected Goods. Subject to the provisions of the immediately preceding section on perishables if the seller gives no instructions within a reasonable time after notification of rejection the buyer may store the rejected goods for the seller's account or reship them to him or resell them for the seller's account with reimbursement as provided in the preceding section. Such action is not acceptance or conversion.

§2–605. Waiver of Buyer's Objections by Failure to Particularize. (1) The buyer's failure to state in connection with rejection a particular defect which is ascertainable by reasonable inspection precludes him from relying on the unstated defect to justify rejection or to establish breach

(a) where the seller could have cured it if stated seasonably; or

(b) between merchants when the seller has after rejection made a request in writing for a full and final written statement of all defects on which the buyer proposes to rely.

(2) Payment against documents made without reservation of rights precludes recovery of the payment for defects apparent on the face of the documents.

§2–606. What Constitutes Acceptance of Goods. (1) Acceptance of goods occurs when the buyer

(a) after a reasonable opportunity to inspect the goods signifies to the seller that the goods are conforming or that he will take or retain them in spite of their non-conformity; or

(b) fails to make an effective rejection (subsection (1) of Section 2–602), but such acceptance does not occur until the buyer has had a reasonable opportunity to inspect them; or

(c) does any act inconsistent with the seller's ownership; but if such act is wrongful as against the seller it is an acceptance only if ratified by him.

(2) Acceptance of a part of any commercial unit is acceptance of that entire unit.

§2–607. Effect of Acceptance; Notice of Breach; Burden of Establishing Breach After Acceptance; Notice of Claim or Litigation to Person Answerable Over. (1) The buyer must pay at the contract rate for any goods accepted.

(2) Acceptance of goods by the buyer precludes rejection of the goods accepted and if made with knowledge of a non-conformity cannot be revoked because of it unless the acceptance was on the reasonable assumption that the non-conformity would be seasonably cured but acceptance does not of itself impair any other remedy provided by this Article for non-conformity.

(3) Where a tender has been accepted

(a) the buyer must within a reasonable time after he discovers or should have discovered any breach notify the seller of breach or be barred from any remedy; and

(b) if the claim is one for infringement or the like (subsection (3) of Section 2-312) and the buyer is sued as a result of such a breach he must so notify the seller within a reasonable time after he receives notice of the litigation or be barred from any remedy over for liability established by the litigation.

(4) The burden is on the buyer to establish any breach with respect to the goods accepted.

(5) Where the buyer is sued for breach of a warranty or other obligation for which his seller is answerable over

(a) he may give his seller written notice of the litigation. If the notice states that the seller may come in and defend and that if the seller does not do so he will be bound in any action against him by his buyer by any determination of fact common to the two litigations, then unless the seller after seasonable receipt of the notice does come in and defend he is so bound.

(b) if the claim is one for infringement or the like (subsection (3) of Section 2-312) the original seller may demand in writing that his buyer turn over to him control of the litigation including settlement or else be barred from any remedy over and if he also agrees to bear all expense and to satisfy any adverse judgment, then unless the buyer after seasonable receipt of the demand does turn over control the buyer is so barred.

(6) The provisions of subsections (3), (4) and (5) apply to any obligation of a buyer to hold the seller harmless against infringement or the like (subsection (3) of Section 2-312).

§2-608. Revocation of Acceptance in Whole or in Part. (1) The buyer may revoke his acceptance of a lot or commercial unit whose non-conformity substantially impairs its value to him if he has accepted it

(a) on the reasonable assumption that its non-conformity would be cured and it has not been seasonably cured; or

(b) without discovery of such non-conformity if his acceptance was reasonably induced either by the difficulty of discovery before acceptance or by the seller's assurances.

(2) Revocation of acceptance must occur within a reasonable time after the buyer discovers or should have discovered the ground for it and before any substantial change in condition of the goods which is not caused by their own defects. It is not effective until the buyer notifies the seller of it.

(3) A buyer who so revokes has the same rights and duties with regard to the goods involved as if he had rejected them.

§2-609. Right to Adequate Assurance of Performance. (1) A contract for sale imposes an obligation on each party that the other's expectation of receiving due performance will not be impaired. When reasonable grounds for insecurity arise with respect to the performance of either party the other may in writing demand adequate assurance of due performance and until he receives such assurance may if commercially reasonable suspend any performance for which he has not already received the agreed return.

(2) Between merchants the reasonableness of grounds for insecurity and the

adequacy of any assurance offered shall be determined according to commercial standards.

(3) Acceptance of any improper delivery or payment does not prejudice the aggrieved party's right to demand adequate assurance of future performance.

(4) After receipt of a justified demand failure to provide within a reasonable time not exceeding thirty days such assurance of due performance as is adequate under the circumstances of the particular case is a repudiation of the contract.

§2–610. Anticipatory Repudiation. When either party repudiates the contract with respect to a performance not yet due the loss of which will substantially impair the value of the contract to the other, the aggrieved party may

(a) for a commercially reasonable time await performance by the repudiating party; or

(b) resort to any remedy for breach (Section 2–703 or Section 2–711), even though he has notified the repudiating party that he would await the latter's performance and has urged retraction; and

(c) in either case suspend his own performance or proceed in accordance with the provisions of this Article on the seller's right to identify goods to the contract notwithstanding breach or to salvage unfinished goods (Section 2–704).

§2–611. Retraction of Anticipatory Repudiation. (1) Until the repudiating party's next performance is due he can retract his repudiation unless the aggrieved party has since the repudiation cancelled or materially changed his position or otherwise indicated that he considers the repudiation final.

(2) Retraction may be by any method which clearly indicates to the aggrieved party that the repudiating party intends to perform, but must include any assurance justifiably demanded under the provisions of this Article (Section 2–609).

(3) Retraction reinstates the repudiating party's rights under the contract with due excuse and allowance to the aggrieved party for any delay occasioned by the repudiation.

§2–612. "Installment Contract"; Breach. (1) An "installment contract" is one which requires or authorizes the delivery of goods in separate lots to be separately accepted, even though the contract contains a clause "each delivery is a separate contract" or its equivalent.

(2) The buyer may reject any installment which is non-conforming if the non-conformity substantially impairs the value of that installment and cannot be cured or if the non-conformity is a defect in the required documents; but if the non-conformity does not fall within subsection (3) and the seller gives adequate assurance of its cure the buyer must accept that installment.

(3) Whenever non-conformity or default with respect to one or more installments substantially impairs the value of the whole contract there is a breach of the whole. But the aggrieved party reinstates the contract if he accepts a non-conforming installment without seasonably notifying of cancellation or if he brings an action with respect only to past installments or demands performance as to future installments.

§2–613. Casualty to Identified Goods. Where the contract requires for its performance goods identified when the contract is made, and the goods suffer casualty without fault of either party before the risk of loss passes to the buyer, or in a proper case under a "no arrival, no sale" term (Section 2–324) then

(a) if the loss is total the contract is avoided; and

(b) if the loss is partial or the goods have so deteriorated as no longer to conform to the contract the buyer may nevertheless demand inspection and at his option either treat the contract as avoided or accept the goods with due allowance from the contract price for the deterioration or the deficiency in quantity but without further right against the seller.

§2–614. Substituted Performance. (1) Where without fault of either party the agreed berthing, loading, or unloading facilities fail or an agreed type of carrier becomes unavailable or the agreed manner of delivery otherwise becomes commercially impracticable but a commercially reasonable substitute is available, such substitute performance must be tendered and accepted.

(2) If the agreed means or manner of payment fails because of domestic or foreign governmental regulation, the seller may withhold or stop delivery unless the buyer provides a means or manner of payment which is commercially a substantial equivalent. If delivery has already been taken, payment by the means or in the manner provided by the regulation discharges the buyer's obligation unless the regulation is discriminatory, oppressive or predatory.

§2–615. Excuse by Failure of Presupposed Conditions. Except so far as a seller may have assumed a greater obligation and subject to the preceding section on substituted performance:

(a) Delay in delivery or non-delivery in whole or in part by a seller who complies with paragraphs (b) and (c) is not a breach of his duty under a contract for sale if performance as agreed has been made impracticable by the occurrence of a contingency the non-occurrence of which was a basic assumption on which the contract was made or by compliance in good faith with any applicable foreign or domestic governmental regulation or order whether or not it later proves to be invalid.

(b) Where the causes mentioned in paragraph (a) affect only a part of the seller's capacity to perform, he must allocate production and deliveries among his customers but may at his option include regular customers not then under contract as well as his own requirements for further manufacture. He may so allocate in any manner which is fair and reasonable.

(c) The seller must notify the buyer seasonably that there will be delay or non-delivery and, when allocation is required under paragraph (b), of the estimated quota thus made available for the buyer.

§2–616. Procedure on Notice Claiming Excuse. (1) Where the buyer receives notification of a material or indefinite delay or an allocation justified under the preceding section he may by written notification to the seller as to any delivery concerned, and where the prospective deficiency substantially impairs the value of the whole contract under the provisions of this Article relating to breach of installment contracts (Section 2–612), then also as to the whole,

(a) terminate and thereby discharge any unexecuted portion of the contract; or

(b) modify the contract by agreeing to take his available quota in substitution.

(2) If after receipt of such notification from the seller the buyer fails so to modify the contract within a reasonable time not exceeding thirty days the contract lapses with respect to any deliveries affected.

(3) The provisions of this section may not be negated by agreement except in so far as the seller has assumed a greater obligation under the preceding section.

Part 7

Remedies

§2–701. Remedies for Breach of Collateral Contracts Not Impaired. Remedies for breach of any obligation or promise collateral or ancillary to a contract for sale are not impaired by the provisions of this Article.

§2–702. Seller's Remedies on Discovery of Buyer's Insolvency. (1) Where the seller discovers the buyer to be insolvent he may refuse delivery except for cash including payment for all goods theretofore delivered under the contract, and stop delivery under this Article (Section 2–705).

(2) Where the seller discovers that the buyer has received goods on credit while insolvent he may reclaim the goods upon demand made within ten days after the receipt, but if misrepresentation of solvency has been made to the particular seller in writing within three months before delivery the ten day limitation does not apply. Except as provided in this subsection the seller may not base a right to reclaim goods on the buyer's fraudulent or innocent misrepresentation of solvency or of intent to pay.

(3) The seller's right to reclaim under subsection (2) is subject to the rights of a buyer in ordinary course or other good faith purchaser or lien creditor under this Article (Section 2–403). Successful reclamation of goods excludes all other remedies with respect to them.

§2–703. Seller's Remedies in General. Where the buyer wrongfully rejects or revokes acceptance of goods or fails to make a payment due on or before delivery or repudiates with respect to a part or the whole, then with respect to any goods directly affected and, if the breach is of the whole contract (Section 2–612), then also with respect to the whole undelivered balance, the aggrieved seller may

(a) withhold delivery of such goods;

(b) stop delivery by any bailee as hereafter provided (Section 2–705);

(c) proceed under the next section respecting goods still unidentified to the contract;

(d) resell and recover damages as hereafter provided (Section 2–706);

(e) recover damages for non-acceptance (Section 2–708) or in a proper case the price (Section 2–709);

(f) cancel.

§2–704. Seller's Right to Identify Goods to the Contract Notwithstanding Breach or to Salvage Unfinished Goods. (1) An aggrieved seller under the preceding section may

(a) identify to the contract conforming goods not already identified if at the time he learned of the breach they are in his possession or control;

(b) treat as the subject of resale goods which have demonstrably been intended for the particular contract even though those goods are unfinished.

(2) Where the goods are unfinished an aggrieved seller may in the exercise of reasonable commercial judgment for the purposes of avoiding loss and of effective realization either complete the manufacture and wholly identify the goods to the contract or cease manufacture and resell for scrap or salvage value or proceed in any other reasonable manner.

§2–705. Seller's Stoppage of Delivery in Transit or Otherwise. (1) The seller may stop delivery of goods in the possession of a carrier or other bailee when he discovers the buyer to be insolvent (Section 2–702) and may stop delivery of carload, truckload, planeload or larger shipments of express or freight when the buyer repudiates or fails to make a payment due before delivery or if for any other reason the seller has a right to withhold or reclaim the goods.

(2) As against such buyer the seller may stop delivery until

(a) receipt of the goods by the buyer; or

(b) acknowledgment to the buyer by any bailee of the goods except a carrier that the bailee holds the goods for the buyer; or

(c) such acknowledgment to the buyer by a carrier by reshipment or as warehouseman; or

(d) negotiation to the buyer of any negotiable document of title covering the goods.

(3) (a) To stop delivery the seller must so notify as to enable the bailee by reasonable diligence to prevent delivery of the goods.

(b) After such notification the bailee must hold and deliver the goods according to the directions of the seller but the seller is liable to the bailee for any ensuing charges or damages.

(c) If a negotiable document of title has been issued for goods the bailee is not obliged to obey a notification to stop until surrender of the document.

(d) A carrier who has issued a non-negotiable bill of lading is not obliged to obey a notification to stop received from a person other than the consignor.

§2–706. Seller's Resale Including Contract for Resale. (1) Under the conditions stated in Section 2–703 on seller's remedies, the seller may resell the goods concerned or the undelivered balance thereof. Where the resale is made in good faith and in a commercially reasonable manner the seller may recover the difference between the resale price and the contract price together with any incidental damages allowed under the provisions of this Article (Section 2–710), but less expenses saved in consequence of the buyer's breach.

(2) Except as otherwise provided in subsection (3) or unless otherwise agreed resale may be at public or private sale including sale by way of one or more contracts to sell or of identification to an existing contract of the seller. Sale may be as a unit or in parcels and at any time and place and on any terms but every aspect of the sale including the method, manner, time, place and terms must be commercially reasonable. The resale must be reasonably identified as referring to the broken contract, but it is not necessary that the goods

be in existence or that any or all of them have been identified to the contract before the breach.

(3) Where the resale is at private sale the seller must give the buyer reasonable notification of his intention to resell.

(4) Where the resale is at public sale

(a) only identified goods can be sold except where there is a recognized market for a public sale of futures in goods of the kind; and

(b) it must be made at a usual place or market for public sale if one is reasonably available and except in the case of goods which are perishable or threaten to decline in value speedily the seller must give the buyer reasonable notice of the time and place of the resale; and

(c) if the goods are not to be within the view of those attending the sale the notification of sale must state the place where the goods are located and provide for their reasonable inspection by prospective bidders; and

(d) the seller may buy.

(5) A purchaser who buys in good faith at a resale takes the goods free of any rights of the original buyer even though the seller fails to comply with one or more of the requirements of this section.

(6) The seller is not accountable to the buyer for any profit made on any resale. A person in the position of a seller (Section 2–707) or a buyer who has rightfully rejected or justifiably revoked acceptance must account for any excess over the amount of his security interest, as hereinafter defined (subsection (3) of Section 2–711).

§2–707. **"Person in the Position of a Seller".** (1) A "person in the position of a seller" includes as against a principal an agent who has paid or become responsible for the price of goods on behalf of his principal or anyone who otherwise holds a security interest or other right in goods similar to that of a seller.

(2) A person in the position of a seller may as provided in this Article withhold or stop delivery (Section 2–705) and resell (Section 2–706) and recover incidental damages (Section 2–710).

§2–708. **Seller's Damages for Non-acceptance or Repudiation.** (1) Subject to subsection (2) and to the provisions of this Article with respect to proof of market price (Section 2–723), the measure of damages for non-acceptance or repudiation by the buyer is the difference between the market price at the time and place for tender and the unpaid contract price together with any incidental damages provided in this Article (Section 2–710), but less expenses saved in consequence of the buyer's breach.

(2) If the measure of damages provided in subsection (1) is inadequate to put the seller in as good a position as performance would have done then the measure of damages is the profit (including reasonable overhead) which the seller would have made from full performance by the buyer, together with any incidental damages provided in this Article (Section 2–710), due allowance for costs reasonably incurred and due credit for payments or proceeds of resale.

§2–709. **Action for the Price.** (1) When the buyer fails to pay the price as it becomes due the seller may recover, together with any incidental damages under the next section, the price

(a) of goods accepted or of conforming goods lost or damaged within a commercially reasonable time after risk of their loss has passed to the buyer; and

(b) of goods identified to the contract if the seller is unable after reasonable effort to resell them at a reasonable price or the circumstances reasonably indicate that such effort will be unavailing.

(2) Where the seller sues for the price he must hold for the buyer any goods which have been identified to the contract and are still in his control except that if resale becomes possible he may resell them at any time prior to the collection of the judgment. The net proceeds of any such resale must be credited to the buyer and payment of the judgment entitles him to any goods not resold.

(3) After the buyer has wrongfully rejected or revoked acceptance of the goods or has failed to make a payment due or has repudiated (Section 2–610), a seller who is held not entitled to the price under this section shall nevertheless be awarded damages for non-acceptance under the preceding section.

§2–710. Seller's Incidental Damages. Incidental damages to an aggrieved seller include any commercially reasonable charges, expenses or commissions incurred in stopping delivery, in the transportation, care and custody of goods after the buyer's breach, in connection with return or resale of the goods or otherwise resulting from the breach.

§2–711. Buyer's Remedies in General; Buyer's Security Interest in Rejected Goods. (1) Where the seller fails to make delivery or repudiates or the buyer rightfully rejects or justifiably revokes acceptance then with respect to any goods involved, and with respect to the whole if the breach goes to the whole contract (Section 2–612), the buyer may cancel and whether or not he has done so may in addition to recovering so much of the price as has been paid

(a) "cover" and have damages under the next section as to all the goods affected whether or not they have been identified to the contract; or

(b) recover damages for non-delivery as provided in this Article (Section 2–713).

(2) Where the seller fails to deliver or repudiates the buyer may also

(a) if the goods have been identified recover them as provided in this Article (Section 2–502); or

(b) in a proper case obtain specific performance or replevy the goods as provided in this Article (Section 2–716).

(3) On rightful rejection or justifiable revocation of acceptance a buyer has a security interest in goods in his possession or control for any payments made on their price and any expenses reasonably incurred in their inspection, receipt, transportation, care and custody and may hold such goods and resell them in like manner as an aggrieved seller (Section 2–706).

§2–712. "Cover"; Buyer's Procurement of Substitute Goods. (1) After a breach within the preceding section the buyer may "cover" by making in good faith and without unreasonable delay any reasonable purchase of or contract to purchase goods in substitution for those due from the seller.

(2) The buyer may recover from the seller as damages the difference between the cost of cover and the contract price together with any incidental or consequential damages as hereinafter defined (Section 2–715), but less expenses saved in consequence of the seller's breach.

(3) Failure of the buyer to effect cover within this section does not bar him from any other remedy.

§2–713. Buyer's Damages for Non-Delivery or Repudiation. (1) Subject to the provisions of this Article with respect to proof of market price (Section 2–723), the measure of damages for non-delivery or repudiation by the seller is the difference between the market price at the time when the buyer learned of the breach and the contract price together with any incidental and consequential damages provided in this Article (Section 2–715), but less expenses saved in consequence of the seller's breach.

(2) Market price is to be determined as of the place for tender or, in cases of rejection after arrival or revocation of acceptance, as of the place of arrival.

§2–714. Buyer's Damages for Breach in Regard to Accepted Goods. (1) Where the buyer has accepted goods and given notification (subsection (3) of Section 2–607) he may recover as damages for any non-conformity of tender the loss resulting in the ordinary course of events from the seller's breach as determined in any manner which is reasonable.

(2) The measure of damages for breach of warranty is the difference at the time and place of acceptance between the value of the goods accepted and the value they would have had if they had been as warranted, unless special circumstances show proximate damages of a different amount.

(3) In a proper case any incidental and consequential damages under the next section may also be recovered.

§2–715. Buyer's Incidental and Consequential Damages. (1) Incidental damages resulting from the seller's breach include expenses reasonably incurred in inspection, receipt, transportation and care and custody of goods rightfully rejected, any commercially reasonable charges, expenses or commissions in connection with effecting cover and any other reasonable expense incident to the delay or other breach.

(2) Consequential damages resulting from the seller's breach include

(a) any loss resulting from general or particular requirements and needs of which the seller at the time of contracting had reason to know and which could not reasonably be prevented by cover or otherwise; and

(b) injury to person or property proximately resulting from any breach of warranty.

§2–716. Buyer's Right to Specific Performance or Replevin. (1) Specific performance may be decreed where the goods are unique or in other proper circumstances.

(2) The decree for specific performance may include such terms and conditions as to payment of the price, damages, or other relief as the court may deem just.

(3) The buyer has a right of replevin for goods identified to the contract if after reasonable effort he is unable to effect cover for such goods or the circum-

stances reasonably indicate that such effort will be unavailing or if the goods have been shipped under reservation and satisfaction of the security interest in them has been made or tendered.

§2–717. Deduction of Damages From the Price. The buyer on notifying the seller of his intention to do so may deduct all or any part of the damages resulting from any breach of the contract from any part of the price still due under the same contract.

§2–718. Liquidation or Limitation of Damages; Deposits. (1) Damages for breach by either party may be liquidated in the agreement but only at an amount which is reasonable in the light of the anticipated or actual harm caused by the breach, the difficulties of proof of loss, and the inconvenience or non-feasibility of otherwise obtaining an adequate remedy. A term fixing unreasonably large liquidated damages is void as a penalty.

(2) Where the seller justifiably withholds delivery of goods because of the buyer's breach, the buyer is entitled to restitution of any amount by which the sum of his payments exceeds

(a) the amount to which the seller is entitled by virtue of terms liquidating the seller's damages in accordance with subsection (1), or

(b) in the absence of such terms, twenty per cent of the value of the total performance for which the buyer is obligated under the contract or $500, whichever is smaller.

(3) The buyer's right to restitution under subsection (2) is subject to offset to the extent that the seller establishes

(a) a right to recover damages under the provisions of this Article other than subsection (1), and

(b) the amount or value of any benefits received by the buyer directly or indirectly by reason of the contract.

(4) Where a seller has received payment in goods their reasonable value or the proceeds of their resale shall be treated as payments for the purposes of subsection (2); but if the seller has notice of the buyer's breach before reselling goods received in part performance, his resale is subject to the conditions laid down in this Article on resale by an aggrieved seller (Section 2–706).

§2–719. Contractual Modification or Limitation of Remedy. (1) Subject to the provisions of subsections (2) and (3) of this section and of the preceding section on liquidation and limitation of damages,

(a) the agreement may provide for remedies in addition to or in substitution for those provided in this Article and may limit or alter the measure of damages recoverable under this Article, as by limiting the buyer's remedies to return of the goods and repayment of the price or to repair and replacement of non-conforming goods or parts; and

(b) resort to a remedy as provided is optional unless the remedy is expressly agreed to be exclusive, in which case it is the sole remedy.

(2) Where circumstances cause an exclusive or limited remedy to fail of its essential purpose, remedy may be had as provided in this Act.

(3) Consequential damages may be limited or excluded unless the limitation or exclusion is unconscionable. Limitation of consequential damages for in-

jury to the person in the case of consumer goods is prima facie unconscionable but limitation of damages where the loss is commercial is not.

§2–720. Effect of "Cancellation" or "Rescission" on Claims for Antecedent Breach. Unless the contrary intention clearly appears, expressions of "cancellation" or "rescission" of the contract or the like shall not be construed as a renunciation or discharge of any claim in damages for an antecedent breach.

§2–721. Remedies for Fraud. Remedies for material misrepresentation or fraud include all remedies available under this Article for non-fraudulent breach. Neither rescission or a claim for rescission of the contract for sale nor rejection or return of the goods shall bar or be deemed inconsistent with a claim for damages or other remedy.

§2–722. Who Can Sue Third Parties for Injury to Goods. Where a third party so deals with goods which have been identified to a contract for sale as to cause actionable injury to a party to that contract

(a) a right of action against the third party is in either party to the contract for sale who has title to or a security interest or a special property or an insurable interest in the goods; and if the goods have been destroyed or converted a right of action is also in the party who either bore the risk of loss under the contract for sale or has since the injury assumed that risk as against the other;

(b) if at the time of the injury the party plaintiff did not bear the risk of loss as against the other party to the contract for sale and there is no arrangement between them for disposition of the recovery, his suit or settlement is, subject to his own interest, as a fiduciary for the other party to the contract;

(c) either party may with the consent of the other sue for the benefit of whom it may concern.

§2–723. Proof of Market Price: Time and Place. (1) If an action based on anticipatory repudiation comes to trial before the time for performance with respect to some or all of the goods, any damages based on market price (Section 2–708 or Section 2–713) shall be determined according to the price of such goods prevailing at the time when the aggrieved party learned of the repudiation.

(2) If evidence of a price prevailing at the times or places described in this Article is not readily available the price prevailing within any reasonable time before or after the time described or at any other place which in commercial judgment or under usage of trade would serve as a reasonable substitute for the one described may be used, making any proper allowance for the cost of transporting the goods to or from such other place.

(3) Evidence of a relevant price prevailing at a time or place other than the one described in this Article offered by one party is not admissible unless and until he has given the other party such notice as the court finds sufficient to prevent unfair surprise.

§2–724. Admissibility of Market Quotations. Whenever the prevailing price or value of any goods regularly bought and sold in any established commodity market is in issue, reports in official publications or trade journals or in newspapers or periodicals of general circulation published as the reports of such market shall be admissible in evidence. The circumstances of the preparation of such a report may be shown to affect its weight but not its admissibility.

§2–725. Statute of Limitations in Contracts for Sale. (1) An action for breach of any contract for sale must be commenced within four years after the cause of action has accrued. By the original agreement the parties may reduce the period of limitation to not less than one year but may not extend it.

(2) A cause of action accrues when the breach occurs, regardless of the aggrieved party's lack of knowledge of the breach. A breach of warranty occurs when tender of delivery is made, except that where a warranty explicitly extends to future performance of the goods and discovery of the breach must await the time of such performance the cause of action accrues when the breach is or should have been discovered.

(3) Where an action commenced within the time limited by subsection (1) is so terminated as to leave available a remedy by another action for the same breach such other action may be commenced after the expiration of the time limited and within six months after the termination of the first action unless the termination resulted from voluntary discontinuance or from dismissal for failure or neglect to prosecute.

(4) This section does not alter the law on tolling of the statute of limitations nor does it apply to causes of action which have accrued before this Act becomes effective.

Article 3: Commercial Paper

Part 1

Short Title, Form and Interpretation

§3–101. Short Title. This Article shall be known and may be cited as Uniform Commercial Code—Commercial Paper.

§3–102. Definitions and Index of Definitions. (1) In this Article unless the context otherwise requires

(a) "Issue" means the first delivery of an instrument to a holder or a remitter.

(b) An "order" is a direction to pay and must be more than an authorization or request. It must identify the person to pay with reasonable certainty. It may be addressed to one or more such persons jointly or in the alternative but not in succession.

(c) A "promise" is an undertaking to pay and must be more than an acknowledgment of an obligation.

(d) "Secondary party" means a drawer or endorser.

(e) "Instrument" means a negotiable instrument.

(2) Other definitions applying to this Article and the sections in which they appear are:

"Acceptance". Section 3–410.

"Accommodation party". Section 3–415.

"Alteration". Section 3–407.

"Certificate of deposit". Section 3–104.

"Certification". Section 3–411.

"Check". Section 3–104.

"Definite time". Section 3–109.

"Dishonor". Section 3–507.

"Draft". Section 3–104.

"Holder in due course". Section 3–302.

"Negotiation". Section 3–202.

"Note". Section 3–104.

"Notice of dishonor". Section 3–508.

"On demand". Section 3–108.

"Presentment". Section 3–504.

"Protest". Section 3–509.

"Restrictive Indorsement". Section 3–205.

"Signature". Section 3–401.

(3) The following definitions in other Articles apply to this Article:

"Account". Section 4–104.

"Banking Day". Section 4–104.

"Clearing house". Section 4–104.

"Collecting bank". Section 4–105.

"Customer". Section 4–104.

"Depositary Bank". Section 4–105.

"Documentary Draft". Section 4–104.

"Intermediary Bank". Section 4–105.

"Item". Section 4–104.

"Midnight deadline". Section 4–104.

"Payor bank". Section 4–105.

(4) In addition Article 1 contains general definitions and principles of construction and interpretation applicable throughout this Article.

§3–103. Limitations on Scope of Article. (1) This article does not apply to money, documents of title or investment securities.

(2) The provisions of this Article are subject to the provisions of the Article on Bank Deposits and Collections (Article 4) and Secured Transactions (Article 9).

§3–104. Form of Negotiable Instruments; "Draft"; "Check"; "Certificate of Deposit"; "Note". (1) Any writing to be a negotiable instrument within this Article must

(a) be signed by the maker or drawer; and

(b) contain an unconditional promise or order to pay a sum certain in money and no other promise, order, obligation or power given by the maker or drawer except as authorized by this Article; and

(c) be payable on demand or at a definite time; and

(d) be payable to order or to bearer.

(2) A writing which complies with the requirements of this section is

(a) a "draft" ("bill of exchange") if it is an order;

(b) a "check" if it is a draft drawn on a bank and payable on demand;

(c) a "certificate of deposit" if it is an acknowledgment by a bank of receipt of money with an engagement to repay it;

(d) a "note" if it is a promise other than a certificate of deposit.

(3) As used in other Articles of this Act, and as the context may require, the terms "draft", "check", "certificate of deposit" and "note" may refer to instruments which are not negotiable within this Article as well as to instruments which are so negotiable.

§3–105. When Promise or Order Unconditional. (1) A promise or order otherwise unconditional is not made conditional by the fact that the instrument

(a) is subject to implied or constructive conditions; or

(b) states its consideration, whether performed or promised, or the transaction which gave rise to the instrument, or that the promise or order is made or the instrument matures in accordance with or "as per" such transaction; or

(c) refers to or states that it arises out of a separate agreement; or

(d) states that it is drawn under a letter of credit; or

(e) states that it is secured, whether by mortgage, reservation of title or otherwise; or

(f) indicates a particular account to be debited or any other fund or source from which reimbursement is expected; or

(g) is limited to payment out of a particular fund or the proceeds of a particular source, if the instrument is issued by a government or governmental agency or unit; or

(h) is limited to payment out of the entire assets of a partnership, unincorporated association, trust or estate by or on behalf of which the instrument is issued.

(2) A promise or order is not unconditional if the instrument

(a) states that it is subject to or governed by any other agreement; or

(b) states that it is to be paid only out of a particular fund or source except as provided in this section.

§3–106. Sum Certain. (1) The sum payable is a sum certain even though it is to be paid

(a) with stated interest or by stated installments; or

(b) with stated different rates of interest before and after default or a specified date; or

(c) with a stated discount or addition if paid before or after the date fixed for payment; or

(d) with exchange or less exchange, whether at a fixed rate or at the current rate; or

(e) with costs of collection or an attorney's fee or both upon default.

(2) Nothing in this section shall validate any term which is otherwise illegal.

§3–107. Money. (1) An instrument is payable in money if the medium of exchange in which it is payable is money at the time the instrument is made. An instrument payable in "currency" or "current funds" is payable in money.

(2) A promise or order to pay a sum stated in a foreign currency is for a sum certain in money and, unless a different medium of payment is specified in the instrument, may be satisfied by payment of that number of dollars which the stated foreign currency will purchase at the buying sight rate for that currency on the day on which the instrument is payable or, if payable on demand, on

the day of demand. If such an instrument specifies a foreign currency as the medium of payment the instrument is payable in that currency.

§3–108. Payable on Demand. Instruments payable on demand include those payable at sight or on presentation and those in which no time for payment is stated.

§3–109. Definite Time. (1) An instrument is payable at a definite time if by its terms it is payable

(a) on or before a stated date or at a fixed period after a stated date; or

(b) at a fixed period after sight; or

(c) at a definite time subject to any acceleration; or

(d) at a definite time subject to extension at the option of the holder, or to extension to a further definite time at the option of the maker or acceptor or automatically upon or after a specified act or event.

(2) An instrument which by its terms is otherwise payable only upon an act or event uncertain as to time of occurrence is not payable at a definite time even though the act or event has occurred.

§3–110. Payable to Order. (1) An instrument is payable to order when by its terms it is payable to the order or assigns of any person therein specified with reasonable certainty, or to him or his order, or when it is conspicuously designated on its face as "exchange" or the like and names a payee. It may be payable to the order of

(a) the maker or drawer; or

(b) the drawee; or

(c) a payee who is not maker, drawer or drawee; or

(d) two or more payees together or in the alternative; or

(e) an estate, trust or fund, in which case it is payable to the order of the representative of such estate, trust or fund or his successors; or

(f) an office, or an officer by his title as such in which case it is payable to the principal but the incumbent of the office or his successors may act as if he or they were the holder; or

(g) a partnership or unincorporated association, in which case it is payable to the partnership or association and may be indorsed or transferred by any person thereto authorized.

(2) An instrument not payable to order is not made so payable by such words as "payable upon return of this instrument properly indorsed."

(3) An instrument made payable both to order and to bearer is payable to order unless the bearer words are handwritten or typewritten.

§3–111. Payable to Bearer. An instrument is payable to bearer when by its terms it is payable to

(a) bearer or the order of bearer; or

(b) a specified person or bearer; or

(c) "cash" or the order of "cash", or any other indication which does not purport to designate a specific payee.

§3–112. Terms and Omissions Not Affecting Negotiability. (1) The negotiability of an instrument is not affected by

(a) the omission of a statement of any consideration or of the place where the instrument is drawn or payable; or

(b) a statement that collateral has been given for the instrument or in case of default on the instrument the collateral may be sold; or

(c) a promise or power to maintain or protect collateral or to give additional collateral; or

(d) a term authorizing a confession of judgment on the instrument if it is not paid when due; or

(e) a term purporting to waive the benefit of any law intended for the advantage or protection of any obligor; or

(f) a term in a draft providing that the payee by indorsing or cashing it acknowledges full satisfaction of an obligation of the drawer; or

(g) a statement in a draft drawn in a set of parts (Section 3–801) to the effect that the order is effective only if no other part has been honored.

(2) Nothing in this section shall validate any term which is otherwise illegal.

§3–113. Seal. An instrument otherwise negotiable is within this Article even though it is under a seal.

§3–114. Date, Antedating, Postdating. (1) The negotiability of an instrument is not affected by the fact that it is undated, antedated or postdated.

(2) Where an instrument is antedated or postdated the time when it is payable is determined by the stated date if the instrument is payable on demand or at a fixed period after date.

(3) Where the instrument or any signature thereon is dated, the date is presumed to be correct.

§3–115. Incomplete Instruments. (1) When a paper whose contents at the time of signing show that it is intended to become an instrument is signed while still incomplete in any necessary respect it cannot be enforced until completed, but when it is completed in accordance with authority given it is effective as completed.

(2) If the completion is unauthorized the rules as to material alteration apply (Section 3–407), even though the paper was not delivered by the maker or drawer; but the burden of establishing that any completion is unauthorized is on the party so asserting.

§3–116. Instruments Payable to Two or More Persons. An instrument payable to the order of two or more persons

(a) if in the alternative is payable to any one of them and may be negotiated, discharged or enforced by any of them who has possession of it;

(b) if not in the alternative is payable to all of them and may be negotiated, discharged or enforced only by all of them.

§3–117. Instruments Payable With Words of Description. An instrument made payable to a named person with the addition of words describing him

(a) as agent or officer of a specified person is payable to his principal but the agent or officer may act as if he were the holder;

(b) as any other fiduciary for a specified person or purpose is payable to the payee and may be negotiated, discharged or enforced by him;

(c) in any other manner is payable to the payee unconditionally and the additional words are without effect on subsequent parties.

§3–118. Ambiguous Terms and Rules of Construction. The following rules apply to every instrument:

(a) Where there is doubt whether the instrument is a draft or a note the holder may treat it as either. A draft drawn on the drawer is effective as a note.

(b) Handwritten terms control typewritten and printed terms, and typewritten control printed.

(c) Words control figures except that if the words are ambiguous figures control.

(d) Unless otherwise specified a provision for interest means interest at the judgment rate at the place of payment from the date of the instrument, or if it is undated from the date of issue.

(e) Unless the instrument otherwise specifies two or more persons who sign as maker, acceptor or drawer or indorser and as a part of the same transaction are jointly and severally liable even though the instrument contains such words as "I promise to pay."

(f) Unless otherwise specified consent to extension authorizes a single extension for not longer than the original period. A consent to extension, expressed in the instrument, is binding on secondary parties and accommodation makers. A holder may not exercise his option to extend an instrument over the objection of a maker or acceptor or other party who in accordance with Section 3–604 tenders full payment when the instrument is due.

§3–119. Other Writings Affecting Instrument. (1) As between the obligor and his immediate obligee or any transferee the terms of an instrument may be modified or affected by any other written agreement executed as a part of the same transaction, except that a holder in due course is not affected by any limitation of his rights arising out of the separate written agreement if he had no notice of the limitation when he took the instrument.

(2) A separate agreement does not affect the negotiability of an instrument.

§3–120. Instruments "Payable Through" Bank. An instrument which states that it is "payable through" a bank or the like designates that bank as a collecting bank to make presentment but does not of itself authorize the bank to pay the instrument.

§3–121. Instruments Payable at Bank. Note: *If this Act is introduced in the Congress of the United States this section should be omitted. (States to select either alternative)*

Alternative A—

A note or acceptance which states that it is payable at a bank is the equivalent of a draft drawn on the bank payable when it falls due out of any funds of the maker or acceptor in current account or otherwise available for such payment.

Alternative B—

A note or acceptance which states that it is payable at a bank is not of itself an order or authorization to the bank to pay it.

§3–122. Accrual of Cause of Action. (1) A cause of action against a maker or an acceptor accrues

  (a) in the case of a time instrument on the day after maturity;

  (b) in the case of a demand instrument upon its date or, if no date is stated, on the date of issue.

(2) A cause of action against the obligor of a demand or time certificate of deposit accrues upon demand, but demand on a time certificate may not be made until on or after the date of maturity.

(3) A cause of action against a drawer of a draft or an indorser of any instrument accrues upon demand following dishonor of the instrument. Notice of dishonor is a demand.

(4) Unless an instrument provides otherwise, interest runs at the rate provided by law for a judgment

  (a) in the case of a maker of a demand note, from the date of demand;

  (b) in all other cases from the date of accrual of the cause of action.

Part 2

Transfer and Negotiation

§3–201. Transfer: Right to Indorsement. (1) Transfer of an instrument vests in the transferee such rights as the transferor has therein, except that a transferee who has himself been a party to any fraud or illegality affecting the instrument or who as a prior holder had notice of a defense or claim against it cannot improve his position by taking from a later holder in due course.

(2) A transfer of a security interest in an instrument vests the foregoing rights in the transferee to the extent of the interest transferred.

(3) Unless otherwise agreed any transfer for value of an instrument not then payable to bearer gives the transferee the specifically enforceable right to have the unqualified indorsement of the transferor. Negotiation takes effect only when the indorsement is made and until that time there is no presumption that the transferee is the owner.

§3–202. Negotiation. (1) Negotiation is the transfer of an instrument in such form that the transferee becomes a holder. If the instrument is payable to order it is negotiated by delivery with any necessary indorsement; if payable to bearer it is negotiated by delivery.

(2) An indorsement must be written by or on behalf of the holder and on the instrument or on a paper so firmly affixed thereto as to become a part thereof.

(3) An indorsement is effective for negotiation only when it conveys the entire instrument or any unpaid residue. If it purports to be of less it operates only as a partial assignment.

(4) Words of assignment, condition, waiver, guaranty, limitation or disclaimer of liability and the like accompanying an indorsement do not affect its character as an indorsement.

§3–203. Wrong or Misspelled Name. Where an instrument is made payable to a person under a misspelled name or one other than his own he may indorse in that name or his own or both; but signature in both names may be required by a person paying or giving value for the instrument.

§3–204. Special Indorsement; Blank Indorsement. (1) A special indorsement specifies the person to whom or to whose order it makes the instrument payable. Any instrument specially indorsed becomes payable to the order of the special indorsee and may be further negotiated only by his indorsement.

(2) An indorsement in blank specifies no particular indorsee and may consist of a mere signature. An instrument payable to order and indorsed in blank becomes payable to bearer and may be negotiated by delivery alone until specially indorsed.

(3) The holder may convert a blank indorsement into a special indorsement by writing over the signature of the indorser in blank any contract consistent with the character of the indorsement.

§3–205. Restrictive Indorsements. An indorsement is restrictive which either

(a) is conditional; or

(b) purports to prohibit further transfer of the instrument; or

(c) includes the words "for collection", "for deposit", "pay any bank", or like terms signifying a purpose of deposit or collection; or

(d) otherwise states that it is for the benefit or use of the indorser or of another person.

§3–206. Effect of Restrictive Indorsement. (1) No restrictive indorsement prevents further transfer or negotiation of the instrument.

(2) An intermediary bank, or a payor bank which is not the depositary bank, is neither given notice nor otherwise affected by a restrictive indorsement of any person except the bank's immediate transferor or the person presenting for payment.

(3) Except for an intermediary bank, any transferee under an indorsement which is conditional or includes the words "for collection", "for deposit", "pay any bank", or like terms (subparagraphs (a) and (c) of Section 3–205) must pay or apply any value given by him for or on the security of the instrument consistently with the indorsement and to the extent that he does so he become a holder for value. In addition such transferee is a holder in due course if he otherwise complies with the requirements of Section 3–302 on what constitutes a holder in due course.

(4) The first taker under an indorsement for the benefit of the indorser or another person (subparagraph (d) of Section 3–205) must pay or apply any value given by him for or on the security of the instrument consistently with the indorsement and to the extent that he does so he becomes a holder for value. In addition such taker is a holder in due course if he otherwise complies with the requirements of Section 3–302 on what constitutes a holder in due course. A later holder for value is neither given notice nor otherwise affected by such restrictive indorsement unless he has knowledge that a fiduciary or other person has negotiated the instrument in any transaction for his own benefit or otherwise in breach of duty (subsection (2) of Section 3–304).

§3–207. Negotiation Effective Although It May Be Rescinded. (1) Negotiation is effective to transfer the instrument although the negotiation is

(a) made by an infant, a corporation exceeding its powers, or any other person without capacity; or

(b) obtained by fraud, duress or mistake of any kind; or

(c) part of an illegal transaction; or

(d) made in breach of duty.

(2) Except as against a subsequent holder in due course such negotiation is in an appropriate case subject to rescission, the declaration of a constructive trust or any other remedy permitted by law.

§3–208. Reacquisition. Where an instrument is returned to or reacquired by a prior party he may cancel any indorsement which is not necessary to his title and reissue or further negotiate the instrument, but any intervening party is discharged as against the reacquiring party and subsequent holders not in due course and if his indorsement has been cancelled is discharged as against subsequent holders in due course as well.

Part 3

Rights of a Holder

§3–301. Rights of a Holder. The holder of an instrument whether or not he is the owner may transfer or negotiate it and, except as otherwise provided in Section 3–603 on payment or satisfaction, discharge it or enforce payment in his own name.

§3–302. Holder in Due Course. (1) A holder in due course is a holder who takes the instrument

(a) for value; and

(b) in good faith; and

(c) without notice that it is overdue or has been dishonored or of any defense against or claim to it on the part of any person.

(2) A payee may be a holder in due course.

(3) A holder does not become a holder in due course of an instrument:

(a) by purchase of it at judicial sale or by taking it under legal process; or

(b) by acquiring it in taking over an estate; or

(c) by purchasing it as part of a bulk transaction not in regular course of business of the transferor.

(4) A purchaser of a limited interest can be a holder in due course only to the extent of the interest purchased.

§3–303. Taking for Value. A holder takes the instrument for value

(a) to the extent that the agreed consideration has been performed or that he acquires a security interest in or a lien on the instrument otherwise than by legal process; or

(b) when he takes the instrument in payment of or as security for an antecedent claim against any person whether or not the claim is due; or

(c) when he gives a negotiable instrument for it or makes an irrevocable commitment to a third person.

§3–304. Notice to Purchaser. (1) The purchaser has notice of a claim or defense if

(a) the instrument is so incomplete, bears such visible evidence of forgery or alteration, or is otherwise so irregular as to call into question its validity, terms or ownership or to create an ambiguity as to the party to pay; or

(b) the purchaser has notice that the obligation of any party is voidable in whole or in part, or that all parties have been discharged.

(2) The purchaser has notice of a claim against the instrument when he has knowledge that a fiduciary has negotiated the instrument in payment of or as security for his own debt or in any transaction for his own benefit or otherwise in breach of duty.

(3) The purchaser has notice that an instrument is overdue if he has reason to know

(a) that any part of the principal amount is overdue or that there is an uncured default in payment of another instrument of the same series; or

(b) that acceleration of the instrument has been made; or

(c) that he is taking a demand instrument after demand has been made or more than a reasonable length of time after its issue. A reasonable time for a check drawn and payable within the states and territories of the United States and the District of Columbia is presumed to be thirty days.

(4) Knowledge of the following facts does not of itself give the purchaser notice of a defense or claim

(a) that the instrument is antedated or postdated;

(b) that it was issued or negotiated in return for an executory promise or accompanied by a separate agreement, unless the purchaser has notice that a defense or claim has arisen from the terms thereof;

(c) that any party has signed for accommodation;

(d) that an incomplete instrument has been completed, unless the purchaser has notice of any improper completion;

(e) that any person negotiating the instrument is or was a fiduciary;

(f) that there has been default in payment of interest on the instrument or in payment of any other instrument, except one of the same series.

(5) The filing or recording of a document does not of itself constitute notice within the provisions of this Article to a person who would otherwise be a holder in due course.

(6) To be effective notice must be received at such time and in such manner as to give a reasonable opportunity to act on it.

§3–305. Rights of a Holder in Due Course. To the extent that a holder is a holder in due course he takes the instrument free from

(1) all claims to it on the part of any person; and

(2) all defenses of any party to the instrument with whom the holder has not dealt except

(a) infancy, to the extent that it is a defense to a simple contract; and

(b) such other incapacity, or duress, or illegality of the transaction, as renders the obligation of the party a nullity; and

(c) such misrepresentation as has induced the party to sign the instrument with neither knowledge nor reasonable opportunity to obtain knowledge of its character or its essential terms; and

(d) discharge in insolvency proceedings; and

(e) any other discharge of which the holder has notice when he takes the instrument.

§3–306. Rights of One Not Holder in Due Course. Unless he has the rights of a holder in due course any person takes the instrument subject to

(a) all valid claims to it on the part of any person; and

(b) all defenses of any party which would be available in an action on a simple contract; and

(c) the defenses of want or failure of consideration, non-performance of any condition precedent, non-delivery, or delivery for a special purpose (Section 3–408); and

(d) the defense that he or a person through whom he holds the instrument acquired it by theft, or that payment or satisfaction to such holder would be inconsistent with the terms of a restrictive indorsement. The claim of any third person to the instrument is not otherwise available as a defense to any party liable thereon unless the third person himself defends the action for such party.

§3–307. Burden of Establishing Signatures, Defenses and Due Course. (1) Unless specifically denied in the pleadings each signature on an instrument is admitted. When the effectiveness of a signature is put in issue

(a) the burden of establishing it is on the party claiming under the signature; but

(b) the signature is presumed to be genuine or authorized except where the action is to enforce the obligation of a purported signer who has died or become incompetent before proof is required.

(2) When signatures are admitted or established, production of the instrument entitles a holder to recover on it unless the defendant establishes a defense.

(3) After it is shown that a defense exists a person claiming the rights of a holder in due course has the burden of establishing that he or some person under whom he claims is in all respects a holder in due course.

Part 4

Liability of Parties

§3–401. Signature. (1) No person is liable on an instrument unless his signature appears thereon.

(2) A signature is made by use of any name, including any trade or assumed name, upon an instrument, or by any word or mark used in lieu of a written signature.

§3–402. Signature in Ambiguous Capacity. Unless the instrument clearly indicates that a signature is made in some other capacity it is an indorsement.

§3–403. Signature by Authorized Representative. (1) A signature may be made by an agent or other representative, and his authority to make it may be established as in other cases of representation. No particular form of appointment is necessary to establish such authority.

(2) An authorized representative who signs his own name to an instrument

(a) is personally obligated if the instrument neither names the person represented nor shows that the representative signed in a representative capacity;

(b) except as otherwise established between the immediate parties, is personally obligated if the instrument names the person represented but does not show that the representative signed in a representative capacity, or if the instrument does not name the person represented but does show that the representative signed in a representative capacity.

(3) Except as otherwise established the name of an organization preceded or followed by the name and office of an authorized individual is a signature made in a representative capacity.

§3–404. Unauthorized Signatures. (1) Any unauthorized signature is wholly inoperative as that of the person whose name is signed unless he ratifies it or is precluded from denying it; but it operates as the signature of the unauthorized signer in favor of any person who in good faith pays the instrument or takes it for value.

(2) Any unauthorized signature may be ratified for all purposes of this Article. Such ratification does not of itself affect any rights of the person ratifying against the actual signer.

§3–405. Impostors; Signature in Name of Payee. (1) An indorsement by any person in the name of a named payee is effective if

(a) an impostor by use of the mails or otherwise has induced the maker or drawer to issue the instrument to him or his confederate in the name of the payee; or

(b) a person signing as or on behalf of a maker or drawer intends the payee to have no interest in the instrument; or

(c) an agent or employee of the maker or drawer has supplied him with the name of the payee intending the latter to have no such interest.

(2) Nothing in this section shall affect the criminal or civil liability of the person so indorsing.

§3–406. Negligence Contributing to Alteration or Unauthorized Signature. Any person who by his negligence substantially contributes to a material alteration of the instrument or to the making of an unauthorized signature is precluded from asserting the alteration or lack of authority against a holder in due course or against a drawee or other payor who pays the instrument in good faith and in accordance with the reasonable commercial standards of the drawee's or payor's business.

§3–407. Alteration. (1) Any alteration of an instrument is material which changes the contract of any party thereto in any respect, including any such change in

(a) the number or relations of the parties; or

(b) an incomplete instrument, by completing it otherwise than as authorized; or

(c) the writing as signed, by adding to it or by removing any part of it.

(2) As against any person other than a subsequent holder in due course

(a) alteration by the holder which is both fraudulent and material discharges any party whose contract is thereby changed unless that party assents or is precluded from asserting the defense;

(b) no other alteration discharges any party and the instrument may be enforced according to its original tenor, or as to incomplete instruments according to the authority given.

(3) A subsequent holder in due course may in all cases enforce the instrument according to its original tenor, and when an incomplete instrument has been completed, he may enforce it as completed.

§3–408. Consideration. Want or failure of consideration is a defense as against any person not having the rights of a holder in due course (Section 3–305), except that no consideration is necessary for an instrument or obligation thereon given in payment of or as security for an antecedent obligation of any kind. Nothing in this section shall be taken to displace any statute outside this Act under which a promise is enforceable notwithstanding lack or failure of consideration. Partial failure of consideration is a defense pro tanto whether or not the failure is in an ascertained or liquidated amount.

§3–409. Draft Not an Assignment. (1) A check or other draft does not of itself operate as an assignment of any funds in the hands of the drawee available for its payment, and the drawee is not liable on the instrument until he accepts it.

(2) Nothing in this section shall affect any liability in contract, tort or otherwise arising from any letter of credit or other obligation or representation which is not an acceptance.

§3–410. Definition and Operation of Acceptance. (1) Acceptance is the drawee's signed engagement to honor the draft as presented. It must be written on the draft, and may consist of his signature alone. It becomes operative when completed by delivery or notification.

(2) A draft may be accepted although it has not been signed by the drawer or is otherwise incomplete or is overdue or has been dishonored.

(3) Where the draft is payable at a fixed period after sight and the acceptor fails to date his acceptance the holder may complete it by supplying a date in good faith.

§3–411. Certification of a Check. (1) Certification of a check is acceptance. Where a holder procures certification the drawer and all prior indorsers are discharged.

(2) Unless otherwise agreed a bank has no obligation to certify a check.

(3) A bank may certify a check before returning it for lack of proper indorsement. If it does so the drawer is discharged.

§3–412. Acceptance Varying Draft. (1) Where the drawee's proffered acceptance in any manner varies the draft as presented the holder may refuse the acceptance and treat the draft as dishonored in which case the drawee is entitled to have his acceptance cancelled.

(2) The terms of the draft are not varied by an acceptance to pay at any particular bank or place in the continental United States, unless the acceptance states that the draft is to be paid only at such bank or place.

(3) Where the holder assents to an acceptance varying the terms of the draft each drawer and indorser who does not affirmatively assent is discharged.

§3–413. Contract of Maker, Drawer and Acceptor. (1) The maker or acceptor engages that he will pay the instrument according to its tenor at the time of his engagement or as completed pursuant to Section 3–115 on incomplete instruments.

(2) The drawer engages that upon dishonor of the draft and any necessary notice of dishonor or protest he will pay the amount of the draft to the holder or to any indorser who takes it up. The drawer may disclaim this liability by drawing without recourse.

(3) By making, drawing or accepting the party admits as against all subsequent parties including the drawee the existence of the payee and his then capacity to indorse.

§3–414. Contract of Indorser; Order of Liability. (1) Unless the indorsement otherwise specifies (as by such words as "without recourse") every indorser engages that upon dishonor and any necessary notice of dishonor and protest he will pay the instrument according to its tenor at the time of his indorsement to the holder or to any subsequent indorser who takes it up, even though the indorser who takes it up was not obligated to do so.

(2) Unless they otherwise agree indorsers are liable to one another in the order in which they indorse, which is presumed to be the order in which their signatures appear on the instrument.

§3–415. Contract of Accommodation Party. (1) An accommodation party is one who signs the instrument in any capacity for the purpose of lending his name to another party to it.

(2) When the instrument has been taken for value before it is due the accommodation party is liable in the capacity in which he has signed even though the taker knows of the accommodation.

(3) As against a holder in due course and without notice of the accommodation oral proof of the accommodation is not admissible to give the accommodation party the benefit of discharges dependent on his character as such. In other cases the accommodation character may be shown by oral proof.

(4) An indorsement which shows that it is not in the chain of title is notice of its accommodation character.

(5) An accommodation party is not liable to the party accommodated, and if he pays the instrument has a right of recourse on the instrument against such party.

§3–416. Contract of Guarantor. (1) "Payment guaranteed" or equivalent words added to a signature mean that the signer engages that if the instrument is not paid when due he will pay it according to its tenor without resort by the holder to any other party.

(2) "Collection guaranteed" or equivalent words added to a signature mean that the signer engages that if the instrument is not paid when due he will pay it according to its tenor, but only after the holder has reduced his claim against the maker or acceptor to judgment and execution has been returned unsatisfied, or after the maker or acceptor has become insolvent or it is otherwise apparent that it is useless to proceed against him.

(3) Words of guaranty which do not otherwise specify guarantee payment.

(4) No words of guaranty added to the signature of a sole maker or acceptor affect his liability on the instrument. Such words added to the signature of one of two or more makers or acceptors create a presumption that the signature is for the accommodation of the others.

(5) When words of guaranty are used presentment, notice of dishonor and protest are not necessary to charge the user.

(6) Any guaranty written on the instrument is enforceable notwithstanding any statute of frauds.

§3–417. **Warranties on Presentment and Transfer.** (1) Any person who obtains payment or acceptance and any prior transferor warrants to a person who in good faith pays or accepts that

(a) he has a good title to the instrument or is authorized to obtain payment or acceptance on behalf of one who has a good title; and

(b) he has no knowledge that the signature of the maker or drawer is unauthorized, except that this warranty is not given by a holder in due course acting in good faith

(i) to a maker with respect to the maker's own signature; or

(ii) to a drawer with respect to the drawer's own signature, whether or not the drawer is also the drawee; or

(iii) to an acceptor of a draft if the holder in due course took the draft after the acceptance or obtained the acceptance without knowledge that the drawer's signature was unauthorized; and

(c) the instrument has not been materially altered, except that this warranty is not given by a holder in due course acting in good faith

(i) to the maker of a note; or

(ii) to the drawer of a draft whether or not the drawer is also the drawee; or

(iii) to the acceptor of a draft with respect to an alteration made prior to the acceptance if the holder in due course took the draft after the acceptance, even though the acceptance provided "payable as originally drawn" or equivalent terms; or

(iv) to the acceptor of a draft with respect to an alteration made after the acceptance.

(2) Any person who transfers an instrument and receives consideration warrants to his transferee and if the transfer is by indorsement to any subsequent holder who takes the instrument in good faith that

(a) he has a good title to the instrument or is authorized to obtain payment or acceptance on behalf of one who has a good title and the transfer is otherwise rightful; and

(b) all signatures are genuine or authorized; and

(c) the instrument has not been materially altered; and

(d) no defense of any party is good against him; and

(e) he has no knowledge of any insolvency proceeding instituted with respect to the maker or acceptor or the drawer of an unaccepted instrument.

(3) By transferring "without recourse" the transferor limits the obligation stated in subsection (2) (d) to a warranty that he has no knowledge of such a defense.

(4) A selling agent or broker who does not disclose the fact that he is acting only as such gives the warranties provided in this section, but if he makes such disclosure warrants only his good faith and authority.

§3–418. Finality of Payment or Acceptance. Except for recovery of bank payments as provided in the Article on Bank Deposits and Collections (Article 4) and except for liability for breach of warranty on presentment under the preceding section, payment or acceptance of any instrument is final in favor of a holder in due course, or a person who has in good faith changed his position in reliance on the payment.

§3–419. Conversion of Instrument; Innocent Representative. (1) An instrument is converted when

(a) a drawee to whom it is delivered for acceptance refuses to return it on demand; or

(b) any person to whom it is delivered for payment refuses on demand either to pay or to return it; or

(c) it is paid on a forged indorsement.

(2) In an action against a drawee under subsection (1) the measure of the drawee's liability is the face amount of the instrument. In any other action under subsection (1) the measure of liability is presumed to be the face amount of the instrument.

(3) Subject to the provisions of this Act concerning restrictive indorsements a representative, including a depositary or collecting bank, who has in good faith and in accordance with the reasonable commercial standards applicable to the business of such representative dealt with an instrument or its proceeds on behalf of one who was not the true owner is not liable in conversion or otherwise to the true owner beyond the amount of any proceeds remaining in his hands.

(4) An intermediary bank or payor bank which is not a depositary bank is not liable in conversion solely by reason of the fact that proceeds of an item indorsed restrictively (Sections 3–205 and 3–206) are not paid or applied consistently with the restrictive indorsement of an indorser other than its immediate transferor.

Part 5

Presentment, Notice of Dishonor and Protest

§3–501. When Presentment, Notice of Dishonor, and Protest Necessary or Permissible. (1) Unless excused (Section 3–511) presentment is necessary to charge secondary parties as follows:

(a) presentment for acceptance is necessary to charge the drawer and indorsers of a draft where the draft so provides, or is payable elsewhere than at the residence or place of business of the drawee, or its date of payment depends upon such presentment. The holder may at his option present for acceptance any other draft payable at a stated date;

(b) presentment for payment is necessary to charge any indorser;

(c) in the case of any drawer, the acceptor of a draft payable at a bank or the maker of a note payable at a bank, presentment for payment is necessary, but failure to make presentment discharges such drawer, acceptor or maker only as stated in Section 3–502(1) (b).

(2) Unless excused (Section 3–511)

(a) notice of any dishonor is necessary to charge any indorser;

(b) in the case of any drawer, the acceptor of a draft payable at a bank or the maker of a note payable at a bank, notice of any dishonor is necessary, but failure to give such notice discharges such drawer, acceptor or maker only as stated in Section 3–502(1) (b).

(3) Unless excused (Section 3–511) protest of any dishonor is necessary to charge the drawer and indorsers of any draft which on its face appears to be drawn or payable outside of the states and territories of the United States and the District of Columbia. The holder may at his option make protest of any dishonor of any other instrument and in the case of a foreign draft may on insolvency of the acceptor before maturity make protest for better security.

(4) Notwithstanding any provision of this section, neither presentment nor notice of dishonor nor protest is necessary to charge an indorser who has indorsed an instrument after maturity.

§3–502. Unexcused Delay; Discharge. (1) Where without excuse any necessary presentment or notice of dishonor is delayed beyond the time when it is due

(a) any indorser is discharged; and

(b) any drawer or the acceptor of a draft payable at a bank or the maker of a note payable at a bank who because the drawee or payor bank becomes insolvent during the delay is deprived of funds maintained with the drawee or payor bank to cover the instrument may discharge his liability by written assignment to the holder of his rights against the drawee or payor bank in respect of such funds, but such drawer, acceptor or maker is not otherwise discharged.

(2) Where without excuse a necessary protest is delayed beyond the time when it is due any drawer or indorser is discharged.

§3–503. Time of Presentment. (1) Unless a different time is expressed in the instrument the time for any presentment is determined as follows:

(a) where an instrument is payable at or a fixed period after a stated date any presentment for acceptance must be made on or before the date it is payable;

(b) where an instrument is payable after sight it must either be presented for acceptance or negotiated within a reasonable time after date or issue whichever is later;

(c) where an instrument shows the date on which it is payable presentment for payment is due on that date;

(d) where an instrument is accelerated presentment for payment is due within a reasonable time after the acceleration;

(e) with respect to the liability of any secondary party presentment for acceptance or payment of any other instrument is due within a reasonable time after such party becomes liable thereon.

(2) A reasonable time for presentment is determined by the nature of the

instrument, any usage of banking or trade and the facts of the particular case. In the case of an uncertified check which is drawn and payable within the United States and which is not a draft drawn by a bank the following are presumed to be reasonable periods within which to present for payment or to initiate bank collection:

(a) with respect to the liability of the drawer, thirty days after date or issue whichever is later; and

(b) with respect to the liability of an indorser, seven days after his indorsement.

(3) Where any presentment is due on a day which is not a full business day for either the person making presentment or the party to pay or accept, presentment is due on the next following day which is a full business day for both parties.

(4) Presentment to be sufficient must be made at a reasonable hour, and if at a bank during its banking day.

§3–504. How Presentment Made. (1) Presentment is a demand for acceptance or payment made upon the maker, acceptor, drawee or other payor by or on behalf of the holder.

(2) Presentment may be made

(a) by mail, in which event the time of presentment is determined by the time of receipt of the mail; or

(b) through a clearing house; or

(c) at the place of acceptance or payment specified in the instrument or if there be none at the place of business or residence of the party to accept or pay. If neither the party to accept or pay nor anyone authorized to act for him is present or accessible at such place presentment is excused.

(3) It may be made

(a) to any one of two or more makers, acceptors, drawees or other payors; or

(b) to any person who has authority to make or refuse the acceptance or payment.

(4) A draft accepted or a note made payable at a bank in the continental United States must be presented at such bank.

(5) In the cases described in Section 4–210 presentment may be made in the manner and with the result stated in that section.

§3–505. Rights of Party to Whom Presentment Is Made. (1) The party to whom presentment is made may without dishonor require

(a) exhibition of the instrument; and

(b) reasonable identification of the person making presentment and evidence of his authority to make it if made for another; and

(c) that the instrument be produced for acceptance or payment at a place specified in it, or if there be none at any place reasonable in the circumstances; and

(d) a signed receipt on the instrument for any partial or full payment and its surrender upon full payment.

(2) Failure to comply with any such requirement invalidates the presentment but the person presenting has a reasonable time in which to comply and the time for acceptance or payment runs from the time of compliance.

§3–506. Time Allowed for Acceptance or Payment. (1) Acceptance may be deferred without dishonor until the close of the next business day following presentment. The holder may also in a good faith effort to obtain acceptance and without either dishonor of the instrument or discharge of secondary parties allow postponement of acceptance for an additional business day.

(2) Except as a longer time is allowed in the case of documentary drafts drawn under a letter of credit, and unless an earlier time is agreed to by the party to pay, payment of an instrument may be deferred without dishonor pending reasonable examination to determine whether it is properly payable, but payment must be made in any event before the close of business on the day of presentment.

§3–507. Dishonor; Holder's Right of Recourse; Term Allowing Re-Presentment. (1) An instrument is dishonored when

(a) a necessary or optional presentment is duly made and due acceptance or payment is refused or cannot be obtained within the prescribed time or in case of bank collections the instrument is seasonably returned by the midnight deadline (Section 4–301); or

(b) presentment is excused and the instrument is not duly accepted or paid.

(2) Subject to any necessary notice of dishonor and protest, the holder has upon dishonor an immediate right of recourse against the drawers and indorsers.

(3) Return of an instrument for lack of proper indorsement is not dishonor.

(4) A term in a draft or an indorsement thereof allowing a stated time for re-presentment in the event of any dishonor of the draft by nonacceptance if a time draft or by nonpayment if a sight draft gives the holder as against any secondary party bound by the term an option to waive the dishonor without affecting the liability of the secondary party and he may present again up to the end of the stated time.

§3–508. Notice of Dishonor. (1) Notice of dishonor may be given to any person who may be liable on the instrument by or on behalf of the holder or any party who has himself received notice, or any other party who can be compelled to pay the instrument. In addition an agent or bank in whose hands the instrument is dishonored may give notice to his principal or customer or to another agent or bank from which the instrument was received.

(2) Any necessary notice must be given by a bank before its midnight deadline and by any other person before midnight of the third business day after dishonor or receipt of notice of dishonor.

(3) Notice may be given in any reasonable manner. It may be oral or written and in any terms which identify the instrument and state that it has been dishonored. A misdescription which does not mislead the party notified does not vitiate the notice. Sending the instrument bearing a stamp, ticket or writing stating that acceptance or payment has been refused or sending a notice of debit with respect to the instrument is sufficient.

(4) Written notice is given when sent although it is not received.

(5) Notice to one partner is notice to each although the firm has been dissolved.

(6) When any party is in insolvency proceedings instituted after the issue of the instrument notice may be given either to the party or to the representative of his estate.

(7) When any party is dead or incompetent notice may be sent to his last known address or given to his personal representative.

(8) Notice operates for the benefit of all parties who have rights on the instrument against the party notified.

§3–509. Protest; Noting for Protest. (1) A protest is a certificate of dishonor made under the hand and seal of a United States consul or vice consul or a notary public or other person authorized to certify dishonor by the law of the place where dishonor occurs. It may be made upon information satisfactory to such person.

(2) The protest must identify the instrument and certify either that due presentment has been made or the reason why it is excused and that the instrument has been dishonored by nonacceptance or nonpayment.

(3) The protest may also certify that notice of dishonor has been given to all parties or to specified parties.

(4) Subject to subsection (5) any necessary protest is due by the time that notice of dishonor is due.

(5) If, before protest is due, an instrument has been noted for protest by the officer to make protest, the protest may be made at any time thereafter as of the date of the noting.

§3–510. Evidence of Dishonor and Notice of Dishonor. The following are admissible as evidence and create a presumption of dishonor and of any notice of dishonor therein shown:

(a) a document regular in form as provided in the preceding section which purports to be a protest;

(b) the purported stamp or writing of the drawee, payor bank or presenting bank on the instrument or accompanying it stating that acceptance or payment has been refused for reasons consistent with dishonor;

(c) any book or record of the drawee, payor bank, or any collecting bank kept in the usual course of business which shows dishonor, even though there is no evidence of who made the entry.

§3–511. Waived or Excused Presentment, Protest or Notice of Dishonor or Delay Therein. (1) Delay in presentment, protest or notice of dishonor is excused when the party is without notice that it is due or when the delay is caused by circumstances beyond his control and he exercises reasonable diligence after the cause of the delay ceases to operate.

(2) Presentment or notice or protest as the case may be is entirely excused when

(a) the party to be charged has waived it expressly or by implication either before or after it is due; or

(b) such party has himself dishonored the instrument or has countermanded payment or otherwise has no reason to expect or right to require that the instrument be accepted or paid; or

(c) by reasonable diligence the presentment or protest cannot be made or the notice given.

(3) Presentment is also entirely excused when

(a) the maker, acceptor or drawee of any instrument except a documentary draft is dead or in insolvency proceedings instituted after the issue of the instrument; or

(b) acceptance or payment is refused but not for want of proper presentment.

(4) Where a draft has been dishonored by nonacceptance a later presentment for payment and any notice of dishonor and protest for nonpayment are excused unless in the meantime the instrument has been accepted.

(5) A waiver of protest is also a waiver of presentment and of notice of dishonor even though protest is not required.

(6) Where a waiver of presentment or notice of protest is embodied in the instrument itself it is binding upon all parties; but where it is written above the signature of an indorser it binds him only.

Part 6

Discharge

§3–601. Discharge of Parties. (1) The extent of the discharge of any party from liability on an instrument is governed by the sections on

(a) payment or satisfaction (Section 3–603); or

(b) tender of payment (Section 3–604); or

(c) cancellation or renunciation (Section 3–605); or

(d) impairment of right of recourse or of collateral (Section 3–606); or

(e) reacquisition of the instrument by a prior party (Section 3–208); or

(f) fraudulent and material alteration (Section 3–407); or

(g) certification of a check (Section 3–411); or

(h) acceptance varying a draft (Section 3–412); or

(i) unexcused delay in presentment or notice of dishonor or protest (Section 3–502).

(2) Any party is also discharged from his liability on an instrument to another party by any other act or agreement with such party which would discharge his simple contract for the payment of money.

(3) The liability of all parties is discharged when any party who has himself no right of action or recourse on the instrument

(a) reacquires the instrument in his own right; or

(b) is discharged under any provision of this Article, except as otherwise provided with respect to discharge for impairment of recourse or of collateral (Section 3–606).

§3–602. Effect of Discharge Against Holder in Due Course. No discharge of any party provided by this Article is effective against a subsequent holder in due course unless he has notice thereof when he takes the instrument.

§3–603. Payment or Satisfaction. (1) The liability of any party is discharged to the extent of his payment or satisfaction to the holder even though it is made with knowledge of a claim of another person to the instrument unless prior to such payment or satisfaction the person making the claim either supplies indemnity deemed adequate by the party seeking the discharge or enjoins payment or satisfaction by order of a court of competent jurisdiction in an action in which the adverse claimant and the holder are parties. This subsection does not, however, result in the discharge of the liability

(a) of a party who in bad faith pays or satisfies a holder who acquired the instrument by theft or who (unless having the rights of a holder in due course) holds through one who so acquired it; or

(b) of a party (other than an intermediary bank or a payor bank which is not a depositary bank) who pays or satisfies the holder of an instrument which has been restrictively indorsed in a manner not consistent with the terms of such restrictive indorsement.

(2) Payment or satisfaction may be made with the consent of the holder by any person including a stranger to the instrument. Surrender of the instrument to such a person gives him the rights of a transferee (Section 3-201).

§3-604. **Tender of Payment.** (1) Any party making tender of full payment to a holder when or after it is due is discharged to the extent of all subsequent liability for interest, costs and attorney's fees.

(2) The holder's refusal of such tender wholly discharges any party who has a right of recourse against the party making the tender.

(3) Where the maker or acceptor of an instrument payable otherwise than on demand is able and ready to pay at every place of payment specified in the instrument when it is due, it is equivalent to tender.

§3-605. **Cancellation and Renunciation.** (1) The holder of an instrument may even without consideration discharge any party

(a) in any manner apparent on the face of the instrument or the indorsement, as by intentionally cancelling the instrument or the party's signature by destruction or mutilation, or by striking out the party's signature; or

(b) by renouncing his rights by a writing signed and delivered or by surrender of the instrument to the party to be discharged.

(2) Neither cancellation nor renunciation without surrender of the instrument affects the title thereto.

§3-606. **Impairment of Recourse or of Collateral.** (1) The holder discharges any party to the instrument to the extent that without such party's consent the holder

(a) without express reservation of rights releases or agrees not to sue any person against whom the party has to the knowledge of the holder a right of recourse or agrees to suspend the right to enforce against such person the instrument or collateral or otherwise discharges such person, except that failure or delay in effecting any required presentment, protest or notice of dishonor with respect to any such person does not discharge any party as to whom presentment, protest or notice of dishonor is effective or unnecessary; or

(b) unjustifiably impairs any collateral for the instrument given by or on behalf of the party or any person against whom he has a right of recourse.

(2) By express reservation of rights against a party with a right of recourse the holder preserves

(a) all his rights against such party as of the time when the instrument was originally due; and

(b) the right of the party to pay the instrument as of that time; and

(c) all rights of such party to recourse against others.

Part 7

Advice of International Sight Draft

§3–701. Letter of Advice of International Sight Draft. (1) A "letter of advice" is a drawer's communication to the drawee that a described draft has been drawn.

(2) Unless otherwise agreed when a bank receives from another bank a letter of advice of an international sight draft the drawee bank may immediately debit the drawer's account and stop the running of interest pro tanto. Such a debit and any resulting credit to any account covering outstanding drafts leaves in the drawer full power to stop payment or otherwise dispose of the amount and creates no trust or interest in favor of the holder.

(3) Unless otherwise agreed and except where a draft is drawn under a credit issued by the drawee, the drawee of an international sight draft owes the drawer no duty to pay an unadvised draft but if it does so and the draft is genuine, may appropriately debit the drawer's account.

Part 8

Miscellaneous

§3–801. Drafts in a Set. (1) Where a draft is drawn in a set of parts, each of which is numbered and expressed to be an order only if no other part has been honored, the whole of the parts constitutes one draft but a taker of any part may become a holder in due course of the draft.

(2) Any person who negotiates, indorses or accepts a single part of a draft drawn in a set thereby becomes liable to any holder in due course of that part as if it were the whole set, but as between different holders in due course to whom different parts have been negotiated the holder whose title first accrues has all rights to the draft and its proceeds.

(3) As against the drawee the first presented part of a draft drawn in a set is the part entitled to payment, or if a time draft to acceptance and payment. Acceptance of any subsequently presented part renders the drawee liable thereon under subsection (2). With respect both to a holder and to the drawer payment of a subsequently presented part of a draft payable at sight has the same effect as payment of a check notwithstanding an effective stop order (Section 4–407).

(4) Except as otherwise provided in this section, where any part of a draft in a set is discharged by payment or otherwise the whole draft is discharged.

§3–802. Effect of Instrument on Obligation for Which It Is Given. (1) Unless otherwise agreed where an instrument is taken for an underlying obligation

(a) the obligation is pro tanto discharged if a bank is drawer, maker or acceptor of the instrument and there is no recourse on the instrument against the underlying obligor; and

(b) in any other case the obligation is suspended pro tanto until the instrument is due or if it is payable on demand until its presentment. If the instrument is dishonored action may be maintained on either the instrument or the obligation; discharge of the underlying obligor on the instrument also discharges him on the obligation.

(2) The taking in good faith of a check which is not postdated does not of itself so extend the time on the original obligation as to discharge a surety.

§3–803. Notice to Third Party. Where a defendant is sued for breach of an obligation for which a third person is answerable over under this Article he may give the third person written notice of the litigation, and the person notified may then give similar notice to any other person who is answerable over to him under this Article. If the notice states that the person notified may come in and defend and that if the person notified does not do so he will in any action against him by the person giving the notice be bound by any determination of fact common to the two litigations, then unless after seasonable receipt of the notice the person notified does come in and defend he is so bound.

§3–804. Lost, Destroyed or Stolen Instruments. The owner of an instrument which is lost, whether by destruction, theft or otherwise, may maintain an action in his own name and recover from any party liable thereon upon due proof of his ownership, the facts which prevent his production of the instrument and its terms. The court may require security indemnifying the defendant against loss by reason of further claims on the instrument.

§3–805. Instruments Not Payable to Order or to Bearer. This Article applies to any instrument whose terms do not preclude transfer and which is otherwise negotiable within this Article but which is not payable to order or to bearer, except that there can be no holder in due course of such an instrument.

[ARTICLES 4 AND 5 OMITTED]

ARTICLE 6: BULK TRANSFERS

§6–101. Short Title. This Article shall be known and may be cited as Uniform Commercial Code—Bulk Transfers.

§6–102. "Bulk Transfer"; Transfers of Equipment; Enterprises Subject to This Article; Bulk Transfers Subject to This Article. (1) A "bulk transfer" is any transfer in bulk and not in the ordinary course of the transferor's business of a major part of the materials, supplies, merchandise or other inventory (Section 9–109) of an enterprise subject to this Article.

(2) A transfer of a substantial part of the equipment (Section 9–109) of such an enterprise is a bulk transfer if it is made in connection with a bulk transfer of inventory, but not otherwise.

(3) The enterprises subject to this Article are all those whose principal business is the sale of merchandise from stock, including those who manufacture what they sell.

(4) Except as limited by the following section all bulk transfers of goods located within this state are subject to this Article.

§6–103. Transfers Excepted From This Article. The following transfers are not subject to this Article:

(1) Those made to give security for the performance of an obligation;

(2) General assignments for the benefit of all the creditors of the transferor, and subsequent transfers by the assignee thereunder;

(3) Transfers in settlement or realization of a lien or other security interest;

(4) Sales by executors, administrators, receivers, trustees in bankruptcy, or any public officer under judicial process;

(5) Sales made in the course of judicial or administrative proceedings for the dissolution or reorganization of a corporation and of which notice is sent to the creditors of the corporation pursuant to order of the court or administrative agency;

(6) Transfers to a person maintaining a known place of business in this State who becomes bound to pay the debts of the transferor in full and gives public notice of that fact, and who is solvent after becoming so bound;

(7) A transfer to a new enterprise organized to take over and continue the business, if public notice of the transaction is given and the new enterprise assumes the debts of the transferor and he receives nothing from the transaction except an interest in the new enterprise junior to the claims of creditors;

(8) Transfers of property which is exempt from execution.

§6–104. Schedule of Property, List of Creditors. (1) Except as provided with respect to auction sales (Section 6–108), a bulk transfer subject to this Article is ineffective against any creditor of the transferor unless:

(a) The transferee requires the transferor to furnish a list of his existing creditors prepared as stated in this section; and

(b) The parties prepare a schedule of the property transferred sufficient to identify it; and

(c) The transferee preserves the list and schedule for six months next following the transfer and permits inspection of either or both and copying therefrom at all reasonable hours by any creditor of the transferor, or files the list and schedule in (*a public office to be here identified*).

(2) The list of creditors must be signed and sworn to or affirmed by the transferor or his agent. It must contain the names and business addresses of all creditors of the transferor, with the amounts when known, and also the names of all persons who are known to the transferor to assert claims against him even though such claims are disputed.

(3) Responsibility for the completeness and accuracy of the list of creditors rests on the transferor, and the transfer is not rendered ineffective by errors or omissions therein unless the transferee is shown to have had knowledge.

§6–105. Notice to Creditors. In addition to the requirements of the preceding section, any bulk transfer subject to this Article except one made by auction sale (Section 6–108) is ineffective against any creditor of the transferor unless at least ten days before he takes possession of the goods or pays for them, whichever happens first, the transferee gives notice of the transfer in the manner and to the persons hereafter provided (Section 6–107).

[**§6–106. Application of the Proceeds.** In addition to the requirements of the two preceding sections:

(1) Upon every bulk transfer subject to this Article for which new consideration becomes payable except those made by sale at auction it is the duty of the transferee to assure that such consideration is applied so far as necessary to pay those debts of the transferor which are either shown on the list furnished by the transferor (Section 6–104) or filed in writing in the place stated in the notice (Section 6–107) within thirty days after the mailing of such notice. This duty of the transferee runs to all the holders of such debts, and may be enforced by any of them for the benefit of all.

(2) If any of said debts are in dispute the necessary sum may be withheld from distribution until the dispute is settled or adjudicated.

(3) If the consideration payable is not enough to pay all of the said debts in full distribution shall be made pro rata.]

Note: *This section is bracketed to indicate division of opinion as to whether or not it is a wise provision, and to suggest that this is a point on which State enactments may differ without serious damage to the principle of uniformity.*

In any State where this section is omitted, the following parts of sections, also bracketed in the text, should also be omitted, namely:

Section 6–107(2)(e).

6–108(3)(c).

6–109(2).

In any State where this section is enacted, these other provisions should be also.

§6–107. The Notice. (1) The notice to creditors (Section 6–105) shall state:

(a) that a bulk transfer is about to be made; and

(b) the names and business addresses of the transferor and transferee, and all other business names and addresses used by the transferor within three years last past so far as known to the transferee; and

(c) whether or not all the debts of the transferor are to be paid in full as they fall due as a result of the transaction, and if so, the address to which creditors should send their bills.

(2) If the debts of the transferor are not to be paid in full as they fall due or if the transferee is in doubt on that point then the notice shall state further:

(a) the location and general description of the property to be transferred and the estimated total of the transferor's debts;

(b) the address where the schedule of property and list of creditors (Section 6–104) may be inspected;

(c) whether the transfer is to pay existing debts and if so the amount of such debts and to whom owing;

(d) whether the transfer is for new consideration and if so the amount of such consideration and the time and place of payment; [and]

[(e) if for new consideration the time and place where creditors of the transferor are to file their claims.]

(3) The notice in any case shall be delivered personally or sent by registered mail to all the persons shown on the list of creditors furnished by the transferor (Section 6–104) and to all other persons who are known to the transferee to hold or assert claims against the transferor.

§6–108. Auction Sales; "Auctioneer". (1) A bulk transfer is subject to this Article even though it is by sale at auction, but only in the manner and with the results stated in this section.

(2) The transferor shall furnish a list of his creditors and assist in the preparation of a schedule of the property to be sold, both prepared as before stated (Section 6–104).

(3) The person or persons other than the transferor who direct, control or are responsible for the auction are collectively called the "auctioneer". The auctioneer shall:

(a) receive and retain the list of creditors and prepare and retain the schedule of property for the period stated in this Article (Section 6–104);

(b) give notice of the auction personally or by registered mail at least ten days before it occurs to all persons shown on the list of creditors and to all other persons who are known to him to hold or assert claims against the transferor; [and]

[(c) assure that the net proceeds of the auction are applied as provided in this Article (Section 6–106).]

(4) Failure of the auctioneer to perform any of these duties does not affect the validity of the sale or the title of the purchasers, but if the auctioneer knows that the auction constitutes a bulk transfer such failure renders the auctioneer liable to the creditors of the transferor as a class for the sums owing to them from the transferor up to but not exceeding the net proceeds of the auction. If the auctioneer consists of several persons their liability is joint and several.

§6–109. What Creditors Protected; [Credit for Payment to Particular Creditors]. (1) The creditors of the transferor mentioned in this Article are those holding claims based on transactions or events occurring before the bulk transfer, but creditors who become such after notice to creditors is given (Sections 6–105 and 6–107) are not entitled to notice.

[(2) Against the aggregate obligation imposed by the provisions of this Article concerning the application of the proceeds (Section 6–106 and subsection (3) (c) of 6–108) the transferee or auctioneer is entitled to credit for sums paid to particular creditors of the transferor, not exceeding the sums believed in good faith at the time of the payment to be properly payable to such creditors.]

§6–110. Subsequent Transfers. When the title of a transferee to property is subject to a defect by reason of his non-compliance with the requirements of this Article, then:

(1) a purchaser of any of such property from such transferee who pays no value or who takes with notice of such non-compliance takes subject to such defect, but

(2) a purchaser for value in good faith and without such notice takes free of such defect.

§6–111. Limitation of Actions and Levies. No action under this Article shall be brought nor levy made more than six months after the date on which the transferee took possession of the goods unless the transfer has been concealed. If the transfer has been concealed, actions may be brought or levies made within six months after its discovery.

ARTICLE 7: WAREHOUSE RECEIPTS, BILLS OF LADING
AND OTHER DOCUMENTS OF TITLE

Part 1

General

§7–101. Short Title. This Article shall be known and may be cited as Uniform Commercial Code—Documents of Title.

§7–102. Definitions and Index of Definitions. (1) In this Article, unless the context otherwise requires:

(a) "Bailee" means the person who by a warehouse receipt, bill of lading or other document of title acknowledges possession of goods and contracts to deliver them.

(b) "Consignee" means the person named in a bill to whom or to whose order the bill promises delivery.

(c) "Consignor" means the person named in a bill as the person from whom the goods have been received for shipment.

(d) "Delivery order" means a written order to deliver goods directed to a warehouseman, carrier or other person who in the ordinary course of business issues warehouse receipts or bills of lading.

(e) "Document" means document of title as defined in the general definitions in Article 1 (Section 1–201).

(f) "Goods" means all things which are treated as movable for the purposes of a contract of storage or transportation.

(g) "Issuer" means a bailee who issues a document except that in relation to an unaccepted delivery order it means the person who orders the possessor of goods to deliver. Issuer includes any person for whom an agent or employee purports to act in issuing a document if the agent or employee has real or apparent authority to issue documents, notwithstanding that the issuer received no goods or that the goods were misdescribed or that in any other respect the agent or employee violated his instructions.

(h) "Warehouseman" is a person engaged in the business of storing goods for hire.

(2) Other definitions applying to this Article or to specified Parts thereof, and the sections in which they appear are:

"Duly negotiate". Section 7-501.

"Person entitled under the document". Section 7–403(4).

(3) Definitions in other Articles applying to this Article and the sections in which they appear are:

"Contract for sale". Section 2–106.

"Overseas". Section 2–323.

"Receipt" of goods. Section 2–103.

(4) In addition Article 1 contains general definitions and principles of construction and interpretation applicable throughout this Article.

§7–103. **Relation of Article to Treaty, Statute, Tariff, Classification or Regulation.** To the extent that any treaty or statute of the United States, regulatory statute of this State or tariff, classification or regulation filed or issued pursuant thereto is applicable, the provisions of this Article are subject thereto.

§7–104. **Negotiable and Non-Negotiable Warehouse Receipt, Bill of Lading or Other Document of Title.** (1) A warehouse receipt, bill of lading or other document of title is negotiable

(a) if by its terms the goods are to be delivered to bearer or to the order of a named person; or

(b) where recognized in overseas trade, if it runs to a named person or assigns.

(2) Any other document is non-negotiable. A bill of lading in which it is stated that the goods are consigned to a named person is not made negotiable by a provision that the goods are to be delivered only against a written order signed by the same or another named person.

§7–105. **Construction Against Negative Implication.** The omission from either Part 2 or Part 3 of this Article of a provision corresponding to a provision made in the other Part does not imply that a corresponding rule of law is not applicable.

Part 2

Warehouse Receipts: Special Provisions

§7–201. **Who May Issue a Warehouse Receipt; Storage Under Government Bond.** (1) A warehouse receipt may be issued by any warehouseman.

(2) Where goods including distilled spirits and agricultural commodities are stored under a statute requiring a bond against withdrawal or a license for the issuance of receipts in the nature of warehouse receipts, a receipt issued for the goods has like effect as a warehouse receipt even though issued by a person who is the owner of the goods and is not a warehouseman.

§7–202. **Form of Warehouse Receipt; Essential Terms; Optional Terms.** (1) A warehouse receipt need not be in any particular form.

(2) Unless a warehouse receipt embodies within its written or printed terms each of the following, the warehouseman is liable for damages caused by the omission to a person injured thereby:

(a) the location of the warehouse where the goods are stored;

(b) the date of issue of the receipt;

(c) the consecutive number of the receipt;

(d) a statement whether the goods received will be delivered to the bearer, to a specified person, or to a specified person or his order;

(e) the rate of storage and handling charges, except that where goods are stored under a field warehousing arrangement a statement of that fact is sufficient on a non-negotiable receipt;

(f) a description of the goods or of the packages containing them;

(g) the signature of the warehouseman, which may be made by his authorized agent;

(h) if the receipt is issued for goods of which the warehouseman is owner, either solely or jointly or in common with others, the fact of such ownership; and

(i) a statement of the amount of advances made and of liabilities incurred for which the warehouseman claims a lien or security interest (Section 7–209). If the precise amount of such advances made or of such liabilities incurred is, at the time of the issue of the receipt, unknown to the warehouseman or to his agent who issues it, a statement of the fact that advances have been made or liabilities incurred and the purpose thereof is sufficient.

(3) A warehouseman may insert in his receipt any other terms which are not contrary to the provisions of this Act and do not impair his obligation of delivery (Section 7–403) or his duty of care (Section 7–204). Any contrary provisions shall be ineffective.

§7–203. Liability for Non-Receipt or Misdescription. A party to or purchaser for value in good faith of a document of title other than a bill of lading relying in either case upon the description therein of the goods may recover from the issuer damages caused by the non-receipt or misdescription of the goods, except to the extent that the document conspicuously indicates that the issuer does not know whether any part or all of the goods in fact were received or conform to the description, as where the description is in terms of marks or labels or kind, quantity or condition, or the receipt or description is qualified by "contents, condition and quality unknown", "said to contain" or the like, if such indication be true, or the party or purchaser otherwise has notice.

§7–204. Duty of Care; Contractual Limitation of Warehouseman's Liability.
(1) A warehouseman is liable for damages for loss of or injury to the goods caused by his failure to exercise such care in regard to them as a reasonably careful man would exercise under like circumstances but unless otherwise agreed he is not liable for damages which could not have been avoided by the exercise of such care.

(2) Damages may be limited by a term in the warehouse receipt or storage agreement limiting the amount of liability in case of loss or damage, and setting forth a specific liability per article or item, or value per unit of weight, beyond which the warehouseman shall not be liable; provided, however, that such liability may on written request of the bailor at the time of signing such storage agreement or within a reasonable time after receipt of the warehouse receipt be increased on part or all of the goods thereunder, in which event increased rates may be charged based on such increased valuation, but that no such increase shall be permitted contrary to a lawful limitation of liability contained in the warehouseman's tariff, if any. No such limitation is effective with respect to the warehouseman's liability for conversion to his own use.

(3) Reasonable provisions as to the time and manner of presenting claims and

instituting actions based on the bailment may be included in the warehouse receipt or tariff.

(4) This section does not impair or repeal . . .

Note: *Insert in subsection (4) a reference to any statute which imposes a higher responsibility upon the warehouseman or invalidates contractual limitations which would be permissible under this Article.*

§7–205. Title Under Warehouse Receipt Defeated in Certain Cases. A buyer in the ordinary course of business of fungible goods sold and delivered by a warehouseman who is also in the business of buying and selling such goods takes free of any claim under a warehouse receipt even though it has been duly negotiated.

§7–206. Termination of Storage at Warehouseman's Option. (1) A warehouseman may on notifying the person on whose account the goods are held and any other person known to claim an interest in the goods require payment of any charges and removal of the goods from the warehouse at the termination of the period of storage fixed by the document, or, if no period is fixed, within a stated period not less than thirty days after the notification. If the goods are not removed before the date specified in the notification, the warehouseman may sell them in accordance with the provisions of the section on enforcement of a warehouseman's lien (Section 7–210).

(2) If a warehouseman in good faith believes that the goods are about to deteriorate or decline in value to less than the amount of his lien within the time prescribed in subsection (1) for notification, advertisement and sale, the warehouseman may specify in the notification any reasonable shorter time for removal of the goods and in case the goods are not removed, may sell them at public sale held not less than one week after a single advertisement or posting.

(3) If as a result of a quality or condition of the goods of which the warehouseman had no notice at the time of deposit the goods are a hazard to other property or to the warehouse or to persons, the warehouseman may sell the goods at public or private sale without advertisement on reasonable notification to all persons known to claim an interest in the goods. If the warehouseman after a reasonable effort is unable to sell the goods he may dispose of them in any lawful manner and shall incur no liability by reason of such disposition.

(4) The warehouseman must deliver the goods to any person entitled to them under this Article upon due demand made at any time prior to sale or other disposition under this section.

(5) The warehouseman may satisfy his lien from the proceeds of any sale or disposition under this section but must hold the balance for delivery on the demand of any person to whom he would have been bound to deliver the goods.

§7–207. Goods Must Be Kept Separate; Fungible Goods. (1) Unless the warehouse receipt otherwise provides, a warehouseman must keep separate the goods covered by each receipt so as to permit at all times identification and delivery of those goods except that different lots of fungible goods may be commingled.

(2) Fungible goods so commingled are owned in common by the persons entitled thereto and the warehouseman is severally liable to each owner for that

owner's share. Where because of overissue a mass of fungible goods is insufficient to meet all the receipts which the warehouseman has issued against it, the
persons entitled include all holders to whom overissued receipts have been duly
negotiated.

§7–208. Altered Warehouse Receipts. Where a blank in a negotiable warehouse
receipt has been filled in without authority, a purchaser for value and without
notice of the want of authority may treat the insertion as authorized. Any other
unauthorized alteration leaves any receipt enforceable against the issuer according to its original tenor.

§7–209. Lien of Warehouseman. (1) A warehouseman has a lien against the
bailor on the goods covered by a warehouse receipt or on the proceeds thereof
in his possession for charges for storage or transportation (including demurrage
and terminal charges), insurance, labor, or charges present or future in relation
to the goods, and for expenses necessary for preservation of the goods or reasonably incurred in their sale pursuant to law. If the person on whose account
the goods are held is liable for like charges or expenses in relation to other
goods whenever deposited and it is stated in the receipt that a lien is claimed
for charges and expenses in relation to other goods, the warehouseman also has
a lien against him for such charges and expenses whether or not the other
goods have been delivered by the warehouseman. But against a person to whom
a negotiable warehouse receipt is duly negotiated a warehouseman's lien is
limited to charges in an amount or at a rate specified on the receipt or if no
charges are so specified then to a reasonable charge for storage of the goods covered by the receipt subsequent to the date of the receipt.

(2) The warehouseman may also reserve a security interest against the bailor
for a maximum amount specified on the receipt for charges other than those
specified in subsection (1), such as for money advanced and interest. Such a
security interest is governed by the Article on Secured Transactions (Article 9).

(3) A warehouseman's lien for charges and expenses under subsection (1) or
a security interest under subsection (2) is also effective against any person who
so entrusted the bailor with possession of the goods that a pledge of them by him
to a good faith purchaser for value would have been valid but is not effective
against a person as to whom the document confers no right in the goods covered by it under Section 7–503.

(4) A warehouseman loses his lien on any goods which he voluntarily delivers
or which he unjustifiably refuses to deliver.

§7–210. Enforcement of Warehouseman's Lien. (1) Except as provided in subsection (2), a warehouseman's lien may be enforced by public or private sale
of the goods in bloc or in parcels, at any time or place and on any terms which
are commercially reasonable, after notifying all persons known to claim an interest in the goods. Such notification must include a statement of the amount due,
the nature of the proposed sale and the time and place of any public sale. The
fact that a better price could have been obtained by a sale at a different time or
in a different method from that selected by the warehouseman is not of itself
sufficient to establish that the sale was not made in a commercially reasonable
manner. If the warehouseman either sells the goods in the usual manner in any

recognized market therefor, or if he sells at the price current in such market at the time of his sale, or if he has otherwise sold in conformity with commercially reasonable practices among dealers in the type of goods sold, he has sold in a commercially reasonable manner. A sale of more goods than apparently necessary to be offered to insure satisfaction of the obligation is not commercially reasonable except in cases covered by the preceding sentence.

(2) A warehouseman's lien on goods other than goods stored by a merchant in the course of his business may be enforced only as follows:

(a) All persons known to claim an interest in the goods must be notified.

(b) The notification must be delivered in person or sent by registered letter to the last known address of any person to be notified.

(c) The notification must include an itemized statement of the claim, a description of the goods subject to the lien, a demand for payment within a specified time not less than ten days after receipt of the notification, and a conspicuous statement that unless the claim is paid within that time the goods will be advertised for sale and sold by auction at a specified time and place.

(d) The sale must conform to the terms of the notification.

(e) The sale must be held at the nearest suitable place to that where the goods are held or stored.

(f) After the expiration of the time given in the notification, an advertisement of the sale must be published once a week for two weeks consecutively in a newspaper of general circulation where the sale is to be held. The advertisement must include a description of the goods, the name of the person on whose account they are being held, and the time and place of the sale. The sale must take place at least fifteen days after the first publication. If there is no newspaper of general circulation where the sale is to be held, the advertisement must be posted at least ten days before the sale in not less than six conspicuous places in the neighborhood of the proposed sale.

(3) Before any sale pursuant to this section any person claiming a right in the goods may pay the amount necessary to satisfy the lien and the reasonable expenses incurred under this section. In that event the goods must not be sold, but must be retained by the warehouseman subject to the terms of the receipt and this Article.

(4) The warehouseman may buy at any public sale pursuant to this section.

(5) A purchaser in good faith of goods sold to enforce a warehouseman's lien takes the goods free of any rights of persons against whom the lien was valid, despite noncompliance by the warehouseman with the requirements of this section.

(6) The warehouseman may satisfy his lien from the proceeds of any sale pursuant to this section but must hold the balance, if any, for delivery on demand to any person to whom he would have been bound to deliver the goods.

(7) The rights provided by this section shall be in addition to all other rights allowed by law to a creditor against his debtor.

(8) Where a lien is on goods stored by a merchant in the course of his business the lien may be enforced in accordance with either subsection (1) or (2).

(9) The warehouseman is liable for damages caused by failure to comply with

the requirements for sale under this section and in case of willful violation is liable for conversion.

Part 3

Bills of Lading: Special Provisions

§7–301. Liability for Non-Receipt or Misdescription; "Said to Contain"; "Shipper's Load and Count"; Improper Handling. (1) A consignee of a non-negotiable bill who has given value in good faith or a holder to whom a negotiable bill has been duly negotiated relying in either case upon the description therein of the goods, or upon the date therein shown, may recover from the issuer damages caused by the misdating of the bill or the non-receipt or misdescription of the goods, except to the extent that the document indicates that the issuer does not know whether any part or all of the goods in fact were received or conform to the description, as where the description is in terms of marks or labels or kind, quantity, or condition or the receipt or description is qualified by "contents or condition of contents of packages unknown", "said to contain", "shipper's weight, load and count" or the like, if such indication be true.

(2) When goods are loaded by an issuer who is a common carrier, the issuer must count the packages of goods if package freight and ascertain the kind and quantity if bulk freight. In such cases "shipper's weight, load and count" or other words indicating that the description was made by the shipper are ineffective except as to freight concealed by packages.

(3) When bulk freight is loaded by a shipper who makes available to the issuer adequate facilities for weighing such freight, an issuer who is a common carrier must ascertain the kind and quantity within a reasonable time after receiving the written request of the shipper to do so. In such cases "shipper's weight" or other words of like purport are ineffective.

(4) The issuer may by inserting in the bill the words "shipper's weight, load and count" or other words of like purport indicate that the goods were loaded by the shipper; and if such statement be true the issuer shall not be liable for damages caused by the improper loading. But their omission does not imply liability for such damages.

(5) The shipper shall be deemed to have guaranteed to the issuer the accuracy at the time of shipment of the description, marks, labels, number, kind, quantity, condition and weight, as furnished by him; and the shipper shall indemnify the issuer against damage caused by inaccuracies in such particulars. The right of the issuer to such indemnity shall in no way limit his responsibility and liability under the contract of carriage to any person other than the shipper.

§7–302. Through Bills of Lading and Similar Documents. (1) The issuer of a through bill of lading or other document embodying an undertaking to be performed in part by persons acting as its agents or by connecting carriers is liable to anyone entitled to recover on the document for any breach by such other persons or by a connecting carrier of its obligation under the document but to the extent that the bill covers an undertaking to be performed overseas or in territory not contiguous to the continental United States or an undertaking including matters other than transportation this liability may be varied by agreemen of the parties.

(2) Where goods covered by a through bill of lading or other document embodying an undertaking to be performed in part by persons other than the issuer are received by any such person, he is subject with respect to his own performance while the goods are in his possession to the obligation of the issuer. His obligation is discharged by delivery of the goods to another such person pursuant to the document, and does not include liability for breach by any other such persons or by the issuer.

(3) The issuer of such through bill of lading or other document shall be entitled to recover from the connecting carrier or such other person in possession of the goods when the breach of the obligation under the document occurred, the amount it may be required to pay to anyone entitled to recover on the document therefor, as may be evidenced by any receipt, judgment, or transcript thereof, and the amount of any expense reasonably incurred by it in defending any action brought by anyone entitled to recover on the document therefor.

§7–303. Diversion; Reconsignment; Change of Instructions. (1) Unless the bill of lading otherwise provides, the carrier may deliver the goods to a person or destination other than that stated in the bill or may otherwise dispose of the goods on instructions from

(a) the holder of a negotiable bill; or

(b) the consignor on a non-negotiable bill notwithstanding contrary instructions from the consignee; or

(c) the consignee on a non-negotiable bill in the absence of contrary instructions from the consignor, if the goods have arrived at the billed destination or if the consignee is in possession of the bill; or

(d) the consignee on a non-negotiable bill if he is entitled as against the consignor to dispose of them.

(2) Unless such instructions are noted on a negotiable bill of lading, a person to whom the bill is duly negotiated can hold the bailee according to the original terms.

§7–304. Bills of Lading in a Set. (1) Except where customary in overseas transportation, a bill of lading must not be issued in a set of parts. The issuer is liable for damages caused by violation of this subsection.

(2) Where a bill of lading is lawfully drawn in a set of parts, each of which is numbered and expressed to be valid only if the goods have not been delivered against any other part, the whole of the parts constitute one bill.

(3) Where a bill of lading is lawfully issued in a set of parts and different parts are negotiated to different persons, the title of the holder to whom the first due negotiation is made prevails as to both the document and the goods even though any later holder may have received the goods from the carrier in good faith and discharged the carrier's obligation by surrender of his part.

(4) Any person who negotiates or transfers a single part of a bill of lading drawn in a set is liable to holders of that part as if it were the whole set.

(5) The bailee is obliged to deliver in accordance with Part 4 of this Article

against the first presented part of a bill of lading lawfully drawn in a set. Such delivery discharges the bailee's obligation on the whole bill.

§7–305. Destination Bills. (1) Instead of issuing a bill of lading to the consignor at the place of shipment a carrier may at the request of the consignor procure the bill to be issued at destination or at any other place designated in the request.

(2) Upon request of anyone entitled as against the carrier to control the goods while in transit and on surrender of any outstanding bill of lading or other receipt covering such goods, the issuer may procure a substitute bill to be issued at any place designated in the request.

§7–306. Altered Bills of Lading. An unauthorized alteration or filling in of a blank in a bill of lading leaves the bill enforceable according to its original tenor.

§7–307. Lien of Carrier. (1) A carrier has a lien on the goods covered by a bill of lading for charges subsequent to the date of its receipt of the goods for storage or transportation (including demurrage and terminal charges) and for expenses necessary for preservation of the goods incident to their transportation or reasonably incurred in their sale pursuant to law. But against a purchaser for value of a negotiable bill of lading a carrier's lien is limited to charges stated in the bill or the applicable tariffs, or if no charges are stated then to a reasonable charge.

(2) A lien for charges and expenses under subsection (1) on goods which the carrier was required by law to receive for transportation is effective against the consignor or any person entitled to the goods unless the carrier had notice that the consignor lacked authority to subject the goods to such charges and expenses. Any other lien under subsection (1) is effective against the consignor and any person who permitted the bailor to have control or possession of the goods unless the carrier had notice that the bailor lacked such authority.

(3) A carrier loses his lien on any goods which he voluntarily delivers or which he unjustifiably refuses to deliver.

§7–308. Enforcement of Carrier's Lien. (1) A carrier's lien may be enforced by public or private sale of the goods, in bloc or in parcels, at any time or place and on any terms which are commercially reasonable, after notifying all persons known to claim an interest in the goods. Such notification must include a statement of the amount due, the nature of the proposed sale and the time and place of any public sale. The fact that a better price could have been obtained by a sale at a different time or in a different method from that selected by the carrier is not of itself sufficient to establish that the sale was not made in a commercially reasonable manner. If the carrier either sells the goods in the usual manner in any recognized market therefore or if he sells at the price current in such market at the time of his sale or if he has otherwise sold in conformity with commercially reasonable practices among dealers in the type of goods sold he has sold in a commercially reasonable manner. A sale of more goods than apparently necessary to be offered to ensure satisfaction of the obligation is not commercially reasonable except in cases covered by the preceding sentence.

(2) Before any sale pursuant to this section any person claiming a right in the goods may pay the amount necessary to satisfy the lien and the reasonable expenses incurred under this section. In that event the goods must not be sold, but must be retained by the carrier subject to the terms of the bill and this Article.

(3) The carrier may buy at any public sale pursuant to this section.

(4) A purchaser in good faith of goods sold to enforce a carrier's lien takes the goods free of any rights of persons against whom the lien was valid, despite noncompliance by the carrier with the requirements of this section.

(5) The carrier may satisfy his lien from the proceeds of any sale pursuant to this section but must hold the balance, if any, for delivery on demand to any person to whom he would have been bound to deliver the goods.

(6) The rights provided by this section shall be in addition to all other rights allowed by law to a creditor against his debtor.

(7) A carrier's lien may be enforced in accordance with either subsection (1) or the procedure set forth in subsection (2) of Section 7–210.

(8) The carrier is liable for damages caused by failure to comply with the requirements for sale under this section and in case of willful violation is liable for conversion.

§7–309. Duty of Care; Contractual Limitation of Carrier's Liability. (1) A carrier who issues a bill of lading whether negotiable or non-negotiable must exercise the degree of care in relation to the goods which a reasonably careful man would exercise under like circumstances. This subsection does not repeal or change any law or rule of law which imposes liability upon a common carrier for damages not caused by its negligence.

(2) Damages may be limited by a provision that the carrier's liability shall not exceed a value stated in the document if the carrier's rates are dependent upon value and the consignor by the carrier's tariff is afforded an opportunity to declare a higher value or a value as lawfully provided in the tariff, or where no tariff is filed he is otherwise advised of such opportunity; but no such limitation is effective with respect to the carrier's liability for conversion to its own use.

(3) Reasonable provisions as to the time and manner of presenting claims and instituting actions based on the shipment may be included in a bill of lading or tariff.

Part 4

Warehouse Receipts and Bills of Lading: General Obligations

§7–401. Irregularities in Issue of Receipt or Bill or Conduct of Issuer. The obligations imposed by this Article on an issuer apply to a document of title regardless of the fact that

(a) the document may not comply with the requirements of this Article or of any other law or regulation regarding its issue, form or content; or

(b) the issuer may have violated laws regulating the conduct of his business; or

(c) the goods covered by the document were owned by the bailee at the time the document was issued; or

(d) the person issuing the document does not come within the definition of warehouseman if it purports to be a warehouse receipt.

§7–402. Duplicate Receipt or Bill; Overissue. Neither a duplicate nor any other document of title purporting to cover goods already represented by an outstanding document of the same issuer confers any right in the goods, except as provided in the case of bills in a set, overissue of documents for fungible goods and substitutes for lost, stolen or destroyed documents. But the issuer is liable for damages caused by his overissue or failure to identify a duplicate document as such by conspicuous notation on its face.

§7–403. Obligation of Warehouseman or Carrier to Deliver; Excuse. (1) The bailee must deliver the goods to a person entitled under the document who complies with subsections (2) and (3), unless and to the extent that the bailee establishes any of the following:

(a) delivery of the goods to a person whose receipt was rightful as against the claimant;

(b) damage to or delay, loss or destruction of the goods for which the bailee is not liable [, but the burden of establishing negligence in such cases is on the person entitled under the document];

Note: *The brackets in (1) (b) indicate that State enactments may differ on this point without serious damage to the principle of uniformity.*

(c) previous sale or other disposition of the goods in lawful enforcement of a lien or on warehouseman's lawful termination of storage;

(d) the exercise by a seller of his right to stop delivery pursuant to the provisions of the Article on Sales (Section 2–705);

(e) a diversion, reconsignment or other disposition pursuant to the provisions of this Article (Section 7–303) or tariff regulating such right;

(f) release, satisfaction or any other fact affording a personal defense against the claimant;

(g) any other lawful excuse.

(2) A person claiming goods covered by a document of title must satisfy the bailee's lien where the bailee so requests or where the bailee is prohibited by law from delivering the goods until the charges are paid.

(3) Unless the person claiming is one against whom the document confers no right under Sec. 7–503 (1), he must surrender for cancellation or notation of partial deliveries any outstanding negotiable document covering the goods, and the bailee must cancel the document or conspicuously note the partial delivery thereon or be liable to any person to whom the document is duly negotiated.

(4) "Person entitled under the document" means holder in the case of a negotiable document, or the person to whom delivery is to be made by the terms of or pursuant to written instructions under a non-negotiable document.

§7–404. No Liability for Good Faith Delivery Pursuant to Receipt or Bill. A bailee who in good faith including observance of reasonable commercial standards has received goods and delivered or otherwise disposed of them according to the terms of the document of title or pursuant to this Article is not liable therefor. This rule applies even though the person from whom he received the goods had no authority to procure the document or to dispose of the goods and even though the person to whom he delivered the goods had no authority to receive them.

Part 5

Warehouse Receipts and Bills of Lading: Negotiation and Transfer

§7–501. Form of Negotiation and Requirements of "Due Negotiation". (1) A negotiable document of title running to the order of a named person is negotiated by his indorsement and delivery. After his indorsement in blank or to bearer any person can negotiate it by delivery alone.

(2) (a) A negotiable document of title is also negotiated by delivery alone when by its original terms it runs to bearer.

(b) When a document running to the order of a named person is delivered to him the effect is the same as if the document had been negotiated.

(3) Negotiation of a negotiable document of title after it has been indorsed to a specific person requires indorsement by the special indorsee as well as delivery.

(4) A negotiable document of title is "duly negotiated" when it is negotiated in the manner stated in this section to a holder who purchases it in good faith without notice of any defense against or claim to it on the part of any person and for value, unless it is established that the negotiation is not in the regular course of business or financing or involves receiving the document in settlement or payment of a money obligation.

(5) Indorsement of a non-negotiable document neither makes it negotiable nor adds to the transferee's rights.

(6) The naming in a negotiable bill of a person to be notified of the arrival of the goods does not limit the negotiability of the bill nor constitute notice to a purchaser thereof of any interest of such person in the goods.

§7–502. Rights Acquired by Due Negotiation. (1) Subject to the following section and to the provisions of Section 7–205 on fungible goods, a holder to whom a negotiable document of title has been duly negotiated acquires thereby:

(a) title to the document;

(b) title to the goods;

(c) all rights accruing under the law of agency or estoppel, including rights to goods delivered to the bailee after the document was issued; and

(d) the direct obligation of the issuer to hold or deliver the goods according to the terms of the document free of any defense or claim by him except those arising under the terms of the document or under this Article. In the case of a delivery order the bailee's obligation accrues only upon acceptance and the obligation acquired by the holder is that the issuer and any indorser will procure the acceptance of the bailee.

(2) Subject to the following section, title and rights so acquired are not defeated by any stoppage of the goods represented by the document or by surrender of such goods by the bailee, and are not impaired even through the negotiation or any prior negotiation constituted a breach of duty or even though

any person has been deprived of possession of the document by misrepresentation, fraud, accident, mistake, duress, loss, theft or conversion, or even though a previous sale or other transfer of the goods or document has been made to a third person.

§7-503. Document of Title to Goods Defeated in Certain Cases. (1) A document of title confers no right in goods against a person who before issuance of the document had a legal interest or a perfected security interest in them and who neither

(a) delivered or entrusted them or any document of title covering them to the bailor or his nominee with actual or apparent authority to ship, store or sell or with power to obtain delivery under this Article (Section 7-403) or with power of disposition under this Act (Sections 2-403 and 9-307) or other statute or rule of law; nor

(b) acquiesced in the procurement by the bailor or his nominee of any document of title.

(2) Title to goods based upon an unaccepted delivery order is subject to the rights of anyone to whom a negotiable warehouse receipt or bill of lading covering the goods has been duly negotiated. Such a title may be defeated under the next section to the same extent as the rights of the issuer or a transferee from the issuer.

(3) Title to goods based upon a bill of lading issued to a freight forwarder is subject to the rights of anyone to whom a bill issued by the freight forwarder is duly negotiated; but delivery by the carrier in accordance with Part 4 of this Article pursuant to its own bill of lading discharges the carrier's obligation to deliver.

§7-504. Rights Acquired in the Absence of Due Negotiation; Effect of Diversion; Seller's Stoppage of Delivery. (1) A transferee of a document, whether negotiable or non-negotiable, to whom the document has been delivered but not duly negotiated, acquires the title and rights which his transferor had or had actual authority to convey.

(2) In the case of a non-negotiable document, until but not after the bailee receives notification of the transfer, the rights of the transferee may be defeated

(a) by those creditors of the transferor who could treat the sale as void under Section 2-402; or

(b) by a buyer from the transferor in ordinary course of business if the bailee has delivered the goods to the buyer or received notification of his rights; or

(c) as against the bailee by good faith dealings of the bailee with the transferor.

(3) A diversion or other change of shipping instructions by the consignor in a non-negotiable bill of lading which causes the bailee not to deliver to the consignee defeats the consignee's title to the goods if they have been delivered to a buyer in ordinary course of business and in any event defeats the consignee's rights against the bailee.

(4) Delivery pursuant to a non-negotiable document may be stopped by a seller under Section 2-705, and subject to the requirement of due notification there provided. A bailee honoring the seller's instructions is entitled to be indemnified by the seller against any resulting loss or expense.

§7–505. Indorser Not a Guarantor for Other Parties. The indorsement of a document of title issued by a bailee does not make the indorser liable for any default by the bailee or by previous indorsers.

§7–506. Delivery Without Indorsement: Right to Compel Indorsement. The transferee of a negotiable document of title has a specifically enforceable right to have his transferor supply any necessary indorsement but the transfer becomes a negotiation only as of the time the indorsement is supplied.

§7–507. Warranties on Negotiation or Transfer of Receipt or Bill. Where a person negotiates or transfers a document of title for value otherwise than as a mere intermediary under the next following section, then unless otherwise agreed he warrants to his immediate purchaser only in addition to any warranty made in selling the goods

(a) that the document is genuine; and

(b) that he has no knowledge of any fact which would impair its validity or worth; and

(c) that his negotiation or transfer is rightful and fully effective with respect to the title to the document and the goods it represents.

§7–508. Warranties of Collecting Bank as to Documents. A collecting bank or other intermediary known to be entrusted with documents on behalf of another or with collection of a draft or other claim against delivery of documents warrants by such delivery of the documents only its own good faith and authority. This rule applies even though the intermediary has purchased or made advances against the claim or draft to be collected.

§7–509. Receipt or Bill: When Adequate Compliance With Commercial Contract. The question whether a document is adequate to fulfill the obligations of a contract for sale or the conditions of a credit is governed by the Articles on Sales (Article 2) and on Letters of Credit (Article 5).

Part 6

Warehouse Receipts and Bills of Lading: Miscellaneous Provisions

§7–601. Lost and Missing Documents. (1) If a document has been lost, stolen or destroyed, a court may order delivery of the goods or issuance of a substitute document and the bailee may without liability to any person comply with such order. If the document was negotiable the claimant must post security approved by the court to indemnify any person who may suffer loss as a result of non-surrender of the document. If the document was not negotiable, such security may be required at the discretion of the court. The court may also in its discretion order payment of the bailee's reasonable costs and counsel fees.

(2) A bailee who without court order delivers goods to a person claiming under a missing negotiable document is liable to any person injured thereby, and if the delivery is not in good faith becomes liable for conversion. Delivery in good faith is not conversion if made in accordance with a filed classification or tariff or, where no classification or tariff is filed, if the claimant posts security with the bailee in an amount at least double the value of the goods at the time

of posting to indemnify any person injured by the delivery who files a notice of claim within one year after the delivery.

§7–602. Attachment of Goods Covered by a Negotiable Document. Except where the document was originally issued upon delivery of the goods by a person who had no power to dispose of them, no lien attaches by virtue of any judicial process to goods in the possession of a bailee for which a negotiable document of title is outstanding unless the document be first surrendered to the bailee or its negotiation enjoined, and the bailee shall not be compelled to deliver the goods pursuant to process until the document is surrendered to him or impounded by the court. One who purchases the document for value without notice of the process or injunction takes free of the lien imposed by judicial process.

§7–603. Conflicting Claims; Interpleader. If more than one person claims title or possession of the goods, the bailee is excused from delivery until he has had a reasonable time to ascertain the validity of the adverse claims or to bring an action to compel all claimants to interplead and may compel such interpleader, either in defending an action for non-delivery of the goods, or by original action, whichever is appropriate.

ARTICLE 8: INVESTMENT SECURITIES

Part 1

Short Title and General Matters

§8–101. Short Title. This Article shall be known and may be cited as Uniform Commercial Code—Investment Securities.

§8–102. Definitions and Index of Definitions. (1) In this Article unless the context otherwise requires

(a) A "security" is an instrument which

(i) is issued in bearer or registered form; and

(ii) is of a type commonly dealt in upon securities exchanges or markets or commonly recognized in any area in which it is issued or dealt in as a medium for investment; and

(iii) is either one of a class or series or by its terms is divisible into a class or series of instruments; and

(iv) evidences a share, participation or other interest in property or in an enterprise or evidences an obligation of the issuer.

(b) A writing which is a security is governed by this Article and not by Uniform Commercial Code—Commercial Paper even though it also meets the requirements of that Article. This Article does not apply to money.

(c) A security is in "registered form" when it specifies a person entitled to the security or to the rights it evidences and when its transfer may be registered upon books maintained for that purpose by or on behalf of an issuer or the security so states.

(d) A security is in "bearer form" when it runs to bearer according to its terms and not by reason of any indorsement.

(2) "Proper form" means regular on its face with regard to all formal matters.

(3) A "subsequent purchaser" is a person who takes other than by original issue.

(4) Other definitions applying to this Article or to specified Parts thereof and the sections in which they appear are:

"Adverse claim". Section 8–301.

"Bona fide purchaser". Section 8–302.

"Broker". Section 8–303.

"Guarantee of the signature". Section 8–402.

"Intermediary Bank". Section 4–105.

"Issuer". Section 8–201.

"Overissue". Section 8–104.

(5) In addition Article 1 contains general definitions and principles of construction and interpretation applicable throughout this Article.

§8–103. Issuer's Lien. A lien upon a security in favor of an issuer thereof is valid against a purchaser only if the right of the issuer to such lien is noted conspicuously on the security.

§8–104. Effect of Overissue; "Overissue." (1) The provisions of this Article which validate a security or compel its issue or reissue do not apply to the extent that validation, issue or reissue would result in overissue; but

(a) if an identical security which does not constitute an overissue is reasonably available for purchase, the person entitled to issue or validation may compel the issuer to purchase and deliver such a security to him against surrender of the security, if any, which he holds; or

(b) if a security is not so available for purchase, the person entitled to issue or validation may recover from the issuer the price he or the last purchaser for value paid for it with interest from the date of his demand.

(2) "Overissue" means the issue of securities in excess of the amount which the issuer has corporate power to issue.

§8–105. Securities Negotiable; Presumptions. (1) Securities governed by this Article are negotiable instruments.

(2) In any action on a security

(a) unless specifically denied in the pleadings, each signature on the security or in a necessary indorsement is admitted;

(b) when the effectiveness of a signature is put in issue the burden of establishing it is on the party claiming under the signature but the signature is presumed to be genuine or authorized;

(c) when signatures are admitted or established production of the instrument entitles a holder to recover on it unless the defendant establishes a defense or a defect going to the validity of the security; and

(d) after it is shown that a defense or defect exists the plaintiff has the burden of establishing that he or some person under whom he claims is a person against whom the defense or defect is ineffective (Section 8–202).

§8–106. Applicability. The validity of a security and the rights and duties of the issuer with respect to registration of transfer are governed by the law (including the conflict of laws rules) of the jurisdiction of organization of the issuer.

Part 2

Issue—Issuer

§8–201. "Issuer." (1) With respect to obligations on or defenses to a security "issuer" includes a person who

(a) places or authorizes the placing of his name on a security (otherwise than as authenticating trustee, registrar, transfer agent or the like) to evidence that it represents a share, participation or other interest in his property or in an enterprise or to evidence his duty to perform an obligation evidenced by the security; or

(b) directly or indirectly creates fractional interests in his rights or property which fractional interests are evidenced by securities; or

(c) becomes responsible for or in place of any other person described as an issuer in this section.

(2) With respect to obligations on or defenses to a security a guarantor is an issuer to the extent of his guaranty whether or not his obligation is noted on the security.

(3) With respect to registration of transfer (Part 4 of this Article) "issuer" means a person on whose behalf transfer books are maintained.

§8–202. Issuer's Responsibility and Defenses; Notice of Defect or Defense. (1) Even against a purchaser for value and without notice, the terms of a security include those stated on the security and those made part of the security by reference to another instrument, indenture or document or to a constitution, statute, ordinance, rule, regulation, order or the like to the extent that the terms so referred to do not conflict with the stated terms. Such a reference does not of itself charge a purchaser for value with notice of a defect going to the validity of the security even though the security expressly states that a person accepting it admits such notice.

(2) (a) A security other than one issued by a government or governmental agency or unit even though issued with a defect going to its validity is valid in the hands of a purchaser for value and without notice of the particular defect unless the defect involves a violation of constitutional provisions in which case the security is valid in the hands of a subsequent purchaser for value and without notice of the defect.

(b) The rule of subparagraph (a) applies to an issuer which is a government or governmental agency or unit only if either there has been substantial compliance with the legal requirements governing the issue or the issuer has received a substantial consideration for the issue as a whole or for the particular security and a stated purpose of the issue is one for which the issuer has power to borrow money or issue the security.

(3) Except as otherwise provided in the case of certain unauthorized signatures

on issue (Section 8–205), lack of genuineness of a security is a complete defense even against a purchaser for value and without notice.

(4) All other defenses of the issuer including nondelivery and conditional delivery of the security are ineffective against a purchaser for value who has taken without notice of the particular defense.

(5) Nothing in this section shall be construed to affect the right of a party to a "when, as and if issued" or a "when distributed" contract to cancel the contract in the event of a material change in the character of the security which is the subject of the contract or in the plan or arrangement pursuant to which such security is to be issued or distributed.

§8–203. Staleness as Notice of Defects or Defenses. (1) After an act or event which creates a right to immediate performance of the principal obligation evidenced by the security or which sets a date on or after which the security is to be presented or surrendered for redemption or exchange, a purchaser is charged with notice of any defect in its issue or defense of the issuer.

(a) if the act or event is one requiring the payment of money or the delivery of securities or both on presentation or surrender of the security and such funds or securities are available on the date set for payment or exchange and he takes the security more than one year after that date; and

(b) if the act or event is not covered by paragraph (a) and he takes the security more than two years after the date set for surrender or presentation or the date on which such performance became due.

(2) A call which has been revoked is not within subsection (1).

§8–204. Effect of Issuer's Restrictions on Transfer. Unless noted conspicuously on the security a restriction on transfer imposed by the issuer even though otherwise lawful is ineffective except against a person with actual knowledge of it.

§8–205. Effect of Unauthorized Signature on Issue. An unauthorized signature placed on a security prior to or in the course of issue is ineffective except that the signature is effective in favor of a purchaser for value and without notice of the lack of authority if the signing has been done by

(a) an authenticating trustee, registrar, transfer agent or other person entrusted by the issuer with the signing of the security or of similar securities or their immediate preparation for signing; or

(b) an employee of the issuer or of any of the foregoing entrusted with responsible handling of the security.

§8–206. Completion or Alteration of Instrument. (1) Where a security contains the signatures necessary to its issue or transfer but is incomplete in any other respect

(a) any person may complete it by filling in the blanks as authorized; and

(b) even though the blanks are incorrectly filled in, the security as completed is enforceable by a purchaser who took it for value and without notice of such incorrectness.

(2) A complete security which has been improperly altered even though fraudulently remains enforceable but only according to its original terms.

§8–207. Rights of Issuer With Respect to Registered Owners. (1) Prior to due presentment for registration of transfer of a security in registered form the issuer or indenture trustee may treat the registered owner as the person exclusively entitled to vote, to receive notifications and otherwise to exercise all the rights and powers of an owner.

(2) Nothing in this Article shall be construed to affect the liability of the registered owner of a security for calls, assessments or the like.

§8–208. Effect of Signature of Authenticating Trustee, Registrar or Transfer Agent. (1) A person placing his signature upon a security as authenticating trustee, registrar, transfer agent or the like warrants to a purchaser for value without notice of the particular defect that

(a) the security is genuine and in proper form; and

(b) his own participation in the issue of the security is within his capacity and within the scope of the authorization received by him from the issuer; and

(c) he has reasonable grounds to believe that the security is within the amount the issuer is authorized to issue.

(2) Unless otherwise agreed, a person by so placing his signature does not assume responsibility for the validity of the security in other respects.

Part 3

Purchase

§8–301. Rights Acquired by Purchaser; "Adverse Claim"; Title Acquired by Bona Fide Purchaser. (1) Upon delivery of a security the purchaser acquires the rights in the security which his transferor had or had actual authority to convey except that a purchaser who has himself been a party to any fraud or illegality affecting the security or who as a prior holder had notice of an adverse claim cannot improve his position by taking from a later bona fide purchaser. "Adverse claim" includes a claim that a transfer was or would be wrongful or that a particular adverse person is the owner of or has an interest in the security.

(2) A bona fide purchaser in addition to acquiring the rights of a purchaser also acquires the security free of any adverse claim.

(3) A purchaser of a limited interest acquires rights only to the extent of the interest purchased.

§8–302. "Bona Fide Purchaser." A "bona fide purchaser" is a purchaser for value in good faith and without notice of any adverse claim who takes delivery of a security in bearer form or of one in registered form issued to him or indorsed to him or in blank.

§8–303. "Broker." "Broker" means a person engaged for all or part of his time in the business of buying and selling securities, who in the transaction concerned acts for, or buys a security from or sells a security to a customer. Nothing in this Article determines the capacity in which a person acts for purposes of any other statute or rule to which such person is subject.

§8–304. Notice to Purchaser of Adverse Claims. (1) A purchaser (including a broker for the seller or buyer but excluding an intermediary bank) of a security is charged with notice of adverse claims if

(a) the security whether in bearer or registered form has been indorsed "for collection" or "for surrender" or for some other purpose not involving tansfer; or

(b) the security is in bearer form and has on it an unambiguous statement that it is the property of a person other than the transferor. The mere writing of a name on a security is not such a statement.

(2) The fact that the purchaser (including a broker for the seller or buyer) has notice that the security is held for a third person or is registered in the name of or indorsed by a fiduciary does not create a duty of inquiry into the rightfulness of the transfer or constitute notice of adverse claims. If, however, the purchaser (excluding an intermediary bank) has knowledge that the proceeds are being used or that the transaction is for the individual benefit of the fiduciary or otherwise in breach of duty, the purchaser is charged with notice of adverse claims.

§8–305. Staleness as Notice of Adverse Claims. An act or event which creates a right to immediate performance of the principal obligation evidenced by the security or which sets a date on or after which the security is to be presented or surrendered for redemption or exchange does not of itself constitute any notice of adverse claims except in the case of a purchase

(a) after one year from any date set for such presentment or surrender for redemption or exchange; or

(b) after six months from any date set for payment of money against presentation or surrender of the security if funds are available for payment on that date.

§8–306. Warranties on Presentment and Transfer. (1) A person who presents a security for registration of transfer or for payment or exchange warrants to the issuer that he is entitled to the registration, payment or exchange. But a purchaser for value without notice of adverse claims who receives a new, reissued or re-registered security on registration of transfer warrants only that he has no knowledge of any unauthorized signature (Section 8–311) in a necessary indorsement.

(2) A person by transferring a security to a purchaser for value warrants only that

(a) his transfer is effective and rightful; and

(b) the security is genuine and has not been materially altered; and

(c) he knows no fact which might impair the validity of the security.

(3) Where a security is delivered by an intermediary known to be entrusted with delivery of the security on behalf of another or with collection of a draft or other claim against such delivery, the intermediary by such delivery warrants only his own good faith and authority even though he has purchased or made advances against the claim to be collected against the delivery. A broker is not an intermediary within the meaning of this subsection.

(4) A pledgee or other holder for security who redelivers the security received, or after payment and on order of the debtor delivers that security to a third person makes only the warranties of an intermediary under subsection (3).

(5) A broker gives to his customer and to the issuer and a purchaser the warranties provided in this section and has the rights and privileges of a purchaser under this section. The warranties of and in favor of the broker acting as an agent are in addition to applicable warranties given by and in favor of his customer.

§8–307. Effect of Delivery Without Indorsement; Right to Compel Indorsement. Where a security in registered form has been delivered to a purchaser without a necessary indorsement he may become a bona fide purchaser only as of the time the indorsement is supplied, but against the transferor the transfer is complete upon delivery and the purchaser has a specially enforceable right to have any necessary indorsement supplied.

§8–308. Indorsement, How Made; Special Indorsement; Indorser Not a Guarantor; Partial Assignment. (1) An indorsement of a security in registered form is made when an appropriate person signs on it or on a separate document an assignment or transfer of the security or a power to assign or transfer it or when the signature of such person is written without more upon the back of the security.

(2) An indorsement may be in blank or special. An indorsement in blank includes an indorsement to bearer. A special indorsement specifies the person to whom the security is to be transferred, or who has power to transfer it. A holder may convert a blank indorsement into a special indorsement.

(3) "An appropriate person" in subsection (1) means

(a) the person specified by the security or by special indorsement to be entitled to the security; or

(b) where the person so specified is described as a fiduciary but is no longer serving in the described capacity,—his successor; or

(c) where the security or indorsement so specifies more than one person as fiduciaries and one or more are no longer serving in the described capacity,— the remaining fiduciary or fiduciaries, whether or not a successor has been appointed or qualified; or

(d) where the person so specified is an individual and is without capacity to act by virtue of death, incompetence, infancy or otherwise,—his executor, administrator, guardian or like fiduciary; or

(e) where the security or indorsement so specifies more than one person as tenants by the entirety or with right of survivorship and by reason of death all cannot sign,—the survivor or survivors; or

(f) a person having power to sign under applicable law or controlling instrument; or

(g) to the extent that any of the foregoing persons may act through an agent, —his authorized agent.

(4) Unless otherwise agreed the indorser by his indorsement assumes no obligation that the security will be honored by the issuer.

(5) An indorsement purporting to be only of part of a security representing

units intended by the issuer to be separately transferable is effective to the extent of the indorsement.

(6) Whether the person signing is appropriate is determined as of the date of signing and an indorsement by such a person does not become unauthorized for the purposes of this Article by virtue of any subsequent change of circumstances.

(7) Failure of a fiduciary to comply with a controlling instrument or with the law of the state having jurisdiction of the fiduciary relationship, including any law requiring the fiduciary to obtain court approval of the transfer, does not render his indorsement unauthorized for the purposes of this Article.

§8–309. Effect of Indorsement Without Delivery. An indorsement of a security whether special or in blank does not constitute a transfer until delivery of the security on which it appears or if the indorsement is on a separate document until delivery of both the document and the security.

§8–310. Indorsement of Security in Bearer Form. An indorsement of a security in bearer form may give notice of adverse claims (Section 8–304) but does not otherwise affect any right to registration the holder may possess.

§8–311. Effect of Unauthorized Indorsement. Unless the owner has ratified an unauthorized indorsement or is otherwise precluded from asserting its ineffectiveness

(a) he may assert its ineffectiveness against the issuer or any purchaser other than a purchaser for value and without notice of adverse claims who has in good faith received a new, reissued or re-registered security on registration of transfer; and

(b) an issuer who registers the transfer of a security upon the unauthorized indorsement is subject to liability for improper registration (Section 8–404).

§8–312. Effect of Guaranteeing Signature or Indorsement. (1) Any person guaranteeing a signature of an indorser of a security warrants that at the time of signing

(a) the signature was genuine; and

(b) the signer was an appropriate person to indorse (Section 8–308); and

(c) the signer had legal capacity to sign.

But the guarantor does not otherwise warrant the rightfulness of the particular transfer.

(2) Any person may guarantee an indorsement of a security and by so doing warrants not only the signature (subsection 1) but also the rightfulness of the particular transfer in all respects. But no issuer may require a guarantee of indorsement as a condition to registration of transfer.

(3) The foregoing warranties are made to any person taking or dealing with the security in reliance on the guarantee and the guarantor is liable to such person for any loss resulting from breach of the warranties.

§8–313. When Delivery to the Purchaser Occurs; Purchaser's Broker as Holder. (1) Delivery to purchaser occurs when

(a) he or a person designated by him acquires possession of a security; or

(b) his broker acquires possession of a security specially indorsed to or issued in the name of the purchaser; or

(c) his broker sends him confirmation of the purchase and also by book entry or otherwise identifies a specific security in the broker's possession as belonging to the purchaser; or

(d) with respect to an identified security to be delivered while still in the possession of a third person when that person acknowledges that he holds for the purchaser.

(2) Except as specified in subparagraphs (b) and (c) of subsection (1) the purchaser is not the holder of securities held for him by his broker despite a confirmation of purchase and a book entry and other indication that the security is part of a fungible bulk held for customers and despite the customer's acquisition of a proportionate property interest in the fungible bulk.

§8–314. Duty to Deliver, When Completed. (1) Unless otherwise agreed where a sale of a security is made on an exchange or otherwise through brokers

(a) the selling customer fulfills his duty to deliver when he places such a security in the possession of the selling broker or of a person designated by the broker or if requested causes an acknowledgment to be made to the selling broker that it is held for him; and

(b) the selling broker including a correspondent broker acting for a selling customer fulfills his duty to deliver by placing the security or a like security in the possession of the buying broker or a person designated by him or by effecting clearance of the sale in accordance with the rules of the exchange on which the transaction took place.

(2) Except as otherwise provided in this section and unless otherwise agreed, a transferor's duty to deliver a security under a contract of purchase is not fulfilled until he places the security in form to be negotiated by the purchaser in the possession of the purchaser or of a person designated by him or at the purchaser's request causes an acknowledgment to be made to the purchaser that it is held for him. Unless made on an exchange a sale to a broker purchasing for his own account is within this subsection and not within subsection (1).

§8–315. Action Against Purchaser Based Upon Wrongful Transfer. (1) Any person against whom the transfer of a security is wrongful for any reason, including his incapacity, may against anyone except a bona fide purchaser reclaim possession of the security or obtain possession of any new security evidencing all or part of the same rights or have damages.

(2) If the transfer is wrongful because of an unauthorized indorsement, the owner may also reclaim or obtain possession of the security or new security even from a bona fide purchaser if the ineffectiveness of the purported indorsement can be asserted against him under the provisions of this Article on unauthorized indorsements (Section 8–311).

(3) The right to obtain or reclaim possession of a security may be specifically enforced and its transfer enjoined and the security impounded pending the litigation.

§8–316. Purchaser's Right to Requisites for Registration of Transfer on Books. Unless otherwise agreed the transferor must on due demand supply his purchaser with any proof of his authority to transfer or with any other requisite which may be necessary to obtain registration of the transfer of the security but if the transfer is not for value a transferor need not do so unless the purchaser furnishes the necessary expenses. Failure to comply with a demand made within a reasonable time gives the purchaser the right to reject or rescind the transfer.

§8–317. **Attachment or Levy Upon Security.** (1) No attachment or levy upon a security or any share or other interest evidenced thereby which is outstanding shall be valid until the security is actually seized by the officer making the attachment or levy but a security which has been surrendered to the issuer may be attached or levied upon at the source.

(2) A creditor whose debtor is the owner of a security shall be entitled to such aid from courts of appropriate jurisdiction, by injunction or otherwise, in reaching such security or in satisfying the claim by means thereof as is allowed at law or in equity in regard to property which cannot readily be attached or levied upon by ordinary legal process.

§8–318. **No Conversion by Good Faith Delivery.** An agent or bailee who in good faith (including observance of reasonable commercial standards if he is in the business of buying, selling or otherwise dealing with securities) has received securities and sold, pledged or delivered them according to the instructions of his principal is not liable for conversion or for participation in breach of fiduciary duty although the principal had no right to dispose of them.

§8–319. **Statute of Frauds.** A contract for the sale of securities is not enforceable by way of action or defense unless

(a) there is some writing signed by the party against whom enforcement is sought or by his authorized agent or broker sufficient to indicate that a contract has been made for sale of a stated quantity of described securities at a defined or stated price; or

(b) delivery of the security has been accepted or payment has been made but the contract is enforceable under this provision only to the extent of such delivery or payment; or

(c) within a reasonable time a writing in confirmation of the sale or purchase and sufficient against the sender under paragraph (a) has been received by the party against whom enforcement is sought and he has failed to send written objection to its contents within ten days after its receipt; or

(d) the party against whom enforcement is sought admits in his pleading, testimony or otherwise in court that a contract was made for sale of a stated quantity of described securities at a defined or stated price.

Part 4

Registration

§8–401. **Duty of Issuer to Register Transfer.** (1) Where a security in registered form is presented to the issuer with a request to register transfer, the issuer is under a duty to register the transfer as requested if

(a) the security is indorsed by the appropriate person or persons (Section 8–308); and

(b) reasonable assurance is given that those indorsements are genuine and effective (Section 8–402); and

(c) the issuer has no duty to inquire into adverse claims or has discharged any such duty (Section 8–403); and

(d) any applicable law relating to the collection of taxes has been complied with; and

(e) the transfer is in fact rightful or is to a bona fide purchaser.

(2) Where an issuer is under a duty to register a transfer of a security the issuer is also liable to the person presenting it for registration or his principal for loss resulting from any unreasonable delay in registration or from failure or refusal to register the transfer.

§8–402. Assurance that Indorsements Are Effective. (1) The issuer may require the following assurance that each necessary indorsement (Section 8–308) is genuine and effective

(a) in all cases, a guarantee of the signature (subsection (1) of Section 8–312) of the person indorsing; and

(b) where the indorsement is by an agent, appropriate assurance of authority to sign;

(c) where the indorsement is by a fiduciary, appropriate evidence of appointment or incumbency;

(d) where there is more than one fiduciary, reasonable assurance that all who are required to sign have done so;

(e) where the indorsement is by a person not covered by any of the foregoing, assurance appropriate to the case corresponding as nearly as may be to the foregoing.

(2) A "guarantee of the signature" in subsection (1) means a guarantee signed by or on behalf of a person reasonably believed by the issuer to be responsible. The issuer may adopt standards with respect to responsibility provided such standards are not manifestly unreasonable.

(3) "Appropriate evidence of appointment or incumbency" in subsection (1) means

(a) in the case of a fiduciary appointed or qualified by a court, a certificate issued by or under the direction or supervision of that court or an officer thereof and dated within sixty days before the date of presentation for transfers; or

(b) in any other case, a copy of a document showing the appointment or a certificate issued by or on behalf of a person reasonably believed by the issuer to be responsible or, in the absence of such a document or certificate, other evidence reasonably deemed by the issuer to be appropriate. The issuer may adopt standards with respect to such evidence provided such standards are not manifestly unreasonable. The issuer is not charged with notice of the contents of any document obtained pursuant to this paragraph (b) except to the extent that the contents relate directly to the appointment or incumbency.

(4) The issuer may elect to require reasonable assurance beyond that specified in this section but if it does so and for a purpose other than that specified in subsection 3(b) both requires and obtains a copy of a will, trust, indenture,

articles of co-partnership, by-laws or other controlling instrument it is charged with notice of all matters contained therein affecting the transfer.

§8–403. Limited Duty of Inquiry. (1) An issuer to whom a security is presented for registration is under a duty to inquire into adverse claims if

(a) a written notification of an adverse claim is received at a time and in a manner which affords the issuer a reasonable opportunity to act on it prior to the issuance of a new, reissued or re-registered security and the notification identifies the claimant, the registered owner and the issue of which the security is a part and provides an address for communications directed to the claimant; or

(b) the issuer is charged with notice of an adverse claim from a controlling instrument which it has elected to require under subsection (4) of Section 8–402,

(2) The issuer may discharge any duty of inquiry by any reasonable means, including notifying an adverse claimant by registered or certified mail at the address furnished by him or if there be no such address at his residence or regular place of business that the security has been presented for registration of transfer by a named person, and that the transfer will be registered unless within thirty days from the date of mailing the notification, either

(a) an appropriate restraining order, injunction or other process issues from a court of competent jurisdiction; or

(b) an indemnity bond sufficient in the issuer's judgment to protect the issuer and any transfer agent, registrar or other agent of the issuer involved, from any loss which it or they may suffer by complying with the adverse claim is filed with the issuer.

(3) Unless an issuer is charged with notice of an adverse claim from a controlling instrument which it has elected to require under subsection (4) of Section 8–402 or receives notification of an adverse claim under subsection (1) of this section, where a security presented for registration is indorsed by the appropriate person or persons the issuer is under no duty to inquire into adverse claims. In particular

(a) an issuer registering a security in the name of a person who is a fiduciary or who is described as a fiduciary is not bound to inquire into the existence, extent, or correct description of the fiduciary relationship and thereafter the issuer may assume without inquiry that the newly registered owner continues to be the fiduciary until the issuer receives written notice that the fiduciary is no longer acting as such with respect to the particular security;

(b) an issuer registering transfer on an indorsement by a fiduciary is not bound to inquire whether the transfer is made in compliance with a controlling instrument or with the law of the state having jurisdiction of the fiduciary relationship, including any law requiring the fiduciary to obtain court approval of the transfer; and

(c) the issuer is not charged with notice of the contents of any court record or file or other recorded or unrecorded document even though the document is in its possession and even though the transfer is made on the indorsement of a fiduciary to the fiduciary himself or to his nominee.

§8–404. Liability and Non-Liability for Registration. (1) Except as otherwise provided in any law relating to the collection of taxes, the issuer is not liable to the owner or any other person suffering loss as a result of the registration of a transfer of a security if

(a) there were on or with the security the necessary indorsements (Section 8–308); and

(b) the issuer had no duty to inquire into adverse claims or has discharged any such duty (Section 8–403).

(2) Where an issuer has registered a transfer of a security to a person not entitled to it the issuer on demand must deliver a like security to the true owner unless

(a) the registration was pursuant to subsection (1); or

(b) the owner is precluded from asserting any claim for registering the transfer under subsection (1) of the following section; or

(c) such delivery would result in overissue, in which case the issuer's liability is governed by Section 8–104.

§8–405. Lost, Destroyed and Stolen Securities. (1) Where a security has been lost, apparently destroyed or wrongfully taken and the owner fails to notify the issuer of that fact within a reasonable time after he has notice of it and the issuer registers a transfer of the security before receiving such a notification, the owner is precluded from asserting against the issuer any claim for registering the transfer under the preceding section or any claim to a new security under this section.

(2) Where the owner of a security claims that the security has been lost, destroyed or wrongfully taken, the issuer must issue a new security in place of the original security if the owner

(a) so requests before the issuer has notice that the security has been acquired by a bona fide purchaser; and

(b) files with the issuer a sufficient indemnity bond; and

(c) satisfies any other reasonable requirements imposed by the issuer.

(3) If, after the issue of the new security, a bona fide purchaser of the original security presents it for registration of transfer, the issuer must register the transfer unless registration would result in overissue, in which event the issuer's liability is governed by Section 8–104. In addition to any rights on the indemnity bond, the issuer may recover the new security from the person to whom it was issued or any person taking under him except a bona fide purchaser.

§8–406. Duty of Authenticating Trustee, Transfer Agent or Registrar. (1) Where a person acts as authenticating trustee, transfer agent, registrar, or other agent for an issuer in the registration of transfers of its securities or in the issue of new securities or in the cancellation of surrendered securities

(a) he is under a duty to the issuer to exercise good faith and due diligence in performing his functions; and

(b) he has with regard to the particular functions he performs the same obligation to the holder or owner of the security and has the same rights and privileges as the issuer has in regard to those functions.

(2) Notice to an authenticating trustee, transfer agent, registrar or other such agent is notice to the issuer with respect to the functions performed by the agent.

ARTICLE 9: SECURED TRANSACTIONS; SALES OF ACCOUNTS, CONTRACT RIGHTS AND
CHATTEL PAPER

Part 1

Short Title, Applicability and Definitions

§9–101. Short Title. This Article shall be known and may be cited as Uniform
Commercial Code—Secured Transactions.

§9–102. Policy and Scope of Article. (1) Except as otherwise provided in Section
9–103 on multiple state transactions and in Section 9–104 on excluded transactions, this Article applies so far as concerns any personal property and fixtures
within the jurisdiction of this state

(a) to any transaction (regardless of its form) which is intended to create a
security interest in personal property or fixtures including goods, documents,
instruments, general intangibles, chattel paper, accounts or contract rights; and
also

(b) to any sale of accounts, contract rights or chattel paper.

(2) This Article applies to security interests created by contract including
pledge, assignment, chattel mortgage, chattel trust, trust deed, factor's lien, equipment trust, conditional sale, trust receipt, other lien or title retention contract
and lease or consignment intended as security. This Article does not apply
to statutory liens except as provided in Section 9–310.

(3) The application of this Article to a security interest in a secured obligation is not affected by the fact that the obligation is itself secured by a transaction or interest to which this Article does not apply.

Note: *The adoption of this Article should be accompanied by the repeal of
existing statutes dealing with conditional sales, trust receipts, factor's liens
where the factor is given a non-possessory lien, chattel mortgages, crop mortgages, mortgages on railroad equipment, assignment of accounts and generally
statutes regulating security interests in personal property.*

*Where the state has a retail installment selling act or small loan act, that
legislation should be carefully examined to determine what changes in those acts
are needed to conform them to this Article. This Article primarily sets out rules
defining rights of a secured party against persons dealing with the debtor; it
does not prescribe regulations and controls which may be necessary to curb
abuses arising in the small loan business or in the financing of consumer purchases on credit. Accordingly there is no intention to repeal existing regulatory acts in those fields. See Section 9–203(2) and the Note thereto.*

**§9–103. Accounts, Contract Rights, General Intangibles and Equipment Relat-
ing to Another Jurisdiction; and Incoming Goods Already Subject to a Security
Interest.** (1) If the office where the assignor of accounts or contract rights keeps
his records concerning them is in this state, the validity and perfection of a
security interest therein and the possibility and effect of proper filing is gov-

erned by this Article; otherwise by the law (including the conflict of laws rules) of the jurisdiction where such office is located.

(2) If the chief place of business of a debtor is in this state, this Article governs the validity and perfection of a security interest and the possibility and effect of proper filing with regard to general intangibles or with regard to goods of a type which are normally used in more than one jurisdiction (such as automotive equipment, rolling stock, airplanes, road building equipment, commercial harvesting equipment, construction machinery and the like) if such goods are classified as equipment or classified as inventory by reason of their being leased by the debtor to others. Otherwise, the law (including the conflict of laws rules) of the jurisdiction where such chief place of business is located shall govern. If the chief place of business is located in a jurisdiction which does not provide for perfection of the security interest by filing or recording in that jurisdiction, then the security interest may be perfected by filing in this state.

(3) If personal property other than that governed by subsections (1) and (2) is already subject to a security interest when it is brought into this state, the validity of the security interest in this state is to be determined by the law (including the conflict of laws rules) of the jurisdiction where the property was when the security interest attached. However, if the parties to the transaction understood at the time that the security interest attached that the property would be kept in this state and it was brought into this state within 30 days after the security interest attached for purposes other than transportation through this state, then the validity of the security interest in this state is to be determined by the law of this state. If the security interest was already perfected under the law of the jurisdiction where the property was when the security interest attached and before being brought into this state, the security interest continues perfected in this state for four months and also thereafter if within the four month period it is perfected in this state. The security interest may also be perfected in this state after the expiration of the four month period; in such case perfection dates from the time of perfection in this state. If the security interest was not perfected under the law of the jurisdiction where the property was when the security interest attached and before being brought into this state, it may be perfected in this state; in such case perfection dates from the time of perfection in this state.

(4) Notwithstanding subsections (2) and (3), if personal property is covered by a certificate of title issued under a statute of this state or any other jurisdiction which requires indication on a certificate of title of any security interest in the property as a condition of perfection, then the perfection is governed by the law of the jurisdiction which issued the certificate.

§9–104. Transactions Excluded From Article. This Article does not apply

(a) to a security interest subject to any statute of the United States such as the Ship Mortgage Act, 1920, to the extent that such statute governs the rights of parties to and third parties affected by transactions in particular types of property; or

(b) to a landlord's lien; or

(c) to a lien given by statute or other rule of law for services or materials except as provided in Section 9–310 on priority of such liens; or

(d) to a transfer of a claim for wages, salary or other compensation of an employee; or

(e) to an equipment trust covering railway rolling stock; or

(f) to a sale of accounts, contract rights or chattel paper as part of a sale of the business out of which they arose, or an assignment of accounts, contract rights or chattel paper which is for the purpose of collection only, or a transfer of a contract right to an assignee who is also to do the performance under the contract; or

(g) to a transfer of an interest or claim in or under any policy of insurance; or

(h) to a right represented by a judgment; or

(i) to any right of set-off; or

(j) except to the extent that provision is made for fixtures in Section 9–313, to the creation or transfer of an interest in or lien on real estate, including a lease or rents thereunder; or

(k) to a transfer in whole or in part of any of the following: any claim arising out of tort; any deposit, savings, passbook or like account maintained with a bank, savings and loan association, credit union or like organization.

§9–105. Definitions and Index of Definitions. (1) In this Article unless the context otherwise requires:

(a) "Account debtor" means the person who is obligated on an account, chattel paper, contract right or general intangible;

(b) "Chattel paper" means a writing or writings which evidence both a monetary obligation and a security interest in or a lease of specific goods. When a transaction is evidenced both by such a security agreement or a lease and by an instrument or a series of instruments, the group of writings taken together constitutes chattel paper;

(c) "Collateral" means the property subject to a security interest, and includes accounts, contract rights and chattel paper which have been sold;

(d) "Debtor" means the person who owes payment or other performance of the obligation secured, whether or not he owns or has rights in the collateral, and includes the seller of accounts, contract rights or chattel paper. Where the debtor and the owner of the collateral are not the same person, the term "debtor" means the owner of the collateral in any provision of the Article dealing with the collateral, the obligor in any provision dealing with the obligation, and may include both where the context so requires;

(e) "Document" means document of title as defined in the general definitions of Article 1 (Section 1–201);

(f) "Goods" includes all things which are movable at the time the security interest attaches or which are fixtures (Section 9–313), but does not include money, documents, instruments, accounts, chattel paper, general intangibles, contract rights and other things in action. "Goods" also include the unborn young of animals and growing crops;

(g) "Instrument" means a negotiable instrument (defined in Section 3–104), or a security (defined in Section 8–102) or any other writing which evidences a right to the payment of money and is not itself a security agreement or lease and is of a type which is in ordinary course of business transferred by delivery with any necessary indorsement or assignment;

(h) "Security agreement" means an agreement which creates or provides for a security interest;

(i) "Secured party" means a lender, seller or other person in whose favor there is a security interest, including a person to whom accounts, contract rights or chattel paper have been sold. When the holders of obligations issued under an indenture of trust, equipment trust agreement or the like are represented by a trustee or other person, the representative is the secured party.

(2) Other definitions applying to this Article and the sections in which they appear are:

"Account". Section 9–106.

"Consumer goods". Section 9–109(1).

"Contract right". Section 9–106.

"Equipment". Section 9–109(2)

"Farm products". Section 9–109(3).

"General intagibles". Section 9–106.

"Inventory". Section 9–109(4).

"Lien creditor". Section 9–301(3).

"Proceeds". Section 9–306(1).

"Purchase money security interest". Section 9–107.

(3) The following definitions in other Articles apply to this Article:

"Check". Section 3–104.

"Contract for sale". Section 2–106.

"Holder in due course". Section 3–302.

"Note". Section 3–104.

"Sale". Section 2–106.

(4) In addition Article 1 contains general definitions and principles of construction and interpretation applicable throughout this Article.

§9–106. Definitions: "Account"; "Contract Right"; "General Intangibles". "Account" means any right to payment for goods sold or leased or for services rendered which is not evidenced by an instrument or chattel paper. "Contract right" means any right to payment under a contract not yet earned by performance and not evidenced by an instrument or chattel paper. "General intangibles" means any personal property (including things in action) other than goods, accounts, contract rights, chattel paper, documents and instruments.

§9–107. Definitions: "Purchase Money Security Interest". A security interest is a "purchase money security interest" to the extent that it is

(a) taken or retained by the seller of the collateral to secure all or part of its price; or

(b) taken by a person who by making advances or incurring an obligation gives value to enable the debtor to acquire rights in or the use of collateral if such value is in fact so used.

§9–108. When After-Acquired Collateral Not Security for Antecedent Debt. Where a secured party makes an advance, incurs an obligation, releases a perfected security interest, or otherwise gives new value which is to be secured in whole or in part by after-acquired property his security interest in the after-acquired collateral shall be deemed to be taken for new value and not as security for an antecedent debt if the debtor acquires his rights in such collateral either in the ordinary course of his business or under a contract of purchase made pursuant to the security agreement within a reasonable time after new value is given.

§9–109. Classification of Goods; "Consumer Goods"; "Equipment"; "Farm Products"; "Inventory". Goods are

(1) "consumer goods" if they are used or bought for use primarily for personal, family or household purposes;

(2) "equipment" if they are used or bought for use primarily in business (including farming or a profession) or by a debtor who is a non-profit organization or a governmental subdivision or agency or if the goods are not included in the definitions of inventory, farm products or consumer goods;

(3) "farm products" if they are crops or livestock or supplies used or produced in farming operations or if they are products of crops or livestock in their unmanufactured states (such as ginned cotton, wool-clip, maple syrup, milk and eggs), and if they are in the possession of a debtor engaged in raising, fattening, grazing or other farming operations. If goods are farm products they are neither equipment nor inventory;

(4) "inventory" if they are held by a person who holds them for sale or lease or to be furnished under contracts of service or if he has so furnished them, or if they are raw materials, work in process or materials used or consumed in a business. Inventory of a person is not to be classified as his equipment.

§9–110. Sufficiency of Description. For the purposes of this Article any description of personal property or real estate is sufficient whether or not it is specific if it reasonably identifies what is described.

§9–111. Applicability of Bulk Transfer Laws. The creation of a security interest is not a bulk transfer under Article 6 (see Section 6–103).

§9–112. Where Collateral Is Not Owned by Debtor. Unless otherwise agreed, when a secured party knows that collateral is owned by a person who is not the debtor, the owner of the collateral is entitled to receive from the secured party any surplus under Section 9–502(2) or under Section 9–504(1), and is not liable for the debt or for any deficiency after resale, and he has the same right as the debtor

(a) to receive statements under Section 9–208;

(b) to receive notice of and to object to a secured party's proposal to retain the collateral in satisfaction of the indebtedness under Section 9–505;

(c) to redeem the collateral under Section 9–506;

(d) to obtain injunctive or other relief under Section 9–507(1); and

(e) to recover losses caused to him under Section 9–208(2).

§9–113. Security Interests Arising Under Article on Sales. A security interest arising solely under the Article on Sales (Article 2) is subject to the provisions of this Article except that to the extent that and so long as the debtor does not have or does not lawfully obtain possession of the goods

(a) no security agreement is necessary to make the security interest enforceable; and

(b) no filing is required to perfect the security interest; and

(c) the rights of the secured party on default by the debtor are governed by the Article on Sales (Article 2).

Part 2

Validity of Security Agreement and Rights of Parties Thereto

§9–201. General Validity of Security Agreement. Except as otherwise provided by this Act a security agreement is effective according to its terms between the parties, against purchasers of the collateral and against creditors. Nothing in this Article validates any charge or practice illegal under any statute or regulation thereunder governing usury, small loans, retail installment sales, or the like, or extends the application of any such statute or regulation to any transaction not otherwise subject thereto.

§9–202. Title to Collateral Immaterial. Each provision of this Article with regard to rights, obligations and remedies applies whether title to collateral is in the secured party or in the debtor.

§9–203. Enforceability of Security Interest; Proceeds, Formal Requisites. (1) Subject to the provisions of Section 4–208 on the security interest of a collecting bank and Section 9–113 on a security interest arising under the Article on Sales, a security interest is not enforceable aaginst the debtor or third parties unless

(a) the collateral is in the possession of the secured party; or

(b) the debtor has signed a security agreement which contains a description of the collateral and in addition, when the security interest covers crops or oil, gas or minerals to be extracted or timber to be cut, a description of the land concerned. In describing collateral, the word "proceeds" is sufficient without further description to cover proceeds of any character.

(2) A transaction, although subject to this Article, is also subject to ....*, and in the case of conflict between the provision of this Article and any such statute, the provisions of such statute control. Failure to comply with any applicable statute has only the effect which is specified therein.

Note: *At * in subsection (2) insert reference to any local statute regulating small loans, retail installment sales and the like.*

The foregoing subsection (2) is designed to make it clear that certain transactions, although subject to this Article, must also comply with other applicable legislation.

This Article is designed to regulate all the "security" aspects of transactions within its scope. There is, however, much regulatory legislation, particularly in the consumer field, which supplements this Article and should not be repealed by its enactment. Examples are small loan acts, retail installment selling acts and the like. Such acts may provide for licensing and rate regulation and may prescribe particular forms of contract. Such provisions should remain in force despite the enactment of this Article. On the other hand if a Retail Installment Selling Act contains provisions on filing, rights on default, etc., such provisions should be repealed as inconsistent with this Article.

§9–204. When Security Interest Attaches; After-Acquired Property; Future Advances. (1) A security interest cannot attach until there is agreement (subsection (3) of Section 1–201) that it attach and value is given and the debtor has rights in the collateral. It attaches as soon as all of the events in the preceding sentence have taken place unless explicit agreement postpones the time of attaching.

(2) For the purposes of this section the debtor has no rights

(a) in crops until they are planted or otherwise become growing crops, in the young of livestock until they are conceived;

(b) in fish until caught, in oil, gas or minerals until they are extracted, in timber until it is cut;

(c) in a contract right until the contract has been made;

(d) in an account until it comes into existence.

(3) Except as provided in subsection (4) a security agreement may provide that collateral, whenever acquired, shall secure all obligations covered by the security agreement.

(4) No security interest attaches under an after-acquired property clause

(a) to crops which become such more than one year after the security agreement is executed except that a security interest in crops which is given in conjunction with a lease or a land purchase or improvement transaction evidenced by a contract, mortgage or deed of trust may if so agreed attach to crops to be grown on the land concerned during the period of such real estate transaction;

(b) to consumer goods other than accessions (Section 9–314) when given as additional security unless the debtor acquires rights in them within ten days after the secured party gives value.

(5) Obligations covered by a security agreement may include future advances or other value whether or not the advances or value are given pursuant to commitment.

§9–205. Use or Disposition of Collateral Without Accounting Permissible. A security interest is not invalid or fraudulent against creditors by reason of liberty in the debtor to use, commingle or dispose of all or part of the collateral (including returned or repossessed goods) or to collect or compromise accounts, contract rights or chattel paper, or to accept the return of goods or make repossessions, or to use, commingle or dispose of proceeds, or by reason of the failure of the secured party to require the debtor to account for proceeds or replace collateral. This section does not relax the requirements of possession where perfection of a security interest depends upon possession of the collateral by the secured party or by a bailee.

§9–206. Agreement Not to Assert Defenses Against Assignee; Modification of Sales Warranties Where Security Agreement Exists. (1) Subject to any statute or decision which establishes a different rule for buyers of consumer goods, an agreement by a buyer that he will not assert against an assignee any claim or defense which he may have against the seller is enforceable by an assignee who takes his assignment for value, in good faith and without notice of a claim or defense, except as to defenses of a type which may be asserted against a holder in due course of a negotiable instrument under the Article on Commercial Paper (Article 3). A buyer who as part of one transaction signs both a negotiable instrument and a security agreement makes such an agreement.

(2) When a seller retains a purchase money security interest in goods the Article on Sales (Article 2) governs the sale and any disclaimer, limitation or modification of the seller's warranties.

§9–207. Rights and Duties When Collateral Is in Secured Party's Possession. (1) A secured party must use reasonable care in the custody and preservation of collateral in his possession. In the case of an instrument or chattel paper reasonable care includes taking necessary steps to preserve rights against prior parties unless otherwise agreed.

(2) Unless otherwise agreed, when collateral is in the secured party's possession

(a) reasonable expenses (including the cost of any insurance and payment of taxes or other charges) incurred in the custody, preservation, use or operation of the collateral are chargeable to the debtor and are secured by the collateral;

(b) the risk of accidental loss or damage is on the debtor to the extent of any deficiency in any effective insurance coverage;

(c) the secured party may hold as additional security any increase or profits (except money) received from the collateral, but money so received, unless remitted to the debtor, shall be applied in reduction of the secured obligation;

(d) the secured party must keep the collateral identifiable but fungible collateral may be commingled;

(e) the secured party may repledge the collateral upon terms which do not impair the debtor's right to redeem it.

(3) A secured party is liable for any loss caused by his failure to meet any obligation imposed by the preceding subsections but does not lose his security interest.

(4) A secured party may use or operate the collateral for the purpose of preserving the collateral or its value or pursuant to the order of a court of appropriate jurisdiction or, except in the case of consumer goods, in the manner and to the extent provided in the security agreement.

§9–208. Request for Statement of Account or List of Collateral. (1) A debtor may sign a statement indicating what he believes to be the aggregate amount of unpaid indebtedness as of a specified date and may send it to the secured party with a request that the statement be approved or corrected and returned to the debtor. When the security agreement or any other record kept by the secured party identifies the collateral a debtor may similarly request the secured party to approve or correct a list of the collateral.

(2) The secured party must comply with such a request within two weeks after receipt by sending a written correction or approval. If the secured party claims a security interest in all of a particular type of collateral owned by the debtor he may indicate that fact in his reply and need not approve or correct an itemized list of such collateral. If the secured party without reasonable excuse fails to comply he is liable for any loss caused to the debtor thereby; and if the debtor has properly included in his request a good faith statement of the obligation or a list of the collateral or both the secured party may claim a security interest only as shown in the statement against persons misled by his failure to comply. If he no longer has an interest in the obligation or collateral at the time the request is received he must disclose the name and address of any successor in interest known to him and he is liable for any loss caused to the debtor as a result of failure to disclose. A successor in interest is not subject to this section until a request is received by him.

(3) A debtor is entitled to such a statement once every six months without charge. The secured party may require payment of a charge not exceeding $10 for each additional statement furnished.

Part 3

Rights of Third Parties; Perfected and Unperfected Security Interests; Rules of Priority

§9–301. Persons Who Take Priority Over Unperfected Security Interests; "Lien Creditor". (1) Except as otherwise provided in subsection (2), an unperfected security interest is subordinate to the rights of

(a) persons entitled to priority under Section 9–312;

(b) a person who becomes a lien creditor without knowledge of the security interest and before it is perfected;

(c) in the case of goods, instruments, documents, and chattel paper, a person who is not a secured party and who is a transferee in bulk or other buyer not in ordinary course of business to the extent that he gives value and receives delivery of the collateral without knowledge of the security interest and before it is perfected;

(d) in the case of accounts, contract rights, and general intangibles, a person who is not a secured party and who is a transferee to the extent that he gives value without knowledge of the security interest and before it is perfected.

(2) If the secured party files with respect to a purchase money security interest before or within ten days after the collateral comes into possession of the debtor, he takes priority over the rights of a transferee in bulk or of a lien creditor which arise between the time the security interest attaches and the time of filing.

(3) A "lien creditor" means a creditor who has acquired a lien on the property involved by attachment, levy or the like and includes an assignee for benefit of creditors from the time of assignment, and a trustee in bankruptcy from the date of the filing of the petition or a receiver in equity from the time of appointment. Unless all the creditors represented had knowledge of the

security interest such a representative of creditors is a lien creditor without knowledge even though he personally has knowledge of the security interest.

§9–302. When Filing Is Required to Perfect Security Interest; Security Interests to Which Filing Provisions of This Article Do Not Apply. (1) A financing statement must be filed to perfect all security interests except the following:

(a) a security interest in collateral in possession of the secured party under Section 9–305;

(b) a security interest temporarily perfected in instruments or documents without delivery under Section 9–304 or in proceeds for a 10 day period under Section 9–306;

(c) a purchase money security interest in farm equipment having a purchase price not in excess of $2500; but filing is required for a fixture under Section 9–313 or for a motor vehicle required to be licensed;

(d) a purchase money security interest in consumer goods; but filing is required for a fixture under Section 9–313 or for a motor vehicle required to be licensed;

(e) an assignment of accounts or contract rights which does not alone or in conjunction with other assignments to the same assignee transfer a significant part of the outstanding accounts or contract rights of the assignor;

(f) a security interest of a collecting bank (Section 4–208) or arising under the Article on Sales (see Section 9–113) or covered in subsection (3) of this section.

(2) If a secured party assigns a perfected security interest, no filing under this Article is required in order to continue the perfected status of the security interest against creditors of and transferees from the original debtor.

(3) The filing provisions of this Article do not apply to a security interest in property subject to a statute

(a) of the United States which provides for a national registration or filing of all security interests in such property; or

Note: *States to select either Alternative A or Alternative B.*

Alternative A—

(b) of this state which provides for central filing of, or which requires indication on a certificate of title of, such security interests in such property.

Alternative B—

(b) of this state which provides for central filing of security interests in such property, or in a motor vehicle which is not inventory held for sale for which a certificate of title is required under the statutes of this state if a notation of such a security interest can be indicated by a public official on a certificate or a duplicate thereof.

(4) A security interest in property covered by a statute described in subsection (3) can be perfected only by registration or filing under that statute or by indication of the security interest on a certificate of title or a duplicate thereof by a public official.

§9–303. When Security Interest Is Perfected; Continuity of Perfection. (1) A security interest is perfected when it has attached and when all of the applicable steps required for perfection have been taken. Such steps are specified in Sections 9–302, 9–304, 9–305 and 9–306. If such steps are taken before the security interest attaches, it is perfected at the time when it attaches.

(2) If a security interest is originally perfected in any way permitted under this Article and is subsequently perfected in some other way under this Article, without an intermediate period when it was unperfected, the security interest shall be deemed to be perfected continuously for the purposes of this Article.

§9–304. **Perfection of Security Interest in Instruments, Documents, and Goods Covered by Documents; Perfection by Permissive Filing; Temporary Perfection Without Filing or Transfer of Possession.** (1) A security interest in chattel paper or negotiable documents may be perfected by filing. A security interest in instruments (other than instruments which constitute part of chattel paper) can be perfected only by the secured party's taking possession, except as provided in subsections (4) and (5).

(2) During the period that goods are in the possession of the issuer of a negotiable document therefor, a security interest in the goods is perfected by perfecting a security interest in the document, and any security interest in the goods otherwise perfected during such period is subject thereto.

(3) A security interest in goods in the possession of a bailee other than one who has issued a negotiable document therefor is perfected by issuance of a document in the name of the secured party or by the bailee's receipt of notification of the secured party's interest or by filing as to the goods.

(4) A security interest in instruments or negotiable documents is perfected without filing or the taking of possession for a period of 21 days from the time it attaches to the extent that it arises for new value given under a written security agreement.

(5) A security interest remains perfected for a period of 21 days without filing where a secured party having a perfected security interest in an instrument, a negotiable document or goods in possession of a bailee other than one who has issued a negotiable document therefor

(a) makes available to the debtor the goods or documents representing the goods for the purpose of ultimate sale or exchange or for the purpose of loading, unloading, storing, shipping, transshipping, manufacturing, processing or otherwise dealing with them in a manner preliminary to their sale or exchange; or

(b) delivers the instrument to the debtor for the purpose of ultimate sale or exchange or of presentation, collection, renewal or registration of transfer.

(6) After the 21 day period in subsections (4) and (5) perfection depends upon compliance with applicable provisions of this Article.

§9–305. **When Possession by Secured Party Perfects Security Interest Without Filing.** A security interest in letters of credit and advices of credit (subsection (2) (a) of Section 5–116), goods, instruments, negotiable documents or chattel paper may be perfected by the secured party's taking possession of the collateral. If such collateral other than goods covered by a negotiable document is held by a bailee, the secured party is deemed to have possession from the time the bailee receives notification of the secured party's interest. A security interest is perfected by possession from the time possession is taken without relation back and continues only so long as possession is retained, unless otherwise specified in this Article. The security interest may be otherwise perfected as provided in this Article before or after the period of possession by the secured party.

§9–306. "Proceeds"; Secured Party's Rights on Disposition of Collateral. (1) "Proceeds" includes whatever is received when collateral or proceeds is sold, exchanged, collected or otherwise disposed of. The term also includes the account arising when the right to payment is earned under a contract right. Money, checks and the like are "cash proceeds". All other proceeds are "non-cash proceeds".

(2) Except where this Article otherwise provides, a security interest continues in collateral notwithstanding sale, exchange or other disposition thereof by the debtor unless his action was authorized by the secured party in the security agreement or otherwise, and also continues in any identifiable proceeds including collections received by the debtor.

(3) The security interest in proceeds is a continuously perfected security interest if the interest in the original collateral was perfected but it ceases to be a perfected security interest and becomes unperfected ten days after receipt of the proceeds by the debtor unless

(a) a filed financing statement covering the original collateral also covers proceeds; or

(b) the security interest in the proceeds is perfected before the expiration of the ten day period.

(4) In the event of insolvency proceedings instituted by or against a debtor, a secured party with a perfected security interest in proceeds has a perfected security interest

(a) in identifiable non-cash proceeds;

(b) in identifiable cash proceeds in the form of money which is not commingled with other money or deposited in a bank account prior to the insolvency proceedings;

(c) in identifiable cash proceeds in the form of checks and the like which are not deposited in a bank account prior to the insolvency proceedings; and

(d) in all cash and bank accounts of the debtor, if other cash proceeds have been commingled or deposited in a bank account, but the perfected security interest under this paragraph (d) is

(i) subject to any right of set-off; and

(ii) limited to an amount not greater than the amount of any cash proceeds received by the debtor within ten days before the institution of the insolvency proceedings and commingled or deposited in a bank account prior to the insolvency proceedings less the amount of cash proceeds received by the debtor and paid over to the secured party during the ten day period.

(5) If a sale of goods results in an account or chattel paper which is transferred by the seller to a secured party, and if the goods are returned to or are repossessed by the seller or the secured party, the following rules determine priorities:

(a) If the goods were collateral at the time of sale for an indebtedness of the seller which is still unpaid, the original security interest attaches again to the goods and continues as a perfected security interest if it was perfected at the time when the goods were sold. If the security interest was originally perfected by a filing which is still effective, nothing further is required to continue the perfected status; in any other case, the secured party must take possession of the returned or repossessed goods or must file.

(b) An unpaid transferee of the chattel paper has a security interest in the goods against the transferor. Such security interest is prior to a security interest asserted under paragraph (a) to the extent that the transferee of the chattel paper was entitled to priority under Section 9–308.

(c) An unpaid transferee of the account has a security interest in the goods against the transferor. Such security interest is subordinate to a security interest asserted under paragraph (a).

(d) A security interest of an unpaid transferee asserted under paragraph (b) or (c) must be perfected for protection against creditors of the transferor and purchasers of the returned or repossessed goods.

§9–307. Protection of Buyers of Goods. (1) A buyer in ordinary course of business (subsection (9) of Section 1–201) other than a person buying farm products from a person engaged in farming operations takes free of a security interest created by his seller even though the security interest is perfected and even though the buyer knows of its existence.

(2) In the case of consumer goods and in the case of farm equipment having an original purchase price not in excess of $2500 (other than fixtures, see Section 9–313), a buyer takes free of a security interest even though perfected if he buys without knowledge of the security interest, for value and for his own personal, family or household purposes or his own farming operations unless prior to the purchase the secured party has filed a financing statement covering such goods.

§9–308. Purchase of Chattel Paper and Non-Negotiable Instruments. A purchaser of chattel paper or a non-negotiable instrument who gives new value and takes possession of it in the ordinary course of his business and without knowledge that the specific paper or instrument is subject to a security interest has priority over a security interest which is perfected under Section 9–304 (permissive filing and temporary perfection). A purchaser of chattel paper who gives new value and takes possession of it in the ordinary course of his business has priority over a security interest in chattel paper which is claimed merely as proceeds of inventory subject to a security interest (Section 9–306), even though he knows that the specific paper is subject to the security interest.

§9–309. Protection of Purchasers of Instruments and Documents. Nothing in this Article limits the rights of a holder in due course of a negotiable instrument (Section 3–302) or a holder to whom a negotiable document of title has been duly negotiated (Section 7–501) or a bona fide purchaser of a security (Section 8–301) and such holders or purchasers take priority over an earlier security interest even though perfected. Filing under this Article does not constitute notice of the security interest to such holders or purchasers.

§9–310. Priority of Certain Liens Arising by Operation of Law. When a person in the ordinary course of his business furnishes services or materials with respect to goods subject to a security interest, a lien upon goods in the possession of such person given by statute or rule of law for such materials or services takes priority over a perfected security interest unless the lien is statutory and the statute expressly provides otherwise.

§9–311. Alienability of Debtor's Rights: Judicial Process. The debtor's rights in collateral may be voluntarily or involuntarily transferred (by way of sale, creation of a security interest, attachment, levy, garnishment or other judicial process) notwithstanding a provision in the security agreement prohibiting any transfer or making the transfer constitute a default.

§9–312. Priorities Among Conflicting Security Interests in the Same Collateral.
(1) The rules of priority stated in the following sections shall govern where applicable: Section 4–208 with respect to the security interest of collecting banks in items being collected, accompanying documents and proceeds; Section 9–301 on certain priorities; Section 9–304 on goods covered by documents; Section 9–306 on proceeds and repossessions; Section 9–307 on buyers of goods; Section 9–308 on possessory against non-possessory interests in chattel paper or non-negotiable instruments; Section 9–309 on security interests in negotiable instruments, documents or securities; Section 9–310 on priorities between perfected security interests and liens by operation of law; Section 9–313 on security interests in fixtures as against interests in real estate; Section 9–314 on security interests in accessions as against interest in goods; Section 9–315 on conflicting security interests where goods lose their identity or become part of a product; and Section 9–316 on contractual subordination.

(2) A perfected security interest in crops for new value given to enable the debtor to produce the crops during the production season and given not more than three months before the crops become growing crops by planting or otherwise takes priority over an earlier perfected security interest to the extent that such earlier interest secures obligations due more than six months before the crops become growing crops by planting or otherwise, even though the person giving new value had knowledge of the earlier security interest.

(3) A purchase money security interest in inventory collateral has priority over a conflicting security interest in the same collateral if
(a) the purchase money security interest is perfected at the time the debtor receives possession of the collateral; and
(b) any secured party whose security interest is known to the holder of the purchase money security interest or who, prior to the date of the filing made by the holder of the purchase money security interest, had filed a financing statement covering the same items or type of inventory, has received notification of the purchase money security interest before the debtor receives possession of the collateral covered by the purchase money security interest; and
(c) such notification states that the person giving the notice has or expects to acquire a purchase money security interest in inventory of the debtor, describing such inventory by item or type.

(4) A purchase money security interest in collateral other than inventory has priority over a conflicting security interest in the same collateral if the

purchase money security interest is perfected at the time the debtor receives possession of the collateral or within ten days thereafter.

(5) In all cases not governed by other rules stated in this section (including cases of purchase money security interests which do not qualify for the special priorities set forth in subsections (3) and (4) of this section), priority between conflicting security interests in the same collateral shall be determined as follows:

(a) in the order of filing if both are perfected by filing, regardless of which security interest attached first under Section 9–204(1) and whether it attached before or after filing;

(b) in the order of perfection unless both are perfected by filing, regardless of which security interest attached first under Section 9–204(1) and, in the case of a filed security interest, whether it attached before or after filing; and

(c) in the order of attachment under Section 9–204(1) so long as neither is perfected.

(6) For the purpose of the priority rules of the immediately preceding subsection, a continuously perfected security interest shall be treated at all times as if perfected by filing if it was originally so perfected and it shall be treated at all times as if perfected otherwise than by filing if it was originally perfected otherwise than by filing.

§9–313. **Priority of Security Interests in Fixtures.** (1) The rules of this section do not apply to goods incorporated into a structure in the manner of lumber, bricks, tile, cement, glass, metal work and the like and no security interest in them exists under this Article unless the structure remains personal property under applicable law. The law of this state other than this Act determines whether and when other goods become fixtures. This Act does not prevent creation of an encumbrance upon fixtures or real estate pursuant to the law applicable to real estate.

(2) A security interest which attaches to goods before they become fixtures takes priority as to the goods over the claims of all persons who have an interest in the real estate except as stated in subsection (4).

(3) A security interest which attaches to goods after they become fixtures is valid against all persons subsequently acquiring interests in the real estate except as stated in subsection (4) but is invalid against any person with an interest in the real estate at the time the security interest attaches to the goods who has not in writing consented to the security interest or disclaimed an interest in the goods as fixtures.

(4) The security interests described in subsections (2) and (3) do not take priority over

(a) a subsequent purchaser for value of any interest in the real estate; or

(b) a creditor with a lien on the real estate subsequently obtained by judicial proceedings; or

(c) a creditor with a prior encumbrance of record on the real estate to the extent that he makes subsequent advances

if the subsequent purchase is made, the lien by judicial proceedings is obtained, or the subsequent advance under the prior encumbrance is made or contracted for without knowledge of the security interest and before it is perfected. A purchaser of the real estate at a foreclosure sale other than an encumbrancer purchasing at his own foreclosure sale is a subsequent purchaser within this section.

(5) When under subsections (2) or (3) and (4) a secured party has priority over the claims of all persons who have interests in the real estate, he may, on default, subject to the provisions of Part 5, remove his collateral from the real estate but he must reimburse any encumbrancer or owner of the real estate who is not the debtor and who has not otherwise agreed for the cost of repair of any physical injury, but not for any diminution in value of the real estate caused by the absence of the goods removed or by any necessity for replacing them. A person entitled to reimbursement may refuse permission to remove until the secured party gives adequate security for the performance of this obligation.

§9-314. Accessions. (1) A security interest in goods which attaches before they are installed in or affixed to other goods takes priority as to the goods installed or affixed (called in this section "accessions") over the claims of all persons to the whole except as stated in subsection (3) and subject to Section 9-315(1).

(2) A security interest which attaches to goods after they become part of a whole is valid against all persons subsequently acquiring interests in the whole except as stated in subsection (3) but is invalid against any person with an interest in the whole at the time the security interest attaches to the goods who has not in writing consented to the security interest or disclaimed an interest in the goods as part of the whole.

(3) The security interests described in subsections (1) and (2) do not take priority over

(a) a subsequent purchaser for value of any interest in the whole; or

(b) a creditor with a lien on the whole subsequently obtained by judicial proceedings; or

(c) a creditor with a prior perfected security interest in the whole to the extent that he makes subsequent advances

if the subsequent purchase is made, the lien by judicial proceedings obtained or the subsequent advance under the prior perfected security interest is made or contracted for without knowledge of the security interest and before it is perfected. A purchaser of the whole at a foreclosure sale other than the holder of a perfected security interest purchasing at his own foreclosure sale is a subsequent purchaser within this section.

(4) When under subsections (1) or (2) and (3) a secured party has an interest in accessions which has priority over the claims of all persons who have interests in the whole, he may on default subject to the provisions of Part 5 remove his collateral from the whole but he must reimburse any encumbrancer or owner of the whole who is not the debtor and who has not otherwise agreed for the cost of repair of any physical injury but not for any diminution in value of the whole caused by the absence of the goods removed or by any necessity for replacing them. A person entitled to reimbursement may refuse permission to

remove until the secured party gives adequate security for the performance of this obligation.

§9–315. Priority When Goods Are Commingled or Processed. (1) If a security interest in goods was perfected and subsequently the goods or a part thereof have become part of a product or mass, the security interest continues in the product or mass if

(a) the goods are so manufactured, processed, assembled or commingled that their identity is lost in the product or mass; or

(b) a financing statement covering the original goods also covers the product into which the goods have been manufactured, processed or assembled.

In a case to which paragraph (b) applies, no separate security interest in that part of the original goods which has been manufactured, processed or assembled into the product may be claimed under Section 9–314.

(2) When under subsection (1) more than one security interest attaches to the product or mass, they rank equally according to the ratio that the cost of the goods to which each interest originally attached bears to the cost of the total product or mass.

§9–316. Priority Subject to Subordination. Nothing in this Article prevents subordination by agreement by any person entitled to priority.

§9–317. Secured Party Not Obligated on Contract of Debtor. The mere existence of a security interest or authority given to the debtor to dispose of or use collateral does not impose contract or tort liability upon the secured party for the debtor's acts or omissions.

§9–318. Defenses Against Assignee; Modification of Contract After Notification of Assignment; Term Prohibiting Assignment Ineffective; Identification and Proof of Assignment. (1) Unless an account debtor has made an enforceable agreement not to assert defenses or claims arising out of a sale as provided in Section 9–206 the rights of an assignee are subject to

(a) all the terms of the contract between the account debtor and assignor and any defense or claim arising therefrom; and

(b) any other defense or claim of the account debtor against the assignor which accrues before the account debtor receives notification of the assignment.

(2) So far as the right to payment under an assigned contract right has not already become an account, and notwithstanding notification of the assignment, any modification of or substitution for the contract made in good faith and in accordance with reasonable commercial standards is effective against an assignee unless the account debtor has otherwise agreed but the assignee acquires corresponding rights under the modified or substituted contract. The assignment may provide that such modification or substitution is a breach by the assignor.

(3) The account debtor is authorized to pay the assignor until the account debtor receives notification that the account has been assigned and that payment is to be made to the assignee. A notification which does not reasonably identify the rights assigned is ineffective. If requested by the account debtor, the assignee must seasonably furnish reasonable proof that the assignment has been made and unless he does so the account debtor may pay the assignor.

(4) A term in any contract between an account debtor and an assignor which

prohibits assignment of an account or contract right to which they are parties is ineffective.

Part 4

Filing

§9–401. Place of Filing; Erroneous Filing; Removal of Collateral. (1) The proper place to file in order to perfect a security interest is as follows:
Optional paragraph (a)

(a) when the collateral is equipment used in farming operations, or farm products, or accounts, contract rights or general intangibles arising from or relating to the sale of farm products by a farmer, or consumer goods, then in the office of the .... in the county of the debtor's residence or if the debtor is not a resident of this state then in the office of the .... in the county where the goods are kept, and in addition when the collateral is crops in the office of the .... in the county where the land on which the crops are growing or to be grown is located;

(b) when the collateral is goods which at the time the security interest attaches are or are to become fixtures, then in the office where a mortgage on the real estate concerned would be field or recorded;
Optional paragraph (c)

(c) in all other cases, in the office of the [Secretary of State] [and in addition, if the debtor has a place of business in only one county of this state, also in the office of .... of such county, or, if the debtor has no place of business in this state, but resides in the state, also in the office of .... of the county in which he resides.]

Note: *Paragraph (a) may be omitted, in which case all of the subject matter thereof will be governed by new paragraph (c), and only filing in the office of the Secretary of State will be required. In that case, the optional language in paragraph (c) requiring local filing should be omitted. If paragraph (a) is omitted, the subsequent paragraphs should be relettered.*

If, however, paragraph (a) is adopted, paragraph (c) can be adopted with or without the optional language requiring local filing under the conditions specified.

(2) A filing which is made in good faith in an improper place or not in all of the places required by this section is nevertheless effective with regard to any collateral as to which the filing complied with the requirements of this Article and is also effective with regard to collateral covered by the financing statement against any person who has knowledge of the contents of such financing statement.

(3) A filing which is made in the proper place in this state continues effective even though the debtor's residence or place of business or the location of the collateral or its use, whichever controlled the original filing, is thereafter changed.
Alternative subsection (3)

[(3) A filing which is made in the proper county continues effective for four months after a change to another county of the debtor's residence or place of business or the location of the collateral, whichever controlled the original filing. It becomes ineffective thereafter unless a copy of the financing statement signed by the secured party is filed in the new county within said period. The security interest may also be perfected in the new county after the expiration of the four-month period; in such case perfection dates from the time of perfection in the new county. A change in the use of the collateral does not impair the effectiveness of the original filing.]

(4) If collateral is brought into this state from another jurisdiction, the rules stated in Section 9–103 determine whether filing is necessary in this state.

§9–402. Formal Requisites of Financing Statement; Amendments. (1) A financing statement is sufficient if it is signed by the debtor and the secured party, gives an address of the secured party from which information concerning the security interest may be obtained, gives a mailing address of the debtor and contains a statement indicating the types, or describing the items, of collateral. A financing statement may be filed before a security agreement is made or a security interest otherwise attaches. When the financing statement covers crops growing or to be grown or goods which are or are to become fixtures, the statement must also contain a description of the real estate concerned. A copy of the security agreement is sufficient as a financing statement if it contains the above information and is signed by both parties.

(2) A financing statement which otherwise complies with subsection (1) is sufficient although it is signed only by the secured party when it is filed to perfect a security interest in

(a) collateral already subject to a security interest in another jurisdiction when it is brought into this state. Such a financing statement must state that the collateral was brought into this state under such circumstances.

(b) proceeds under Secion 9–306 if the security interest in the original collateral was perfected. Such a financing statement must describe the original collateral.

(3) A form substantially as follows is sufficient to comply with subsection (1):

Name of debtor (or assignor) ....

Address ....

Name of secured party (or assignee) ....

Address ....

1. This financing statement covers the following types (or items) of property:
   (Describe) ....

2. (If collateral is crops) The above described crops are growing or are to be grown on:
   (Describe Real Estate) ....

3. (If collateral is goods which are or are to become fixtures) The above described goods are affixed or to be affixed to:
   (Describe Real Estate) ....

4. (If proceeds or products of collateral are claimed) Proceeds—Products of the collateral are also covered.
   Signature of Debtor (or Assignor) ....
   Signature of Secured Party (or Assignee) ....

(4) The term "financing statement" as used in this Article means the original financing statement and any amendments but if any amendment adds collateral, it is effective as to the added collateral only from the filing date of the amendment.

(5) A financing statement substantially complying with the requirements of this section is effective even though it contains minor errors which are not seriously misleading.

§9–403. What Constitutes Filing; Duration of Filing; Effect of Lapsed Filing; Duties of Filing Officer. (1) Presentation for filing of a financing statement and tender of the filing fee or acceptance of the statement by the filing officer constitutes filing under this Article.

(2) A filed financing statement which states a maturity date of the obligation secured of five years or less is effective until such maturity date and thereafter for a period of sixty days. Any other filed financing statement is effective for a period of five years from the date of filing. The effectiveness of a filed financing statement lapses on the expiration of such sixty day period after a stated maturity date or on the expiration of such five year period, as the case may be, unless a continuation statement is filed prior to the lapse. Upon such lapse the security interest becomes unperfected.

(3) A continuation statement may be filed by the secured party (i) within six months before and sixty days after a stated maturity date of five years or less, and (ii) otherwise within six months prior to the expiration of the five year period specified in subsection (2). Any such continuation statement must be signed by the secured party, identify the original statement by file number and state that the original statement is still effective. Upon timely filing of the continuation statement, the effectiveness of the original statement is continued for five years after the last date to which the filing was effective whereupon it lapses in the same manner as provided in subsection (2) unless another continuation statement is filed prior to such lapse. Succeeding continuation statements may be filed in the same manner to continue the effectiveness of the original statement. Unless a statute on disposition of public records provides otherwise, the filing officer may remove a lapsed statement from the files and destroy it.

(4) A filing officer shall mark each statement with a consecutive file number and with the date and hour of filing and shall hold the statement for public inspection. In addition the filing officer shall index the statements according to the name of the debtor and shall note in the index the file number and the address of the debtor given in the statement.

(5) The uniform fee for filing, indexing and furnishing filing data for an original or a continuation statement shall be $. . . . .

§9–404. Termination Statement. (1) Whenever there is no outstanding secured obligation and no commitment to make advances, incur obligations or otherwise give value, the secured party must on written demand by the debtor send the debtor a statement that he no longer claims a security interest under the financing statement, which shall be identified by file number. A termination statement signed by a person other than the secured party of record must include or be accompanied by the assignment or a statement by the secured party of record that he has assigned the security interest to the signer of the termination statement. The uniform fee for filing and indexing such an assignment or statement thereof shall be $......... If the affected secured party fails to send such a termination statement within ten days after proper demand therefor he shall be liable to the debtor for one hundred dollars, and in addition for any loss caused to the debtor by such failure.

(2) On presentation to the filing officer of such a termination statement he must note it in the index. The filing officer shall remove from the files, mark "terminated" and send or deliver to the secured party the financing statement and any continuation statement, statement of assignment or statement of release pertaining thereto.

(3) The uniform fee for filing and indexing a termination statement including sending or delivering the financing statement shall be $........

§9–405. Assignment of Security Interest; Duties of Filing Officer; Fees. (1) A financing statement may disclose an assignment of a security interest in the collateral described in the statement by indication in the statement of the name and address of the assignee or by an assignment itself or a copy thereof on the face or back of the statement. Either the original secured party or the assignee may sign this statement as the secured party. On presentation to the filing officer of such a financing statement the filing officer shall mark the same as provided in Section 9–403(4). The uniform fee for filing, indexing and furnishing filing data for a financing statement so indicating an assignment shall be $........

(2) A secured party may assign of record all or a part of his rights under a financing statement by the filing of a separate written statement of assignment signed by the secured party of record and setting forth the name of the secured party of record and the debtor, the file number and the date of filing of the financing statement and the name and address of the assignee and containing a description of the collateral assigned. A copy of the assignment is sufficient as a separate statement if it complies with the preceding sentence. On presentation to the filing officer of such a separate statement, the filing officer shall mark such separate statement with the date and hour of the filing. He shall note the assignment on the index of the financing statement. The uniform fee for filing, indexing and furnishing filing data about such a separate statement of assignment shall be $........

(3) After the disclosure or filing of an assignment under this section, the assignee is the secured party of record.

§9–406. Release of Collateral; Duties of Filing Officer; Fees. A secured party of record may by his signed statement release all or a part of any collateral described in a filed financing statement. The statement of release is sufficient if it contains a description of the collateral being released, the name and address of the debtor, the name and address of the secured party, and the file number of the financing statement. Upon presentation of such a statement to the filing officer he shall mark the statement with the hour and date of filing and shall note the same upon the margin of the index of the filing of the financing statement. The uniform fee for filing and noting such a statement of release shall be $.........

[**§9–407. Information From Filing Officer.** (1) If the person filing any financing statement, termination statement, statement of assignment, or statement of release, furnishes the filing officer a copy thereof, the filing officer shall upon request note upon the copy the file number and date and hour of the filing of the original and deliver or send the copy to such person.

(2) Upon request of any person, the filing officer shall issue his certificate showing whether there is on file on the date and hour stated therein, any presently effective financing statement naming a particular debtor and any statement of assignment thereof and if there is, giving the date and hour of filing of each such statement and the names and addresses of each secured party therein. The uniform fee for such a certificate shall be $...... plus $...... for each financing statement and for each statement of assignment reported therein. Upon request the filing officer shall furnish a copy of any filed financing statement or statement of assignment for a uniform fee of $...... per page.]

Note: *This new section is proposed as an optional provision to require filing officers to furnish certificates. Local law and practices should be consulted with regard to the advisability of adoption.*

Part 5

Default

§9–501. Default; Procedure When Security Agreement Covers Both Real and Personal Property. (1) When a debtor is in default under a security agreement, a secured party has the rights and remedies provided in this Part and except as limited by subsection (3) those provided in the security agreement. He may reduce his claim to judgment, foreclose or otherwise enforce the security interest by any available judicial procedure. If the collateral is documents the secured party may proceed either as to the documents or as to the goods covered thereby. A secured party in possession has the rights, remedies and duties provided in Section 9–207. The rights and remedies referred to in this subsection are cumulative.

(2) After default, the debtor has the rights and remedies provided in this Part, those provided in the security agreement and those provided in Section 9–207.

(3) To the extent that they give rights to the debtor and impose duties on the secured party, the rules stated in the subsections referred to below may not be waived or varied except as provided with respect to compulsory disposition of collateral (Subsection (1) of Section 9–505) and with respect to redemption of collateral (Section 9–506) but the parties may by agreement determine the standards by which the fulfillment of these rights and duties is to be measured if such standards are not manifestly unreasonable:

(a) subsection (2) of Section 9–502 and subsection (2) of Section 9–504 insofar as they require accounting for surplus proceeds of collateral;

(b) subsection (3) of Section 9–504 and subsection (1) of Section 9–505 which deal with disposition of collateral;

(c) subsection (2) of Section 9–505 which deals with acceptance of collateral as discharge of obligation;

(d) Section 9–506 which deals with redemption of collateral; and

(e) subsection (1) of Section 9–507 which deals with the secured party's liability for failure to comply with this Part.

(4) If the security agreement covers both real and personal property, the secured party may proceed under this Part as to the personal property or he may proceed as to both the real and the personal property in accordance with his rights and remedies in respect of the real property in which case the provisions of this Part do not apply.

(5) When a secured party has reduced his claim to judgment the lien of any levy which may be made upon his collateral by virtue of any execution based upon the judgment shall relate back to the date of the perfection of the security interest in such collateral. A judicial sale, pursuant to such execution, is a foreclosure of the security interest by judicial procedure within the meaning of this section, and the secured party may purchase at the sale and thereafter hold the collateral free of any other requirements of this Article.

§9–502. Collection Rights of Secured Party. (1) When so agreed and in any event on default the secured party is entitled to notify an account debtor or the obligor on an instrument to make payment to him whether or not the assignor was theretofore making collections on the collateral, and also to take control of any proceeds to which he is entitled under Section 9–306.

(2) A secured party who by agreement is entitled to charge back uncollected collateral or otherwise to full or limited recourse against the debtor and who undertakes to collect from the account debtors or obligors must proceed in a commercially reasonable manner and may deduct his reasonable expenses of realization from the collections. If the security agreement secures an indebtedness, the secured party must account to the debtor for any surplus, and unless otherwise agreed, the debtor is liable for any deficiency. But, if the underlying transaction was a sale of accounts, contract rights, or chattel paper, the debtor is entitled to any surplus or is liable for any deficiency only if the security agreement so provides.

§9–503. Secured Party's Right to Take Possession After Default. Unless otherwise agreed a secured party has on default the right to take possession of the collateral. In taking possession a secured party may proceed without judicial process if this can be done without breach of the peace or may proceed by action. If the security agreement so provides the secured party may require the debtor to assemble the collateral and make it available to the secured party at a place to be designated by the secured party which is reasonably convenient to both parties. Without removal a secured party may render equipment unusable, and may dispose of collateral on the debtor's premises under Section 9–504.

§9–504. Secured Party's Right to Dispose of Collateral After Default; Effect of Disposition. (1) A secured party after default may sell, lease or otherwise dispose of any or all of the collateral in its then condition or following any commercially reasonable preparation or processing. Any sale of goods is subject to the Article on Sales (Article 2). The proceeds of disposition shall be applied in the order following to

(a) the reasonable expenses of retaking, holding, preparing for sale, selling and the like and, to the extent provided for in the agreement and not prohibited by law, the reasonable attorneys' fees and legal expenses incurred by the secured party;

(b) the satisfaction of indebtedness secured by the security interest under which the disposition is made;

(c) the satisfaction of indebtedness secured by any subordinate security interest in the collateral if written notification of demand therefor is received before distribution of the proceeds is completed. If requested by the secured party, the holder of a subordinate security interest must seasonably furnish reasonable proof of his interest, and unless he does so, the secured party need not comply with his demand.

(2) If the security interest secures an indebtedness, the secured party must account to the debtor for any surplus, and, unless otherwise agreed, the debtor is liable for any deficiency. But if the underlying transaction was a sale of accounts, contract rights, or chattel paper, the debtor is entitled to any surplus or is liable for any deficiency only if the security agreement so provides.

(3) Disposition of the collateral may be by public or private proceedings and may be made by way of one or more contracts. Sale or other disposition may be as a unit or in parcels and at any time and place and on any terms but every aspect of the disposition including the method, manner, time, place and terms must be commercially reasonable. Unless collateral is perishable or threatens to decline speedily in value or is of a type customarily sold on a recognized market, reasonable notification of the time and place of any public sale or reasonable notification of the time after which any private sale or other intended disposition is to be made shall be sent by the secured party to the debtor, and except in the case of consumer goods to any other person who has a security interest in the collateral and who has duly filed a financing statement indexed in the name of the debtor in this state or who is known by the secured party to have a security interest in the collateral. The secured party may buy at any public sale and if the collateral is of a type customarily sold in a recognized market or is of a type which is the subject of widely distributed standard price quotations he may buy at private sale.

(4) When collateral is disposed of by a secured party after default, the disposition transfers to a purchaser for value all of the debtor's rights therein, discharges the security interest under which it is made and any security interest or lien subordinate thereto. The purchaser takes free of all such rights and interests even though the secured party fails to comply with the requirements of this Part or of any judicial proceedings

(a) in the case of a public sale, if the purchaser has no knowledge of any defects in the sale and if he does not buy in collusion with the secured party, other bidders or the person conducting the sale; or

(b) in any other case, if the purchaser acts in good faith.

(5) A person who is liable to a secured party under a guaranty, indorsement, repurchase agreement or the like and who receives a transfer of collateral from the secured party or is subrogated to his rights has thereafter the rights and duties of the secured party. Such a transfer of collateral is not a sale or disposition of the collateral under this Article.

§9–505. Compulsory Disposition of Collateral; Acceptance of the Collateral as Discharge of Obligation. (1) If the debtor has paid sixty per cent of the cash price in the case of a purchase money security interest in consumer goods or sixty per cent of the loan in the case of another security interest in consumer goods, and has not signed after default a statement renouncing or modifying his rights under this Part a secured party who has taken possession of collateral must dispose of it under Section 9–504 and if he fails to do so within ninety days after he takes possession the debtor at his option may recover in conversion or under Section 9–507(1) on secured party's liability.

(2) In any other case involving consumer goods or any other collateral a secured party in possession may, after default, propose to retain the collateral in satisfaction of the obligation. Written notice of such proposal shall be sent to the debtor and except in the case of consumer goods to any other secured party who has a security interest in the collateral and who has duly filed a financing statement indexed in the name of the debtor in this state or is known by the secured party in possession to have a security interest in it. If the debtor or other person entitled to receive notification objects in writing within thirty days from the receipt of the notification or if any other secured party objects in writing within thirty days after the secured party obtains possession the secured party must dispose of the collateral under Section 9–504. In the absence of such written objection the secured party may retain the collateral in satisfaction of the debtor's obligation.

§9–506. Debtor's Right to Redeem Collateral. At any time before the secured party has disposed of collateral or entered into a contract for its disposition under Section 9–504 or before the obligation has been discharged under Section 9–505(2) the debtor or any other secured party may unless otherwise agreed in writing after default redeem the collateral by tendering fulfillment of all obligations secured by the collateral as well as the expenses reasonably incurred by the secured party in retaking, holding and preparing the collateral for disposition, in arranging for the sale, and to the extent provided in the agreement and not prohibited by law, his reasonable attorneys' fees and legal expenses.

§9–507. Secured Party's Liability for Failure to Comply With This Part. (1) If it is established that the secured party is not proceeding in accordance with the provisions of this Part disposition may be ordered or restrained on appropriate terms and conditions. If the disposition has occurred the debtor or any person entitled to notification or whose security interest has been made known to the secured party prior to the disposition has a right to recover from the secured party any loss caused by a failure to comply with the provisions of this Part. If the collateral is consumer goods, the debtor has a right to recover in any event an amount not less than the credit service charge plus ten per cent of the principal amount of the debt or the time price differential plus ten per cent of the cash price.

(2) The fact that a better price could have been obtained by a sale at a different time or in a different method from that selected by the secured party is not of itself sufficient to establish that the sale was not made in a commercially reasonable manner. If the secured party either sells the collateral in the usual manner in any recognized market therefor or if he sells at the price current in such market at the time of his sale or if he has otherwise sold in conformity with reasonable commercial practices among dealers in the type of property sold he has sold in a commercially reasonable manner. The principles stated in the two preceding sentences with respect to sales also apply as may be appropriate to other types of disposition. A disposition which has been approved in any judicial proceeding or by any bona fide creditors' committee or representative of creditors shall conclusively be deemed to be commercially reasonable, but this sentence does not indicate that any such approval must be obtained in any case nor does it indicate that any disposition not so approved is not commercially reasonable.

Uniform Partnership Act

PART I

Preliminary Provisions

§1. Name of Act. This act may be cited as Uniform Partnership Act.

§2. Definition of Terms. In this act, "Court" includes every court and judge having jurisdiction in the case.

"Business" includes every trade, occupation, or profession.

"Person" includes individuals, partnerships, corporations, and other associations.

"Bankrupt" includes bankrupt under the Federal Bankruptcy Act or insolvent under any state insolvent act.

"Conveyance" includes every assignment, lease, mortgage, or encumbrance.

"Real property" includes land and any interest or estate in land.

§3. Interpretation of Knowledge and Notice. (1) A person has "knowledge" of a fact within the meaning of this act not only when he has actual knowledge thereof, but also when he has knowledge of such other facts as in the circumstances shows bad faith.

(2) A person has "notice" of a fact within the meaning of this act when the person who claims the benefit of the notice

(a) States the fact to such person, or

(b) Delivers through the mail, or by other means of communication, a written statement of the fact to such person or to a proper person at his place of business or residence.

§4. Rules of Construction. (1) The rule that statutes in derogation of the common law are to be strictly construed shall have no application to this act.

Reprinted with permission of the National Conference of Commissioners on Uniform State Laws.

(2) The law of estoppel shall apply under this act.

(3) The law of agency shall apply under this act.

(4) This act shall be so interpreted and construed as to effect its general purpose to make uniform the law of those states which enact it.

(5) This act shall not be construed so as to impair the obligations of any contract existing when the act goes into effect, nor to affect any action or proceedings begun or right accrued before this act takes effect.

§5. Rules for Cases not Provided for in this Act. In any case not provided for in this act the rules of law and equity, including the law merchant, shall govern.

PART II

Nature of a Partnership

§6. Partnership Defined. (1) A partnership is an association of two or more persons to carry on as co-owners a business for profit.

(2) But any association formed under any other statute of this state, or any statute adopted by authority, other than the authority of this state, is not a partnership under this act, unless such association would have been a partnership in this state prior to the adoption of this act; but this act shall apply to limited partnerships except in so far as the statutes relating to such partnerships are inconsistent herewith.

§7. Rules for Determining the Existence of a Partnership. In determining whether a partnership exists, these rules shall apply:

(1) Except as provided by Section 16 persons who are not partners as to each other are not partners as to third persons.

(2) Joint tenancy, tenancy in common, tenancy by the entireties, joint property, common property, or part ownership does not of itself establish a partnership, whether such co-owners do or do not share any profits made by the use of the property.

(3) The sharing of gross returns does not of itself establish a partnership, whether or not the persons sharing them have a joint or common right or interest in any property from which the returns are derived.

(4) The receipt by a person of a share of the profits of a business is prima facie evidence that he is a partner in the business, but no such inference shall be drawn if such profits were received in payment:

(a) As a debt by installments or otherwise,

(b) As wages of an employee or rent to a landlord,

(c) As an annuity to a widow or representative of a deceased partner,

(d) As interest on a loan, though the amount of payment vary with the profits of the business,

(e) As the consideration for the sale of a good-will of a business or other property by installments or otherwise.

§8. Partnership Property. (1) All property originally brought into the partnership stock or subsequently acquired by purchase or otherwise, on account of the partnership, is partnership property.

(2) Unless the contrary intention appears, property acquired with partnership funds is partnership property.

(3) Any estate in real property may be acquired in the partnership name. Title so acquired can be conveyed only in the partnership name.

(4) A conveyance to a partnership in the partnership name, though without words of inheritance, passes the entire estate of the grantor unless a contrary intent appears.

PART III

Relations of Partners to Persons Dealing with the Partnership

§9. Partner Agent of Partnership as to Partnership Business. (1) Every partner is an agent of the partnership for the purpose of its business, and the act of every partner, including the execution in the partnership name of any instrument, for apparently carrying on in the usual way the business of the partnership of which he is a member binds the partnership, unless the partner so acting has in fact no authority to act for the partnership in the particular matter, and the person with whom he is dealing has knowledge of the fact that he has no such authority.

(2) An act of a partner which is not apparently for the carrying on of the business of the partnership in the usual way does not bind the partnership unless authorized by the other partners.

(3) Unless authorized by the other partners or unless they have abandoned the business, one or more but less than all the partners have no authority to:

(a) Assign the partnership property in trust for creditors or on the assignee's promise to pay the debts of the partnership,

(b) Dispose of the good-will of the business,

(c) Do any other act which would make it impossible to carry on the ordinary business of a partnership,

(d) Confess a judgment,

(e) Submit a partnership claim or liability to arbitration or reference.

(4) No act of a partner in contravention of a restriction on authority shall bind the partnership to persons having knowledge of the restriction.

§10. Conveyance of Real Property of the Partnership. (1) Where title to real property is in the partnership name, any partner may convey title to such property by a conveyance executed in the partnership name; but the partnership may recover such property unless the partner's act binds the partnership under the provisions of paragraph (1) of section 9 or unless such property has been conveyed by the grantee or a person claiming through such grantee to a holder for value without knowledge that the partner, in making the conveyance, has exceeded his authority.

(2) Where title to real property is in the name of the partnership, a conveyance executed by a partner, in his own name, passes the equitable interest of the partnership, provided the act is one within the authority of the partner under the provisions of paragraph (1) of section 9.

(3) Where title to real property is in the name of one or more but not all the partners, and the record does not disclose the right of the partnership, the partners in whose name the title stands may convey title to such property, but the partnership may recover such property if the partners' act does not bind the partnership under the provisions of paragraph (1) of section 9, unless the purchaser or his assignee, is a holder for value, without knowledge.

(4) Where the title to real property is in the name of one or more or all the partners, or in a third person in trust for the partnership, a conveyance executed by a partner in the partnership name, or in his own name, passes the equitable interest of the partnership, provided the act is one within the authority of the partner under the provisions of paragraph (1) of section 9.

(5) Where the title to real property is in the names of all the partners a conveyance executed by all the partners passes all their rights in such property.

§11. **Partnership Bound by Admission of Partner.** An admission or representation made by any partner concerning partnership affairs within the scope of his authority as conferred by this act is evidence against the partnership.

§12. **Partnership Charged with Knowledge of or Notice to Partner.** Notice to any partner of any matter relating to partnership affairs, and the knowledge of the partner acting in the particular matter, acquired while a partner or then present to his mind, and the knowledge of any other partner who reasonably could and should have communicated it to the acting partner, operate as notice to or knowledge of the partnership, except in the case of a fraud on the partnership committed by or with the consent of that partner.

§13. **Partnership Bound by Partner's Wrongful Act.** Where, by any wrongful act or omission of any partner acting in the ordinary course of the business of the partnership or with the authority of his co-partners, loss or injury is caused to any person, not being a partner in the partnership, or any penalty is incurred, the partnership is liable therefor to the same extent as the partner so acting or omitting to act.

§14. Partnership Bound by Partner's Breach of Trust. The partnership is bound to make good the loss:

(a) Where one partner acting within the scope of his apparent authority receives money or property of a third person and misapplies it; and

(b) Where the partnership in the course of its business receives money or property of a third person and the money or property so received is misapplied by any partner while it is in the custody of the partnership.

§15. Nature of Partner's Liability. All partners are liable.

(a) Jointly and severally for everything chargeable to the partnership under sections 13 and 14.

(b) Jointly for all other debts and obligations of the partnership; but any partner may enter into a separate obligation to perform a partnership contract.

§16. Partner by Estoppel. (1) When a person, by words spoken or written or by conduct, represents himself, or consents to another representing him to any one, as a partner in an existing partnership or with one or more persons not actual partners, he is liable to any such person to whom such representation has been made, who has, on the faith of such representation, given credit to the actual or apparent partnership, and if he has made such representation or consented to its being made in a public manner he is liable to such person, whether the representation has or has not been made or communicated to such person so giving credit by or with the knowledge of the apparent partner making the representation or consenting to its being made.

(a) When a partnership liability results, he is liable as though he were an actual member of the partnership.

(b) When no partnership liability results, he is liable jointly with the other persons, if any, so consenting to the contract or representation as to incur liability, otherwise separately.

(2) When a person has been thus represented to be a partner in an existing partnership, or with one or more persons not actual partners, he is an agent of the persons consenting to such representation to bind them to the same extent and in the same manner as though he were a partner in fact, with respect to persons who rely upon the representation. Where all the members of the existing partnership consent to the representation, a partnership act or obligation results; but in all other cases it is the joint act or obligation of the person acting and the persons consenting to the representation.

§17. Liability of Incoming Partner. A person admitted as a partner into an existing partnership is liable for all the obligations of the partnership arising before his admission as though he had been a partner when such obligations were incurred, except that this liability shall be satisfied only out of partnership property.

PART IV

Relations of Partners to One Another

§18. Rules Determining Rights and Duties of Partners. The rights and duties of the partners in relation to the partnership shall be determined, subject to any agreement between them, by the following rules:

(a) Each partner shall be repaid his contributions, whether by way of capital or advances to the partnership property and share equally in the profits and surplus remaining after all liabilities, including those to partners, are satisfied; and must contribute towards the losses, whether of capital or otherwise, sustained by the partnership according to his share in the profits.

(b) The partnership must indemnify every partner in respect of payments made and personal liabilities reasonably incurred by him in the ordinary and proper conduct of its business, or for the preservation of its business or property.

(c) A partner, who in aid of the partnership makes any payment or advance beyond the amount of capital which he agreed to contribute, shall be paid interest from the date of the payment or advance.

(d) A partner shall receive interest on the capital contributed by him only from the date when repayment should be made.

(e) All partners have equal rights in the management and conduct of the partnership business.

(f) No partner is entitled to remuneration for acting in the partnership business, except that a surviving partner is entitled to reasonable compensation for his services in winding up the partnership affairs.

(g) No person can become a member of a partnership without the consent of all the partners.

(h) Any difference arising as to ordinary matters connected with the partnership business may be decided by a majority of the partners; but no act in contravention of any agreement between the partners may be done rightfully without the consent of all the partners.

§19. Partnership Books. The partnership books shall be kept, subject to any agreement between the partners, at the principal place of business of the partnership, and every partner shall at all times have access to and may inspect and copy any of them.

§20. Duty of Partners to Render Information. Partners shall render on demand true and full information of all things affecting the partnership to any partner or the legal representative of any deceased partner or partner under legal disability.

§21. Partner Accountable as a Fiduciary. (1) Every partner must account to the partnership for any benefit, and hold as trustee for it any profits derived by him without the consent of the other partners from any transaction connected with the formation, conduct, or liquidation of the partnership or from any use by him of its property.

(2) This section applies also to the representatives of a deceased partner engaged in the liquidation of the affairs of the partnership as the personal representatives of the last surviving partner.

§22. Right to an Account. Any partner shall have the right to a formal account as to partnership affairs:

(a) If he is wrongfully excluded from the partnership business or possession of its property by his co-partners,

(b) If the right exists under the terms of any agreement,

(c) As provided by section 21,

(d) Whenever other circumstances render it just and reasonable.

§23. Continuation of Partnership Beyond Fixed Term. (1) When a partnership for a fixed term or particular undertaking is continued after the termination of such term or particular undertaking without any express agreement, the rights and duties of the partners remain the same as they were at such termination, so far as is consistent with a partnership at will.

(2) A continuation of the business by the partners or such of them as habitually acted therein during the term, without any settlement or liquidation of the partnership affairs, is prima facie evidence of a continuation of the partnership.

PART V

Property Rights of a Partner

§24. Extent of Property Rights of a Partner. The property rights of a partner are (1) his rights in specific partnership property, (2) his interest in the partnership, and (3) his right to participate in the management.

§25. Nature of a Partner's Right in Specific Partnership Property.

(1) A partner is co-owner with his partners of specific partnership property holding as a tenant in partnership.

(2) The incidents of this tenancy are such that:

(a) A partner, subject to the provisions of this act and to any agreement between the partners, has an equal right with his partners to possess specific partnership property for partnership purposes; but he has no right to possess such property for any other purpose without the consent of his partners.

(b) A partner's right in specific partnership property is not assignable except in connection with the assignment of rights of all the partners in the same property.

(c) A partner's right in specific partnership property is not subject to attachment or execution, except on a claim against the partnership. When partnership property is attached for a partnership debt the partners, or any of them, or the representatives of a deceased partner, cannot claim any right under the homestead or exemption laws.

(d) On the death of a partner his right in specific partnership property vests in the surviving partner or partners, except where the deceased was the last surviving partner, when his right in such property vests in his legal representative. Such surviving partner or partners, or the legal representative of the last surviving partner, has no right to possess the partnership property for any but a partnership purpose.

(e) A partner's right in specific partnership property is not subject to dower, curtesy, or allowances to widows, heirs, or next of kin.

§26. Nature of Partner's Interest in the Partnership. A partner's interest in the partnership is his share of the profits and surplus, and the same is personal property.

§27. Assignment of Partner's Interest. (1) A conveyance by a partner of his interest in the partnership does not of itself dissolve the partnership, nor, as against the other partners in the absence of agreement, entitle the assignee, during the continuance of the partnership to interfere in the management or administration of the partnership business or affairs, or to require any information or account of partnership transactions, or to inspect the partnership books; but it merely entitles the assignee to receive in accordance with his contract the profits to which the assigning partner would otherwise be entitled.

(2) In case of a dissolution of the partnership, the assignee is entitled to receive his assignor's interest and may require an account from the date only of the last account agreed to by all the partners.

§28. Partner's Interest Subject to Charging Order. (1) On due application to a competent court by any judgment creditor of a partner, the court which entered the judgment, order, or decree, or any other court, may charge the interest of the debtor partner with payment of the unsatisfied amount of such judgment debt with interest thereon; and may then or later appoint a receiver of his share of the profits, and of any other money due or to fall due to him in respect of the partnership, and make all other orders, directions, accounts and inquiries which the debtor partner might have made, or which the circumstances of the case may require.

(2) The interest charged may be redeemed at any time before fore-

closure, or in case of a sale being directed by the court may be purchased without thereby causing a dissolution:

(a) With separate property, by any one or more of the partners, or

(b) With partnership property, by any one or more of the partners with the consent of all the partners whose interests are not so charged or sold.

(3) Nothing in this act shall be held to deprive a partner of his right, if any, under the exemption laws, as regards his interest in the partnership.

PART VI

Dissolution and Winding Up

§29. Dissolution Defined. The dissolution of a partnership is the change in the relation of the partners caused by any partner ceasing to be associated in the carrying on as distinguished from the winding up of the business.

§30. Partnership Not Terminated by Dissolution. On dissolution the partnership is not terminated, but continues until the winding up of partnership affairs is completed.

§31. Causes of Dissolution. Dissolution is caused: (1) Without violation of the agreement between the partners,

(a) By the termination of the definite term or particular undertaking specified in the agreement,

(b) By the express will of any partner when no definite term or particular undertaking is specified,

(c) By the express will of all the partners who have not assigned their interests or suffered them to be charged for their separate debts, either before or after the termination of any specified term or particular undertaking,

(d) By the expulsion of any partner from the business bona fide in accordance with such a power conferred by the agreement between the partners;

(2) In contravention of the agreement between the partners, where the circumstances do not permit a dissolution under any other provision of this section, by the express will of any partner at any time;

(3) By any event which makes it unlawful for the business of the partnership to be carried on or for the members to carry it on in partnership;

(4) By the death of any partner;

(5) By the bankruptcy of any partner or the partnership;

(6) By decree of court under section 32.

§32. Dissolution by Decree of Court. (1) On application by or for a partner the court shall decree a dissolution whenever:

(a) A partner has been declared a lunatic in any judicial proceeding or is shown to be of unsound mind,

(b) A partner becomes in any other way incapable of performing his part of the partnership contract,

(c) A partner has been guilty of such conduct as tends to affect prejudicially the carrying on of the business,

(d) A partner wilfully or persistently commits a breach of the partnership agreement, or otherwise so conducts himself in matters relating to the partnership business that it is not reasonably practicable to carry on the business in partnership with him,

(e) The business of the partnership can only be carried on at a loss,

(f) Other circumstances render a dissolution equitable.

(2) On the application of the purchaser of a partner's interest under sections 27 or 28:

(a) After the termination of the specified term or particular undertaking,

(b) At any time if the partnership was a partnership at will when the interest was assigned or when the charging order was issued.

§33. General Effect of Dissolution on Authority of Partner. Except so far as may be necessary to wind up partnership affairs or to complete transactions begun but not then finished, dissolution terminates all authority of any partner to act for the partnership,

(1) With respect to the partners,

(a) When the dissolution is not by the act, bankruptcy or death of a partner; or

(b) When the dissolution is by such act, bankruptcy or death of a partner, in cases where section 34 so requires.

(2) With respect to persons not partners, as declared in section 35.

§34. Right of Partner to Contribution From Copartners After Dissolution. Where the dissolution is caused by the act, death or bankruptcy of a partner, each partner is liable to his copartners for his share of any liability created by any partner acting for the partnership as if the partnership had not been dissolved unless

(a) The dissolution being by act of any partner, the partner acting for the partnership had knowledge of the dissolution, or

(b) The dissolution being by the death or bankruptcy of a partner, the partner acting for the partnership had knowledge or notice of the death or bankruptcy.

§35. Power of Partner to Bind Partnership to Third Persons After Dis-

solution. (1) After dissolution a partner can bind the partnership except as provided in Paragraph (3)

(a) By any act appropriate for winding up partnership affairs or completing transactions unfinished at dissolution;

(b) By any transaction which would bind the partnership if dissolution had not taken place, provided the other party to the transaction

(I) Had extended credit to the partnership prior to dissolution and had no knowledge or notice of the dissolution; or

(II) Though he had not so extended credit, had nevertheless known of the partnership prior to dissolution, and, having no knowledge or notice of dissolution, the fact of dissolution had not been advertised in a newspaper of general circulation in the place (or in each place if more than one) at which the partnership business was regularly carried on.

(2) The liability of a partner under paragraph (1b) shall be satisfied out of partnership assets alone when such partner had been prior to dissolution.

(a) Unknown as a partner to the person with whom the contract is made; and

(b) So far unknown and inactive in partnership affairs that the business reputation of the partnership could not be said to have been in any degree due to his connection with it.

(3) The partnership is in no case bound by any act of a partner after dissolution

(a) Where the partnership is dissolved because it is unlawful to carry on the business, unless the act is appropriate for winding up partnership affairs; or

(b) Where the partner has become bankrupt; or

(c) Where the partner has no authority to wind up partnership affairs; except by a transaction with one who

(I) Had extended credit to the partnership prior to dissolution and had no knowledge or notice of his want of authority; or

(II) Had not extended credit to the partnership prior to dissolution, and, having no knowledge or notice of his want of authority, the fact of his want of authority has not been advertised in the manner provided for advertising the fact of dissolution in paragraph (1bII).

(4) Nothing in this section shall affect the liability under section 16 of any person who after dissolution represents himself or consents to another representing him as a partner in a partnership engaged in carrying on business.

§36. Effect of Dissolution on Partner's Existing Liability. (1) The dissolution of the partnership does not of itself discharge the existing liability of any partner.

(2) A partner is discharged from any existing liability upon dissolution of the partnership by an agreement to that effect between himself, the partnership creditor and the person or partnership continuing the business; and such agreement may be inferred from the course of dealing between the creditor having knowledge of the dissolution and the person or partnership continuing the business.

(3) Where a person agrees to assume the existing obligations of a dissolved partnership, the partners whose obligations have been assumed shall be discharged from any liability to any creditor of the partnership who, knowing of the agreement, consents to a material alteration in the nature or time of payment of such obligations.

(4) The individual property of a deceased partner shall be liable for all obligations of the partnership incurred while he was a partner but subject to the prior payment of his separate debts.

§37. **Right to Wind Up.** Unless otherwise agreed the partners who have not wrongfully dissolved the partnership or the legal representative of the last surviving partner, not bankrupt, has the right to wind up the partnership affairs; provided, however, that any partner, his legal representative or his assignee, upon cause shown, may obtain winding up by the court.

§38. **Rights of Partners to Application of Partnership Property.** (1) When dissolution is caused in any way, except in contravention of the partnership agreement, each partner as against his co-partners and all persons claiming through them in respect of their interests in the partnership, unless otherwise agreed, may have the partnership property applied to discharge its liabilities, and the surplus applied to pay in cash the net amount owing to the respective partners. But if dissolution is caused by expulsion of a partner, bona fide under the partnership agreement and if the expelled partner is discharged from all partnership liabilities, either by payment or agreement under section 36 (2), he shall receive in cash only the net amount due him from the partnership.

(2) When dissolution is caused in contravention of the partnership agreement the rights of the partners shall be as follows:

(a) Each partner who has not caused dissolution wrongfully shall have,

(I) All the rights specified in paragraph (1) of this section, and

(II) The right, as against each partner who has caused the dissolution wrongfully, to damages for breach of the agreement.

(b) The partners who have not caused the dissolution wrongfully, if they all desire to continue the business in the same name, either by themselves or jointly with others, may do so, during the agreed term for the partnership and for that purpose may possess the partnership property, provided they secure the payment by bond approved by the court, or pay to any partner who has caused the dissolution wrongfully, the value of his interest in the partnership at the dissolution, less any damages recoverable under clause (2aII) of this section, and in like manner indemnify him against all present or future partnership liabilities.

(c) A partner who has caused the dissolution wrongfully shall have:

(I) If the business is not continued under the provisions of paragraph (2b) all the rights of a partner under paragraph (1), subject to clause (2aII), of this section,

(II) If the business is continued under paragraph (2b) of this section the right as against his co-partners and all claiming through them in respect of their interests in the partnership, to have the value of his interest in the partnership, less any damages caused to his co-partners by the dissolution, ascertained and paid to him in cash, or the payment secured by bond approved by the court, and to be released from all existing liabilities of the partnership; but in ascertaining the value of the partner's interest the value of the good-will of the business shall not be considered.

§39. **Rights Where Partnership is Dissolved for Fraud or Misrepresentation.** Where a partnership contract is rescinded on the ground of the fraud or misrepresentation of one of the parties thereto, the party entitled to rescind is, without prejudice to any other right, entitled,

(a) To a lien on, or right of retention of, the surplus of the partnership property after satisfying the partnership liabilities to third persons for any sum of money paid by him for the purchase of an interest in the partnership and for any capital or advances contributed by him; and

(b) To stand, after all liabilities to third persons have been satisfied, in the place of the creditors of the partnership for any payments made by him in respect of the partnership liabilities; and

(c) To be indemnified by the person guilty of the fraud or making the representation against all debts and liabilities of the partnership.

§40. **Rules for Distribution.** In settling accounts between the partners after dissolution, the following rules shall be observed, subject to any agreement to the contrary:

(a) The assets of the partnership are:

(I) The partnership property,

(II) The contributions of the partners necessary for the payment of all the liabilities specified in clause (b) of this paragraph.

(b) The liabilities of the partnership shall rank in order of payment, as follows:

(I) Those owing to creditors other than partners,

(II) Those owing to partners other than for capital and profits,

(III) Those owing to partners in respect of capital,

(IV) Those owing to partners in respect of profits.

(c) The assets shall be applied in the order of their declaration in clause (a) of this paragraph to the satisfaction of the liabilities.

(d) The partners shall contribute, as provided by section 18 (a) the amount necessary to satisfy the liabilities; but if any, but not all, of the partners are insolvent, or, not being subject to process, refuse to contribute, the other partners shall contribute their share of the liabilities, and, in the relative proportions in which they share the profits, the additional amount necessary to pay the liabilities.

(e) An assignee for the benefit of creditors or any person appointed by the court shall have the right to enforce the contributions specified in clause (d) of this paragraph.

(f) Any partner or his legal representative shall have the right to enforce the contributions specified in clause (d) of this paragraph, to the extent of the amount which he has paid in excess of his share of the liability.

(g) The individual property of a deceased partner shall be liable for the contributions specified in clause (d) of this paragraph.

(h) When partnership property and the individual properties of the partners are in possession of a court for distribution, partnership creditors shall have priority on partnership property and separate creditors on individual property, saving the rights of lien or secured creditors as heretofore.

(i) Where a partner has become bankrupt or his estate is insolvent the claims against his separate property shall rank in the following order:

(I) Those owing to separate creditors,

(II) Those owing to partnership creditors,

(III) Those owing to partners by way of contribution.

§41. Liability of Persons Continuing the Business in Certain Cases. (1) When any new partner is admitted into an existing partnership, or when any partner retires and assigns (or the representative of the deceased partner assigns) his rights in partnership property to two or more of the partners, or to one or more of the partners and one or more third persons, if the business is continued without liquidation of the partnership affairs, creditors of the first or dissolved partnership are also creditors of the partnership so continuing the business.

(2) When all but one partner retire and assign (or the representative of a deceased partner assigns) their rights in partnership property to the remaining partner, who continues the business without liquidation of partnership affairs, either alone or with others, creditors of the dissolved partnership are also creditors of the person or partnership so continuing the business.

(3) When any partner retires or dies and the business of the dissolved

partnership is continued as set forth in paragraphs (1) and (2) of this section, with the consent of the retired partners or the representative of the deceased partner, but without any assignment of his right in partnership property, rights of creditors of the dissolved partnership and of the creditors of the person or partnership continuing the business shall be as if such assignment had been made.

(4) When all the partners or their representatives assign their rights in partnership property to one or more third persons who promise to pay the debts and who continue the business of the dissolved partnership, creditors of the dissolved partnership are also creditors of the person or partnership continuing the business.

(5) When any partner wrongfully causes a dissolution and the remaining partners continue the business under the provisions of section 38 (2b), either alone or with others, and without liquidation of the partnership affairs, creditors of the dissolved partnership are also creditors of the person or partnership continuing the business.

(6) When a partner is expelled and the remaining partners continue the business either alone or with others, without liquidation of the partnership affairs, creditors of the dissolved partnership are also credtors of the person or partnership continuing the business.

(7) The liability of a third person becoming a partner in the partnership continuing the business, under this section, to the creditors of the dissolved partnership shall be satisfied out of partnership property only.

(8) When the business of a partnership after dissolution is continued under any conditions set forth in this section the creditors of the dissolved partnership, as against the separate creditors of the retiring or deceased partner or the representative of the deceased partner, have a prior right to any claim of the retired partner or the representative of the deceased partner against the person or partnership continuing the business, on account of the retired or deceased partner's interest in the dissolved partnership or on account of any consideration promised for such interest or for his right in partnership property.

(9) Nothing in this section shall be held to modify any right of creditors to set aside any assignment on the ground of fraud.

(10) The use by the person or partnership continuing the business of the partnership name, or the name of a deceased partner as part thereof, shall not of itself make the individual property of the deceased partner liable for any debts contracted by such person or partnership.

§42. Rights of Retiring or Estate of Deceased Partner When the Business is Continued. When any partner retires or dies, and the business is continued under any of the conditions set forth in section 41 (1, 2, 3, 5, 6), or section 38 (2b), without any settlement of accounts as between him or his estate and the person or partnership continuing the business, unless otherwise agreed, he or his legal representative as against such persons or partnership may have the value of his interest at the date of dissolution ascertained, and shall receive as an ordinary creditor an amount equal to the value of his interest in the dissolved partnership with interest, or, at his option or at the option of his legal representative, in lieu of interest, the profits attributable to the use of his right in the property of the dissolved partnership; provided that the creditors of the dissolved partnership as against the separate creditors, or the representative of the retired or deceased partner, shall have priority on any claim arising under this section, as provided by section 41 (8) of this act.

§43. Accrual of Actions. The right to an account of his interest shall accrue to any partner, or his legal representative, as against the winding up partners or the surviving partners or the person or partnership continuing the business, at the date of dissolution, in the absence of any agreement to the contrary.

Glossary

(Other legal terms are defined elsewhere in the text. Refer to the Index for them. Definitions also appear in the Uniform Commercial Code and the Uniform Partnership Act which are included in the Appendix.)

abrogate   To annul, repeal, or abolish; such as to make a former rule, order, law, or treaty void or inoperative.

abstract of title   A summary of the history of the title to land, containing a synopsis of all conveyances and transactions which affect the title, as well as a statement of all liens, encumbrances, and claims which are outstanding against the land.

acceptance   Assent to the act or proposal of another; as the acceptance of an offer to make a contract, of a bill of exchange, or of a deed for real property.

accession   An enlargement of or addition to a chattel or the enhancement of its value by the addition of labor or materials; also the principle that property is acquired by its incorporation or union with other property.

accommodation paper   A negotiable instrument signed by a party as maker, drawer, acceptor or indorser, without receiving value and for the purpose of enabling another party to obtain money or credit.

accord and satisfaction   An agreement to substitute a new agreement and performance for that provided for in the contract and the performance of the new agreement.

adjective law   The branch of law comprised of the rules of procedure and practice according to which the substantive law is administered.

adjudication   A judgment or determination by a court or similar body.

administrative law The law relating to the powers and the procedures of governmental bodies; other than courts and legislatures, which affect the rights of private persons through investigations, hearings, rule making and adjudication.

administrator A person appointed by a probate court to settle the estate of an intestate and such estates as have no competent executor designated by the testator.

adverse possession Possession of real property by one who is not the owner but whose possession is actual, hostile to the owner, and made under a claim of right, open, and notorious, exclusive and continuous, and if the possession continues for the prescribed statutory period, the possessor acquires title to the real property.

affirmative relief Relief, benefit, or compensation which may be granted to the defendant in a judgment or decree in accordance with the facts established in his favor.

agency A legal relationship in which one person, an agent, acts for another person, the principal.

allegations The assertion, declaration, or statement of a party to a lawsuit, made in a pleading, setting out what he expects to prove.

ancillary Auxiliary or incidental to something which is primary, as an ancillary administrator of the assets of a decedent as are found within a state other than that of his domicil.

answer The pleading of a defendant in which he takes issue with any or all allegations set out in the plaintiff's declaration, complaint, or petition.

anticipatory breach A breach of contract that occurs in advance of the time for performance as called for in the contract.

appellate court A court that hears appeals from the decisions of lower courts. Alleged errors by the lower court in applying the law afford the basis for an appeal. The appealing party is called the appellant; the other party is called the appellee.

assent Consent or agreement.

assignment The transfer of rights, such as those present in a contract, lease, or mortgage from one person, the assignor, to another person, the assignee.

arbitration The submission of some disputed matter to selected persons, and the substitution of their decision or award for the judgment of the established tribunals of justice, thus avoiding the formalities, the delay, and the expense of ordinary litigation.

attachment A process under law which directs the seizure of property of a defendant by an officer to prevent the defendant from disposing of the property during a lawsuit.

attorney in fact Denotes all agents, but technically the term denotes only an agent whose power is conferred by a formal writing known as a power of attorney; distinguished from an attorney at law or lawyer who performs acts for others requiring that he be admitted to the practice of law by the state.

auction A public sale of property to the highest bidder.

bailment The delivery of personal property by one person, the bailor, to another, the bailee, for a special purpose, on condition that the property be returned or otherwise disposed of pursuant to agreement.

bankruptcy A procedure by which one unable to pay his debts may be declared a bankrupt, after which his assets, in excess of certain exemptions, are surrendered to the court for distribution to his creditors, and the bankrupt is given a discharge releasing him from further liability on most debts.

barter To trade one article of property for another.

beneficiary A person who is entitled to the benefits of a trust or the proceeds of an insurance policy. In contract law, a third party beneficiary is a person for whose benefit a contract is made, although he is not a party to the contract.

bilateral contract A contract in which there is a mutual exchange of promises by the parties.

bill of lading A document issued by a carrier as a receipt for goods delivered to the carrier and a contract for their transportation and delivery to a specified place to a person named or his order.

bill of sale A document evidencing the sale of personal property to the party named in the document.

bona fide Good faith; absence of decit or fraud.

bona fide purchaser One who buys property without notice that some other person has rights to the property.

breach of contract The unjustified failure of a party to a contract to fulfill a duty he has assumed under the contract.

burden of proof The duty of proving a fact or facts in dispute in relation to an issue raised between the parties to a lawsuit.

bylaws A set of rules and regulations for controlling the internal affairs of a corporation or organization.

capacity In contract law, the legal ability to enter into binding contractual relationships.

capital Net assets of a corporation; in a partnership, the permanent investment that the partners make in the business.

capital stock The declared money value of the outstanding stock of the corporation.

cause of action A claim that has a sufficient legal basis to give the claimant the right to seek a remedy in court.

caveat emptor Let the buyer beware.

chancery Denotes the high court of Chancery in England and refers to the equity courts and proceedings in the United States.

chattel An article of tangible personal property.

chose in action An intangible right or action not reduced to possession but recoverable by a suit at law.

c.i.f. A mercantile term meaning "cost, insurance, and freight."

circuit The territory in which a court possesses jurisdiction or travels from place to place to hear and decide cases.

civil law The branch of law governing private rights and remedies, used in contradistinction to the criminal law branch. Term also used to describe the legal systems of countries whose law stems from Roman law as distinguished from those legal systems referred to as common-law systems.

civil wrong An act, or omission to act, which violates a legal duty, and which gives the victim of the wrong the right to bring a civil action for a remedy.

code A systematic compilation of statutes enacted by a legislature.

commission merchant A factor.

common law The body of law referred to as the unwritten law and found in court decisions based on precedents, originally derived from the usages and customs of the community.

compensatory damages A sum of money which will pay for the amount of actual loss a person has suffered as the result of an infringement of his legal right.

complaint The first pleading filed by the plaintiff in a lawsuit, alleging the facts upon which his cause of action is based; also known as a petition and declaration.

composition An agreement by a debtor with his creditors whereby each creditor agrees to take a lesser amount than is owed to him, in complete satisfaction of the total debt due.

conditional sale A sale of goods in which the title to the goods remains in the seller until the price has been paid or until other conditions have been met, in the meantime the buyer to have the possession of the goods.

condition precedent An express or implied provision of a contract calling for the happening of some event or the performance of some act, before the contract will be binding upon the parties.

condition subsequent A provision in a contract that describes an event or act, upon the happening of which certain obligations under the contract terminate.

condominium A form of co-ownership of real property in which a person owns specific property, such as an apartment or dwelling in fee simple, and he also owns an undivided share in certain common facilities, such as land, parking space, and elevators.

confusion The mixing of goods of different owners into a common mass.

consideration Something of value given or promised in exchange for an act or promise so as to make an agreement a binding contract.

consignment A bailment of goods by a consignor to a consignee who is to sell the goods if he can.

constitution The basic law, usually embodied in a single document, establishing a framework of government and limitations upon the powers of the branches and levels of government, with the definition of basic rights held by the people.

constructive notice Knowledge of a fact imputed by law to a person and binding on him as though he had actual notice of the information.

contract An enforceable agreement; the essential elements being mutual assent (offer and acceptance), consideration, competent parties, and legal object.

conversion An act of dominion wrongfully exercised over another's personal property.

conveyance A written instrument which transfers title to property, usually real estate.

corporation An artificial person existing as a legal entity by virtue of incorporation under the law.

corporeal Tangible, possessing a physical substance so as to be perceptible to the senses.

counterclaim A cross demand by a defendant which if established constitutes a distinct cause of action that can be used in opposition to, or deduction from, the plaintiff's claim.

court of record A court in which the pleadings and proceedings, along with a record of its judgments are made a matter of written record.

covenant A promise contained in a deed, lease, mortgage, or other instrument executed by signing, sealing, and delivery; also commonly used as a synonym for a contractual promise.

creditor Used to describe one who has a right to recover money from a debtor or to enforce some other right of action.

crime Any breach of a law established for the protection of the public, as distinguished from an infringement of mere private rights, although the same act may constitute both a crime and a private or civil wrong, called a tort.

culpable act Censurable, blameworthy; also sometimes used to mean criminal.

damages Sum of money which may be recovered by a person who has suffered loss or injury through the unlawful act, omission, or negligence of another.

debtor A person obligated on a debt owed to a creditor.

declaration Same as complaint.

deceit A fradulent misrepresentation or contrivance which misleads another person to his injury.

deed A formal writing, sealed and delivered by a party; a legal instrument transferring the ownership of real property.

de facto In fact as distinguished from "de jure," by right. For example, a de facto corporation is one that has failed to comply with the law governing its formation, but is nevertheless recognized as a corporation in fact and its existence may be challenged only by the state in a direct action for the purpose; others who deal with the corporation may not attack the corporation's existence.

default judgment A judgment granted against a party to a lawsuit when he fails to file a necessary pleading within the time allowed by law for that purpose.

defendant In a lawsuit the plaintiff is the complaining party and the defendant is the adverse party.

de jure By right. For example, a de jure corporation is one that has been formed in full compliance with the state incorporation law and all other legal requirements.

del credere agent An agent who guarantees to his principal against the default of those with whom contracts are made.

demurrer A pleading which admits the facts stated in an opposing pleading but declares that the pleading objected to is insufficient to state a cause of action or is otherwise defective.

de novo trial Anew. A trial de novo is a new trial in which the entire case is retried, including a determination of the facts as well as the application of the law to the facts.

devise A gift of real property by will.

directed verdict A direction by the trial judge ordering the jury to return a verdict in favor of a party to the action.

disaffirm To repudiate; to disclaim intention of being obligated; as, to disaffirm a voidable contract.

donee A person who receives a gift.

donor A person who makes a gift.

dower The right of a widow to the use or ownership of some portion of the real estate owned by the husband.

drawee The person upon whom a bill of exchange, draft, or check is drawn.

drawer The person who draws and issues a bill of exchange, draft, or check.

duress Unlawful conduct that deprives a person of his free will in making a contract or doing an act and which generally gives the victim the right to rescind the transaction entered into under such circumstances.

easement A right of one person to use the land of another person for some special purpose.

ejectment A writ granted by a court to oust a person who is unlawfully in possession of real property.

emancipation Occurs when parents release their right to claim their minor child's services and earnings.

embezzlement The fraudulent conversion of another's personal property by one to whom it has been entrusted.

equity The branch of law which was developed and administered in England by the high court of Chancery because of the inadequacy of the rules then applied by the common-law courts and which now affords relief in the courts of the United States when the remedy at law is inadequate.

escheat   The principle by which property reverts to the state because of the nonexistence of legal heirs.

estoppel   Arises when one does an act which in fairness will preclude him from averring anything to the contrary, as where another has been innocently mislead into some injurious change of position.

evidence   Whatever tends to establish matters of fact, the truth of which is submitted to judicial investigation and includes oral testimony of witnesses, documents, exhibits, and every other thing which may properly give information to the court upon the issues presented.

executed   1. Used to indicate that a legal instrument has been signed or otherwise validated or 2. Signifies that a transaction has been completed as where the obligations under a contract have been performed.

execution   A writ or process afforded by law for the enforcement of a judgment. Also refers to the signing, sealing, and delivery of a written contract or the performance of a contract.

executor   A person who is named in a will as one who is to administer the estate of the testator.

executory   Unperformed, as where the obligations under a contract remain unfulfilled, wholly or in part.

factor   An agent authorized to sell goods on a commission basis; also called a commission merchant.

f.a.s.   A shipping term meaning "free alongside" a named vessel.

fee simple   The entire interest in property in land and which is an estate of inheritance.

felony   A major crime, generally punishable by death or imprisonment in a penitentiary.

fiduciary   One who holds a position of trust and confidence in his dealings with another person.

fixture   A chattel which has been attached to land with the intention of making it a permanent addition to the land and thus has become real property.

f.o.b.   A shipping term meaning "free on board."

franchise   A special privilege granted to an individual or corporation by law, as a franchise for a utility company.

fraud A false statement or conduct about a past or existing material fact with knowledge of its falsity or with reckless disregard as to its truth with the intent to cause another to rely thereon, and he does justifiably rely thereon to his injury.

freehold Any estate of inheritance or a life estate in land.

fungible goods Goods of which any unit is by its nature or by mercantile usage treated as the equivalent of any other unit, usually sold by weight or measure.

garnishment A process provided for by statute under which a judgment creditor obtains by court order the judgment debtor's money or property held by a third person.

gift causa mortis A transfer of property by a person who faces impending death, with intention that the donee shall become the owner of the property, but on condition that the donor's failure to die shall revoke the gift.

gift inter vivos A transfer of property to a donee during the life of the donor, for no consideration, with the intention on the part of the donor to divest himself of control or dominion over the subject of the gift.

good will The value attached to the name of a business on the basis of the community's favorable regard for the business and the likelihood of continued patronage by its customers.

guaranty A contract by which one person is to be responsible for the debt or default of another person.

guardian One to whom the law entrusts the care of the person or property of another.

habeus corpus Literally, "you have the body." A writ is issued by a court ordering the individual who has custody of a person to produce such person at a given time and place, in order that the court may inquire into the legality of the detention or custody.

heirs Those persons designated by statute to receive the estate of a decedent where the estate is not disposed of by will.

homestead The right of the owner of a dwelling to claim certain limited statutory exemptions or rights; for example, with respect to seizure and sale of such property upon levy of execution.

implied in fact contract A contract deduced from the conduct of the parties or from the facts, as distinguished from an express oral or written contract.

indemnity An obligation or duty resting on one person to compensate for any loss or damage another has incurred at his request or for his benefit.

injunction   A judicial command to do or refrain from doing a particular act.

in pari delicto   In equal fault or guilt.

in personam   Against the person.

in rem   Against the thing or status.

insurable interest   A person's interest in or relation to a thing or person where the person in possession of it will derive pecuniary benefit or advantage from its preservation.

intestate   A person who dies without leaving a will.

judgment   A final determination by a court of the rights of the parties to an action.

judgment lien   The lien upon the real property of a judgment debtor which arises under statute by virtue of the judgment itself.

jurisdiction   The power of a court to hear, determine, and render final judgment in a case.

jurisprudence   The science of law.

jury   A body of laymen, legally selected, to inquire into matters of fact under the guidance of a judge, and to render their verdict according to the evidence.

laches   An equity doctrine which holds that unreasonable delay in bringing action on a claim will bar recovery on it.

lease   An agreement by which an owner, the lessor, gives the possession of his property to another person, the lessee, for a stated period for a consideration called rent.

legacy   A bequest or gift of personal property by will.

legal right   An interest which the law will protect.

legal tender   All coins and currencies of the United States.

legal wrong   An invasion of a legal right.

libel   Written and published matter, calculated to defame another by bringing him into ridicule, hatred, or contempt.

license   A personal privilege to do some act or series of acts upon the land of another, without possessing any estate therein. A permit to do some act, such as carry on a business or practice a profession, without which the carrying on of the enterprise would be unlawful.

lien   A charge upon real or personal property for the payment or discharge of a debtor's duty.

liquidated damages An amount of money agreed upon by the parties to a contract in advance, to be paid in case of a breach.

liquidated debt A debt undisputed as to its existence or amount.

litigants The parties to a lawsuit.

locus sigilli; l.s. Place of the seal.

mandamus A writ issued by a court to compel a natural person, corporation, public officer, or inferior court to do some particular thing pertaining to their office or duty.

misdemeanor A minor crime, usually punishable by a fine.

mitigation of damages The principle that an injured party who claims damages must make reasonable efforts to reduce the damages as much as possible.

necessaries With reference to infants, necessaries include whatever is reasonably necessary for his proper and suitable maintenance, as related to his station in life.

negligence The failure to do what a reasonable and prudent man would ordinarily have done under the circumstances of the situation, or doing what such a person, under the existing circumstances, would not have done.

negotiable instrument An instrument which may be transferred or negotiated, so as to give the holder the right to sue on the instrument in his own name.

nominal damages The law infers some damage from the breach of an agreement, or the invasion of a right, and if no evidence is given of any particular amount of loss, it declares the right by the award of "nominal damages," being some small sum of money.

novation A mutual agreement among all parties concerned for the discharge of a valid existing obligation by the substitution of a new valid obligation on the part of the debtor or another, or a like agreement for the discharge of a debtor to his creditor by the substitution of a new creditor.

nuisance Anything which endangers life or health, gives offense to the senses, violates the laws of decency, or obstructs the reasonable and comfortable use of property.

offer A proposal by one person, the offeror, to another, the offeree, which is intended to create a contract on acceptance by the offeree.

option A contract by which one party in consideration of the payment of a certain sum to the other party acquires the privilege of buying from or otherwise acquiring or selling to such other party an interest in specified property at a fixed price within a stated time.

ordinance A legislative enactment; usually applied to the acts or laws passed by a municipal or local government legislative body.

parol Oral; verbal; spoken as opposed to written.

partnership An association of two or more persons to carry on as co-owners a business for profit.

payee The person to whom a note, bill of exchange, or check is made payable.

perjury Intentional false swearing as to something material in a proceeding before a court, tribunal, or officer, or in a matter to which an oath is authorized by law.

per se By itself; intrinsically.

petition Same as complaint.

plaintiff A person who brings a lawsuit.

pleadings The written allegations setting forth the claims and defenses of the parties to a lawsuit.

pledge A bailment of personal property by a pledgor to a pledgee as security for a debt.

power of attorney A written authorization to an agent to perform specified acts in behalf of his principal.

preponderance of the evidence The greater weight of the evidence.

presumption An inference as to the existence of a fact not actually known, arising from its usual connection with another fact which is known.

prima facie Literally, "at the first appearance." Prima facie evidence of a fact in law means it is sufficient to establish the fact, unless rebutted or contradicted.

privity A succession or chain of relationship to the same thing, right or interest, as a privity of contract, privity of estate, privity of possession.

probate To prove; used to describe the proceeding in a probate or similar court, whereby a will is established as the last will and testament of the person who purported to sign it; also applied to matters generally over which probate courts have jurisdiction.

proxy A written authorization by a stockholder to another person to vote the stock owned by the stockholder; also refers to the person who holds such a written authorization.

punitive damages Also referred to as exemplary damages and are those assessed as punishment of a party on account of the wanton, reckless, malicious, or oppressive nature of his wrongful act.

quantum meruit Literally, "as much as he has earned;" reasonable value.

quasi As if; almost; similar to.

quasi contract An obligation imposed by law, independent of agreement or intention of the parties, to prevent unjust enrichment; also called a contract implied in law or constructive contract.

quo warranto By what authority. The name of a writ and proceeding by which the government brings an action to recover an office or franchise from the person or corporation who holds it.

ratification The approval or confirmation by a person of a previous contract or other act that would not otherwise be binding on him in the absence of such approval.

recission The cancellation of a contract and the restoration of the parties to their original positions prior to the making of the contract.

recognizance An obligation of record entered into before some court of record, or before a duly authorized magistrate, conditioned for the performance of some particular act, usually to appear and answer to a criminal charge.

reformation The remedy by which a written instrument is corrected to express the real agreement or intention of the parties.

remedies The relief available from a court by which the violation of a legal right is prevented or a legal wrong is redressed.

replevin An action by which the owner, or other proper person, recovers possession of goods wrongfully taken or withheld.

res judicata The principle which holds that once a lawsuit has been adjudicated on its merits and all appeals exhausted, the parties may not raise the same issues in a subsequent lawsuit between themselves.

respondeat superior The doctrine that a principal or employer is responsible for the losses and injuries of third persons due to the torts committed by an agent or an employee in the course of his employment.

scienter   knowingly; wilfully.

seal   An impression on an instrument, or any mark not ordinarily part of the signature, or the word "Seal" or the letters "L.S.," stated or intended to represent a seal.

secured note   A promissory note that has some form of security, such as a mortgage on property, for the obligation represented by the note.

setoff   A defendant's counter demand for an amount arising out of a cause of action not connected with the plaintiff's claim, but which is set up as a deduction from the plaintiff's claim.

slander   Defamation of character by spoken words or gestures.

specific performance   An equitable remedy in contract law consisting of a court order directing a party to perform his contractual obligation instead of just paying damages.

stare decisis   To stand by decided cases. The doctrine that courts should follow the precedents established by earlier court decisions in analogous cases, so as to give a degree of certainty, predictability, and continuity to the law.

status quo   The existing state of things. In contract law, recission of a contract is dependent upon the status quo being restored, i.e., the parties must be placed in their original positions prior to the making of the contract.

statute   An act of the legislature, referred to as written law.

statute of frauds   A statute providing that certain kinds of contracts are not enforceable unless they are in writing, or evidenced by a memorandum signed by the party sought to be held.

statute of limitations   A statute which prescribes the period of time within which an action may be brought.

subrogation   The right of a party secondarily liable to be substituted in the place of the creditor after he has made payment to the creditor and to enforce the creditor's right against the primary debtor in order to obtain indemnity from such debtor.

substantive law   The branch of law which defines legal rights and duties.

summons   A writ or process notifying a person that an action has been brought against him and requiring him to appear and answer the allegations in such action.

surety   A party who by an agreement with a principal undertakes to perform an obligation of the principal if the principal defaults.

tenant A lessee. Also a person who owns an interest in property.

tender An unconditional offer of money or goods in extinguishment of a contractual obligation.

testator A male who dies leaving a will.

testatrix A female who dies leaving a will.

toll the statute To stop the running of the period of a statute of limitations because of some act of the debtor.

tort Any private or civil wrong other than a breach of contract. Arises from a breach of a duty created by law and for which the injured party is granted a remedy against the wrongdoer called the tortfeasor.

treason An attempt to overthrow or betray the government to which one owes allegiance.

trespass Any unauthorized entry on another's property.

trust A legal arrangement by which one person called a trustee holds property in trust for the benefit of another person called the cestui que trust or beneficiary.

ultra vires Beyond the power. In corporation law, denotes corporate acts or contracts which are outside its legal power to do or make.

undue influence Assertion of control over the will of another and causing him to contract or act in a way he would not do if left to act according to his own free will.

unilateral contract A contract in which one party performs an act in return for the promise of the other party.

usury Unlawful interest. The lending of money at a rate of interest in excess of the lawful rate.

vendee A purchaser or buyer.

vendor A seller of property to a vendee.

void A nullity; of no legal effect; not binding.

voidable Capable of being avoided, as where a party to a contract has the election of disaffirming the contract and thus avoiding performance.

waiver A voluntary and intentional relinquishment of a known right.

warranty An undertaking or agreement to assume responsibility for losses caused by the failure of certain things to turn out as represented.

will A legal instrument by which a person provides for the disposition of his property after his death.

Index

NOTES

NOTES

NOTES

NOTES

NOTES

NOTES

NOTES

NOTES

NOTES

NOTES